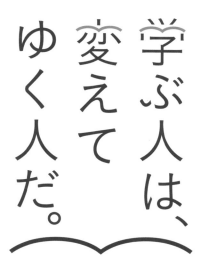

学ぶ人は、
変えて
ゆく人だ。

目の前にある問題はもちろん、

人生の問いや、

社会の課題を自ら見つけ、

挑み続けるために、人は学ぶ。

「学び」で、

少しずつ世界は変えてゆける。

いつでも、どこでも、誰でも、

学ぶことができる世の中へ。

旺文社

JN040753

全国高校入試問題正解 2025年受験用

分野別過去問 358題

英語

長文読解・英作文・リスニング

旺文社

≪ 2025 年受験用　全国高校入試問題正解 ≫

分野別過去問 英語

はじめに

　本書は，2021 年から 2023 年に実施された公立高校入試問題を厳選し，分野別に並べ替えた問題集です。小社刊行『全国高校入試問題正解』に掲載された問題，解答・解き方が収録されています。

◆特長◆

①入試の出題傾向を知る！

　本書をご覧いただければ，類似した問題が複数の都道府県で出題されていることは一目瞭然です。本書に取り組むことにより，入試の出題傾向を知ることができます。

②必要な問題を必要なだけ解く！

　本書は様々な分野に渡ってたくさんの問題を掲載しています。苦手意識のある分野や，攻略しておきたい分野の問題を集中的に演習することができます。

　本書が皆さんの受験勉強の一助となれば幸いです。

旺文社

目　　　次

【リスニング問題の音声について】

本書の英文を読み上げた音声を，専用ウェブサイトで聞くことができます。 音声 1 のように示しています。
指示文やポーズの間隔は，実際の試験よりも短縮したり，省略したりしてあります。また，本来英文が2回読まれている場合でも，1回だけにとどめています。聞き取りにくいところがありましたら，別冊解答の【放送内容】を参考にして練習してください。

・以下のサイトにアクセスし，パスワードを入力してください。
　https://service.obunsha.co.jp/tokuten/kseikai/
　パスワード：022170

ご利用可能期間：刊行日〜 2029 年 3 月 31 日
※本サービスは予告なく変更，終了することがあります。

・右の 2 次元コードからも簡単にアクセスできます。
・音声ファイルをダウンロードするか，ウェブ上で再生するかが選べます。

＜ご注意ください＞
・ダウンロードの音声の再生には，MP3 を再生できる機器が別途必要です。
・スマートフォンやタブレットでは音声ファイルをダウンロードできません。パソコンで音声ファイルをダウンロードしてから機器に転送するか，音声をウェブ上で再生する方法をご利用ください。
・音声をウェブ上で再生する際の通信料にご注意ください。

［編集協力］弘田春美　［デザイン］土屋真郁（丸屋）

第1章　**知識問題**

a．文中空欄の補充・選択

1 次の(ア)～(ウ)の文の(　　　)の中に入れるのに最も適するものを，あとの1～4の中からそれぞれ一つずつ選び，その番号を答えなさい。

(ア) I can't carry the table because it's very (　　　). Will you help me?
　1．bright　　2．deep　　3．heavy　　4．glad

(イ) I hope the (　　　) will be sunny tomorrow because I'm going to go fishing.
　1．company　　　2．festival
　3．health　　　　4．weather

(ウ) Let me (　　　) my friend. His name is Taro. He is from Kamome Junior High School. He likes playing basketball.
　1．communicate　　2．improve
　3．introduce　　　　4．respect
　　　　　　　　　　　　　　　　　　＜神奈川県＞

2 次の問いに答えなさい。

問1．次の(1), (2)の英文の[　　　]に入る最も適当な英語1語をそれぞれ語群から選んで書きなさい。

(1) Hi, my name is Takuya. Please [　　　] me Taku.
　語群

show	ask	call	give

(2) Let's go to the [　　　] and play soccer there.
　語群

park	library	station	restaurant

問2．次の絵の場面に合うように，(1), (2)の[　　　]に入る適当な英語1語をそれぞれ書きなさい。

(1) Please [　　　] quiet here.
(2) You [　　　] eat here.
　　　　　　　　　　　　　　　　　　＜北海道＞

3 次の(1)・(2)の対話の内容から考えて，それぞれの[　　　]に当てはまる適切な英語1語を書きなさい。ただし，[　　　]内に示した文字で書き始めること。

(1) *Kai* : What do you do in your free time?
　Lucy : I like listening to music.
　Kai : What [k　　　] of music do you listen to?
　Lucy : My favorite is classical music.

(2) *Shigeo* : Linda, you have a new bag.
　Linda : Yes. I bought this last week.
　Shigeo : Why did you choose it?
　Linda : Because it is [p　　　] among young girls.
　　　　　　　　　　　　　　　　　　＜高知県＞

4 次は，Yukoと留学生のTomとの対話である。(　①　)～(　③　)に，あとの[　　　]内の[説明]が示す英語1語をそれぞれ書け。

Yuko : Hi, Tom. How are you?
Tom : Fine, but a little hungry. I got up late this morning, so I couldn't eat (　①　).
Yuko : Oh, no! Please remember to eat something next Sunday morning.
Tom : I know, Yuko. We're going to Kirishima to (　②　) mountains again. Do you remember when we went there last time?
Yuko : Yes. We went there in (　③　). It was in early spring.

[説明] ① the food people eat in the morning after they get up
　　　 ② to go up to a higher or the highest place
　　　 ③ the third month of the year
　　　　　　　　　　　　　　　　　　＜鹿児島県＞

5 次は，Johnと父のOliverとの自宅での対話である。(　①　)～(　③　)に，下の[　　　]内の[説明]が示す英語1語をそれぞれ書け。

John : Good morning, Dad.
Oliver : Good morning, John. Oh, you will have a party here tonight with your friends, right?
John : Yes. I'm very happy. Ben and Ron will come.
Oliver : What time will they come?
John : They will (　①　) at the station at 5:30 p.m. So, maybe they will come here at 5:45 p.m. or 5:50 p.m.
Oliver : I see.
John : Can we use the (　②　)? We will cook pizza together.
Oliver : That's good. You can use all the (　③　) on the table.
John : Thank you. We will use the potatoes and onions.

[説明] ① to get to the place
　　　 ② the room that is used for cooking
　　　 ③ plants that you eat, for example, potatoes, carrots, and onions
　　　　　　　　　　　　　　　　　　＜鹿児島県＞

6 次の(1)・(2)の対話の内容から考えて，それぞれの　　　　に当てはまる適切な英語1語を書け。ただし，　　　内に示した文字で書き始めること。

(1) *Kana*：I'm looking forward to P.E. class today. I really like P.E. What is your favorite s　　　　, Ben?

Ben：I like science.

Kana：Wow. You like science!　I'm not good at it.

(2) *Shota*：What time do you u　　　　 get up?

Judy：From Monday to Friday, I always get up at six in the morning.

〈高知県〉

7 次の対話の（ 1 ）～（ 4 ）に入る最も適切なものを，それぞれア～エから1つずつ選び，記号で答えなさい。

A：Whose watch（ 1 ）this?

B：It's（ 2 ）. My father bought it for me.

A：It's cool. Please tell me（ 3 ）he bought it.

B：It was（ 4 ）at a shop in Himuka Station.

（ 1 ）　ア．is　　　イ．are
　　　　ウ．do　　　エ．does
（ 2 ）　ア．him　　イ．his
　　　　ウ．my　　　エ．mine
（ 3 ）　ア．what　イ．where
　　　　ウ．when　エ．why
（ 4 ）　ア．sell　　イ．sells
　　　　ウ．sold　　エ．selling

〈宮崎県〉

8 次の会話の（　　　）に入る最も適切な英語を，1語書きなさい。ただし，（　　　）内に示されている文字で書き始め，その文字も含めて答えること。

Shin　：Hello, Martha. Are you free next Saturday?

Martha：Yes. I have（n　　　　）to do on that day. What's up?

Shin　：I have two concert tickets. Would you like to come with me?

Martha：Of course!

〈岐阜県〉

9 次の㋐～㋓の文の（　　　）の中に入れるのに最も適するものを，あとの1～4の中からそれぞれ一つずつ選び，その番号を答えなさい。

㋐ One of the boys you met at the park yesterday（　　　）my brother.

1．am　　　　　2．is
3．are　　　　 4．were

㋑ Which school event do you like（　　　）?

1．good　　　　2．well
3．better than　4．the best

㋒ This is a school which（　　　）in 1980.

1．is building　　2．built
3．was built　　 4．were building

㋓ I have been reading this book（　　　）10 o'clock this morning.

1．at　　　　　2．before
3．for　　　　 4．since

〈神奈川県〉

10 次の問いに答えなさい。

問1．次の(1)，(2)の英文が，それぞれの日本語と同じ意味になるように，　　　　に入る最も適当な英語1語をそれぞれ語群から選んで書きなさい。

(1) Sit　　　　, please.
座ってください。

語群

of	to	down	from

(2) May I　　　　you?
いらっしゃいませ。

語群

help	come	thank	call

問2．次の(1)，(2)の英文の　　　　に入る最も適当な英語1語をそれぞれ語群から選んで書きなさい。

(1) We usually go to the　　　　to see many kinds of animals.

語群

station	factory	gym	zoo

(2) Blue, red, and green are the words for　　　　.

語群

weeks	families	colors	numbers

問3．次の(1)，(2)の対話が成り立つように，　　　　に入る適当な英語1語をそれぞれ書きなさい。ただし，　　　　内の＿には記入例にならい，1文字ずつ書くものとします。

記入例　| b | o | o | k |

(1) A：When did you buy this racket?
　　B：I bought it two years ＿＿＿.

(2) A：Here's a birthday ＿＿＿＿＿＿＿ for you.
　　B：Oh, it's a nice watch!　Thank you very much.

問4．次のグラフは，北海道のある都市の月ごとの降水量を表しています。グラフから考えて，(1)，(2)の　　　　に入る適当な英語1語をそれぞれ書きなさい。

(1) It rains the　　　　in September.

(2) It rains about 80 mm in March and　　　　.

〈北海道〉

11 次の1～3の対話文の　　　　に入れるのに最も適当なものを，それぞれ下のア～エから一つ選び，記号で答えなさい。

1．A：Mom, will you　　　　me to the zoo?
　　I want to see the animals there.

　　B：OK, but didn't we go there two weeks ago?

ア．ask　イ．go　ウ．take　エ．visit

２．A：Which restaurant is the 　　　　　 from here? I'm very hungry.
　　B：How about ABC restaurant? We can get there in only a few minutes.
　ア．fastest　　イ．highest
　ウ．latest　　エ．nearest
３．A：Wow, their performance is exciting! That girl on the stage is my classmate.
　　B：Really? The boy 　　　　　 the guitar is my friend.
　ア．is playing　　　イ．playing
　ウ．plays　　　エ．who play
＜熊本県・選択問題Ｂ＞

12 次の各問いの会話文について，（　　）に入る最も適切なものを次のア〜エのうちから１つ選び，その記号を書きなさい。
問１．A：What did you do last weekend?
　　　B：I went to a temple and （　　　　） a lot of pictures.
　　ア．take　　イ．taken　　ウ．taking　　エ．took
問２．A：Did you see Mike at school yesterday?
　　　B：I think he （　　　　） come to school because he was sick yesterday.
　　ア．didn't　　イ．doesn't　　ウ．isn't　　エ．wasn't
問３．A：Did you see the pictures painted by the famous artist?
　　　B：I wanted to see （　　　　）, but I couldn't because there were many people in front of me.
　　ア．her　　イ．him　　ウ．it　　エ．them
＜沖縄県＞

13 次の１〜３の対話文の 　　　　 に入れるのに最も適当なものを，それぞれ下のア〜エから一つ選び，記号で答えなさい。
　１．A：Your shopping bag looks 　　　　　 and you look tired. Do you want me to carry it for you?
　　　B：Thank you very much.
　　ア．heavy　　イ．light　　ウ．new　　エ．old
　２．A：Look at the man over there! He's playing basketball very well.
　　　B：Right. He's so cool! I wish I 　　　　　 play like him.
　　ア．will　　イ．can　　ウ．could　　エ．should
　３．A：Do you know where we'll practice singing?
　　　B：No. I'll ask our teacher and 　　　　　 you know later.
　　ア．show　　イ．let　　ウ．tell　　エ．want
＜熊本県＞

14 次の各問いの会話文について，（　　）に入る最も適切なものをア〜エのうちから１つ選び，その記号を書きなさい。
問１．A：Thank you for your help.
　　　B：No problem. I'm so happy （　　　　） you.
　　ア．to help　　イ．help
　　ウ．helped　　エ．can help
問２．A：Wow! That's a cool bike! Whose bike is that?
　　　B：It's （　　　　）. I bought it last week.
　　ア．my　　イ．me　　ウ．mine　　エ．I

問３．A：Do you have any sisters?
　　　B：Yes, look at this picture! These girls dancing on the stage （　　　　） my sisters.
　　ア．be　　イ．is　　ウ．am　　エ．are
＜沖縄県＞

15 次の(ア)〜(エ)の文の（　　　）の中に入れるのに最も適するものを，あとの１〜４の中からそれぞれ一つずつ選び，その番号を答えなさい。
(ア) A：Tom, you speak Japanese well.
　　 B：I （　　　　） in Japan with my family for three years when I was a child.
　　１．lived　　２．have lived　　３．live　　４．lives
(イ) A：Which would you like to drink, apple juice or orange juice?
　　 B：Well, it's difficult for me to choose because I like （　　　　） apple juice and orange juice.
　　１．between　　２．about　　３．both　　４．than
(ウ) A：I want to be a doctor and help many people. How about you?
　　 B：I haven't decided （　　　　） I want to do in the future.
　　１．whose　　２．what　　３．when　　４．why
(エ) A：Why do you like your English class?
　　 B：Because I can learn a lot of things by （　　　　） with my friends in English.
　　１．to talk　　２．have talked
　　３．talked　　４．talking
＜神奈川県＞

16 次の対話文の（　　）の中に最も適する英語を，それぞれ１語ずつ書きなさい。
(1) *Rumi*：Which do you like better, coffee （　　　　） tea?
　　Harry：I like tea better. I always drink it with milk.
(2) *Isamu*：It will be rainy today. Take an （　　　　） when you go out.
　　Freddie：I'll take the blue one. I can't use the red one because it doesn't open.
(3) *Woman*：Sorry, Mr. Okada cannot go to the meeting tomorrow.
　　Man　：Oh, really? Well, we want someone to come to the meeting （　　　　） of him.
＜山形県＞

17 次の対話の（　１　）〜（　４　）に入る最も適切なものを，それぞれア〜エから１つずつ選び，記号で答えなさい。
A：（　１　） you seen this movie yet?
B：Yes. I saw it with my family （　２　）.
A：Wow, （　３　） was it?
B：It was fantastic! You （　４　） watch it.
（１）ア．Are　　イ．Did　　ウ．Do　　エ．Have
（２）ア．next week　　イ．last week
　　　ウ．tomorrow　　エ．now
（３）ア．how　　イ．what
　　　ウ．which　　エ．who
（４）ア．could　　イ．couldn't
　　　ウ．should　　エ．shouldn't
＜宮崎県＞

18 次の会話文について，（　）に入る最も適切なもの
を次のア～カのうちから１つ選び，その記号を書き
なさい。ただし，文頭にくる文字も小文字になっています。

A :（　①　） was your speaking test in English
　class? It was difficult for me.
B : I did OK. Did you prepare well?
A : Yes, but I should study harder next time.
B : Well, I have a good idea. I have a friend
　（　②　） speaks English very well. He
　（　③　） English in Australia when he was
　little.
A : Ah, I know him.
　ア．studied　　イ．has studied　　ウ．who
　エ．whose　　オ．which　　　　　カ．how
＜沖縄県＞

19 次の対話の（　１　）～（　４　）に入る最も適切なもの
を，それぞれア～エから１つずつ選び，記号で答え
なさい。

A : Those pictures on the wall（　１　）good.
B : Thanks. I（　２　）them on New Year's Day
　this year.
A : That's nice. Who's the man（　３　）a
　kimono?
B : He's my（　４　）. He's my mother's brother.
（　１　）ア．am　　　　イ．is
　　　　　ウ．are　　　　エ．be
（　２　）ア．take　　　 イ．took
　　　　　ウ．taken　　 エ．am taking
（　３　）ア．wear　　　イ．wore
　　　　　ウ．worn　　 エ．wearing
（　４　）ア．uncle　　 イ．aunt
　　　　　ウ．son　　　エ．daughter
＜宮崎県＞

20 次の１～３の対話文の｜￣￣｜に入れるのに最も適
当なものを，それぞれ下のア～エから一つ選び，記
号で答えなさい。

1．A : Where is Taro now? I'm looking for him.
　　B : I saw him at the ｜￣￣｜. He was
　　　waiting for a train for Aso.
　ア．hospital　　　　イ．library
　ウ．museum　　　　エ．station
2．A : Do you know this book?
　　B : Yes. It's *Kusamakura*. It ｜￣￣｜ *Natsume
　　　Soseki* more than 100 years ago.
　ア．is written by　　イ．was written by
　ウ．is writing　　　 エ．was writing
3．A : Should I bring something to the party?
　　B : Everything is ready, so you ｜￣￣｜
　　　bring anything.
　ア．must　　　　　 イ．should
　ウ．don't have to　 エ．didn't
＜熊本県＞

21 次の(ア)～(エ)の文の（　）の中に入れるのに最も適す
るものを，あとの１～４の中からそれぞれ一つずつ
選び，その番号を答えなさい。

(ア)（　　　） do you have for breakfast, rice or
　*bread?
　1．When　　　2．Which
　3．Why　　　 4．How

(イ) The new library near the station（　　　）
　great.
　1．looks　　　 2．sees
　3．gives　　　 4．takes
(ウ) She（　　　） cold water when she arrived at
　school.
　1．drinks　　　 2．is drinking
　3．drank　　　　4．has drunk
(エ) My grandfather lives in Osaka, and I（　　　）
　him for two months.
　1．don't see　　　2．was seeing
　3．was seen　　　4．haven't seen
　(注) bread　パン
＜神奈川県＞

22 次の英文中の ｜(1)｜ から ｜(6)｜ に入る語として，下
の(1)から(6)のア，イ，ウ，エのうち，それぞれ最も
適切なものはどれか。

　Hello, everyone. Do you like ｜(1)｜ movies?
Me? Yes, I ｜(2)｜. I'll introduce my favorite
movie. It is "The Traveling of the Amazing Girl."
The story is ｜(3)｜ a girl who travels through
time. Some troubles happen, but she can solve
｜(4)｜. The story is ｜(5)｜, and the music
is also exciting. The movie was made a long time
ago, but even now it is very popular. It is a great
movie. If you were the girl, what ｜(6)｜ you
do?

(1)　ア．watch　　　　 イ．watches
　　 ウ．watching　　　エ．watched
(2)　ア．am　 イ．do　 ウ．is　 エ．does
(3)　ア．about　 イ．in　 ウ．to　 エ．with
(4)　ア．they　 イ．their　 ウ．them　 エ．theirs
(5)　ア．empty　　　　イ．fantastic
　　 ウ．narrow　　　 エ．terrible
(6)　ア．can　 イ．may　 ウ．must　 エ．would
＜栃木県＞

23 次の①～③は，それぞれAとBの対話です。（　　）
に入る最も適当なものを，ア～エの中からそれぞれ
一つずつ選びなさい。

①　〔*In a party*〕
　A : Wow! Your bag is really pretty.
　B : Thanks. This is（　　　）. I borrowed it
　　from her today.
　ア．mine　　　　 イ．yours
　ウ．my sister's　 エ．my bag
②　〔*In the morning*〕
　A : Oh, I'll be late! I need more time to eat
　　breakfast.
　B : Get up earlier,（　　　）you'll have more
　　time.
　ア．and　 イ．or　 ウ．but　 エ．that
③　〔*In a classroom*〕
　A : Hi, my name is Yumi. If you have any
　　questions,（　　　）.
　B : Thank you. I'm John. Well, could you tell me
　　how to get to the computer room?
　ア．you will play the guitar with me
　イ．please feel free to ask me
　ウ．I would get along with you
　エ．let me give you some examples
＜福島県＞

24 次の対話文(1)〜(4)の　□　に入る最も適当な英語を，下のア〜エのうちからそれぞれ一つずつ選び，その記号を書きなさい。　（各2点，計8点）

(1) A : Do you like reading books, Tom?
　　B : Yes. I want to read Japanese manga. □ there a library in this town?
　　A : Yes. You can enjoy reading many Japanese manga there.
　　ア. Do　イ. Does　ウ. Are　エ. Is

(2) A : We'll have a party this Friday. Everything is ready.
　　B : Oh, is it?
　　A : Yes. So you □ have to bring anything for the party.
　　B : OK. I can't wait!
　　ア. aren't　イ. can　ウ. don't　エ. should

(3) A : Do you know where Mary is?
　　B : Yes. She's at home. She didn't come to school today.
　　A : What happened?
　　B : She □ sick since last week. I hope she'll come to school tomorrow.
　　ア. didn't have　イ. has been
　　ウ. isn't feeling　エ. was felt

(4) A : Do you sometimes want to go back to the past?
　　B : Yes, but of course we can't do that now.
　　A : If you □ go back to the past, what would you do?
　　B : I would say to myself, "You should do everything you want to do."
　　ア. could　イ. didn't　ウ. had　エ. weren't
　　　　　　　　　　　　　　　　　〈岩手県〉

25 次は，*Taro*と留学生の*Ann*との対話の一部である。これを読んで，下の(1)，(2)に答えなさい。

Ann : How do you usually spend New Year's Day?
Taro : Well, I go to my grandmother's house with my family ___(A)___ we have special food such as *ozoni*. Have you ever (B)(eat) *ozoni*?
Ann : No. What's that?
Taro : It's a Japanese traditional soup dish for New Year's Day. We ___(C)___ it *ozoni*.
Ann : A special dish for New Year's Day? That sounds interesting.
Taro : On New Year's Day this year, my aunt came to see us with her son. He was too little to eat *ozoni* well, so I helped him. I like to ___(D)___ little children. We enjoyed *ozoni* together.
　（注）spend 〜　〜を過ごす

(1) 下線部(A)，(C)，(D)に入る最も適切なものを，それぞれ1〜4から選び，記号で答えなさい。
　(A) 1. that　2. while　3. which　4. and
　(C) 1. give　2. call　3. try　4. show
　(D) 1. come from　2. arrive at
　　　 3. take care of　4. be famous for

(2) 下線部(B)の( )の中の単語を，適切な形にして書きなさい。
　　　　　　　　　　　　　　　　　　〈山口県〉

26 次の①〜③は，それぞれAとBの対話です。（ ）に入る最も適当なものを，ア〜エの中からそれぞれ一つずつ選びなさい。

① 〔*In a house*〕
　A : I'm hungry, Mom. What is today's lunch?
　B : I'm ( ) spaghetti. You said you wanted to eat it yesterday.
　ア. cook　イ. cooked
　ウ. cooks　エ. cooking

② 〔*In a classroom*〕
　A : What do you want to do when you visit your friend, Jane, in Australia?
　B : I want to show her ( ) make curry and rice because she likes it very much.
　ア. when to　イ. how to
　ウ. where to　エ. what to

③ 〔*At a shopping mall*〕
　A : Hey, Steve. ( ).
　B : Oh, Mike! Me, too! What are you going to buy here today?
　ア. You bought a very nice watch
　イ. I've never been there before
　ウ. I'm surprised to see you here
　エ. You took a lot of pictures there
　　　　　　　　　　　　　　　　　　〈福島県〉

27 次の対話文(1)〜(4)の　□　に入る最も適当な英語を，下のア〜エのうちからそれぞれ一つずつ選び，その記号を書きなさい。

(1) A : I had a good time with my friends yesterday.
　　B : What □ you do?
　　A : I saw an exciting movie with them.
　　ア. are　イ. did　ウ. do　エ. were

(2) A : What time do you usually start to study and take a bath?
　　B : I usually start to study at seven o'clock and take a bath at nine thirty.
　　A : So you take a bath □ you study, right?
　　B : Yes.
　　ア. after　イ. before
　　ウ. between　エ. during

(3) A : Do you have any pets?
　　B : Yes. I have a cat. How about you?
　　A : Well, I have a dog □ *Pochi*. What's the name of your cat?
　　B : It's *Tama*. She's very cute.
　　ア. said　イ. spoken
　　ウ. called　エ. talked

(4) A : Hi, Tom. You sang well at the chorus festival.
　　B : Thank you. I practice every day.
　　A : Are you going to try any contests?
　　B : Yes. I am going to □ a singing contest next week.
　　ア. get back from　イ. get up
　　ウ. take off　エ. take part in
　　　　　　　　　　　　　　　　　　〈岩手県〉

28 次は，ニュージーランド(New Zealand)で留学を始める*Kenji*と，留学先の学校の*Lee*先生との対話の一部である。これを読んで，下の(1)，(2)に答えなさい。

Ms. Lee : Hello, Kenji. Welcome to our school! You arrived ___(A)___ the airport this morning, right? How are you?

Kenji : I'm fine. But it's really hot here.

Ms. Lee : Oh, I know what you mean. It's winter in Japan now, right?

Kenji : Yes. Last week, I enjoyed skiing with my friends.

Ms. Lee : Really? I love skiing. I wish I (B)(　be　) in Japan now.

Kenji : 　(C)　, I saw a lot of unique street names on the way here.

Ms. Lee : Oh, they come from the 　(D)　 that Maori people speak. Maori people are indigenous to our country. We respect their culture.

Kenji : I see. Now I want to know more about New Zealand!

（注）skiing　スキー
　　　Maori　マオリ（ニュージーランドの先住民）の
　　　indigenous to～　～に先住している

(1) 下線部(A)，(C)，(D)に入る最も適切なものを，それぞれ1～4から1つずつ選び，記号で答えなさい。
　(A) 1．at　　2．for　　3．of　　4．to
　(C) 1．Every year　　2．As a result
　　　 3．By the way　　4．For example
　(D) 1．art　　　　2．language
　　　 3．school　　4．nature
(2) 下線部(B)の（　）の中の語を，適切な形にして書きなさい。

〈山口県〉

29 次のNo.1～No.3の会話を読み，（　）にあてはまる適切な英語を，それぞれ1語で答えなさい。
No.1
　Salesperson : Hello. May I help you?
　John　　　　 : Yes, I want to buy a T-shirt.
　Salesperson　 : (　　) about this blue one?
　　（注）salesperson　店員
No.2
　A man : Excuse me. Could you tell me the way to the nearest station?
　Kaori : Sure. Go down this street and (　　) right at the next corner. You'll find it on your left.
　A man : Thank you.
No.3
　Kate : It's very hot today. I want something to (　　).
　Mother : Sure. Here's some orange juice.
　Kate : Thank you.
問2．次のNo.1，No.2の英文を読み，（　）にあてはまる最も適切な語を，次のア～エからひとつずつ選び，記号で答えなさい。
No.1
　Erika likes (　　) at the store next to the library because things are not expensive there.
　　ア．studying　　イ．singing
　　ウ．reading　　エ．shopping
No.2
　I wanted to watch that TV program yesterday, (　　) I had no time to watch it.
　　ア．because　　イ．but　　ウ．if　　エ．or

〈鳥取県〉

30 次の英文中の　(1)　から　(6)　に入る語句として，下の(1)から(6)のア，イ，ウ，エのうち，それぞれ最も適切なものはどれか。
Sunday, May 10
　I went fishing in the Tochigi River with my brother, Takashi. It was the 　(1)　 time for me to fish in a river. Takashi 　(2)　 me how to fish. In the morning, he caught many fish, 　(3)　 I couldn't catch any fish. At noon, we had lunch which my mother made for 　(4)　. We really enjoyed it. In the afternoon, I tried again. I saw a big fish behind a rock. I waited for a chance for a long time, and finally I caught it! It was 　(5)　 than any fish that Takashi caught. I was 　(6)　 and had a great time.
　(1) ア．one　　　イ．first
　　　 ウ．every　　エ．all
　(2) ア．taught　　イ．called
　　　 ウ．helped　　エ．knew
　(3) ア．if　　　イ．because
　　　 ウ．or　　　エ．but
　(4) ア．we　　　イ．our
　　　 ウ．us　　　エ．ours
　(5) ア．big　　　イ．bigger
　　　 ウ．biggest　エ．more big
　(6) ア．boring　　イ．bored
　　　 ウ．exciting　エ．excited

〈栃木県〉

31 恵子(Keiko)と留学生のレオン(Leon)が話しています。二人の対話が成り立つように，下線部①から③までのそれぞれの（　）内に最も適当な語を入れて，英文を完成させなさい。ただし，（　）内に示されている文字で始まる語を解答すること。

Keiko : Hi, Leon. How are you enjoying your new life in Nagoya?

Leon : Hi, Keiko. It's great. I traveled a lot. ①It's not (d　　　) to travel (b　　　) train. I can find some train stations near my host family's house, so it's convenient.

Keiko : I see your point. How about your school life?

Leon : It's exciting because I have new classmates. ②They often (h　　　) me (l　　　) Japanese. Thanks to them, I understand many Japanese words and enjoy my life here.

Keiko : Sounds good. What do you think about our school uniform?

Leon : I like it and I think school uniforms save time. ③We don't (h　　　) to (c　　　) clothes every morning!

〈愛知県・Bグループ〉

32 次の対話文(1)～(4)の　　　　に入る最も適当な英語を，下のア～エのうちからそれぞれ一つずつ選び，その記号を書きなさい。
(1) A : What time do you usually get up?
　　B : I usually get up at seven o'clock, but I got up at six this morning.
　　A : Oh, 　　　　 you? I got up at six, too.
　　ア．are　　　　イ．were
　　ウ．does　　　エ．did

— 9 —

(2) A : Let's clean the classroom.
　　B : OK. Oh, there is a dictionary on the desk.
　　A : _____ dictionary is it?
　　B : It's Tony's. His name is on it.
　ア．Where　　　イ．Which
　ウ．Whose　　　エ．Why

(3) A : Do you like Japanese movies, John?
　　B : Yes, I love them.
　　A : Is English _____ on the screen?
　　B : Yes, so I can enjoy watching Japanese movies.
　ア．shown　　　イ．showing
　ウ．speaking　　エ．spoke

(4) A : I have been sick since this morning.
　　B : Oh, really?　How do you feel now?
　　A : Not so good. I will go to bed earlier.
　　B : If I _____ you, I would go to the doctor.
　ア．am　　　　イ．were
　ウ．wish　　　エ．wished
　　　　　　　　　　　　　　　　　　　　　〈岩手県〉

33 次の①〜③は，それぞれAとBの対話です。（　）に入る最も適当なものを，ア〜エの中からそれぞれ一つずつ選びなさい。

① 〔After school〕
　A : You started learning the piano, right? When do you have piano lessons?
　B : Well, I have piano lessons (　　　) weekends.
　ア．with　　イ．for　　ウ．on　　エ．under

② 〔In a classroom〕
　A : My father will take me to the zoo this Saturday. Would you like to come with us?
　B : I'd love to, but I can't. I (　　　) my homework.
　ア．have to do　　イ．have done
　ウ．have to play　エ．have played

③ 〔At lunchtime〕
　A : Hey, Mike. Our baseball team got the trophy.
　B : Really? (　　　) Tell me more about it.
　ア．Guess what!
　イ．You are welcome.
　ウ．I'm sorry to buy that.
　エ．What a surprise!
　　　　　　　　　　　　　　　　　　　　　〈福島県〉

34 モリ先生（Mr. Mori）が留学生のティナ（Tina），ジム（Jim）と話をしています。次の会話文を読んで，下の(1)，(2)の問いに答えなさい。

Mr. Mori : Tina, your Japanese is very good. How long have you been studying Japanese?
Tina : Thank you. For three years. I talk a lot with my *host family in Japanese but it is difficult to read Japanese, especially *kanji*. I ①(w　　　) I could read all the *kanji* *characters.
Mr. Mori : I see. *Kanji* will help you understand Japanese better. Jim, you have lived in Japan longer than Tina. You are good at ②(b　　　) speaking and reading Japanese. How do you usually ③(p　　　) reading Japanese?

Jim : I read many books ④(　write　) in easy Japanese. You can learn a lot of Japanese little by little. Now, I often read *manga*. Reading it is ⑤(　easy　) than reading other kinds of books.
Mr. Mori : That's good not only for ⑥(　child　) but also for adults. It is very important to enjoy studying.
　　(注) host family　ホストファミリー
　　　　character(s)　文字　　*manga*　マンガ

(1) 会話文が完成するように，文中の①〜③の（　）内に，最も適切な英語を，それぞれ1語ずつ書きなさい。なお，答えはすべて，（　）内に示されている文字で書き始めるものとします。

(2) 会話文が完成するように，文中の④〜⑥の（　）の中の語を，それぞれ1語で適切な形に直して書きなさい。
　　　　　　　　　　　　　　　　　　　　　〈茨城県〉

35 次の(1)〜(2)の問いに答えなさい。

(1) 次の①〜④について，（例）を参考にして，〔説明〕が示す英語1語を（　）に書き，英文を完成させなさい。ただし，答えは（　）内に示されている文字で書き始めること。

　（例）　He likes (h　　　) very much. He's interested in old foreign events.
　〔説明〕　all the events that have already happened
　　　　　　　　　　　　　　　〔答え〕（history）

① I have a friend who lives in Midori City. I visited him last (S　　　).
　〔説明〕　the day of the week before Sunday
② If you want to borrow some books, you should go to a (l　　　).
　〔説明〕　a building which has many books, newspapers and so on
③ That supermarket has become (p　　　) because it sells many kinds of vegetables.
　〔説明〕　liked or enjoyed by a lot of people
④ I like to (c　　　) cards of this anime character. I have many cards of the character.
　〔説明〕　to get things from different places

(2) 次の①〜③について，（例）を参考にして，〈　　　〉の状況の会話がそれぞれ成り立つように _____ 内の語に必要な2語を加え，正しい語順で英文を完成させなさい。ただし，文頭にくる語は，最初の文字を大文字にすること。

　（例）　〈留学生と教室で〉
　Mike : _____ pen _____ this?
　Naoki : Oh, it's mine. Thank you, Mike.
　　　　　　　　　　　　〔答え〕　Whose pen is

① 〈ALTの先生との授業中のやり取りで〉
　Kana : I visited Kyoto last week.
　Ms. Smith : Good. _____ you _____ go there?
　Kana : I went there by train. I had a lot of fun there.
② 〈留学生と休日に〉
　Ben : I'll go skiing next month.
　Kanako : Nice!　I think skiing is the _____ exciting _____ all winter sports.

③〈留学生と職員室の前で〉
Kevin ：What did Mr. Sato say to you, Takeru?
Takeru ：He told 　go　 to the science room after lunch.

〈秋田県〉

36 次の各問いに答えなさい。

問1．次のNo.1～No.3の会話を読み，（　）にあてはまる最も適切な英語を，それぞれ1語で答えなさい。
No.1
George ：What（　　）did you get up today?
Emi 　 ：At seven thirty. I was late for school this morning.
No.2
Sachie ：How long have you lived in Tottori?
Daniel ：I have been here（　　）five years.
No.3
Henry 　：Look! That mountain is beautiful.
Kimiko ：Yes.（　　）is also fun to climb it. Let's go together someday.

問2．次のNo.1，No.2の英文を読み，（　）にあてはまる最も適切な英語を，次のア～エからひとつずつ選び，記号で答えなさい。
No.1
I bought this computer yesterday, but it doesn't （　　）. What should I do?
　ア．use　　イ．break　　ウ．work　　エ．go
No.2
I have decided（　　）to go next summer. I will go to Okinawa to swim in the sea.
　ア．where　　イ．when
　ウ．how　　エ．which way

問3．次のマット（Matt）さんと，はるき（Haruki）さんの会話を読み，（　）内の語を必要に応じて適切な形に変えたり，不足している語を補ったりして，会話が成り立つように英語を完成させなさい。
〈はるきさんの家で〉
Matt 　：You have very nice cups.
Haruki ：Thank you.
　　　　I bought these cups last year.
　　　　（make）by a famous *artist in my town.
　　（注）artist　芸術家

〈鳥取県〉

37 次の各問いに答えなさい。

問1．次のNo.1～No.3の会話を読み，（　）にあてはまる最も適切な英語を，それぞれ1語で答えなさい。
No.1
Mother ：I saw an English book on the table. Is it yours?
Son 　 ：Yes, it's（　　）. I bought it yesterday.
Mother ：Really? It looks interesting. Can I borrow it?
No.2
Meg 　　　　　　：Hello. This is Meg. May I（　　）to Yuto, please?
Yuto's father ：Sorry, he's not here. Do you want to leave a message?
Meg 　　　　　　：Yes. Could you tell him to come to my house at four o'clock?

No.3
Miki ：This is a new kind of rice made in Tottori.
Bob 　：Wow! It's so good. Does this rice have a name?
Miki ：We（　　）it Hoshizora-mai. The name comes from Tottori's beautiful sky which has many stars.

問2．次のNo.1，No.2の英文を読み，（　）にあてはまる最も適当な英語を，次のア～エからひとつずつ選び，記号で答えなさい。
No.1
I usually walk in the park in the evening. Then I start cooking dinner.
Walking（　　）dinner always makes me hungry.
　ア．after　　イ．before
　ウ．with　　エ．over
No.2
Don't take any food to the school library. You （　　）eat there.
　ア．should
　イ．can
　ウ．don't have to
　エ．must not

問3．次の会話を読み，（　）内の語を適切な形に変えたり，不足している語を補ったりして，会話が成り立つように英語を完成させなさい。
〈週明けに教室で〉
A ：What did you do last weekend?
B ：I went to the park with my friend.（ enjoy ） playing soccer together for two hours.

〈鳥取県〉

38 次の問いに答えなさい。

1．次の対話文の（　）の中に最も適する英語を，それぞれ1語ずつ書きなさい。
(1) *Lucy* ：You are a good baseball player. How （　　）have you been playing it?
　　Akira ：Since I was six. It's my favorite sport.
(2) *Bill* ：How was the（　　）in Kyoto yesterday?
　　Keiko ：It was sunny at first, but it started to rain when I left Kyoto.
(3) *Sakura* ：According to our research, forty-eight percent of our class comes to school by bike.
　　Kevin ：Does about（　　）of the class ride a bike to get here? That's a lot.

2．次の対話文の（　）の中に最も適するものを，あとのア～エからそれぞれ一つずつ選び，記号で答えなさい。
(1) *Kate* 　：Have you read this book yet?
　　Shinji ：No, I haven't. How about you?
　　Kate 　：I read it yesterday. It was very exciting because...
　　Shinji ：Please stop!（　　）
　ア．I also read the book yesterday.
　イ．I have already read it.
　ウ．I will read the book again soon.
　エ．I am going to read it tomorrow.
(2) *Peter* ：I brought too many sandwiches for my lunch.

— 11 —

Hitomi : Wow! Did you think you could eat all of them?

Peter : Yes. I thought I could when I bought them, but now I can't. Can you eat some for me?

Hitomi : OK. (　　　　　)

ア．I am surprised that you love making so many sandwiches.

イ．I will have one, but you should also ask others to help you.

ウ．I don't think you can eat more, but you still say you can.

エ．I should buy some for you because you ate all of them.

<山形県>

39 次の(1)〜(3)に答えなさい。

(1) 次の英文(a)・(b)の意味が通るように，(　　　)に最も適するものを，それぞれア〜エから1つずつ選びなさい。

(a) My sister likes curry and rice very much, (　　　) I don't.
　ア．so　イ．or　ウ．and　エ．but

(b) Mr. Brown often washes his car when he (　　　) free time.
　ア．has　イ．feels　ウ．saves　エ．studies

(2) 次の対話文(a)〜(c)を読んで，　　　　に最も適するものを，それぞれア〜エから1つずつ選びなさい。

(a) A : Are you using your dictionary now?
　B : 　　　　　 You can use it.
　A : Oh, thank you. I forgot mine at home.
　ア．Yes, I am.　イ．Yes, I can.
　ウ．No, I'm not.　エ．No, I can't.

(b) A : Did you watch the weather report? It will be rainy this afternoon.
　B : Oh, no. 　　　　　
　A : Well, why don't we watch a movie at home?
　B : OK. Then let's play tennis next Sunday.
　ア．We have to leave home soon.
　イ．We should play tennis at the park.
　ウ．We should cook at home.
　エ．We have to change our plans.

(c) A : I read a very exciting book last weekend.
　B : Did you? 　　　　　
　A : It's a true story about a doctor who saved a lot of people.
　ア．Where can you get it?
　イ．Who wrote the book?
　ウ．What kind of book is it?
　エ．Which one is your favorite?

(3) 次の対話が成り立つように，(　　　)の中のア〜エを並べかえなさい。ただし，文頭の語も小文字で示してある。

A : From tomorrow, I have summer vacation for one week.
B : Great. (ア．were　イ．you　ウ．if　エ．I), I would go abroad.

<徳島県>

40 次の(1)〜(3)に答えなさい。

(1) 次の英文(a)・(b)の意味が通るように，(　　　)に最も適するものを，それぞれア〜エから1つずつ選びなさい。

(a) The Midori Festival is the biggest (　　　　　) in our town.
　ア．event　イ．forest　ウ．park　エ．school

(b) I had a great time with my friends in Kyoto. I'll never (　　　) about it.
　ア．know　イ．hear　ウ．enjoy　エ．forget

(2) 次の対話文(a)〜(c)を読んで，　　　　に最も適するものを，それぞれア〜エから1つずつ選びなさい。

(a) A : Do you and your brother play baseball?
　B : 　　　　　 We play on the same team.
　ア．Yes, I do.　イ．No, I don't.
　ウ．Yes, we do.　エ．No, we don't.

(b) A : If you have any questions about history, you should ask Emma. She is a walking dictionary.
　B : A walking dictionary? 　　　　　
　A : A walking dictionary is someone who knows a lot. Emma knows a lot about history.
　ア．What do you think?
　イ．What do you mean?
　ウ．What do you have?
　エ．What do you need?

(c) A : Why don't we eat lunch at the new Chinese restaurant? I hear we can try various kinds of noodles.
　B : I'm sorry. 　　　　　 How about tomorrow?
　A : OK. Let's meet in front of Aoba Station at eleven thirty.
　ア．I've just finished my lunch.
　イ．I don't usually make my lunch.
　ウ．I don't like eating noodles.
　エ．I've never been to China before.

(3) 次の対話が成り立つように，(　　　)の中のア〜エを並べかえなさい。

A : Do you know (ア．your mother　イ．talking　ウ．with　エ．the man)?
B : Yes, he's my uncle.

<徳島県>

41 次の問いに答えなさい。

1．次の対話文の(　　　)の中に最も適する英語を，それぞれ1語ずつ書きなさい。

(1) *Ichiro* : In Japan, we have four (　　　　　), and I like spring.
　Dave : I like winter because I can go skiing.

(2) *Paul* : Please tell me (　　　　) to carry this table.
　Nanami : To the room on the third floor.

(3) *Student* : I learned a new word. If a child is a boy, he is a 'son' to his father and mother.
　Teacher : Yes. If a child is a girl, she is a '(　　　　)'.

2．次の対話文の(　　　)の中に最も適するものを，あとのア〜エからそれぞれ一つずつ選び，記号で答えなさい。

(1) *Student* : Mr. Kato, we want to choose a song which our class will sing at the chorus contest.

Mr. Kato : OK. Please make groups of four students and talk about it.

Student : But there are thirty-three students in our class.

Mr. Kato : (　　　　　　　)

ア．Then, let's sing some of the songs.

イ．Then, let's make ideas in the groups.

ウ．Then, let's listen to thirty-three songs.

エ．Then, let's make one group of five students.

(2) *Haruka* : Did you read the e-mail about the New Year's party?

Brian : Yes, I did. Thank you for sending me the e-mail. I will go to the party.

Haruka : Great. I really want to join it, too. (　　　　　　　)

Brian : I hope you can come.

ア．I couldn't write the e-mail because my computer was very old.

イ．I didn't send you the e-mail because I was so busy.

ウ．I couldn't go to the party last year because I was sick.

エ．I didn't invite you to the party because you had homework to do.

〈山形県〉

42 Choose the phrase that best completes each sentence below.

(1) I'm (　　　　　　　) are kind to you.

ア．glad to all that your neighbors hear

イ．glad that hear to your neighbors all

ウ．glad to hear that all your neighbors

エ．your neighbors that glad to hear all

(2) The book (　　　　　　　) a difficult math question.

ア．answer me helped my father gave me

イ．gave me answer me helped my father

ウ．helped my father gave me answer me

エ．my father gave me helped me answer

(3) I could play basketball (　　　　　　　) to practice.

ア．as well as my brother if I had more time

イ．well if I had more time as my brother as

ウ．if time more I had as well as my brother

エ．if I had time my brother as more well as

(4) The soccer player (　　　　　　　) Japan.

ア．came to many people who is loved by

イ．loved by many people who is came to

ウ．is loved to many people who came by

エ．who is loved by many people came to

(5) (　　　　　　　) wonderful.

ア．The idea sounds in our group shared

イ．Our group sounds the idea shared in

ウ．The idea shared in our group sounds

エ．Our group shared the idea sounds in

(6) I want to know (　　　　　　　) by plane.

ア．London takes many hours how to go to it

イ．how many hours it takes to go to London

ウ．how to go to London it takes many hours

エ．how many it takes hours to go to London

〈大阪府・Ｃ問題〉

43 Choose the phrase that best completes each sentence below.

(1) The boy (　　　　　　　) is my brother.

ア．who the contest won twice

イ．won who the contest twice

ウ．who won the contest twice

エ．won the contest twice who

(2) The students were (　　　　　　　) the school gate.

ア．excited to find a sleeping cat beside

イ．sleeping to excited find a cat beside

ウ．excited beside to a sleeping cat find

エ．sleeping excited to beside a cat find

(3) I want to know (　　　　　　　) every day.

ア．that singer practices how many hours

イ．how many hours practices that singer

ウ．that singer how many hours practices

エ．how many hours that singer practices

(4) The present (　　　　　　　) to get for a long time.

ア．she gave me I was wanted the one

イ．was the one I wanted she gave me

ウ．she gave me was the one I wanted

エ．was she gave me the one I wanted

(5) The book gave (　　　　　　　) prepare for the trip abroad.

ア．enough information to learn to me what

イ．me enough to learn information to what

ウ．enough to me what information to learn

エ．me enough information to learn what to

(6) I will (　　　　　　　) me until the exam is over.

ア．keep to watch the DVDs from I want away

イ．watch the DVDs I keep away from want to

ウ．keep the DVDs I want to watch away from

エ．watch the DVDs to keep I want from away

〈大阪府・Ｃ問題〉

44 Choose the phrase that best completes each sentence below.

(1) Do you (　　　　　　　) your bag?

ア．have everything in you need that

イ．need that have everything in you

ウ．have everything that you need in

エ．need everything have you that in

(2) The officer (　　　　　　　) to go.

ア．standing there will show you which way

イ．will you show which way standing there

ウ．standing which way there you will show

エ．will show you way there which standing

(3) The machine (　　　　　　　).

ア．easily clean my room helps me

イ．helps me my room clean easily

ウ．easily clean me helps my room

エ．helps me clean my room easily

(4) I wish I (　　　　　　　).

ア．speak you could as fluently as French

イ．could speak French as fluently as you

ウ．speak you as fluently as could French

エ．could you speak French as fluently as

(5) The letter (　　　　　　　) in his house.

ア．which he lost many years ago was found

イ．was found which many years lost ago he

— 13 —

ウ．which was lost found he many years ago
エ．was lost many years ago he found which

(6) I will (　　　　) the piano in the festival.
　ア．play to my teacher let me ask
　イ．ask my teacher to let me play
　ウ．play my teacher let me ask to
　エ．ask to let me my teacher play

＜大阪府・C問題＞

45

次の1～3の各組の対話が成り立つように，□A□～□D□にあてはまる最も適当なものを，それぞれのア～エから一つ選び，記号を書け。

1. {
　John　：Will you watch the rugby game on TV next Sunday?
　Takumi：Oh, the Japanese national team?
　John　：Yes. You should watch it! □A□
　Takumi：How about watching it together at my house?
}

A. {
　ア．I have already watched the game.
　イ．I think the game will be exciting.
　ウ．I will play rugby in the game.
　エ．I wanted you to win the game.
}

2. {
　Mother：Tom! Emily! Please help me carry these bags.
　Tom　：Sure. You bought a lot of food today.
　Mother：Yes, for our party tomorrow. Where is Emily?
　Tom　：She is in her room. □B□
　Mother：Wow, she is very interested in that book.
}

B. {
　ア．She has been to parties many times.
　イ．She has no book to read there.
　ウ．She has to buy more food at the shop.
　エ．She has been reading a book for three hours.
}

3. {
　Kumi　：Ms. Beck, I have a question for my report. What do you do for your health every day?
　Ms. Beck：I run for 50 minutes every morning.
　Kumi　：Sounds hard. □C□
　Ms. Beck：Yes. I feel good and can sleep well.
　Kumi　：How can you keep doing it?
　Ms. Beck：□D□ So, I can see something new when I run.
　Kumi　：How wonderful! Thank you for your time, Ms. Beck.
}

C. {
　ア．Are there any good points about running for you?
　イ．Is it difficult for me to run every day?
　ウ．Do you have any problems when you run?
　エ．Do you want to stop running in the future?
}

D. {
　ア．Running is a good topic for my report.
　イ．Running in the morning is boring for me.
　ウ．I take different running courses every day.
　エ．I feel tired after running in the morning.
}

＜福岡県＞

46

次の1～3の各組の対話が成り立つように，□A□～□D□にあてはまる最も適当なものを，それぞれのア～エから一つ選び，記号を書け。

1. {
　Fumiko　：Mr. Jones, I received some big news today. Did you hear about Shelly?
　Mr. Jones：Big news about Shelly? □A□
　Fumiko　：She decided to go back to Canada this winter. I'm so sad.
　Mr. Jones：Oh, I didn't know that.
}

A. {
　ア．What do you mean?
　イ．When will you get the news?
　ウ．OK. Here you are.
　エ．Of course, you are.
}

2. {
　Ken　：I can't go shopping with you tomorrow. Can we change the day?
　Daniel：No problem. When is good for you?
　Ken　：□B□
　Daniel：Sure, that's good because we have club activities in the morning.
　Ken　：Thanks, Daniel.
}

B. {
　ア．How will the weather be on Saturday?
　イ．How about next Saturday afternoon?
　ウ．I will be busy on Saturday morning.
　エ．I think Saturday is the best for studying.
}

3. {
　Satoru：Hi, Kacy. Are you going to play in the piano contest next week?
　Kacy　：Yes, I am. How did you know that?
　Satoru：□C□ She told me about it then. Are you nervous?
　Kacy　：I was nervous one month ago, but now I think I will enjoy playing the piano in front of everyone in the hall.
　Satoru：Wow! □D□ Why can you think that way?
　Kacy　：Because I practiced many times. Now I believe I can do well.
　Satoru：How wonderful!
}

C. {
　ア．My sister didn't know about the contest.
　イ．I don't know how to play the piano.
　ウ．Your sister will come to my house tomorrow.
　エ．I met your sister at the station yesterday.
}

D. {
　ア．If I were you, I couldn't think like that.
　イ．I know you're still nervous.
　ウ．I think you worry too much.
　エ．I wish you could join the contest.
}

＜福岡県＞

b．そのほかの問題

1 次のクリスマスカードは，中学生のSachikoが，オーストラリアにいる友人Judyからもらったものです。また，後の英文は，Sachikoが送ったお礼のメールです。これを読んで，英文の意味が通るように，（ア）～（オ）に当てはまる単語を後の〔　　〕内からそれぞれ1語選び，必要があれば適切な形に変えて書きなさい。

Hi Judy,

I've just（　ア　）your Christmas card. Thank you very much. I like the picture of *Santa Claus. He is（　イ　）with fish and looks so happy!

In the card, you say that you will go to the sea with your family on Christmas. That's amazing! If I（　ウ　）in Australia, I could go to the sea with you.

Please tell me more about Christmas in summer. How does Santa Claus bring presents to children? Are there any popular Christmas songs（　エ　）by many people in Australia?

I'll（　オ　）a New Year's card to you soon.

Sachiko

（注）Santa Claus　サンタクロース

〔begin　live　receive　send　sing
swim　win〕

<群馬県>

2 次の各問いの会話文について，（　　）に入る1語を語群から選び，自然な会話になるように，適切な形に変えて書きなさい。ただし，語群の単語はそれぞれ1度しか使えません。

問1．A：I have three cats. Their names are Shiro, Tama, and Mike.
　　　B：So cute!　Are they the same age?
　　　A：No, Shiro is the（　　　　）of the three.
問2．A：What did you buy at the store?
　　　B：I got a book（　　　　）in English.
問3．A：Welcome to our party, Ryo!
　　　B：Hi, Bob. Thank you for（　　　　）me.
問4．A：I really like this band.
　　　B：Oh, I have never（　　　　）their music before.

語群：long　old　hear　write　watch
　　　invite

<沖縄県>

3 次の各問いの会話文について，（　　）に入る1語をあとの語群から選び，自然な会話になるように適切な形に変えて1語で書きなさい。ただし，語群の単語はそれぞれ1度しか使えません。

問1．A：I visited Hokkaido last month for the first time.
　　　B：Really?　I have never（　　　　）there.
問2．A：It was very hot yesterday.
　　　B：Yes, it was, but today is（　　　　）than yesterday.
問3．A：Did you know that French is（　　　　）in Canada?
　　　B：Really?　I had no idea.
問4．A：I saw a man who won ￥100,000 on the quiz show yesterday.
　　　B：Wow!　If I had that money, I（　　　　）buy a new smartphone.

語群：can　hot　speak　be

<沖縄県>

4 次の英文は，高校1年生の生徒が，英語の授業について書いた感想です。
　　① ～ ③ に入る英語を，あとの語群から選び，必要に応じて適切な形に変えたり，不足している語を補ったりして，英文を完成させなさい。ただし，2語以内で答えること。

Our class had a speech contest. Before the contest, I needed　①　very hard for it. I felt relaxed when I finally　②　making my speech during the contest. By　③　to the speeches of my classmates, I learned how to make a better speech for the next time.

| finish　get　listen　practice　receive |

<兵庫県>

5 (1)～(3)について，下の〔例〕を参考にしながら，（　　）内の語を含めて3語以上使用して，英文を完成させよ。ただし，（　　）内の語は必要に応じて形を変えてもよい。また，文頭に来る語は，最初の文字を大文字にすること。

〔例〕

〈教室で〉
A：What were you doing when I called you yesterday?
B：（study）in my room.　　（答）I was studying

(1)　〈教室で〉
　　A：When did you see the movie?
　　B：（see）yesterday.
(2)　〈教室で〉
　　A：It's rainy today. How about tomorrow?
　　B：I hear that it（sunny）tomorrow.
(3)　〈家で〉
　　A：Can you use this old camera?
　　B：No, but our father knows（use）it.

<鹿児島県>

6 次の各問いの会話文について，（　　）に入る単語を語群から選び，自然な会話になるように必要であれば適切な形に変えて1語で書きなさい。ただし，語群の単語はそれぞれ1度しか使えません。

問1．A：Look!　There is Mt. Fuji.
　　　B：Wow!　I have never （　　　） such a beautiful mountain.
問2．A：It's cold today.
　　　B：Really?　I think it's （　　　） than yesterday.
問3．A：Who is the man （　　　） the guitar on the bench?　He is making a beautiful sound.
　　　B：Oh, he is my brother.　He loves music.
問4．A：Will it （　　　） a fine day tomorrow?
　　　B：I have no idea.　Let's check the weather news.

> 語群：be　warm　easy　play　see
> 　　　come

〈沖縄県〉

7 次は，中学生の未来(Miku)と留学生のルーシー(Lucy)が，お互いの持ち物について会話をしている場面です。（　　）内の①～④の語を，それぞれ適切な形に直して英語1語で書き，会話を完成させなさい。

Miku：Oh, you have a nice bag. Where did you find it?
Lucy：I （① find） it at the new shop near my house last week. This is my favorite *brand.
Miku：I know that brand. I like the design. It's very famous, so （② get） it is difficult, right?
Lucy：Yes. Oh, you have a new bag, too. I've never seen this kind of design.
Miku：This small bag was made by my grandmother. She （③ give） it to me last month. This type of small bag is called *gamaguchi* in Japan.
Lucy：*Gamaguchi*?　What's that?
Miku：It means a *toad's mouth. It opens *wide, so it's easy to put small things into it. I think this *gamaguchi* is （④ good） than my old bag.

（注）brand　銘柄
　　　toad's mouth　ヒキガエルの口
　　　wide　広く

〈茨城県〉

8 次はSotaと留学生のLucyとの対話である。①～③について，［例］を参考にしながら，（　　）内の語に必要な2語を加えて，英文を完成させよ。ただし，（　　）内の語は必要に応じて形を変えてもよい。また，文頭に来る語は，最初の文字を大文字にすること。

> ［例］　A：What were you doing when I called you yesterday?
> 　　　　B：（study） in my room.
> 　　　　　　　　　　　（答）I was studying

Sota：Hi, Lucy. What books are you reading?　Oh, are they history books?
Lucy：Yes. ①（like）. They are very interesting.

Sota：Then, maybe you will like this. This is a picture of an old house in Izumi.
Lucy：Wow!　It's very beautiful. Did you take this picture?
Sota：No, my father did. ②（visit） it many times to take pictures. I hear it's the oldest building there.
Lucy：How old is the house?
Sota：③（build） more than 250 years ago.
Lucy：Oh, I want to see it soon.

〈鹿児島県〉

9 次の各問いに答えなさい。

1．次の英文は，高校1年生の生徒が，英語の授業で放課後の予定について話した内容です。　①　～　③　に入る英語を，あとの語群から選び，必要に応じて適切な形に変えたり，不足している語を補ったりして，英文を完成させなさい。ただし，2語以内で答えること。

　　Today, my parents are very busy. So I'm going 　①　 curry and rice for them tonight. I'll use fresh vegetables my grandmother 　②　 to us yesterday. I'll go shopping when school 　③　. I hope they'll like my curry and rice.

> cook　eat　finish　give　grow

2．次の表の右側には，左側の語のグループに属する語が並んでいます。（①）～（③）に入る語を，例を参考にしながら，それぞれ英語1語で書きなさい。

例	weather	cloudy,　rainy,　snowy,　sunny　など

（　①　）	spring,　summer,　fall,　winter
meal	（　②　），　lunch,　dinner　など
（　③　）	blue,　brown,　purple,　red,　yellow　など

〈兵庫県〉

10 次の(1)～(5)の対話文を完成させなさい。(1), (2)については，それぞれの（　　）の中の語を最も適当な形にしなさい。ただし，英単語1語で答えること。また，(3)～(5)については，それぞれの（　　）の中のア～オを正しい語順に並べかえ，その順序を符号で示しなさい。

(1)　A：Good job!　That was a great dance!
　　　B：Thank you. The （perform） was difficult, but it was exciting.
(2)　A：I hear Oliver broke his leg and couldn't play in the soccer game.
　　　B：If I were you, I （will） visit his house and cheer him up.
(3)　A：What a wonderful idea Luna had!
　　　B：I think so, too. She （ア. good　イ. making　ウ. is　エ. plans　オ. at ）.
(4)　A：Do you （ア. a towel　イ. looking　ウ. someone　エ. for　オ. know ）?
　　　B：Yes, Kevin has lost his towel.
(5)　A：Will you （ア. the　イ. show　ウ. you　エ. pictures　オ. me ） took on your trip?

B：OK！ I have many happy memories from the trip.

11 次の(1)～(5)のそれぞれの対話文を完成させなさい。(1)，(2)については，（ ）内の語を最も適当な形にしなさい。ただし，1語で答えること。

また，(3)～(5)については，それぞれの（ ）の中のア～オを正しい語順に並べかえ，その順序を符号で示しなさい。

(1) A：There (be) many trees around here 20 years ago.
　　B：Really？ We can only see tall buildings now.
(2) A：I hear that tomorrow will be the (hot) day of this month.
　　B：Wow！ I don't like hot days.
(3) A：I like this cake. Where did you buy it？
　　B：I made it myself. To be a chef (ア．of　イ．dreams　ウ．my　エ．one　オ．is).
(4) A：What (ア．do　イ．like　ウ．to　エ．sports　オ．you) watch on TV？
　　B：I often watch baseball.
(5) A：Who introduced this book to you？
　　B：Roy did. It (ア．made　イ．interested　ウ．me　エ．in　オ．recycling).

12 次の(1)～(5)のそれぞれの対話文を完成させなさい。(1)，(2)については，（ ）の中の語を最も適当な形にしなさい。ただし，1語で答えること。また，(3)～(5)については，それぞれの（ ）の中のア～オを正しい語順に並べかえ，その順序を符号で示しなさい。なお，文頭に来るべき語も小文字で示してあります。

(1) A：What kind of book is that？
　　B：This is my new dictionary. It is very (use).
(2) A：Your bag is beautiful.
　　B：Thank you！ My mother (buy) it for me last week.
(3) A：(ア．your　イ．old　ウ．is　エ．sister　オ．how)？
　　B：She is nineteen, four years older than I.
(4) A：Do you know that we will get two new classmates next week？
　　B：Yes, I do. I (ア．was　イ．the news　ウ．at　エ．very　オ．surprised).
(5) A：Do (ア．are　イ．who　ウ．they　エ．you　オ．know)？
　　B：They are popular dancers.

13 次のAとBの英文は，茨城県に住む高校生のサチコ(Sachiko)と，ニューヨーク市に住むマーサ(Martha)がやり取りしたメールです。それぞれの英文を読んで，下の(1)，(2)の問いに答えなさい。

A.

Hello, Sachiko.
How are you？ I'm happy that I can visit you this summer. I have never ①(be) to Japan. Everything will be new to me. I'm very interested in Japanese culture. I'd like to go to famous places and talk with you a lot. I'm sure that I can have a lot of good ②(memory). Now I have one question. Is Ibaraki ③(hot) than New York in summer？

B.

Hi, Martha.
Thank you for your e-mail. I don't know about the summer in New York, but Ibaraki is very hot in summer. There is a festival in my town on ④(A　　　) 10. My friends and I will ⑤(t　　　) you to the festival. Last year, my father ⑥(b　　　) a *yukata for me as a present at a kimono shop. This summer you can wear my yukata in the festival. I hope you will enjoy staying in Ibaraki. See you soon.

　（注）yukata 浴衣（ゆかた）

(1) Aの英文が完成するように，文中の①～③の（ ）の中の語を，それぞれ1語で適切な形に直して書きなさい。
(2) Bの英文が完成するように，文中の④～⑥の（ ）内に，最も適切な英語を，それぞれ1語ずつ書きなさい。なお，答えはすべて（ ）内に示されている文字で書き始めるものとします。

14 次のAとBの英文は，日本に住む高校生のモモコ(Momoko)と，モモコの家でホームステイをする予定のマレーシア(Malaysia)に住むソフィア(Sophia)がやりとりしたメールです。それぞれの英文を読んで，下の(1)，(2)の問いに答えなさい。

A.

Hi, Momoko.

My name is Sophia, and I'm fifteen years old. It is always hot in Malaysia, but I learned that Japan has four ①(s　　　). When I go to Japan next ②(D　　　), I can enjoy winter in Japan, right？ I hope I can go skiing with you.

In my school, I play sports ③(s　　　) as tennis and *netball. I don't think netball is popular in Japan. Do you play any sports？ I can't wait to meet you.

　（注）netball ネットボール（バスケットボールに似た球技）

B.

Hi, Sophia.

It will be fun to spend next winter with you. Let's go skiing together. I have never ④(hear) of netball, so please show me how to play it when you come to Japan. I like playing sports, too. I have been on the basketball team for five years. Last month, ⑤(we) team won a tournament, and now we are practicing ⑥(hard) than before. I can't wait to play sports together.

(1) Aの英文が完成するように，文中の①～③の（ ）内に，最も適切な英語を，それぞれ1語ずつ書きなさい。なお，答えはすべて（ ）内に示されている文字で書き始めるものとします。
(2) Bの英文が完成するように，文中の④～⑥の（ ）の中の語を，それぞれ1語で適切な形に直して書きなさい。

15 次は，小学校で職場体験をした留学生の*Emily*と，受け入れ先の小学校の担当者である岡先生(*Mr. Oka*)との対話の一部である。2人は，その日の体験について話をしている。これを読んで，下の(1)～(3)に答えなさい。

Mr. Oka : Emily, you worked very hard today.

Emily : Thank you. I'm tired because I have (A)(　be　) busy since this morning.

Mr. Oka : In the English class, you found (B)(couldn't / who / a boy / speak) English well and you helped him.

Emily : Yes, it was hard ____(C)____ him to talk in English. But he began to enjoy talking in English after I helped him. I was glad because he looked happy.

Mr. Oka : Good. Did you have a good time today?

Emily : Yes! I think I did my ____(D)____!

(1) 下線部(A)の(　)の中の語を，適切な形にして，英語1語で書きなさい。

(2) 下線部(B)の(　)の中の語句を，本文の内容に合うように並べかえて書きなさい。

(3) 下線部(C), (D)に入る最も適切なものを，それぞれ1～4から選び，記号で答えなさい。
   (C) 1. in　　2. by　　3. under　　4. for
   (D) 1. best　　　2. problem
   　　3. health　　4. nothing

〈山口県・選択問題〉

16 次は，*Naoko*と留学生の*Sindy*との対話の一部である。2人は，古い町並みを散策しながら話をしている。これを読んで，下の(1)～(3)に答えなさい。

Naoko : Sindy, look at that. It's the (A)(　old　) house in this city.

Sindy : I can feel its history. Do you know (B)(built / it / when / was)?

Naoko : About two hundred years ago.

Sindy : Wow! Is there anyone ____(C)____ in the house now?

Naoko : No, but Mr. Yamada once lived there.

Sindy : Who is Mr. Yamada?

Naoko : He was born in this city, and later, he was known ____(D)____ a great doctor. He saved many people.

Sindy : I see. I want to know more about him.

(1) 下線部(A)の(　)の中の語を，適切な形にして，英語1語で書きなさい。

(2) 下線部(B)の(　)の中の語句を，本文の内容に合うように並べかえて書きなさい。

(3) 下線部(C), (D)に入る最も適切なものを，それぞれ1～4から選び，記号で答えなさい。
   (C) 1. live　　　2. lives
   　　3. living　　4. to live
   (D) 1. as　　2. at　　3. from　　4. on

〈山口県・選択問題〉

17 次の(1)～(3)の問いについて答えなさい。

(1) 次は，中学生の麻衣子(Maiko)とアメリカ出身の留学生のアンナ(Anna)が，書店で，血液型(blood type)について会話をしている場面です。(　)内の①～④の語を，それぞれ適切な形に直して英語1語で書き，会話を完成させなさい。

Anna : There are so many kinds of books here.

Maiko : This is the (①　large) of all bookstores in this city.

Anna : I'm surprised that many books about blood types are (②　sell) here.

Maiko : It's a popular topic. We often enjoy (③　talk) about our blood types. In Japan, "What is your blood type?" is a common question.

Anna : We don't usually ask such a question in America. Actually, most of us don't know our blood types. Why is it necessary to know them?

Maiko : In Japan, people sometimes connect blood types to *personalities. Look at this magazine. It (④　say) that type A people are kind to others.

Anna : Sounds interesting.

(注) personality　性格

(2) 次の①～④について，〔説明〕が示す英語1語を(　)に書き，英文を完成させなさい。ただし，答えは(　)内に示されている文字で書き始めること。

① During (w　　　　) vacation, many people in Japan send New Year's cards.
   〔説明〕 the season between autumn and spring

② It's important to be (q　　　　) in the library.
   〔説明〕 peaceful, without big sounds or voices

③ If your friend has a different (o　　　　) from yours, you should listen to it.
   〔説明〕 an idea or a feeling about something

④ I'll go to bed early because I couldn't (s　　　　) well last night.
   〔説明〕 to close your eyes and rest

(3) 次の①～③について，〈　〉内の状況の会話がそれぞれ成り立つように，[　]内の語に必要な2語を加え，正しい語順で英文を完成させなさい。ただし，文頭にくる語は，最初の文字を大文字にすること。

① 〈留学生と休み時間に写真を見ながら〉
   Paul : This is my grandfather, Eric.
   Hitoshi : He looks young. [　　how　　] he?
   Paul : He's seventy years old.

② 〈アメリカのレストランで〉
   Taro : Excuse me. Could [　　show　　] a menu? I want something sweet.
   Woman : Sure. Here you are.
   Taro : Thank you.

③ 〈ALTとスキー場で〉
   Mr. Lee : You're tired, aren't you? How [　　you　　] been skiing?
   Rumi : For about four hours, but I'm still fine.

〈秋田県〉

第2章 **長文読解問題**

a．スピーチ・発表原稿

① 日常・文化・社会

1 主人公である修二(Shuji)と，その同級生の竜也(Tatsuya)について書かれた次の英文を読んで，1から5までの問いに答えなさい。

　I met Tatsuya when I was 7 years old. We joined a badminton club then. I was good at sports, so I improved my *skills for badminton soon. Tatsuya was not a good player, but he always practiced hard and said, "I can do it! I will win next time." He even said, "I will be the *champion of badminton in Japan." I also had a dream to become the champion, but I ☐ such words because I thought it was *embarrassing to do that. When I won against him, he always said to me, "Shuji, let's play one more game. I will win next time." I never lost against him, but I felt he was improving his skills.

　When we were 11 years old, the situation changed. In a city tournament, I played a badminton game against Tatsuya. Before the game, he said to me, "Shuji, I will win this time." I thought I would win against him easily because I never lost against him. However, I couldn't. I lost against him *for the first time. I never thought <u>that</u> would happen so soon. He smiled and said, "I finally won!" Then I started to practice badminton harder because I didn't want to lose again.

　When we were junior high school students, we played several badminton games, but I couldn't win even once. Tatsuya became strong and joined the *national badminton tournament, so I went to watch his games. In the tournament, his play was great. Sometimes he *made mistakes in the games, but then, he said, "It's OK! I will not make the same mistake again!" He even said, "I will be the champion!" I thought, "He hasn't changed since he was a beginner."

　Finally, Tatsuya really became the champion of badminton in Japan. After the tournament, I asked him why he became so strong. He said, "Shuji, I always say that I will be the champion. Do you know why? When we *say our goals out loud, our *mind and body move to *reach the goals. In fact, by saying that I will be the champion, I can practice hard, and that helps me play better. The words I say make me strong." I realized that those words gave him the (p　　　　) to reach the goal. On that day, I decided to say my goal and practice hard to reach it.

　Now I am 18 years old and I am ready to win the national tournament. Now I am standing on the *court to play a game against Tatsuya in the *final of the national badminton tournament. I have changed. I am going to say to Tatsuya, "I will win this time. I will be the champion."

　(注) skill 技術　　champion　チャンピオン
　　　 embarrassing　恥ずかしい
　　　 for the first time　初めて　　national　全国の
　　　 make a mistake　ミスをする
　　　 say ～ out loud　～を声に出す　　mind　心
　　　 reach ～　～を達成する　　court　コート
　　　 final　決勝

1．本文中の☐に入る適切な英語を2語または3語で書きなさい。

2．本文中の下線部の指す内容は何か。日本語で書きなさい。

3．本文中の(　)に入る適切な英語を1語で書きなさい。ただし，(　)内に示されている文字で書き始め，その文字も含めて答えること。

4．次の文は，本文中の最後の段落に書かれた出来事の翌日に，竜也が修二に宛てて送ったメールの内容である。(　A　)，(　B　)に入る語の組み合わせとして，最も適切なものはどれか。

> Hi Shuji,
>
> *Congratulations!
> Now you are the champion, my friend.
> You've become my goal again.
> You were always my goal when I was little.
> I remember I was very (　A　) when I won against you for the first time.
>
> At that time, you told me that it was embarrassing for you to say your goal.
> So I was (　B　) when you said to me, "I will be the champion."
> This time I lost, but I will win next time.
>
> Your friend,
> Tatsuya

　(注) congratulations　おめでとう

ア．A：sorry　　—　B：bored
イ．A：sad　　　—　B：excited
ウ．A：happy　　—　B：lonely
エ．A：glad　　　—　B：surprised

5．本文の内容と一致するものはどれか。

　ア．Shuji played badminton better than Tatsuya when they began to play it.

　イ．Tatsuya asked Shuji to practice hard and become the champion in Japan.

　ウ．Shuji thought Tatsuya would win against Shuji in the national tournament.

　エ．Tatsuya decided to say his goal out loud because Shuji told Tatsuya to do so.

〈栃木県〉

2 次の英文は，高校生の奈菜(Nana)が，英語の授業で行ったスピーチの原稿です。これを読み，〔問1〕～〔問6〕に答えなさい。

Today, I'd like to talk about my dream. But before telling you what my dream is, [A] There are seven members in my family. The oldest member of the seven is my great-grandfather. He is now 98 years old. When he was young, he was in the battlefields overseas for two years during World War Ⅱ. A few months ago, my great-grandfather and I were watching TV news about wars in foreign countries. Then he told me about his own sad experiences in World War Ⅱ. He also told me, "Wars make many people sad. Please try to imagine their feelings. It's something everyone can do."

ⓐAfter talking with my great-grandfather, (learn, began, about, to, I) wars in the world. I visited many websites for world peace. I also read many newspaper articles about wars. I was surprised to learn there are so many people feeling sad because of wars. And I have realized I should think about wars more. [B]

I've also learned there are many kinds of online activities to support world peace. Even high school students can join some of them. Actually, I joined an online international forum for peace last week. Many foreign high school students joined it. We talked about peace and shared our ideas. After the forum, I told my great-grandfather about ⓑmy good experience in the forum. He looked very happy.

ⓒNow my friends, my dream is to (peaceful, the world, make, more). Some of you may think it's very difficult for high school students to do something for world peace. But that's not true. After the forum, I received many e-mails from the high school students who joined the forum. In the e-mails, some of the students say they have groups for peace in their schools. The members of the group work together to take actions for peace, such as making messages and songs. Some groups have peace events at their school festivals. It's cool! Even high school students can do many things for world peace.

Joining the forum was just the first action to reach my dream. And my next action is to make a group for peace in our school. ⓓThese actions may be small, but I believe even a small action can make the world better if many people try. Why don't we work together?

(注) great-grandfather　祖父母の父
　　　battlefield　戦場
　　　World War Ⅱ　第二次世界大戦
　　　online　オンラインで行われる
　　　forum　フォーラム，討論会

〔問1〕　本文の流れに合うように，文中の [A]，[B] にあてはまる最も適当なものを，それぞれア～エの中から1つずつ選び，その記号を書きなさい。

[A]
ア．let me ask you about a member of your family.
イ．let me ask you about your dream.
ウ．let me tell you about a member of my family.
エ．let me tell you about my dream.

[B]
ア．This is an interesting message from the TV news.
イ．This is an important message from my great-grandfather.
ウ．This is an international experience in our daily lives.
エ．This is a sad experience in World War Ⅱ.

〔問2〕　下線部ⓐ，ⓒについて，それぞれ本文の流れに合うように，( )の中の語句を並べかえ，英文を完成させなさい。

〔問3〕　下線部ⓑmy good experienceの内容を，日本語で具体的に書きなさい。

〔問4〕　次の(1)，(2)の答えを，それぞれ英語で書きなさい。
(1)　How many members are there in Nana's family?
(2)　What do some groups of the students do at their school festivals?

〔問5〕　次のア～エの英文を，奈菜のスピーチの流れに合うよう並べかえると，どのような順序になりますか。その記号を順に書きなさい。
ア．She joined an online international forum for peace.
イ．She received e-mails about peace actions from high school students.
ウ．She was surprised to learn so many people were feeling sad because of wars.
エ．She watched TV news about wars with her great-grandfather.

〔問6〕　下線部ⓓThese actionsの内容を，日本語で具体的に書きなさい。

〈和歌山県〉

3 次の英文は，中学生の武(Takeshi)が，中学校での最後の英語の授業で，中学校生活を振り返って書いたものです。これを読んで，問いに答えなさい。

When I entered junior high school, I was very excited to make new friends and join a club activity. In my second year, I was still having a good time. I [ ] the *captain of the soccer team and also [ ] the classroom *leader. But I *gradually began to feel too busy and tired because I felt I had too much work to do. For example, I had to make the *training schedule every week as the captain of the soccer team. And as the classroom leader, I had to listen to many ideas from my classmates and decide what to do at the school festival.

I didn't know what I should do, so I talked about it with Ms. Kato, my *homeroom teacher, at lunch time. Then, Ms. Kato told me about *time management. She said that I should make *to-do lists when I felt too busy and wanted to use my time well. She taught me how to make the list.

First, Ms. Kato asked me what I must do on the day and ①she [ ] write them on the paper. After I wrote them, I was surprised to see so many things on the paper. Then she said to me, "Choose the especially important things from them. After ②that, you have to think about when you should do them. During lunch time? After school? After dinner? This is also important." I made my to-do list *as Ms. Kato told me.

Now I understand that making to-do lists is a good way to know what to do and when to do them. So I make my to-do list every day. I think I can use my time better than before. To-do lists are so useful!

*Thanks to Ms. Kato, I [　　　　] *positive about my school life again. I'll enjoy the *rest of my time here.

（注）captain　主将，キャプテン
　　　leader　リーダー
　　　gradually　徐々に
　　　training schedule　練習計画
　　　homeroom teacher　担任
　　　time management　時間の管理
　　　to-do list(s)　やるべきことをまとめたリスト
　　　as　〜のとおりに
　　　thanks to　〜のおかげで
　　　positive　前向きな
　　　rest of　残りの〜

問1．本文の内容から考えて，[　　　]に共通して入る英語として最も適当なものを次の中から選び，正しい形に直して書きなさい。

see	know	become	get

問2．下線部①が，加藤先生が武に対して，紙に書くよう指示した英文となるように，[　　　]に入る英語を3語以上で書きなさい。

問3．下線部②の示す内容を具体的に表す英語として最も適当なものを，ア〜エから選びなさい。
　ア．choosing the especially important things
　イ．seeing so many things on the paper
　ウ．making the to-do list every day
　エ．teaching how to make the list

問4．本文の内容に合うものを，ア〜オから2つ選びなさい。
　ア．Takeshi felt he had too much work to do in his first year of junior high school.
　イ．Takeshi was taught how to make to-do lists by Ms. Kato at lunch time.
　ウ．Takeshi was surprised because Ms. Kato wrote many things on the paper.
　エ．Takeshi had to do all the important things after school as Ms. Kato told him.
　オ．Takeshi feels he can use his time well now because he talked with Ms. Kato.

問5．次の英文は，武が中学3年生のある日のリストを英語にしたものの一部です。あなたが武になったつもりで，[　　　]に入る英語を2語以上で自由に書きなさい。

〈to-do list on the day of *graduation〉
　□　to check what to take to school
　□　to [　　　　　　] to my friends and teachers to show my thanks

（注）graduation　卒業

<北海道>

4 次の英文は，ミキ（Miki）が書いたスピーチの原稿です。この英文を読んで，(1)〜(5)の問いに答えなさい。

"Miki, be ready to move to a new house! You can't take many books." My mother kept saying this. We were going to leave town and move abroad in two months. I had too many books on the *bookshelf. I said, "But, Mom, these are my *treasures. I want to keep these books." [　ア　] I read them many times when I was a little child and they are full of good memories. Though I was a junior high school student, I still loved those books very much.

My mother said, "I understand how you feel. But Miki, I'm sure that those books will meet some new people in the future, and you will, too." [　イ　] I asked my mother, "Will my books meet new people?" I thought, "What does she mean?" I knew it would be hard to take all of those books to the new house. But I wanted to keep all my treasures.

One Saturday, I went to the city library to say goodbye to my favorite place and to an old woman who worked there. I said to her, "This will be the last time here." She looked surprised. I spent some time in the library and talked with her. When I left the library, the old woman ran after me. She gave me an old book.

After I got home, I started to read the book. Soon I found that it was very interesting. I continued reading it for two hours and finally finished it. The book was about a girl who had to move. [　ウ　] She became stronger through meeting new people. Her story gave me great *courage. I remembered my mother's words.

The next day, I went to the library and said "thank you" to the old woman. She smiled and looked happy. She said, "I moved to this town when I was as old as you. I read that book and it gave me courage. Good luck at your new place."

I never thought that I would *let go of my favorite books, but I understood my mother's words. I decided to give them to other people *like the old woman did. I wanted my books to make someone feel excited or *encouraged.

A few days later, I went to a *used-book store with my mother. [　エ　] I sold some of my treasures. My books would meet someone. I hoped that they would become *someone else's treasures.

Before we moved, the bookshelf in my room became a little lighter. And my heart did, too.

（注）bookshelf　本棚　　treasure(s)　宝物
　　　courage　勇気　　let go of 〜　〜を手放す
　　　like 〜　〜のように　　encouraged　励まされた
　　　used-book store　古本屋
　　　someone else's　誰か他の人の

(1) 本文の内容に合う文を，次のア〜クの中から3つ選んで，その記号を書きなさい。
　ア．Miki and her family moved to a new house in the same town.
　イ．Miki's mother had a lot of books about treasures.
　ウ．Miki's books were her treasures because they gave her good memories.
　エ．Miki soon agreed with her mother's idea about letting go of all of her books.
　オ．One Saturday, Miki went to the library to look for some books.
　カ．Miki was given a book by the old woman at school.

キ．Miki finished reading the book which the old woman gave her in two hours.

ク．The old woman moved when she was a junior high school student.

(2) 次の文は，文中の　ア　～　エ　のどこに入るのが最も適切か，記号で答えなさい。

I thought she was like me.

(3) 次の①，②の文を，本文の内容と合うように完成させるには，□の中に，それぞれ下のア～エのどれを入れるのが最も適切か，記号で答えなさい。

① The old book given by the old woman made □.

ア．Miki nervous
イ．Miki encouraged
ウ．Miki's mother angry
エ．Miki's mother surprised

② On Sunday, Miki went □.

ア．to the library to say "thank you" to the old woman
イ．to the used-book store to say goodbye to her town
ウ．to the library to give her treasures to other people
エ．to the used-book store to read a book

(4) 下線部の内容を次の□内のように表したとき，（　）に入る適切な英語を，本文から4語で抜き出して書きなさい。

And my heart (　　　　　　　　　), too.

(5) 次の質問の答えとなるように，（　）内に適切な英語を1語ずつ書きなさい。

① When Miki decided to let go of some of her books, what did she understand?

She understood (　　) (　　) (　　) words meant.

② When Miki sold some of her books, what did she hope?

She hoped that (　　) (　　) (　　) someone else's treasures.

〈茨城県〉

5 次の英文は，中学生の正太(Shota)が，同級生の亜希(Aki)と良(Ryo)とのできごとを振り返って書いたものである。この英文を読んで，(1)～(7)の問いに答えなさい。

Every year in May, we have the sports day in our school. Each class shows a dance performance on that day. When I became one of the dance leaders in my class, I ⓐ(feel) excited. Aki and Ryo became leaders, too.

One day in April, Aki, Ryo, and I had the first meeting in the classroom. We wanted to decide what kind of music to use for our dance. First, Aki said to us, "We should choose a famous Japanese song. By using a song that □A□, our classmates can dance easily. Also, the audience will have more fun if they hear famous melody." I didn't agree with her. I said to Aki, "If we use a popular Japanese song, our dance may be the same as dances of other classes. I want to use old American rock music to □B□. I think the audience will be interested in it." Aki said, "You mean we use a song ⓑ(write) in English? We shouldn't do that. I

like old American rock music, but no class used it for the performance last year."

During the meeting, Aki never changed her opinion, and I didn't change my opinion, either. Ryo was just listening to us. Finally, Aki and I stopped talking, and the classroom became quiet.

After a few minutes, Ryo started talking. "Well, the music you want to use is different, but Aki and Shota want to do the same thing." I was surprised and said, "The same thing?" Ryo answered, "Yes. Both of you want □　　□, and I agree. Your opinions are great, so let's put them together. How about using two songs?" Aki and I looked at each other.

Then, Aki said, "That's a good idea! Let's begin our dance with old American rock music. I'm sure the audience will be surprised." I said, "Great! After they are surprised, let's use a popular Japanese song. They can enjoy our dance together." Ryo said, "OK. Now let's talk about how to tell our plan to our classmates."

After the meeting, I said, "Ryo, you made us a good team." Ryo smiled and said, "No, you and Aki did it. Both of you had your own ideas and weren't afraid to say them to improve our dance. That influenced me."

On the next day, I told our plan to our classmates, but some students didn't like the plan. They said, "Old American rock music isn't cool." So Aki showed a CD of old American rock music to our classmates. We listened to it together, and Ryo danced. Thanks to their support, all of the classmates agreed with us, and we chose an old American rock song and a popular Japanese song. I said to Aki and Ryo, "I realized that things which I can do without your help are limited. Let's create a wonderful dance performance together."

(注) sports day　運動会　　leader　リーダー
meeting　会議　　melody　メロディー
rock music　ロック音楽
put ～ together　～をまとめる
influence　～に影響を与える
thanks to ～　～のおかげで

(1) 本文中のⓐ，ⓑの（　）の中の語を，それぞれ適切な形に直しなさい。

(2) 次の質問に対して，英語で答えなさい。

① What did the dance leaders want to decide at the first meeting?

② What was Ryo doing before Shota and Aki stopped talking?

(3) 本文中の　A　，　B　の中に補う英語の組み合わせとして，次のア～エの中から最も適切なものを1つ選び，記号で答えなさい。

ア．A：many students already know
　　B：follow the other classes
イ．A：many students already know
　　B：make our dance unique
ウ．A：only a few students know
　　B：follow the other classes
エ．A：only a few students know
　　B：make our dance unique

(4) 本文中の□の中に補う英語として，次のア～エの中から最も適切なものを1つ選び，記号で答えなさい。

ア．to use a famous English song for our dance

イ．to show other students that you're good at dancing

ウ．our classmates to dance quickly

エ．people watching our dance to enjoy it

(5) 良は，正太と亜希のどのようなようすが自分に影響を与えたと述べているか，日本語で書きなさい。

(6) 正太がクラスメートに計画を話した日，正太はどのようなことに気付いたと亜希と良に伝えているか。亜希と良に伝えている，正太が気付いたことを，日本語で書きなさい。

(7) 次のア～エの中から，本文の内容と合うものを１つ選び，記号で答えなさい。

ア．Aki, Ryo, and Shota had the first meeting, and they told all of the classmates to join it.

イ．Ryo told Shota that popular Japanese songs were always used at the dance performance.

ウ．Aki and Shota had different opinions at first, but Ryo helped them have a better idea.

エ．Shota's class chose two Japanese songs because some students didn't like English songs.

＜静岡県＞

6 次は，高校生の絵里（Eri）が，英語の授業でスピーチをするために書いたものである。英文を読んで，１～５の問いに答えなさい。

Today, I want to talk about my pet and some benefits of having pets. I have had a small dog since I was a little girl. His name is Koro. Ten years ago, my parents and I went to a pet shop. When I first saw him there, he was very cute and small. I really loved him, and wanted to have him. So I asked my parents, "Can I have this dog as a pet?" They thought for a while and said, "OK, Eri. You can have this dog, but you have to take good care of him." I was very ___①___ to have him and we have been good friends since then.

What are the benefits of having animals as pets? I looked for information about them in some books and on the Internet. I found many good points, but today I'll tell you three benefits of having pets.

First, we can feel happy or relaxed. When we live with pets, we can forget about our bad things or busy lives. For example, when I feel lonely or sad, Koro always comes to me and makes me happy. When I am very busy and tired, I feel relaxed to be with him.

Second, we can learn the responsibility for having pets. In my family, I have to give food to Koro every day. I also take a walk with him after coming home from school. It is sometimes hard for me to do everything by myself, but it is necessary for him. So I feel the responsibility for taking care of him.

Third, we can have a lot of chances for ___②___ with other people when we have pets. For example, pet owners have many chances to meet and talk with other people because they often walk with their dogs. Many pet owners also take a lot of pictures of their pets, show them on the Internet, and share a lot of information about their pets with others.

I found many good points of having pets, and I know many pet owners have a good time with their pets. Through taking care of my pet, I have learned that every animal has a life as we do, and their lives are as important as ours. To be a good pet owner, we should think more about the lives of pets and give a lot of love to them. At the same time, they will give you a lot of wonderful memories as my pet, Koro, does. So if you have a chance, why don't you get a pet and follow my advice?

(注) benefit　恩恵
for a while　しばらくの間
relaxed　落ち着いた
responsibility　責任
pet owner　ペットの飼い主
advice　助言

１．___①___に入れるのに最も適当なものを，次のア～エから一つ選び，記号で答えなさい。
ア．nervous　　イ．funny
ウ．sad　　　　エ．glad

２．本文の内容について，次の質問に英語で答えなさい。
When and where did Eri meet Koro for the first time?

３．本文の流れに合うように，___②___に当てはまる英語を１語で書きなさい。

４．本文の内容と合っているものを，次のア～オからすべて選び，記号で答えなさい。

ア．Eri's parents said Eri was too young to have a dog when she first met Koro.

イ．Eri used books and the Internet to find the good points about having pets.

ウ．Eri always stays with Koro when she thinks he is sad or lonely.

エ．Eri usually walks with Koro before she goes to school.

オ．Eri has learned, through having her pet, that all animals have lives as we do.

５．下の英文は，絵里のスピーチを聞いた後，クラスメートの健二（Kenji）が絵里に書いた感想である。英文中の____に当てはまる英語を，10語以内で書きなさい。ただし，短縮形（I'mやisn'tなど）は１語と数え，ピリオド（.），コンマ（,）などの符号は語数に含めないものとする。

健二が書いた感想

> To Eri,
> 　Your speech was very interesting. I agree that pets make us happy and relaxed. From your speech, I learned other benefits of having pets. I have a cat, so I should have more responsibility for taking care of my cat. As you said at the end of your speech, when we take care of pets, we should ____. So I will follow your advice and try to be a good pet owner.
> 　　　　　　　　　　　　　　　Kenji

＜熊本県・選択問題Ｂ＞

7 次の英文は，中学生のハルカ（Haruka）が，英語の授業で行ったスピーチの原稿である。これを読んで，問１～問５に答えなさい。

Did you have breakfast this morning? I know breakfast is important. When I thought about what to talk about in this English class, I remembered a day two weeks ago. On that day, I *overslept and had no time to eat breakfast. Then, I couldn't study very well and got tired quickly at school. So ①I wanted to learn more about breakfast. Today, I would like to talk about the good points of breakfast and easy ways to have breakfast during busy mornings.

I want to show that breakfast is important for us. In a book, it says that breakfast has two good points. First, ②breakfast is good for our bodies. Bodies get warmer by having breakfast, and we can play sports well without *getting injured.

I will tell you wonderful news as the second point. If you have breakfast every day, you may get higher test *scores. The *graph of "Having Breakfast and the *Average Correct Answer Rate of a Test" on the Internet says that the Average Correct Answer Rate on the Japanese of students having breakfast is the highest of the six. On all the three subjects, the Average Correct Answer Rate of students who have breakfast is higher than the Average Correct Answer Rate of students who don't have breakfast. The *difference on the Math between the Average Correct Answer Rate of students who have breakfast and the Average Correct Answer Rate of students who don't have breakfast is the biggest of the three subjects. So this graph shows that students having breakfast every day may get higher scores. But be careful because only having breakfast is not enough. Of course, you should study hard, too.

Though we know the good points of breakfast, some of us often *skip breakfast. Now, I will tell you how you can make and have breakfast every day. When you make dinner, it is good to make more food for breakfast. If you do so, you can easily eat it in the morning.

Then, what should we have for breakfast? I think a Japanese traditional breakfast such as rice, miso soup, *natto* and fish is the best. It takes a little long time to cook it, but I don't get hungry for a long time when I eat it for breakfast.

I will be glad if you can now understand that breakfast is important. Of course, not only breakfast but also lunch and dinner are important, too. So when you have *meals, say "thank you" for everything. We have wonderful *phrases in Japanese to show our *gratitude: "*itadakimasu*" and "*gochisosama*."

　　(注) oversleep (overslept)　寝坊する
　　　　 get(ting) injured　ケガをする
　　　　 score(s)　得点
　　　　 graph　グラフ
　　　　 average correct answer rate　平均正答率
　　　　 difference　差，違い
　　　　 skip 〜　〜を抜く
　　　　 meal(s)　食事
　　　　 phrase(s)　表現，言い方
　　　　 gratitude　感謝の気持ち

問１．下線部①について，ハルカが朝食について調べようと思ったのはなぜか。最も適当なものを，次のア〜エの中から一つ選び，記号を書きなさい。
　ア．Because Haruka's English teacher told her to write about breakfast.
　イ．Because Haruka remembered her friends when she thought about breakfast.
　ウ．Because Haruka didn't eat breakfast and had trouble in school.
　エ．Because Haruka didn't have breakfast and couldn't sleep well at night.

問２．下線部②とは具体的にどのようなことか。次の文がその説明になるように，（　　）に適当な日本語を書きなさい。
　（　　　　　　　　）。また，ケガをすることなく運動ができる。

問３．次の【グラフ(graph)】の（　１　）〜（　３　）には本文中の教科名が入る。本文の内容に合う教科名の組み合わせとして最も適当なものを，下のア〜エの中から一つ選び，記号を書きなさい。
【グラフ(graph)】

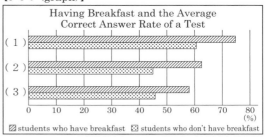

文部科学省ホームページ『平成31年度（令和元年度）
全国学力・学習状況調査』より作成

　ア．（　１　）Japanese　　（　２　）Math
　　　（　３　）English
　イ．（　１　）Japanese　　（　２　）English
　　　（　３　）Math
　ウ．（　１　）Math　　　　（　２　）English
　　　（　３　）Japanese
　エ．（　１　）Math　　　　（　２　）Japanese
　　　（　３　）English

問４．ハルカがスピーチの中で勧(すす)めていることで，手軽に朝食を食べるための工夫は何か。日本語で書きなさい。

問５．ハルカが日本の伝統的な朝食が好ましいと思っているのはなぜか。日本語で書きなさい。
　　　　　　　　　　　　　　　　　　　　＜佐賀県＞

8 次は，中学生の聡(Satoshi)が，ユネスコ無形文化遺産(UNESCO Intangible Cultural Heritage)に登録された和食(*washoku*)について，英語の授業でスピーチをするために書いたものである。英文を読んで，１〜５の問いに答えなさい。

Do you like *washoku*? I love it. I sometimes cook *washoku* for my family. In my speech, I want to tell you about *washoku*, traditional Japanese dishes. It was registered as a UNESCO Intangible Cultural Heritage in 2013. As you know, *washoku* is very ＿＿①＿＿ all over the world, and there are many *washoku* restaurants abroad. Now, many people in the world like to eat *washoku*. There are many reasons for this. Today, let's think about three wonderful points of *washoku*.

First, Japan is rich in nature and *washoku* has many kinds of foods, both from the mountains and from the sea. There are also many ways to cook them, so we can ＿＿②＿＿ the rich taste of the food.

Second, *washoku* is well-balanced in nutrition, so eating *washoku* is very good for our health. I hear that Japanese people live longer than people in many other countries. I think one of the reasons is that they eat *washoku* almost every day.

Third, we can see the beautiful parts of nature and changing of the seasons in *washoku*. For example, we can feel the seasons ③ the dishes of *washoku* often have some flowers from each season. When *washoku* is served, it also looks very beautiful because the designs and the colors of the foods are wonderful. I hear that many people from abroad are often surprised to see the beautiful designs of *washoku*.

We have such wonderful *washoku* culture in our lives, but we sometimes forget about the good points of *washoku*. So I think [　　　] and tell more about it to people both in our country and in other countries. I also think we should pass this great culture on to people in the future.

(注) register 登録する　　rich 豊かな
　　　nature 自然　　taste 味わい
　　　well-balanced in nutrition 栄養バランスがよい
　　　serve （食事などを）出す
　　　pass ～ on to ... ～を…に伝えていく

1. ① ～ ③ に入れるのに最も適当なものを，それぞれ次のア～ウから一つ選び，記号で答えなさい。
　① ア. difficult　　イ. expensive
　　　ウ. popular
　② ア. enjoy　　　イ. teach
　　　ウ. spend
　③ ア. before　　　イ. because
　　　ウ. but

2. 次は，下線部の内容をまとめたものである。本文の内容に合うように，A ～ C にそれぞれ適当なことばを日本語で書きなさい。

和食の三つの特長
・食材の A が豊富で，調理方法もたくさんある。
・栄養バランスがとれているので，とても B 。
・自然の美しさや C の変化が表れている。

3. [　　　] に入れるのに最も適当なものを，次のア～ウから一つ選び，記号で答えなさい。
　ア. it is necessary to change this wonderful part of our culture
　イ. it is important to understand this wonderful part of our culture
　ウ. it is difficult to choose this wonderful part of our culture

4. 本文の内容について，次の質問に英語で答えなさい。
　Do many people in the world like to eat *washoku* now?

5. 本文の内容に合っているものを，次のア～ウから一つ選び，記号で答えなさい。
　ア. Satoshi sometimes cooks *washoku* for his family but he doesn't like to eat it.
　イ. Satoshi is often surprised to see the designs and the colors of *washoku*.
　ウ. Satoshi thinks we should keep the wonderful *washoku* culture in the future.

〈熊本県・選択問題A〉

9 次の英文は，蔵之介(Kuranosuke)が書いたスピーチの原稿です。これを読んで，⑴～⑹の問いに答えなさい。

Last year, I made a big decision to become a member of *the student council. I worked hard for my school every day. However, I wasn't *sure if I was *making some contributions to my school. I often asked myself, "What should I do to make a better school for students?" However, I didn't think of any answers. One day, Mr. Watanabe, the teacher who leads the student council, told me about a *meeting for students in my village. He said, "If you attend the meeting, you can *share ideas about how to make your village better with other students and some village officers." I thought this was a big *chance to learn something important A . So, I decided to attend the meeting.

At the meeting, there were twenty students. Ten of them were high school students. Six were junior high school students like me. The other students were elementary school students. The high school students *confidently shared their ideas with others. Some junior high school students and even some elementary school students confidently talked, too. However, I couldn't *express my ideas B I was not sure if my ideas were "the right answers."

During the meeting, one of the village officers asked us, "What action should the village take to make our places better for future *generations?" That was a very difficult question. Everyone couldn't say anything. Then, I thought, "I have to say something for my local *community." After a while, I raised my hand and said, "I have no idea what action the village should take. The only thing I can say is..., well..., I love my community. I love watching *fireflies in the *rice field near my house. They are so beautiful. But the number of the fireflies is decreasing now, I guess. I mean, it's hard to find fireflies these days. I think that's our big problem. We're losing something that makes our community special. What can we do about that?" After I said so, I thought, "Everyone will laugh at me."

However, a high school student said, "When I was a child, I visited your local community to watch fireflies. They were so beautiful. I want to do something *so that future generations can enjoy watching fireflies there." After this, one of the village officers said, "Fireflies can live only in places with clean water. If the number of the fireflies is decreasing, I want to do something for your community with you. Thanks for sharing your problem."

From this experience, I learned something important. If I want to make a better place, I should first look for a problem. If I can find a problem and share it with others, they will help me find an answer.

Now, I will try to find a problem about our school and share it with other members of the student council so that we can find an answer together.

(注) the student council 生徒会

sure if 〜　〜かどうか確信して
making some contributions　貢献している
meeting　会議　　share 〜　〜を共有する
chance　機会
confidently　自信をもって
express 〜　〜を表現する
generations　世代　　community　地域社会
fireflies　ホタル　　rice field　田んぼ
so that 〜 can ...　〜が…できるように

(1) 本文中の　A　に入る英語として最も適当なものを，ア〜エの中から一つ選びなさい。
　ア．for the most convenient device
　イ．by cleaning the classrooms in our school
　ウ．about holding the meeting
　エ．as a member of the student council

(2) 本文中の　B　に入る英語として最も適当なものを，ア〜エの中から一つ選びなさい。
　ア．because　イ．if　ウ．though　エ．but

(3) 本文中の下線部thatの内容を示した英文として最も適当なものを，ア〜エの中から一つ選びなさい。
　ア．Kuranosuke is thinking about what to do to make a better school for students.
　イ．Kuranosuke loves watching fireflies in the rice field near his house.
　ウ．Kuranosuke's community is losing something that makes it special.
　エ．A high school student could enjoy watching fireflies in Kuranosuke's community.

(4) 本文の内容に合っているものを，ア〜エの中から一つ選びなさい。
　ア．Kuranosuke wanted to make a better village for Mr. Watanabe before the meeting.
　イ．Five elementary school students attended the meeting and had their own opinions.
　ウ．All of the members laughed at Kuranosuke after he told his opinion to them.
　エ．Kuranosuke learned from the meeting that it was important to find a problem first.

(5) 本文の内容に合うように，次の①と②のQuestionに答えなさい。ただし，答えはAnswerの下線部に適当な英語を書きなさい。
　① Question：What does Mr. Watanabe say about the meeting for students in Kuranosuke's village?
　　Answer：He says Kuranosuke can ＿＿＿＿＿＿＿ with other people if he attends it.
　② Question：According to the village officer, where can fireflies live?
　　Answer：They can live only in ＿＿＿＿＿＿＿.

(6) 次は，蔵之介のスピーチを聞いた後の遥(Haruka)と蔵之介の対話です。下線部に適当な英文を１文で書きなさい。
　Haruka　　　：Your speech was great. May I ask you a question about our school?
　Kuranosuke：Sure, Haruka. What's your question?
　Haruka　　　：＿＿＿＿＿＿＿
　Kuranosuke：Yes, I did. Actually, there are some problems.
　Haruka　　　：Oh, give me an example, please.
　Kuranosuke：OK. For example, I found that some

classrooms in our school were not very clean. I think I have to talk about this problem with other students.
　Haruka　　　：I see. I hope our school will be a better place.

<福島県>

10 次の英文は，中学生の久美(Kumi)が，最近印象に残ったできごとについて，英語の授業でスピーチをしたときのものです。1〜7の問いに答えなさい。

Last Saturday, our softball team had an important game. ＿ア＿ I practiced very hard with my team members to win. However, I didn't play well in the game, and we lost. Other members encouraged me after the game, but I could not stop crying.

After I came back home, I told my father how much I wanted to win. He said, "I know how you feel, Kumi. You've tried hard to win that game for such a long time." Then he continued, "Well, I'm going to climb a mountain tomorrow. How about going together, Kumi?" "Climbing a mountain? I don't want to go, because I'm ①exhausted now," I answered. He said, "If you walk in a mountain, you may feel better. Why don't you come?" I thought for a minute. I felt it would be nice for a change, and decided to go with him. ＿イ＿

The next morning, it was cloudy, but soon after we began to climb, it started to rain. I said to myself, "Yesterday I lost the game, and today it's raining. Nothing is good to me." When we got to the top, I was disappointed that I could not see anything from there. But my father looked happy in the rain. When we were eating lunch there, I asked him why. He said, "We cannot stop the rain by complaining, Kumi. I just enjoy climbing whether it is rainy or sunny. When it rains, you can enjoy the rain." "Enjoy the rain? How can you enjoy when it rains?" I asked. He answered, "See the trees when they're wet with rain. They're very beautiful." I said, "But I want to enjoy walking in the sun. Climbing on a rainy day is like losing games. It's no fun. ＿ウ＿ Then he said, "I know what you mean, Kumi. But there is no winner or loser in climbing. I feel happy in the mountains even on rainy days because I really like mountains." When I heard his words, I remembered the time when I started to play softball at the age of ten. At that time, (②). But now I play softball just to win. My father smiled and said, "Well, when you have a hard time, you have three things to do. First, you can do your best and run for success. You may think this is always the best choice. But you sometimes need to stop and think about what you have done. This is the second thing you can do." "Stop and think about what I have done," I repeated. He said, "I think this is also important because it's impossible to have success all the time. And there is one more thing you can do." "What's that?" I asked. He said, "Accept the situation and walk step by step. If you continue to walk, you may find something wonderful along the way." While I was listening to him, I remembered the faces of my team members. 　エ

In the afternoon, it stopped raining. When we started to go down the mountain, my father said, "Look over there!" A rainbow was in the clear sky. My father and I looked at each other. He said, "See? That is 'something wonderful along the way'." I said, "You're right. I can see it only after the rain. No rain, no rainbow!"

（注）encourage　励ます　　for a change　気分転換に
　　　complain　不平を言う
　　　whether 〜　〜であろうとも　　loser　敗者
　　　the time when 〜　〜したときのこと
　　　success　成功　　situation　状況
　　　step by step　一歩一歩　　rainbow　虹

1．久美が登山した日の天気はどのように変化したかを，ア〜エから1つ選び，符号で書きなさい。

2．次の英文が入る最も適切な箇所を，本文中の　ア　〜　エ　から1つ選び，符号で書きなさい。
　　Though I lost the game, I had a lot of experiences with them.

3．本文中の下線部①と，ほぼ同じ意味を表すものを，ア〜エから1つ選び，符号で書きなさい。
　ア．excited　　　イ．interested
　ウ．pleased　　　エ．tired

4．本文中の（　②　）に入る最も適切なものを，ア〜エから1つ選び，符号で書きなさい。
　ア．I didn't enjoy playing it
　イ．I didn't play it well
　ウ．I just enjoyed playing it with my friends
　エ．I tried to win the game with my friends

5．次の質問に対する答えを，本文の内容に即して，英語で書きなさい。ただし，　　　　の部分には1語ずつ書くこと。
　(1)　Did Kumi win the softball game on Saturday?
　　　　　　　　, she　　　　　　　.
　(2)　What did Kumi remember while she was talking with her father on the top of the mountain?
　　　She remembered the time when she 　　　　　　to play softball and the 　　　　　　of her team members.

6．本文の内容に合っているものを，ア〜オから1つ選び，符号で書きなさい。
　ア．Kumi was happy when her father asked her to go to the mountain with him.
　イ．Kumi's father said he liked to climb mountains even in the rain.
　ウ．Kumi and her father ate lunch after they went down the mountain.
　エ．Kumi's father thought that it is important to win the game all the time.
　オ．Kumi was not happy though she saw a rainbow from the mountain.

7．次の英文は，登山を終えた久美が父に書いた手紙の一部を，英語にしたものです。（③　　　），（④　　　）に入る最も適切な英語を，1語ずつ書きなさい。ただし，（　）内に示されている文字で書き始め，その文字も含めて答えること。

Thank you for taking me to the mountain on （③S　　）. Though I could not see anything from the top, I really enjoyed climbing with you. I felt that climbing a mountain is like playing softball. While we were climbing, you taught me three important things to do when we had a hard time: run, stop, and （④w　　　） step by step. Now I think they are all important. When I play the game next time, I can enjoy playing softball with my team members. Please come to watch me!

〈岐阜県〉

11 次の英文は，高校1年生のまどか(Madoka)が，英語の授業で食品ロス(food loss)について発表したときの原稿です。これを読んで，1から6の問いに答えなさい。なお，本文中の【1】〜【5】は発表した原稿の段落番号を表します。
（*は(注)の語を示す。）

Food Loss

【1】 Hello, everyone. Today, I'd like to talk about the problem of food loss. I think many of you have heard of it, but through my presentation, I want you to learn more about this problem.

【2】 Food loss means *wasting food that we can still eat. Many people know throwing away food is *mottainai*, but I guess many people don't think that food loss is a big problem because there is a lot of food around us. At first, I wasn't interested in this problem, either. However, last week, in social studies class, we learned that there are more than 8 million hungry people in the world, but at the same time over 1.3 *billion *tons of food is thrown away every year. I felt very sad to hear this. After the class, I wanted to know about food loss in Japan. So, I tried to get more information on the Internet. Then, I found a good website. It shows that in Japan in one year, about 6 million tons of food that can still be eaten is thrown away, and about half of it comes from homes. It was very surprising to me. Also, I learned that throwing away food means wasting the water and energy used to make the food, and if we *burn a lot of *food waste, it makes CO_2. So, wasting food is bad for the environment, too.

【3】 Why do people waste so much food? For example, in a supermarket, people may buy too much food, but they sometimes forget to eat it. Then it becomes food waste. In a restaurant or at home, people sometimes order or cook too much food, so they don't eat all of it and then they waste it like this. Also, some people want to buy *fruits or vegetables which look good. So, some fruits and vegetables are thrown away just because their color or shape is bad for selling.

【4】 So, what can we do to stop food loss? First, we can stop buying too much food. Before going shopping, we should check 　　　　　　.

Second, we can stop ordering or cooking too much food. Then we can eat everything and don't waste food. Third, we can give food to *food banks. Do you know food banks? Food banks collect food which was not sold or eaten. Then they give it to people who don't have *enough food. So, if we have much food which we don't need, by sending it to food banks, we can save people without wasting food.

【5】 I believe we all can do something to solve many problems and help many people. I think it is important to start with small things that we can do in our daily lives. One small thing I can do is to join a volunteer activity. So, I have decided to help at a food bank to stop food loss. How about you? Let's do something small to make our lives better. Thank you for listening.

(注) waste 無駄にする　 billion 十億
ton(s) トン(重さの単位)　 burn 燃やす
food waste 食品廃棄物　 fruit(s) 果物
food bank(s) フードバンク
enough 十分な

1．次の①，②の問いに答えるとき，本文の内容に合う最も適当なものをア～エから一つずつ選び，その記号を書きなさい。
① What does Madoka want her classmates to do through her presentation?
ア．She wants them to do their presentation.
イ．She wants them to listen to many people.
ウ．She wants them to learn more about food loss.
エ．She wants them to stop using the Internet.
② How much food loss comes from homes in Japan in one year?
ア．About 1 million tons.
イ．About 3 million tons.
ウ．About 6 million tons.
エ．About 8 million tons.

2．次のア～オのうち，本文の内容と合っているものを二つ選び，その記号を書きなさい。
ア．Food loss means throwing away food that can't be eaten.
イ．Madoka wasn't interested in food loss before she learned about it in class.
ウ．The problem of food loss can be solved by burning a lot of food waste.
エ．Some fruits and vegetables are thrown away because they don't look good and aren't sold.
オ．Madoka told everyone to decide to join a volunteer activity to stop food loss.

3．次のア～オは，本文の【1】～【5】のいずれかの段落の内容を表した見出しです。各段落にふさわしい見出しを，ア～オから一つずつ選び，それぞれ記号を書きなさい。
ア．Things that we can do about food loss
イ．Examples showing why food loss happens
ウ．The beginning of the presentation about food loss
エ．Doing something small to solve problems and help people
オ．Information about food loss happening in the world and in Japan

4．本文の内容から考えて，本文中の□□□に入る最も適当な英語を，次のア～エから一つ選び，その記号を書きなさい。
ア．how much food we have at home
イ．how much information there is on the Internet
ウ．how many people sell food at the supermarket
エ．how many restaurants are found in our town

5．次の英文は，まどか(Madoka)の発表をもとに，あるクラスメイトがまとめたものです。(A)～(D)に当てはまる最も適当な英語を１語ずつ書きなさい。

Madoka taught us that food loss is a very big (A), so now I'm (B) in food loss, too. I learned a lot of food is wasted even in Japan. I think if we don't throw away food and we give it to hungry people, we can save them. Also, I learned wasting food is (C) for the environment. So, I want to do small things to stop food loss. I'll try to buy only food that I need and I want to enjoy eating (D) wasting food.

6．下線部One small thing I can doについて，あなたなら人のため，または社会のために，どのようなことができると思いますか。下の条件に従って書きなさい。

条件・一つのことについて，具体的に書くこと。
・35語以上50語以内の英語で書くこと。文の数はいくつでもよい。
なお，短縮形(I'veやisn'tなど)は１語と数え，符号(，や？など)は語数に含めない。

<山梨県>

12 次の英文は，中学生のさやか(Sayaka)さんが，留学生のリアム(Liam)さんを迎えるまでの間に取り組んだことについて，スピーチコンテストで発表するために書いた原稿である。これを読んで，(1)～(6)に答えなさい。

"We'll have a new student from abroad after summer vacation. His name is Liam, and he'll be a member of this class." When our teacher Ms. Tanaka told us the news, we were all very surprised. We asked her a lot of questions to learn about the new student.

Then Ms. Tanaka said to us, "Now, here's my question. It's his first time to come and live in a foreign country. If you were Liam, how would you feel before leaving your country?" Eita answered, "I would be very excited, but also worry about living abroad without my family." Ms. Tanaka continued, "Then, is there anything we can do for Liam? I want you to think about it and decide what to do."

We had various good ideas, but Wataru's idea was the □□□. He said, "Let's take videos to introduce our school life and send them to Liam in America! He can watch them and get some information about our school before coming to Japan." "Sounds great! I'm sure it will help him start his school life smoothly," said Chiho. Everyone agreed with Wataru's idea too.

We thought about what to tell Liam, such as the schedules, rules, school buildings, and club activities. Ms. Tanaka told us to work in groups, and each group had to choose a different topic to introduce. My group decided to introduce the school buildings. First, we chose some of the rooms or places in our school, and wrote the explanations in Japanese. However, it was very difficult for us to say everything in English. Then our ALT Grace gave us a hint. She said, "I know you have a lot to tell Liam, but try to give him only the most important information." So, we wrote shorter explanations for each place and took videos. All the groups tried hard to make useful videos for Liam, and we hoped he would like them.

After sending our videos, Liam also sent a video to us. We were glad to know that he enjoyed watching our videos. He wanted to know about the town too, so we took more videos to introduce our favorite shops and restaurants, the park, and the station near our school, and sent them to Liam.

Now Liam is in Japan and has been enjoying his school life with us. The other day, he said, "Your videos gave me a lot of information about the school and the town. They were really helpful, and now I have nothing to worry about. You're all very kind and I'm so happy to be a member of this class." His words made us happy too.

It was great to think about Liam and work together with my group members. We could actually help him start his new life smoothly. Through this experience, I learned helping others makes us happy. So, I hope we will always keep trying to find something we can do for others.

　（注）smoothly　スムーズに
　　　schedule(s)　時間割
　　　school building(s)　校舎
　　　explanation(s)　説明
　　　the other day　先日

(1)　次の(a)・(b)の問いに対する答えを，それぞれ3語以上の英文1文で書きなさい。ただし，符号は語数に含めない。
　(a)　Is it Liam's first time to live abroad?
　(b)　What did Sayaka and her group members decide to introduce in their video?

(2)　下線部について，あなたがさやかさんのクラスメートならどのような質問をするか，あなたから田中先生（Ms. Tanaka）への質問の形で，英文1文で書きなさい。

(3)　本文の内容に合うように，　　　　　に最も適する1語の英語を書きなさい。

(4)　本文の内容に合うように，次の英文の　　　　　に最も適するものをア〜エから選びなさい。

　Sayaka and her classmates sent the second videos to Liam because 　　　　　　.
　ア．Wataru wanted Liam to know more about club activities
　イ．everyone wanted to watch another video from Liam
　ウ．each group got a hint from their ALT to make useful videos
　エ．Liam asked them to give him information about the town

(5)　次の英文は，さやかさんとALTのグレイス（Grace）先生が，スピーチのタイトル（title）について交わしている対話の一部である。対話が成り立つように，　ⓐ　には最も適するものをア〜エから選び，　ⓑ　には最も適する1語の英語を本文中から抜き出して書きなさい。

Sayaka：I can't think of a good title for my speech. Could you help me?
Grace：Sure. Try to use the words from the most important part. How about "　ⓐ　", for example? In the last part of your speech, you say thinking about 　ⓑ　 and doing something for them is great. That's the thing you really wanted to tell, right?
Sayaka：Yes! That title can tell people what I'm going to talk about in my speech too. Thanks for your idea.

　ア．Sending our videos to America
　イ．Working together for our new friend
　ウ．Introducing our school in English
　エ．Enjoying our school life together

(6)　本文の内容と合うものをア〜カから2つ選びなさい。
　ア．Everyone in Sayaka's class was so surprised to hear about a new student.
　イ．Ms. Tanaka's first question made her students think about Eita's feelings.
　ウ．Chiho thought introducing their school life to Liam was a very good idea.
　エ．All the groups in Sayaka's class had to choose the same topic to introduce.
　オ．Grace told Sayaka's group to write more explanations in English for Liam.
　カ．Liam is glad to be in Sayaka's class, but he still worries about living in Japan.

〈徳島県〉

13　次の英文は，高校生の涼真（Ryoma）が英語の授業で書いた作文である。これを読んで，問い(1)〜(8)に答えよ。

I have ①(meet) many people in my life, and there is a person who I will never forget among them. He was one of my classmates. He came to our school when I was a junior high school student.

One morning, our teacher said to us, "We will have a new student from a foreign country next week. He will come to our school because his family will stay in this town. He will spend two months here." ②[(ア) hear / (イ) that / (ウ) to / (エ) were / (オ) we / (カ) surprised]. I talked about the new student with my friends after school. One of my friends asked me, "What language does he speak?" I said to him, "English? Japanese? I'm not sure, but I can't wait to see the new student."

The day came. He came into our classroom and we welcomed him. His name was *Mauro. He introduced himself in English. He spoke English slowly for us and we could understand what he said. After that, he introduced himself in Japanese, too. His Japanese was not *fluent, but he tried hard to speak Japanese, and I liked ③that way of introducing himself. So, I thought I could *get along with him.

He sat next to me in the classroom. He studied very hard in every class in Japanese. I asked him,

"Do you sometimes feel studying in Japanese is hard?" He smiled and said to me, "No, I don't. Every class is interesting." I understood how hard he studied, so I respected him. When he had a Japanese word he couldn't understand, he always asked people around him ④a question. Also, he often tried to speak Japanese with us, and his Japanese became better.

One day, every student made a speech in our English class. The topic was "What is the most important in your life?" Each speaker went to the front of the classroom. We made our speeches when our *turns came. Finally, my turn came after many speakers made their speeches. I started ⑤my speech. "I think friends are the most important in my life. I have three reasons. First, they *cheer me up when I am sad. Second, they help me solve problems that I have. Third, it is important for me to talk with them every day because we can share our opinions with each other." I was so nervous during my speech, but I *did my best.

Soon, Mauro's turn came and it was the last speech in our class. He went to the front and ⑥(begin) his speech. He said, "Education is the most important in my life. In my country, some children can't study though they want to study. I think education can give us many things. For example, if we get new *knowledge through education, we can have wide *views and many ways of thinking, and we can solve our problems with the knowledge. And we can get many *skills and have a lot of *choices for our jobs in the future. So, we can *expand our *possibilities in the future." After I listened to his speech, I understood why he studied so hard in every class even in Japanese. I thought everyone in the world had a chance to get education, but that was wrong. After I got home, I talked about his speech with my mother. I said, "For the first time, I thought how important education is. *From now on, I will study harder. Education can help us make our future better." I *took it for granted that I got education but I understood it was special and necessary for my future.

Two months *passed and the last day at our school came for him. He had to go back to his country the next day. We were so sad and told him how we were feeling. I said to him, "Thank you for the good time. I will never forget your speech in the English class. Next time, I want to see you in your country." He said to us, "Thank you for your words. I had a good time in Japan. It is my treasure."

Now I study hard in every class, and I am trying to do my best in my school life and enjoy it because he taught us an important thing. I think education has the power to expand our possibilities for our future.

(注) Mauro　マウロ(男性の名)
　　　fluent　流ちょうな
　　　get along with ～　～と仲良くやっていく
　　　turn　順番
　　　cheer ～ up　～を元気づける
　　　do my best　最善を尽くす
　　　knowledge　知識

view　見方　　skill　技術
choice　選択　　expand ～　～を広げる
possibility　可能性
from now on　今後は
take it for granted that ～　～ということを当然のことと思う
pass　(時が)過ぎる

(1) 下線部①(meet)・⑥(begin)を，文章から考えて，それぞれ正しい形にかえて１語で書け。

(2) 下線部②の[　　]内の(ア)～(カ)を，文意が通じるように正しく並べかえ，記号で書け。ただし，文頭に来る語も小文字で示されている。

(3) 下線部③が指す内容として最も適当なものを，次の(ア)～(エ)から１つ選べ。
　(ア) マウロが，つたなくても英語で自己紹介をしたこと。
　(イ) マウロが，自己紹介を日本語でした後に英語でもしたこと。
　(ウ) マウロが，日本語で流ちょうに自己紹介をしたこと。
　(エ) マウロが，日本語で懸命に自己紹介をしたこと。

(4) 下線部④は具体的にはどのような発言と考えられるか，次の(ア)～(エ)のうち最も適当なものを，１つ選べ。
　(ア) "Can you tell me what this Japanese word means?"
　(イ) "Do you want to know what this word means in English?"
　(ウ) "Are there many people learning English in your country?"
　(エ) "How often do you speak Japanese in your house?"

(5) 次の英文は，下線部⑤に関して説明したものである。これを読んで，下の問い(a)・(b)に答えよ。

> Ryoma made a speech in his English class. The topic was "What is the most important in your life?" He felt 　　i 　　 when he was making his speech, but he tried hard. He told his classmates that friends are the most important, and as one of the reasons, he told it is important for him to talk with his friends every day because 　　ii 　　.

　(a) 本文の内容から考えて，　i　に入る最も適当な語を，本文中から１語で抜き出して書け。
　(b) 本文の内容から考えて，　ii　に入る表現として最も適当なものを，次の(ア)～(エ)から１つ選べ。
　　(ア) he can give them his ideas and also get theirs
　　(イ) they cheer him up when he is sad
　　(ウ) he enjoys talking with them
　　(エ) they help him solve a problem

(6) 本文の内容から考えて，次の〈質問〉に対して下の〈答え〉が成り立つように，　　　　に入る最も適当なものを，次の(ア)～(エ)から１つ選べ。
　〈質問〉　What did Mauro tell his classmates on his last day at Ryoma's school?
　〈答え〉　He told them that 　　　　　　 after saying "Thank you."
　　(ア) he had to go back to his country soon
　　(イ) he remembered Ryoma's speech in the English class
　　(ウ) his days in Japan were his treasure
　　(エ) his dream was to see his friends in Japan next time

(7) 本文の内容と一致する英文として最も適当なものを，

次の(ア)～(エ)から1つ選べ。

(ア) Ryoma heard from his teacher that Mauro was going to stay in Japan for a month.

(イ) Ryoma didn't know what language Mauro spoke before seeing him.

(ウ) Ryoma didn't think Mauro studied hard in some classes in Japanese.

(エ) Ryoma was the last student to make a speech in his English class.

(8) 次の英文は，この作文を読んだ高校生の裕次郎 (Yujiro)と留学生のミラ(Mira)が交わしている会話の一部である。これを読んで，あとの問い(a)・(b)に答えよ。

Yujiro：Let's talk about the things Ryoma learned from Mauro's speech.

Mira ：OK. He thought ⬚⬚⬚ i ⬚⬚⬚ before listening to it, but he understood that was not true.

Yujiro：You are right. Also, Mauro said in his speech that we can get many things through education.

Mira ：Yes, and Ryoma thought how important education was after listening to Mauro's speech.

Yujiro：I see. Ryoma realized we can ⬚⬚⬚ ii ⬚⬚⬚ through education, and he has been studying hard after he listened to the speech.

Mira ：Yes. I'll also try to do my best in my school life and enjoy it.

(a) 本文の内容から考えて，⬚ i ⬚ に入る表現として最も適当なものを，次の(ア)～(エ)から1つ選べ。

(ア) he could share it with his family

(イ) everyone in the world could understand each other

(ウ) he could not get along with Mauro

(エ) everyone in the world could get education

(b) 本文の内容から考えて，⬚ ii ⬚ に入る表現として最も適当な部分を，本文中から4語で抜き出して書け。

〈京都府〉

14 次の文章を読んで，あとの各問に答えなさい。
（＊印のついている単語・語句には，本文のあとに(注1)がある。また，＊＊印のついている単語には，本文のあとに(注2)があり，英語で意味が説明されている。）

Hello, my name is Lisa Smith. My friends call me Lisa. I'm fifteen years old. I live with my parents and my brother in a small town in Canada. The other day, something important happened and I have realized that pet animals have special powers. Why do I think pet animals have special powers? I'll tell you why.

I'm a junior high school student. I walk to and from school every day. I enjoy walking to school and it takes about half an hour. One warm spring day, when I was on my way home from school, a small friend was following me. This friend was different from any other friend. She was very small. "What a cute **kitten!" She had no *identifying marks of any kind. "Is she a *stray cat?" I thought. She followed me all the way. When I arrived home, she was just behind me.

When my parents came back home from work that evening, they were surprised to see the kitten. I told them that my friend gave her to me, but it was a *lie. My parents knew that I was telling a lie. My parents love cats but told me that we should find the owner and give her back. They said I should think of the owner. "What should I do?" I thought. I thought about a *notice in the town newspaper. However, that was the last thing I wanted to do. "If I put a notice in the town newspaper, her owner may appear," I thought. The kitten was so cute. I started to think, "⬚⬚⬚ (1) ⬚⬚⬚" I did not want to lose her.

My brother said that the kitten was maybe about six months old. The cat liked us right away. After dinner she climbed on to my legs and watched TV with us. By now I was asking my parents to keep her.

By the end of the week, the new cat was part of our family. She was very smart and good with me. My parents started to change their minds about the cat. My father said to me, "Lisa, I think no one is looking for this cat. Now, it's time for you to take *responsibility for another life. This will be a good chance for you to learn something important. You'll learn something you'll need when you become a parent in the future."

The next week, something told me to check the town newspaper. One very small notice jumped out at me. When I saw it, I was surprised. A woman near my house was looking for her lost cat. My hands were shaking. I knew I should call the woman, but I couldn't pick up the phone. Instead, I tried to believe that I didn't see the notice. I quickly threw the newspaper away in the closet in my room and continued to do my homework. I ⬚⬚ (2) ⬚⬚ said a word about it to my parents.

We gave a name to the kitten. She was all white like snow, so we decided to call her Snow. When I was studying at my desk, she was quiet. However, when I went into the garden, she followed me and asked me to play with her. When I was doing the dishes, she was there to lend a hand (or should I say **paw?).

There was only one problem with this perfect picture. I could not forget the notice in the town newspaper. One day, I started to think what I really should do. I knew in my heart that I should call the woman. I knew she really wanted to see her cat again. I thought, "Is our Snow the cat the woman wants to see?" I didn't sleep well that night.

The next morning, I talked about the notice to my parents, and, at last, I started to push the numbers on my phone. In my heart, I was hoping no one would answer, but someone did. "Hello." It was the voice of a young woman. I explained to her about the cat and she asked me a lot of questions. She said she really wanted to come. After the phone call, I was very nervous. I asked my parents to stay with me.

I was with my parents at the kitchen table. I hoped a *miracle would happen. Snow was sitting at my feet the whole time and sometimes looked up at me with those pretty eyes. (3)Snow noticed something was wrong.

Within minutes the woman was at the front door. I saw her through the window. She was standing there with a map in her hand. She *knocked on the front door. "Excuse me, is this the home of Mr. and Mrs. Smith?" she asked. When she knocked on the door again, a thousand *thoughts crossed my mind. I could say to her, "[_____(4)_____]" But it was too late; my mother opened the door. I also went there to face my fear.

The woman looked at Snow and the woman's face changed. I saw a big smile on her face. "Here, Lucy," she called. "Come to me, girl." Now I realized the cat was called Lucy by the woman. The cat looked very happy at the woman's voice. It was clear that she belonged to the woman.

I was in tears. I couldn't do anything. I wanted to run away with Snow. Instead, I smiled a little and my parents asked the young woman to come in.

The young woman was already holding Snow up into her arms. She opened her *purse and tried to give my parents some money.

"For your trouble," she said.

My parents shook their heads. My mother said, "Oh, we can't. She has been a joy. We should pay you some money." With that, the woman smiled and *hugged Snow again.

Snow was really happy to see the woman again. I knew it was time for them to go home. I opened the front door. When the woman was leaving, I noticed a little girl with her father. The girl was sitting in the front seat of the car. When the girl saw the kitten, I saw a big smile on her face. The girl said, "Come here, Lucy!"

Before I said something, the woman started to explain. "My family moved to this town last month. The girl in the car is my daughter. She did not know anyone in this town and she felt very lonely every day. Lucy was given to her because my husband and I know that she loves cats."

The woman continued, "When Lucy *disappeared, my daughter was very shocked. She was crying all day. She was in her room all the time. Every day she said she wanted to see Lucy again. Lucy is her only friend at this new place. She has a special *bond with the kitten."

Suddenly I realized that I was thinking only about myself. My heart went out to that little girl. When I saw the car going away, the smile on my face was real. I knew I did the right thing. I knew that the kitten was exactly at the right place. (5)I learned something important from the cat.

（注１）identifying mark　身元を示すしるし
　stray cat　のら猫　　lie　うそ　　notice　告知
　responsibility　責任感　　miracle　奇跡
　knock　ノックする　　thought　考え　　purse　財布
　hug　抱きしめる　　disappear　いなくなる
　bond　きずな

（注２）kitten—A kitten is a very young cat.
　paw—The paws of an animal such as a cat or dog are its feet.

〔問１〕　本文の流れに合うように，[　(1)　]に英語を入れるとき，最も適切なものは次の中ではどれか。
　ア．I have to find her owner and give her back as soon as I can.
　イ．I must go and check the newspaper at the school library now.
　ウ．I really want to know why my friend gave me such a pretty cat.
　エ．I cannot understand why her owner did not watch her enough.

〔問２〕　本文の流れに合うように，[　(2)　]に英語１語を入れるとき，入るべき英語１語は何か。

〔問３〕　(3)Snow noticed something was wrong.とあるが，この文とほぼ同じ意味を持つものは次の中ではどれか。
　ア．Snow felt something was going to happen.
　イ．Snow thought she made a terrible mistake.
　ウ．Snow thought she should feel sorry for me.
　エ．Snow felt we should think more carefully.

〔問４〕　本文の流れに合うように，[　(4)　]に英語を入れるとき，最も適切なものは次の中ではどれか。
　ア．Hello, welcome. Open the door, please.
　イ．I'm afraid you have the wrong address.
　ウ．Sorry, I don't know anything about Lucy.
　エ．Who is it?　My mother is coming soon.

〔問５〕　(5)I learned something important from the cat.とあるが，Lisaはこの日の晩に，次の日記を書いた。日記を読んで，あとの〔質問Ａ〕〔質問Ｂ〕に対する答えを自分で考えて，それぞれ20語以上の英語で書きなさい。英文は二つ以上にしてもよい。なお，「,」「.」「!」「?」などは語数に含めないものとする。I'llのような「'」を使った語やe-mailのような「-」で結ばれた語はそれぞれ１語と扱うこととする。

> I have learned something important from Snow. Now, she is not here. I really miss her. I really want to see her again, but I know I did the right thing. The kitten is now at the right place. I can now look at the world in a different way.

〔質問Ａ〕　Lisa wrote in her diary, "I have learned something important from Snow." What did she learn from the cat?

〔質問B〕　Lisa wrote in her diary, "The kitten is now at the right place." What does this sentence mean?

〔問6〕　本文の内容と合っているものを，次のア～カから二つ選びなさい。

ア．Lisa walks to junior high school with her small friend every day. She spends about thirty minutes going to school.

イ．At first, Lisa's parents told Lisa to return the cat to the owner because they thought Lisa was still a child and should not keep a cat.

ウ．Finally, Lisa agreed to meet a woman who was looking for her cat, so her mother made a phone call to the woman.

エ．The woman who came was the owner of the cat. She said "thank you" and gave some money to Lisa's parents.

オ．The kitten was called Snow by Lisa because it was all white, and the same cat was called Lucy by the girl in the car.

カ．For the girl in the car, the cat was her only friend in the town. She had no other friend there because she was new there.

〔問7〕　次の単語のうちで，下線の引かれている部分の発音が他と異なるものを，次のア～オから一つ選びなさい。

ア．learn　　イ．word　　ウ．perfect
エ．heart　　オ．girl

<東京都立国立高等学校>

②　自然・産業・科学技術

1　次の英文は，高校生の武志(Takeshi)が，英語の授業で行った，惑星についてのスピーチの原稿です。これを読み，〔問1〕～〔問3〕に答えなさい。

Today, I'd like to talk about some planets in space. I love planets. Last year, my father gave me a book about planets with beautiful pictures. It was great. The book made me happy. Since then, I've been interested in planets.

When I talked with our science teacher, Ms. Suzuki, she said, "There are many planets in space. And they have their own features. Do you know Venus? Venus is a beautiful planet which is smaller than the Earth." I knew the names of some planets, but I didn't know much about them. So I wanted to know about planets more.

Last weekend, I researched the four planets which are close to the Sun. They are Mercury, Venus, Earth and Mars. I got data about them from books and websites. I wanted to share the data, so I made charts. Please look at these charts. Chart 1 shows the order of the four planets from the Sun. Chart 2 shows the order of their size. From these charts, we can see that Mercury is the closest to the Sun and it is the smallest of the four. From the Sun, Mars is farther than the Earth.

Of these four planets, I thought that the largest planet was Mars because it's the farthest from the Sun. But I was not right. Mars is the second smallest planet of the four. I learned new things from making these charts. I love to learn about planets because there are many things I don't know. In the future, I'll continue to learn about them.

図

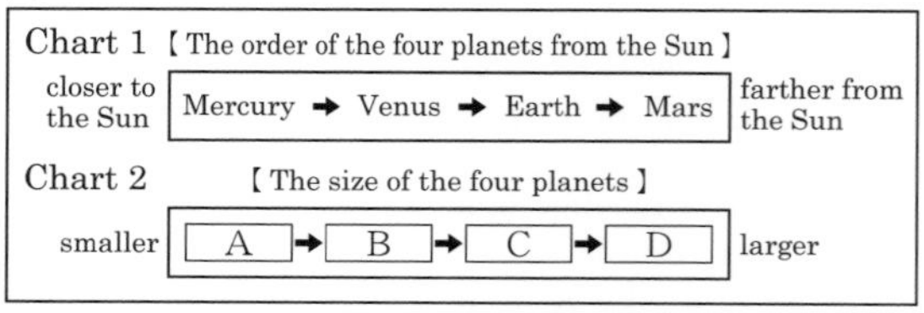

Chart 1 【 The order of the four planets from the Sun 】
closer to the Sun　Mercury ➡ Venus ➡ Earth ➡ Mars　farther from the Sun

Chart 2 　【 The size of the four planets 】
smaller　A ➡ B ➡ C ➡ D　larger

(注) space 宇宙　feature 特徴　Venus 金星
research 調べる　close to ～　～に近い
Sun 太陽　Mercury 水星　Mars 火星
chart 図　order 順番　size 大きさ
farther：farの比較級
farthest：farの最上級

〔問1〕　本文の内容に合うように，次の(1)，(2)の（　　）にあてはまる最も適切なものを，それぞれア～エの中から1つ選び，その記号を書きなさい。

(1) Takeshi is interested in planets because （　　）.

ア．the book his father gave him was great

イ．his science teacher gave him a book about them

ウ．there are many planets in space

エ．he learned about planets in space in his

science class
(2) Takeshi (　　　　).
　　ア．thought that the largest planet in space was Venus
　　イ．thought that there are only four planets in space
　　ウ．loves planets and wants to learn about planets in the future
　　エ．loves planets because he knows everything about them

〔問2〕 文中の下線部Chart 2について，本文の内容に合うように，図の　A　～　D　にあてはまるものを，次のア～エの中から1つずつ選び，その記号を書きなさい。
　　ア．Mercury　　イ．Venus
　　ウ．Earth　　　エ．Mars

〔問3〕 武志は，スピーチの後，ALT(外国語指導助手)のジェシー(Jessy)と話をしました。次の対話文は，そのやりとりの一部です。これを読み，あとの(1)，(2)に答えなさい。

Jessy	：Your speech about planets was interesting.
Takeshi	：Oh, really?　Thank you.
Jessy	：From listening to your speech, I know you really like to learn about planets. So, 　①
Takeshi	：Well, actually, it's one of my future dreams.
Jessy	：Wow!　That's exciting. You can do it! I hope you can visit some planets such as Mars in the future.
Takeshi	：I hope so.
Jessy	：　②　 if you could go to Mars tomorrow?
Takeshi	：If I could go there tomorrow, I would look at the Earth from it.
Jessy	：Sounds good!

(1) 対話の流れに合うように，文中の　①　にあてはまる最も適切なものを，次のア～エの中から1つ選び，その記号を書きなさい。
　　ア．I want to tell you about my dream for the future.
　　イ．I want you to tell me about your dream for the future.
　　ウ．I want to become a space scientist in the future.
　　エ．I want you to become a space scientist in the future.

(2) 対話の流れに合うように，文中の　②　にふさわしい英語を書きなさい。ただし，語数は4語以上とし，符号(．，?！など)は語数に含まないものとする。
　　　　　　　　　　　　　　　　　　＜和歌山県＞

2 次の英文は，中学生のミホ(Miho)がお気に入りのものについて紹介したスピーチです。これを読んで，あとの(1)～(3)に答えなさい。＊印の語句には，スピーチのあとに(注)があります。

Do you know the children's picture book, "The Very Hungry *Caterpillar" by *Eric Carle?　A little green caterpillar was born from an egg, ate one apple on Monday, three *plums on Wednesday, five oranges on Friday... and finally grew into a big, beautiful *butterfly!　If you read it, you may feel

that you want to try something new and improve yourself. The original book was written in America in 1969. The book was written in more than 70 different languages. A lot of people in the world have bought the book. Some of you may have it, but did you know that it was created by using Japanese *technology?

You can find "*Printed in Japan" on the first book's last *page. Why was it printed in Japan? The book has many colors, different page sizes, and even some holes on the pages. You can see a hole on some fruits in the book. It shows that the caterpillar has already eaten them. This is one of Eric's interesting ideas. Children can enjoy reading by putting their fingers into these holes. They were difficult to make in America. Then a Japanese man said to Eric, "We will help you. Our company's technology can do it." This is why the book was printed in Japan.

Eric's new idea and Japanese technology made this book famous. He died last May, but his book has *influenced many people around the world and will be always with us.

　(注) caterpillar　イモムシ
　　　 Eric Carle　エリック・カール(人名)
　　　 plum(s)　スモモ　　 butterfly　チョウ
　　　 technology　技術　　 print(ed)　～を印刷する
　　　 page(s)　ページ　　 influence(d)　～に影響を与える

(1) 次の文章は，ミホのスピーチの内容に関する生徒のメモです。スピーチの内容と合うように，(ア)～(ウ)に入る最も適切な日本語をそれぞれ書きなさい。
【メモ】

・「The Very Hungry Caterpillar」という絵本を読むと，(ア)に挑戦して自分を高めていきたい気持ちになる。
・果物の絵に開いている穴は，イモムシがすでに(イ)ことを表している。
・エリック氏は昨年(ウ)に亡くなったが，彼の本はこれからも私たちのそばにあり続ける。

(2) ミホのスピーチの内容と合うように，次の1～3の質問に対する答えをそれぞれ一つの英文で書きなさい。
　1．When was the original book written in America?
　2．How can children enjoy reading with the holes in the book?
　3．Was it easy to make the holes on the pages in America?

(3) 「あなたのお気に入りのもの」一つについて，その理由を含めて英語20語以上で書きなさい。文の数はいくつでもかまいません。
　　　　　　　　　　　　　　　　　　＜青森県＞

3 智也さんは，立山に生息する天然記念物(special natural monument)のライチョウ(ptarmigan)が富山の県鳥であることを知り，興味をもちました。智也さんが書いた次の英文レポートを読んで，あとの問いに答えなさい。

The ptarmigans are special natural monuments of Japan, and live only in cold places like high mountains. You can't find them in their *natural habitat so often, but you can see them on Tateyama if you have good luck. People often think the ptarmigans live only on high mountains. However, some of them spend winter by the sea in countries like Russia. Did you know that they change color each season? They become dark brown in summer and white in winter. When the birds change color like that, it is hard for other animals to find them.

The ptarmigan was first called "*rai no tori*" in the Heian period, but it was changed to *raicho* in the Edo period. When it is written in kanji, it means "*thunder bird." People in the Edo period believed that these birds protected them from fire and thunder, so the number of birds didn't *decrease for a long time. ☐ After the *order, the birds became special natural monuments of Japan.

The number of ptarmigans decreased for other reasons too. One reason is *changes in temperature. When it got hot, it was easy for strong animals that ate ptarmigans, like *foxes, to live on high mountains.

Another reason is the people who visited the mountain. They brought plastic bags and bottles that had *bacteria to the mountain. Many ptarmigans got sick and died because of the bacteria, so people started working to protect the ptarmigans. They built *fences for the birds and cleaned the mountains, but it wasn't easy to *increase the number of birds. Please look at the *chart I made with numbers from the Internet. There were more ptarmigans on Tateyama in 1991 than in 1981. However, it became more difficult to find the birds in 2001. After that, the number of birds increased because people worked harder to protect them.

I think we can also do something to protect the ptarmigans. For example, we can do volunteer work to keep their natural habitat clean. I heard that a lot of money is necessary to protect the ptarmigans, so we can also collect money to help the birds.

Through writing this report, I became more interested in the birds and I learned that a lot of effort is needed to protect them. I would like to go to Tateyama this summer to see their natural habitat and learn more about them.

(注) natural habitat　自然生息地　　thunder　雷
　　　decrease　減る　　order　命令
　　　change in temperature　気温の変化
　　　foxes：fox(キツネ)の複数形
　　　bacteria　細菌　　fence　柵(㟴)
　　　increase　増やす，増える　　chart　表

(1) 本文中の☐には，次のA～Cの文を並べ替えたものが入ります。本文の内容に合うように適切な順に並べ，記号で答えなさい。
　A. Because of this, the number of birds on the mountains decreased.
　B. However, some people started catching them for food.
　C. So, people were told to stop catching them.

(2) 下線部the chartについて，智也さんが示した表として最も適切なものを，次のア～エから1つ選んで記号で答えなさい。

ア.
年	1981	1991	2001	2011
生息数	244	333	167	284

イ.
年	1981	1991	2001	2011
生息数	284	167	244	333

ウ.
年	1981	1991	2001	2011
生息数	333	244	284	167

エ.
年	1981	1991	2001	2011
生息数	167	284	333	244

(3) 本文の内容に合うものを，次のア～エから1つ選んで記号で答えなさい。
　ア. You can see the ptarmigans by the sea in some parts of Japan.
　イ. Some ptarmigans died because the weather got too hot for them.
　ウ. The ptarmigans become dark brown in summer, so finding them is difficult for other animals.
　エ. *Rai no tori*" and *raicho* are different kinds of birds.

(4) 智也さんは，ライチョウを保護するために私たちができることを2つ述べています。その内容を日本語で書きなさい。
　　　　　　　　　　　　　　　　　　　＜富山県＞

4 次の英文は，高校1年生のコウスケ(Kosuke)が，英語の授業で発表した内容です。これを読んで，あとの(1)～(3)に答えなさい。

I gave my five-year-old sister a toy on her birthday. Then she brought the toy's box with a *2D code and asked me, "What's this? I always see this around me." Before I answered, I put my smartphone's camera over it. Then, information about the toy appeared on my phone. She was very surprised with this new world behind the 2D code. I said to her, "If we have this 2D code, we can easily get this information from it."

*Innovation sometimes comes from simple, easy answers and improves our lives. The 2D code was invented by a Japanese man. His company kept many boxes with *barcodes, but there was a problem. It was not easy to know all the box's information without any trouble. One day, workers were playing a traditional game, *igo. Don't you think it looks similar to a 2D code? He focused on its *pattern of black and white pieces. This gave him the great idea about how to keep a lot of information, and he thought what good change this would bring to his daily life. 2D codes have more information than barcodes. They are now found in textbooks, video games, and websites. This shows some people tried to find better ways to use them in their daily lives. Through this story, I respect this Japanese man and how he invented the 2D code, and I also respect people who want to make it better.

The 2D code is a good example of innovation and helped me realize an important thing. We can get great ideas from anything, anywhere, and at any time. So, innovation doesn't need to come from something big and special. There are *inconvenient things and simple problems around us. Sometimes, answers to them can be very easy. They can be the key to innovation. We just need to look around and ask ourselves, "What can be improved?" Do we look for new ideas or do we stay with only old ideas?

When I thought about this more, I found I often heard, "If I had…" or "If there were…" around me. Before, I thought these "If" *sentences would not create anything, but now I believe they can be the first step to innovation. We don't need to keep listening to and saying "If" without doing anything. Look around you to see what you can improve. How many doors of innovation have been waiting to be opened around you? You can be on the way to discover and create something better. Use people's "If" to open the doors and make our society better in ways we have never imagined.

（注）2D code(s) 二次元コード
innovation 革新
barcode(s) バーコード
igo 囲碁
pattern 模様
inconvenient 不便な
sentence(s) 文

(1) 本文の内容と合うように英文を完成させるとき，次のア～エに続く最も適切なものを，１～４の中からそれぞれ一つ選び，その番号を書きなさい。

ア．When Kosuke talked with his sister about 2D codes,
　１．it was her first time to see them.
　２．he didn't know anything about them.
　３．she saw some of them before.
　４．he let her put his smartphone over them.

イ．2D codes
　１．were born because many Japanese people tried hard to invent them.
　２．have less information than barcodes.
　３．were used in a company to keep many boxes.
　４．became popular because there were people who wanted to find ways to use them.

ウ．The thing Kosuke learned is that
　１．innovation is only born from something big and special.
　２．answers to inconvenient things can sometimes be very easy.
　３．he doesn't need to look for new ideas and should stay with old ideas.
　４．a great idea can spread in the society even if we especially don't do anything.

エ．Kosuke is thinking that
　１．he can create a better society by focusing on "If" around him.
　２．it is important to keep listening to "If" from people and waiting for innovation.
　３．the society around him has no doors of innovation, so he has to make them.
　４．"If" will create nothing and people should stop saying "If."

(2) 下線部an important thingが表している内容を日本語で書きなさい。

(3) 本文の内容をふまえて，次の英文の（ ア ）～（ ウ ）に入る最も適切な語を，下の１～７の中からそれぞれ一つ選び，その番号を書きなさい。

When a Japanese man had（ ア ）in keeping a lot of information in his work, he found an answer from an *igo* board in his daily life. Kosuke understood that he could use a（ イ ）way of thinking to make the society around him better. We should look around and（ ウ ）what we can improve without keeping only old ideas. Each of us will be one of the people who will make a good change in the future.

１．stay　　　　２．similar　　　３．easy
４．convenience　５．trouble　　　６．find
７．traditional

<青森県>

5 次の英文を読んで，問いに答えなさい。

　ハヤトが睡眠についてスライド(Slide)を使って，プレゼンテーションをしています。

How long do you sleep every day? Do you think that everyone needs almost the same sleeping hours? Please look at Slide 1. It shows how long you need to sleep. Do you sleep for around 9 hours every day? New-born babies need to sleep for more than 10 hours. Adults need to sleep about 30% of the day. You should sleep enough for your health.

Do you know how long animals sleep? Now, let's look at Slide 2. It shows that koalas sleep the longest. They sleep for more than 22 hours in a day! During the day, they sleep in trees, and then move at night. Tigers and lions sleep for more than half of the day. Tigers sleep a little longer than lions. On the other hand, giraffes sleep for the shortest time of the animals on this slide.

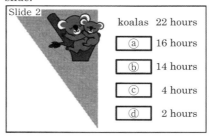

Why are they different? I'll show you two reasons. First, animals like giraffes or elephants are plant-eating animals. They need a lot of time to find food and they have to eat a lot to be （ B ）. Second, plant-eating animals can't sleep for a long time because other animals may try to eat them while they are sleeping. It is （ C ） for them. However, animals like tigers or lions are so strong that they can sleep longer than giraffes or elephants. I found some other interesting information. Some scientists say that plant-eating animals sleep longer when they are in a safe place, for example, in a zoo.

How about koalas? They are plant-eating animals, but they sleep for a long time. They are active for only 2 hours in a day. Why?

Slide 3

（注）new-born baby　新生児　　adult　大人
　　　on the other hand　一方
　　　plant-eating animals　草食動物

① 本文の内容と合うように，Slide 1 の（ A ）に入る最も適当なものを，次のア〜エのうちから一つ選び，その符号を書きなさい。
　　ア．3〜4　　　イ．5〜6
　　ウ．7〜8　　　エ．10〜11

② 本文の内容と合うように，Slide 2 の　ⓐ　〜　ⓓ　に入るものの組み合わせとして最も適当なものを，次のア〜エのうちから一つ選び，その符号を書きなさい。

Tigers

Giraffes

Lions

Elephants

	ⓐ	ⓑ	ⓒ	ⓓ
ア	Tigers	Lions	Giraffes	Elephants
イ	Tigers	Lions	Elephants	Giraffes
ウ	Lions	Tigers	Giraffes	Elephants
エ	Lions	Tigers	Elephants	Giraffes

③ 本文中の（ B ）に入る最も適当なものを，次のア〜エのうちから一つ選び，その符号を書きなさい。
　　ア．full　　イ．tired　　ウ．hungry　　エ．sleepy

④ 本文中の（ C ）に適する英単語1語を書きなさい。
　　　　　　　　　　　　　　　　　　　＜千葉県＞

6 次は，中学生のKenが英語の授業で発表した鳥と湿地（wetlands）についてのプレゼンテーションである。英文を読み，あとの問いに答えなさい。

Hello everyone. Do you like birds? I love birds so much. Today, I'd like to talk about birds and their favorite places, wetlands.

①Today, I will talk about four points. First, I want to talk about birds in Japan. Second, I will explain favorite places of birds. Third, I will tell you ②the problem about their favorite places, and then, I will explain why wetlands are important for us, too.

Do you know how many kinds of birds there are in Japan? Bird lovers in Japan work together to learn about birds every year. From 2016 to 2020, 379 kinds of birds were found. ③Please look at this *graph. The three birds seen often in Japan are *Hiyodori*, *Uguisu*, and *Suzume*. We have seen *Hiyodori*

the most often. From 1997 to 2002, we could see *Suzume* more often than *Uguisu*, but *Suzume* became the third from 2016 to 2020.

Second, I will talk about birds' favorite places, "wetlands." Have you ever heard about wetlands? Wetlands are *areas of *lands which are covered with water. Why do birds love wetlands?

Wetlands can give the best environment for many kinds of living things. There is a lot of water in wetlands. So, many kinds of plants live there. These plants are home and food for many *insects and fish. Birds eat those plants, insects, and fish. Wetlands are the best environment for birds because there is a lot of (④) for birds.

Wetlands are now getting smaller and that's a big problem. You can find information on the website of *the United Nations. It says, "In just 50 years — since 1970 — 35% of the world's wetlands have been lost." Why are they getting smaller? Each wetland has different reasons for this. People are using too much (⑤). For example, they use it for drinking, *agriculture and *industry. *Global warming is hurting wetlands, too. Wetlands are lost faster than forests because of these reasons. This is very serious for birds.

Do we have to solve this? Yes, we do. Those birds' favorite places are very important for humans, too. They support both our lives and environment. I'll tell you ⑥two things that wetlands do for us. First, wetlands make water clean. After the rain, water stays in wetlands. Then, *dirt in the water goes down, and the clean water goes into the river. We use that clean water in our comfortable lives. Second, wetlands can hold CO_2. Plants there keep CO_2 in their bodies even after they die. Actually, wetlands are better at holding CO_2 than forests. They are very useful to stop global warming.

Why don't you do something together to protect birds and wetlands? Thank you for listening.

（注）graph　グラフ
　　　area(s)　地域
　　　land　陸地
　　　insect(s)　昆虫
　　　the United Nations　国際連合
　　　agriculture　農業
　　　industry　産業
　　　global warming　地球温暖化
　　　dirt　泥

1．次は，下線部①でKenが見せたスライドである。Kenが発表した順になるようにスライドの（ A ）〜（ C ）に入る最も適当なものを下のア〜ウの中からそれぞれ一つずつ選び，その記号を書け。

Birds and Wetlands	
1.	（ A ）
2.	（ B ）
3.	（ C ）
4.	Why Wetlands are Important

ア．The Problem about Wetlands
イ．Birds' Favorite Places
ウ．Birds in Japan

２．下線部②の内容を最もよく表している英語５語を，本文中から抜き出して書け。

３．下線部③でKenが見せたグラフとして最も適当なものを次のア〜ウの中から一つ選び，その記号を書け。

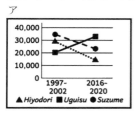
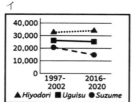

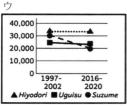

※各グラフの縦軸は鳥の数を，横軸は調査期間を示す。
（「全国鳥類繁殖分布調査」をもとに作成）

４．（ ④ ），（ ⑤ ）に入る語の組み合わせとして，最も適当なものを下のア〜エから一つ選び，その記号を書け。

	④	⑤
ア	money	water
イ	money	air
ウ	food	air
エ	food	water

５．下線部⑥の内容を具体的に25字程度の日本語で書け。

６．次は，Annが自分の発表で使うグラフと，それを見ながら話しているAnnとKenとの対話である。Annに代わって，対話中の□□□に15語程度の英文を書け。２文以上になってもかまわない。

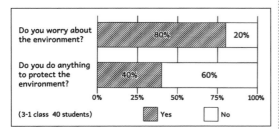

Do you worry about the environment? 80% 20%
Do you do anything to protect the environment? 40% 60%
0% 25% 50% 75% 100%
(3-1 class 40 students) ▨ Yes □ No

Ann : Your presentation was good. I'll speak in the next class. Please look at this. 80% of our classmates worry about the environment, but more than half of them don't do anything to save the environment. I don't think it is good. We should do something to change this.

Ken : What can we do?

Ann :

Ken : That's a good idea.

〈鹿児島県〉

7 次の英文を読んで，後の(1)〜(4)の問いに答えなさい。なお，本文中の【１】〜【５】は，Kojiが発表した内容の段落番号を示しています。

A junior high school student, Koji, reads news on the Internet every day. One day, he found interesting news about convenience stores. Now *robots are working at some convenience stores in Japan! Koji wanted to know more about this news and found interesting things about convenience stores. He *gave a presentation about them in an English class.

【１】 The history of convenience stores started in the U.S.A. in 1927. About 45 years later, convenience stores in Japan opened. At that time, they didn't have many *services, and they didn't sell many kinds of things. For example, they were not open for 24 hours, and they didn't sell *onigiri*. When they started to sell *onigiri*, it was a new idea. There were just a few people who bought them. Since then, convenience stores have changed a lot.

【２】 Now in Japan, there are about 58,000 convenience stores. Each store sells about 3,000 kinds of things and has a lot of services. They sell many kinds of *onigiri* and *bento* every day. At convenience stores, we can also buy *stamps, so they are like post offices. My mother *pays electricity bills at a convenience store. She says, "I don't have to go to a *bank, and I can pay at night." These services started about 30 years ago, and there are many other services now.

【３】 Convenience stores have changed because our *society has changed. There are more old people in our society, so customers at convenience stores have changed, too. About 30 years ago, most of the customers were young people. □□□□□ Convenience stores sell food in small sizes. Old people who don't eat so much think the size is perfect for them.

【４】 Convenience stores have many important *roles, but there is a problem for them because of changes in society. There are not so many people who can work. If convenience stores cannot find *enough workers, they have to close. What should they do about this problem?

【５】 Using robots may be an answer to this question. It is a new idea now. There are just a few robots at convenience stores in Japan. They are just learning how to move, and they are not working very much yet. But in the future, there will be more robots, and those robots may □□□□□□□ at convenience stores. Then convenience stores don't have to close. Convenience stores are small shops, but they have big roles in our society. They will change more because our society will change, too.

（注）robot ロボット
give a presentation 発表する
service サービス　　stamp 切手
pay an electricity bill 電気料金を支払う
bank 銀行　society 社会　role 役割
enough 十分な

(1) Kojiは，【１】〜【５】の各段落のタイトルを示しながら発表しました。次のア〜オは，【１】〜【５】のいずれかの段落のタイトルを表しています。【１】，【２】，【４】の段落の内容を表すタイトルとして最も適切なものを，それぞれア〜オから選びなさい。

<table>
<tr><td>

ア.

The future of
convenience stores

</td><td>

イ.

A change in
customers at
convenience stores

</td></tr>
</table>

ア.	イ.
The future of convenience stores	A change in customers at convenience stores
ウ.	エ.
The services at convenience stores now	A problem for convenience stores

オ.

Convenience stores in
old days

(2) 【3】の段落の[＿＿]には，次のア～ウが入ります。英文の流れを考えて，最も適切な順序になるように，ア～ウを並べなさい。

　ア．Also, if they buy food like *onigiri* or *bento* there, they don't have to cook.

　イ．Convenience stores near their houses are very useful because they can walk to the store and don't have to drive.

　ウ．But now there are many old customers.

(3) 【5】の段落の[＿＿]の部分に当てはまる内容を考えて，Kojiの発表の流れに合うように，4語以上の英語で書きなさい。

(4) 本文の内容と合っているものを，次のア～オから2つ選びなさい。

　ア．Koji saw interesting news about robots working at convenience stores on TV.

　イ．When convenience stores started selling *onigiri*, those *onigiri* weren't very popular.

　ウ．When convenience stores first opened in Japan, they sold stamps like post offices.

　エ．Now it is not difficult for convenience stores to find people who can work there.

　オ．Using robots is a new idea for a problem which convenience stores in Japan have now.

〈群馬県〉

8 高校1年生の生徒が，英語の授業での発表に向けて，次の英文を読んでポスターを作成しました。あとの問いに答えなさい。

Do you know what a *fishfinder* is? It is a machine *fishers use to find groups of fish in the sea. The first fishfinder was invented about 70 years ago. With this machine, they were able to catch more fish than before because they could see where the groups of fish were on the screen.

However, the old fishfinder caused a problem. Fishers sometimes caught too many young fish because they could not see the size of each fish. As a result, the number of fish became smaller in some areas, and fishers could not catch enough fish.

A Japanese man who used to study dolphins got an idea to improve this problem. He knew how

dolphins could swim fast and were good at catching fish. They have a special skill for hunting with sound waves. Dolphins *emit sound waves many times very quickly. These sound waves will reach the fish and come back. So, dolphins can easily find where the fish are. They can see the shape, size, and speed of the fish, too.

He *applied the dolphins' skill to his fishfinder. It was a great success. Today, his new fishfinder can show the image more clearly than the old one. So, fishers can even see how large each fish is. When they find that the fish are too young, they can stop fishing and go to another place. This is helpful to save young fish in that area. Fishers can keep catching fish there for many years.

He said, "The sea has given us a lot of good things for a long time. I'd like to give something back to it. I believe we have to learn from nature around us. The dolphins' skill is one of the examples. From dolphins, I got the idea and invented the new fishfinder. I want to continue inventing useful machines for our daily lives. If more children like the sea because of my work, I'll be very happy."

(注) fishfinder　魚群探知機
　　　fishers　漁師
　　　emit　出す
　　　apply　応用する

Poster

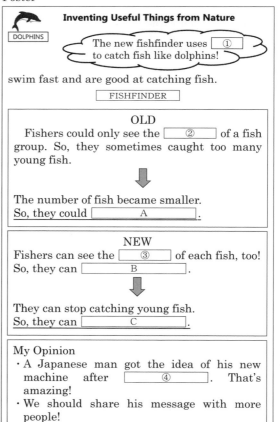

Inventing Useful Things from Nature

DOLPHINS

The new fishfinder uses ① to catch fish like dolphins!

swim fast and are good at catching fish.

FISHFINDER

OLD
Fishers could only see the ② of a fish group. So, they sometimes caught too many young fish.

The number of fish became smaller.
So, they could 　A 　.

NEW
Fishers can see the ③ of each fish, too!
So, they can 　B 　.

They can stop catching young fish.
So, they can 　C 　.

My Opinion
・A Japanese man got the idea of his new machine after ④ . That's amazing!
・We should share his message with more people!

1．ポスターの □①□ に入る適切なものを，次のア～エから１つ選んで，その符号を書きなさい。
　ア．large screens　　　イ．old machines
　ウ．swimming skills　　エ．sound waves

2．ポスターの □②□ ，□③□ に入る語の組み合わせとして適切なものを，次のア～エから１つ選んで，その符号を書きなさい。
　ア．② place　　③ speed
　イ．② speed　　③ place
　ウ．② place　　③ size
　エ．② speed　　③ shape

3．ポスターの □A□ ～□C□ に入る適切なものを，次のア～エからそれぞれ１つ選んで，その符号を書きなさい。
　ア．choose the fish they want to catch
　イ．continue catching fish for many years
　ウ．learn how to catch fish from dolphins
　エ．catch only a small number of fish

4．ポスターの □④□ に入る適切なものを，次のア～エから１つ選んで，その符号を書きなさい。
　ア．inventing something useful in our daily lives
　イ．paying attention to the hunting skills of dolphins
　ウ．catching a lot of fish with the new machine
　エ．improving the machine to get many kinds of fish

〈兵庫県〉

9 次の英文は，高校生の次郎が，校内英語スピーチコンテストで発表したときの原稿です。これに関して，あとの１～６に答えなさい。

What are you interested in? Music, video games, or sports? When I was five years old, I found the most interesting thing in a forest near my house. It was a mushroom. I remember exactly how the mushroom I first found looked. It was red and looked beautiful. I tried to pick it, but my father stopped me. He said to me, "It is a poisonous mushroom." He taught me that there are dangerous mushrooms. After I got home, I read a book about mushrooms and was surprised. The book had pictures of more than 700 different mushrooms. I thought, "Why are there so many beautiful mushrooms?" and "Why are there some poisonous mushrooms?" This was the beginning of my curiosity about mushrooms.

Since then, I have read many books about mushrooms and learned that there are many mushrooms in the world. I have also learned that there are still a lot of mushrooms that have no names. I often walk in the forest near my house and try to find such mushrooms.

Now, I'll introduce two of my favorite mushrooms. The first one is *yakoutake*. The mushrooms are found on some islands in Japan and emit a beautiful green light. Many people travel to the islands to see them. Why do they emit a beautiful green light? ①We don't have a clear answer, but some people say the mushrooms may do it to attract insects which carry the spores of the mushrooms. Spores are necessary for new mushrooms to grow.

My other favorite mushroom is *benitengutake*. This is the mushroom I first found in the forest near my house. The caps of the mushrooms are a beautiful red, and people in some countries believe that the mushrooms bring happiness. However, they are poisonous and dangerous for many animals. For example, if a dog eats them, it will feel sick. Why are they poisonous? Maybe they don't want animals to eat them.

I feel each mushroom has different messages to insects and animals. For example, the message of *yakoutake* is "Come to me!" and the message of *benitengutake* is "Don't □ me!" Insects and animals cannot hear these messages, but they can feel them.

By the way, how do mushrooms communicate with each other? A scientist says that mushrooms use electrical signals. I don't know the truth, but maybe they are talking with each other to protect themselves. ②It (if　fun　I　be　would) could understand what mushrooms are talking about.

I'd like to study more about mushrooms at university. My dream is to visit many places around the world and find mushrooms that I have never seen. I also want to learn more about their way of communicating. I have not lost the curiosity that I had when I was a child. It led me to my dream for the future. Now, I'll ask you the question again. "What are you interested in?" Your curiosity will help you find your dreams.

（注）forest　森　　mushroom　キノコ
　exactly　正確に　　poisonous　有毒な
　curiosity　好奇心　　emit　発する　　clear　明確な
　attract　引き寄せる　　insect　昆虫　　spore　胞子
　grow　育つ　　cap　(キノコの)かさ
　happiness　幸福　　electrical　電気の
　signal　信号　　truth　真実
　themselves　彼ら自身を　　led　導いた

1．次の(1)・(2)に対する答えを，それぞれ英文で書きなさい。
　(1) Did Jiro find the most interesting thing when he was five years old?
　(2) Who stopped Jiro when he tried to pick the mushroom he first found?

2．下線部①について，その内容を表している最も適切な英文を，次のア～エの中から選び，その記号を書きなさい。
　ア．We do not know exactly where we can see *yakoutake*.
　イ．We want to know when the beautiful green light of *yakoutake* can be seen.
　ウ．We do not know exactly why a beautiful green light is emitted by *yakoutake*.
　エ．We want to know how we can get *yakoutake*.

3．本文中の □ に適切な語を１語補って，英文を完成しなさい。

4．下線部②が意味の通る英文になるように，(　　)内の語を並べかえなさい。

5．次のア～エの中で，本文の内容に合っているものを２つ選び，その記号を書きなさい。
　ア．There are many mushrooms which do not have names.
　イ．*Yakoutake* and *benitengutake* are Jiro's favorite mushrooms.
　ウ．Some people believe that *yakoutake* and

benitengutake bring happiness.

エ．Jiro's dream is to protect all of the mushrooms around the world.

6．校内英語スピーチコンテストに聴衆として参加した生徒たちは，英語の授業で，発表者にあててスピーチの感想を書くことになりました。あなたなら，次郎がスピーチで話した内容についてどのような感想を書きますか。25語程度の英文で書きなさい。なお，2文以上になっても構いません。

〈広島県〉

10 次の英文は，健太（Kenta）が英語の時間に発表したものである。これを読んで，1〜6の問いに答えなさい。

I love the sea. I was born near the beautiful sea. When I was a small child, I often enjoyed swimming and playing with sea animals there. I cannot think about living without the sea. But now marine ecosystems are not in good condition. I worry about that. What can we do about that? Many people work together to protect marine ecosystems. I will tell you some examples from books which I _____(A)_____ from the library last week.

In Australia, people have started a project for green sea turtles on an island. They go there to lay eggs on the beach. [　ア　] There is a problem. The sea level is getting higher. If their eggs are under water, their babies cannot come out of the eggs. So people thought about what to do for green sea turtles and tried to protect them by _____(B)_____ the island's beach taller.

We can see projects to protect marine ecosystems also in Japan. In Aichi, people have started their *amamo* project. *Amamo* is a kind of plant. It is very important for small sea animals. [　イ　] It gives them oxygen. Also, it helps them stay away from bigger sea animals. We can say that it is home for (C)them because it is a safe place. However, the amount of *amamo* got smaller. So people have started to put *amamo* at the bottom of the sea. They hope that it will give a good life to small sea animals. Many projects like this are done in other parts of Japan, too.

In Chiba, (D)a fisherman has started his "sustainable fishing" project. He worries that the number of some kinds of fish living in the sea near Tokyo is getting smaller. So he doesn't catch fish with eggs and young fish. They are put back into the sea. Also, he visits a lot of places to let people know what he is doing. He hopes that people in the future can also enjoy eating many kinds of fish from the sea near Tokyo.

In Okinawa, people have started a project to protect coral. Some coral there died because of the red soil. Strong typhoons often come to the islands, and the red soil on the fields goes into the sea. When coral is under the red soil, it often dies. [　ウ　] If the fields are surrounded with plants which have strong roots, the red soil can stay on the fields. Many people have joined this project, and now much coral there is protected from the red soil.

I want to have a job that is related to marine ecosystems in the future. [　エ　] Many kinds of sea animals have been extinct. I am very sad about that. I am interested in starting my own project, and I want many people to join it. If we work together, we can do more things to protect marine ecosystems. I hope that everyone will think about what to do for marine ecosystems.

（注）marine ecosystem(s)　海洋生態系
　　be in good condition　良い状態である
　　protect 〜　〜を守る　　project(s)　計画
　　green sea turtle(s)　アオウミガメ
　　island(s)　島　　lay 〜　〜を産む　　beach　浜辺
　　level　高さ　　baby (babies)　赤ちゃん
　　amamo　アマモ　　plant(s)　植物　　oxygen　酸素
　　safe　安全な　　amount　量　　bottom　底
　　fisherman　漁師
　　sustainable fishing　持続可能な漁業
　　coral　サンゴ　　red soil　赤土　　typhoon(s)　台風
　　field(s)　畑
　　be surrounded with 〜　〜で囲まれる
　　root(s)　根　　be related to 〜　〜と関係がある
　　extinct　絶滅した

1．本文中の(A)，(B)に入る英語として最も適当なものを，次の中から一つずつ選び，それぞれ正しい形の1語に直して書け。

become	borrow	forget	make
sell	wash	write	

2．次の1文が入る最も適当な場所を，本文中のア〜エの中から一つ選び，その記号を書け。

To stop that, a junior high school student gave people there a good idea.

3．本文中の(C)が指すものを，3語で本文中からそのまま抜き出して書け。

4．下の文は，本文中の(D)が行っている活動をまとめたものである。本文の内容に合うように，文中の（　①　）〜（　③　）にそれぞれ当てはまる適当な日本語を書け。（①，②の順序は問わない。）

（　①　）や（　②　）を捕らずに海に戻す。また，自分の取り組みを（　③　）ために，多くの場所を訪れる。

5．本文中に書かれている内容と一致するものを，次のア〜キの中から二つ選び，その記号を書け。

ア．Kenta likes the sea very much and thinks that it is important in his life.

イ．Green sea turtles in Australia don't come out of the sea when they lay eggs.

ウ．*Amamo* is a kind of plant which needs more oxygen than other plants in the sea.

エ．The fisherman in Chiba wants many people to eat a lot of fish for their health.

オ．Coral in Okinawa cannot live without the red soil which goes into the sea.

カ．Plants which have strong roots can help the red soil stay on the fields.

キ．Kenta hopes that many people will need him for their own projects.

6．この発表の題名として最も適当なものを，次のア〜エの中から一つ選び，その記号を書け。

ア．A way to become a good fisherman in the future

イ．Working together for better marine ecosystems

ウ．Many kinds of plants which have been extinct

エ．Swimming with green sea turtles in the world
＜愛媛県＞

11
次の英文は，高校生のカイト（Kaito）が英語の授業で行った人工知能についての発表の原稿です。英文を読んで，あとの（ア）～（ウ）の問いに答えなさい。

Hi, I'm Kaito. Today, I will talk about AI *devices. We use many kinds of AI devices like *robots, *drones, and *smartphones. AI devices collect a lot of information, remember it, and use it to do work given by humans. I think AI devices can make our lives better. There is still a lot of work AI devices cannot do, but they can do some work to make our lives easier. Through my speech, I want you to learn more about AI devices and to imagine how we can live with them in the future.

I didn't know anything about AI devices before I joined an event about them this summer. It *was held by Kamome City. At the event, I learned about many kinds of AI devices. I saw a robot that worked like a doctor. When a woman told the robot that she had some problems with her body, it asked her some questions, and gave her *suggestions to make her feel better. A man from Kamome *City Office said to me, "Though this robot can work like a doctor, (①). It cannot *replace a doctor. But there will be more robots working in hospitals in the future." At the event, I started thinking about the ways to make AI devices that can help humans.

After I went to the event, I started to learn more about AI devices. I've learned that AI devices are used in many different ways. For example, AI devices help farmers. Look at this *graph. It shows the *changes in the number of farmers in 2010, 2015, and 2020 in Japan and how old they were in each year. The number of farmers became smaller, and the *percentage of the farmers who were 60 years old and older than 60 years old became larger. And now, AI devices *are expected to be a great help to farmers.

I went to another event to learn how AI devices actually help farmers. One robot I saw there helped farmers pick tomatoes. The robot has a *camera on it to collect a lot of information about the tomatoes. It remembers the shapes and *colors of *ripe tomatoes and decides when to pick the tomatoes. When it decides to pick the tomatoes, it picks them with its arms. Farmers send the tomatoes that the robot has picked to the stores. At this event, I talked with a farmer who used the *tomato-picking robot. I asked him, "What do you think about working with the robot?" He said, "I don't think robots and humans can do all of the same work. But (②). Today, robots have become very important. The number of young people who want to be farmers has become smaller, because a farmer's work is hard and needs much experience. If robots can do the hard work for farmers, they will improve farmers' lives. I hope more young people will want to become farmers."

AI devices are used in our lives in many ways. I've learned that it is difficult for us to live without AI devices in today's world. However, we need to remember AI devices are not perfect. AI devices can remember all the information they collect, but (③). So, we always have to think about effective ways of using them. I hope that more AI devices will be used to help people. AI devices, like the doctor robot and the tomato-picking robot, can improve our lives. So, I want to make AI devices that can work well with humans to make our lives better in the future. That's my dream. Thank you for listening.

（注）devices 機器　robots ロボット
　　　drones ドローン
　　　smartphones スマートフォン
　　　was held 開催された　　suggestions 提案
　　　City Office 市役所
　　　replace ～　～に取って代わる
　　　graph グラフ　changes in ～　～の変化
　　　percentage 割合
　　　are expected to ～　～と思われている
　　　camera カメラ　colors 色　ripe 熟した
　　　tomato-picking robot トマト摘みロボット

（ア）本文中の＿＿＿線部が表す内容として最も適するものを，次の１～４の中から一つ選び，その番号を答えなさい。

1.
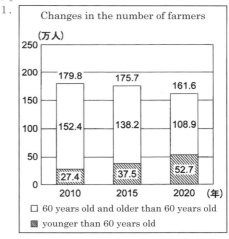
Changes in the number of farmers
（万人）
179.8　175.7　161.6
152.4　138.2　108.9
27.4　37.5　52.7
2010　2015　2020　（年）
□ 60 years old and older than 60 years old
▨ younger than 60 years old

2.
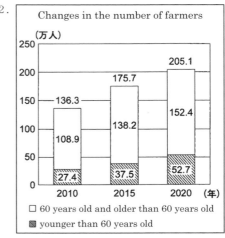
Changes in the number of farmers
（万人）
136.3　175.7　205.1
108.9　138.2　152.4
27.4　37.5　52.7
2010　2015　2020　（年）
□ 60 years old and older than 60 years old
▨ younger than 60 years old

3.

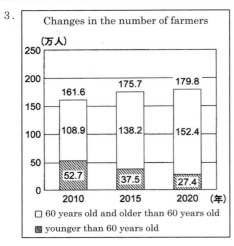

Changes in the number of farmers

(万人)

	2010	2015	2020 (年)
60 years old and older than 60 years old	161.6 (108.9)	175.7 (138.2)	179.8 (152.4)
younger than 60 years old	52.7	37.5	27.4

□ 60 years old and older than 60 years old
▨ younger than 60 years old

4.

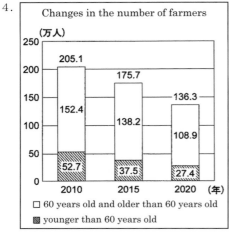

Changes in the number of farmers

(万人)

	2010	2015	2020 (年)
60 years old and older than 60 years old	205.1 (152.4)	175.7 (138.2)	136.3 (108.9)
younger than 60 years old	52.7	37.5	27.4

□ 60 years old and older than 60 years old
▨ younger than 60 years old

(イ)　本文中の（　①　）～（　③　）の中に，次のA～Cを意味が通るように入れるとき，その組み合わせとして最も適するものを，あとの１～６の中から一つ選び，その番号を答えなさい。

A．there are things it cannot do
B．humans have to teach the devices how to use it
C．robots can do some work humans do

1．①−A　②−B　③−C
2．①−A　②−C　③−B
3．①−B　②−A　③−C
4．①−B　②−C　③−A
5．①−C　②−A　③−B
6．①−C　②−B　③−A

(ウ)　次のa～fの中から，本文の内容に合うものを二つ選んだときの組み合わせとして最も適するものを，あとの１～８の中から一つ選び，その番号を答えなさい。

a．Kaito wants his audience to imagine a future with AI devices in his speech.
b．Kaito found at the event he joined that the doctor robot couldn't give a woman suggestions.
c．Kaito learned at the event he joined that Japanese farmers didn't like using AI devices.
d．The tomato-picking robot does a lot of work such as sending tomatoes to the stores.

e．Robots will improve farmers' lives by doing the hard work that farmers do.
f．Kaito's dream is to make AI devices that can replace humans.

1．aとc　　2．aとe
3．aとf　　4．bとd
5．bとe　　6．cとd
7．cとf　　8．dとe

<神奈川県>

12 次は，高校生の雅代(Masayo)が英語の授業で行ったスピーチの原稿です。彼女が書いたこの原稿を読んで，あとの問いに答えなさい。

Do you like scallops? A scallop is a kind of shellfish with two shells. Scallops are delicious and they are my favorite food. One day, after I ate them for dinner, I saw an amazing scene on TV. Many scallops were swimming and jumping in the sea! When I saw it, I was very surprised ＿＿①＿＿ I didn't know that shellfish could move quickly. I thought, "How can they move like that?" I became interested and looked for information on the Internet. ＿＿②＿＿

ホタテガイの貝殻 (a shell) を示す写真

scallops（ホタテガイ）

How do scallops move? Scallops move by taking water into their shells and pushing it out quickly. They can go forward or turn by changing how they push the water out. For example, if they want to go to the right, they push the water out to the left. This means scallops can move by pushing the water out quickly to the ＿＿③＿＿ side of the way they want to go. By using this way of moving, when other sea animals try to eat scallops, scallops swim away from ⒶＴＨＥＭ to protect their lives. Scallops also move to find a good place for getting their food, and some of them move 500 meters in one night. Scallops are the most active of all shellfish with two shells.

写真

scallops in the sea

Well, I want to ask your experience. ＿＿④＿＿ the two shells with your hands? When I did that for the first time, I noticed it was not easy. ＿＿⑤＿＿ According to the books, they have a strong muscle to keep closing their shells. When shellfish with two shells live in the ocean, to keep closing their shells, they usually keep using the strong muscle. For us, it is like holding a heavy bag for a long time. If we do that, we will be very tired because it needs a lot of energy. However, shellfish with two shells don't become tired. Their muscle needs very little energy to keep closing their shells. It has a special protein that we don't have. To keep closing the shells, the special protein connects with each other. When the proteins are in that condition, shellfish with two shells don't become tired by using the muscle. This means, if we had the same muscle that shellfish with two shells have, ＿＿⑥＿＿ by holding a heavy bag for a long time. When I learned about this, I thought it was very interesting and also very useful.

貝の写真

shellfish with two shells

— 44 —

Now I know shellfish like scallops are not just delicious food. Scallops are active shellfish which can move quickly. In addition, I understand the muscle of shellfish with two shells has an amazing power that we don't have. If science and technology improve more in the future, we can use the power of the strong muscle. I think it will help people carry some heavy things or take care of people who need help. I believe we can support many people with difficulties. Thank you for listening.

（注）shellfish （生き物としての）貝（複数形もshellfish）
　　　muscle　筋肉
　　　protein　タンパク質

(1) 本文の内容から考えて，次のうち，本文中の ① に入れるのに最も適しているものはどれですか。一つ選び，記号で答えなさい。

　ア. because　　イ. if　　ウ. though　　エ. until

(2) 本文中の ② が，「いくつかのレポートを読むことで，私はそれらがどのようにして動くことができるのかを理解しました。」という内容になるように，次の〔　　〕内の語を並べかえて，英文を完成させなさい。

　By reading some reports, I〔could　they how　move　understood〕.

(3) 本文の内容から考えて，次のうち，本文中の ③ に入れるのに最も適しているものはどれですか。一つ選び，記号で答えなさい。

　ア. same　　イ. similar
　ウ. open　　エ. opposite

(4) 本文中のⒶthemの表している内容に当たるものとして最も適しているひとつづきの英語３語を，本文中から抜き出して書きなさい。

(5) 本文中の ' ④ the two shells with your hands?' が，「あなたはその２枚の貝殻を手で開けようとしたことがありますか。」という内容になるように，英語５語を書き入れ，英文を完成させなさい。

(6) 本文中の ⑤ に，次の(i)〜(ⅲ)の英文を適切な順序に並べかえ，前後と意味がつながる内容となるようにして入れたい。あとのア〜エのうち，英文の順序として最も適しているものはどれですか。一つ選び，記号で答えなさい。

　(i) I remembered this experience, and wanted to know why shellfish could keep closing their shells.
　(ⅱ) It was hard work and it took a long time, and finally I couldn't.
　(ⅲ) So, I went to a library, read some books, and then found the answer to the question.
　　ア．(i)→(ⅲ)→(ⅱ)
　　イ．(ⅱ)→(i)→(ⅲ)
　　ウ．(ⅱ)→(ⅲ)→(i)
　　エ．(ⅲ)→(i)→(ⅱ)

(7) 本文の内容から考えて，次のうち，本文中の ⑥ に入れるのに最も適しているものはどれですか。一つ選び，記号で答えなさい。

　ア．the shellfish are tired
　イ．the shellfish are not tired
　ウ．we would be tired
　エ．we would not be tired

(8) 次のうち，本文で述べられている内容と合うものはどれですか。一つ選び，記号で答えなさい。

　ア．Masayo got the information about the muscle of shellfish with two shells by watching TV.
　イ．Some scallops move 500 meters in one night

and look for a good place for getting their food.
　ウ．Masayo thinks scallops are just delicious food and her thought wasn't changed after she read some reports and books.
　エ．Shellfish with two shells become tired when the special protein in their muscle connects with each other.

(9) 本文の内容と合うように，次の問いに対する答えをそれぞれ英語で書きなさい。ただし，①は３語，②は９語の英語で書くこと。
　① Are scallops the most active of all shellfish with two shells?
　② If science and technology improve more in the future, what can we use?

<大阪府・Ｂ問題>

13 次は，高校１年生のMayumiが書いた英文です。これを読んで，問１〜問６に答えなさい。＊印のついている語句には，本文のあとに（注）があります。

How do you *deal with rainy days? I use an umbrella. *Whenever I use an umbrella, I wonder why the shape of umbrellas never changes. I wish there were an umbrella that I didn't have to hold with my hands. But there are no umbrellas like that. Umbrellas still keep the same shape. When I use an umbrella, I open it and hold it. When did people start using umbrellas? How do people in other countries deal with rainy days? Why hasn't the shape of the umbrella changed? I researched the history and culture of umbrellas to answer my questions.

Picture 1

Early umbrellas looked like a *canopy with a stick and could not close (Picture 1). It *seems that they were used to A the *authority of the owner, such as a king.

The earliest *evidence of umbrellas in Japan is from the Kofun period. However, it is hard to find where Japanese umbrellas were born. Some say umbrellas came from other countries. Others say umbrellas were made in Japan a long time ago.

Picture 2

After reading some articles and books, I learned that people began to use umbrellas after the middle of the Edo period. Japanese umbrellas were made from bamboo *shafts and bones covered with oil paper. They were very expensive, so only rich people could buy them. They could open and close but were heavy and easily B . So, until the Edo period, most people used *mino* and *sugegasa* on rainy days (Picture 2). After the way of making Japanese umbrellas spread, they became easier and cheaper to make. Umbrella culture was found in *Kabuki* and *Ukiyo-e*, so it spread to many people. Japanese umbrella makers thought their umbrellas would be popular, but the *introduction of Western umbrellas to Japan changed the situation.

Many Japanese people first saw Western umbrellas when *Commodore Perry came to Japan by ship. Some staff who came with him to Japan used them. After the Meiji period, Western umbrellas were brought to and sold in Japan. They became popular because of their light weight and cool design, and soon they spread around Japan.

In the twentieth century, some makers in Japan kept making Japanese umbrellas, and others started making Western umbrellas. However, some makers tried hard to create their own umbrellas. Around 1950, some makers created folding umbrellas, *based on the ones developed in Germany. About 10 years later, an umbrella maker invented the *vinyl umbrella. It was first seen by people around the world at the 1964 Tokyo Olympics. It became popular in Japan and overseas. Maybe the *transparency and good visibility made it popular. In this way, ①

By the way, how do people in other countries deal with rainy days? In some countries, the rainy and dry seasons are *distinct. In the rainy season, it rains suddenly and stops after a short time. For this reason, many people say, "We don't use umbrellas because ② "

How about Japan? Of course, it rains a lot in Japan, and Japan has a rainy season. But, I found an interesting news article on the Internet. It said each person has an *average of 3.3 umbrellas in Japan and the average for other countries is 2.4 umbrellas. This means that Japanese people *tend to use umbrellas more often when it rains. However, in New Zealand, people don't use umbrellas very often when it rains, though ③ What is the reason for this difference? I *compared the *humidity of the two countries and found that Japan has higher humidity. In my opinion, because of the high humidity, it takes longer to dry off if they get wet, so Japanese people use umbrellas more often than people in other countries. It seems that the way of thinking about umbrellas depends on the weather of the country which you live in.

Before reading the articles and books about umbrellas, I didn't think that the shape of umbrellas has changed. However, when I researched the history of umbrellas, I learned that they have actually changed shape. Early umbrellas were a canopy with a stick. But now, umbrellas can open and close, and there are folding umbrellas, too. Umbrellas will continue to change shape in the future. Sometimes〔I / in / be / like / will / what / imagine / umbrellas〕the future. For example, there may be umbrellas that fly above our heads and *provide a barrier. When I was thinking about future umbrellas, I *noticed something interesting. The umbrella I imagined might be a *sugegasa* with a different shape. We may get a hint for creating a new umbrella by learning about its history.

（注）deal with ～　～に対処する
　　　whenever ～　～するときはいつでも
　　　canopy with a stick　棒のついた天蓋
　　　seem ～　～のようである
　　　authority of the owner　所有者の権威
　　　evidence　形跡　　shaft and bone　軸と骨
　　　introduction　伝来
　　　Commodore Perry　ペリー提督
　　　based on ～　～をもとに　　vinyl　ビニール

transparency and good visibility　透明で良好な視界
distinct　はっきりしている　　average　平均
tend to ～　～する傾向にある
compare ～　～を比べる　　humidity　湿度
provide a barrier　バリアを張る
notice ～　～に気づく

問1．本文の内容に関する次の質問に，英語で答えなさい。
　　Why did Western umbrellas become popular in Japan after the Meiji period?
問2．Mayumiは，自分の意見として，日本人が，他国の人々と比べて傘を使う頻度が高いのはなぜだと述べていますか。日本語で書きなさい。
問3．空欄　A ，　B にあてはまる最も適切なものを，次の中から一つずつ選び，必要に応じて，それぞれ正しい形にかえて書きなさい。

break	surprise	show	sell
worry	buy	learn	know

問4．空欄　① ～　③ にあてはまる最も適切な文を，次のア～カの中から一つずつ選び，その記号を書きなさい。なお，同じ記号を2度以上使うことはありません。
ア．many umbrella makers stopped making new umbrellas.
イ．it is sold at a higher price.
ウ．some types of umbrellas were made by Japanese makers.
エ．it rains as much as in Japan.
オ．everyone uses an umbrella when it rains.
カ．it will soon stop raining.
問5．〔　　　〕内のすべての語を，本文の流れに合うように，正しい順序に並べかえて書きなさい。
問6．次の英文は，本文の内容をまとめたものです。次の（　1　）～（　3　）に適切な英語を，それぞれ2語で書きなさい。

　　Mayumi wondered why umbrellas have not changed their shape. She researched the history and culture of umbrellas. She learned that people in Japan started（　1　）after the middle of the Edo period. After the Meiji period, some Japanese makers tried hard to make their own umbrellas. She also learned that Japanese people have（　2　）from people in other countries about using umbrellas. After she finished her research, she found that umbrellas have actually changed shape. She sometimes imagined future umbrellas. She noticed that the umbrella she imagined could be *sugegasa* with a different shape. She thought learning the history of umbrellas would（　3　）a hint for creating a new umbrella.

＜埼玉県・学校選択問題＞

b．Eメール・手紙文

1 あなたは夏休みにニュージーランドでホームステイをすることになりました。ホストファミリーの一員である大学生のMichaelから，次の【メール】を受け取りました。あなたはこの【メール】を読んで，返信します。【返信】の中の［　　］に入る最も適切なものを，ア～エから一つ選び，その記号を書きなさい。

【メール】

> Hi ○○○，
>
> How are you? I'm Michael. I'm very happy to hear that you will stay with us next year. I want to make a plan for you. So, please tell me what you are interested in and what you want to do in New Zealand.
> Please send me a message.
>
> Thanks,
> Michael

【返信】

> Dear Michael,
>
> Thank you for your e-mail. I'm happy to receive it. I'll answer your questions.
> I'm interested in the culture of New Zealand.
> ［　　］
> I'm looking forward to seeing you soon.
>
> Thanks,
> ○○○

ア．There are many cows and sheep in New Zealand. You can visit a farm.
イ．I have two brothers and both of them have been to New Zealand.
ウ．Japanese comic books are very interesting. I hope you will like them.
エ．I would like to try traditional dancing with local people there.

<高知県>

2 次の２つの電子メール（email）は里穂（Riho）さんと留学生のビクトリア（Victoria）さんとのやりとりです。これらの電子メールの内容から分かることを，ア～エから１つ選んで記号で答えなさい。

> Hi Victoria,
> I heard that you went to the doctor today. Are you OK?
> Today, in English class, the teacher talked about the presentation. We have to make groups of three or four people and choose a country as a topic. In today's class, Michiko and I talked about making a group together. Can you join us?　　　Riho

> Hi Riho,
> Thank you for your email. I felt sick this morning but I feel better now.
> Sure! I will join you. Michiko also told me about the presentation on the phone. She wants to choose China. If we are going to talk about China, how about showing pictures of famous places? I have a book with a lot of pictures taken in China.
> I will go to school tomorrow. Let's talk more about it then.　　　Victoria

ア．Victoria and Michiko were not at school today because they felt sick.
イ．Both Riho and Michiko sent an email to Victoria to tell her about the presentation.
ウ．Each group will talk about a country in the presentation in English class.
エ．Riho has a book that has a lot of pictures taken in China.

<富山県>

3 次の英文を読んで，あとの(1)～(6)の問いに答えなさい。

Hikari is a high school student. She likes English and she enjoys communicating with her American friend, Fred. One day, she sent an e-mail to him.

【E-mail from Hikari to Fred】

> Hello, Fred. How are you? I'm enjoying my high school life, but I have ᴬa big question now, and I want your opinion.
> Today, my friend, Yuri, and I talked about our future. Now I'm interested in art history and I want to study about it after I finish high school. When I said so to Yuri, she asked me, "Will you be a teacher or a researcher in the future?" I said, "I have no idea about my future job now. I just want to study about art history because I'm interested in it." Yuri was really surprised to hear my answer. She decided her goal first before she decided what she would study.
> Fred, you want to be a doctor and you are studying hard to achieve your goal, right? Should I decide my future job before I decide what to study?

【E-mail from Fred to Hikari】

> Thank you for your e-mail, Hikari. I'm doing well.
> Your question is difficult. Now I'm studying to achieve my goal, but I will keep studying after I become a doctor. And I also enjoy studying subjects which are not related to my dream. For

example, in the U.S., many schools have drama classes. Most students will not be actors, but drama class is very popular. I like it. I think we can improve some skills through drama classes. For example, we sometimes make our own stories. My drama teacher says we can be good at creating something new through this activity. Also, now I can talk more clearly than before.

My brother studies math at university, but he is taking a music class, too. He says he can learn good teamwork in the class. You should study your favorite subjects. You can improve some skills by doing so.

Hikari thought Fred's opinion was interesting. She also likes music though she won't be a musician. "If 　　　B　　　 through learning, I'll be happy," she thought.

One week later, Fred introduced a website article to Hikari. It was an article for students written by a university professor.

【The website article】

You may think like this. "Why do I have to study this subject? I don't like it. It isn't related to my goal." I can understand your feelings, but is it really a good idea to study only your favorite things?

Let me tell you about ^Cone good example, Florence Nightingale. She is one of the most famous nurses in the world. She tried to make clean hospitals. She needed to show that it was important to make clean environments to save people's lives. She had the knowledge of math and statistics. By using that knowledge, she created her original graphs and showed that dirty environments would threaten people's lives.

Do you understand what this story means? You don't know what will be useful in the future. For example, in the future, you may find problems you want to solve. Then, some knowledge may help you. Or you can create something new by using that knowledge. You may not use it in the future, but it will be so fun to learn something new. Enjoy learning a lot of things. By doing so, you can broaden your world.

My father was a science teacher. He is 75 years old, but now, he is studying classic literature at university. He says he is so happy to learn something new.

"　　　D　　　," Hikari thought. "^EI'll write an e-mail to Fred tonight."

（注）achieve ～　～を達成する
　　　be related to ～　～と関連する
　　　skill　技能
　　　clearly　はっきりと
　　　take ～ class　～の授業を受ける
　　　teamwork　チームワーク
　　　article　記事
　　　professor　教授　　knowledge　知識
　　　statistics　統計学　　graph　グラフ
　　　threaten ～　～をおびやかす

broaden ～　～を広げる
classic literature　古典文学

(1) 下線部分Aについて，その内容を，具体的に日本語で書きなさい。

(2) 文中のBの　　　　　に当てはまる内容を，4語以上の英語で書きなさい。

(3) 下線部分Cについて，フローレンス・ナイチンゲール (Florence Nightingale)の例で，記事の筆者が最も伝えたいことを表している1文を，本文から探して抜き出しなさい。

(4) 文中のDの　　　　　の中に入る最も適当なものを，次のア～エから一つ選び，その符号を書きなさい。
　ア．People have different reasons for learning
　イ．We should study for our dreams
　ウ．There is only one reason for learning
　エ．It is important to learn useful things

(5) 次の①～③の問いに対する答えを，それぞれ3語以上の英文で書きなさい。
　①　Has Hikari already decided her future job?
　②　How did Yuri decide what she would study?
　③　In the drama class at Fred's school, what do students do to be good at creating something new?

(6) 下線部分Eについて，ヒカリ (Hikari)になったつもりで，フレッド (Fred)に対するメールを "Hello, Fred. Thank you for your e-mail and the interesting article." に続けて，　　　　　の中に，4行以内の英文で書きなさい。

Hello, Fred.
Thank you for your e-mail and the interesting article.

Your friend, Hikari

<新潟県>

4 次の英文を読んで，あとの(1)～(6)の問いに答えなさい。

Mike is from America and he studied about Japanese culture at university in Japan. Now he is an ALT at Hikari High School. He puts his "Question Box" on the table in front of the teachers' room. Students can put letters into it when they have questions. They ask him about America, how to learn English, and so on. Mike likes his "Question Box" because it is a good way to communicate with students.

One day in October, he got two long letters. One letter was from Kana, a girl in the English club. The other letter was from Leo, a student from France.

【The letter from Kana】

Hello, Mike. I'm Kana. Do you know Leo, a student from France? He has been in our class for two months. He is kind and everyone likes him. But now, I am worrying about him a little.

He doesn't speak Japanese well and sometimes cannot understand our Japanese. But ᴬthat is not the problem. We can communicate with him in English. He is a great English speaker and we learn a lot from him. Last month, he looked very happy when he talked with us. But these days, he doesn't look so happy when we talk to him. Why does he look like that?

Well, sometimes we cannot understand Leo's English because he talks very fast and uses difficult words. Also it is difficult for us to express everything in English. Is it making him disappointed? If we improve our English, will he be happy?

When I ask him, "Are you OK?", he always says he is OK. But if he has any trouble, I want to help him. Mike, can you guess what ᴮhis problem is? Please give me some advice and help us become good friends.

【The letter from Leo】

Hello, Mike. I'm Leo. I came to Japan in August. I'm writing this letter because you may be the only person who can understand my feelings.

I cannot speak Japanese well, so my classmates talk to me in English. They may think that all foreign people speak great English. My English may be better than theirs, but I'm not a great English speaker. I love talking with my classmates but sometimes I feel as if my classmates talk to me only because they want to practice English.

I came to Japan to learn Japanese. I study Japanese every day, and have learned some words. If my classmates speak slowly, I can understand their Japanese a little. But they try to say everything in English.

I know English is our common language. We can communicate with each other in English though it is not the language we usually speak. In the future, my classmates and I can share ideas with people in the world by using English. That's wonderful, but now, I want to communicate with my classmates in Japanese. I cannot improve my Japanese if I don't use it at school.

Mike, should I tell my classmates my feelings? I know they are trying to be kind to me, and I don't want to hurt their feelings. What would you do if you were me?

Mike remembered his university days. He really understood their feelings. He thought, "Some friends talked to me in English to help me. They were good friends and thanks to them, I enjoyed life in Japan. But I wanted to ____C____ and improve my Japanese. Leo, I had the same wish."

However, Mike didn't worry too much. He said to himself, "Sometimes it is difficult to communicate with other people, but both Kana and Leo ____D____. They will be good friends." Mike started

to write letters to them.

（注）〜 and so on　〜など
communicate　意思を伝え合う
disappointed　がっかりする
feel as if 〜　まるで〜であるかのように感じる
only because 〜　ただ〜だから
slowly　ゆっくりと
common　共通の
thanks to 〜　〜のおかげで
wish　願い
say to himself　彼自身の心の中で考える

(1) 下線部分Aについて，その内容を，具体的に日本語で書きなさい。

(2) 次の英文は，下線部分Bについてのカナ(Kana)の考えをまとめたものです。X，Yの〔　　〕の中に入るものの組合せとして，最も適当なものを，ア～エから一つ選び，その符号を書きなさい。

Leo〔　X　〕because〔　Y　〕.

	X	Y
ア	isn't happy when he talks with us	our English is not as good as Leo's
イ	isn't happy when he talks with us	we talk to him in English
ウ	cannot improve his Japanese	our English is not as good as Leo's
エ	cannot improve his Japanese	we talk to him in English

(3) 文中のCの□□□に当てはまる内容を，5語以上の英語で書きなさい。

(4) 文中のDの□□□の中に入る最も適当なものを，次のア～エから一つ選び，その符号を書きなさい。
ア．practice English very hard
イ．enjoy talking in Japanese
ウ．tell their true feelings with each other
エ．think about each other

(5) 次の①～③の問いに対する答えを，それぞれ3語以上の英文で書きなさい。
① Can students ask Mike questions by putting letters into his "Question Box"?
② Why is Kana worrying about Leo these days?
③ According to Leo, what can Leo and his classmates do in the future by using English?

(6) あなたが，カナとレオ(Leo)の2人から，マイク(Mike)先生への手紙と同じ内容の手紙をもらったとしたら，どのような返事を書きますか。返事を書く相手として，カナかレオのどちらかを選び，KanaかLeoを書き，それに続けて，4行以内の英文で返事を書きなさい。ただし，＊＊＊の部分には，あなたの名前が書かれているものとします。

Hello,〔　　　　〕. I'm ＊＊＊.

<新潟県>

5 千葉県に住む中学3年生のトモミ(Tomomi)は，国内で遠く離れて暮らす祖母のフサコ(Fusako)に電子メールを送りました。トモミが送った電子メールと祖母からの手紙による返事を読んで，あとの(1)～(4)の問いに答えなさい。

From: tomomi-17@abc.jp　　To: fusako-smile@abc.jp
Sunday, July 10th
Dear Grandmother,

　Hello. I haven't seen you for six years. How are you? I'm fine, but I am very busy these days. I am going to have a piano concert next Saturday, so I will do my best!

　By the way, I heard that you bought a computer, so I decided to send an e-mail to you! E-mail is a very convenient tool because we can communicate with each other very quickly. I know that you worked in America a long time ago. You can use English very well, so I am writing this e-mail in English! English is one of my favorite subjects, and I want to use English when I get a job. This is a good chance for me to practice writing in English.

　I remember that I took the train to your house with Mom for four hours when I was in elementary school. I enjoyed looking at the beautiful sea from the window. At your house, I was surprised to see many books written in English in your room. I didn't understand English then, but I think I can read them a little more now. I have liked reading stories from America since I was little. I have read some of them in Japanese. When I visit you next, I want to read them in English.

　I am looking forward to seeing you again.

From Tomomi

Monday, July 11th
Dear Tomomi,

　Thank you very much for your e-mail. I was very happy to read your e-mail in English!

　English is a wonderful tool for communicating with people around the world. What do you really want to do with English? The answer will give you some ideas. Please keep studying, and enjoy writing, speaking, and reading English!

　You said that e-mail is very convenient, but I am writing this letter by hand. A letter can do some things that an e-mail cannot do. First, it takes time to write and send a letter, so I can share my feelings with you through it better. Second, I am using the pen you gave me six years ago, because I want to remember the time with you. Third, I can put a pressed flower in the envelope. You can use it as a bookmark when you read books. The flower is a gerbera. In the language of flowers, gerbera means "hope." So, I hope that you can have a good piano concert.

　I also hope to see you soon. A lot of ☐☐☐☐☐ are waiting for you in my room with me. Because now you can use English better than before, you can enjoy them!

Love, Fusako

（注）by the way　ところで　　convenient　便利な
　　　tool　道具　　communicate　コミュニケーションをとる
　　　pressed flower　押し花　　envelope　封筒
　　　bookmark　しおり　　gerbera　ガーベラ(花の名前)
　　　language of flowers　花言葉

(1)　祖母の家に行った時のトモミの様子を表した絵として最も適当なものを，次のア～エのうちから一つ選び，その符号を書きなさい。

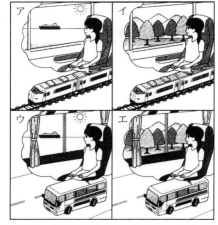

(2)　本文の内容に関する次の質問に，英語で答えなさい。
　　Why did Fusako use the pen Tomomi gave her to write the letter?

(3)　本文の内容に合っているものを，次のア～エのうちから一つ選び，その符号を書きなさい。
　　ア．Tomomi bought a computer and sent it to Fusako.
　　イ．Fusako worked in a foreign country a long time ago.
　　ウ．Tomomi understood English well when she was in elementary school.
　　エ．Fusako thinks that a bookmark is useful when Tomomi sends an e-mail.

(4)　本文中の ☐☐☐☐☐ に適する英単語2語を書きなさい。
　　　　　　　　　　　　　　　　＜千葉県＞

6 次の英文は，日本に住む高校生の太一(Taichi)とインドネシア(Indonesia)に住む友人のレオ(Leo)とのインターネット上でのやり取りです。これを読んで，あとの(1)〜(3)の問いに答えなさい。

〈August 18th, 2020〉

Hi, Leo. Now I am *searching for a Japanese *product used in foreign countries to make an English speech. I have found something interesting on the Internet. Look at this.
 Taichi

Old Japanese trains in the world!
　Many people in Indonesia use trains in their daily lives. A *railway company in Indonesia has *imported Japanese trains. It had about 1,500 Japanese trains in 2019. *Thanks to the Japanese trains, more people can go to work. It is also good for Japanese railway companies. Japanese *workers can have a good experience by living and working abroad.
電車の写真
 Taichi

Have you ever seen these trains in Indonesia?
 Taichi

 Leo
Hi, Taichi. Yes. In my country I often see trains with Japanese words. ①

Really? How are the trains?
 Taichi

 Leo
The *air conditioners in Japanese trains make me feel good. The idea is very nice.

Sounds good! I have decided to make a speech about the trains. I'll show you after I finish writing the speech.
 Taichi

 Leo
OK.

〈August 25th, 2020〉

I have not finished writing the speech, but I added new information about the trains. Can you check it?
 Taichi

　I am going to talk about a Japanese product used in the world: Old Japanese trains in Indonesia. I have never imagined how the old trains were used. But I was surprised that there were about 1,500 Japanese trains in the year 2019 in Indonesia. Using these trains is good for both Indonesia and Japan. More people in Indonesia can use them when they go to work. Japanese railway companies can give workers a chance to work outside Japan. However, *according to a newspaper, Indonesia will stop importing trains. It also says that Indonesia will try to use trains made in Indonesia.
...
Thank you for listening.
 Taichi

 Leo
I was surprised to see the new information. It is interesting to know that Indonesia will try to use trains made in Indonesia. I hope Indonesia can develop more.

Me too. At first I felt sad, but I am happy to know that ② .
 Taichi

(注) search(ing) for 〜を探す　product 製品
　railway company (companies) 鉄道会社
　import(ed/ing) 輸入する
　thanks to 〜 〜のおかげで　worker(s) 労働者
　air conditioner(s) 冷房
　according to 〜 〜によると

(1) 文中の ① に入る英語は何ですか。次のア〜エのうちから最も適当なものを一つ選び，その記号を書きなさい。
　ア．Also, I have actually used the trains.
　イ．Also, I have never made the trains.
　ウ．I will never introduce the trains to everyone.
　エ．I will watch the trains someday.

(2) 文中の下線部I added new information about the trainsについて，太一が付け加えた情報は何ですか。次のア〜エのうちから最も適当なものを一つ選び，その記号を書きなさい。
　ア．There were about 1,500 Japanese trains in the year 2019 in Indonesia.
　イ．More people in Indonesia can use the trains when they go to work.
　ウ．Japanese railway companies can give workers a chance to work outside Japan.
　エ．Indonesia will try to use trains made in Indonesia.

(3) 文中の ② には，どんな英語が入りますか。太一とLeoのやり取りを踏まえて，4語以上の英語で書きなさい。

〈岩手県〉

c．グラフ・資料

① グラフ・表

1 次は，高校生の絵梨(Eri)と，留学生のサム(Sam)との対話である。英文を読んで，1，2の問いに答えなさい。

Sam：Eri, what are you going to talk about for the presentation in our English class?

Eri：I'll talk about studying abroad. I'm surprised about the results of this graph and table about high school students in Japan.

Sam：What did you find out?

Eri：Look at the graph. For high school students, the most popular reason to study abroad is to improve their foreign language skills. Then, ①　　　 of them want to make friends with people in other countries.

Sam：I see. Then, do you want to study abroad, Eri?

Eri：Yes, of course! I'm interested in living and studying in other countries. I'm surprised that only about ②　　　 percent of high school students are interested in doing that. How about you, Sam? Why did you come to Japan?

Sam：Because I　　　　. I really wanted to join a judo club in Japan. I'm happy that about thirty-eight percent have the same idea. By the way, if you study abroad, where do you want to go?

Eri：I want to go to ③　　　. Look at the table. It's not the most popular country, but the number of students who went there is a little larger than nine hundred. I want to go there and experience the way of life in that country.

Sam：That's a good idea. I hope you can go there in the future.

　(注) presentation 発表　　study abroad 留学する
　　　 graph グラフ　　table 表　　skill 技能

Graph 日本の高校生の海外に留学したい理由(複数回答)[一部抜粋]

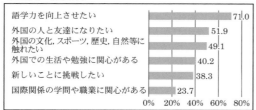

語学力を向上させたい	71.0
外国の人と友達になりたい	51.9
外国の文化，スポーツ，歴史，自然等に触れたい	49.1
外国での生活や勉強に関心がある	40.2
新しいことに挑戦したい	38.3
国際関係の学問や職業に関心がある	23.7

（平成29年度文部科学省資料による）

Table 日本の高校生の留学（3か月以上）

留学先(国)	生徒数(人)
アメリカ	1,151
カナダ	937
ニュージーランド	704
オーストラリア	522
その他	762

（平成29年度文部科学省資料による）

1． ①　～　③ に入れるのに最も適当な組み合わせを，次のア〜カから一つ選び，記号で答えなさい。
ア． ① about seventy percent　② forty
　　③ New Zealand
イ． ① about seventy percent　② twenty
　　③ Canada
ウ． ① about seventy percent　② twenty
　　③ New Zealand
エ． ① more than half　② forty
　　③ Canada
オ． ① more than half　② forty
　　③ New Zealand
カ． ① more than half　② twenty
　　③ Canada
2． 　　　に，対話が成り立つような英語を7語以内で書きなさい。

〈熊本県・選択問題B〉

2 次の英文は，春樹(Haruki)が，キャンプ場(camping site)での経験をきっかけに，キャンプについて調べ，英語の授業で発表したときのものです。1〜3の問いに答えなさい。

During summer vacation this year, I went camping with my father for the first time. At night, we ate delicious food and looked at the beautiful stars. My father said, "When I was your age, I often went camping." He also said, "We're lucky to live in Gifu because we have many good camping sites. Each camping site has its own good points." On that day, I became a big fan of camping. Then I used the Internet and some books to learn about camping.

Look at the table. This shows five prefectures with the largest number of camping sites in Japan in 2021. I am glad to find that Gifu is one of them. Hokkaido has more than 200 camping sites. The second is Nagano. You can see the number of camping sites in Yamanashi is a little larger than the number in Gifu. I think all of these five prefectures have great nature.

Next, look at the graph. This shows the number of people who went camping from 1989 to 2019 in Japan. The largest number was in 1994. It is called the first camping boom. But the number ☐①☐ in 1999. In 2009, the number became about a ☐②☐ of the number in 1994. However, from 2009 to 2019, it kept ☐③☐ again.

Why is camping becoming popular again? I read an article and found two reasons. First, many young people think camping is cool and attractive. Because of camping anime and camping videos of famous people, they are interested in camping now. Second, a lot of people who experienced camping in the first camping boom have become parents, and started to go camping again with their children today. My father is one of them.

When I go camping, I can relax in nature. I hope the beautiful nature will continue to grow into the future.

Table

First	A	222
Second	B	149
Third	C	99
Fourth	D	93
Fifth	Niigata	79

Graph

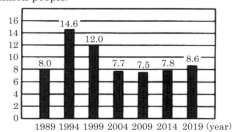

(million people)

1989 8.0 / 1994 14.6 / 1999 12.0 / 2004 7.7 / 2009 7.5 / 2014 7.8 / 2019 8.6 (year)

（注）table　表
　　　prefecture　都道府県
　　　first camping boom　第一次キャンプブーム

1．Tableの ☐C☐ に入る最も適切なものを，ア〜エから１つ選び，符号で書きなさい。
　ア．Gifu　　　　イ．Hokkaido
　ウ．Nagano　　エ．Yamanashi
2．本文中の ☐①☐ 〜 ☐③☐ に入る英語の組み合わせとして最も適切なものを，ア〜エから１つ選び，符号で書きなさい。
　ア．①—increased　　②—half　　③—decreasing
　イ．①—increased　　②—third　　③—decreasing
　ウ．①—decreased　　②—half　　③—increasing
　エ．①—decreased　　②—third　　③—increasing
3．本文の内容に合っているものを，ア〜エから１つ選び，符号で書きなさい。
　ア．Haruki found that the number of people who went camping kept increasing from 1989 and it never decreased.
　イ．Haruki found that many people who went camping in the first camping boom go camping again with their children today.
　ウ．Haruki said that his father went camping this summer for the first time because he thought it was cool.

エ．Haruki said that the first camping boom happened because of camping anime and videos of famous people.

<岐阜県>

3 次の英文は，中学生のKoharuが，鹿児島中央駅のJR利用者数と鹿児島県内のバス利用者数について英語の授業で行った発表である。これをもとに，Koharuが使用したグラフをア〜エの中から二つ選び，発表した順に記号で書け。

Good morning, everyone. Do you like trains and buses? I love them. Now I'm going to talk about the number of people who used them from 2009 to 2014. Please look at this *graph. Many people used JR trains at Kagoshima Chuo Station. We can find the biggest change from 2010 to 2011. In 2011, about fifteen million people used trains. The Kyushu Shinkansen started running from Kagoshima Chuo Station to Hakata Station that year. So I think many people began to use the Shinkansen. Now, I'm going to talk about buses. Please look at the next graph. Many people used buses, but the number of bus *users went down almost every year. I think many people used cars. Thank you for listening.

（注）graph　グラフ　　users　利用者

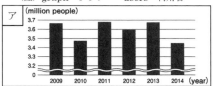

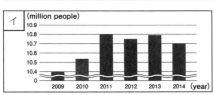

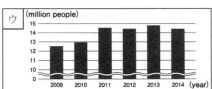

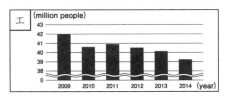

（鹿児島市「鹿児島市公共交通ビジョン改定版」から作成）
※グラフのタイトルは省略

<鹿児島県>

4 次の英文は，高校生の由衣(Yui)が，販売実習について，英語の授業で行ったスピーチの原稿です。これを読み，〔問１〕～〔問４〕に答えなさい。

In our school, we can study agriculture. I'm in the agriculture course. I learn how to grow good vegetables, flowers, and fruits. I grow them with my classmates. At school, we sometimes make processed products like juice.

In June, we started to sell vegetables, flowers, fruits, and processed products. Every Friday, we sold them at the station near our school. When we sold them, I recorded the sales there. I was happy when many people came to the station to buy our products. I sometimes asked them how they liked our products.

At the end of each month, I made a pie chart to check the percentage of all sales in the month. Today, I'll show you the pie charts of June and July. In those months, we sold vegetables the most. In June, the percentage of processed products was higher than fruits and flowers. However, in July, processed products weren't so popular. Compared to June, the percentage of fruits became higher and the percentage of flowers was the same.

It has been a great experience for me to make and sell products. At the station, people tell me what they think about our products. And the pie charts show me the popular products in different seasons. I'm glad I have some useful information now.

Well, here is the thing which I want to tell you the most. I want to improve our products by making use of the things I learned.

（注）agriculture　農業　　course　学科
grow　育てる　　processed product　加工製品
sold：sellの過去形
record　記録する　　sales　売上げ　　end　終わり
pie chart　円グラフ　　percentage　割合
compared to ～　　～と比較すると
make use of ～　　～を生かす

円グラフ

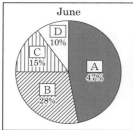
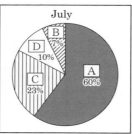

〔問１〕　本文の内容に合うように，次の(　　　)にあてはまる最も適切なものを，ア～エの中から１つ選び，その記号を書きなさい。
　　Yui (　　　　).
　　ア．sold the products in her school
　　イ．made juice at the station
　　ウ．wanted to teach agriculture at school
　　エ．recorded the sales at the station
〔問２〕　文中の下線部the pie chartsについて，本文の内容に合うように，円グラフのA～Dにあてはまる最も適切なものを，次のア～エの中から１つずつ選び，その記号を書きなさい。
　　ア．vegetables

イ．flowers
ウ．fruits
エ．processed products
〔問３〕　由衣が，スピーチを通して一番伝えたいことはどのようなことですか。最も適切なものを，次のア～エの中から１つ選び，その記号を書きなさい。
　　ア．Yui wants to make better products.
　　イ．Yui wants to show her pie charts.
　　ウ．Yui wants to record the sales.
　　エ．Yui wants to think about more products.
〔問４〕　由衣は，スピーチの後，ALT（外国語指導助手）のトム(Tom)と話をしました。次の対話文は，そのやりとりの一部です。これを読み，あとの(1)，(2)に答えなさい。

Tom：That was a wonderful speech. It's a good idea to sell products at the station.
Yui ：Yes. People look happy when they buy our products. So I become happy.
Tom：Good. I want to buy some fruits next Friday.
Yui ：Please come to the station. I want more people to come.
Tom：Well, what can you do about that?
Yui ：I think I can 　　　　　　　　.
Tom：That's a good idea. If you do it, more people will come to the station.

(1)　対話の流れに合うように，文中の　　　　　にふさわしい英語を書きなさい。ただし，語数は２語以上とし，符号（．，?!など）は語数に含まないものとする。
(2)　対話の内容に合う最も適切なものを，次のア～エの中から１つ選び，その記号を書きなさい。
　　ア．Yui could buy some fruits on Sunday.
　　イ．Yui wants people to enjoy the products.
　　ウ．Tom was sad to hear Yui's speech.
　　エ．Tom has a question about fruits.

〈和歌山県〉

5 中学生の健(Ken)さんは，ALTのミラ(Mila)さんの話を聞いて，ヨーロッパにおける日本語学習者(Japanese-language learner)について調べ，表(table)とグラフ(graph)にまとめました。次は，表とグラフを見ている，健さんとミラさんの対話です。表とグラフおよび対話について，あとの問いに答えなさい。

表　国別の日本語学習者数（人）

国　　名	2015年	2018年	2015年からの増減
X	20,875	24,150	3,275
イギリス	20,093	20,040	-53
Y	13,256	15,465	2,209
Z	5,122	8,495	3,373
イタリア	7,031	7,831	800

グラフ　日本語学習の理由

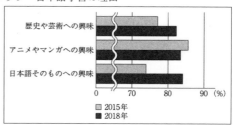

国際交流基金「海外の日本語教育の現状」から作成

Ken : I knew you started learning Japanese when you were in your country, *the U.K., and last week you told us that there were many Japanese-language learners in Europe. I wanted to learn more about them, so I made this table and this graph.

Mila : The table is interesting. I didn't know the U.K. had so many Japanese-language learners. More people learned Japanese in my country than in *Germany in 2018.

Ken : In France, you can see a big change from 2015 to 2018. More than three thousand learners *were added.

Mila : The number increased a lot in Spain, too. I also found that Spain had the smallest number of the five countries in 2015. Now, does this graph show why people in Europe learned Japanese?

Ken : Yes. I know anime is popular there, but I'm surprised that over eighty percent of the learners were interested in the Japanese language in 2018.

Mila : I started learning Japanese because I was a big fan of anime, but soon I became interested in the language, too. I still read the Japanese-language textbook I used in the U.K.

Ken : Really?　①I'd like to look at it!

Mila : OK. I'll bring it tomorrow.

(注) the U.K.　イギリス
　　　Germany　ドイツ
　　　(were) added　加えられた

1．表中のX〜Zには，ドイツ，フランス，スペインのいずれかの国名が入ります。対話の内容に即して，X〜Zのそれぞれにあてはまる国名を，日本語で書きなさい。

2．下線部①について，健さんが見たいものは何ですか。対話の内容に即して日本語で書きなさい。

3．表とグラフおよび対話の内容に合うものを，次のア〜オから二つ選び，記号で答えなさい。

　ア．Ken found that Mila learned Japanese in the U.K. after making the table and the graph.

　イ．Mila looks at the table and says that the U.K. didn't have many Japanese-language learners.

　ウ．The table shows that more people learned Japanese in the U.K. in 2015 than in 2018.

　エ．Over eighty percent of the learners in Europe were interested in history and art in 2015.

　オ．Mila says that she became an anime fan before she got interested in the Japanese language.

<山形県>

6 次の英文は，真衣(Mai)が，平均睡眠時間(average sleep hours)について，英語の授業で発表したときのものです。1〜3の問いに答えなさい。

Some of you may count sheep when you can't sleep. Do you know why? The sound "sheep" and "sleep" are similar, so counting sheep may be one of the good ways to sleep. Sleep is important for all of us. We can't live without sleeping. But many Japanese people say that they want to sleep longer if they can. How many hours do people sleep in Japan and around the world?

Look at the graph. This is the average sleep hours in Japan and the four other countries in 2018. You can see that people in Japan sleep 7 hours and 22 minutes on average. You may think that 7 hours of sleep is enough, but when you look at the graph, you will find that it is very short. The graph shows that people in China sleep the longest of all, and people in India sleep almost as long as people in America. People in Germany sleep shorter than people in those three countries, but I was surprised that they sleep about one hour longer than us.

Now look at the table. This is the average sleep hours of people in Japan in 2007, 2011 and 2015. What can you see from this table? In 2007, about one third of the people sleep 7 hours or longer. But in 2015, almost 40% of the people sleep less than 6 hours, and only about a quarter of the people sleep 7 hours or longer. It means that more people in Japan sleep (①s　　　　　) than before.

You may watch TV or use the Internet until late at night. But we need to sleep longer especially when we are young. Sleep is important not only for our bodies but also for our minds. To make our bodies and minds more active, let's go to bed earlier and count sheep tonight.

Graph

A	9 hours and 1 minute	
India	8 hours and 48 minutes	
B	8 hours and 45 minutes	
C	8 hours and 18 minutes	
D	7 hours and 22 minutes	

4　5　6　7　8　9 (hour)

Table

	Less than 6 hours	Between 6 and 7 hours	7 hours or longer
2007	28.4%	37.8%	33.8%
2011	34.1%	36.7%	29.2%
2015	39.4%	34.1%	26.5%

(注) sheep　羊　　similar　似ている
　　　on average　平均して
　　　one hour longer　1時間長く　　table　表
　　　mind　心

1．Graphの[B]に入る最も適切なものを，ア〜エから1つ選び，符号で書きなさい。

　ア．America　　　　イ．China
　ウ．Germany　　　　エ．Japan

2．本文中の(①　　　)に入る最も適切な英語を，本文中から抜き出して1語書きなさい。ただし，(　)内に示されている文字で書き始め，その文字も含めて答えること。

3．本文の内容に合っているものを，ア〜エから1つ選び，符号で書きなさい。

　ア．Mai is surprised that people in China sleep the shortest in the five countries.

　イ．Mai says that people need to sleep longer especially when they are young.

ウ．Mai thinks that watching TV and using the Internet are more important than sleeping.

エ．Mai uses the table which shows how long people in the five countries sleep from 2007 to 2015.

<岐阜県>

7 Read the passage and choose the answer which best completes each blank ① and ②, and choose the answer which best completes sentence (3).

In 2021, Osaka Prefecture did research to know what people thought about using a smartphone while walking. The members of the research group asked some questions to 1,000 people over 17 years old. To answer each question, the respondents chose their answers from the choices prepared by the research group. "Do you use a smartphone while walking?" was the first question. 332 of the 1,000 respondents chose "Yes," and the other respondents chose "No." The respondents who chose "Yes" were also asked other questions. "Why do you use a smartphone while walking?" was one of the questions. The table shows what respondents in each age group chose as their answers to this question. Each respondent chose only one answer.

We can learn some things from the table. First, in each age group, the percentage of the respondents who chose "To send or read messages" was the highest. More than half of the respondents who were ［　　①　　］ chose that answer. Then, if we compare the percentages of the respondents who chose ［　　②　　］ the percentage of the respondents who were 60-84 years old was the highest.

According to the research, more than 80% of the respondents who chose "Yes" to the first question also chose "Yes" to the question "Do you think using a smartphone while walking is dangerous?" Let's stop using a smartphone while walking.

【Table】

Question: "Why do you use a smartphone while walking?"						
answers ＼ ages	18-84 years old	18-29 years old	30-39 years old	40-49 years old	50-59 years old	60-84 years old
To send or read messages.	46.1%	50.6%	40.8%	48.6%	43.9%	45.0%
To see a map or a timetable.	14.8%	21.2%	11.8%	11.4%	19.5%	10.0%
To get information.	9.6%	4.7%	11.8%	12.9%	9.8%	10.0%
To play a game.	7.5%	2.4%	7.9%	8.6%	7.3%	13.3%
To play, stop or choose music.	6.9%	5.9%	11.8%	5.7%	4.9%	5.0%
To watch videos or movies.	1.8%	1.2%	2.6%	2.9%	0.0%	1.7%
Without thinking anything.	10.8%	12.9%	13.2%	8.6%	9.8%	8.3%
For other reasons.	2.4%	1.2%	0.0%	1.4%	4.9%	6.7%

（大阪府「大阪府政策マーケティング・リサーチ「おおさかＱネット」（令和３年度）」により作成）

（注）Osaka Prefecture　大阪府
smartphone　スマートフォン
while ～ ing　～している間に
over 17 years old　17歳より年上の，18歳以上の

respondent　回答者　　table　表
percentage　割合　　timetable　時刻表
video　動画

(1) ①　ア．18-29 years old　　イ．30-39 years old
　　　　ウ．40-49 years old　　エ．50-59 years old
(2) ②　ア．"To get information,"
　　　　イ．"To play a game,"
　　　　ウ．"To play, stop or choose music,"
　　　　エ．"To watch videos or movies,"
(3) According to the research,
　　ア．Osaka Prefecture did research to know the percentage of people who have their own smartphone.
　　イ．more than half of all the respondents chose "No" to the question "Do you use a smartphone while walking?".
　　ウ．less than 10% of the respondents in each age group chose "Without thinking anything" to the question "Why do you use a smartphone while walking?".
　　エ．more than 80% of the respondents who chose "Yes" to the first question didn't choose "Yes" to the question "Do you think using a smartphone while walking is dangerous?".

<大阪府・Ｃ問題>

8 Read the passage and choose the answer which best completes each blank ①～③.

"What are the important factors when you choose food?" This was one of the questions in research which was done on health and food in 2018. The research was done on people over 19 years old. The people who joined the research answered this question by choosing one or more factors from several choices. The following table shows eight factors and the percentages of people who chose them. From all the people who answered the question, the table shows three generations: people who were 20-29, 40-49, and 60-69 years old.

Look at the table. For each generation, the two factors which show the highest and the lowest percentages are same. They are ［　　①　　］ However, the table also shows that people in each generation had different views on choosing food. If you rank the factors of each generation in order from the highest percentages to the lowest ones, there are some differences in the factors which were ranked second and third among the three generations. ［　　②　　］ was ranked second by people who were 20-29 and 40-49 years old though it was ranked third by people who were 60-69 years old. For each factor, there are some differences in percentage points between the generations. Of all the factors, the biggest difference in percentage points is 38.7, and it is found on ［　　③　　］

（注）factor　要素
over 19 years old　19歳より年上の，20歳以上の
choice　選択肢　table　表　percentage　割合
generation　世代　rank　並べる
difference in percentage points　割合の差

【Table】

factors \ ages	20-29	40-49	60-69
taste（おいしさ）	79.5%	78.1%	75.8%
price（価格）	60.2%	68.5%	68.1%
freshness（鮮度）	32.8%	57.3%	71.5%
safety（安全性）	31.0%	52.1%	62.7%
amount and size（量・大きさ）	45.8%	41.4%	34.6%
nutrition（栄養価）	29.1%	41.9%	46.3%
season（季節感・旬）	20.9%	38.6%	48.6%
how easy and convenient（簡便性）	16.1%	16.1%	16.1%

Question: "What are the important factors when you choose food?"
Eight factors and the percentages of people who chose them

（厚生労働省「国民健康・栄養調査」（令和２年）により作成）

(1) ① ア．"taste" and "price."
 イ．"taste" and "how easy and convenient."
 ウ．"price" and "freshness."
 エ．"amount and size" and "nutrition."

(2) ② ア．"Taste" イ．"Price"
 ウ．"Freshness" エ．"Amount and size"

(3) ③ ア．"freshness." イ．"safety."
 ウ．"nutrition." エ．"season."

〈大阪府・Ｃ問題〉

9 次の英文は，中学３年生のTakashi，Aya，Emi，Yutaの班が英語の授業で，自分たちが調べたことを発表している場面のものです。グラフ（Graph），スライド（Slide）および英文をもとにして，(1)〜(5)の問いに答えなさい。

Graph

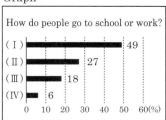

How do people go to school or work?

（コペンハーゲン市の資料を参考に作成）

Slide

Convenient for people

Takashi : What will our city look like in the future? We hope our city will be a better place for everyone. Today our group will tell you about "   ①   ."

Aya : Do you know the city, *Copenhagen? It is the *capital city of *Denmark. Please look at ②this graph. It shows how people in this city go to school or go to work. About half of the people in the city use bicycles. Using cars comes next, and 18% of them take buses or trains. The other people walk to school or work.

Emi : Why are bicycles popular in this city? Please look at this slide. ③I am surprised to find these things. For example, there are some roads and traffic lights only for bicycles. Also, people can bring their bicycles with them on the train. This city is convenient for people who use bicycles. So a lot of people can enjoy riding bicycles.

Yuta : Using bicycles has some good points for our lives. I'll show you ④three slides. The first slide shows that riding bicycles is good for the environment. The *amount of CO2 is smaller when we use bicycles. So if we go to school or work by bicycle, it will keep the environment clean. The second slide shows that riding bicycles gives us a chance to *exercise. I'm afraid people don't have enough time to exercise. However, if we often ride bicycles, we will make our health better. The last slide shows that our city is trying to create a new style of *sightseeing. Our city has beautiful *nature and some famous places. More people can come to our city and visit those famous places by bicycle. They will enjoy visiting those places.

Takashi : Using bicycles will give us a good chance to make our city better for the environment and the people. To enjoy our lives with bicycles, we should be careful of *accidents when we ride bicycles. Wearing a *helmet is one of the ways. ⑤There are other ways to be *safe when we ride bicycles. What should you do? Let's think about it. Thank you for listening!

（注）Copenhagen コペンハーゲン
 capital city 首都 Denmark デンマーク
 amount of CO2 二酸化炭素の量
 exercise 運動する
 sightseeing 観光
 nature 自然 accidents 事故
 helmet ヘルメット safe 安全な

(1) 英文中の ① に入る発表のタイトルとして最も適当なものを，ア〜エから１つ選び，記号を書きなさい。
 ア．A long history of bicycles
 イ．The most popular road for bicycles
 ウ．A better life with bicycles
 エ．A new way to invent bicycles

(2) 下線部②が示すグラフ内の（ Ⅰ ）〜（ Ⅳ ）に入る語句の組み合わせとして最も適当なものを，ア〜エから１つ選び，記号を書きなさい。

	Ⅰ	Ⅱ	Ⅲ	Ⅳ
ア	bicycles	buses or trains	cars	walk
イ	bicycles	cars	buses or trains	walk
ウ	bicycles	cars	walk	buses or trains
エ	buses or trains	bicycles	walk	cars

(3) 下線部③について，Emiが発言した理由になるように，次の英文の□□□□に入る最も適当なものを，ア～エから1つ選び，記号を書きなさい。

　Emi is surprised to learn that □□□□□.

ア．there are a lot of people who use cars to go to work in Japan

イ．there are some festivals many people from abroad can join in Copenhagen

ウ．there are some roads for people riding bicycles in Japan

エ．there are some ways to help people who use bicycles in Copenhagen

(4) 下線部④について，Yutaが示したスライドをア～エから3つ選び，発表の順番に並べかえ，記号を書きなさい。

ア
Good for our health
・Having a chance to exercise

イ
The rules when we ride bicycles
・Wearing a helmet

ウ
Safe for the environment
・Keeping the environment clean

エ
A new way of sightseeing
・Visiting famous places by bicycle

(5) 下線部⑤について，次の条件にしたがって，あなたの考えを書きなさい。

条件

① 自転車を安全に運転するために注意すべきことについて，主語と動詞を含む5語以上の英語で書くこと。ただし，英文中で述べられていない内容を書くこと。

② 英文の数はいくつでもよい。

③ 短縮形（I'mなど）は1語として数えることとし，ピリオド，コンマなどの符号は語数に含めないこと。

〈大分県〉

10 次の対話は，高校生の太郎と留学生のエリックが，太郎の自宅でキャッシュレス決済について話したときのものです。また，グラフ1とグラフ2は，そのとき太郎たちが見ていたウェブページの一部です。これらに関して，あとの1～5に答えなさい。

Taro：Erik, my aunt told me that most payments in many countries will be cashless in the future. Can you imagine that?

Erik：Yes. Cashless payments are very ☐ A ☐ in my country, Sweden. A lot of families don't use notes or coins. For example, my parents usually use smartphones for payments and I have a debit card.

Taro：Really?　I think many people still use cash in Japan. ☐ B ☐.

Erik：Then, how about looking for some information about cashless payments on the Internet?

Taro：That's a good idea. Oh, look at this graph. It shows that cashless payments are increasing in Japan. Over 30% of payments were cashless in ☐ C ☐.

Erik：I see. Look!　I found a graph about payments in my country. Only 13% of people used cash for their most recent payments in 2018.

Taro：Oh!　Why do so many people choose cashless payments? [　あ　]

Erik：Because it is easier to pay without cash. You don't have to carry a wallet when you go shopping and don't spend so much time when you pay.

Taro：I think it is easier for people from abroad to buy things without cash. [　い　]

Erik：Cashless payments are also good for store staff. They don't have to prepare change and check notes and coins in the register, so they can save time.

Taro：That's great. Cashless payments have a lot of good points, but I think there are some problems, too. [　う　]

Erik：What are they?

Taro：If you lose your smartphone or debit card, someone who finds them may spend your money.

Erik：Oh, that's right. We should be careful. Anything else?

Taro：You can't see notes and coins when you use cashless payments, so you sometimes don't realize you are spending too much money. [　え　]

Erik：I think so, too. Especially, children may not be able to have a sense of money.

Taro：I see. I will try to find more information about cashless payments to use them in the future.

(注) most たいていの　　payment 支払い
cashless 現金のいらない　　imagine 想像する
Sweden スウェーデン　　note 紙幣　　coin 硬貨
smartphone スマートフォン
debit card デビットカード　　cash 現金
increase 増える　　recent 最近の　　wallet 財布
spend 使う　　staff 従業員　　prepare 準備する
change つり銭　　register レジ　　save 節約する
be able to ～　　～することができる　　sense 感覚

グラフ1

（経済産業省ウェブページにより作成。）

グラフ2

（財務省財務総合政策研究所「デジタル時代のイノベーションに関する研究会」報告書（2019年）により作成。）

1．本文中の　Ａ　に当てはまる最も適切な語を，次のア〜エの中から選び，その記号を書きなさい。
　　ア．exciting　　イ．expensive
　　ウ．popular　　エ．weak
2．本文中の　Ｂ　に当てはまる最も適切な英語を，次のア〜エの中から選び，その記号を書きなさい。
　　ア．I can't imagine life with cash
　　イ．I can't imagine life without cash
　　ウ．I know how to live without cash in Sweden
　　エ．I know how to use cash in Sweden
3．本文中の　Ｃ　に当てはまる最も適切な数字を，次のア〜エの中から選び，その記号を書きなさい。
　　ア．2010　　イ．2012　　ウ．2020　　エ．2021
4．次の英文は，本文中から抜き出したものです。この英文を入れる最も適切なところを本文中の［　あ　］〜［　え　］の中から選び，その記号を書きなさい。
　　They don't have to bring a lot of notes and coins from their countries.
5．太郎は，英語の授業で，「日本はキャッシュレス決済を推進すべきである」というテーマでディベートを行うことになりました。次のメモは，太郎がその準備として，エリックと話した内容をまとめたものの一部です。このメモ中の（　ａ　）〜（　ｄ　）に当てはまる最も適切な英語を，あとのア〜エの中からそれぞれ選び，その記号を書きなさい。

> Good points of cashless payments
> 　for us
>
> | We don't need a wallet for shopping. |
> | We（　　ａ　　）quickly. |
>
> 　for store staff
> 　・They don't need change.
> 　・They don't need to check the money in the register.
> 　　　　　　　　↓
> | They（　　ｂ　　）. |
>
> Bad points of cashless payments
> 　for us
>
> | If we lose our smartphone or debit card, someone（　　ｃ　　）and we may lose our money. |
>
> 　・We can't see notes and coins when we pay.
> 　　　　　　　　↓
> | We may spend too much money and may not realize it. |
> | It（　　ｄ　　）to understand how important money is. |

　　ア．can save time　　　イ．can pay
　　ウ．may be difficult　　エ．may use them
〈広島県〉

---

11 次の英文は，博（Hiroshi）が，食料自給率（food self-sufficiency rate）について，グラフ（Graph）と表（Table）を作り，英語の授業で発表したときのものです。1〜3の問いに答えなさい。

I made *okonomiyaki* with my mother last week. While we were cooking, she said, "Do you think *okonomiyaki* is Japanese food?" I answered, "Of course!" Then she said, "You are right, but some of the ingredients come from other countries. For example, the pork and the shrimps that we're using now are imported from overseas. We depend on foreign countries for a lot of ingredients." Then I remembered the word 'food self-sufficiency rate'. I learned at school that Japan's food self-sufficiency rate is less than half.

Then, where does the food we eat come from? Look at the two graphs first. You can see that we import pork and shrimps from these countries. The left graph shows that about half of pork is imported from America and Canada. When you look at the right graph, you can see shrimps come from some countries in Asia. I was surprised that we import them from so many different countries.

Now look at the table. This is about the food self-sufficiency rate of four countries in 1963 and 2013. You can see that the food self-sufficiency rate of Canada is the highest both in 1963 and 2013. And in 2013, the rate of France and America is about the same, though the rate of America is higher than the rate of France in 1963. When you compare the rate in 1963 and 2013, only the rate of Japan gets smaller from 1963 to 2013. The table shows that Japan imports about 60% of food from foreign countries in 2013. If we cannot import any food, we may have a difficult time.

I thought *okonomiyaki* was 'Japanese' food. But you can also say it is '（　①　）' food. I guess there are many other things we import. So when you go to a supermarket next time, why don't you check where they come from?

Graph

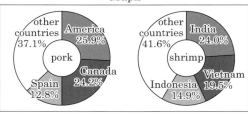

Table

Country	1963	2013
Ａ	161%	264%
Ｂ	120%	130%
Ｃ	98%	127%
Ｄ	72%	39%

（注）ingredient　材料　　pork　豚肉　　shrimp　エビ
　　　import　輸入する　　Vietnam　ベトナム
　　　Indonesia　インドネシア

1．Tableの　Ｃ　に入る最も適切なものを，ア〜エから1つ選び，符号で書きなさい。

ア．America　　イ．Canada
ウ．France　　エ．Japan

2．本文中の（　①　）に入る最も適切なものを，ア～エから
1つ選び，符号で書きなさい。
ア．delicious　　イ．expensive
ウ．fast　　　　エ．international

3．本文の内容に合っているものを，ア～エから1つ選び，
符号で書きなさい。
ア．Hiroshi found that Japan imports pork and shrimps from many different countries.
イ．Hiroshi learned about 'food self-sufficiency rate' from his mother.
ウ．The right graph shows that we import about half of shrimps from Vietnam.
エ．The table shows the percentage of pork and shrimps that the four countries import.

＜岐阜県＞

12 中学生のなおや(Naoya)さんとアメリカから来た留学生のジョン(John)さんがいるクラスで，来週，環境問題について，全員がそれぞれテーマを設定して発表することになりました。次の会話は，なおやさんとジョンさんが，発表に向けての話をしたときのものです。あとのグラフ(Graph 1, Graph 2)は，ジョンさんが発表用に準備したものです。また，あとのスピーチは，なおやさんが実際に行った発表の内容です。これらを読み，あとの各問いに答えなさい。

Naoya：What are you going to talk about for your speech in English class next week?
John　：I'm going to talk about the problem of *plastic. We use a lot of plastic every day, like shopping bags and water bottles. When we throw them away, some of them go into the river, and then go into the sea. Small pieces of plastic look like food to fish, so a lot of fish eat the plastic.
Naoya：That's a big problem! How much plastic *waste do people throw away?
John　：Look at ①these two graphs. Graph 1 shows how much plastic waste these four countries produced in 2010. Graph 2 shows how much plastic waste each person in each of these countries produced in 2010. China, as a country, produced the most *amount of plastic waste. America is second. It is said that about 8 *million tons of plastic waste is going into the sea every year.
Naoya：It is the（　②　）amount of the plastic waste which Japan produced as a country!
John　：That's true.
Naoya：In India, people produced the *least amount of plastic waste as a country and *per person. I want to know why.
John　：Me too. ③I want to check the Internet and learn more about it. Then I can finish writing my speech this weekend. What are you going to talk about for your speech, Naoya?
Naoya：I will talk about plastic too. Plastic is making our life better, but it is *causing *serious problems for the *environment. I think we need to do something. I'm going to talk about plastic bags.

（注）plastic　プラスチック(の)，ビニール(の)
　　　waste　ごみ，廃棄物　　amount of　～の量
　　　million ton(s)　百万トン(重さの単位)
　　　least：little「少ない」の最上級
　　　per person　一人あたり
　　　causing：cause「～を生じさせる」の現在分詞形
　　　serious　深刻な　　environment　環境

Graph 1

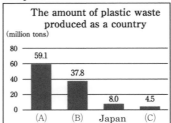

Graph 2

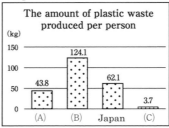

「ハナ・リッチー＆マックス・ローザーによる2010年に実施したプラスチック汚染に関する調査報告(2018年)」より作成

スピーチ

Do you use plastic bags when you go shopping? Now we must *pay for plastic bags if we want them at the store. I think that this is good because we need to stop using plastic bags to *reduce plastic waste for the environment. Many people take their own bags to the store now. I have started to take my own bag too.

However, there are still some people who use plastic bags. These people say, "Plastic bags are only 2% of the plastic waste produced in the world.（　④　）?"

My answer is this. If you stop using plastic bags, you can make a small difference. It is only a small *step, but if all of us take small steps to make the environment better, we will take a big step together. Our world will be a better place for all people and animals.

（注）pay　(お金を)支払う　　reduce　～を減らす
　　　step　一歩

問1．2人の会話で指摘されていることとして最も適切なものを，次のア～エからひとつ選び，記号で答えなさい。
ア．People have stopped throwing plastic away.
イ．Plastic helps fish in many ways.
ウ．Some animals produce the plastic in the sea.
エ．Fish think the plastic in the sea is food.

問2．会話の下線部①について，会話の内容から判断して，Graph 1, 2の(A)～(C)にあてはまる国名の組み合わせとして最も適切なものを，次のア～エからひとつ選び，記

号で答えなさい。
ア．(A) America　(B) India　(C) China
イ．(A) China　(B) America　(C) India
ウ．(A) China　(B) India　(C) America
エ．(A) India　(B) America　(C) China

問３．会話の内容から判断して，（　②　）にあてはまる適切な英語を，１語で答えなさい。

問４．会話の下線部③について，会話の内容から判断して，ジョンさんがインターネットで調べたいと思っていることは何ですか。次の(　　　)にあてはまるように，30字以内の日本語で答えなさい。ただし，句読点も１字に数えることとします。

> グラフ中の４か国のうち，(　　　　　　　　　)こと。

問５．スピーチの内容から判断して，（　④　）にあてはまる最も適切な英文を，次のア〜エからひとつ選び，記号で答えなさい。
ア．What are the plastic bags made of
イ．How should we ask more people to use plastic
ウ．Where does the other plastic go
エ．Why do we have to stop using plastic bags

問６．スピーチにおいて，なおやさんが伝えたい内容と一致する英文として最も適切なものを，次のア〜エからひとつ選び，記号で答えなさい。
ア．We don't have to worry about plastic because it is only a part of the problem for the environment.
イ．The problems of plastic are so difficult that we should stop thinking about what to do.
ウ．Taking our own bags to the store may be a small thing to do, but it will make a difference if everyone does it.
エ．People will not be able to stop using plastic bags, so it is too late to do something for the environment.

　　　　　　　　　　　　　　　　　　　＜鳥取県＞

13 七海(Nanami)さんと翔太(Shota)さんの学級では，英語の授業で，田中先生(Mr. Tanaka)が次の話をしました。また，翌週の授業で，七海さんが発表をしました。【田中先生の話】【二人の会話】【七海さんの発表】を読んで，後の１から７までの各問いに答えなさい。

【田中先生の話】
I'd like to talk about your future jobs today. Look at chart 1 and chart 2. Chart 1 is the list of the jobs which were popular about fifty years ago, in 1970. Chart 2 shows what the students in this class want to be in the future.

〈Chart 1〉
Popular Jobs in 1970

Baseball Player	Cartoonist
Doctor	Engineer
Fashion Designer	Flight Attendant
Nurse	Pilot
Scientist	Teacher

〈Chart 2〉
What Do You Want to Be in the Future?

Job	Number of Students
Programmer	5
Illustrator	4
Doctor	4
Game Designer	3
Nurse	3
Athlete	2
Hairstylist	2
Teacher	2
Dancer	1
Fashion Designer	1
Engineer	1
Voice Actor	1
Writer	1
Not Decided Yet	5
Total	35

What do these charts show us? Doctor and nurse are popular in both chart 1 and chart 2, but there are jobs which you can find only in chart 1 or in chart 2. It means that different jobs are popular in different times. Future generations may have different dreams.

According to chart 2, programmer is the most popular job in this class. Illustrator is as popular as doctor. You should make efforts to make your great dreams true.

Some students haven't decided their dreams yet. That's not a problem. You still have many things that you haven't experienced. Your dream may change if you have new experiences. So, it is important to learn more.

Now, your task is to interview a person who has a job and write a report. You have to ask questions about the job, such as "Why have you chosen your job?" You'll make a presentation next week. I'm looking forward to it.

（注）programmer　プログラマー
illustrator　イラストレーター

１．【田中先生の話】の内容として合っているものを，次のアからカまでの中から２つ選びなさい。
ア．Mr. Tanaka will ask students about their dreams in the next lesson.
イ．Hairstylist is popular in both chart 1 and chart 2.
ウ．Some popular jobs in 1970 are related to airplanes.
エ．All the students in the class have decided their future jobs.
オ．Mr. Tanaka believes that new experiences may change dreams.
カ．Students should interview each other about their dreams by next week.

田中先生の話を聞いて，七海さんと翔太さんが話しました。
【二人の会話】
Nanami：Shota, have you decided your goal?
Shota　：Yes. I want to be a nurse.
Nanami：Why do you want to be a nurse?

Shota : When I was a child, I had an operation. While I was in the hospital, I felt lonely and sometimes cried. Then, a nurse came to talk to me, and I felt relieved. I'll never forget his (①), and I want to be a nurse like him.

Nanami : That's wonderful.

Shota : How about you?

Nanami : I haven't found my goal yet. I ②【 find / how / it / to / wonder 】.

Shota : You can find your dream if you learn about people's experiences. (③) will you interview?

Nanami : Well, I will ask my father. He is a police officer, but I don't know why he wanted to be one. I want to know more about his job.

Shota : You may find some hints for your dream. Good luck!

2. (①)に入る語として最も適当なものを，次のアからエまでの中から1つ選びなさい。
　ア. happiness　イ. information
　ウ. innovation　エ. kindness

3. ②【　　　】内の語を，意味が通るように並べかえなさい。

4. (③)に入る適当な英語1語を書きなさい。

七海さんは，翌週の授業で発表をしました。
【七海さんの発表】

　Hello, everyone. I interviewed my father. My father has been a police officer for twenty-five years, but I didn't know why he chose this job.

　He said to me, "I feel happy when I can help people who need help. I do this job (④) their smiles always make me happy."

　When I said to him, "I haven't found my dream," he gave some advice to me. "You should get more knowledge, and you can imagine many things. It will give you more choices for your future."

　I haven't decided what I will do, but, like my father, I want to help people who need help. I will [⑤] to find my dream. Now, I'm so excited to find a way to my dream. Thank you.

（注）choice(s) 選択肢

5. 【七海さんの発表】について，次の質問に対する答えになるように，（　）に入る適当な英語を，3語以上で書きなさい。
　How long has Nanami's father worked as a police officer?
　→（　　　　　　　　　　　　　　　　　　）.

6. (④)に入る語として最も適当なものを，次のアからエまでの中から1つ選びなさい。
　ア. because　イ. before
　ウ. if　エ. though

7. [⑤]に入る適当な英語を，3語以上で書きなさい。
　　　　　　　　　　　　　　　　　　＜滋賀県＞

14 知美(Tomomi)さんと健太(Kenta)さんの学級では，英語の授業で興味のある社会的な問題についての意見発表を行いました。次は，【知美さんの発表】【知美さんの発表資料】【健太さんの感想】です。これらを読んで，後の1から6までの各問いに答えなさい。

【知美さんの発表】

　Hello, everyone. Have you ever thought about the food you eat every day? Where does it come from? How does it come to you? I believe food and the environment are important.

　Look at graph 1. Japan's food self-sufficiency rate is 37%. It means that Japan imports more than 60% of its food. I didn't know that, but I understood it when I thought about my breakfast. I ate rice, grilled fish, and miso soup. The rice was grown in Japan, but the fish was (①) in a foreign country. The miso and tofu are made from soybeans. However, most of the soybeans are imported from other countries. The breakfast was *washoku*, traditional Japanese cooking, but it was international.

　Look at graph 2. Do you know how far your food traveled to get to you? You can see the food mileage here. Food mileage is calculated by multiplying weight and distance and it tells how much fuel is used to transport food. Japan's food mileage is higher than the other countries' food mileage in the graph. Japan buys a lot of food from many countries and a lot of fuel is used when the food is transported. Using too much fuel is not good for the environment, so we need to think about this. If we buy locally produced food, we don't use much fuel. I think buying locally produced food is one of the good ways to solve this problem.

　There is another problem. There are ②【 around / from / hunger / many / suffer / people / who 】 the world. However, food waste in Japan is more than six million tons a year. According to graph 3, [③]. I think we should do something to solve this problem. If we reduce food waste from home, it can make all the difference. When I opened the refrigerator last week, I found some food that was too old to eat. I had to throw it away and I felt very sorry. We should buy only the food we will eat.

　Food is very important for us. We should think about the food we eat every day. I believe that we can find answers to our environmental problems. What is your opinion?
　Thank you.

（注）food mileage　フード・マイレージ（単位はt・km（トン・キロメートル））
　　　calculate(d)　計算する
　　　multiplying：multiply（かける）のing形
　　　weight　重さ
　　　distance　距離
　　　fuel　燃料
　　　locally produced food　地元でつくられた食べ物
　　　refrigerator　冷蔵庫

【知美さんの発表資料】

[Graph 1]

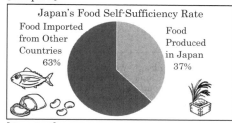

Japan's Food Self-Sufficiency Rate

Food Imported from Other Countries 63%

Food Produced in Japan 37%

[Graph 2]

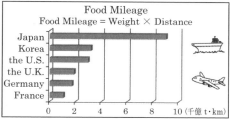

Food Mileage

Food Mileage ＝ Weight × Distance

Japan
Korea
the U.S.
the U.K.
Germany
France

0　2　4　6　8　10 (千億 t・km)

[Graph 3]

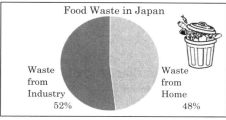

Food Waste in Japan

Waste from Industry 52%

Waste from Home 48%

グラフ1は農林水産省「平成30年度食料自給率・食料自給力指標について」，グラフ2はウェブサイト「フード・マイレージ」資料室（データは2001年），グラフ3は農林水産省「食品廃棄物等の利用状況等（平成25年度推計）」より作成

【健太さんの感想】

　　Thank you, Tomomi. Your presentation is great. You say that buying locally produced food is good for the environment and it has other good points, too. A few days ago, I went to the market near my house. A lot of vegetables grown in my town are sold there. The vegetables are fresh and we can get them in season. Sometimes the farmers who grew the vegetables come to the market to sell them. I met a farmer and enjoyed talking with him. He also taught me how to cook the vegetables. I ate them for dinner and they were delicious. If I know who grows the vegetables, I feel safe about my food. ④I think it is good to buy the food produced in our local area not only for the environment but also for us.

1．【知美さんの発表】について，次の(1)，(2)の質問に対する答えになるように，（　　）に入る適当な英語を2語以上で書きなさい。
　(1)　Does Japan import more than 60% of its food from foreign countries?
　　　→（　　　　　　　　　　　　　　　）．
　(2)　What food in Tomomi's breakfast was produced in Japan?
　　　→（　　　　　　　　　　　　　　　）．
2．（　①　）に入る最も適当なものを，次のアからエまでの

中から1つ選びなさい。
　　ア．caught　　イ．eaten
　　ウ．swum　　エ．thought
3．②【　　　】内の語を，意味が通るように並べかえなさい。
4．[　③　]に入る最も適当なものを，次のアからエまでの中から1つ選びなさい。
　　ア．the food waste from home is larger than the food waste from industry
　　イ．the food waste from home is half of the food waste from industry
　　ウ．the food waste from home is more than six million tons a year
　　エ．the food waste from home is almost half of all the food waste
5．【知美さんの発表】の内容として合っているものを，次のアからオまでの中から1つ選びなさい。
　　ア．All of the food we eat in Japan comes from foreign countries.
　　イ．The food mileage of Japan is the lowest of the six countries in graph 2.
　　ウ．Tomomi says locally produced food needs less fuel than imported food.
　　エ．Tomomi believes that reducing the food waste from industry is more important.
　　オ．We can do nothing to solve the food waste problem because it is too serious.
6．下線部④の健太さんの意見について，あなたの考えとその理由を10語以上の英語で書きなさい。2文以上になってもかまいません。ただし，知美さんが話したこととは違う内容で，書き出しは次のどちらかを用いることとし，書き出しの語句は語数に含めるものとする。
　　書き出し　I agree / I disagree
＜滋賀県＞

15　昨年の秋，英語の授業で，中学生の剛（Takeshi）さんが，クラスの生徒にプレゼンテーションをしました。その時に使ったグラフ（graph）と発表の原稿を読んで，あとの各問に答えなさい。

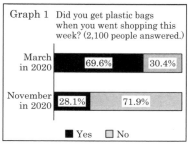

Graph 1　Did you get plastic bags when you went shopping this week? (2,100 people answered.)

March in 2020　69.6%　30.4%

November in 2020　28.1%　71.9%

■ Yes　□ No

Graph 2　Are you more interested in plastic garbage problems than you were before the system started?

27.4%　29.5%　21.1%　22.0%

□ I was interested and started taking action before the system started.
■ Yes, and I've started to take action.
□ Yes, but I haven't started to take action yet.
■ No. I haven't started to take action yet.

(Graph 1, Graph 2は環境省ホームページより作成)

On a sunny summer day, when I was taking a walk along a beach, I came to a pretty small store and found works of art which looked ▢▢▢▢ sea animals. They were so cute and I bought some. Then, a woman came up to me and told me she made them. She collected plastic garbage on the beach and made those dolphins out of it. When she saw a lot of plastic garbage there, she thought she should do something. She said, "Plastic garbage in the sea causes serious problems around the world. More people should know this fact."

I became interested in the garbage problem and read the magazine she gave me. ▢▢▢▢
(1)
After reading this magazine, I thought we should work hard to solve this problem.

First, we should stop throwing away plastic garbage because it may go to the sea. However, it is more important to decrease the amount of plastic we use. The Japanese government started a new system in July 2020, and now we have to pay for plastic shopping bags. Look at Graph 1. It shows how many people got plastic bags in a week when they did shopping. From the graph, we can say this system is ▢ あ ▢ because ▢ い ▢ people got plastic bags in November than in March. Other research says when people get plastic bags, about 80% of the people use them again.

Now, look at Graph 2. It shows how people have changed since the system started. Some people have started to take action. There are some companies that have started to use less plastic. A famous coffee shop began to use paper straws instead of plastic straws. However, ▢▢▢ (2) ▢▢▢. How can we change these people?

The woman ▢▢ (3) ▢▢ said, "I like art, so making works of art is the easiest way for me to let more people know about plastic garbage in the sea." The best way to solve this problem is to start with things we can enjoy.

I will introduce a good example. Last year, I joined "*Supo-GOMI*" with my brother and sister. During this event, people enjoyed collecting garbage on the beach as a sport. People made groups of three to five and collected garbage for an hour. Winners were decided by how much and what kind of garbage they got. We picked up many kinds of garbage on the beach. We were surprised to learn there was more plastic garbage than we thought.

I'm thinking of holding "*Supo-GOMI*" on a beach near our school. I hope everyone will have a good time and be interested in the plastic garbage problem. It will take a long time to (A) it, so we should do things that we can (B). Our actions may be (C), but if more people join us, the future of the sea will be (D). What can you do for sea animals and fish? Everyone, let's take the first step to protect life in the sea.

　(注) system 制度　　amount 量　　straw ストロー
　　　　winner 勝者

問1．▢▢▢の中に入る語として，次のア～エから最も適切なものを1つ選び，その符号を書きなさい。
　ア．at　　イ．for　　ウ．into　　エ．like

問2．▢(1)▢の中には次のア～エが入る。文章の意味が通じるように最も適切な順に並べ替え，その符号を書きなさい。
　ア．In it, I found the expression "disasters of sea animals."
　イ．It continued, "If we do not stop this, there will be no sea animals or fish in the sea."
　ウ．It means more and more sea animals and fish die because of the plastic garbage they eat in the sea.
　エ．The article also said there will be more plastic garbage than fish in 2050.

問3．▢ あ ▢，▢ い ▢の中に入る英語の組み合わせとして，次のア～エから最も適切なものを1つ選び，その符号を書きなさい。
　ア．▢ あ ▢ successful　　▢ い ▢ fewer
　イ．▢ あ ▢ successful　　▢ い ▢ more
　ウ．▢ あ ▢ not successful　　▢ い ▢ fewer
　エ．▢ あ ▢ not successful　　▢ い ▢ more

問4．▢(2)▢の中に入る英語として，次のア～エから最も適切なものを1つ選び，その符号を書きなさい。
　ア．about 20% of the people haven't taken any action yet
　イ．about 30% of the people have already started to take action
　ウ．more than 40% of the people haven't taken any action yet
　エ．more than half of the people have already started to take action

問5．▢(3)▢の中に，4語以上の適切な内容の英語を書きなさい。

問6．英文の意味が通じるように，(A)～(D)に入る語として，次のア～カから最も適切なものをそれぞれ1つ選び，その符号を書きなさい。
　ア．continue　　イ．different　　ウ．increase
　エ．same　　オ．small　　カ．solve

問7．プレゼンテーションの後にALTのベーカー先生(Mr. Baker)が剛さんに質問しました。(a)に入る英語として，下のア～エから最も適切なものを1つ選び，その符号を書きなさい。また，(b)には4文以上のまとまりのある英文を書きなさい。

Mr. Baker：What is the main point of your presentation?
Takeshi　：I want more people to be interested in ＿＿(a)＿＿.
Mr. Baker：For that reason, you're going to hold "*Supo-GOMI*" at your school.
Takeshi　：Yes. I'm also interested in other problems such as global warming and air pollution.
Mr. Baker：What else can you do to protect the environment?
Takeshi　：＿＿＿(b)＿＿＿
　ア．artworks　　　イ．paper straws
　ウ．plastic garbage　　エ．shopping bags

＜石川県＞

② ポスター・案内など

1 次の英文は，ホテルの予約サイトに載っている，Nagisa Hotelに対する評価（review）です。海外からの観光客がそれを読んで，このホテルに泊まるかどうかを考えているところです。それぞれの評価を読み，(1)・(2)の問いの答えとして最も適切なものを，それぞれのア～エから一つ選び，その記号を書きなさい。

Nagisa Hotel ★★★★☆

2.5 km (30 minutes on foot) from Nagisa Station

Review from Dreaming of Traveling ★★★★☆

When I visit Nagisa City, I always stay at this hotel because the view is wonderful. I enjoy watching the beautiful sea from my room. If you like nice views, Nagisa Hotel is the one you should choose!

Review from Sally ★★★☆☆

I stayed at this hotel because a friend of mine said that he loved it. I think he was right. It was a good hotel with clean rooms, friendly staff, and nice views. But it was too far from the station. I didn't have a car, so I had to take a taxi. If I have a chance to visit Nagisa City again, I will probably choose a hotel near the station.

Review from Good Dad Eric ★★★★★

My family and I really enjoyed our stay at Nagisa Hotel. It is in front of Nagisa Beach, so my kids were able to play there all day. We loved the restaurant in the hotel, too. Food was fresh. I had tasty fish for dinner and cake for dessert. If you are looking for a hotel in Nagisa City, you definitely should choose this hotel. I'm sure you will have a great time.

---

(1) What is one thing that both Dreaming of Traveling and Sally liked about this hotel?
　ア．The view from the hotel.
　イ．The beach near the hotel.
　ウ．The people working at the hotel.
　エ．The distance from the station.

(2) Which is not true about this hotel?
　ア．You can eat good seafood in the restaurant.
　イ．It takes half an hour to walk there from the station.
　ウ．You have to take a taxi to go to the beach.
　エ．The staff are friendly and the rooms are clean.

<高知県>

2 あなたは，夏休みに語学講座に参加したいと考えており，次の【広告】のどのコース（course(s)）が良いか検討している。この【広告】の内容に合う適当な英文を，あとのア～カの中から二つ選び，記号を書きなさい。

【広告】

★GABAI Summer English Event★
July 25 — August 31, 2023

ONLINE *CONVERSATION COURSE

Age: all ages
Place / Time:
　*anywhere / every day, 10:00-22:00 (1 hour *per *lesson, 1 lesson per day)

*Content and *Fee:
・You can practice conversation anywhere with teachers from all over the world.
・You can choose the time to take the lesson from 10:00 to 22:00.
・You have to join *at least 10 lessons.
・5,000 yen for this course

---

*BUSINESS COURSE

Age: over 18 years old
Place / Time:
　Sagan Meeting Room / every Monday and Friday, 19:00-21:00 (2 hours per lesson)
Content and Fee:
・You can learn how to talk on the phone and how to write e-mails for business.
・You have to join at least 3 lessons.
・2,000 yen for one lesson

CULTURE COURSE

Age: 12 years old or older
Place / Time:
　Hagakure Cooking Room / every Saturday, 11:00-14:00 (3 hours per lesson)
Content and Fee:
・You can cook traditional food from some countries and speak in English.
・4,000 yen for one lesson

〈MORE INFORMATION〉
Phone: 0120－●●－◆◆◆◆　　Mail: gabaisee@example.jp

(注) conversation　会話
　　anywhere　どこでも
　　per ～　～につき
　　lesson(s)　レッスン，講座
　　content　内容
　　fee　料金
　　at least　少なくとも
　　business　仕事，ビジネス

ア．In the Online Conversation Course, you can take the lessons every day.
イ．You can take three lessons in the Online Conversation Course for 3,000 yen.
ウ．You have to join all lessons in the Business Course.
エ．You can join the Culture Course in the evening.
オ．If you are 15 years old, you can take all the courses.
カ．If you want more information about this event, you can call or send an e-mail.

<佐賀県>

3 次は，高校生の健太(Kenta)が，留学先のリバータウン高校(River Town High School)で見つけたサッカーチームのポスターである。1，2の問いに答えなさい。

Let's Enjoy Soccer Together!
River Town High School Soccer Team

We are looking for new members who will enjoy soccer with us. You don't need any experience in soccer. Our coaches will teach you everything. Just come and enjoy soccer!!

Practice Plan for the Week

Day	Time	Place to Practice
Monday	4:00 p.m. ～ 6:00 p.m.	River Town Park
Wednesday	4:00 p.m. ～ 6:00 p.m.	River Town High School
Friday	4:00 p.m. ～ 6:00 p.m.	River Town Stadium
Saturday	9:00 a.m. ～ 11:00 a.m.	River Town Stadium

You can come all four days or choose one, two, or three days for practice.
・Bring your soccer shoes and some drinks.
・You can join us as a player or a supporter.
If you are interested in our activity, please tell Mr. White, the P.E. teacher, or just visit one of our practices.

(注) coach　コーチ
　　　supporter　サポーター

1. ポスターの内容として最も適当なものを，次のア～エから一つ選び，記号で答えなさい。
　ア．You can join the team without any experience in soccer.
　イ．You don't need your own soccer shoes because you can borrow them from the team.
　ウ．You have to play soccer if you want to join the team.
　エ．You must meet Mr. White first if you want to join the team,

2. 健太は，友達のトム(Tom)とポスターを見ながら話をしています。　①　と　②　に入れるのに最も適当なものを，それぞれ下のア～ウから一つ選び，記号で答えなさい。

This soccer team looks nice. How about joining the soccer practice?
Kenta

 Tom
Sounds good. I'm interested in playing soccer, but I have another club meeting every Monday and Wednesday after school.

I have English lessons on Saturday morning. So, how about joining the practice next 　①　? Let's meet at the River Town 　②　 at 3:50 p.m.

---

① ア．Monday　　イ．Wednesday
　 ウ．Friday
② ア．High School　イ．Park
　 ウ．Stadium

<熊本県>

4 次は，アメリカに留学中のNamiと，友人のChrisとの対話の一部である。対話文と【ウェブサイト】を読んで，(1)～(3)に答えなさい。

Chris：Nami, what are you looking at?
Nami：This is a website about a photo book. I'll make a photo book with the pictures I took in this city.
Chris：That's a good idea. What kind of photo book will you make?
Nami：Well, I think I'll order a medium photo book.
Chris：How about a cover?
Nami：I know soft covers of all sizes are (c　　　　) than hard covers. But I'll choose a hard cover photo book. And I'll make it gloss-finished.
Chris：Sounds good. I'm sure it'll be nice.

(注) photo book(s) フォトブック(写真を各ページに印刷し製本したもの)
　　　order ～ ～を注文する
　　　cover(s) 表紙
　　　hard 硬い，厚手の
　　　gloss-finished つや出し加工の

【ウェブサイト】

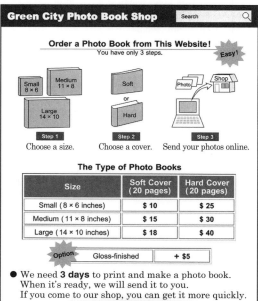

(注) online　オンラインで
　　　inch(es)　インチ(長さの単位，1インチはおよそ2.5センチメートル)
　　　option　オプション(追加メニュー)

(1) 【ウェブサイト】の内容に合うように，対話文中の下線部に入る適切な英語1語を書きなさい。ただし，(　　　)内に与えられた文字で書き始めなさい。

(2) 対話と【ウェブサイト】の内容によると，Namiが購入しようとしているフォトブックの値段はいくらになるか。次の1～4から1つ選び，記号で答えなさい。
　1. 20 dollars
　2. 30 dollars
　3. 35 dollars
　4. 40 dollars

(3) 【ウェブサイト】から読み取れる内容と一致するもの

を，次の１〜６から２つ選び，記号で答えなさい。

1. People can order a photo book through the Internet.
2. Sending pictures is the first step to make a photo book.
3. There are four different sizes of photo books.
4. All the photo books people can order have thirty pages.
5. The shop needs a week to finish making a photo book.
6. People can receive a photo book at the shop.

〈山口県〉

5 カナダでホームステイ中の由佳（Yuka）さんは同級生のケイ（Kay）さんと話をしています。次の対話文とポスターの内容について，あとの問いに答えなさい。

Kay : Next Saturday is my brother's birthday.
Yuka : Happy birthday to him. How old will he be?
Kay : He will be ten years old. He likes science, so my father and mother will take him and me to the science museum on his birthday.
Yuka : Sounds nice! I like science too. Is it the museum near our junior high school?
Kay : Yes. Will you join us?
Yuka : I want to go. I will buy a present for him at the museum's shop.
Kay : Thank you. He will be happy.
Yuka : When can we go to the museum's shop?
Kay : We are going to join the special event after we have lunch at the museum's restaurant. Let's go to the shop after the special event.

Welcome to The Science Museum			
*Fees		Monday – Friday	Weekend
	*Adults (18 〜)	15 dollars	20 dollars
	Children(6 〜 17)	8 dollars	10 dollars

Special Event
*Virtual Space Tour
① 11:00 − 12:00   ② 14:00 − 15:00
Please come to the Special Event Room
5 minutes before each time.

Museum Shop 10:00 − 16:00	Museum Restaurant 11:00 − 14:00

(注) fee 入場料金　　adult 大人
　　Virtual Space Tour　バーチャル宇宙旅行

(1) ケイさんの家族と由佳さんの入場料金は合計でいくらですか。その金額を書きなさい。
　　＿＿＿＿ドル

(2) 由佳さんたちがバーチャル宇宙旅行に参加するためには，いつまでに会場へ行く必要がありますか。その時刻を書きなさい。
　　＿＿＿＿時＿＿＿＿分

〈富山県〉

6 第一中学校の２年生は職業体験(work experience)へ行くことになっています。各体験場所での予定表が配られ，マサ(Masa)とカイ(Kai)はどの体験場所を選ぶか考えているところです。以下の資料と２人の会話を参考に，各問いに答えなさい。

Daiichi Junior High School's Work Experience Plan

Dates：November 18th-November 20th

Tell your teacher your *choice by November 4th.

Sakura *Nursery School

7:30 Clean the children's classroom
8:00 Play with the children
9:30 Take the children to the park
11:30 Lunch

Sunshine Restaurant

9:00 Clean the floor and tables
10:00 Welcome customers and take orders
11:00 Wash the dishes
12:00 Lunch

South Fire Station

8:30 Go running on the road
9:30 Practice climbing buildings
10:30 Practice using *fire extinguishers
12:00 Lunch

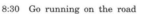

City Library

8:00 Clean the floor and desks
9:00 Return books to the shelves
10:30 Read books to children
12:00 Lunch

(注) choice　選択　　Nursery School　保育園
　　fire extinguisher　消火器

Masa : Hey, Kai, have you decided which place you want to go?
Kai : Why don't we go to the same place? How about the South Fire Station? I like to run and I want to become a firefighter.
Masa : Really? I don't like running. I am interested in (　①　), but I am worried about reading books well to the children.
Kai : I see. You are really shy.
Masa : What should I do?
Kai : You should go and talk to our teacher. Maybe

she can help you.

Masa：OK.

問1．この職業体験は何月に何日間行われますか。次のア〜エのうちから1つ選び、その記号を書きなさい。
　ア．10月の2日間　　イ．11月の2日間
　ウ．10月の3日間　　エ．11月の3日間

問2．空欄（　①　）に入るマサが最初に興味を持った場所はどこですか。次のア〜エのうちから1つ選び、その記号を書きなさい。
　ア．Sakura Nursery School
　イ．Sunshine Restaurant
　ウ．South Fire Station
　エ．City Library

問3．次のア〜オのうち、予定表及び会話文の内容と一致するものを2つ選び、その記号を書きなさい。
　ア．Both Masa and Kai want to be firefighters.
　イ．Both Masa and Kai need help from their teacher.
　ウ．Students who choose the Sakura Nursery School have lunch the earliest.
　エ．Students who choose the Sunshine Restaurant can learn how to cook.
　オ．Students who choose the South Fire Station will go running outside.

<沖縄県>

7 里香（Rika）が、里香の家にホームステイ中のナンシー（Nancy）と話をしています。【案内】と【二人の対話】をもとに、下の1〜4の問いに答えなさい。

【案内】

Collecting *Garbage and Recycling Information		
Types of Garbage	Day (Time)	Other Information
*Burnable Garbage	Monday and Friday (by 8:30 a.m.)	Put your garbage in a garbage bag made by this city.
Old Clothes	Wednesday (by 8:30 a.m.)	Don't *dispose of it on a rainy day.
Plastics	Thursday (by 9:00 a.m.)	Only plastics with 🈁.

○ City garbage bags (Each *pack has 10 bags in it.)
　・Large size pack:400 yen
　・Medium size pack:300 yen
　・Small size pack:200yen
○ For large size waste such as chairs and bikes, please put a special card on it.
　When you dispose of large size waste, please call 0120-XXX-XXX.
　・Special card:500yen

（注）garbage　ごみ
　　　burnable　燃やせる
　　　dispose of　〜を捨てる
　　　pack　包み

【二人の対話】

Rika：Thanks for your help. We've cleaned our house and collected lots of garbage.

Nancy：You're welcome. But how can we dispose of that large chair?

Rika：Well. Look at this information. We need to put a special card on the chair and 　①　 to dispose of it.

Nancy：I see. Let's look at the information again.

Today is Thursday. So tomorrow is the day for the 　②　. Oh, we have no city garbage bags. I guess we need one medium size pack.

Rika：Let's see. We have lots of garbage. I think one large size pack is better.

Nancy：OK. Then why don't we go out to buy one card and one pack of that size?

Rika：Sure. We must pay（　　　　）yen for them, right?

Nancy：That's right. Before we go out, let's dispose of the 　③　.

Rika：Wait. It's almost 11:00. So we should dispose of them next week.

1．次の質問の答えとして、下線部に入る適切な語を、英語1語で書きなさい。
　（質問）How many times is burnable garbage collected in this city?
　（答え）It's collected ＿＿＿＿＿＿＿ a week.

2．【二人の対話】の 　①　 に入る最も適切なものを、次のア〜エから1つ選び、記号で答えなさい。
　ア．clean our house
　イ．collect garbage
　ウ．recycle it
　エ．call this number

3．【二人の対話】の 　②　 と 　③　 に入る最も適切なものを、それぞれ次のア〜エから1つずつ選び、記号で答えなさい。
　ア．burnable garbage
　イ．old clothes
　ウ．plastics
　エ．large size waste

4．【二人の対話】の（　　　）に入る適切な数字を答えなさい。

<宮崎県>

8 高校生のタクヤ（Takuya）とニュージーランドからの留学生のクリス（Chris）が、次のウェブサイトを見ながら話をしています。下の対話文を読んで、(1), (2)の問いに答えなさい。

Takuya：Hi, Chris. What are you doing on your computer?

Chris：I'm just looking for a place to play basketball.

Takuya：There are some *courts at Asahi Sports Park.

Chris：Really? I'll see its website. Oh, the park has（　①　）, so we can play at the park.

Takuya：Are you going to play with your classmates?

Chris：Yes, but we only have nine people now. We need another person. Can you join us?

Takuya：Sure. It will be fun.

Chris：Thank you, Takuya. Oh, look here. （　②　）. Do you have any balls?

Takuya：I have some balls, so we can use mine.

Chris：Really? That's nice.

Takuya：When are we going to play?

Chris：I want to play next Sunday.

Takuya：I'm so sorry. I have a swimming lesson on that day. How about next Monday?

Chris：I'm free, but look at this website again. ＿＿＿＿＿＿＿ because it is *closed.

Takuya : Well, then let's go there on Saturday morning.

Chris : That's a great idea. I think the other members can come on Saturday.

Takuya : What time shall we meet?

Chris : Let's meet in front of the park entrance when the park opens.

Takuya : Do you mean at（　③　）?

Chris : Yes.

Takuya : I see. How long will we play? I have to meet my sister at the station at one o'clock.

Chris : Are you going to take the bus to the station?

Takuya : Yes.

Chris :（　④　）.

Takuya : All right. I can arrive there before she comes.

Chris : Then we can play for three hours. We need money to use a court. We will use just one court, so each of us needs（　⑤　）yen.

Takuya : OK. See you on Saturday.

（注）court(s)（テニスなどの）コート
closed　閉まっている

Asahi Sports Park	
Opening Hours	
Tuesday － Friday	8:00 － 20:00
Saturday	9:00 － 18:00
Sunday	10:00 － 19:00

Closed Days
Every Monday
December 30 － January 3

How many courts
3 badminton courts
4 tennis courts
2 basketball courts
2 volleyball courts

How much
To use one court for one hour each group needs...
Badminton － 500 yen
Tennis － 500 yen
Basketball － 1,000 yen
Volleyball － 1,000 yen

Bus					
Station → Park (about 20 minutes)					
7:20	7:50	8:20	8:50	9:50	10:50
11:50	12:50	13:50	14:50	15:50	
Park → Station (about 20 minutes)					
9:30	10:15	11:00	11:45	12:30	13:15
14:00	14:45	15:30	16:15	17:15	

※We don't have any balls or rackets.
※You must not eat on the courts.

(1) 対話中の（　①　）～（　⑤　）に入る最も適切なものを，ア～エの中から一つ選んで，その記号を書きなさい。

① ア．three badminton courts
　 イ．four tennis courts
　 ウ．two basketball courts
　 エ．two volleyball courts

② ア．We can't borrow basketballs from the park
　 イ．We need money to use basketballs at the park
　 ウ．We can only borrow tennis balls from the park
　 エ．Someone has already borrowed basketballs from the park

③ ア．seven　　イ．eight
　 ウ．nine　　エ．ten

④ ア．You should leave the park at eleven fifty
　 イ．You should leave the park at twelve forty
　 ウ．You should take the bus at eleven forty-five
　 エ．You should take the bus at twelve thirty

⑤ ア．100　　イ．300
　 ウ．1,000　　エ．3,000

(2) 対話の流れに合うように，文中の　　　に入る適切な英語を，4語以上，8語以内で書き，英文を完成させなさい。

<茨城県>

9 次の英文は，高校生のまみ（Mami）と留学生のジーナ（Gina）が交わしている会話である。あとのリスト（list）を参考にして英文を読み，あとの問い(1)～(4)に答えよ。

Gina : What are you looking at, Mami?

Mami : I'm looking at a list of English books. Our English teacher Ms. Smith gave this to me yesterday. I started reading English books last month and asked her to tell me good books. The *comments on the list are her comments about each book. I'll go shopping tomorrow and buy some of the books on the list.

Gina : Can I see it? Oh, I think you should read this book. I haven't read it, but look at the comment. You are interested in the U.S., right? You can learn about many famous places there if you read it.

Mami : Wow, that's nice. I'll buy it.

Gina : How about "The Blue Sky"? I first read it when I was little and it was very interesting. You should also buy it.

Mami : Then, I'll buy it, 　①　.

Gina : I heard the writer of the book is liked by a lot of people in Japan. Look at the comment. The same writer wrote "The White Sea". I like the writer, so I want to read it someday. Have you read it before?

Mami : No, but this story is in our English *textbook. We will read the story in the class, so I will not buy it. Well, I want to read "Our Memory", but I think it is difficult. Have you ever read it?

Gina : No, but if you want to read it, you should read it. I'll help you if you can't understand the book.

Mami : Thank you. I'll also buy it.

Gina : How about this book? I haven't read it, but I think you can learn a lot about English.

Mami : I have read it before, so I will not buy it. It tells us many interesting facts about

English words and I learned about the *origin of the names of the months. For example, September means "the seventh month."

Gina : Wait. Today, September is the ninth month of the year, right?

Mami : Yes. Let me talk about the history ____②____. When people began to use a *calendar, there were only ten months in a year, and the year started in March. September was really the seventh month then. The book says that there are some *theories, but it introduces this theory.

Gina : I see.

Mami : Oh, I think I chose ____③____ many books. I don't think I have enough money.

Gina : Well, look at the list. I don't think you need to buy ④this book. I found it at the library in our school. I've liked it since I first read it, so I was happy when I found it there.

Mami : I see. So, I will not buy it tomorrow and I'll visit the library next week. Thank you.

リスト (list)

Name of Book	Comment
(ア)　Lily	A girl called Lily visits many famous places in the U.S. You can learn a lot about them with pictures taken by the writer.
(イ)　Our Memory	A girl goes abroad and studies about AI. There are some difficult words in this book.
(ウ)　The Blue Sky	This is a story about a boy who goes to the future. The writer of this book is liked by many people in Japan and the writer also wrote "The White Sea".
(エ)　The Past	A boy travels to the past and learns about the origin of English words.
(オ)　The White Sea	A small cat visits a city in the sea. There are many pictures in this book. The writer drew them and they will help you understand the situations.

（注）comment　コメント
textbook　教科書
origin　起源　　calendar　暦
theory　説

(1)　①・③に共通して入る最も適当な1語を書け。

(2)　②に入る表現として最も適当なものを，次の(ア)〜(エ)から1つ選べ。
(ア)　to tell you the reason
(イ)　to buy the book tomorrow
(ウ)　to write a comment about each book
(エ)　to learn about Japanese words

(3)　本文とリスト(list)の内容から考えて，下線部④にあたるものとして最も適当なものを，リスト(list)の中の(ア)〜(オ)から1つ選べ。

(4)　本文とリスト(list)の内容と一致する英文として最も適当なものを，次の(ア)〜(エ)から1つ選べ。
(ア)　Mami says that she decided to start reading English books because Ms. Smith gave her the list.
(イ)　The writer of "The Blue Sky" is popular in Japan and Gina knew that before she talks with Mami.
(ウ)　Through the comments, Ms. Smith tells Mami that there are some difficult words in "The Past".
(エ)　Many pictures taken by the writer help people understand the situations in "The White Sea".

<京都府>

③ 複合資料

1 次の㋐の英文とリスト（List），㋑の英文とポスター（Poster）やリストについて，それぞれあとの質問の答えとして最も適するものを，１～５の中からそれぞれ一つずつ選び，その番号を答えなさい。

㋐ *Becky is a high school student in Australia. She is going to stay at Miki's house in Kamome City. Miki and Becky are sending messages to each other on their *smartphones.*

| Miki
5:30p.m. | I'm excited to see you here in Japan! You said you wanted to eat *tempura*. I've just sent a list of the *tempura* restaurants in my city. Will you go to one with me on Saturday or Sunday? |

| Sure. How about going for lunch on Sunday? | Becky
5:40p.m. |

| Miki
6:00p.m. | OK. Let's choose a restaurant! |

| I want to go to the one with the *cheapest lunch. If the lunch is cheap, I can use my money for other activities. I want to try many things in Japan. | Becky
6:20p.m. |

| Miki
6:30p.m. | OK. Look at the list. We can use a *discount at *lunchtime. What kind of *tempura* would you like? |

| I'd like to eat vegetable *tempura*. I want to go to the restaurant which uses local vegetables. | Becky
6:40p.m. |

| Miki
7:00p.m. | I see. Let's go to ⬚⬚⬚⬚⬚. |

| Sure. After we eat, please show me around your city. | Becky
7:10p.m. |

List

Restaurant	*Business hours	*Price of lunch	Discount at lunchtime	Miki's opinion
Wakaba 	It's closed on Sundays.	1,600 yen	Everyone can get a 20% discount.	The vegetable *tempura* is very good. The *chef makes *tempura* in front of us.
Momiji 	It's closed on Tuesdays.	1,600 yen	Groups of four *or more get a 20% discount.	You can make your own *tempura*. You can eat very good fish *tempura*.
Kaede 	It's closed on Mondays.	1,500 yen	Everyone can get a 10% discount.	The fish *tempura* is very good. The chef makes *tempura* in front of us.
Komachi 	It's closed on Tuesdays.	1,500 yen	Groups of two or more get a 10% discount.	The vegetable *tempura* is very good. This restaurant uses vegetables from Kamome City.
Sakura 	It's closed on Mondays.	1,500 yen	Groups of four or more get a 10% discount.	The vegetable *tempura* is very good. This restaurant uses vegetables from Kamome City.

（注） smartphones　スマートフォン
cheapest　（値段が）最も安い　　discount　割引
lunchtime　ランチタイム
Business hours　営業時間　　Price　価格
chef　料理人　　～ or more　～以上

質問：What will be in ⬚⬚⬚⬚⬚⬚？
 1．Wakaba 　　 2．Momiji 　　 3．Kaede
 4．Komachi 　　 5．Sakura

㋑ *Daisuke is a high school student. He is talking with Mr. Green at school.*

Mr. Green：Hi, Daisuke. What are you doing?

Daisuke　：I'm looking at this poster. I'm going to join this speech *contest.

Mr. Green：That's great! You have one week before the *deadline. Have you sent the things to take part in the first *round?

Daisuke　：No, I haven't. I have just got an *application form and I have decided the topic of my speech.

Mr. Green：Oh, what is the topic of your speech?

Daisuke　：I will talk about Japanese culture. I have already found some interesting books about it and I have read them. I'll write a *summary of my speech next.

Mr. Green：Well, I think you should write your *script first. When your script is finished, you can write the summary quickly.

Daisuke　：OK. I'll do that. After that, I will practice how to *gesture during my speech. I think gesturing well is important in an English speech.

Mr. Green：I think that is important, too. But speaking well is more important. So, you should practice speaking English before the voice *recording. You should practice gesturing after sending the voice recording for the second round.

Daisuke　：Thank you. I'll make a list of the things to do for the speech contest now.

Mr. Green：That's good!　Good luck!

Poster
Kamome City English Speech Contest 2022 KAMOME

Rounds	Things to send	*Details	Deadlines
First round	An application form	Get from our website. Write the speech topic.	*By September 12
	A summary of your speech	50～60 words	
	A script of your speech	400～500 words	
Second round	A voice recording of your speech	5 minutes	By September 26
*Final		Give your speech in front of the audience at Kamome Hall on October 9.	

List

Things to do by September 12	Things to do by September 26	Things to do by October 9
□ (①)	□ (③)	□ (⑤)
↓	↓	
□ (②)	□ (④)	

(ア) To practice speaking English.
(イ) To write a summary.
(ウ) To practice gesturing.
(エ) To make a voice recording.
(オ) To write a script.

(注) contest コンテスト　deadline 締め切り
〜 round 〜回戦　application form 応募用紙
summary 概要　script 原稿
gesture 身振りで示す　recording 録音
Details 詳細　By 〜 〜までに　Final 本戦

質問： What will be in (①), (②),
(③), (④), and (⑤) on the
list?

1．①－(イ) ②－(オ) ③－(ア) ④－(エ) ⑤－(ウ)
2．①－(イ) ②－(オ) ③－(ウ) ④－(エ) ⑤－(ア)
3．①－(オ) ②－(イ) ③－(ア) ④－(ウ) ⑤－(エ)
4．①－(オ) ②－(イ) ③－(ア) ④－(エ) ⑤－(ウ)
5．①－(オ) ②－(イ) ③－(ウ) ④－(エ) ⑤－(ア)

<神奈川県>

2 次の英文は，中学生の真奈（Mana）と，イギリス（the U.K.）からの留学生アリス（Alice）との対話の一部である。また，あとのそれぞれの図は，総合的な学習の時間で二人が作成している，ツバメ（swallow）に関する発表資料である。これらに関して，1から6までの問いに答えなさい。

Mana : Where do swallows in the U.K. come from in spring, Alice?
Alice : Some of them come from *Southern Africa. They travel about 10,000 km.
Mana : Really? They can fly so far! ☐ A ☐ do they fly to go to the U.K.?
Alice : I'm not sure, but for more than three weeks.
Mana : Wow. In Japan, swallows come from *Southeast Asia. It may take about a week. Then, they make their *nests under the *roof of a house.
Alice : Why do they choose people's houses for making nests?
Mana : There are many people around the houses, so other animals don't come close to their nests.
Alice : I see. Do Japanese people like swallows?
Mana : Yes, and there are some words about swallows in Japan. One of them is, "If a swallow flies low in the sky, ___(1)___." I'll draw a picture of it later.
Alice : Interesting! Swallows are popular in my country, too. We have a story called *The Happy Prince*. One day, there was a gold *statue of a prince in a city. The prince wanted to help poor people. He asked a swallow to give his *jewelry to them. ___(2)___ *Oscar Wilde.
Mana : Let's introduce the story to everyone. I also want to show (3)this graph. It says 36,000 swallows were found in our city in 1985. But only 9,500 swallows were found in 2020. *On the other hand, the number of houses has been growing for these 35 years.
Alice : You said a human's house was a safe place for swallows, right? If there are many houses, that is good for them.
Mana : Well, actually, more people in Japan like to live in Western style houses. Traditional Japanese houses are good for swallows because those houses usually have wide *space under the roof. So, it ___(4)___ to make their nests. However, some Western style houses don't have space under the roof.
Alice : I see. Well, I think many swallows have (5)other problems when they grow their babies. Their nests are sometimes broken by people. Also, baby swallows fall from their nests. They need a safe place.
Mana : You're right, Alice. Our city has got bigger, and its *nature was lost in many places. Living in this city is not easy for swallows ☐ B ☐ they can't find their food. We have to know more about *environmental problems.
Alice : That's true. (6)We have to live in a nature-friendly way.

(注) Southern Africa アフリカ南部
Southeast Asia 東南アジア
nest 巣　roof 屋根
The Happy Prince 『幸福な王子』（イギリスの童話）
statue 像　jewelry 宝石
Oscar Wilde オスカー・ワイルド（イギリスの作家）
on the other hand 一方で　space 空間
nature 自然　environmental 環境の

図1

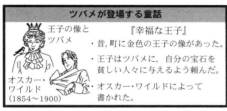

図2

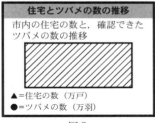

図3

図4

1．二人の対話が成り立つよう，本文中の　Ａ　に入る適切な英語2語を書きなさい。

2．二人の対話が成り立つよう，図1，図2，図4を参考に，下線部(1)，(2)，(4)に適切な英語を書きなさい。

3．下線部(3)について，図3の▨の位置に入るグラフとして，最も適切なものはどれか。

ア

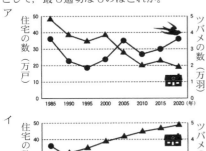

イ

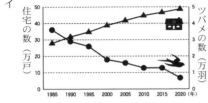

ウ

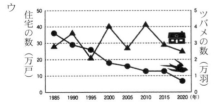

エ

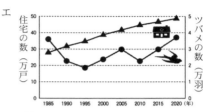

4．下線部(5)について，本文中で述べられている具体例を二つ挙げて，20字以上30字以内の日本語で書きなさい。ただし，句読点も字数に加えるものとする。

5．本文中の　Ｂ　に入る語として，最も適切なものはどれか。
ア．because　　イ．but　　ウ．though　　エ．until

6．下線部(6)について，自然環境に優しい生活を送るために，あなたが普段行っていること，またはこれから行おうと思うことは何ですか。まとまりのある5文程度の英語で書きなさい。

<栃木県>

3 次の各問に答えよ。
（＊印の付いている単語には，本文のあとに(注)がある。）

1．高校生のRikuとイギリスからの留学生Tonyは，Rikuが授業で公園について発表するために調べて作成した資料を見ながら話をしている。　(A)　及び　(B)　の中に，それぞれ入る語句の組み合わせとして正しいものは，ア〜エのうちではどれか。ただし，次のＩは，二人が見ている資料である。

Ⅰ

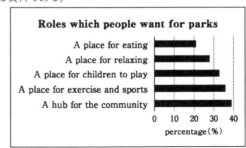

Tony：What are you going to *present in the next class?

Riku：I'm going to present my idea for a new park. I think people want many *roles for parks. They are important. I want to make a wonderful new park in my town in the future.

Tony：Great!

Riku：What is the most important role for parks to you?

Tony：Well, I think 　(A)　 is the most important.

Riku：I think that is important, too. But the *percentage for it is the lowest in this *graph.

Tony：Interesting. In my country. I often enjoy eating lunch in a park.

Riku：I think 　(B)　 is the most important. Many other people also want that role.

Tony：Yes. The percentage for it is a little lower than the percentages for "A place for *exercise and sports" and "A *hub for the "*community." But it's higher than the percentages for the other *items.

Riku：Parks can *play a lot of roles in a town. I'll try to make a park that plays important roles. There are many *possible roles for a park in a town. I hope people find good roles for my park.

Tony：Great! I think your presentation will be really interesting. I want to know more about parks and towns.

（注）present 発表する　　role 役割
　　percentage パーセンテージ　　graph グラフ
　　exercise 運動　　hub 拠点
　　community 地域社会　　item 項目　　play 果たす
　　possible あり得る

ア．(A) A place for eating
　　(B) A hub for the community
イ．(A) A place for relaxing
　　(B) A place for children to play
ウ．(A) A place for eating
　　(B) A place for children to play
エ．(A) A place for relaxing
　　(B) A hub for the community

2．都市と公園についてさらに学びたいと思ったRikuとTonyは，インターネットの画面を見ながら話をしている。 (A) 及び (B) の中に，それぞれ入る語句の組み合わせとして正しいものは，ア〜エのうちではどれか。ただし，次のⅡは，二人が見ている，海外のある大学のオンライン講義の予定表であり，表中の時間は日本時間である。

Ⅱ

Date	Day	Time	Class
August 2	Monday	10:00 - 12:00	How to *Design a City (☆)
		14:00 - 16:00	Making Parks in Towns (○)
August 3	Tuesday	10:00 - 12:00	Making Parks in Towns (○)
		14:00 - 16:00	City Planning (○)
August 4	Wednesday	10:00 - 12:00	Making Parks in Towns (☆)
		14:00 - 16:00	How to Design a City (○)
August 5	Thursday	10:00 - 12:00	How to Design a City (☆)
		14:00 - 16:00	City Planning (○)
August 6	Friday	10:00 - 12:00	Making Parks in Towns (○)
		14:00 - 16:00	City Planning (☆)

（☆）…Advanced class　　（○）…Basic class

Riku：Tony, look! We can join some *online classes of the university.

Tony：Sounds interesting. I want to take one. I'm interested in City Planning.

Riku：Do you want to take a *Basic class or an *Advanced class?

Tony：I want to take a Basic class. But I talk with my family on the Internet every Thursday afternoon, so I can't take it on that day.

Riku：Really? But you can take it on (A) , right?

Tony：Yes. I'll take it. Riku, which class are you interested in the most?

Riku：I'm interested in Making Parks in Towns the most. In the future, I want to make some parks in Tokyo.

Tony：Great! But, Riku, can you take that class?

I think you are busy with the tennis club.

Riku：We practice every Monday, Wednesday, and Friday in the afternoon. So I can take a morning class.

Tony：OK. Do you want to take a Basic class or an Advanced class?

Riku：I want to take an Advanced class.

Tony：So you're going to take an online class on (B) , right?

Riku：Yes!

（注）design デザインする　　online オンラインの
　　basic 基本的な　　advanced 発展的な

ア．(A) Tuesday afternoon
　　(B) Wednesday morning
イ．(A) Thursday afternoon
　　(B) Wednesday morning
ウ．(A) Tuesday afternoon
　　(B) Friday morning
エ．(A) Thursday afternoon
　　(B) Friday morning

3．次の文章は，イギリスに帰国したTonyがRikuに送ったEメールの内容である。

Dear Riku,

Thank you for your help during my stay in Japan. Taking an online class of the university is a special memory for me. In the class, we learned how parks could make our lives better. Now I am very interested in parks and towns. Now I realize that parks are very important for towns.

After returning to my country, I *researched about parks in my town. I knew some big festivals were held in the parks. But I didn't know that many other events were also held in them. I was a little surprised to learn that. I will tell my sister about those events. She will enjoy talking with people at them. I think parks are wonderful places for people to *communicate.

I'm going to join an online meeting about City Planning next week. I want to know more about parks and towns. What are some good points to you about having parks in towns? Please tell me some of your ideas.

Yours,
Tony

（注）research 調べる
　　communicate 意志の疎通をする

(1) このEメールの内容と合っているのは，次のうちではどれか。
　ア．Tony realized that online classes could make his life better.
　イ．Tony was a little surprised that many other events were also held in the parks in his town.
　ウ．Tony's sister researched about parks in her town because she wanted to take online

classes.

エ．Tony's sister joined an event in a park and enjoyed talking with Tony there.

(2) RikuはTonyに返事のEメールを送ることにしました。あなたがRikuだとしたら，Tonyにどのような返事のEメールを送りますか。次の〈条件〉に合うように，下の□□□□の中に，三つの英語の文を書きなさい。

〈条件〉

○前後の文につながるように書き，全体としてまとまりのある返事のEメールとすること。
○Tonyに伝えたい内容を一つ取り上げ，それを取り上げた理由などを含めること。

Hello, Tony,

Thank you for your e-mail. I learned a lot from a class, too. I'm glad to hear that you are very interested in parks and towns. The online meeting you're going to join sounds very interesting.

I'll try to answer your question. You asked me, "What are some good points to you about having parks in towns?" I'll tell you one good point.

I hope my idea can help you.

I'm looking forward to seeing you again.

Your friend,
Riku

〈東京都〉

---

4 次の各問いに答えなさい。

問1．中学生のかおるさんは，英語の授業で図書委員会の活動について紹介することになり，校内の読書に関するアンケート調査をもとに発表しました。次の資料1および資料2は，1年生(first-year)，2年生(second-year)，3年生(third-year)の各学年(each year)100人ずつの生徒に行ったアンケート調査の結果をまとめたものです。資料1および資料2を見て，あとの(1)，(2)の各問いに答えなさい。

資料1

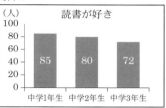

資料2

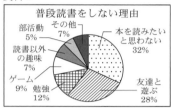

(1) 資料1の結果からわかることとして，最も適切なものを，次のア〜エからひとつ選び，記号で答えなさい。

ア．More than 80 percent of the students in each year like to read books.

イ．The first-year students like to read books more than the third-year students.

ウ．Older students are more interested in reading books than younger students.

エ．The second-year students don't like to read books as much as the third-year students.

(2) かおるさんは，発表の中で，資料2をもとに校内の生徒が普段読書をしない理由について説明しました。次の説明中の(①)と(②)にあてはまる最も適切なものを，あとのア〜エからそれぞれひとつ選び，記号で答えなさい。ただし，説明中の(①)には同じ語句が入ります。

説明

Among the students who don't read books, more than 30% said that they do not want to read books. I thought many students would answer that they do not read books because of (①). However, only 5% of the students *gave (①) as their *reason. Another reason that more than 20% of the students gave was (②).

（注）gave：give「(理由を)述べる」の過去形
reason　理由

ア．club activities
イ．playing games
ウ．playing with friends
エ．studying

問2．ジョシュア(Joshua)先生は，サイクリング(cycling)に興味があり，英語の授業の中でホワイトボードアプリを使ってA〜Dのどのサイクリングルートがよいかについて質問(Question)しました。グループ(Group)1〜3の生徒たちは，各サイクリングルートについて調べ，ホワイトボードアプリ上の付箋に書き込みました。生徒たちが書き込んだ付箋を読んだジョシュア先生は，どのルートに決めたのかを生徒に伝えました。先生の結論中の(　　)にあてはまる最も適切なものを，あとのア〜エからひとつ選び，記号で答えなさい。

生徒たちが書き込んだ付箋

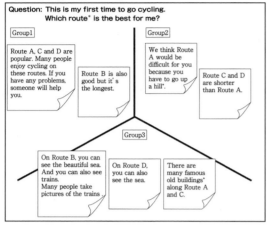

Question: This is my first time to go cycling.
Which route* is the best for me?

Group1

Route A, C and D are popular. Many people enjoy cycling on these routes. If you have any problems, someone will help you.

Route B is also good but it's the longest.

Group2

We think Route A would be difficult for you because you have to go up a hill*.

Route C and D are shorter than Route A.

Group3

On Route B, you can see the beautiful sea. And you can also see trains. Many people take pictures of the trains.

On Route D, you can also see the sea.

There are many famous old buildings* along Route A and C.

(注) route(s)　ルート　　hill　坂道
building(s)　建物

先生の結論

Thank you. I think a short and easy route is the best for me. I think I will need help if I have any problems. I also like taking pictures of nature, like the sea and mountains. So, I will choose (　　　　). Joshua

ア．Route A　　イ．Route B
ウ．Route C　　エ．Route D

問3．中学生のあゆみさんとみきさんの学校に，新しくグリーン先生(Ms. Green)が着任することになりました。グリーン先生が安心して生活できるように，あゆみさんとみきさんのふたりは，防災マップ(hazard map)の作り方(英語版)をもとに，グリーン先生のための防災マップを作り，英語の授業で発表することになりました。あとの(1)，(2)の各問いに答えなさい。

■防災マップの作り方(英語版)■
How To Make Your Own Hazard Map
1．*Dangerous *Areas Near Your House
Look at the hazard map your town made and find where the dangerous areas are. Please be careful if there have been any *landslides or *flooding in the past.
2．*Evacuation Sites
Look for the evacuation sites near your house. *Check the names and phone numbers of the evacuation sites. Draw a map that shows your house and the evacuation sites.
3．*Evacuation Routes
Draw two or three evacuation routes from your house to each evacuation site on the map. There may be an evacuation route you

can't use after a big earthquake or a landslide.
4．Dangerous Areas Along The Evacuation Routes
Walk along the evacuation routes with your family and look for any dangerous areas. Find how long it takes to walk from your house to each evacuation site and write it on your hazard map.
5．Your Own Hazard Map
Write phone numbers you may need to call *in an emergency on your map. For example, *city hall, *police station, and *fire station. Show your family the map you made.
(注) dangerous　危険な　　area(s)　区域
landslide(s)　土砂災害(の)　　flooding　洪水
evacuation site(s)　避難所　　check　〜を確かめる
evacuation route(s)　避難ルート
in an emergency　緊急時に　　city hall　市役所
police station　警察署　　fire station　消防署

■グリーン先生のための防災マップ■

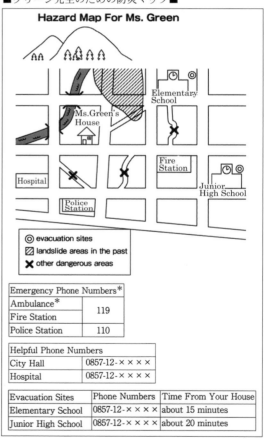

Hazard Map For Ms. Green

Elementary School

Ms.Green's House

Hospital

Fire Station

Junior High School

Police Station

◎ evacuation sites
▨ landslide areas in the past
✖ other dangerous areas

Emergency Phone Numbers*	
Ambulance*	119
Fire Station	
Police Station	110

Helpful Phone Numbers	
City Hall	0857-12-×××××
Hospital	0857-12-×××××

Evacuation Sites	Phone Numbers	Time From Your House
Elementary School	0857-12-×××××	about 15 minutes
Junior High School	0857-12-×××××	about 20 minutes

(注) emergency phone number(s)　緊急連絡先
ambulance　救急車

(1)　防災マップの作り方(英語版)の内容に合うものとして，最も適切なものを，次のア〜エからひとつ選び，記号で答えなさい。
ア．You should draw the supermarkets near your house.
イ．You should show your hazard map to your

friends.

ウ．You should look at your town's hazard map to check dangerous areas.

エ．You should draw a map from your house to the nearest hospital.

(2) あゆみさんとみきさんは，防災マップの作り方（英語版）と，グリーン先生のための防災マップについて英語の授業で発表しました。授業担当の佐藤先生は，発表後にあゆみさんとみきさんにアドバイスしました。佐藤先生のアドバイスとして，最も適切なものを，次のア～エからひとつ選び，記号で答えなさい。

ア．Write how long it takes from Ms. Green's house to the schools.

イ．Draw evacuation routes from Ms. Green's house to each evacuation site.

ウ．Draw the landslide areas in the past and other dangerous areas.

エ．Write the phone numbers Ms. Green may need in an emergency.

〈鳥取県〉

5 次の各問に答えよ。

（＊印の付いている単語・語句には，本文のあとに(注)がある。）

1. 高校生のHirotoと，Hirotoの家にホームステイしているアメリカからの留学生のMikeは，夏休みのある土曜日の予定について話をしている。 (A) 及び (B) の中に，それぞれ入る語句の組み合わせとして正しいものは，ア～エのうちではどれか。ただし，次のⅠは，二人が見ている，東京都内のある地域を紹介したパンフレットの一部である。

Ⅰ

	Things You Can Do	More Information
Forest Area	・Visiting old buildings ・Enjoying beautiful views of nature from the buildings	・There are two buses every hour. ・The buildings are in beautiful forests.
Mountain Area	・Walking across a long bridge ・Feeling cool wind from *valleys	・To get to the bridge from the nearest bus stop takes about one hour.
Onsen Area	・Enjoying famous *onsen ・Eating delicious local food	・This area is near the station. ・You can walk to it.
Park Area	・Watching birds and animals in the park ・Seeing beautiful views of nature from the park	・There are six buses every hour. ・The park has a lot of stairs.

Hiroto : Look at this. There are four areas here. My father says we can visit three of them on our one-day trip in Tokyo. There is a *shuttle bus service to and from the station. Which areas do you want to visit, Mike?

Mike : I want to enjoy beautiful views of nature.

Hiroto : I see. How about visiting the (A) ? We can go there by bus.

Mike : That's nice. I like watching birds and walking in places that are rich in nature. I don't *mind going up and down a lot of stairs. Let's go there.

Hiroto : Yes, let's. Where shall we visit next?

Mike : Both the Mountain Area and the *Onsen* Area look good to me. I would also like to enjoy local food.

Hiroto : Well, that sounds nice. Which of the two shall we visit first?

Mike : Shall we visit the (B) first? If we do that, we can enjoy hot springs at the end of our one-day trip.

Hiroto : That's a good idea. Let's do that.

Mike : Thank you. I'm looking forward to having a good time.

Hiroto : Me, too. I'll tell my father about our plan.

（注）shuttle bus 往復バス
mind 気にする
valley 谷

ア．(A) Forest Area (B) *Onsen* Area
イ．(A) Park Area (B) *Onsen* Area
ウ．(A) Forest Area (B) Mountain Area
エ．(A) Park Area (B) Mountain Area

2. 東京都内のある地域を訪れることにしたHirotoとMikeは，インターネットの画面を見ながら話をしている。 (A) 及び (B) の中に，それぞれ入る語句の組み合わせとして正しいものは，ア～エのうちではどれか。ただし，次のⅡは，二人が見ている，東京都内のある地域の施設別来訪者数を示したグラフである。

Ⅱ

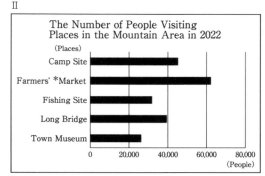

The Number of People Visiting Places in the Mountain Area in 2022

Hiroto : There are many places to visit in the Mountain Area.

Mike : They all look interesting.

Hiroto : Yes. Here is a *guide book about this area. It recommends the (A) . The book says we can buy fresh vegetables and also enjoy eating *grilled fish there.

Mike : Grilled fish? That sounds delicious. And the *graph says it is the most popular place in this area. Let's go there.

Hiroto : Yes, let's. And I think we can visit two more places after that. What other places shall we visit?

Mike : I want to visit the Long Bridge. I've heard it's the most exciting place in this area.

Hiroto : The book also recommends that place. I want to go there, too.

Mike : OK. Let's go there. Look at the graph again. There are three other places.

Hiroto : Yes. How about going to the *Camp Site? It's the most popular of the three.

Mike : That sounds nice, but I'm very interested in the history of this area. Shall we visit the (B) ?

Hiroto : Sure. The building was built in the *Edo* period. It looks interesting.

Mike　：I can't wait to go.
　（注）market　市場
　　　　guide　案内
　　　　grilled　焼いた
　　　　graph　グラフ
　　　　camp　キャンプ
ア．(A)　Farmers' Market　　(B)　Long Bridge
イ．(A)　Fishing Site　　　　(B)　Town Museum
ウ．(A)　Farmers' Market　　(B)　Town Museum
エ．(A)　Fishing Site　　　　(B)　Long Bridge

3．次の文章は，アメリカに帰国したMikeがHirotoに
送ったEメールの内容である。

Dear Hiroto,

Thank you for helping me a lot during my stay
in Japan. I enjoyed visiting various places with
you. The Mountain Area was one of them.
Walking across the bridge in the valley was
especially exciting. I enjoyed visiting places
that were rich in nature.

Since coming back to my country, I have read
many books to learn more about Japan. There
are a lot of beautiful places to see in your
country. After I talked about that with my
father, he made a plan for our family to visit
Japan next spring. I was really surprised!

Next time, I want to visit many new places. My
parents said Japan is famous for its traditional
culture. And they want to enjoy it. What should
we do in Japan? Do you have any ideas? If
you do, please tell me about them. I'm looking
forward to seeing you in Tokyo next spring.

Yours,
Mike

(1)　このEメールの内容と合っているのは，次のうちで
はどれか。
　ア．Mike was very surprised when his father
　　　made a plan to visit Japan the next spring.
　イ．Mike visited the Mountain Area with his
　　　father and enjoyed walking across the bridge.
　ウ．Mike read many books to learn more about
　　　nature in Japan before he went back to his
　　　country.
　エ．Mike showed his father a plan to visit Japan
　　　because he wanted to meet Hiroto again in
　　　Tokyo.
(2)　HirotoはMikeに返事のEメールを送ることにしま
した。あなたがHirotoだとしたら，Mikeにどのよう
な返事のEメールを送りますか。次の〈条件〉に合うよ
うに，次の □□□□ の中に，三つの英語の文を書きなさ
い。
　〈条件〉

　　○前後の文につながるように書き，全体としてまと
　　　まりのある返事のEメールとすること。
　　○Mikeに伝えたい内容を一つ取り上げ，それを取
　　　り上げた理由などを含めること。

Hello, Mike,

Thank you for your e-mail. I enjoyed reading
it. While you were in Japan, we visited many
places.
I had a good time when we visited the places
that were rich in nature. I have special
memories of our time together.

In Japan, you can enjoy traditional Japanese
culture in many places. You can have
interesting experiences. I'll tell you one idea.

I hope to visit some places with you when we
meet again next spring.
I'm looking forward to it.

Your friend,
Hiroto

＜東京都＞

d. 会話文

1 次の英文は、晴(Haru)とクリス博士(Dr. Chris)とのオンラインでの対話の一部です。晴は、「宇宙での生活」に関する英語の発表活動に向けた準備をしていて、宇宙に詳しいクリス博士にインタビューをしています。これを読んで、あとの(1)〜(3)の問いに答えなさい。

Dr. Chris：How was your *research about space?

Haru：I read books about food in space. *Astronauts can't eat their favorite foods easily, right?

Dr. Chris：That's right. Food from many countries is sent to space, but astronauts can't enjoy many kinds of foods.

Haru：Vegetables are good for their health, but they can't often eat fresh vegetable in space.

Dr. Chris：That's a good point. The big reason is money. About 1,000,000 yen is needed to send about 500 *grams of food to space. Also, some people think it isn't easy to grow vegetables in space.

Haru：I don't think it's a difficult thing to do.

Dr. Chris：Actually, you're right, Haru. One vegetable was grown in a space *experiment.

Haru：I want to know how the vegetable was grown in space.

Dr. Chris：I'll tell you about an interesting machine. Its name is "Veggie."

Haru："Veggie!" That's an interesting name.

Dr. Chris：It uses *LED lights. Vegetables can't get *sunlight at night, but "Veggie" can give light to them *all day. Also, it needs *less water than a farm on the *earth.

Haru：How useful! What vegetable was grown in the experiment?

Dr. Chris：*Lettuce was.

Haru：Lettuce! Let me think about ①the reasons for growing lettuce. Well…, I think it's very easy to eat because we don't often cook it.

Dr. Chris：That's true. Astronauts can do other things if they can *save time. Also, lettuce can grow faster than other vegetables in space.

Haru：I see. I'm glad to learn about those things.

Dr. Chris：Living in space isn't easy and food is important. So we should grow food in space to stay there for a long time.

Haru：Experiments in space may make life there easier in the future. Then maybe I'll be able to live there someday. That's my dream.

Dr. Chris：Haru, you can become a person who will ②do so.

Haru：Thanks, Dr. Chris. Next time I'd like to talk with you about astronauts' clothes.

Dr. Chris：Sure.

(注) research 研究　astronaut(s) 宇宙飛行士　gram(s) グラム(重さの単位)　experiment 実験　LED light(s) LEDライト　sunlight 太陽光　all day 一日中　less より少ない　earth 地球　lettuce レタス　save 節約する

(1) 次のスライドは、晴が発表用に作成したものの一部です。スライド中の Ⅰ , Ⅱ に入る英語は何ですか。本文の内容に合うように、あとのア〜エのうちから、その英語の組み合わせとして最も適当なものを一つ選び、その記号を書きなさい。

【スライド】

Foods in Space

Astronauts can't often eat fresh vegetables
・Carrying them to space is [　Ⅰ　].
・It is difficult to grow them in space.

Machine to grow vegetables : Veggie

・The LED lights of Veggie give light to vegetables for a [　Ⅱ　] time than the sun.
・Veggie needs less water than a farm on the earth.

	ア	イ	ウ	エ
Ⅰ	cheap	cheap	expensive	expensive
Ⅱ	longer	shorter	longer	shorter

(2) 文中の下線部①the reasons for growing lettuceについて、次のア〜エのうち、その内容として正しいものはどれですか。一つ選び、その記号を書きなさい。

ア．Astronauts can eat lettuce without cooking it and lettuce can grow fast.

イ．Astronauts can enjoy eating delicious lettuce after they cook it.

ウ．Astronauts have to cook lettuce because it grows fast.

エ．Astronauts have to learn how to get sunlight all day.

(3) 次のア〜エのうち、文中の下線部②do soが指し示す内容として正しいものはどれですか。一つ選び、その記号を書きなさい。

ア．make astronauts' clothes

イ．live in space

ウ．grow space vegetables

エ．create space foods

〈岩手県〉

2 次の文章は、中学校のALTのナターシャ(Natasha)先生と、英語教師のサキナ(Sakina)先生の会話です。英文を読み、各問いに答えなさい。

Natasha：Look outside the window, Sakina. There is a rainbow. I feel lucky!

Sakina：Yes, I do, too. It's beautiful! But I heard a story from my grandmother about ①rainbows in the old days in Okinawa. She said they were believed to be big red snakes and drank all the water in the sky, so a *drought happened after that. Maybe, a rainbow was a bad sign and *negative to them.

Natasha : Really? That's interesting. In my country, a rainbow is a good sign. It usually has a meaning of hope. Do you know Charlie Chaplin? He is a famous comedian and a movie actor. He said, "You'll never find a rainbow if you're looking down." (　ア　)

Sakina : Wow, I like that!

Natasha : It means that you should always be *positive. There are a lot of positive *images about the rainbow.

Sakina : Yes! I have just *searched rainbows on the internet, and I found so many other positive ideas about them! Some people say, "You are my rainbow on a cloudy day," to people they love.

Natasha : That's so cute. I want to be someone's rainbow on a cloudy day. Then, I can make them happy when they are sad. (　イ　)

Sakina : Me, too. Oh, I also like this idea, "Your true colors are beautiful like a rainbow." I think it means that everyone is different and special.

Natasha : Many people feel happy when they think of a rainbow. (　ウ　)

Sakina : Hmm, let me see. This *article is talking about how many colors are in a rainbow. It's interesting! Natasha, you are from America, right? How many colors do you see in a rainbow?

Natasha : Let me count. Red, Orange, Yellow, Green, Blue, Purple. Why do you ask? Is it different for you?

Sakina : Yes! In Japan, we see one more color than you do! This article says that different cultures see different numbers of colors in the rainbow. Wow, in some countries, such as *Indonesia, people see only four colors, and some people in Africa see eight colors! (　エ　)

Natasha : I didn't know that! It's very interesting. Do we learn that when we are children?

Sakina : Yes. The article says every culture teaches different ideas about rainbows.

(注) drought　干ばつ
negative　悲観的な　　positive　前向きな
image　イメージ
search　検索する
article　記事
Indonesia　インドネシア

問1．下線部①について，昔の沖縄の人々にとって虹はどのようなものでしたか。次のア〜エのうちから1つ選び，その記号を書きなさい。
ア．People thought a rainbow had six colors.
イ．People thought "big red snakes" actually drank all the water in the sky.
ウ．Most people thought a rainbow was beautiful.
エ．People thought a rainbow was a bad sign.

問2．次のグラフはSakinaが見つけた記事に記載されているグラフである。本文及びグラフを参考に次の各問いに答えなさい。
(1)　Natashaの出身地を表すのは，グラフ中のア，イ，ウのうちどれですか。1つ選んでその記号を書きなさい。

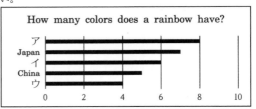

問2．（グラフ）
How many colors does a rainbow have?

(2)　本文及びグラフの内容に一致している文として適切なものを，次のア〜エのうちから1つ選び，その記号を書きなさい。
ア．People in China see more colors than Japanese.
イ．Some people in Africa see the most colors in rainbow.
ウ．People have the same image about rainbows all over the world.
エ．People in Indonesia think a rainbow has more than seven colors.

問3．次の英文が入る最も適切な箇所を，本文中の（　ア　）〜（　エ　）のうちから1つ選び，記号で答えなさい。
　　Have you found any other interesting information about rainbows?

問4．2人の会話をまとめた表現として最も適切なものを，次のア〜エのうちから1つ選び，その記号を書きなさい。
ア．Bad images about rainbows
イ．The big red snakes in the sky
ウ．Colors of the rainbows
エ．Different ideas and images about rainbows
〈沖縄県〉

3 次の英文は，静岡県でホームステイをしているジュディ（Judy）と，クラスメートの京子（Kyoko）との会話である。この英文を読んで，(1)〜(5)の問いに答えなさい。
(After winter vacation, Judy and Kyoko are talking at school.)

Judy : Thank you for your New Year's card, *nengajo*. It was very beautiful, so I showed it to all of my host family.

Kyoko : ［　　　A　　　］ It is made of traditional Japanese paper called *washi*.

Judy : I like *washi*, and my host family showed me an interesting video about it.

Kyoko : A video? ［　　　B　　　］

Judy : The video was about old paper documents in Shosoin. The paper documents were made of *washi* about 1,300 years ago. People have used *washi* since then.

Kyoko : That's very long! I didn't know that.

Judy : When we read a variety (　ⓐ　) information written on *washi*, we can find things about the life in the past.

Kyoko : I see. *Washi* is important because we can (　ⓑ　) the long history of Japan, right? I've never thought of that. I'm happy I can understand Japanese culture more.

Judy : By the way, where did you get the beautiful postcard?

Kyoko : I made it at a history museum.

Judy : Do you mean you made *washi* by yourself?

Kyoko : [___C___] I made a small size of *washi*, and used it as a postcard.

Judy : Wonderful! But making *washi* isn't easy. (ⓒ) I were you, I would buy postcards at shops.

Kyoko : Well... You love traditional Japanese things, so I wanted to make a special thing for you by using *washi*. It was fun to [ア．how イ．think about ウ．could エ．create オ．I] a great *nengajo*.

Judy : Your *nengajo* was amazing! The *nengajo* gave me a chance to know an interesting part of Japanese culture. I found *washi* is not only beautiful but also important in your culture.

Kyoko : You taught me something new about *washi*, and I enjoyed talking about it with you. If you want, let's go to the museum. [_____]

Judy : Yes, of course!

(注) card あいさつ状　host family ホストファミリー
be made of ～から作られている　document 文書
Shosoin 正倉院(東大寺の宝庫)　past 過去
think of ～について考える　by the way ところで
postcard はがき　by yourself （あなたが）自分で
chance 機会

(1) 会話の流れが自然になるように，本文中の[___A___]～[___C___]の中に補う英語として，それぞれア～ウの中から最も適切なものを1つ選び，記号で答えなさい。

[___A___] ア．I'm glad to hear that.
　　　イ．Don't be angry.
　　　ウ．I'll do my best.

[___B___] ア．Here you are.
　　　イ．You're welcome.
　　　ウ．Tell me more.

[___C___] ア．That's right.　イ．Did you?
　　　ウ．I don't think so.

(2) 本文中の(ⓐ)～(ⓒ)の中に補う英語として，それぞれア～エの中から最も適切なものを1つ選び，記号で答えなさい。

(ⓐ) ア．for　イ．of　ウ．at　エ．with
(ⓑ) ア．borrow　イ．lose
　　　ウ．finish　エ．learn
(ⓒ) ア．Because　イ．When
　　　ウ．If　エ．Before

(3) 本文中の[　]の中のア～オを，意味が通るように並べかえ，記号で答えなさい。

(4) 本文中の[_____]で，京子は，今度の日曜日の都合はよいかという内容の質問をしている。その内容となるように，[_____]の中に，適切な英語を補いなさい。

(5) 次の英文は，ジュディがこの日に書いた日記の一部である。本文の内容と合うように，次の[_____]の中に補うものとして，本文中から最も適切な部分を3語で抜き出しなさい。

During winter vacation, Kyoko sent me a *nengajo* made of *washi* and I watched a video about it. So, I found *washi* is beautiful and important. Today, I told her about the video, and she found *washi* has a long history. I think her *nengajo* helped

us [_____] very well. Also, she wanted to send me something special. She is wonderful!

〈静岡県〉

4 次の英文を読んで，あとの(1)～(6)の問いに答えなさい。

Luis is a junior high school student from Mexico. He is staying with a family in Niigata. Now he is talking with Keita, the father of the family, in the home vegetable garden.

Keita : Luis, let's plant tomatoes in the garden together. Do you like tomatoes?

Luis : Yes. In Mexico, we use tomatoes for many dishes. I'll cook some dishes for you tomorrow.

Keita : Great! First, let's plant tomatoes and then, plant some marigolds near them.

Luis : Marigolds? They are very popular in Mexico. We use the flowers in a traditional festival in November.

Keita : What kind of festival is it?

Luis : We decorate graves with a lot of marigolds. We believe that our ancestors come back (A) the strong smell of marigolds.

Keita : It's like Japanese *obon*. We also believe our ancestors come back and we offer some flowers to them. We have the event in summer.

Luis : Wow, I thought your culture and our culture were different, but we have the same kind of traditional event. ᴮHow interesting! By the way, why do you plant marigolds near tomatoes?

Keita : Good question! The marigolds ᶜ[me, make, help] a safe vegetable garden.

Luis : Really? Why do marigolds do such a thing?

Keita : Again, the reason is their strong smell. Insects which eat tomato leaves don't like the smell, so [___D___].

Luis : Great! We don't have to use agricultural chemicals.

Keita : Right. I want to choose safe ways for the environment when I plant vegetables. (E) marigolds is one good way.

Luis : I see. ᶠCan you tell me another example?

Keita : Yes, of course. For example, can you see the flowers over there? They are called *renge-sou* in Japanese. They will be natural fertilizers.

Luis : Amazing! I want to learn more about such ways. What should I do?

Keita : Well, ᴳ[you, I, if, were], I would ask people who know about them very well.

Luis : That's a good idea. Can you introduce such people to me?

Keita : OK, some of my friends are farmers, so I'll ask them.

Luis : Thank you! At school, I'll start a research project with my classmates next month. It may be interesting to do research about eco-friendly ways to plant vegetables.

Keita : That will be an interesting research topic. I

think my friends will help you a lot. Some of them also have machines which use less energy. You may also be interested in them.

Luis ： Sounds interesting! Thank you.

Keita ： You're welcome. Do your best in your research project.

Luis ： I will. Can I find new eco-friendly ways?

Keita ： It's not so easy, but I believe you can do it in the future if you work hard.

Luis ： I hope so. My teacher told us that some human activities damage the environment. I think it is important for us to make the situation better.

Keita ： That's right. Humans have been developing the civilization by using nature, but if we keep using things in nature, we will destroy the environment.

Luis ： Yes. We should look for ways to live with nature.

(注) plant〜　〜を植える
　　marigold　マリーゴールド(花の名前)
　　decorate〜　〜を飾りつける　　grave 墓
　　ancestor　先祖　　smell　におい
　　obon　お盆
　　offer〜　〜を供える　　insect　昆虫
　　agricultural chemical　農薬
　　renge-sou　れんげ草(花の名前)
　　natural fertilizer　天然肥料
　　eco-friendly　環境にやさしい
　　civilization　文明
　　destroy〜　〜を破壊する

(1)　文中のA，Eの(　　)に入る最も適当なものを，次のア〜エからそれぞれ一つずつ選び，その符号を書きなさい。
　　A．ア．according to　　イ．because of
　　　　ウ．instead of　　エ．such as
　　E．ア．Use　　イ．Uses　　ウ．Used　　エ．Using

(2)　下線部分Bについて，ルイス(Luis)がそのように感じた理由を，具体的に日本語で書きなさい。

(3)　文中のC，Gの　　　の中の語を，それぞれ正しい順序に並べ替えて書きなさい。

(4)　文中のDの　　　の中に入る最も適当なものを，次のア〜エから一つ選び，その符号を書きなさい。
　　ア．they like to stay on the flowers
　　イ．they fly near the flowers
　　ウ．they don't come to eat tomato leaves
　　エ．they aren't damaged by tomato leaves

(5)　下線部分Fについて，ルイスが教えてほしいと言っているのは，何についての例か。具体的に日本語で書きなさい。

(6)　本文の内容に合っているものを，次のア〜オから二つ選び，その符号を書きなさい。
　　ア．Tomatoes are very popular in Mexico and they are put on graves during the festival in November.
　　イ．Both people in Mexico and people in Japan believe that their ancestors come back in summer.
　　ウ．Keita believes it is good to use safe ways for the environment when he plants vegetables.
　　エ．Luis wants to meet some of Keita's friends to learn how to make delicious vegetables.
　　オ．Luis learned from his teacher that humans

damage the environment through some activities.

〈新潟県〉

5　高校に入学した智(Satoshi)と留学生のアマンダ(Amanda)が話しています。次の対話文を読んで，あとの(1)から(4)までの問いに答えなさい。

Satoshi ： Hello, Amanda. I'm working on my report. Can I ask you some questions?

Amanda ： 【　a　】

Satoshi ： It's about smartphones.

Amanda ： 【　b　】

Satoshi ： Yes, smartphones are very popular today. Now, some high school students can use smartphones in the classroom. I think this topic is interesting. What do you think about it?

Amanda ： Well, I think there are both good points and bad points.

Satoshi ： 【　c　】

Amanda ： These days, most high school students have a smartphone. They have easy access to the internet. ①If the students can use smartphones in the classroom, their school life is more convenient (　　　) before.

Satoshi ： I don't understand your point. Could you give me an example?

Amanda ： Sure! For example, students can surf the internet and work on classroom activities more effectively. Sharing information with classmates and teachers is easy. Using the internet from your smartphones is the fastest.

Satoshi ： 【　d　】

Amanda ： Well, students can find and watch videos about a variety of topics. They can even use it as a calculator or for taking notes in the classroom. A smartphone can be useful for learning.

Satoshi ： ②Well, what do you think about the (　　　) points?

Amanda ： I think that it's easy for students to lose focus when they use a smartphone. They play games and do various things that are not related to school work. If students cannot use their smartphone properly, there will be a lot of problems in the classroom. This situation will (　A　) other people uncomfortable.

Satoshi ： 【　e　】 I understand what you think. We should know how to use smartphones properly.

Amanda ： You're welcome. I'm glad to hear that.

(注) access　アクセス(情報システムへの接続)
　　effectively　効率よく
　　calculator　計算機
　　notes　メモ，覚え書き
　　focus　集中
　　properly　適切に

(1)　次のアからオまでの英文を，対話文中の【　a　】から【　e　】までのそれぞれにあてはめて，対話の文として最も適当なものにするには，【　b　】と【　d　】にどれ

を入れたらよいか，そのかな符号を書きなさい。ただし，いずれも一度しか用いることができません。

ア．I agree. I want to know about the good points first.

イ．I understand. What else can students do with their smartphones?

ウ．Of course. What is your report about?

エ．Sounds exciting. I know a lot of people use smartphones in their daily lives.

オ．Thank you for sharing your opinion. It helped me a lot.

⑵ 下線①，②のついた文が，対話の文として最も適当なものとなるように，それぞれの（　　）にあてはまる語を書きなさい。

⑶ （　A　）にあてはまる最も適当な語を，次のアからエまでの中から選んで，そのかな符号を書きなさい。

ア．become　　　イ．remove
ウ．perform　　　エ．make

⑷ 次の英文は，この対話があった日の夜，智が英語の授業で発表するために書いたスピーチ原稿です。この原稿が対話文の内容に合うように，英文中の（　X　），（　Y　）にそれぞれあてはまる最も適当な語を書きなさい。

Using smartphones in high school

I want to talk about using smartphones in high school. Some high school students can use smartphones in their classroom. I'm interested in this topic. So, I decided to ask Amanda about her opinion.

According to her, there are both good points and bad points. Students can find more information from the internet. They can also （　X　） the information with their classmates and teachers easily. However, if they lose focus, they may start playing games.

I learned from her opinion. I think it is （　Y　） for us to use smartphones properly. Thank you.

<愛知県・Bグループ>

6 この文章は，中学生のひろき（Hiroki）とALT（外国語指導助手）のMr. Jonesとの会話です。これを読んで，1から7の問いに答えなさい。（＊は(注)の語を示す。）

— Outside after school on Friday —

Hiroki ： Oh, Mr. Jones. Are you going home now?

Mr. Jones ： No. I'm going to the library.

Hiroki ： It's going to rain really hard. Do you have an umbrella?

Mr. Jones ： No, I'll be OK without one. In the U.S., we don't often use umbrellas.

Hiroki ： Really?

Mr. Jones ： Sorry, Hiroki. I have to go. ［　　　ⓐ　　　］ See you next week.

— In the teachers' room next Monday —

Hiroki ： Hello, Mr. Jones. I came here to talk with you. ⑴あなたは，この前の金曜日私に会ったことを覚えていますか。

Mr. Jones ： Of course, Hiroki. Thank you ［　A　］ coming.

Hiroki ： At that time, I wanted to ask you why you don't often use an umbrella, but I couldn't. So, I did some *research about

how people use umbrellas abroad by reading some books and websites.

Mr. Jones ： Wow! Please ［　B　］ me know the things you found out.

Hiroki ： According to the books I read, the ①（ ア．color　 イ．history　 ウ．language　 エ．number ） of umbrellas is very long. "Sun umbrellas" were drawn in *ancient *wall paintings about 4,000 years ago. People have been using "sun umbrellas" longer than "rain umbrellas."

Mr. Jones ： Is that so? Oh, Hiroki, did you know the word "umbrella" comes from the *Latin "*umbra*"? It means "*shadow*."

Hiroki ： Well, umbrellas were first used to make shadows on hot and sunny days, right? Anyway, I thought just reading books ②（ ア．weren't　 イ．wasn't　 ウ．couldn't　 エ．wasn't ） helpful enough to understand the use of umbrellas around the world. I actually asked a student who came from the U.K. about it.

Mr. Jones ： ［　　　ⓑ　　　］

Hiroki ： He said when he first came here, it was interesting that a lot of Japanese people use umbrellas on rainy days. He told me there are many rainy days in the U.K., but it stops raining quickly there. ［　　　ⓒ　　　］ He has heard it may be the same in Europe.

Mr. Jones ： I see. In the U.S., we often wear a *raincoat when it rains hard or for a long time. However, some Americans don't worry about *getting wet in the rain. I'm ［　C　］ of them.

Hiroki ： I understand now. Japan is a country that uses umbrellas often. ③（ ア．At first　 イ．For example　 ウ．On the other hand　 エ．As a result ）, some countries don't use them much. From the things I read and heard, I've learned each country has its own way of thinking and living. This research about umbrellas was a lot of fun.

Mr. Jones ： ⑵You've realized something important, Hiroki.

Hiroki ： Thank you, Mr. Jones.

Mr. Jones ： I also respect you because you kept thinking about your question and tried to answer it yourself in various ways. ⑶Can ［　　　　　　　　　　］ in class?

Hiroki ： Sure. I want everyone to enjoy my speech.

(注) research 調査　　ancient 古代の
　　wall paintings 壁画　　Latin ラテン語
　　shadow(s) 影　　raincoat レインコート
　　get wet ぬれる

1．［ⓐ］～［ⓒ］に入る最も適当な英文を，ア～オから一つずつ選び，その記号を書きなさい。

ア．What did the student say?

イ．The library will soon be closed.

ウ．What will you do at the library?

エ．So, most people usually don't use umbrellas.

オ．If you were a student in the U.K., what would you say?

2．本文の会話が成り立つように，下線部⑴あなたは，この前の金曜日私に会ったことを覚えていますか。という内容を表す英文を一つ書きなさい。

3．　A　～　C　に当てはまる最も適当な英語を，本文の内容に合うように，1語ずつ書きなさい。

4．①～③の（　　）に当てはまる最も適当な英語を，本文の内容に合うように，ア～エから一つずつ選び，その記号を書きなさい。

5．下線部⑵You've realized something importantの中のsomething importantが表している内容を，ひとつづきの10語で本文中から抜き出し，始めと終わりの2語を書きなさい。

6．本文の会話が成り立つように，下線部⑶にCanから始まり，in class?で終わる適当な英文を一つ書きなさい。ただし，Canとin class?も書くこと。　　　　（3点）

7．本文とほぼ同じ内容になるように，次の①～③の英文の（　　）に当てはまる最も適当な英語を1語ずつ書きなさい。

①　On Friday, Hiroki wanted to know (　　　　) Mr. Jones doesn't use an umbrella.

②　The umbrellas (　　　　) in ancient wall paintings are "sun umbrellas."

③　Mr. Jones respected Hiroki because Hiroki didn't (　　　　) thinking about his own question and tried to answer it himself in various ways.

<山梨県>

7 次の会話を読んで，あとの問いに答えなさい。なお，あとの(注)を参考にしなさい。

〔高校生のヒロ（Hiro）とALT（外国語指導助手）のスミス先生（Ms. Smith）が話をしています。〕

Hiro : Ms. Smith, what kind of food do you like the best?

Ms. Smith : It's a difficult question. I like Mexican food very much, but, of course, Japanese food is good, too. Wait, Thai food is also delicious. Well, I can't choose one.

Hiro : You like many different foods. But you're from the USA. 　A　

Ms. Smith : Of course I like it. When I was in my country, I often had a very nice sandwich at the restaurant near my house.

Hiro : It sounds good. But you can eat nice sandwiches in Japan, too.

Ms. Smith : Yes, but I think the sandwiches in Japan are 　B　 the sandwiches in the USA. If you come to the USA, you can eat more delicious sandwiches.

Hiro : I want to try them. Well, I'm thinking about my next speech in your English class. Can I talk about foods in different countries?

Ms. Smith : Oh, that's a nice idea. Do you know what the most delicious food in the world is?

Hiro : I don't know. What is it?

Ms. Smith : I've watched a video on the Internet. It shows the world's 20 most delicious foods, and they choose *rendang* as the

most delicious food. *Rendang* is a beef dish in Indonesia.

Hiro : I've never heard about it. Is *sushi* second?

Ms. Smith : No. *Sushi* comes third. They say that *nasi goreng*, fried rice in Indonesia, is better than *sushi*. *Tom Yum Kung*, a famous Thai soup, comes after *sushi*. They have another Thai food called *Pad Thai*. *Pad Thai* is fried noodles like *yakisoba*. *Pad Thai* is fifth.

Hiro : All the foods are from Asia! I'm surprised.

Ms. Smith : I've traveled around Asia and tried those dishes. They're so different from the food we eat in the USA. Many American people like dishes from Asia. It is because they are delicious and we want to try something different. When we try something different, we can find interesting things. So trying new things is 　C　.

Hiro : I agree! Well, I'm looking for the video now.... Oh, I found it.

Ms. Smith : Did you find it? You can find many comments about it, too. Reading them is fun.

Hiro : OK. I will watch the video and read the comments. I'm sure my speech will be great.

〈*Comments*〉

Maria	I'm so happy that my country's food is number one. It's so cool!
David	I tried to make *rendang* before, but it was really difficult! You should just go to a restaurant.
Billy	I will go to Nagasaki in Japan next winter, so I want to try *sushi* there. But my friend told me that *ramen* was the best. Which food should I try?

(注) Mexican　メキシコの　　Thai　タイの
sandwich(es)　サンドイッチ　　video　動画
rendang　ルンダン　　Indonesia　インドネシア
sushi　すし
nasi goreng　ナシゴレン
fried炒（いた）めた
Tom Yum Kung　トムヤムクン
Pad Thai　パッタイ　　noodle(s)　麺
yakisoba　焼きそば　　Asia　アジア
comment(s)　コメント　　*ramen*　ラーメン

問1．会話中の　A　に入る英語として最も適当なものを次のア～エの中から一つ選んで，その記号を書け。

ア．How about American food?

イ．What is your favorite food?

ウ．When did you eat American food?

エ．Why did you cook Mexican food?

問2．会話中の　B　に入る英語として最も適当なものを次のア～エの中から一つ選んで，その記号を書け。

ア．better than　　イ．as good as

ウ．as bad as　　エ．not as good as

問３．会話中に出てくる料理のランキングとして，最も適当なものを次のア〜エの中から一つ選んで，その記号を書け。

ア
1位	ルンダン
2位	すし
3位	ナシゴレン
4位	トムヤムクン
5位	パッタイ

イ
1位	ルンダン
2位	ナシゴレン
3位	すし
4位	トムヤムクン
5位	パッタイ

ウ
1位	ルンダン
2位	すし
3位	ナシゴレン
4位	パッタイ
5位	トムヤムクン

エ
1位	ルンダン
2位	ナシゴレン
3位	すし
4位	パッタイ
5位	トムヤムクン

問４．会話中の　C　に入る英語として最も適当なものを次のア〜エの中から一つ選んで，その記号を書け。
ア．surprised　　イ．difficult
ウ．exciting　　エ．dangerous

問５．会話および〈Comments〉の内容と一致するものを次のア〜オの中から二つ選んで，その記号を書け。
ア．Ms. Smith likes many kinds of food, and she likes Thai food better than Japanese food.
イ．In Ms. Smith's class, Hiro is going to make a speech about foods in different countries.
ウ．Hiro traveled around Asia and got interested in many different foods in the world.
エ．In the comments, Maria is glad her country's food was chosen as the most delicious food.
オ．In the comments, David thinks that it is easy for him to make delicious *rendang*.

問６　〈Comments〉の中の下線部の質問に対して，あなたなら何とコメントするか。*sushi*または*ramen*のいずれかを選び，その理由を（　　）に10語以上の英語で書け。なお，英語が２文以上になってもかまわない。ただし，コンマ(,)やピリオド(.)などは語数に含めない。You should try〔*sushi* / *ramen*〕because（　　　　　　）.

<長崎県>

8 次の英文は，中学生のAyaとその父が，Ayaの家にホームステイしているアメリカ出身のNoraとレストランで交わした会話の一部です。また，【Menu】（メニュー）は，その時３人が見ていたものです。英文と【Menu】を読んで，後の(1)〜(3)の問いに答えなさい。

Aya's father：Nora, here is an English menu.
Nora：Oh, thank you.
Aya's father：　　　　A
Nora：Yes. I can't eat beef. Also, I have an egg *allergy.
Aya's father：You can check what is used in the curries and the information about allergies by reading this *2D code with your phone.
Nora：Let me see. Great!　Now, I know what I can eat.
Aya：Do you like *hot curry?
Nora：Yes. I'll have the hottest one. Then, which set is the best for me?　Well, I want to have ice cream. But I don't need a drink. OK, I've decided.
Aya：I'll have this set because I want to have ice cream and apple juice. I'll eat

vegetable curry. How about you, Dad?
Aya's father：I like beef, and I want to have a cup of coffee. So I'll have B Set.

【Menu】

Use this 2D code for more information about allergies!

Menu
Choose your curry from Vegetable, Beef, or Chicken
Vegetable … Not Hot　　Beef … Hot
Chicken … Very Hot

A Set：800 yen Choose one kind of curry Rice and Salad	B Set：950 yen Choose one kind of curry Rice, Salad, and Drink
C Set：1,100 yen Choose one kind of curry Rice, Salad, and Ice cream	D Set：1,200 yen Choose one kind of curry Rice, Salad, Drink, and Ice cream

Drink：Apple juice, Orange juice, or Coffee

They are talking about the 2D code on the menu when they are waiting for their food.

Nora：I'm glad that this menu has a 2D code. 2D codes are very useful. We can get the information we want very quickly and easily.
Aya：Yes. Now, we can find 2D codes like this in many places.
Aya's father：I heard that a Japanese *engineer created this kind of 2D code. He really wanted to make something that was better than *barcodes.

123456789
Barcode

Nora：What's the problem with barcodes?
Aya's father：They can't *include much information. This is because they are just lines. One day, he got an idea for 2D codes when he was playing a traditional board game with black and white stones. Can you guess what it was?

碁盤の
写真

Go（碁）

Aya：Well, I think it was *Go*.
Aya's father：　　　　B　　　　2D codes look like the board game. In a 2D code, there are many small black and white shapes. By changing them, we can make many different 2D codes. Even a small 2D code can include more information than a barcode.

2D Code

Aya：Interesting!　I see them on TV, on posters, and in textbooks. Also, I've heard they are used in hospitals and *companies, too.
Aya's father：He thought 2D codes were very useful for everyone. So he wanted people around the world to use 2D codes *for free. Now we can use them and make them easily.
Nora：One good idea has improved our lives.
Aya：I really think so, too. Oh, our curries are coming. They smell so good!

　（注）allergy　アレルギー　　2D code　二次元コード

hot　辛い　　engineer　技術者
barcode　バーコード　　include ～　～を含む
company　会社　　for free　無料で

(1) 　A　，　B　に当てはまるものとして最も適当なものを，それぞれ次のア～エから選びなさい。
　A．ア．Can you eat all these curries?
　　　イ．What do you think about curries?
　　　ウ．Do you have anything you can't eat?
　　　エ．Did you come to this restaurant before?
　B．ア．I don't think so.
　　　イ．That's right.
　　　ウ．You're welcome.
　　　エ．You should go there.

(2) 次の問いに対する答えとなるように，①，②の[　　]の内から適切なものをそれぞれ選び，文を完成させなさい。
　問い　Which set and curry did Nora decide to eat?
　答え　She decided to eat ①[A・B・C・D] Set with ②[vegetable・beef・chicken] curry.

(3) 本文の内容と合っているものを，次のア～オから2つ選びなさい。
　ア．By using the 2D code on the menu, Nora got the information she needed.
　イ．Aya wanted to drink apple juice, so she chose B Set.
　ウ．A Japanese engineer got an idea for 2D codes when he was watching TV.
　エ．People can put more information in a barcode than in a 2D code.
　オ．Nora and Aya think that the engineer's idea has changed people's lives in good ways.
　　　　　　　　　　　　　　　　　　　　〈群馬県〉

9 中学3年生の桜(Sakura)は現在アメリカで短期留学をしていて，友人のアダム(Adam)と会話をしながら学校の帰り道を歩いています。次の英文を読み，各問いに答えなさい。

Adam　：Do you want to hear an interesting story? It happened to me last night.
Sakura：What is it?　Tell me.
Adam　：I was doing my homework on the sofa. My three-year-old brother James kept *throwing a ball at me. He wanted to play with me. My mother told him to stop but he didn't. Finally, she got angry and said to him, "Go to your room or have a time-out". James said, "Time-out".
Sakura：What is "time-out"?
Adam　：It's part of American culture. When children do something bad or don't listen to their parents, sometimes their parents tell them to stand in the corner of the room. Children must not talk during time-out. They have to be quiet, because it's time for them to think.
Sakura：Oh, how interesting. So, what happened next?
Adam　：James went to the corner and stood *facing the wall. He was looking at the floor. He was quiet and looked sad. We didn't talk to him. After some time, our pet dog Ricky sat next to him. They stayed there together and were quiet. James still didn't

say anything but *kindly touched Ricky's ear and softly *pulled Ricky toward him. Ricky stayed with him until time-out was finished.
Sakura：What a great story!　They *are like close *human friends.
Adam　：Yes, they are. I think Ricky knew James needed him at that time because they always play together. Ricky often knows James's feelings.
Sakura：They are really good friends. That's nice.
Adam　：Do you miss your friends in Japan?
Sakura：I sometimes do, but I can see and talk with them again when I go back. I'm looking forward to it. I hope I will make good friends here, and after I return to Japan, I can keep in touch with them on the Internet.

　（注）throw ～ at ...　～を…に投げる
　　　　facing　～の方を向きながら
　　　　kindly　優しく
　　　　pulled ～ toward ...　～を…へ引き寄せた
　　　　are like ～　～のようだ
　　　　human　人間の

問1．本文の内容を表す次の英文に続く表現として最も適切なものをア～エのうちから1つ選び，その記号を書きなさい。
　　Adam's mother got angry because...
　ア．James didn't stop throwing a ball at her.
　イ．James told Adam to stop doing his homework.
　ウ．James didn't listen to her.
　エ．James said, "Time-out".

問2．次の質問に対する答えとして最も適切なものをア～エのうちから1つ選び，その記号を書きなさい。
　　Where did James and Ricky stay together when James was in time-out?
　ア．On the wall.
　イ．In the corner of the room.
　ウ．In his bed.
　エ．On the sofa.

問3．"time-out" の際のJamesとRickyの様子を表す絵をア～エのうちから1つ選び，その記号を書きなさい。

問4．下線部の文中のitが指している内容をア～エのうちから1つ選び，その記号を書きなさい。
　ア．missing friends in Japan
　イ．seeing and talking with her friends
　ウ．making friends in America
　エ．talking with her friends on the Internet

問5．本文の内容と一致している文として適切なものをア～オのうちから2つ選び，その記号を書きなさい。
　ア．Adam played with James using a ball last night.
　イ．American parents sometimes tell their pet to go to its room.

ウ．Adam didn't talk to James during time-out.

エ．Adam thought Ricky went to James because Ricky was hungry.

オ．Sakura thinks the Internet will be a good way to talk with her friends in America in the future.

〈沖縄県〉

10 次の英文を読んで，あとの(ア)〜(ウ)の問いに答えなさい。

Ayumi and Masao are Kamome High School students. One day in June, they are talking in their classroom after school. Then, Ms. White, their English teacher, talks to them.

Ms. White : Hi, Ayumi and Masao. What are you doing?

Ayumi : We are talking about the school festival in September. Masao and I are in the cooking club, and our club is going to do something about the future of Japanese rice.

Ms. White : Rice? That's interesting. Why are you so interested in rice?

Masao : Because we think we should eat more rice. My grandfather *grows rice in Tohoku and sends his delicious rice to my family every year. He is always happy when my family says we enjoy eating his rice, but he worries about the future of Japanese rice.

Ms. White : Oh, why does he worry about it?

Masao : He said, "The rice *consumption in Japan has been *decreasing a lot because of *changes in our *eating habits."

Ms. White : Oh, really?

Masao : Yes. After I heard that, I used the Internet and found ①this *graph. It shows the *amount of rice one person ate in a year in Japan from 1962 to 2020. In 1962, one person ate 118.3kg of rice. In 2000, one person ate about 55% of the amount in 1962, and, in 2020, one person ate a smaller amount of rice than in 2000.

Ayumi : After Masao showed me this graph, I became interested, too. So we decided to do something about the future of Japanese rice at the school festival. We wanted everyone to become more interested in Japanese rice.

Ms. White : Then, what are your ideas?

Masao : I joined a *volunteer activity to grow rice last month. The activity began in May and will finish in August. I've been learning how to grow rice. At the school festival, I want to make a presentation about Japanese rice by using the graph and the pictures I took during my volunteer activity.

Ms. White : That's great!

Ayumi : Ms. White, look at ②these two graphs.

To know what the students in my school like to eat, I asked 40 students, "Which do you like the best, bread, noodles, or rice?" Bread is the most popular among them, and more than 80% of them like bread or noodles better than rice. Bread and noodles are *made from *wheat flour. Then, I started to think about making something by using *rice flour *instead of wheat flour.

Masao : Ms. White, look at the other graph. I asked the 40 students, "What do you eat for breakfast?" More than 50% of them eat bread for breakfast. So, our club decided to make rice flour bread. I think eating bread made from rice flour will *increase rice consumption in Japan.

Ayumi : So, our club will talk about Japanese rice in Masao's presentation and sell rice flour bread at the school festival. We hope everyone will be more interested in Japanese rice and like our rice flour bread.

Ms. White : I think that is a very good idea. I can't wait to listen to Masao's presentation and eat your rice flour bread!

One day in September, after the school festival, Ayumi and Masao are talking in the classroom after school. Then, Ms. White talks to them.

Ms. White : Hi, Ayumi and Masao. The rice flour bread was wonderful, and everyone enjoyed Masao's presentation.

Masao : Thank you. After the school festival, I used the Internet and learned more about rice and *wheat. Japan *imports about 90% of the wheat it uses. What will happen if enough wheat doesn't come from foreign countries?

Ms. White : I think bread, noodles, and other food made from wheat flour will become very expensive.

Ayumi : But I don't think Japanese people can _____ because their eating habits have changed a lot, and many Japanese people eat food made from wheat flour.

Ms. White : You may be right. How about rice?

Masao : Oh, we grow enough rice in Japan, and we should eat more rice. Let's find ways to increase our rice consumption.

Ayumi : Let's do that! We can create new *recipes to use rice flour.

Ms. White : When your club members cook next time, please let me know!

Ayumi : Sure.

(注) grows 〜 〜を育てる
consumption 消費量
decreasing 減っている
changes in 〜 〜の変化

eating habits　食生活　　graph　グラフ
amount　量
volunteer activity　ボランティア活動
made from 〜　〜で作られた
wheat flour　小麦粉
rice flour　米粉
instead of 〜　〜の代わりに
increase 〜　〜を増やす
wheat　小麦
imports 〜　〜を輸入する
recipes　調理法

(ア)　本文中の＿＿線①と＿＿線②が表す内容を，①は
ア群，②はイ群の中からそれぞれ選んだときの組み合わ
せとして最も適するものを，あとの１〜９の中から一つ
選び，その番号を答えなさい。

ア群

The amount of rice one person ate in a year

A.
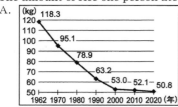

B.
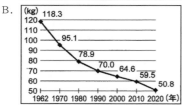

C.
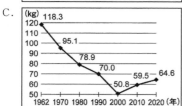

イ群

(a)　Which do you like the best, bread, noodles,
or rice?

(b)　What do you eat for breakfast?

X. (a)　　　　　　　　(b)
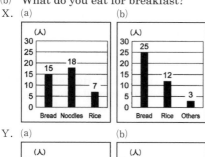

Y. (a)　　　　　　　　(b)
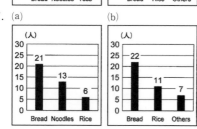

Z. (a)　　　　　　　　(b)
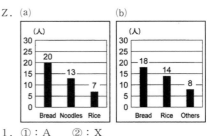

1．①：A　　②：X
2．①：A　　②：Y
3．①：A　　②：Z
4．①：B　　②：X
5．①：B　　②：Y
6．①：B　　②：Z
7．①：C　　②：X
8．①：C　　②：Y
9．①：C　　②：Z

(イ)　本文中の　　　の中に入れるのに最も適するものを，
次の１〜４の中から一つ選び，その番号を答えなさい。
1．stop eating food made from wheat flour
2．continue to eat food made from wheat flour
3．increase their wheat consumption
4．eat more rice and stop using rice flour

(ウ)　次のa〜fの中から，本文の内容に合うものを二つ選
んだときの組み合わせとして最も適するものを，あとの
１〜８の中から一つ選び，その番号を答えなさい。
a．Masao's grandfather always sends his rice to
Kamome High School for the school festival.
b．Masao thinks that changes in people's eating
habits have increased rice consumption in
Japan.
c．Masao decided to make a presentation about
Japanese rice by using his experiences during
his volunteer activity.
d．Ayumi made bread by using wheat flour
because bread was the students' favorite food.
e．Masao thinks that eating more rice flour
bread is a good way to increase rice
consumption in Japan.
f．Ayumi and Masao want to create new recipes
that use wheat flour because rice is not
popular.
1．aとc　　2．aとd
3．bとd　　4．bとf
5．cとe　　6．cとf
7．dとe　　8．eとf

<神奈川県>

11 次の対話の文章を読んで，あとの各問に答えよ。
（＊印の付いている単語・語句には，本文のあとに
(注)がある。）

Rumi, Kenta, and Aika are first-year high school students
in Tokyo. Steve is a high school student from the United
States. They are talking in their classroom after lunch.

Rumi：Hi, Kenta and Steve, what are you doing?
Kenta：Hi, Rumi and Aika. We're talking about how
to *express the numbers of some things in
Japanese.
Steve：Sometimes I don't know what word to add
after a number. For example, "mai" for pages
of paper and "satsu" for books.

Rumi：In English, I often forget to add words before some things. "A piece of cake" is one example.

Aika：(1)I do, too. There are many differences between English and Japanese, and there are a lot of things to remember. Sometimes it is *confusing.

Rumi：Yes, it is. Steve, are there any other difficult things for you about Japanese?

Steve：Yes. Last night, my *host mother said, "... *Murata Sensei ga mieru*...." I thought she could see Mr. Murata, our *homeroom teacher, there. So I looked around, but he wasn't there. (2)That was confusing.

Kenta：She wanted to say that he would come.

Steve：That's right.

Rumi：Is there anything like that in English?

Steve：Yes. I'll give you an example. What do you say when you thank someone for their help?

Aika：I say, "Thank you for your help."

Steve：Yes. We also say "I am grateful for your help," especially in a more *formal *situation.

Rumi：(3)Oh, I remember another expression like that.

Aika：Tell us about it.

Rumi：Sure. When I was a junior high school student, I went to the teachers' room to ask Mr. Brown about a report. When I came into the room, he said to me, "Please have a seat." I couldn't understand what he meant.

Steve：It means "Please sit down." It's also used in formal situations.

Aika：That's interesting. I think we should learn more about formal expressions and use them more often both in English and in Japanese.

Rumi：Should I use them with Steve?

Kenta：Well.... (4)I don't think so.

Aika：What do you think?

Kenta：When I talk with Steve in Japanese, I choose simple expressions because I want him to understand me. He is my close friend.

Aika：I see. We should think about the best expressions to use in different situations.

Steve：And the *speed of speaking, too. Rumi and Aika, you do that for me. And you also use simple expressions. I feel that is very kind. I enjoy talking with you in Japanese.

Aika：I do, too.

Kenta：I also have realized one thing in teaching Japanese to Steve. Japanese is interesting.

Rumi：Why do you think so?

Kenta：Because it has many different ways to express the same thing. For example, when I say "I" in Japanese, I can say "*watashi*," or "*watakushi*," or "*boku*."

Aika：Also, sometimes we don't need to use a word expressing "I."

Kenta：That's right. I have never thought of that. "*Kansha shiteimasu*."

Steve：Wow, that Japanese expression sounds formal.

Kenta：You're right. It means "I am grateful."

Steve：Interesting. I want to learn more Japanese expressions. Would you mind teaching me more?

Rumi：What?

Steve：I mean "Will you teach me more?"

Aika：Of course. And would you mind teaching us more English?

Rumi and Kenta：Yes, please.

Steve：(5)I will be happy to do that.

(注) express　表現する
　　 confusing　混乱させる
　　 host mother　ホームステイ先の母
　　 homeroom teacher　担任の先生
　　 formal　改まった
　　 situation　状況
　　 speed　速さ

〔問１〕 (1)I do, too.の内容を最もよく表しているのは，次のうちではどれか。

ア．Aika remembers that there are many differences between English and Japanese, too.

イ．Aika talks about how to express the number of some things, too.

ウ．Aika adds a word after each number, too.

エ．Aika often forgets to add words before some things, too.

〔問２〕 (2)That was confusing.の内容を最もよく表しているのは，次のうちではどれか。

ア．It was confusing to Steve because his host mother said Mr. Murata, his homeroom teacher, looked like him.

イ．It was confusing because Steve thought his host mother could see Mr. Murata, his homeroom teacher.

ウ．It was confusing to Steve because Mr. Murata, his homeroom teacher, was there.

エ．It was confusing because Steve couldn't see his host mother.

〔問３〕 (3)Oh, I remember another expression like that.の内容を，次のように書き表すとすれば，　　　　の中に，下のどれを入れるのがよいか。

Rumi remembered 　　　　.

ア．another English expression used in a formal situation

イ．another Japanese expression used in a formal situation

ウ．another English expression for saying "Thank you." to people for their help

エ．another Japanese expression for saying "Thank you." to people for their help

〔問４〕 (4)I don't think so.の内容を，次のように書き表すとすれば，　　　　の中に，下のどれを入れるのがよいか。

Kenta doesn't think that 　　　　.

ア．Rumi should use formal expressions with Steve

イ．it is difficult for Rumi to use formal expressions

ウ．Steve should understand what Rumi would like to say

エ．it is important for Rumi to use formal expressions in formal situations

〔問５〕 (5)I will be happy to do that.の内容を，次のように書き表すとすれば，　　　　の中に，下のどれを入れるのがよいか。

Steve will be happy to 　　　　.

ア．use many kinds of Japanese expressions used

in formal situations

イ．give an example of an English expression used in a formal situation

ウ．teach more English to Aika, Rumi, and Kenta

エ．learn Japanese from Aika, Rumi, and Kenta

〔問6〕　次の英語の文を，本文の内容と合うように完成するには，　　　　の中に，下のどれを入れるのがよいか。

When Aika and Rumi talk with Steve in Japanese, they use 　　　　 expressions, and Steve enjoys talking with them.

ア．difficult

イ．simple

ウ．formal

エ．interesting

〔問7〕　次の文章は，Kentaたちと話した日に，Steveが書いた日記の一部である。　(A)　及び　(B)　の中に，それぞれ入る単語の組み合わせとして正しいものは，下のア～エのうちではどれか。

Today, I talked with my friends Rumi, Kenta, and Aika about different expressions, both in Japanese and in English. First we talked about how to express the numbers of things. It is difficult for Rumi and Aika to do that in English. Rumi 　(A)　 me about something difficult in Japanese, and I said that once I couldn't understand one of my host mother's expression in 　(B)　.

After that we talked about English expressions used in formal situations. When we talk in Japanese, their Japanese is usually easy to understand. I enjoy talking with them, both in Japanese and in English. Finally, Kenta said 　(B)　 was interesting. I agree with him. Sometimes it is difficult, but I enjoy studying it. I 　(A)　 them to teach me more Japanese expressions.

ア．(A) asked　　(B) English

イ．(A) told　　(B) English

ウ．(A) asked　　(B) Japanese

エ．(A) told　　(B) Japanese

<東京都>

12 次は，高校生の広志(Hiroshi)，アメリカから来たグリーン先生(Mr. Green)，インドネシア(Indonesia)からの留学生のサリ(Sari)の3人が学校で交わした会話の一部です。会話文を読んで，あとの問いに答えなさい。

Hiroshi ：Hi, Mr. Green. I have a question for you.

Mr. Green ：Hi, Hiroshi. What is your question?

Hiroshi ：Yesterday, I 　①　 for information on the Internet about fermented soybean food, for example, *natto*. Then, I found some interesting information. According to Ⓐit, *natto* is one kind of fermented soybean food and there are many other kinds of fermented soybean food in the world. Are there any kinds of fermented soybean food in America?

Mr. Green ：Well, *natto* is often sold in supermarkets

納豆の写真

natto（納豆）
（複数形も
natto）

in America, but I'm not sure that other kinds of fermented soybean food are sold there. However, I know that there are other kinds of fermented soybean food in Asia.

Hiroshi ：Really?　Why do you know that?

Mr. Green ：Actually, when I visited Thailand three years ago, I ate fermented soybean food made in Thailand. I studied cultures of Asia at university, and learned that some areas and countries in Asia have similar food. They have a similar climate, and similar trees and plants, so people there can make similar food.

Thailand（タイ）

Indonesia（インドネシア）

Hiroshi ：That sounds interesting. You mean 　②　, right?

Mr. Green ：That's right!

Hiroshi ：Thank you, Mr. Green. I will try to find information about fermented soybean food in Asia.

Mr. Green ：I hope you'll find something about it. Oh, Sari is there. She is from Indonesia. Maybe she knows something. 　③　

Hiroshi ：Oh, yes!　I'll do so. Hi, Sari.

Sari ：Hi, Hiroshi. Hi, Mr. Green.

Hiroshi ：Sari, you're from Indonesia, right?　I was talking with Mr. Green about fermented soybean food in the world. In Indonesia, are there any kinds of fermented soybean food?

Sari ：Yes. We have food called "*tempeh*."

テンペの写真

Hiroshi ：*Tempeh*?　Does it look like *natto*?

Sari ：Well, *tempeh* and *natto* look very different. 　④　 of *tempeh* now, I could show it to you.

tempeh（テンペ）
（インドネシアの発酵大豆食品，複数形も*tempeh*）

Hiroshi ：Oh, I've just found a picture on my tablet. Look at this. The food in this picture looks like cake.

Mr. Green ：Is this *tempeh*?

Sari ：Yes, this is *tempeh*. *Tempeh* and *natto* look different, right?　*Tempeh* isn't sticky. When I ate *natto* for the first time, I was surprised that *natto* was sticky!

Hiroshi ：I'm surprised to know that *tempeh* isn't sticky.

Mr. Green ：I can understand how you felt, Sari. I told Hiroshi that I ate fermented soybean food made in Thailand. 　ア　 So, when I first ate *natto*, I was surprised like Sari because eating sticky food was a new experience for

Hiroshi : I see. It's interesting to know how other people feel when they eat *natto*.

Mr. Green : That's true. ［　イ　］

Hiroshi : Is *tempeh* popular food in Indonesia?

Sari : Yes! I think some people in Indonesia always have *tempeh* to cook at home and they eat it almost every day.

Mr. Green : How do they cook *tempeh*?

Sari : We usually fry *tempeh*. For example, my family fries *tempeh* with various vegetables.

Mr. Green : That's interesting. In Japan, *natto* is usually eaten with rice, right? ［　ウ　］ People eat various kinds of fermented soybean food in various ways. ［　エ　］

Hiroshi : I can't imagine the taste of *tempeh*. But, I want to try it someday.

Sari : Now, *tempeh* is getting popular in Japan. ⑤

Hiroshi : Really? I didn't think I could buy *tempeh* in this neighborhood. I want to eat *tempeh*, and compare *tempeh* and *natto*.

Sari : Let's go there this weekend.

Hiroshi : Yes! Thank you, Sari. Learning about various kinds of food in other countries was interesting. And, it made me become more interested in *natto*. I think learning about food in other countries leads me to learning about food in my country.

Sari : I agree with you. ⑥

Mr. Green : Thank you for telling us about *tempeh*, Sari, and thank you for sharing an interesting topic, Hiroshi.

（注）fermented soybean food　発酵大豆食品
climate　気候　　tablet　タブレット
sticky　ねばねばした
fry　（フライパンなどで）炒（いた）める

(1) 本文の内容から考えて，次のうち，本文中の①に入れるのに最も適しているものはどれですか。一つ選び，記号で答えなさい。
　ア．got　イ．looked　ウ．took　エ．used

(2) 本文中のⒶitの表している内容に当たるものとして最も適しているひとつづきの英語3語を，本文中から抜き出して書きなさい。

(3) 本文の内容から考えて，次のうち，本文中の②に入れるのに最も適しているものはどれですか。一つ選び，記号で答えなさい。
　ア．only people living in Japan and Thailand can make fermented soybean food
　イ．people living in various areas tell each other how to make popular food through the Internet
　ウ．people living anywhere in the world can make similar food because the climate isn't important for making food
　エ．even people living in different areas and countries in Asia can make similar food because the climates, trees and plants of those places are similar

(4) 本文の内容から考えて，次のうち，本文中の③に

入れるのに最も適しているものはどれですか。一つ選び，記号で答えなさい。
　ア．How is she today?
　イ．How about asking her?
　ウ．What are you going to do?
　エ．Let's ask her about American food.

(5) 本文中の'④ of *tempeh* now, I could show it to you.'が，「もし今私が1枚のテンペの写真を持っていたら，それをあなたに見せてあげることができるでしょうに。」という内容になるように，＿＿＿に英語5語を書き入れ，英文を完成させなさい。
＿＿＿＿＿＿＿ of *tempeh* now, I could show it to you.

(6) 本文中には次の英文が入ります。本文中の［ア］〜［エ］から，入る場所として最も適しているものを一つ選び，ア〜エの記号で答えなさい。
　And, it wasn't sticky, either.

(7) 本文の内容から考えて，次のうち，本文中の⑤に入れるのに最も適しているものはどれですか。一つ選び，記号で答えなさい。
　ア．I found that *tempeh* was interesting food.
　イ．I found a book about *tempeh* in the school library.
　ウ．I found *tempeh* in the supermarket near our school.
　エ．I found that *tempeh* and *natto* were different when I was in Indonesia.

(8) 本文中の⑥が，「私はあなたにテンペについて話ができてうれしいです。」という内容になるように，次の〔　　〕内の語を並べかえて，英文を完成させなさい。
　I〔am　could　glad　I　that〕tell you about *tempeh*.

(9) 次のうち，本文で述べられている内容と合うものはどれですか。二つ選び，記号で答えなさい。
　ア．Hiroshi asked Mr. Green where people in America went to buy fermented soybean food.
　イ．Mr. Green knows that there are some kinds of fermented soybean food in Asia.
　ウ．Sari knows that *tempeh* and *natto* look different, but she has never eaten *natto* before.
　エ．Sari thinks *tempeh* is popular only among people in Indonesia.
　オ．Hiroshi thinks learning about food in other countries leads him to learning about food in his country.

〈大阪府・B問題〉

13 次の対話の文章を読んで，あとの各問に答えなさい。（＊印の付いている単語・語句には，本文のあとに（注）がある。）

Ken and Risa are Japanese high school students. Ken and Risa have known each other since they were little. George is from the UK. He is doing a homestay at Ken's house. Diane is from France. She is doing a homestay at Risa's house. Ken's family and Risa's family are going to go to Kyoto with George and Diane. They are at Tokyo Station.

Ken : If we go up the stairs, we can get to platform eighteen.

Risa : We'll be able to get on the train there.

George : This is my first time taking a shinkansen in Japan.

Diane : Me too. Look! The *passengers are waiting in line. They're not all over the place.

Ken : Here comes the shinkansen! It leaves at eight thirty.

Risa : It's here. Let's get on!

George : Where are our seats? I hope we can sit by the window.

Ken : Our parents are sitting in the back. Our seat numbers are 5D, 5E, 6D and 6E.

Risa : You can take seats, 5E and 6E! George and Diane should have the window seats. I hope that you two will be able to see some beautiful views.

Diane : [_____(a)_____]

Ken : Oh! Look outside! The train is starting to move!

Diane : How far is it from Tokyo to Kyoto?

Ken : It's about 368 kilometers.

George : And how long does it take from Tokyo to Kyoto by shinkansen?

Ken : It takes about two hours and fifteen minutes.

Diane : The speed on the *screen is increasing quickly! How fast do shinkansen travel?

Risa : They have a top speed of 285 kilometers *per hour.

George : [_____(b)_____]

Ken : The shinkansen is one of the best things Japan has created. Most of Japan's islands, including Honshu, Kyushu and Hokkaido, are served by a network of high speed train lines that connect Tokyo and most of the country's big cities.

Diane : When did people start using shinkansen in Japan?

Risa : They started when the Tokaido Shinkansen line was built in 1964. Since then, Japan has improved shinkansen for over half a century. For example, shinkansen made a lot of *noise, but now they do not.

Ken : I heard that the railway company thought a lot about sound and speed when they designed the shinkansen. The engineers got the idea for the shape from a bird. They designed it to look like a bird's *beak. They thought that to ⁽²⁾【 ア. needed to　イ. the shape of　ウ. very similar to　エ. the shinkansen　オ. and reduce noise　カ. the front of　キ. increase speed　ク. be 】 the beak.

Risa : Yeah! They learned a lot from nature.

*Announcement: We will soon make a *brief stop at Shin-Yokohama Station.*

Diane : We arrived at Shin-Yokohama Station right on time.

George : [_____(c)_____]

Risa : Yes, shinkansen are well known for their *punctuality. The *average *delay time in a year per train is less than one minute.

Ken : Any train *delayed by more than a minute is *officially late.

George : In the UK, any train delayed by more than ten minutes is officially late. Last week, I took the Yamanote line, and there were many people on the platform. I was surprised that there were no delays.

Ken : Yeah, on all Japanese Railway lines if the train arrives even three minutes later, companies *apologize over the speakers.

Diane : Wow, three minutes! In France, any train delayed by more than fifteen minutes is officially late.

George : What is the key to the shinkansen's punctuality?

Ken : The drivers need to stop the shinkansen without the help of computers. The train may be as much as 400 meters long, and the drivers must stop at a stop line. Because of the drivers' hard work, passengers can get on and off quickly.

Diane : Wow! I'm surprised to hear how difficult it is.

Risa : Passengers' *cooperation is important, too. To get on and off in time passengers need to be ready to get off as soon as the doors open, and passengers waiting to get on need to line up outside the doors on the platform.

Ken : Also, shinkansen have few problems because they have good *mechanics. They often check the shinkansen carefully.

George : Ah, so shinkansen's punctuality is all possible because of teamwork from drivers, passengers, and mechanics.

Twenty-five minutes later.

Ken : [_____(d)_____] Mt. Fuji looks beautiful!

Diane : How wonderful! I have only seen photos of Mt. Fuji before.

George : Mt. Fuji looks very beautiful! The windows were cleaned, so we can see outside easily. The whole train is so clean.

Risa : Workers always clean the cars between each trip, so passengers can feel *comfortable.

Ken : And, the seats have a lot of space, so you can relax.

Announcement: The Shinkansen has arrived at Nagoya Station.

George : Wow, we're already in Nagoya. It's only ten after ten. What's the next stop?

Ken : The next station is our stop, Kyoto!

Diane : How many times have you been to Kyoto, Ken?

Ken : This will be my second time, but I often travel by shinkansen.

George : Many people are getting on. How many people can take the shinkansen at a time?

Ken : This shinkansen, for example, has space for over one thousand three hundred people.

Risa : Also, over the shinkansen's fifty-year history, they have carried over one billion passengers. [_____(e)_____]

Diane : The shinkansen is really a safe way to travel!

Twenty-five minutes later.

George : What time is it now?
Risa : It's ten thirty-eight.
George : Really? Time flew by. I can't believe that over two hours passed. We're almost there.
Ken : Soon, we will be able to move faster than we can now. A railway company has developed a shinkansen which can run at speeds of as much as 400 kilometers per hour.
Diane : When I come to Japan next, I want to take it. I think that Japanese companies have been working hard to finish it. I'm sure this news has made many people across Japan excited.
Risa : It has! The *development of the shinkansen is connected to the *cultural importance of punctuality, *comfort, and safety in Japan.
George : That's so interesting!
Announcement: We will soon make a brief stop at Kyoto Station.

Risa : Let's get ready. We'll get to Kyoto Station soon.
Diane : We should clean up. Let's go!

(注) passenger 乗客　　screen スクリーン
per ～　～につき
noise 騒音
beak くちばし
announcement アナウンス
brief stop 停車
punctuality 定時性
average 平均の
delay 遅れ
delayed 遅れた
officially 公式に
apologize 謝罪する
cooperation 協力
mechanic 整備士
comfortable 快適な
development 発展
cultural 文化的な
comfort 快適さ

〔問1〕 本文の流れに合うように，　(a)　～　(e)　の中に，英文を入れるとき，最も適切なものを次の中からそれぞれ一つずつ選びなさい。ただし，同じものは二度使えません。
ア．Really? That's so fast!
イ．Thank you for your kindness!
ウ．And there has not been a single accident during this time.
エ．Have a look outside!
オ．I heard that Japanese trains are almost never late.
〔問2〕 (2)【ア．needed to　イ．the shape of　ウ．very similar to　エ．the shinkansen　オ．and reduce noise　カ．the front of　キ．increase speed　ク．be】とあるが，本文の流れに合うように，【　】内の単語・語句を正しく並べかえたとき，1番目と4番目と8番目にくるものは，それぞれア～クの中

ではどれか。
〔問3〕 本文の内容に合う英文の組み合わせとして最も適切なものは，ア～コの中ではどれか。
① Diane took the shinkansen for the first time and was surprised to see the people in line on the platform at Tokyo Station, but it was not George's first time on a shinkansen.
② Ken and George sat in the window seats to enjoy the good views, and Risa and Diane sat in the window seats on the other side to see the sea.
③ France has a stronger sense of punctuality than the UK, and Japan's is stronger than France's.
④ Not only the hard work of drivers and mechanics but also the cooperation of passengers makes the shinkansen's punctuality possible.
⑤ Workers sometimes clean the cars after every trip and the seats in shinkansen have little space, so we can relax.
⑥ The shinkansen that the four students took arrived at Nagoya Station more than two hours after it left Tokyo Station.
⑦ Shinkansen have carried hundreds of millions of passengers safely for more than fifty years.
⑧ By taking the shinkansen Risa learned that its development is connected to Japanese culture and society.

ア	① ③		イ	② ⑦	
ウ	③ ⑥		エ	④ ⑤	
オ	④ ⑧		カ	① ② ⑤	
キ	① ④ ⑧		ク	② ③ ⑥	
ケ	③ ⑦ ⑧		コ	④ ⑥ ⑦	

〔問4〕 次の文章は，Georgeが日本からイギリスにいる友人に送ったメールの文章である。対話文の内容に一致するように，（ a ）～（ d ）の中に，それぞれ適切な英語1語を入れなさい。
I went to Kyoto with my Japanese friends and another homestay student by shinkansen. We talked a lot about the shinkansen on the train, and I learned that it has four great points. First, the shinkansen runs very fast. The top speed is 285 kilometers per hour. We can travel to many places quickly. Second, it is almost always on (a). The train staff's hard work makes this possible. It is also possible because the train staff and passengers work (b). By using the shinkansen, we can make plans for travel or business easily (c) worrying about delays. Third, we can enjoy comfortable travel because the whole train is clean and the seats have a lot of space. Finally, the shinkansen is (d). There have been no accidents since it was developed over fifty years ago. I think the shinkansen is so popular among people in Japan because of these great points. If you come to Japan, I want you to travel by shinkansen. I think that you will have a great time.

<東京都立西高等学校>

14 次の対話の文章を読んで，あとの各問に答えなさい。
（＊印の付いている単語・語句には，本文のあとに
(注)がある。）

*Rika, Kento and Mick are classmates at Seimei High School in Tokyo. Mick is a student from the United States. They are members of the *biology club. At the beginning of their summer vacation, they are talking about a plan for their science presentation. Their presentation is held in early September. Rika asks them a question in the biology club house.*

Rika	: Guess what sea *creature I want to talk about at the science presentation.
Kento	: What kind of creature?
Rika	: Well, its head looks like an umbrella.
Mick	: An umbrella?
Rika	: It has no *brain and most of the body is made of water.
Kento	: Ah, it's a *jellyfish! But why did you pick it?
Rika	: A few years ago, I went swimming in the sea with my family. I saw some white jellyfish there. They were swimming very slowly. Since then, I have been interested in jellyfish.
Kento	: I see. Do you know why they swim slowly?
Rika	: I'm not sure.
Kento	: They never swim against the *current. They swim with the current.
Rika	: _____(1)-a_____
Mick	: Kento knows well about jellyfish, and Rika is interested in it. How about making a science presentation about jellyfish?
Rika	: Good idea. I have wanted to have a chance to study about jellyfish.
Kento	: Hmm.... I don't think they are exciting for the science presentation.
Mick	: (2)Well, let's ask Mr. Naka, our biology teacher, about jellyfish. He is going to give us a lesson about sea creatures today. He will come back here soon from his trip to the sea. I hope he can give us some good advice.

The three students are sitting around Mr. Naka in the club house. He shows his students several living things. He has caught them in the sea. At the end of his lesson, he tells them to look at a bottle of water in his hand and turns off the lights.

Rika	: Wow! Something is *glowing in the bottle.
Mick	: How beautiful! They look like stars in the night sky.
Mr. Naka	: Does anyone know what is glowing in the bottle?
Kento	: I think there are *sea fireflies glowing in the bottle.
Mr. Naka	: That's right. The sea fireflies are *emitting light. There are a lot of sea fireflies in the sea.
Rika	: Mr. Naka, several sea fireflies have

stopped glowing. Why?

Mr. Naka	: _____(1)-b_____ Does anyone know how they emit their light again?
Kento	: I do. Just shake the bottle.
Mr. Naka	: Great job, Kento. Will you shake it?
Kento	: Sure. Look, the sea fireflies are beginning to glow again.
Rika	: Mr. Naka?
Naka	: Yes, Rika.
Rika	: How did the sea fireflies start to glow again?
Mr. Naka	: The sea fireflies emitted two kinds of *substances into the sea water — a *luminescent material and an *enzyme. Does anyone know what happened with these two?
Kento	: A *chemical reaction happened. So, the sea fireflies began to glow again.
Mr. Naka	: That's correct.
Rika	: Mmm.... I don't understand why the chemical reaction happened. Please tell me a little more about it.
Mr. Naka	: _____(3)_____
Mick	: I'll try it. Imagine that there is an onion. If you don't do anything to the onion, it doesn't produce anything. Then what happens to you soon after you *chop the onion into pieces?
Rika	: Tears come from my eyes.
Mick	: What is happening in the onion then?
Rika	: A chemical reaction happens when it is chopped into pieces.
Mick	: That means _____(4)_____. One is a *raw material and the other is a special substance. The raw material and the special substance will have a chemical reaction, and it will *stimulate your eyes. So, tears come from your eyes.
Rika	: The raw material doesn't meet the special substance in the onion before I chop it, right?
Mick	: That's right. Why (5)【 ① really different ② does ③ change ④ something ⑤ into ⑥ the raw material ⑦ the special substance 】? You've already known it.
Rika	: Ah, it's the chemical reaction. The chemical reaction happened with the help of the special substance, enzyme!
Mr. Naka	: Yes, the enzyme is a special *protein. The enzyme never changes itself through the chemical reaction, while the raw material becomes something quite different. Are there any other questions?
Mick	: Yes, today Rika talked to Kento and me about jellyfish. Are there any jellyfish glowing like the sea fireflies?
Mr. Naka	: Yes, several kinds of jellyfish can glow.
Mick	: I wonder where we can see such a kind of jellyfish.
Mr. Naka	: Why don't you visit the science museum in our town next week? There will be an event about jellyfish. They have a guide

Rika : [(1)-c] Let's go there.

Rika, Mick and Kento visit the science museum in their town. A museum guide explains to them about jellyfish. Her name is Saki.

Saki : What kind of jellyfish would you like to see first?

Rika : We hear that some jellyfish can glow. We can't wait to see them.

Saki : Sure, they are just around the corner.

Mick : Wow, these jellyfish are glowing.

Saki : They are called *crystal jellyfish.

Rika : Beautiful green light.... I wonder how they emit it.

Saki : Would you read the sign here?

Rika : The sign says they can glow with *ultraviolet rays.

Saki : They have a special substance to emit light with ultraviolet rays.

Rika : What is the name of the special substance?

Saki : It is called *Green Fluorescent Protein. We call it GFP.

Kento : Is it a special kind of protein?

Saki : Yes.

Kento : What is [(6)-a] about GFP?

Saki : It has a luminescent material and an enzyme in [(6)-b] place. The crystal jellyfish don't have to get the enzyme from [(6)-c] place when they glow.

Kento : Does that mean they don't produce light like sea fireflies?

Saki : That's right. The sea fireflies have the luminescent material and the enzyme in [(6)-d] places of their body, so these substances need to meet before they glow.

Kento : The crystal jellyfish can emit light more easily than the sea fireflies, right?

Saki : Yes, that's correct. Scientists today know a great way to use GFP.

Mick : How do they use it?

Saki : They use it to find how proteins are moving in the body.

Mick : Does that mean GFP in the crystal jellyfish is used in other creatures?

Saki : Yes, the scientists add it to another creature's proteins and follow the proteins with GFP in the body. Why can the scientists see them clearly?

Rika : The proteins with GFP glow in the body.

Saki : That's true. The scientists in the past didn't get much information about proteins, especially about their movements in the body until GFP was discovered. It is used as one of the most important tools in science and technology.

Kento : Saki, I want to check what we have learned from you. May I ask my friends a question?

Saki : Sure.

Kento : What do the scientists need when they follow the proteins with GFP?

Saki : Oh, that's a good question.

Mick : Let's see. Is it a special protein?

Kento : [(7)-a]

Rika : [(7)-b]

Kento : [(7)-c]

Rika : [(7)-d]

Kento : That's right.

Saki : I'm happy to hear that. You remember what I told you about the crystal jellyfish. Do you know that a Japanese scientist was the first man to discover GFP in the crystal jellyfish? He received the Nobel Prize for his performance.

Rika : Oh, really? Thank you for giving us useful information, Saki.

Saki has gone. They are watching the crystal jellyfish for a while.

Kento : These jellyfish are amazing. I want to show how the Japanese scientist found the special substance at the school festival.

Mick : I hope we can catch a jellyfish for the science presentation.

Rika : [(1)-d]

Mick : Listen, how about showing their pictures or videos?

Rika : Sounds good.

Mick : Let's see every jellyfish here with our own eyes first and then make our plan.

(注) biology 生物　creature 生き物　brain 脳(のう)
jellyfish くらげ　current 水流　glow 光る
sea firefly ウミホタル　emit 出す
substance 物質　luminescent material 蛍光物質
enzyme 酵素(こうそ)　chemical reaction 化学反応
chop 細かく切る　raw material 原料
stimulate 刺激する　protein タンパク質
crystal jellyfish オワンクラゲ
ultraviolet rays 紫外線
Green Fluorescent Protein 緑色蛍光タンパク質

〔問1〕 [(1)-a]～[(1)-d]の中に，それぞれ次のA～Dのどれを入れるのがよいか。その組み合わせが最も適切なものは，下のア～カの中ではどれか。

A．That sounds interesting.

B．Are you kidding?

C．That's new to me.

D．That is a good question.

	(1)-a	(1)-b	(1)-c	(1)-d
ア	A	B	D	C
イ	A	D	B	C
ウ	C	A	D	B
エ	C	D	A	B
オ	D	B	C	A
カ	D	C	B	A

〔問2〕 (2)Well, let's ask Mr. Naka, our biology teacher, about jellyfish.とあるが，このときMickが考えている内容として最も適切なものは，次の中ではどれか。

ア．I don't want to talk to Kento about the science presentation because he thinks jellyfish are so boring.

イ．Kento will join us after Mr. Naka's lesson because Mr. Naka will ask him to do that.

ウ．I'd like to share our information about jellyfish with Mr. Naka and learn something new about jellyfish from him.

エ．We need good advice from Mr. Naka to change our plan for the science presentation.

〔問3〕　本文の流れに合うように，　(3)　に英語を入れるとき，最も適切なものは，次の中ではどれか。

ア．Who can explain the chemical reaction with an easier example?

イ．Will you explain what happens in the body of glowing jellyfish?

ウ．What kind of vegetables do you imagine in addition to sea fireflies?

エ．Will you explain to Rika about a chemical reaction at the presentation?

〔問4〕　本文の流れに合うように，　(4)　に英語を入れるとき，最も適切なものは，次の中ではどれか。

ア．before you chop the onion, one of the two substances changes into a different one

イ．before you chop the onion, there are two different substances in it

ウ．soon after you chop the onion, it makes two quite new substances

エ．when you chop the onion, two substances in it become different ones

〔問5〕　(5)【①　really different　②　does　③　change　④　something　⑤　into　⑥　the raw material　⑦　the special substance】について，本文の流れに合うとき，【　】内の単語・語句を正しく並べかえるとき，【　】内で2番目と4番目と6番目にくるものの組み合わせとして最も適切なものは，次のア～カの中ではどれか。

	2番目	4番目	6番目
ア	④	⑤	③
イ	④	⑤	⑥
ウ	⑥	②	③
エ	⑥	③	①
オ	⑦	⑥	①
カ	⑦	⑥	④

〔問6〕　(6)-a　～　(6)-d　の中に，それぞれ次のA～Dのどれを入れるのがよいか。その組み合わせとして最も適切なものは，下のア～カの中ではどれか。

A．another　　B．different
C．special　　D．the same

	(6)-a	(6)-b	(6)-c	(6)-d
ア	A	C	B	D
イ	A	D	B	C
ウ	B	A	D	C
エ	B	D	C	A
オ	C	A	D	B
カ	C	D	A	B

〔問7〕　(7)-a　～　(7)-d　の中に，それぞれ次のA～Dのどれを入れるのがよいか。その組み合わせとして最も適切なものは，下のア～カの中ではどれか。

A．Of course not.

B．No, it isn't.... They usually come from the sun.

C．Oh, I see.... Ultraviolet rays.

D．People cannot see them in their daily life, right?

	(7)-a	(7)-b	(7)-c	(7)-d
ア	A	C	D	B
イ	A	D	C	B
ウ	B	C	A	D
エ	B	D	A	C
オ	D	A	B	C
カ	D	B	C	A

〔問8〕　本文の内容に合う英文の組み合わせとして最も適切なものは，次のア～シの中ではどれか。

① Mick and Kento decided what to do for the science presentation before they met Rika in the club house at their school in early August.

② Kento knew about jellyfish so well that Rika and Mick were impressed by his quick answers to their questions and deep love of jellyfish.

③ Only Rika realized why several sea fireflies in the bottle didn't have enough energy to produce light.

④ At first Rika didn't understand the chemical reaction well, but Kento carefully taught her about it with another example later.

⑤ When the three students visited the science museum, the crystal jellyfish were glowing there because of the ultraviolet rays.

⑥ Kento found the two sea creatures had different ways to produce light after Saki's talk about them.

⑦ Saki said GFP was among the best tools in scientists' study of proteins, but it was not often used in science and technology before.

⑧ Mick thought it would be good to see all the jellyfish in the science museum and later think about their presentation plan.

ア	①	②		イ	①	⑥	
ウ	②	④		エ	③	⑥	
オ	①	③	⑥	カ	②	④	⑧
キ	④	⑦	⑧	ク	⑤	⑥	⑧
ケ	③	④	⑤ ⑦	コ	③	④	⑦ ⑧
サ	④	⑤	⑥ ⑦	シ	④	⑤	⑥ ⑧

〔問9〕　下の質問について，あなたの考えや意見を，40語以上50語以内の英語で述べなさい。「,」「.」「!」「?」などは，語数に含めません。

What is the most useful animal for people and why?

＜東京都立立川高等学校＞

e．説明文

① 日常・文化・社会

1 次の英文を読んで，1，2，3，4の問いに答えなさい。

When people in Japan want to decide who wins or who goes first quickly, they often play a hand game called *Janken*. They use three hand gestures to play the game. A closed hand means a *rock, an open hand means paper, and a closed hand with the *extended *index and middle fingers means *scissors. A rock breaks scissors, so the rock wins. Also, scissors cut paper, and paper covers a rock. It is （　　　　） the rules, so many people can play *Janken*.

This kind of hand game is played in many countries all around the world. Most of the people use three hand gestures, but some people use more than three. In *France, people use four hand gestures. People in *Malaysia sometimes use five hand gestures.

In other countries, people use hand gestures which are ｜　　A　　｜ from the ones used in Japan. In *Indonesia, a closed hand with the extended *thumb means an elephant, a closed hand with the extended index finger means a person, and a closed hand with the extended *little finger means an *ant. In their rules, an elephant *beats a person, because it is larger and stronger. In the same way, a person beats an ant. But how can a small ant beat a big elephant? Can you imagine the reason? An ant can get into an elephant's ears and nose, and the elephant doesn't like that.

Isn't it interesting to know that there are many kinds of hand games like *Janken* around the world? Even when the hand gestures and their meanings are ｜　　A　　｜, people can enjoy them. If you go to foreign countries in the future, ask the local people how they play their hand games. And why don't you introduce yours and play the games with them? Then that may be ｜　　　B　　　｜.

> （注）*Janken* じゃんけん　　rock 岩，石
> extended 伸ばした
> index and middle fingers 人差し指と中指
> scissors はさみ　　France フランス
> Malaysia マレーシア　　Indonesia インドネシア
> thumb 親指　　little finger 小指
> ant アリ
> beat ～ ～を打ち負かす

1．本文中の（　　　）に入るものとして，最も適切なものはどれか。
　ア．difficult to decide　　イ．easy to understand
　ウ．free to break　　　　　エ．necessary to change

2．本文中の二つの｜　A　｜には同じ英語が入る。適切な英語を1語で書きなさい。

3．本文中の下線部の内容を，次の｜　　　｜が表すように，（　　）に入る25字程度の日本語を書きなさい。ただし，句読点も字数に加えるものとする。

> アリは（　　　　　　　　　　　　　　　　　　　）から，アリがゾウに勝つ。

4．本文中の｜　B　｜に入るものとして，最も適切なものはどれか。
　ア．a good way to learn the culture and history of Japan
　イ．a good way to decide which hand gesture is the best
　ウ．a good start for communicating with people all over the world
　エ．a good start for knowing how you can always win at hand games

<栃木県>

2 次の英文は，智明(Tomoaki)と両親(parents)の間の出来事をもとに書かれたものです。後の1～6の問いに答えなさい。

Tomoaki's parents are farmers. They have a large *farm next to the house. They grow healthy vegetables. The vegetables are very delicious and popular among people （　①　live　） in the town. They *are proud of their job.

However, ｜　　A　　｜ because Tomoaki couldn't go out with his family on the weekends. His friends usually talked *happily about the weekend at school on Mondays. But he had nothing to talk about with his friends. He didn't have time to enjoy the weekends with his family like his friends. His parents worked from morning until night even on the weekends. And when they were very busy, they couldn't have dinner with Tomoaki and his little brothers. Tomoaki felt sad about that.

One day, when Tomoaki came home, he saw many people on the farm. He thought they were local farmers. His parents often had a *meeting to talk about *agricultural *skills to grow healthy vegetables.

However, that day was different. English was （　②　speak　） on the farm. There was a group of foreign people. Tomoaki understood that they were students （　　　　） were learning about Japanese *agriculture. He walked closer to his parents on the farm. His father and mother were talking with the foreign students. Tomoaki was surprised because his parents were communicating in English. His father was explaining about a new *machine they bought for the first time. Then Tomoaki became more surprised to hear their conversation.

A foreign student : I think this machine is very expensive. Why did you decide to buy it?

Tomoaki's father：Because we must make our work easier. We have been too busy.

Tomoaki's mother：This machine will give us more free time to spend with our children.

Tomoaki realized his parents were worried that they didn't have time with their children. He was so glad to know that.

After that, Tomoaki had a good time with his parents and he became interested in agriculture. He sometimes helps his parents on the farm. He learns agricultural skills from them. He is proud of his parents now and studying hard to go to an agricultural high school. He says, "I will be a farmer like my parents. I want to 　　B　　 and make a lot of people happy by selling them." He continues saying, "And I will study English hard in high school. I also want to share our agricultural skills with many people in the world."

（注）farm　農場
　　　be proud of　〜を誇りに思う
　　　happily　楽しそうに
　　　meeting　会合
　　　agricultural　農業の
　　　skill　技術
　　　agriculture　農業
　　　machine　機械

1．次の(1)〜(3)の英文を，本文の内容と合うように完成させるのに，最も適切なものを，それぞれア〜エから1つずつ選び，記号で答えなさい。

(1) Tomoaki felt sad when ＿＿＿＿＿＿＿.
　ア．he could go out with his parents and his little brothers
　イ．his friends didn't talk happily about their weekends
　ウ．he had to work from morning until night even on the weekends
　エ．he and his little brothers had to have dinner without their parents

(2) A group of foreign students came to the farm to ＿＿＿＿＿＿.
　ア．buy the vegetables Tomoaki's parents grew
　イ．teach agriculture in English at Japanese schools
　ウ．learn about Japanese agriculture from Tomoaki's parents
　エ．sell an expensive machine for agriculture

(3) Tomoaki's parents bought the new machine because they wanted to ＿＿＿＿＿＿.
　ア．stop using an old one
　イ．grow more vegetables for foreign people
　ウ．have more time to spend with their children
　エ．share their agricultural skills

2．（ ① ）と（ ② ）の単語を，それぞれ適切な形にして書きなさい。

3．　　A　　に入る最も適切なものを，次のア〜エから1つ選び，記号で答えなさい。
　ア．Tomoaki helped his parents' job
　イ．Tomoaki didn't like his parents' job
　ウ．Tomoaki enjoyed growing vegetables
　エ．Tomoaki didn't want to sell vegetables

4．文中の（　　）に入る最も適切なものを，次のア〜エか

ら1つ選び，記号で答えなさい。
　ア．who　イ．which　ウ．what　エ．how

5．　　B　　に入る最も適切な連続した3語の英語を，本文中からそのまま抜き出して答えなさい。

6．次の対話は，智明の話を読んだ後に二人の中学生が話した内容です。対話が成り立つように，下線部に入る主語と動詞を含む6語以上の英文1文を書きなさい。ただし，符号（ ，．！？など）は語の数に入れないものとします。

A：This is a wonderful story.
B：I agree. I think that Tomoaki is very happy now.
A：Have you had an experience that made you happy?
B：Of course.
A：Please tell me more.
B：I felt happy when ＿＿＿＿＿＿＿＿＿.
A：I see. You felt so happy then.

〈宮崎県〉

3 次の英文を読んで，あとの(1)〜(3)に答えなさい。

Masato and Tom are junior high school students. They have been friends for a year and Tom has learned how to speak Japanese well during his stay in Japan.

Tom is interested in Japanese culture, especially *manga*. Masato also likes it and they often enjoy talking about the stories. Tom is also interested in *kendo*. He often practices it with Masato. They have had a great time together. But Tom is going to leave Japan and go back to London this July.

On Saturday in June, Masato and Tom went to school to practice *kendo*. After they finished practicing *kendo*, they talked about their homework. It was still difficult for Tom to do homework for Japanese classes alone, so they often did it together and Masato helped Tom. The homework for the weekend was to make *tanka*. They learned about *tanka* in a Japanese class. Tom said, "I don't know how to make *tanka* well. Show me your *tanka* first, please!" Masato said, "　ア　 I wish I could show you a good one, but making *tanka* is also not easy for me."

Then, Ms. Oka, the teacher of *kendo*, came to them and said, "　イ　 Are you talking about *tanka*?" Masato remembered that Ms. Oka loved making *tanka*. Masato sometimes saw her good *tanka* in the school newspaper. Masato said, "Yes. We're trying to make *tanka*, but we have no idea. Could you tell us how to make it? It's our homework!" Ms. Oka smiled and said, "OK. 　ウ　 You can make *tanka* freely." "Freely? But *tanka* has a rule about rhythm," Masato said. She said, "Of course it has some rules. 　エ　 But I think the most important thing is to make *tanka* freely with the words born from your heart. Talk with your heart. Then, you can make good *tanka*."

Masato repeated Ms. Oka's words in his heart and remembered the days with Tom. He thought, "We have enjoyed many things. Saying good-bye to Tom will be sad. But we have to grow in each place for our future. It may be hard but I believe we can."

Masato decided to make *tanka* about this feeling and send it to Tom. He thought it would be a good present.

When Masato and Tom left school, Masato looked up at the sky. It was so blue. They stopped and looked at it for a while together. Then, Masato started making his first *tanka* for Tom.

(注) rhythm　リズム（ここでは短歌の５－７－５－７－７のリズムのこと）

heart　心　　good-bye　さようなら

present　贈り物

for a while　しばらくの間

(1) 次の英文が入る最も適切な箇所を，本文中の　ア　～　エ　から選び，記号で答えなさい。

Making *tanka* is not so difficult.

(2) 次の(a)～(d)の質問に対する答えとして，本文の内容に合う最も適切なものを，それぞれ１～４から選び，記号で答えなさい。

(a) What do Masato and Tom usually enjoy together?
1. Creating a story about *kendo*.
2. Studying English.
3. Talking about *manga*.
4. Listening to *tanka*.

(b) Why did Masato and Tom often do homework for Japanese classes together?
1. Because Tom needed Masato's help to do it.
2. Because Masato was interested in teaching.
3. Because Tom liked Japanese classes very much.
4. Because making *tanka* was easy for Masato.

(c) How did Masato know that Ms. Oka made good *tanka*?
1. By buying Ms. Oka's book.
2. By learning about it in a Japanese class.
3. By talking with Tom.
4. By reading the school newspaper.

(d) What did Masato decide to make *tanka* about?
1. About a good present from Masato to Tom.
2. About the memories with Tom and their future.
3. About the beautiful blue sky in July.
4. About Ms. Oka's words to Masato.

(3) 次は，本文の内容についての【質問】である。この【質問】に対する適切な答えとなるように，【答え】の下線部に適切な英語４語を書きなさい。

【質問】

According to Ms. Oka, what should Masato do to make good *tanka*?

【答え】

He should ＿＿＿＿＿＿＿＿＿ and make *tanka* freely.

＜山口県＞

---

4 次の英文は，少年のルーク（Luke）と彼が住む町についての物語です。これを読んで，あとの(1)～(3)の問いに答えなさい。

Some families lived in a small village. They had a good life. Some people grew rice and vegetables, and others went fishing. So they could share food. Also, children could play around the village. The village was so beautiful that many people went there for a picnic. Some of them loved the village and decided to build their own houses there. *Gradually, the number of houses began to *increase.

Several years later, there were many houses and cars. The village *changed into a city. It became very *crowded. Children couldn't play outside, so they had to play *inside their houses. Some children understood that they couldn't play on the streets, but they sometimes did. When they played soccer on the street, they were *scolded by car drivers. "It's dangerous! Don't play here," they were told. Children wanted to play outside, but *nobody shared any places with them.

One day, a 14-year-old boy, Luke, talked with his friends. Luke said, "Let's go to the *city hall. We'll ask the workers to make a park for us." Luke's friends agreed with his idea. They went to the city hall and tried to ask a worker, but the worker said, "Sorry. I have no time to talk with you. We are busy now." They couldn't talk about the park. However, they did not want to *give up.

Then Luke decided to make big *posters which said, "GIVE US A PARK!" Many children who needed a park came together, so they could make a lot of posters. The children brought them to a *main street. They walked along the street and showed the posters to people. Many people weren't interested in the posters. It made Luke sad. However, he continued showing his poster. Little by little, *adults *realized that there were no places for children. The adults began to think about it.

A few days later, an old man gave a *deserted place to Luke. Luke and his friends were able to play soccer on the new ground. Then some people made a *slide for the children, and others *planted some flowers in the ground. Gradually, it became a wonderful park. On the gate there was a message, "This park is for everyone." Anyone could enter the park. Many children and adults came to the new park. Luke always ＿＿＿＿＿ the park with them because it was for everyone.

(注) gradually　徐々に

increase　増える

change(d) into ～　～に変化する

crowded　込み合った

inside ～　～の中で

scold(ed)　叱る　　nobody　誰も～ない

city hall　市役所　　give up　あきらめる

poster(s)　ポスター　　main　主要な

adult(s)　大人　　realize(d)　理解する

deserted place　空き地

slide　すべり台

plant(ed)　植える

(1) 文中の下線部they sometimes didについて，その内

容を示すものは何ですか。次のア〜エのうちから最も適当なものを一つ選び，その記号を書きなさい。

ア．Some children watched soccer games at their homes.

イ．Some children scolded many car drivers.

ウ．Some children played on the streets.

エ．Some children ate many kinds of food.

(2) 次のア〜エのうち，本文の内容と合っているものはどれですか。最も適当なものを一つ選び，その記号を書きなさい。

ア．The workers at the city hall were so kind that they helped Luke.

イ．Luke stopped making a big poster because his friends didn't agree with him.

ウ．Many people walking along the street became interested in Luke's posters quickly.

エ．Some adults understood the children's wish and started to make a park for them.

(3) 文中の [___] に入る最も適当な英語1語を，本文中から抜き出して書きなさい。

<岩手県>

5 次の英文を読んで，問いに答えなさい。

Haruki is a high school student. He has a friend who is also a high school student in America. His name is David. They have been friends for six months. They usually communicate with each other by using online video chat.

One day, Haruki said to his grandfather, "I sometimes get nervous when I talk with David. I make many English mistakes. I'm afraid he doesn't understand my English well." His grandfather said, "Don't worry. If you keep practicing English, you will get better at it."

Later that day, Haruki and David talked online. Haruki said, "David, my school will have a school festival next month. I am a member of the dance team. We want to dance at the festival, but we have a problem." "What is it?" said David. Haruki said, "Our team needs a song for our performance. We have listened to many songs, but they weren't good." David answered that he was a member of a band. He said he would be glad to make a song for Haruki and his dance team. He also said, "We will play the song online when you dance at the festival." Haruki said, "That's great!"

One week later, David sent the song to Haruki by e-mail. Haruki listened to the song with his teammates. Everyone loved it and they started practicing their dance.

The night before the festival, Haruki's grandfather asked, "How do you feel about tomorrow?" Haruki told him that he was worried about it. His grandfather said, "You have practiced a lot. I'm sure you will have fun." Haruki decided to do his best.

The festival day came. Haruki prepared a projector and a computer, and got on the stage with his dance team. Haruki said to the audience, "Please look at the screen. This is David and his band. They will play music for us from America! Please enjoy our performance." The Japanese students and American students started the performance together. The audience thought it was amazing. After the performance, everyone clapped for a long time. Haruki was so happy.

The next day, Haruki talked with David. Haruki said, "Thank you for your help." David told him that he enjoyed making and playing the song. He also said he always enjoyed his conversations with Haruki. Haruki was surprised and said, "Really? I thought it was difficult for you to understand my English." David smiled and said, "You sometimes make small English mistakes, but I can always understand you. I think you are good at speaking English." Haruki felt relieved.

Haruki wrote a message to himself in a notebook. "One mistake is not the end. Mistakes happen when you try. Don't be afraid of making mistakes. Let's keep trying."

(注) online　オンラインの，オンラインで
　　 chat　おしゃべり
　　 mistake(s)　間違い
　　 teammate(s)　チームメート
　　 projector　プロジェクター
　　 clap　拍手する
　　 relieved　安心した

問．本文の内容から考えて，次の1〜4の問いの答えとして最も適切なものを，それぞれ下のア〜エから一つ選び，その記号を書きなさい。

1．What did Haruki's grandfather say about Haruki's English?

ア．Haruki's grandfather said that Haruki was good at speaking English.

イ．Haruki's grandfather said that he couldn't understand Haruki's English.

ウ．Haruki's grandfather said that Haruki made too many English mistakes.

エ．Haruki's grandfather said that Haruki could improve his English by practicing.

2．What happened on the day of the school festival?

ア．The audience prepared a projector and a computer.

イ．The audience saw Haruki on the screen.

ウ．Haruki introduced David and his band to the audience.

エ．Haruki received the song from David by e-mail.

3．Which is true about David?

ア．He is a member of the dance team.

イ．He went to Haruki's school and played music on the stage.

ウ．He gets nervous when he talks with Haruki.

エ．He enjoyed helping Haruki.

4．What does Haruki believe now after his experience?

ア．"It is more interesting to study English at school than at home."

イ．"It is more important to keep trying than to worry."

ウ．"Joining a band with friends is exciting."

エ．"Using online video chat after school is difficult."

<高知県>

6 次の英文は，イギリス出身の教育者であり宣教師（missionary）でもあったエミー・カーマイケル（Amy Carmichael）さんの話です。これを読んで，(1)～(6)の問いに答えなさい。

Amy Carmichael was born in a village in England in 1867. Her parents always worked hard to help other people. She was the oldest of her brothers and sisters. When Amy was a little girl, she liked to do dangerous things outside with her brothers. So, her mother said, "Don't do such things." Amy listened to her mother because she wanted to help people as a missionary like her parents in the future. She decided to be a good girl and helped her parents well. She also *prayed to *God every night with her parents.

One morning, Amy stood in front of the mirror. She was sad because she didn't like her brown eyes. Her mother had clear blue eyes and Amy wanted eyes like her mother's. "Why do I have brown eyes?" Amy wondered. "If I had blue eyes, I would be pretty," Amy said to her mother. "I love your brown eyes," her mother said. That night, Amy prayed to God because she thought that God can do anything. "Please, please give me blue eyes." The next morning, Amy ran to the mirror (A)in anticipation. But her eyes were still brown. Amy cried because God didn't answer her wish. Her mother told her, "Your eyes are so beautiful. You don't have to change the color of your eyes. I love you, Amy."

When Amy was twenty-seven years old, she went to India as a missionary. At that time in India, poor people often left their children at *facilities because they couldn't take care of them. But even in facilities, there was not enough food. One day, Amy met a girl who ran out of a facility. She looked hungry and weak. After talking with her, Amy knew that the girl was seven years old and lived in very difficult conditions at the facility. She said to Amy, "There are a lot of other children like me in the facility." When Amy heard (B)this, she decided to take action to help them.

First, she had to meet and talk with the leader of the facility, but (C)it was hard for her to meet him. In those days, in India, people from other countries couldn't enter the facility. So, she had to change her *skin color and wear Indian clothes. She stood in front of the mirror and put coffee powder on her face to change her skin color.

Then, Amy remembered what she prayed for in her childhood. "If I had (a) eyes, I couldn't be like Indian people. I can change my skin color with coffee powder, but I cannot change the color of my eyes. I don't need blue eyes," she thought. "My mother was right."

After she met the leader of the facility, Amy wrote some books about the children in the facilities. Then people in the world learned about the children and the government in India had to make laws to protect them.

Thanks to her (b) eyes, she could save a lot of children in India. "I'm proud of myself and the color of my eyes. I realize I am worth living," said Amy. When Amy understood this, she loved herself

more.

She spent all her life in India and saved more than 1,000 children.

(注) pray 祈る　God 神　facility 施設　skin 肌

(1) 下線部(A)in anticipationの意味として最も適切なものを，本文の内容から判断して次のア～エから1つ選んで記号を書きなさい。
　ア．反省して　　イ．疲弊して
　ウ．期待して　　エ．回復して

(2) 下線部(B)thisの指している内容を，次のア～エから1つ選んで記号を書きなさい。
　ア．Amy's brothers liked to do dangerous things.
　イ．Amy's eyes were beautiful.
　ウ．The girl was seven years old.
　エ．Many hungry children were in the facility.

(3) 下線部(C)it was hard for her to meet himの理由を，日本語で書きなさい。

(4) 本文の内容から判断して，(a)，(b)に当てはまる最も適切な英語1語を，本文中から抜き出してそれぞれ書きなさい。

(5) 本文の内容と合っているものを，次のア～カから2つ選んで記号を書きなさい。
　ア．Amy liked to play inside with her older brothers and sisters.
　イ．Amy had a color of eyes that was different from her mother's.
　ウ．Amy went to India when she was a little girl.
　エ．Amy used coffee powder to meet the leader of the facility.
　オ．Amy wrote some books to introduce England.
　カ．Amy returned to England after working as a missionary.

(6) 次の英文は，ある生徒が本文を読んで考えをまとめたものです。①，②に当てはまる最も適切な英語1語を，下のア～オから1つずつ選んで記号を書きなさい。

I like two things about Amy's story. First, Amy was strong and learned to (①) everything about herself. Second, Amy didn't (②) helping children even in difficult situations. Amy made many children in India happy. I want to be a person like her.

　ア．hurt　　イ．stop　　ウ．start
　エ．answer　　オ．accept

〈秋田県〉

7 下の英文を読んで，(1)～(4)の問いに答えなさい。

Kazuma is a high school student and studies English very hard. Last year, his teacher, Ms. Aoki, said, "Kazuma, you study English very hard. You can join a special English learning program in a high school in America this summer. I am sure that it will be a wonderful experience. You can learn English with students from other parts of the world." Kazuma *became interested in the program. He thought, "This will be a good chance to learn English in America. It will be exciting." ⬚1⬚ Then, he decided to join the program.

When Kazuma arrived at the school in America, he was very excited because he *was confident in his English. On the first day of the program, Kazuma joined five lessons and studied with twenty-five students from different places around the world. They had their own goals for their future. A few days later, Kazuma thought that the lessons in the school *were very different from the ones in Japan. The students had to read a lot for the lessons. During the lessons, they needed to talk about the books they read at home. They had their own *opinions and shared them during the lessons. Kazuma understood what other students said. ［＿＿＿2＿＿＿］ He felt alone. He lost his *confidence. He remembered Ms. Aoki's words. She said, "It will be a wonderful experience," but he did not think it was wonderful.

One week later, one of Kazuma's teachers talked to him after school. ［＿＿＿3＿＿＿］ He said, "How is your life in America?" Kazuma told the teacher, "Other students really do well in lessons but I can't." The teacher told him, "This school has special teachers who support students. You should go and ask them. I'm sure you can get a lot of *advice from them and find better ways of learning."

The next day, Kazuma went to the special teachers' room. He met one of the teachers, Ms. Smith. ［＿＿＿4＿＿＿］ He told her about his problems and she listened to him carefully. Then she asked some questions about his lessons. He answered the questions *honestly. When he talked with Ms. Smith, Kazuma thought he should change his ways of learning. After that, he tried to read books more carefully to have his own opinions when he was doing his homework. Then he started doing better in lessons because he *became able to share his opinions in English. He became confident again and his English improved. The program was a wonderful experience for him.

(注) become interested in 〜　〜に興味をもつ
be confident in 〜　〜に自信のある
be different from 〜　〜とは異なる
opinion(s)　意見
confidence　自信
advice　助言，アドバイス
honestly　正直に
become able to 〜　〜できるようになる

(1) 本文の内容に合う文を，次のア〜クの中から三つ選んで，その記号を書きなさい。
ア．Ms. Aoki showed Kazuma the English program in Australia.
イ．Kazuma was not interested in joining the program Ms. Aoki talked about.
ウ．Kazuma joined the lessons with the students from different parts of the world in an American school.
エ．Kazuma told his opinions to other students on the first day of the English program.
オ．One of Kazuma's teachers told Kazuma that he should ask the special teachers about his problems.
カ．Kazuma didn't visit the special teacher because he did well in lessons.
キ．Ms. Smith asked a lot of questions when she talked with Kazuma's teacher.

ク．Kazuma thought his experience became wonderful after he talked with Ms. Smith.

(2) 次の文は，文中の ［＿1＿］ 〜 ［＿4＿］ のどこに入るのが最も適切か，番号で答えなさい。
However, he couldn't have his own opinions and didn't say anything.

(3) 次の①，②の質問に，それぞれ指定された語数の英文で答えなさい。ただし，符号（，．？！など）は，語数には含まないものとします。
① How many lessons did Kazuma join on the first day in a high school in America？　（4語）
② What did Kazuma think when he talked with Ms. Smith？　（9語以上）

(4) 次は，本文を読んだ高校生のアツシ（Atsushi）と留学生のケリー（Kelly）の対話文です。①，②に入る英文をあなたの立場で，それぞれ15語程度で書きなさい。ただし，符号（，．？！など）は，語数には含まないものとします。
Kelly　　：I think Kazuma's experience in America was good. Tell me your opinion about his experience, Atsushi.
Atsushi：（　①　）
Kelly　　：I understand. What do you usually do to improve your English？
Atsushi：（　②　）
Kelly　　：Oh, that's different from Kazuma's ways of learning.
＜茨城県＞

8 次の英文は，メアリー（Mary）さんとルーク（Luke）さんの物語です。これを読み，あとの各問いに答えなさい。

Mary and Luke are famous musicians. The music they play is beautiful and they are special. Why are they special？

Luke was a high school student in Australia, and playing the piano was his favorite thing to do. On weekends, he often played for five or six hours. One day, when he was going to school, he *was in a car accident and was taken to the hospital. Four months later, he was able to go home, but his life was changed. He couldn't move the left side of his body. He tried to move his left hand many times, but it didn't move. He thought to himself, "I *cannot play the piano anymore." He felt that his whole world *was over. He felt very（　①　）.

Mary was an Australian student who wanted to be a piano teacher. She practiced the piano every day to make her dream come true. When she was 15 years old, she became sick and had to stay in the hospital for three months. The doctor said to her, "The right side of your body is weak. We will do our best to help you, but you may not be able to use your right hand." ②It was very difficult for her to believe the doctor's words. She still wanted to be a piano teacher.

A few years later, Mary went to a *community center. She wanted to find something she could do. When the *director was *showing her around, she heard the beautiful sound of the piano. ③She started crying. "Are you OK？" the director asked. "The piano brings back memories. It brings back the dreams I had for my future." The director looked at her right hand. Then he said, "Come with me, Mary.

I want you to meet someone." She was surprised to see a man playing the piano beautifully with only one hand. "This is Luke," the director said, "He cannot move the left side of his body because of a car accident, but his love for playing the piano never changed."

Mary walked to Luke and said, "Nice to meet you, Luke. I'm Mary." "Do you know *Polonaise-Fantaisie?" Mary asked Luke. "Yes, I love it," he answered. "Would you like to play it with me?" Luke asked. ④Together they began to play the piano. The music they played was beautiful. They were not （ ⑤ ） anymore.

Mary says, "⑥When one door is closed, another door opens. I lost my music, but I found Luke. Now I have my music again." Luke says, "Life is sometimes difficult. But if you don't give up your dreams, you can find something you really want to do."

　（注）was in a car accident　交通事故にあった
　　　　not ～ anymore　もう～でない
　　　　was over　終わった
　　　　community center　コミュニティセンター(地域の人々が集まってスポーツや文化的な活動ができる場所)
　　　　director　センター長
　　　　show ～ around　～を案内する
　　　　Polonaise-Fantaisie　「ポロネーズ第7番幻想」(ショパンの代表曲の一つ)

問1．本文の内容から判断して，（ ① ）と（ ⑤ ）に共通してあてはまる英語を，1語で答えなさい。

問2．本文の内容から判断して，下線部②の理由として最も適切なものを，次のア～エからひとつ選び，記号で答えなさい。
　ア．Because she was happy with the words of her doctor.
　イ．Because she didn't want to give up her dream.
　ウ．Because she thought she would be able to use her right hand soon.
　エ．Because she was too young to understand the words of her doctor.

問3．本文の内容から判断して，下線部③の理由として最も適切なものを，次のア～エからひとつ選び，記号で答えなさい。
　ア．初めて訪れたコミュニティセンターで，とても緊張していたから。
　イ．コミュニティセンターには，自分がやりたい活動がなかったから。
　ウ．ピアノの音を聞いて，自分がピアノを弾いていた時のことを思い出したから。
　エ．聞こえてきたピアノの演奏がとても上手で，感動したから。

問4．本文の内容から判断して，下線部④の様子を表している絵として，最も適切なものを，
次のア～エからひとつ選び，記号で答えなさい。

問5．下線部⑥について，メアリーさんがこのように述べているのはなぜですか。その理由を，「～から。」に続くように，彼女の経験をふまえて40字以内の日本語で答えなさい。ただし，句読点も1字に数えることとします。

問6．本文の内容をふまえて，次の質問に対するあなたの考えを，10語程度の英語で書きなさい。ただし，I'mのような短縮形は1語として数え，符号（，や．など）は語数に含めないこととします。
質問．What did you learn from the story?
　　　　　　　　　　　　　　　　　　　　　　　＜鳥取県＞

9 次の英文を読み，1～6の問いに答えなさい。

There is a small whiteboard on the *refrigerator at Sarah's house. At first, her mother bought it to write only her plans for the day, but it has a special meaning for Sarah now.

When Sarah was a little girl, she helped her parents as much as she could at home. Her parents worked as nurses. Sarah knew that her parents had many things to do.

When Sarah became a first-year junior high school student, she started to play soccer in a soccer club for girls. Her life changed a lot. She became very busy. Sarah and her mother often went shopping together, but they couldn't after Sarah joined the club. She practiced soccer very hard to be a good player.

One morning, her mother looked sad and said, "We don't have enough time to talk with each other, do we?" Sarah didn't think it was a big problem because she thought it would be the same for other junior high school students. But later ①she remembered her mother's sad face again and again.

Sarah was going to have a soccer game the next Monday. She asked her mother, "Can you come and watch my first game?" Her mother checked her plan and said, "I wish I could go, but I can't. I have to go to work." Then Sarah said, "You may be a good nurse, but you are not a good mother." She knew that it was *mean, but she couldn't stop herself.

On the day of the game, she found a message from her mother on the whiteboard, "Good luck. Have a nice game!" When Sarah saw it, she remembered her words to her mother. "They made her very sad," Sarah thought. ②She didn't like herself.

Two weeks later, Sarah had work experience at a hospital for three days. It was a hospital that her mother once worked at. The nurses helped the *patients and talked to them with a smile. She wanted to be like them, but she could not communicate with the patients well.

On the last day, after lunch, ③she talked about her problem to a nurse, John. He was her mother's friend. "It is difficult for me to communicate with the patients well," Sarah said. "It's easy. If you smile when you talk with them, they will be happy. If you are kind to them, they will be nice to you. I remember your mother. She was always thinking of people around her," John said. When Sarah heard his words, she remembered her mother's face. She thought, "Mom is always busy, but she makes dinner every day and takes me to school. She does a lot of things for me."

That night, Sarah went to the kitchen and took a pen. She was going to write ④her first message to her mother on the whiteboard. At first, she didn't know what to write, but Sarah really wanted to see her mother's happy face. So she decided to write again.

The next morning, Sarah couldn't meet her mother. "Mom had to leave home early. Maybe she hasn't read my message yet," she thought.

That evening, Sarah looked at the whiteboard in the kitchen. The words on it were not Sarah's, instead she found the words of her mother. "Thank you for your message. I was really happy to read it. Please write again." Sarah saw her mother's smile on the whiteboard.

Now, Sarah and her mother talk more often with each other, but they keep writing messages on the whiteboard. It has become a little old, but it *acts as a bridge between Sarah and her mother. They may need it for some years. Sarah hopes she can show her true feelings to her mother without it someday.

（注）refrigerator 冷蔵庫　　mean　意地の悪い
patient(s)　患者　　act(s)　作用する，働く

1．次のア～ウの絵は，本文のある場面を表している。本文の内容に合わないものを一つ選び，その記号を書け。

2．下線部①に関して，次の質問に対する答えを本文の内容に合うように英語で書け。

Why did her mother look sad when she talked to Sarah?

3．下線部②の理由として最も適当なものを下のア～エの中から一つ選び，その記号を書け。
ア．いつも仕事で忙しい母に代わって，Sarahが家事をしなければならなかったから。
イ．Sarahのホワイトボードのメッセージを読んで，母が傷ついたことを知ったから。
ウ．母が書いたホワイトボードのメッセージの内容にSarahがショックを受けたから。
エ．Sarahは，励ましてくれる母に対してひどいことを言ったことを思い出したから。

4．下線部③に関して，SarahがJohnから学んだことを本文の内容に合うように40字程度の日本語で書け。

5．下線部④のメッセージとなるように，Sarahに代わって下の　　　内に15語程度の英文を書け。2文以上になってもかまわない。

Mom,

　　　　　　　　　　　　　　　　Sarah

6．本文の内容に合っているものを，次のア～オの中から二つ選び，その記号を書け。
ア．Sarah and her mother often used the whiteboard to write their plans from the beginning.
イ．Sarah helped her parents do things at home before she began playing soccer with her club.
ウ．During the job experience at the hospital, Sarah talked with John on her last day after lunch.
エ．Sarah wrote her first message to her mother on the whiteboard, but her mother did not answer her.
オ．Sarah can talk with her mother now, so she doesn't write messages on the whiteboard.

〈鹿児島県〉

10 次の文章を読んで，あとの各問いに答えなさい。

Ryota is sixteen and a member of the English club at Hikari High School.

One day after school in July, Ryota and the other members of the English club were going to decide what to do for their next activity. Ryota said, "I like Hikari City, but only a few foreign tourists come to the city. Can we do anything to make foreign tourists more interested in our city?" Mary, one of the members from Australia, said, "Why don't we make a video about Hikari City in English?" All the members said, "(　　①　　)" The leader said, "OK. Let's make a great video and ask the staff members in Hikari City Hall to use it on their website." Then, three members went to Hikari Castle to get information and two members visited Hikari Flower Park to know more about it. Ryota and Mary were talking about Hikari Sunday Market. Mary said, "We can see the market in front of Hikari Station every Sunday. One of my classmates told me about it when I came to this city from Australia last year. I like talking with local people there. We can eat local food." Ryota said, "That's great. We can find something interesting there for our video. Can you go there with me this Sunday?" She said, "Of course."

On the Sunday morning, Ryota and Mary went to Hikari Sunday Market. There were about fifteen stands and some people were buying products there. Mary said, "Look, that is my favorite stand." A woman at the stand was selling juice and cookies. Mary said to her, "Ms. Tanaka, the carrot cookies I bought last week were delicious. What do you recommend today?" The woman smiled and said, "Thank you, Mary. How about fresh tomato juice?" Ryota and Mary had the tomato juice and Ryota said, "Wow, it's delicious. How did you make this delicious juice?" Ms. Tanaka said, "Well, I use my mother's fresh tomatoes. She is a farmer in this city and picks them early in the morning every day." Ryota said to Ms. Tanaka, "I really love this juice." After saying goodbye to Ms. Tanaka, Mary found a new stand. She said, "Look at the stand which sells bags. They are so cute." Ryota agreed and said to Mr. Ito, the man in the stand, "Did you design them?" Mr. Ito said, "Yes. I designed them and the bags' cloth is made in Hikari City." Ryota said, "Sounds interesting." Ryota and Mary walked around the market and enjoyed spending time there.

When Ryota and Mary were going home, he said, "I didn't know about the market at first. However, the people I met there taught me about the market and Hikari City. I understand why you like the market." They decided to go there again the next week and talk to people to get more information.

Four months later, the members of the English club finished making the video and showed it to the staff members in Hikari City Hall. In the video, the members of the club showed some pictures of old walls in the castle, beautiful flowers in the park, and local products in the market, and explained them in English. The leader of the club said to the staff members, "(②   )" Ms. Sato, one of the staff members, said, "We really liked it. We will use it on our city's website for foreign tourists." The leader said, "Thank you." Ryota said, "I hope more foreign tourists will come and enjoy our city."

(Ten years later)

Ryota is a staff member in Hikari City Hall now and helps tourists enjoy the city. Mary is now in Australia, but they are still good friends.

One evening in June, Ryota and Mary were talking online. Mary said, "I'm going to visit Japan with my friend, Kate, next month. Can we meet in Hikari City on the second Sunday of that month?" He said, "Sure. Let's meet at Hikari Station."

That Sunday morning, Mary and Kate were waiting in front of the station, and found Hikari Sunday Market. Then, Ryota came from the market and said to them, "Welcome. Mary, do you remember this market?" Mary said, "Hi! I'm surprised that many foreign tourists are buying local products here. There were only a few foreign tourists ten years ago." He said, "I'm trying to make this market more popular among foreign tourists with some other staff members in the city hall." Mary said to Ryota, "How nice! <u>There are still some stands we showed in the video ten years ago.</u>" He said, "Yes, you can still drink Ms. Tanaka's fresh tomato juice."

(注) activity 活動 leader 部長 stand(s) 屋台
cloth 布 explained 〜 〜を説明した
online オンラインで
remember 〜 〜を覚えている

(1) （ ① ），（ ② ）に入るそれぞれの文として，ア～エから最も適当なものを1つ選び，その記号を書きなさい。

① ア．That's a good idea.
イ．Show me the video you made.
ウ．We didn't know that.
エ．We enjoyed it very much.

② ア．I took the pictures in Hikari City Hall.
イ．I'm going to tell you more about local products.
ウ．We saw a lot of foreign tourists in the city.
エ．We'll be happy if you are interested in our video.

(2) 本文の内容に合うように，下の英文の（ A ），（ B ）のそれぞれに入る最も適当な1語を，本文中から抜（ぬ）き出して書きなさい。

When Ryota was a high school student, he went to Hikari Sunday Market with Mary. Ryota and Mary found some interesting local （ A ）, such as fresh juice and bags. They got more information by （ B ） to people they met in the market.

(3) 下線部にThere are still some stands we showed in the video ten years ago.とあるが，the videoの内容として，ア～エから最も適当なものを1つ選び，その記号を書きなさい。

ア．The video about Hikari High School in English.
イ．The video that shows some places in Hikari City.
ウ．The video taken by foreign tourists in Hikari City.
エ．The video the staff members in Hikari City Hall made.

(4) 本文の内容に合う文として，ア～カから適当なものを2つ選び，その記号を書きなさい。

ア．Ryota asked the other members of the English club to make a video because he wanted foreign tourists to come to Hikari City.
イ．The leader of the English club was going to make a website to show their video to foreign tourists.
ウ．Mary knew about Hikari Sunday Market because one of her classmates told her about it.
エ．Mary bought carrot cookies at Hikari Sunday Market when she went there with Ryota to get information.
オ．After going to Hikari Sunday Market, Ryota asked Mary why she liked the market, but he didn't understand the reason.
カ．When Mary went to Hikari Sunday Market with Kate, she found many foreign tourists there.

＜三重県＞

11 次の文章を読んで，あとの各問に答えよ。
（＊印の付いている単語・語句には，本文のあとに
(注)がある。）

Haruto was a second-year high school student. He had two good friends, Ayaka and Olivia. Olivia was from Australia. One day in May, Ayaka said to Haruto, "I go to a *children's center as a volunteer every Wednesday after school. It's near our school. Some volunteers are needed there. Olivia will join us next week. Can you help us?" Haruto answered, "Me? Do you really think I'll be able to help you? I'm not sure." Ayaka said to him, "Yes, I'm sure you will be able to do that." He finally said yes. Ayaka was happy to hear that.

The next Wednesday, Haruto visited the

children's center with Ayaka and Olivia. There, Ms. Sasaki, one of the *staff members, welcomed them and said, "In our center, please spend a lot of time with the children." She also explained, "This center is used by many children, especially by elementary school students."

In the *playroom, some children were playing. Olivia said to them, "Hi! I'm Olivia, from Australia. I'm studying Japanese, and I want to read picture books to you." Next, Haruto said that he wanted to play together and to teach them math. At that time, one boy was looking down and drawing pictures. Ayaka said, "He is Kazuya, nine years old. He usually comes here after school." Haruto spoke to him with a smile, "Hi! Will you play with me?" Kazuya answered no and continued drawing pictures. Ayaka said to Haruto, "Don't worry." Haruto didn't understand Kazuya's feelings. Ms. Sasaki said, "Kazuya is a very shy boy. To *make friends with him will take a lot of time." Haruto said, "Oh, I see." He said to himself, "It won't be easy to make friends with Kazuya, but I want to build a friendship with him."

One week passed. On the second visit, Haruto and some children were going to play soccer outside. He said to Kazuya, "Join us." Kazuya only said no and kept drawing pictures. That made Haruto disappointed. He thought, "Kazuya doesn't want to talk with me." When he went to the library of the center, Olivia was enjoying reading Japanese picture books with some children there. Ayaka was also helping some children with their homework. They looked happy.

The next week, Haruto didn't try to speak to Kazuya. He helped some children with their homework. That night, Ayaka called him. She said to him, "You didn't speak to Kazuya today. I heard that from him. He looked sad." Haruto was surprised to hear that. He said to himself, "What is the best way to build a friendship with Kazuya? He spends time in drawing pictures in the center. That may be a key." Haruto had an idea about how to build a friendship with Kazuya.

On Wednesday of the next week, Haruto went to the children's center again. It was his fourth visit. He hoped his idea would be *successful. He began to draw pictures on drawing paper. He *noticed that Kazuya was looking at him. Kazuya asked Haruto, "What are you doing?" He looked nervous. Haruto answered, "I'm making *picture-story shows. I'm not good at drawing pictures. Will you help me?" Kazuya thought for a while and said, "Yes, I like drawing pictures." That made Haruto happy. Haruto continued, "After finishing making them, I'll ask Olivia to read them to children here." Kazuya said, "Sounds good."

After that, Kazuya and Haruto started to make picture-story shows together. While drawing, they talked about themselves. Kazuya said, "When I met you for the first time, I was glad that you spoke to me with a smile. But I'm sorry I couldn't say anything." Haruto *nodded and said, "Don't worry about that." Kazuya smiled. Ayaka and some

children came and said, "Your pictures are nice, Kazuya!" Kazuya smiled and said, "Thank you." He looked very happy.

Two weeks later, Kazuya and Haruto finished making their picture-story shows and showed them to Olivia. She said, "They are so beautiful! Good job!" Haruto asked her to read them to children there. She smiled and said, "Of course, I will." Soon, Ms. Sasaki came and said to Kazuya and Haruto, "Oh, wonderful! Now you are good friends!"

(注) children's center　児童館
　　　staff member　職員
　　　playroom　遊戯室(ゆうぎしつ)
　　　make friends with ～　～と友達になる
　　　successful　成功した
　　　notice　気付く
　　　picture-story show　紙芝居(かみしばい)
　　　nod　うなずく

〔問1〕　Haruto didn't understand Kazuya's feelings. の内容を，次のように書き表すとすれば，□□□の中に，下のどれを入れるのがよいか。

　　Haruto didn't understand □□□□.

ア．why Kazuya wanted to speak to him

イ．why Kazuya answered no and continued drawing pictures

ウ．why Kazuya wanted him to play together and to teach math

エ．why Kazuya told Ayaka about drawing pictures

〔問2〕　次のア～エの文を，本文の内容の流れに沿って並べ，記号で答えよ。

ア．Ayaka called Haruto and told him about Kazuya.

イ．Olivia looked happy when she was reading Japanese picture books with some children.

ウ．Olivia said that the picture-story shows made by Kazuya and Haruto were very beautiful.

エ．Ayaka was happy to hear that Haruto decided to go to the children's center.

〔問3〕　次の(1)～(3)の文を，本文の内容と合うように完成するには，□□□の中に，それぞれ下のどれを入れるのがよいか。

(1)　When Ayaka told Haruto about the children's center, □□□□.

　ア．he was not sure that he would be able to help her

　イ．he wanted Olivia to join them every Wednesday after school

　ウ．he hoped that some volunteers were needed at the children's center

　エ．he learned it was used by many children, especially by elementary school students

(2)　When Haruto spoke to Kazuya on the second visit, □□□□.

　ア．he didn't think that making friends with Kazuya would take a lot of time

　イ．he was surprised to hear that Kazuya went to the library of the center

　ウ．he thought Kazuya wanted to play together in the playroom

　エ．he was disappointed that Kazuya said no and kept drawing pictures

(3)　On the fourth visit, Haruto was happy to hear

that _____ .
　ア．Kazuya liked Haruto's pictures
　イ．Kazuya would help him with picture-story shows
　ウ．Kazuya wanted to play with other children
　エ．Kazuya was going to play soccer with him

〔問4〕　次の⑴, ⑵の質問の答えとして適切なものは, それぞれ下のうちではどれか。
⑴　How did Kazuya feel when he met Haruto for the first time?
　ア．He was sad because he wanted to continue drawing pictures.
　イ．He felt that it wouldn't be easy to make friends with Haruto.
　ウ．He felt that it was easy to talk with Haruto.
　エ．He was glad that Haruto spoke to him with a smile.
⑵　How did Haruto build a friendship with Kazuya?
　ア．He did it by reading picture-story shows with other children.
　イ．He did it by asking Olivia to read picture-story shows to children with them.
　ウ．He did it by understanding what Kazuya liked and doing something together.
　エ．He did it by asking Kazuya to play with other children.

〈東京都〉

12 Read the passage and choose the answer which best completes each sentence ⑴, ⑵, ⑷, ⑸ and ⑹, and choose the answer to the question ⑶.

Have you heard the word "nudge"? It is an English word which means "to push someone softly to get the person's attention." People usually nudge someone when they want to make someone do something without talking to the person. However, the word has a wider meaning in the theory called "nudge theory." According to the theory, people tend to choose to do something that is easy. They sometimes don't do something they should do because doing it is a little difficult for them. But, if there is a special situation which makes doing it easy, the special situation has an influence on their actions, and they will do it. In the theory, "nudging" means ____①____

Here is an example of "nudging" which has an influence on many people's actions. In 2020, the Japanese government did research to find how the government could help people reduce the number of plastic bags they use when they shop. In the research, the government made a special situation for the convenience stores which joined the research. In convenience store A, if shoppers don't need a free plastic bag, they show a 'Refusal Card' to a clerk. If they don't show the card, they get a free plastic bag when they pay for their shopping. In convenience store B, if shoppers want to get a free plastic bag, they show a 'Request Card' to a clerk. If they don't show the card, they don't get a free plastic bag. Each convenience store has only

one type of card: 'Refusal Card' or 'Request Card.' Here are the results of the research. In convenience store A, the number of shoppers who didn't get free plastic bags didn't change very much from the number before. However, in convenience store B, the number became clearly bigger than the number before. Before the research, to get a free plastic bag, shoppers did nothing. However, during the research, doing nothing became a part of a special situation. In convenience store A, doing nothing meant shoppers wanted to get a free plastic bag. In convenience store B, doing nothing meant shoppers didn't want to get a free plastic bag. The special situation of convenience store B helped more people reduce the number of plastic bags they use when they shop.

By "nudging," you can also help yourself do something you should do. Please imagine that you want to get up at five and study for one hour before going to school. In the morning, your alarm clock rings at five. If the alarm clock is ____②____ to the bed, you can easily stop it without getting out of the bed. After that, you may sleep again. However, if you make the situation a little different, you can get up at five and study. For example, you put the alarm clock far from the bed and put your textbooks next to the alarm clock before going to bed. The next morning, when the alarm clock rings, you can't stop it if you stay in the bed. ____③____ In this case, to make a special situation means to put the alarm clock far from the bed and the textbooks next to the alarm clock. The special situation can help you get out of the bed and start to study.

Sometimes, "nudging" is to make a small ____④____ in the situation, but it can sometimes have a great influence on people's actions. Now, many people in the world are interested in "nudging." They think "nudging" is one way of solving various problems, and they are trying to learn how they can use "nudging" to solve them.

(注) nudge　(注意をひくために)そっと突く
　　　softly　そっと　　theory　理論
　　　nudge theory　ナッジ理論
　　　tend to ～　～する傾向がある　　shopper　買い物客
　　　Refusal Card　辞退カード
　　　Request Card　要求カード　　result　結果
　　　alarm clock　めざまし時計　　ring　鳴る

⑴　The phrase which should be put in ____①____ is
　ア．"to make a situation which makes something more difficult."
　イ．"to make a special situation which helps someone do something the person should do."
　ウ．"to let someone do something without having any influence on the person's action."
　エ．"to ask someone what the person should do and tell the person how to do it."
⑵　The word which should be put in ____②____ is
　ア．close．　イ．different．
　ウ．open．　エ．similar．
⑶　The following passages ⒤～⒲ should be put in ____③____ in the order that makes the most sense.

(i) After stopping it, you find your textbooks next to the alarm clock and remember that you have to study.

(ii) Then, you don't go back to the bed, and you start to study.

(iii) To stop the alarm clock, you have to get out of the bed, and go to it.
Which is the best order?
ア．(ii) → (iii) → (i)　　イ．(ii) → (i) → (iii)
ウ．(iii) → (i) → (ii)　　エ．(iii) → (ii) → (i)

(4) The word which should be put in 　④　 is
ア．difference.　　イ．mistake.
ウ．technology.　　エ．wish.

(5) According to the passage, in convenience store B,
ア．clerks in the convenience store told shoppers to shop without getting free plastic bags.
イ．shoppers showed a 'Refusal Card' to a clerk if they didn't need a free plastic bag.
ウ．shoppers showed a 'Request Card' to a clerk when they wanted to buy a plastic bag.
エ．the number of shoppers who didn't get free plastic bags became bigger than the number before.

(6) According to the passage,
ア．people talk to someone when they push the person softly.
イ．the nudge theory says that people always do something they should do.
ウ．many people in the world think "nudging" can be used to solve various problems.
エ．the Japanese government did the research to help people get free plastic bags when they shop.

〈大阪府・C問題〉

13 次の文章を読んで，あとの各問に答えなさい。
（＊印のついている単語・語句には，本文のあとに(注)がある。）

When spring comes, I miss "sakura," cherry trees. I'm not talking about the cherry trees in Japan. You can find them along *the Potomac in *Washington, D.C. The image of those beautiful pink and white blossoms still stays in my mind.

When I was nine years old, my father was *transferred to the U.S. and all my family moved to a small town near Washington, D.C. I was very shocked to hear this. I said no. I told my mother that I would stay with my grandparents. I didn't think I could survive because I knew almost no English. I couldn't imagine living in the U.S. and going to elementary school there. Then, my mother said she understood my feelings. However, (1)she 【 ① my father　② to go　③ me　④ wanted　⑤ that　⑥ her and me　⑦ told 】 together. She added, "Living in the United States will be a very precious experience for all of us. If there is a difficulty, I am sure we can solve it together." My father also said, "Don't worry. (2)If it happens, it happens." He is such a positive

person. I only felt worried, but I finally agreed.

Then, in 2017, our family started living in the town with just over 2,000 people. It had only one elementary school, and my parents chose that local school. They thought learning there would be perfect for my future. Imagine this. You are a student who has just moved to a foreign country and you do not understand the language used there. I felt that (3)I was just like a baby deer walking alone in the woods. *Getting used to a new school abroad and understanding most of the classes seemed almost impossible. Surprisingly, however, I quickly found I was wrong. The school had an excellent support program for kids like me. Every student and teacher welcomed and helped me in many ways.

A few months later, in a history class, we had a *pair work activity to write a report about something or someone unique in American history. I worked with Jack. I knew his face because he was our neighbor. However, I had no chance to talk with him. He looked sad, but said, "Jun, I have long wanted to talk to you, but I didn't know what to say." By working together, I soon discovered he was very kind and honest. He was interested in Japanese things. We liked sports, music, and drawings. He said to me, "Why don't we write about *the Lincoln cent? You know the penny, one-cent coin. Lincoln was the sixteenth president and *the Lincoln Memorial is one of the most visited places." (4)I said yes to his idea immediately. This is the report we wrote.

Our topic is about the Lincoln cent. The U.S. has been making the penny since 1793. Since 1909, the penny has had the face of Abraham Lincoln. On the front side, the words "In God we trust" are at the top. The designer of the Lincoln cent said, "I have made a smiling face of Lincoln. I imagined he was talking to children. Of all the U.S. coins, Lincoln is the only president *facing to the right."

In 1959, the back side of the penny was changed to a picture of the Lincoln Memorial, and the penny became the only U.S. coin to show the same person on both sides. Even many Americans do not know that the back of a Lincoln memorial cent has a very tiny President Abraham Lincoln sitting in his chair in the middle of the memorial. If you know he is there, you can find it with your eyes. But you can certainly see it with a good *microscope. When you turn the coin from left to right, the back side is *upside down.

In 2009, the U.S. stopped producing the Lincoln Memorial cent, but the government made four special pennies to celebrate Abraham Lincoln's 200th birthday. The image of Lincoln remained on the front and the back included four different designs from important stages of Lincoln's life. In 2010, a new Lincoln penny with a different back design appeared.

Lincoln did not have an easy life when he was a child. He went to school for only one year. But he loved studying and learned from borrowed books. His love of books changed his life and he changed the world. Even people today respect him as one of the greatest leaders in American history. There is something *nostalgic and sacred about Lincoln pennies, so people love these coins and want to keep using them.

Thanks to this class, Jack and I became very close friends. He helped me with my English. I taught him about Japanese things. We spent most of our time together during my stay in the U.S. *Gradually, my English improved and I *made progress in my subjects. I was really enjoying myself in the U.S.

One day at the end of my first school year, Jack and I decided to *save pennies in bottles to help people in need. Our rule is simple. We can put some pennies in our bottles when we have a happy day, when we get a good grade on a test, get a hit in a baseball game, eat delicious food, and help someone …. Each of us saved over two thousand pennies. We are still saving small coins and our bottles are almost full.

Suddenly, the time to say good-bye came. My family was moving back to Japan in May. I really liked living there, so I thought it was impossible to tell him so. Then, (5)I invited him to the Lincoln Memorial. I decided to let him know there.

Around the Lincoln Memorial, you can see a lot of cherry blossoms from March to April. It was in early April, and a beautiful day. We walked around *the National Mall and enjoyed cherry blossoms a lot. We were able to see the Lincoln Memorial through the cherry blossoms. That was awesome. There I told Jack that my family was leaving America. He kept silent, but we cried and cried. I was remembering that day in history class. He was so kind that he asked me to write about the Lincoln cent together. In the U.S., I found a fantastic friend and learned many valuable things. I really felt I belonged there. When I close my eyes, I can still remember those beautiful cherry blossoms.

Now I am back in Japan. I am in the 9th grade and preparing for the important exam in February. Jack and I exchange e-mails almost every day. We chat a lot online. I feel we are still close neighbors. Through living in America, I have become more positive, curious, and friendly. (6)If you have a problem, there's always a way to get out. You never know until you try. Trust yourself and do your best.

(注) the Potomac　ポトマック川
　　　Washington, D.C.　ワシントンD.C.
　　　transferred to ～　～に転勤になる
　　　get used to ～　～に慣れる
　　　pair work　ペアワーク
　　　the Lincoln cent　リンカーン大統領生誕100年を記念して作られた1セント硬貨
　　　the Lincoln Memorial　リンカーン大統領の功績を記念して，1922年に作られた記念館
　　　facing to ～　～の方を向いている

microscope　顕微鏡
upside down　上下逆さまの
nostalgic　感傷的な
gradually　少しずつ
make progress　進歩する
save　貯（た）める
the National Mall　ワシントンD.C.の中心部に位置する国立公園

〔問1〕 (1)she 【 ① my father　② to go　③ me　④ wanted　⑤ that　⑥ her and me　⑦ told 】together.とあるが，本文の流れに合うように，【　】内の単語・語句を正しく並べかえたとき，2番目と4番目と7番目にくるものの組み合わせとして最も適切なものは次のア〜カの中ではどれか。

	2番目	4番目	7番目
ア	①	③	②
イ	①	⑤	③
ウ	③	①	②
エ	③	④	⑥
オ	⑥	①	⑦
カ	⑥	⑤	③

〔問2〕 (2)If it happens, it happens.とあるが，その表す意味として最も適切なものは次の中ではどれか。
　ア．You need to wait long before you know what will happen in the future.
　イ．You will wait and see what will happen in the future.
　ウ．If you know the future, it can be changed as you like.
　エ．Knowing what will happen in the future is very helpful.

〔問3〕 (3)I was just like a baby deer walking alone in the woods.とあるが，この文の表す内容を20語以上の英語で説明しなさい。英文は二つ以上にしてもよい。
　　なお，「,」「.」「?」などは語数に含めないものとする。I'llのような「'」を使った語やe-mailのような「-」で結ばれた語はそれぞれ1語と扱うこととする。

〔問4〕 (4)I said yes to his idea immediately.とあるが，その内容を次のように書き表すとすれば，　　　　の中にどのような英語を入れるのがよいか。本文中の連続する8語で答えなさい。
　　He asked 　　　　　　　, and I agreed with him right away.

〔問5〕 (5)I invited him to the Lincoln Memorialとあるが，JunはJackに何と言ったのか。文脈に合うように自分で考えて，以下の　　　　に入る表現を，20語以上の英語で書きなさい。英文は二つ以上にしてもよい。
　　なお，I said to Jackと「,」「.」「?」などは語数に含めないものとする。I'llのような「'」を使った語やe-mailのような「-」で結ばれた語はそれぞれ1語と扱うこととする。
　　I said to Jack, "　　　　　　　　"

〔問6〕 (6)If you have a problem, there's always a way to get out.とあるが，この文の内容と，ほぼ同じ意味を持つ発言を本文中から探し，その始めの2語と終わりの2語を答えなさい。なお，「,」「.」「?」などは語数に含めないものとする。

〔問7〕 本文から判断し，次の質問の答えとして正しいものはどれか。
　　If you turn the Lincoln Memorial cent from left to right, which images do you find?

ア
表　　裏

イ
表　　裏

ウ
表　　裏

エ
表　　裏

〔問８〕　本文に書かれている内容に関して，次のように表現したとき，空所に入る適切な英語１語を本文中から探して，その語を答えなさい。

Jack and Jun didn't put any pennies in their bottles when their day was _____ .

〔問９〕本文の内容と合っているものを，次のア〜クの中から一つ選びなさい。

ア．In 2017, Jun's family began to live in a small town with around 1,000 people near Washington, D.C.

イ．Right after Jun started going to school in the U.S., he found his idea about the school there was true.

ウ．Jack wanted to speak to Jun for a long time, but he didn't know how to begin talking to Jun.

エ．It is easy to find Abraham Lincoln on both sides of the Lincoln Memorial cent with your own eyes.

オ．The U.S. government stopped making Lincoln pennies forever in 2010.

カ．Lincoln pennies are respected because they remind American people of his love of books.

キ．Jack and Jun saved almost 4,000 pennies and gave them to people in need.

ク．Jack and Jun are living close to each other now, and they often visit each other's houses.

＜東京都立国立高等学校＞

14 次の文章を読んで，あとの各問に答えなさい。
（＊印の付いている単語・語句には，本文のあとに（注）がある。）

Many students from foreign countries are studying traditional Japanese culture in Tamadaira University. Today, they are listening to a lecture on Rakugo by a Japanese Rakugo *storyteller.

Rakugo is traditional Japanese *storytelling of funny stories about people's lives. Rakugo has a long history. People say that Rakugo first came from a book called "Sei Sui Shou" in 1623. The writer was Sakuden Anrakuan. The book has a lot of funny stories about people's lives. Some stories in it are still told today.

It is difficult to know who the first Rakugo storyteller was. ☐(1)-a ☐(1)-b ☐(1)-c ☐(1)-d

There are two local styles of Rakugo. They are Kamigata Rakugo and Edo Rakugo. Rakugo first became popular around the Kansai area. Then, it also became popular in Tokyo. Today, Rakugo done around the Kansai area is called "Kamigata Rakugo," and Rakugo in Tokyo is called "Edo Rakugo." There are several differences between them. For example, Rakugo storytellers of Kamigata Rakugo use a small desk called *kendai* as a futon, a bathtub, and so on. However, Rakugo storytellers of Edo Rakugo don't use it.

Through its history, Edo Rakugo has decided to use some of the good points of Kamigata Rakugo. One of them is *debayashi*, music played just before Rakugo storytellers go on stage. Kamigata Rakugo was often done outside as a street performance, so *musical instruments such as *taiko*, a Japanese drum, were used to *attract the attention of people walking by the street. During the Taisho period, a lot of Rakugo storytellers in Edo went to Kyoto for work. At that time, they thought using *debayashi* was a nice idea. When they came back to Edo, they started to use it on the stage. Now, *debayashi* is usually used in Edo Rakugo.

Rakugo has a history of about 400 years. (2)Why has it attracted people for such a long time? In my opinion, Rakugo attracts many people because it is about the life of *ordinary people. Many people *empathize with the stories because ordinary people are the main characters. Usually, they aren't very rich, and most of them do their best to live every day. Sometimes, they solve their difficulties or problems because they are *tough or clever. Also, Rakugo stories are often about mistakes or *weaknesses of people. Usually, the characters in Rakugo aren't perfect. When you listen to Rakugo, you feel *relieved to know that no one is perfect.

You can understand Rakugo better if you learn about another traditional storytelling called "Kodan." Kodan and Rakugo seem similar. Both storytellers wear kimono and speak alone on the stage. But there is a great difference between Kodan and Rakugo. Rakugo is about ordinary people, but Kodan is usually about great people. While Rakugo often tells us about mistakes or weaknesses of people, Kodan stories tell us about the histories of great people and encourage us to live like them. Kodan became popular among samurai in the Edo period because it was about how to live as a samurai. It was also used to teach children the history and *courtesy of samurai. Even today, some Kodan stories are made into movies or dramas. Do you know about Chushingura, or the forty-seven ronin? This story is very popular. It is about brave samurai. Forty-seven of the Asano *clan's samurai tried to hurt Kouzukenosuke Kira to show that they were *faithful. We can say that this story is about faithful samurai.

Some Rakugo storytellers, on the other hand, have (3)a different opinion about Chushingura. Danshi Tatekawa, a famous Rakugo storyteller, was one of them. He said, "Do you really believe that the Asano clan only had forty-seven samurai? I don't think so. I think some of the samurai didn't take part in the *attack. Maybe they told a lie like this: 'I'm sick in bed now.' Maybe they stayed at home and didn't join the attack. Nobody wants to *be in danger, right? Some people may say that such samurai were not faithful, but I disagree because sometimes we can't have such a strong *will. It's difficult to be perfect all the time. Rakugo should be about such *aspects of human nature."

I agree with Mr. Tatekawa's opinion. Sometimes, we can't be perfect. We don't have a strong will every day. We sometimes make mistakes in everyday life and worry about them. When we listen to Rakugo stories, we may learn the following lessons: "You made a mistake this time, but don't worry. It's not the end of the world. Everyone makes mistakes," or "Sometimes you cannot realize your goal because of your weakness or *laziness, but it's OK. Everybody is just like you." Rakugo is not about perfect people or great people, but about ordinary people. Through Rakugo, we can laugh our weakness away and know that everything will be OK.

At the end of my speech, (4)【 ① I ② introduce ③ like ④ of ⑤ one ⑥ Rakugo stories ⑦ the most famous ⑧ to ⑨ would 】 to you. This one is very popular among Rakugo fans. This story is about an ordinary man. He is very tough and clever. Let me begin. On a night in summer, a man was sleeping in his room. He kept all the doors open because it was too hot. Then, a *thief was looking for a house to enter, and he realized that all the doors were open. He decided to enter the house to do his job. He walked into a room and found a man sleeping on a futon. The thief said in a quiet voice, "Give me all your money!" But, to his surprise, the man said, "Oh, are you a thief? I don't care. Let me go back to sleep." The thief said with surprise, "I'm a thief. You're *scared, right?" "No! I'm not ⎡ (5)-a ⎦! I have nothing to lose! I am a carpenter, but I have already sold all my *tools. I cannot go to work anymore," the man answered in a loud voice. "Be quiet, will you? Someone will hear us!" the thief said. At this point, the man realized that this thief was not very ⎡ (5)-b ⎦. He had a good idea. The man kept talking in a ⎡ (5)-c ⎦ voice. The thief said, "Don't be so noisy! Please be quiet!" But the man didn't stop. Finally, the thief gave up and said, "OK, OK. I have an idea. How much were all the tools? I will give you money for them if you stop talking." The man became ⎡ (5)-d ⎦ and the thief gave him the money. Before the thief left the house, the man said to the thief, "Hey, thief! Could you come again next month?" The thief said, "Which one of us is really the ⎡ (6) ⎦?"

Did you find this story interesting? I hope you will become interested in Rakugo. Thank you for listening!

(注) storyteller 話し手
storytelling 物語を話すこと
musical instrument 楽器
attract 引きつける
ordinary 普通の
empathize 共感する
tough たくましい

weakness 弱さ
relieved 安心している
courtesy 作法
clan 一族
faithful 忠実である
attack 襲撃
be in danger 危険である
will 意思
aspect 側面
laziness 怠惰(たい)
thief 泥棒
scared 怖い
tool 道具

〔問1〕 ⎡(1)-a⎦ 〜 ⎡(1)-d⎦ の中には次のA〜Dが入る。本文の流れに合うように正しく並べかえたとき，その組み合わせとして最も適切なものは次のア〜カの中ではどれか。

A. But he changed that old style, so this is why they think he was the first Rakugo storyteller.

B. Some people say Shinzaemon Sorori was the first one, but many Rakugo storytellers today don't think so.

C. Before Karaku, Rakugo was usually played on the streets or in *sushi* or *soba* restaurants.

D. They think Sanshotei Karaku was the first one, because he was the first to do Rakugo in a theater.

	(1)-a	(1)-b	(1)-c	(1)-d
ア	B	A	D	C
イ	D	B	C	A
ウ	D	A	C	B
エ	D	C	A	B
オ	B	D	C	A
カ	B	D	A	C

〔問2〕 (2)Why has it attracted people for such a long time?とあるが，このことに関する本文の記述として適切でないものは次の中ではどれか。

ア. Some characters in Rakugo are clever and tough enough to solve their problems.

イ. Some characters in Rakugo do their best to live although they are not very rich.

ウ. The characters in Rakugo sometimes solve difficulties because they are rich.

エ. The characters in Rakugo are often weak and not perfect, so they make some mistakes.

〔問3〕 (3)a different opinion about Chushinguraとあるが，このことに関する本文の記述として適切なものは次の中ではどれか。

ア. Some Rakugo storytellers think that people should live like the characters in Chushingura.

イ. Some Rakugo storytellers think that the samurai were faithful but couldn't have a strong will.

ウ. Some Rakugo storytellers think that Rakugo should be about great samurai.

エ. Some Rakugo storytellers think that some samurai were not faithful or didn't have a strong will.

〔問4〕 (4)【 ① I ② introduce ③ like ④ of ⑤ one ⑥ Rakugo stories ⑦ the most famous ⑧ to ⑨ would 】とあるが，本文の流れに合うように，【 】内の単語・語句を正しく並べかえたとき，3番目と5番目と7番目にくるもの

の組み合わせとして最も適切なものは次のア～カの中ではどれか。

	3番目	5番目	7番目
ア	⑧	②	④
イ	⑧	⑤	⑦
ウ	②	③	④
エ	②	④	⑥
オ	③	②	④
カ	③	⑧	④

〔問5〕　本文の流れに合うように、[5]-a ～ [5]-d の中に、次の単語を入れるとき、その組み合わせとして、最も適切なものは次のア～カの中ではどれか。

ア．(5)-a　scared　　(5)-b　clever
　　(5)-c　loud　　　(5)-d　quiet
イ．(5)-a　scared　　(5)-b　clever
　　(5)-c　quiet　　　(5)-d　loud
ウ．(5)-a　scared　　(5)-b　surprised
　　(5)-c　loud　　　(5)-d　quiet
エ．(5)-a　surprised　(5)-b　scared
　　(5)-c　noisy　　　(5)-d　quiet
オ．(5)-a　surprised　(5)-b　noisy
　　(5)-c　scared　　(5)-d　loud
カ．(5)-a　surprised　(5)-b　scared
　　(5)-c　noisy　　　(5)-d　loud

〔問6〕　本文の流れに合うように、[6] の中に入る最も適切な1語を本文中から抜き出しなさい。

〔問7〕　本文の内容と合っているものを、次のア～カの中から二つ選びなさい。

ア．Edo Rakugo used musical instruments to attract the attention of people on the street.

イ．Rakugo is usually about ordinary people, so it has attracted many people for a very long time.

ウ．Kodan is similar to Rakugo because both of them tell us about mistakes or weaknesses of people.

エ．Some of the Asano clan's samurai didn't take part in the attack because they were sick in bed then.

オ．When we listen to Rakugo, we can laugh our mistakes or weaknesses away and feel relieved.

カ．The thief decided to enter the house because he found a man sleeping on his futon.

〔問8〕　あなたは海外から日本に来た留学生に向けて、落語の魅力（りょく）を伝える紹介文を書くことになりました。本文を参考にし、自身の言葉を用いて40語以上50語以内の英語で書きなさい。ただし、落語の魅力を具体的に挙げ、その理由等を必ず記述すること。「.」「,」「!」「?」などは語数に含めません。

＜東京都立八王子東高等学校＞

---

②　自然・産業・科学技術

1 次の英文を読んで、あとの問いに答えなさい。

[1]　At the train station, we check information on *electric bulletin boards. For example, if the train does not come on time, we will look at them to check where the train is and how ［　①　］ it is. We also get information from the *speakers. For example, when a train is coming to the station, we will hear the message, "The train is ［　②　］. Please stand behind the yellow blocks for your safety." Like these examples, we ［　③　］ to know the situation at the station, and such information is helpful for us.

[2]　One day, a student missed some information from the speakers. It was difficult for him to hear sounds. He said, "I once had a dangerous experience at the station. When I was just getting on the train, the train closed the door. I didn't notice that because I couldn't hear the sound of the *departure bell. To get the information, I must look at the people around me, and then ［　④　］. I wish there was a machine that could *change sounds into letters and images, and show them on a screen!"

[3]　His wish became a real thing. A company listened to his experience, and made the machine for him. It was put on the *platform. There, when the message, "Thank you for using our train," was announced from the speakers, he could see it on the screen. Also, he saw the sound of the closing door on the screen. Because of this machine, he learned the sound of the closing door for the first time. He said, "Now, I can enjoy a sound that I didn't notice before."

[4]　People who experienced this machine said, "It's wonderful and convenient. I think children can enjoy the machine. For example, when the train is moving, they can see the letters of its sounds on the screen. In addition, foreigners can understand information more easily because English is shown to attract their attention there. I hope this machine will ［　⑤　］."

[5]　One student's idea has given us a chance to think about other people. The student said, "When we had meetings for the machine, I talked a lot with many people. By sharing my opinions with them, the station became more friendly to more people. Like this, if we ［　⑥　］, I think we can make our society better."

（注）electric bulletin boards　電光掲示板
　　　speakers　スピーカー（装置）
　　　departure bell　発車ベル

change ～ into ...　～を…に変える
platform　（駅の）プラットホーム

1．文中の　①　，　②　に入る語の組み合わせとして適切なものを，次のア～エから1つ選んで，その符号を書きなさい。

ア．①　late　　②　arriving
イ．①　late　　②　leaving
ウ．①　much　　②　arriving
エ．①　much　　②　leaving

2．文中の　③　～　⑥　に入る適切なものを，次のア～オからそれぞれ1つ選んで，その符号を書きなさい。

ア．accept and respect different ideas
イ．enjoy announcing information by myself
ウ．judge what I should do
エ．see and hear information
オ．spread to other stations in Japan, too

3．次のA～Dのイラストは，段落[3]と[4]で示されている内容を表したものです。文中で具体的に示されている順序として適切なものを，あとのア～カから1つ選んで，その符号を書きなさい。

A

B

C

D

ア．A → B → C → D
イ．A → B → D → C
ウ．A → C → B → D
エ．A → C → D → B
オ．A → D → B → C
カ．A → D → C → B

〈兵庫県〉

2 次の文章を読んで，あとの(1)から(5)までの問いに答えなさい。

For many people living in Japan, it is easy to get water. But have you (　A　) where water comes from? It comes from forests, and they are about two-thirds of Japan's land. Forests release water and we use it for industry, agriculture, our daily lives, and so on. Forests and water are related to each other.

【　a　】 They are a facility that stores rainwater and water from rivers and releases water any time. Forests have the same role. Rainwater goes into the ground under the forests and turns into clean water through the ground. The ground keeps the water as groundwater and it goes out into the rivers slowly.

【　b　】 There are many trees in forests, and the roots of the trees go down into the ground. In case of rain, they absorb rainwater and hold the ground tightly. Without forests, there would be more landslides in Japan when it rains.

【　c　】 One of the main causes of it is carbon dioxide. Scientists say that the amount of carbon dioxide in the air is getting larger and

larger. The Earth is getting warmer and warmer. Trees absorb carbon dioxide and release oxygen while they are growing. They store carbon dioxide inside for years. The same is true for wood which is cut from a tree. So using even a piece of wood is important to protect the environment.

Could you imagine your life without forests? If there were no forests, you would have to worry about more landslides and environmental problems in the future. It would be more difficult to get water. Forests release water for your daily life. You should remember that many forests are protected by forestry. Forestry keeps the forests safe by repeating the cycle, such as growing, cutting, using and planting trees again, in 50-100 years. Forestry is a sustainable industry.

（注）agriculture　農業
　　　groundwater　地下水
　　　root　根
　　　absorb ～　～を吸収する
　　　cause　原因
　　　forestry　林業
　　　repeat a cycle　循環を繰り返す
　　　grow ～　～を育てる
　　　plant ～　～を植える

(1) 文章中の（　A　）にあてはまる最も適当な語を，次のアからエまでの中から選びなさい。

ア．had　　　　イ．finished
ウ．wondered　エ．been

(2) 次のアからウまでの英文を，文章中の【　a　】から【　c　】までのそれぞれにあてはめて文章が成り立つようにするとき，【　b　】にあてはまる最も適当なものを選びなさい。

ア．Forests keep the land safe.
イ．Forests are like dams.
ウ．Forests stop global warming.

(3) 文章中では，森林についてどのように述べられているか。最も適当なものを，次のアからエまでの中から選びなさい。

ア．About two-thirds of Japanese forests are related to each other.
イ．Thanks to forests, rainwater turns into water for our daily lives.
ウ．Forests on the Earth release more and more carbon dioxide.
エ．In forests, water you need in daily life is protected by forestry.

(4) 次のアからエまでの中から，その内容が文章中に書かれていることと一致するものを一つ選びなさい。

ア．The trees in the forest make the water for companies, fields and towns.
イ．Rainwater in the dam goes into the ground under the forest.
ウ．In case of rain, the land with no trees can cause more landslides.
エ．Forestry keeps growing, cutting, using and planting the woods again in one year.

(5) 次の[メモ]は，この文章を読んだ生徒が森林などについて調べ，授業のまとめの活動として英語で発表するために作成したものの一部です。下線部①，②のそれぞれにあてはまる最も適当なことばを，あとのアからエまでの中から選びなさい。なお，2か所ある下線部①，②には，それぞれ同じことばがあてはまる。

［メモ］

○　日本の森林
・人工林…森林の約4割，人が使うために育てている森林
・天然林…森林の約6割，自然に落ちた種などが成長してできた森林
○　木の使用
・木製品…原材料が　①　をたくわえており，使用することが　②　につながる。
・木造建築物…建設後，何年も　①　を閉じ込めておくことができる第2の森林
○　意見
・木づかい(=「木を使う」という気づかい)の心が，②　につながる。

① ア．二酸化炭素　　イ．酸素
　 ウ．地下水　　　　エ．雨水
② ア．労働災害の防止　　イ．水質汚染の防止
　 ウ．土砂災害の防止　　エ．地球温暖化の防止
〈愛知県〉

3 次の(1)〜(2)の英文を読んで，それぞれの問いに答えなさい。

(1) We blink about 15,000 times in a day. Each blink is only 0.3 seconds long. It means that we (　Ａ　) our eyes for 75 minutes each day when we are awake. Most of us blink about 15 times in a minute, but we don't blink so often when we are concentrating. For example, we usually blink about 15 times in a minute when we are talking with our friends, but when we are reading a book, we blink about (　Ｂ　) times in a minute. So, maybe you are not blinking so much right now because you are concentrating on reading this.

(注) blink まばたきする，まばたき　second 秒
　　 awake 起きている　concentrate 集中する

　本文中の(　Ａ　)，(　Ｂ　)に入る最も適当なものを，それぞれ次のア〜エのうちから一つずつ選び，その符号を書きなさい。

Ａ ア．catch　イ．close　ウ．open　エ．show
Ｂ ア．10　　イ．20　　ウ．30　　エ．40

(2) Do you like tomatoes? Tomatoes originally come from the Andes. They were first brought to Europe in the sixteenth century. Tomatoes were used as decorative plants, so people did not eat them at first. The first man to eat them was from Italy. He was very poor and had nothing to eat. He wanted to eat something, so he decided to eat tomatoes. He found that they were very delicious and sweet at that time. After that, tomatoes were first brought to Japan in the seventeenth century. Today they are sold and eaten around the world, and they are often put in salads. Some people say that we can live longer if we eat them every day. We can say "Thank you" to the man from Italy because our lives became better.

(注) originally come from 〜 〜の原産である
　　 the Andes 南米西部のアンデス山脈
　　 decorative plant 観賞用植物
　　 Italy イタリア

① 本文の内容と合うように，次の英文の(　　　)に入る最も適当な英単語1語を書きなさい。

The man from Italy ate tomatoes for the first time because he was very poor and (　　　　).

② 本文の内容に合っているものを，次のア〜エのうちから一つ選び，その符号を書きなさい。
ア．Tomatoes originally come from Europe, and they were brought to the Andes.
イ．People in Europe enjoyed eating tomatoes before the sixteenth century.
ウ．In the sixteenth century, tomatoes were first brought to Japan.
エ．Some people say that our lives become longer by eating tomatoes every day.
〈千葉県〉

4 次の英文を読んで，後の各問に答えよ。

Hiroshi is a junior high school student. One day in an English class, his teacher said, "We have many kinds of new technology around us. Computers, the Internet, and AI are good examples. Do you know any people who use them well? In our next project, I want you to introduce one person in class." So at home that night, Hiroshi asked his mother, and she said to him, "Your grandmother, Toshiko, uses new technology well."

A few days later, Hiroshi talked with Toshiko on the Internet about the project. She said, "Well, you know I am a fruit farmer. I didn't use technology very much in the past. But now, I use it every day. There are many ①benefits of using new technology. I collect information about the weather from websites. I can understand my fruit's growth by keeping records and can share that information with researchers and farmers who live in other parts of Japan. Then I can get good ideas from them and make my fruit bigger and better. Now I don't need to give water to my fruit trees because AI technology can do ②that job. Also, it is easy for me to sell more fruit by using the Internet. In these ways, new technology has changed my way of working and made it better. On my website, I show other farmers how to use new technology which helps us grow better fruit." Hiroshi decided to talk about her to his classmates.

A month later, Hiroshi made a speech in front of his classmates. After the speech, his classmate, Asuka, said, "In your speech, I like the story of your grandmother's website. She shows her ideas about using new technology for agriculture. I hope people will be interested in her website. If they see it, they will learn her ways to grow fruit. Then, they will be influenced by her and start working like her. I really respect her."

Hiroshi was very happy to hear that. He said to Asuka, "Using new technology in effective ways has been changing the lives of many people. I want to learn about this more and create a better society in the future."

(注) technology 科学技術
　　 project 学習課題，プロジェクト
　　 growth 成長
　　 records 記録
　　 researchers 研究者

grow　栽培する　　agriculture　農業
be influenced　影響を受ける
respect　尊敬する
society　社会

問１．次の質問の答えを，4語以上の英語で書け。
　　　What did Hiroshi use to talk with Toshiko?

問２．下線部①を別の語句で表現する場合，最も適当なものを，次のア～エから一つ選び，記号を書け。
　　　ア．difficult points　　イ．good points
　　　ウ．weak points　　　　エ．same points

問３．下線部②の具体的な内容を，英文中から探し，日本語で書け。

問４．英文の内容に合っているものを，次のア～カから二つ選び，記号を書け。
　　　ア．Hiroshi's teacher told him to introduce one person who used English well.
　　　イ．Hiroshi gave Toshiko some ideas by sharing information about fruit and the weather.
　　　ウ．Toshiko changed her way of working as a fruit farmer by using new technology.
　　　エ．Hiroshi talked with Asuka about his grandmother before he made a speech in front of his classmates.
　　　オ．In Asuka's opinion, people who see Toshiko's website will be influenced by Toshiko's ideas about agriculture.
　　　カ．Hiroshi decided to create a better society without new technology in the future.

問５．次の質問にあなたならどう答えるか。5語以上の英語で書け。
　　　How do you use new technology when you study English?

　　　　　　　　　　　　　　　　　　　＜福岡県＞

5 次の英文を読んで，あとの(1)～(3)に答えなさい。

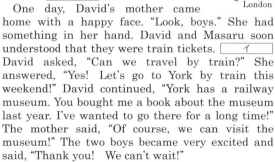

Last summer, Masaru did a homestay in London, the U.K. He stayed with a family with a boy called David. Both Masaru and David were train fans, so they soon became good friends. 　ア　

One day, David's mother came home with a happy face. "Look, boys." She had something in her hand. David and Masaru soon understood that they were train tickets. 　イ　 David asked, "Can we travel by train?" She answered, "Yes! Let's go to York by train this weekend!" David continued, "York has a railway museum. You bought me a book about the museum last year. I've wanted to go there for a long time!" The mother said, "Of course, we can visit the museum!" The two boys became very excited and said, "Thank you! We can't wait!"

On Saturday, they took a train from London to York. On the train, the boys enjoyed seeing cities, mountains and rivers through the windows. Two hours later, they finally got to York and went into the museum just beside the station. The museum was very large, and they were surprised to know that there were about three hundred trains there. Many of them were very old, and they learned many things about the British railway.

Surprisingly, they found a Japanese *Shinkansen*, too. They walked around the museum for almost two hours. 　ウ　

At three, they returned to the station to go home. Then, David suddenly became very excited and said, "Wow, look at that red train!" Masaru asked him, "What's that?" David answered, "It's a train made by a Japanese company. The company designed it with Japanese technology, and it can run very fast. It's so cool!" He continued, "We are very lucky because we can't see it often. We should take it now!" His mother and Masaru agreed, and they got on the train. 　エ　 Masaru learned a lot more about the train from David. Masaru spoke to himself, "The Japanese railway was built 150 years ago with the help of British technology, and now Japanese technology is used to develop the British railway." The strong bond between Japan and the U.K. made him happy.

After his homestay in the U.K., he started to study harder. Now he has a dream of becoming an engineer. He wants to work for a project of the British railway in the future. Japan is now designing a new train that can run the fastest in Europe for the U.K.

(注) homestay　ホームステイ
York　ヨーク(イギリスの都市名)　　railway　鉄道
British　イギリスの　　design ～　　～を設計する
technology　技術　　got on ～　　～に乗り込んだ
bond　絆(きずな)　　Europe　ヨーロッパ

(1)　次の英文が入る最も適切な箇所を，本文中の　ア　～　エ　から選び，記号で答えなさい。
　　　However, the boys didn't feel tired because it was like a dream for them.

(2)　次の(a)～(c)の質問に対する答えとして，本文の内容に合う最も適切なものを，それぞれ１～４から１つずつ選び，記号で答えなさい。

(a)　What did David's mother do to make David and Masaru happy?
　　１．She bought them train tickets to York.
　　２．She gave them movie tickets for train fans.
　　３．She bought them a book with pictures of trains.
　　４．She gave them a book about a railway museum.

(b)　Which was true about the museum Masaru, David and his mother visited?
　　１．It took only an hour from London to the museum by train.
　　２．About three hundred British new trains were seen there.
　　３．It was the best place to learn about the history of London.
　　４．During the stay in the museum, they saw a Japanese train.

(c)　Why did Masaru feel happy when he was on the train from York to London?
　　１．Because so many Japanese *Shinkansen* were running in the U.K.
　　２．Because he liked the train which ran the fastest in Europe.
　　３．Because he learned that Japan worked

together with the U.K.

4．Because the train he took was one of the oldest British trains.

(3) 次の(a)，(b)は，本文の内容についての【質問】と，それに対する【答え】である。(a)の下線部には2語の，(b)の下線部には3語の適切な英語を書き，【答え】を完成させなさい。

(a) 【質問】 What was a special point about the train that Masaru took from York to London?

【答え】 The train was ＿＿＿＿＿＿＿＿ a company with Japanese technology.

(b) 【質問】 Why does Masaru study harder now?

【答え】 To ＿＿＿＿＿＿＿＿ in the future.

〈山口県〉

6 次の英文は，私たちの生活と最新のテクノロジー (technology)の関わりについて述べたものです。これを読んで，あとの(1)～(5)の問いに答えなさい。なお，文中の[1]～[4]は，段落の番号を示しています。

[1] Have you ever thought about new technology in your daily life? Do you have any *items with new technology around you? Our lives have become better and easier because of new technology. However, it may ① ＿＿ cultures or customs. You may lose them in the future.

[2] There are some problems, like our *aging society or many kinds of *disasters in the world. We are trying to find solutions to these problems. One of the solutions is to create ②a new life with new technology. You will be able to do a lot of things you can't do now. Here are some examples. One is *remote *medical care. You can have medical care without going to the hospital. Both *elderly people and young people who can't go to the hospital quickly can have it at home. Another example is that you can get some information about *natural disasters *in advance. By using it, you can be ready for natural disasters and *deal with them *properly. New technology is an important thing to make our lives better. Many people think it is better and easier to live with new technology. However, it sometimes means losing something very important.

[3] Our lives have started to change. Some people can't live in the new way with new technology. So they continue to live in traditional ways. However, other people want to move to a new place with new technology. Many people have moved from their places to new places. So *depopulation has become a problem in some areas. ③Cultures or customs people have in the areas may be lost. So people who live in some towns are trying to protect them. Some people are trying to make food in their traditional way. Others are making their own items with natural resources in the area. Now some people move to these areas because they want to live in a traditional way.

[4] It is important to ④ ＿＿＿ a new life with new technology to make our lives better. Also, it is important to ⑤ ＿＿＿ our traditional things, for example, cultures and customs. We should think about these things for a better future.

(注) item(s) 製品　aging society 高齢化社会　disaster(s) 災害　remote 遠隔の　medical care 医療　elderly 年配の　natural 自然の　in advance 事前に　deal with ～ ～に対応する　properly 適切に　depopulation 人口減少

(1) 文中の ① に入る最も適当な英語は何ですか。次のア～エのうちから一つ選び，その記号を書きなさい。

ア．use　　イ．show　　ウ．live　　エ．change

(2) 文中の下線部②a new lifeについて，本文で述べられていることは何ですか。次のア～エのうちから最も適当なものを一つ選び，その記号を書きなさい。

ア．All people have to go to the hospital when they are sick.

イ．It is one of the problems in the world to create a new life today.

ウ．It is not good for elderly people to live with new technology.

エ．People can know about natural disasters before they happen.

(3) 文中の下線部③Cultures or customs people have in the areas may be lost.について，その原因として段落[2]，[3]で述べられていることは何ですか。次のア～エのうちから最も適当なものを一つ選び，その記号を書きなさい。

ア．In the new places, people have to think about new ways to live because they don't have cultures.

イ．In some areas, people are trying to make their places bigger to create new cultures.

ウ．Many people have moved to new places with new technology because it is easier to live there.

エ．Many people want to keep living in their places because they can't move to new places.

(4) 次のア～エのうち，文中の ④ と ⑤ に入る英語の組み合わせとして最も適当なものはどれですか。一つ選び，その記号を書きなさい。

	④	⑤
ア	create	keep
イ	keep	create
ウ	keep	lose
エ	lose	keep

(5) 次の対話は，本文を読んだ生徒と先生による授業中のやり取りです。対話中の ＿＿＿ に入る最も適当な連続する英語4語は何ですか。本文中から抜き出して書きなさい。

T：Teacher　　S：Student

T：In the future, which do you want, a new life with new technology or a traditional life?

S：It's difficult for me to answer the question.

T：Why?

S：Because now I know that we have to think about the problem of ＿＿＿＿＿＿＿ if we live with new things.

〈岩手県〉

7 次の英文は，京都の２つの会社の取り組みについて述べたものです。これを読んで，あとの(1)〜(5)の問いに答えなさい。なお，文中の①〜④は，段落の番号を示しています。

① What do you do if your favorite things break? Some of you may think, "I should buy a new one." Others may think, "I wish I could use it again." It is true that you can get new things easily today, but is that good? There are companies that *repair old and broken things in Kyoto. They are also trying to protect *traditional Japanese culture. Here are two examples.

montsuki
（紋付）

② One company works hard to keep old clothes and *reuse them by using a traditional Japanese *technique. It is black *dyeing. They have been dyeing *montsuki* for 100 years. *Montsuki* is traditional Japanese *formal wear and its color is black. They hoped their dyeing techniques would be useful for something, so the company started to dye old and dirty clothes in 2013. For the company, it is important to protect their technique, and black is a popular color in fashion. With the company's technique, many people can wear their favorite clothes which are now _____. It is wonderful to continue wearing the clothes without *throwing them away.

③ Second, a *lacquerware company is trying to repair broken things. In Japan, there is a technique called *kintsugi*. It is a technique to repair broken things such as dishes and cups. *Lacquer and *powdered gold are used to *glue the broken parts of the dishes together. Some of you may usually throw away broken things. However, if you repair them by using *kintsugi*, you can use them again and enjoy the beautiful *gold lines. The company also sells a *kintsugi* *kit. When you repair your broken dishes or cups by yourself, you may become more *attached to them. You need many days to repair the cups, but it is easy to understand how to do it by watching a *video. After *kintsugi*, the cups will look more beautiful. So you can have the *kintsugi* experience at home with the kit.

kintsugi
（金継ぎ）

④ Now, there are many cheap things in the world, so you can buy new things easily. However, Japan has traditional techniques to *restore old and broken things. You can use them again if you use these techniques. You will *value your favorite things more than before. Let's think again before throwing away broken things.

(注) repair 修理する　traditional 伝統的な
　　reuse 再使用する　technique(s) 技法
　　dye(ing) 染める　formal wear 正装
　　throw(ing) 〜 away（throw away 〜）〜を捨てる
　　lacquerware 漆器　lacquer 漆
　　powdered gold 金粉
　　glue 〜 together 〜をくっつける
　　gold line(s) 金色のつなぎ目　kit 道具一式
　　attached 愛着がある　video 動画
　　restore 復元する　value 大切にする

(1)　次のア〜エのうち，段落②の内容を示すものとして最

も適当なものはどれですか。一つ選び，その記号を書きなさい。

ア．One company dyes old clothes because new clothes are not cheap.

イ．One company has a traditional technique of dyeing and dyes only *montsuki*.

ウ．One company started to dye and sell *montsuki* in 2013.

エ．One company uses their traditional technique to dye old clothes.

(2)　文中の[　　　]に入る最も適当な英語は何ですか。次のア〜エのうちから一つ選び，その記号を書きなさい。

ア．gold　　イ．cheap　　ウ．broken　　エ．black

(3)　文中の下線部the *kintsugi* experience について，次のア〜エのうち，その内容として正しいものはどれですか。一つ選び，その記号を書きなさい。

ア．People can watch a video to learn how to sell their broken cups.

イ．People can glue the broken parts of their favorite cups together.

ウ．People can dye their favorite clothes to continue wearing the clothes.

エ．People can buy new and beautiful cups from a lacquerware company.

(4)　次の英文は，英語の授業で生徒が*kintsugi*の説明をノートにまとめているものです。[　　　]に入る最も適当な英語５語を書きなさい。

> *Kintsugi* is a traditional Japanese technique to repair broken things. We need lacquer and powdered gold for *kintsugi*. If we use this technique, [　　　　　　].

(5)　次のア〜エのうち，本文の内容に沿ったタイトルとして最も適当なものはどれですか。一つ選び，その記号を書きなさい。

ア．How to Buy Beautiful Things to Protect Japanese Culture

イ．How to Dye Your Favorite Clothes with Japanese Techniques

ウ．How to Reuse Your Favorite Things with Japanese Techniques

エ．How to Throw Away Broken Things to Protect Japanese Culture

〈岩手県〉

8 中学生の絵美(Emi)と彼女の住む町で作られている「あおい焼(Aoi-yaki)」という陶器に関する次の英文を読んで，あとの問いに答えなさい。なお，あとの(注)を参考にしなさい。

One day, when Emi was washing the dishes at home, she dropped a cup and it was broken. Her mother said to her, "Actually, that was your father's favorite cup. He bought it and kept using it for more than ten years. It was *Aoi-yaki*." Emi didn't know (a)that. Emi said to her father, "Sorry. I broke your cup. I will buy a new cup for you." "That's OK. (b)You don't have to do that," he said to Emi. He wasn't angry but looked sad. *Aoi-yaki* is the pottery made in her town. Her town is famous for it. There are many people who like it. But Emi thought it was just old pottery and didn't know why it was so famous.

Two weeks later, the students in her class had a field trip. They were going to visit some places in their town and make a report about the trip. Emi chose an *Aoi-yaki* pottery. It was because she remembered her father's cup and wanted to understand ___A___ .

At the pottery, a young woman, Nao, told the students about *Aoi-yaki*. Nao said, "My dream is to make *Aoi-yaki* more popular among young people. So I have worked with young potters in the town. We are trying to do something new. Look at these. They are new *Aoi-yaki*. Some of the cups and dishes are now used in many restaurants in big cities like Tokyo. Those cups and dishes are loved by people there." Emi was surprised. The designs of the pottery were cool. Emi thought that *Aoi-yaki* was not just an old culture and she wanted to know more about it.

Emi and other students visited a different pottery, too. John worked there. He came from New Zealand. He said, "When I studied art at a university in Tokyo, one of my Japanese friends gave me this *Aoi-yaki* cup on my birthday." He showed the cup to Emi. It didn't look special to her. John said, "I was surprised at such a beautiful cup. Do you know that the color of traditional *Aoi-yaki* is very special? You can see different colors from different angles. After I went back to my country, I often used this and became more interested in *Aoi-yaki*. So I decided to learn how to make *Aoi-yaki* and came to this town. Now, I'm trying to keep this beautiful color for the future. I really enjoy learning about it." Emi thought that (c)*Aoi-yaki* has the power to change someone's life.

Emi found that *Aoi-yaki* is old and new. There are people like John who enjoy making the traditional *Aoi-yaki*. She has also learned that there are new kinds of *Aoi-yaki*. Some young potters like Nao are trying to make *Aoi-yaki* more popular with their new ideas.

After the field trip, Emi talked with her father about it. She said, "I have met some people who love *Aoi-yaki*. Now I understand its good points. It is a great culture of our town." He said, "I'm glad that you have tried to learn about *Aoi-yaki*. When you use it for a long time, you will like it better." Emi said,

"I want to choose a new *Aoi-yaki* cup for you and one for me, too." He looked happy. On the weekend, they are going to visit Nao and John at each pottery again to buy new cups together.

(注) drop　～を落とす　　cup(s)　カップ，ゆのみ
pottery　陶器，陶器製造所　　field trip　校外学習
remember　～を覚えている　　potter(s)　陶芸家
design(s)　デザイン
New Zealand　ニュージーランド
traditional　伝統的な　　angle(s)　角度

問1．次は，下線部(a)の内容を説明したものである。文中の(　　)に入るものとして最も適当なものを下のア～エの中から一つ選んで，その記号を書け。

そのカップは，あおい焼で(　　　　　　　　　)こと。

ア．母親が10年以上前に父親にあげたものだった
イ．父親が気に入って10年以上使っていたものだった
ウ．父親が長い時間をかけて自分で作ったものだった
エ．父親にとってお気に入りのものだと母親が知らなかった

問2．次は，下線部(b)の具体的な内容を説明したものである。空欄に，15字以上20字以内の日本語を書け。

絵美が(　　　　　　　　　)ということ。

問3．本文中の___A___に入る英語として最も適当なものを次のア～エの中から一つ選んで，その記号を書け。
ア．why her father didn't like *Aoi-yaki*
イ．what made her father angry
ウ．why her town didn't have a pottery
エ．what was so good about *Aoi-yaki*

問4．次は，絵美が下線部(c)のように考えた理由を説明したものである。文中の(　①　)，(　②　)に10字以上15字以内で，それぞれあてはまる日本語を書け。なお，句読点も字数に含む。

ニュージーランド出身であるジョン(John)が，誕生日に日本人の友人から(　①　)ことをきっかけに，その美しさに魅了され，(　②　)ことを決心して，この町に来たことを知ったから。

問5．次のア～エの英語を，出来事が起きた順に並べ，記号で答えよ。
ア．Emi talked with the two potters about their pottery.
イ．Emi and her father planned to go to buy their cups.
ウ．Emi decided to go to a pottery on her field trip.
エ．Emi broke her father's cup while she was washing the dishes.

問6．本文の内容と一致するものを次のア～オの中から二つ選んで，その記号を書け。
ア．When Emi broke her father's *Aoi-yaki* cup, she couldn't say sorry to him.
イ．Emi learned from Nao that some people in big cities liked to use *Aoi-yaki*.
ウ．When John showed Emi the cup he made, she thought that it was very special.
エ．Emi's father taught her about *Aoi-yaki*, but she didn't understand its good points.
オ．Emi is going to choose new cups at the places she visited on her field trip.

問7．次は，絵美が校外学習の後に書いたレポートの一部である。文中の(　①　)～(　③　)に入る最も適当な英語を下のア～カの中から一つずつ選んでその記号を書け。た

だし，いずれも一度しか用いることができない。

> I visited two people on our field trip. I met Nao. She is trying to make (　①　) kinds of pottery. She wants to make *Aoi-yaki* more popular. I met John, too. He came from New Zealand. He told me that the (　②　) of *Aoi-yaki* looks different when we see it from different angles. I'm happy that our town has such a great (　③　).

ア．color　　イ．event　　　ウ．culture
エ．new　　　オ．traditional　カ．young

<長崎県>

9 Read the passage and choose the answer which best completes each sentence (1), (2), (4) and (5), and choose the answer to the question (3).

A student in Saitama Prefecture first became interested in the time of blooming for morning glories when she was 12 years old. The student had a question. Why do morning glories bloom in the morning? Later, she learned that the hours of darkness had an influence on the time of blooming. A morning glory blooms about 10 hours after it becomes 　①　 . When she learned the fact, she thought maybe there were some factors which decided the time of blooming. So, she began doing research.

アサガオの写真

a morning glory
（アサガオ）

She kept doing research for five years and found many interesting facts. For example, she found on the white parts of the petal there were very small holes which were called stoma. Many people know that most plants have stomas on their leaves, but she found that morning glories had ②them also on their petals. She did research and made a graph which showed the percentages of opened stomas on petals and leaves. Then, ③the result showed that the stomas on the petals of morning glories opened when it was dark, although the stomas on the leaves opened mainly for photosynthesis when it was light. And, she found that when it got dark and the stomas on the petals opened, water was carried up to the petals from the stems, and the flower bloomed when the petals got enough 　④　 . From this research, she thought that water in petals was a very important factor which decided the time of blooming for morning glories. For her research, she won an international prize in science for high school students in 2018.

The student said that sometimes she could not get the results she wanted, but such results she didn't want encouraged her to think new ideas and try many ways of doing research. Most people know that a morning glory blooms in the morning, but they don't ask why it does. Her research shows how important it is to have questions about the things around us.

(注) Saitama Prefecture　埼玉県
　　bloom　開花する
　　darkness　暗さ　　factor　要因
　　petal　花びら

hole　穴　　stoma　気孔
leaves　葉（leafの複数形）
graph　グラフ
percentage　割合　　result　結果
mainly　主に
photosynthesis　光合成　　stem　茎
prize　賞

(1) The word which should be put in 　①　 is
ア．dark.　イ．late.　ウ．light.　エ．quick.
(2) The word ②them refers to
ア．leaves.　　イ．petals.
ウ．plants.　　エ．stomas.
(3) The graph below shows ③the result of the research which the student in the passage did. Which is the pair of phrases which should be put in 　Ⓐ　 and 　Ⓑ　 on the graph?

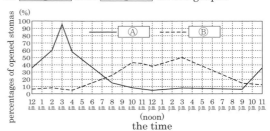

the time

ア．Ⓐ — stomas on leaves
　　Ⓑ — stomas on petals
イ．Ⓐ — stomas on petals
　　Ⓑ — stomas on leaves
ウ．Ⓐ — stomas for photosynthesis
　　Ⓑ — stomas on leaves
エ．Ⓐ — stomas for photosynthesis
　　Ⓑ — stomas on petals
(4) The word which should be put in 　④　 is
ア．light.　　イ．photosynthesis.
ウ．stomas.　エ．water.
(5) According to the passage, the student in Saitama Prefecture
ア．began doing research on morning glories because she got interested in the factors which caused the differences in the colors of petals.
イ．found that on the petals, morning glories had very small holes which were one of the keys to answering her question.
ウ．kept doing research for five years and won a prize in science although the results she didn't want didn't encourage her.
エ．showed the importance of keeping trying to find a correct answer to a question without thinking new ideas through her research.

<大阪府・C問題>

10 次の文章を読んで，あとの各問に答えなさい。
（＊印の付いている単語・語句には，本文のあとに(注)がある。）
These days, it has become quite common to see fake meat in supermarkets, cafes, and restaurants in Japan. It is more common in other countries such as China, the US and the UK. In fact, more and more people are now interested in it and choose it over real meat. The need for fake meat has been growing every year. There is even a report saying

that people will eat more fake meat than real meat for *protein in less than 30 years.

Eating animal meat is, of course, not a new idea. Our *ancestors hunted wild animals and ate their meat in the past. It gave them the energy to survive. These days, most of us do not hunt animals as our ancestors did, but we still eat animal meat for protein. Even people in some countries who did not eat animal meat before eat it in their daily life now, and its *consumption has grown. This means that animal meat is one of the main *sources of protein in the world, and a lot of people probably cannot imagine life without meat.
[____(1)____]

There are several reasons for people to eat fake meat such as health, *ethical and environmental reasons. [__ア__] First, people are beginning to think about the food they eat and trying to eat healthy food. It is true that protein is important for our health and eating animal meat is an effective way to get protein. [__イ__] However, you need to remember that eating too much animal meat may be bad for your health. Second, some people choose fake meat for ethical reasons. The idea of taking the lives of livestock animals such as cows, pigs, and chickens is probably causing people to reduce real meat consumption. [__ウ__] Livestock animals are all living things, just like us humans. So is it OK for us to take livestock's lives and eat their meat? [__エ__] Third, people eat fake meat to protect the environment. As you may know, raising livestock animals uses a lot of water, *grain, and land. [__オ__] Let's take cows as an example. To [__(3)-a__] 1 kilogram of beef, we need 20,600 liters of water and 11 kilograms of grains. And a large amount of land is needed to raise cows, so a lot of trees are cut down to create land for them. Another environmental problem is that when livestock animals such as cows, pigs, and sheep *breathe, they [__(3)-b__] a lot of *methane. This *contributes more to global warming than CO_2. So eating fake meat instead of real meat helps us to protect our environment.

Let's look at fake meat now. There are two kinds of fake meat. One is plant-based meat, and the other is *cultured meat. Plant-based meat is not made from animal meat. It is made from *ingredients such as soybeans, mushrooms, nuts, seeds, and vegetables, so it seems healthier than real meat. It is made into different types of meat such as beef and *chicken breast. So it can be used in various kinds of dishes like hamburgers, salads, and soups. If you see it, you will probably believe that it is real meat. And, when you eat it, you will feel like you are eating real meat. You may think that there is nothing terrible about plant-based meat, but there are some things that you need to worry about. Plant-based meat sometimes has a lot of *artificial ingredients and *additives. A lot of salt and sugar are often added for *seasoning too, so you may think that plant-based meat is a kind of *processed food. Some scientists say that plant-based meat has a smaller amount of *minerals than

real meat. So you may not be able to get enough *nutrients when you eat it.

Scientists have also developed another type of fake meat called cultured meat. It is grown in *cell culture, not inside of animals. First, small cells are taken from animals. Then, scientists feed the cells nutrients. The cells grow and increase to make meat. Cultured meat can be produced without as much pollution as animal meat and without taking animals' lives. You may think that it is an excellent *substitute for real meat, but scientists need a lot of money and time to make just a tiny [____(4)____]. Also, scientists (5)[how / to / cultured meat / the government / is / need / safe / show]. So we may need to wait long until it becomes a substitute for real animal meat.

As we discussed above, [____(6)-a____] people are interested in fake meat for health, ethical, and environmental reasons, but there are both good and bad things about this type of meat. Fake meat may become more common and a good substitute for real meat in the future, but [____(6)-b____] knows about it now. It is true that we need protein to survive, but at the same time we should remember the things discussed above when we get protein from animal meat. How to get enough protein has become a problem these days, so [____(6)-c____] needs to think about a possible solution. Would you eat fake meat as a substitute for real meat? Do you think more people will try fake meat in the future?

(注) protein　タンパク質　　ancestor　祖先
consumption　消費　　source　供給源
ethical　倫理的な　　grain　穀物
breathe　呼吸する　　methane　メタン
contribute　一因となる
cultured meat　培養肉
ingredient　材料
chicken breast　鶏むね肉
artificial　人工の　　additive　添加物
seasoning　味付け　　processed　加工された
mineral　ミネラル　　nutrient　栄養素
cell culture　細胞培養　　substitute　代替物

〔問1〕　本文の流れに合うように，[__(1)__]の中に英文を入れたとき，最も適切なものは，次のア～エの中ではどれか。

ア．So why do a lot of people continue to eat animal meat?

イ．So why did some people start to eat fake meat?

ウ．But why did our ancestors try to get protein only from animal meat?

エ．But why do only a few people eat fake meat?

〔問2〕　次の英文は，[__ア__]～[__オ__]のいずれかに入る。この英文を入れるのに最も適切な場所を選びなさい。

Some people are against this behavior.

〔問3〕　本文の流れに合うように，[__(3)-a__]，[__(3)-b__]の中に共通して入る英語1語を書きなさい。

〔問4〕　本文の流れに合うように，[__(4)__]の中に入る本文中の英語1語を書きなさい。

〔問5〕　(5)[how / to / cultured meat / the government / is / need / safe / show]とあるが，本文の流れに合うように，【　　　】内の単語を正しく並べかえなさい。

〔問6〕 本文の流れに合うように，$\boxed{(6)-a}$，$\boxed{(6)-b}$
$\boxed{(6)-c}$ の中に単語・語句を入れたとき，その組み合わせ
として最も適切なものは，次のア～クの中ではどれか。

	$\boxed{(6)-a}$	$\boxed{(6)-b}$	$\boxed{(6)-c}$
ア	just a few	no one	every one of us
イ	just a few	no one	someone
ウ	just a few	everyone	every one of us
エ	just a few	everyone	someone
オ	quite a few	no one	every one of us
カ	quite a few	no one	someone
キ	quite a few	everyone	every one of us
ク	quite a few	everyone	someone

〔問7〕 次の(A)，(B)について，本文の内容に合っている英
文を全て選ぶとき，最も適切なものは，それぞれ下のア
～コの中ではどれか。

(A)

① Fake meat can be found in more places such
as cafes and restaurants in the UK than in
Japan.
② Eating animal meat is the easiest and most
effective way for people today to get protein.
③ A lot of trees are cut down to create land for
livestock animals such as cows, pigs, and
sheep.
④ Fake meat is better for the environment
because methane has more influence on it
than CO_2.

ア	①	イ	②	ウ	③
エ	④	オ	① ②	カ	① ③
キ	① ④	ク	② ③	ケ	② ④
コ	③ ④				

(B)

① Plant-based meat looks like real meat, so
you cannot tell the difference between them
until you actually eat it.
② Plant-based meat sometimes includes
ingredients that are not from nature but
made by humans.
③ Cultured meat is made outside of animals'
bodies, so producing cultured meat does not
take animals' lives.
④ Cultured meat is more common than plant-
based meat, so it can be found in more
markets now.

ア	①	イ	②	ウ	③
エ	④	オ	① ②	カ	① ③
キ	① ④	ク	② ③	ケ	② ④
コ	③ ④				

〈東京都立西高等学校〉

11 Read the passage and choose the answer
which best completes each sentence (1), (2),
(3), (5) and (6), and choose the answer to the question
(4).

A slime mold is a single-celled
organism. It is a kind of an ameba. We
can find various kinds of slime molds
in a forest. Many scientists in the
world have been $\boxed{①}$ this
interesting creature for many years.

菌の写真

a slime mold
（変形菌）

A slime mold has a strange system for living. It is
born from a spore. A slime mold also explores for
food. A slime mold can get nutrients from the food
and grow. It can change its body shape when it
explores for food. For example, it can shrink and
spread its body. If a slime mold is cut into some
pieces, each piece can $\boxed{②}$ separately and
explore to get food. When one piece of the slime
mold meets another piece of the slime mold, these
pieces can merge and live as one slime mold.

To see how a slime mold gets
nutrients from food which is put at
two different places, a scientist did
a simple experiment. First, he put a
slime mold in the middle of a case.
Then, he put its favorite food at two
places in the case. Some food was
put to the left side and some other
food was put to the right side (see
Picture 1-1). Then, what happened?
The slime mold started to spread its body to both
pieces of the food. The pieces of the food were
covered with the slime mold. After that, its body
shape between the two pieces of the food looked like
a line (see Picture 1-2). The line became the
shortest route between the two places of the food.
This experiment showed that the slime mold could
reach both pieces of the food by $\boxed{③}$ and
could get nutrients from them at one time.

【Picture1-1】
food

a slime mold

【Picture1-2】

The scientist did another experiment by using a
maze. He found that a slime mold could find the
shortest route through the maze. Here are the
things the scientist did. $\boxed{④}$ After
the slime mold filled the maze (see Picture 2-1), the
scientist put the slime mold's favorite food at two
different places of the maze, and waited for a few
hours. The slime mold's body parts which were far
from the food started to shrink and move to the
food put at the two places. After doing such actions,
almost all of the two pieces of the food were covered
with the slime mold and its body shape between the
two places of the food became a line (see Picture
2-2). The line was the shortest route in the maze
between the two places of the food. This experiment
showed that the slime mold found the shortest
route between the two places in the maze.

The slime mold didn't have any
guide to lead it or get any order
from something or someone. The
things the slime mold actually did
were covering the food with most
parts of its body and shrinking its
body parts which were far from the
food. As one slime mold, changing
its body shape was efficient for
getting nutrients. The slime mold
could get most nutrients from the
food put at the two places. The
slime mold may teach us that to be
simple is the key to being efficient.

【Picture2-1】

【Picture2-2】

food

(注) single-celled organism 単細胞生物
ameba アメーバ creature 生き物
spore 胞子 explore 探索する，動き回る

nutrient　養分　　shrink　縮む，縮める
spread　広げる　　cut ~ into ...　~を…に切り分ける
separately　別々に　　merge　融合する
experiment　実験　　route　経路　　maze　迷路
efficient　効率のよい

(1) The expression which should be put in
　　　①　　is
ア．study.　　　　イ．studied.
ウ．studying.　　エ．to study.
(2) The word which should be put in 　②　 is
ア．blow.　　　　イ．count.
ウ．disappear.　　エ．live.
(3) The phrase which should be put in 　③　 is
ア．changing its body shape.
イ．doing a simple experiment.
ウ．learning from a scientist.
エ．cutting its body.
(4) The following passages (i)～(iii) should be put in
　　　④　　in the order that makes the most
sense.
　(i) Each of them started to explore in the maze,
and, when each met another one, they merged.
　(ii) The scientist cut a slime mold into many
pieces and put them in many different places of
the maze.
　(iii) In a few hours, by doing such actions many
times, they became one.
Which is the best order?
　ア．(i)→(ii)→(iii)　　イ．(i)→(iii)→(ii)
　ウ．(ii)→(i)→(iii)　　エ．(ii)→(iii)→(i)
(5) According to the passage, for a slime mold,
ア．being in a maze is an efficient way to live.
イ．spreading its body is the way of reaching the
food put at the two places.
ウ．it is impossible to merge after the slime mold
is cut into many pieces.
エ．it is necessary to know how other creatures
get nutrients from food.
(6) According to the passage,
ア．the life of a slime mold is strange, so no one
can find it in a forest.
イ．a slime mold can teach us that doing nothing
in a difficult situation is efficient.
ウ．a slime mold needs to follow an order from
something or someone when it explores for food.
エ．the shortest route between the food put at the
two places was shown by a slime mold.
〈大阪府・C問題〉

12
次の文章を読んで，あとの各問に答えなさい。
（＊印の付いている単語・語句には，本文のあとに
(注)がある。）

Some people say that we now live in "the
Anthropocene." The Anthropocene is the name of an
*epoch which some scientists started to use at the
beginning of the twenty-first century. *Anthropo*
means "man" in English, and *cene* means "new."
They call the newest period in the Earth's history
the Anthropocene epoch because human activity
has a great influence on the Earth's environment.
Animals are, of course, an example of this.

Every *species of animal has *evolved for billions
of years to survive in their environment. For
example, the process of each species' *evolution has
decided how each animal looks. 　ア　　 Because
of this, each species can better protect itself from
its *predators and survive in the environment
around it. 　イ　　 Since the Anthropocene epoch
started, however, some species have changed how
they look over a very short period of time.
　ウ　　 In this epoch, human activity is causing
quick changes. 　エ　　 One example of these
changes is a species of *moth called the peppered
moth. 　オ　　

Peppered moths live in Europe. Their bodies are
white, with some *marbled patterns on the wings.
Most of the moths that live in England once had
that same light color. In the late nineteenth
century, however, peppered moths began to become
dark especially in factory areas.

(2)Why did this change happen? In the early
nineteenth century, more and more factories were
built. The air pollution *caused by the black smoke
from these factories killed a lot of *lichens on the
*bark of trees that lived near the factories, and the
color of the bark became dark. Peppered moths rest
on these trees during the day. When lichens live on
the bark and the trees look light, it is easy for white
moths to hide themselves from their predators,
birds. When lichens do not cover the bark and the
trees look dark, however, it is hard for birds to find
dark peppered moths. Dark moths have a higher
chance of surviving in this changed environment.
In fact, the same species of the peppered moths
that live in the *countryside, away from factories,
have stayed light.

An English researcher did experiments in 1953
and 1955 to show that it was easier for dark
peppered moths to hide themselves from birds. His
group *released many peppered moths in the woods
both near factory areas and in the countryside.
Then, after some time, they caught the moths that
survived. The results are shown in the table below.
In the table, the numbers show how many light and
dark moths were released and caught again. We
can see that more of the dark peppered moths in
factory areas were able to survive. Where the
peppered moth lives and how it looks is very
important for the species to survive.

area(year)		released / caught again	light moths	dark moths
a	(1953)	released	137	447
		caught again	18	123
b	(1955)	released	64	154
		caught again	16	82
c	(1955)	released	496	473
		caught again	62	30

However, some scientists have said that other
*factors may be influencing the increase of dark
peppered moths. In fact, scientists are now doing
some research on the *genes of these moths, so we
will know more about it someday. Though we are
still researching this, it is clear that the changes in
their environment are connected in some ways to
the changes in the color of the moths. This is one

example to show how during the Anthropocene epoch human activity is influencing on animal life more than before.

In fact, human activity has not only influenced animals but also plants in the Anthropocene epoch. Just like the peppered moth, a species of plant has changed _____(4)_____ in a very short time. In the peppered moth's case, humans changed their environment, and then some of the moths became dark to hide themselves from their predators. But in this plant's case, the predators are humans. This means that human activity influences this plant more *directly. The name of this plant is Fritillaria delavayi.

Fritillaria delavayi grows in China. In the past, its flowers were only bright yellow, and its leaves were only bright green. It has a *herbal component in its *bulbs, so people have picked it to make medicine for at least 2,000 years. In the late twentieth century, however, the need for the medicine started to increase not only in China but also in other countries. Since then, people in China have picked the plants more often. Something strange has started to happen to the plants because of this.

What has happened to Fritillaria delavayi? The answer is this: the colors of its flowers and leaves have become dark. Some of the plants are now grey, and others brown. Why? They grow in mountain areas near rocks and stones, so dark colors like grey or brown are less *noticeable.

```

                           (5)


```

Why has this happened?

According to research done over six years in China, the plants growing in places that humans cannot reach easily, like very high places near the tops of the mountains, stay bright, while the plants growing in places that humans can reach easily are becoming dark. If nobody comes to pick the plants, the next *generations will stay bright because they will not have to make themselves less noticeable. However, the next generations of the plants living near humans will become dark to make themselves less noticeable. Again, where Fritillaria delavayi grows and how it looks is very important for the species to survive.

There may be other factors that have caused these changes in color. Though no researchers have started studying the genes of this plant yet, more and more scientists want to research Fritillaria delavayi because it is one of the very few examples of plants that have experienced quick changes in color.

Many factors have influenced how life on the Earth has evolved for billions of years, but today, the influence that _____(6)_____ is having on it is greater than before. Though some people call this epoch "the Anthropocene", the Earth is not just for humans, but for everything living on it. We should all make every effort to move from the

Anthropocene epoch into a new better epoch in the future. We do not know when we will be able to realize this, but we can say *for sure that it is better to realize it sooner than later.

（注）epoch 時代　species 種(しゅ)
evolve 進化する　evolution 進化
predator 捕食者　moth 蛾(が)
marbled pattern 霜降り模様
cause 引き起こす
lichen 岩石や樹木に生育するコケなどの生物群
bark 樹皮　countryside 田園地帯
release 放つ　factor 要因　gene 遺伝子
directly 直接的に
herbal component 薬草成分
bulb 球根　noticeable 目立つ
generation 世代　for sure 確実に

〔問1〕 次の英文は， ア ～ オ のいずれかに入る。この英文を入れるのに最も適切な場所を選びなさい。

In the Earth's history, such evolutions have usually taken a long time.

〔問2〕 (2)Why did this change happen?とあるが，その答えとして最も適切なものは，次のア〜エの中ではどれか。

ア．Because many lichens on the bark of the trees in the woods near factory areas died and the bark lost the original dark color.

イ．Because more lichens started to cover the bark of the trees in the woods near factory areas after many were built there.

ウ．Because the color of the bark of the trees in the woods near factory areas became dark after a lot of lichens growing on their bark died.

エ．Because the smoke from the factories began to cover the bark of the trees in the woods near them and the color of the trees became light.

〔問3〕 本文の流れに合うように，表中の a ～ c の中に，単語・語句を入れたとき，その組み合わせとして最も適切なものは，次のア〜エの中ではどれか。

	a	b	c
ア	factory area	factory area	countryside
イ	factory area	countryside	factory area
ウ	countryside	factory area	countryside
エ	countryside	countryside	factory area

〔問4〕 本文の流れに合うように， (4) の中に本文中の英語3語を書きなさい。

〔問5〕 (5) の中には，次のA〜Dのうち三つの文が入る。本文の流れに合うように正しく並べかえたとき，その組み合わせとして最も適切なものは，ア〜クの中ではどれか。

A．Some of the plants, however, have stayed as bright as before.

B．Which will be easier for their predators, humans, to find in such places, bright plants or dark plants?

C．Of course, dark plants will be easier for them to find.

D．It is easy to answer this question.

ア．A→B→C　　イ．A→B→D
ウ．B→C→A　　エ．B→D→A
オ．C→B→D　　カ．C→D→A
キ．D→A→C　　ク．D→B→C

〔問6〕　本文の流れに合うように，□(6)□の中に本文中の英語2語を書きなさい。

〔問7〕　本文の内容に合う英文の組み合わせとして最も適切なものは，ア～コの中ではどれか。

① Some scientists started to use the name "the Anthropocene epoch" just after the twentieth century began, because they thought it was an epoch of a new kind of humans.

② We can say by looking at the example of peppered moths that humans started to quickly reduce the speed of the changes in color of some species of animals in the Anthropocene epoch.

③ The color of the peppered moths living in the countryside did not change even after more factories were built in other areas because the color of the bark of the trees there stayed the same as before.

④ Some scientists are studying the genes of peppered moths, so we will know in the future why many peppered moths in the factory areas in England have changed their environment.

⑤ We can say that humans are influencing peppered moths more directly than Fritillaria delavayi because the predators of peppered moths are not birds but humans.

⑥ People in China have thought that Fritillaria delavayi is an important plant for their health for a long time because it has a herbal component in its flowers and leaves.

⑦ How easy it is for people to visit places will decide the colors of the next generations of Fritillaria delavayi which grow in these places.

⑧ The number of scientists who do research on Fritillaria delavayi will increase in the near future because there are very few other plants which have moved to different places.

ア	①	④		イ	②	⑥	
ウ	③	④		エ	③	⑦	
オ	④	⑧		カ	①	②	⑤
キ	②	③	⑦	ク	②	⑦	⑧
ケ	③	④	⑦	コ	⑤	⑥	⑧

〔問8〕　下の質問について，あなたの考えや意見を，40語以上50語以内の英語で述べなさい。「．」「，」「！」「？」などは，語数に含めません。

What is one thing that we should do to reduce our influence on the Earth's environment?　Why is it important to do so?

<東京都立西高等学校>

13　次の文章を読んで，あとの各問に答えよ。
　　　（＊印の付いている単語・語句には，本文のあとに(注)がある。）

You can get information through different kinds of media, such as newspapers, TV, and the Internet. When you read a news story, do you believe it without question?　If so, that may be dangerous. Many of you believe the news is always collected and *directly reported. In fact, [____1____]. If you understand how it is created, then that will be a great help to you.

Take a look at 【Graph 1】 and the two *statements above it.

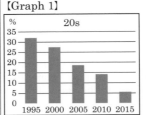

These days young people do not spend much time on newspapers.
This happens because they do not like to read books.

【Graph 1】

1日15分以上新聞を読む20代の割合
（出典：NHK放送文化研究所「2015年国民生活時間調査」）

【Graph 1】 shows that the *percentage of people in their twenties reading newspapers is going down year after year. So, the first statement, "These days young people do not spend much time on newspapers," is a fact and true. However, this graph does not show anything about the *relationship between reading newspapers and reading books. The second statement, "This happens because they do not like to read books," is just the reporter's *assumption without any *data. Facts and assumptions often appear together in a news story, so (2)it is important to be able to tell the difference between facts and assumptions.

【Graph 2】

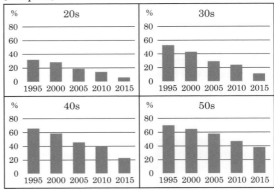

1日15分以上新聞を読む各年代の割合
（出典：NHK放送文化研究所「2015年国民生活時間調査」）

As you can see, people in their twenties do not read newspapers very much. Then, how about older generations?　Look at 【Graph 2】. In fact, older generations today also do not spend much time on newspapers. Are you surprised?　If so, you have made an assumption from 【Graph 1】 and thought only young people do not spend much time on newspapers. To make a news story more *impressive, media can decide which data to use and which to leave out.

The way of showing numbers can make a big difference in your impression. When you look at 【Graph 1】, you see that the percentage of people reading newspapers drops quickly. ___4-a___, if you look at the "20s" in 【Graph 2】, you see the percentage goes down slowly. Both graphs are made from the ___5-a___ data, but each graph gives you a different impression.

___4-b___, how media *describe the situation can make a different impression. For example, if you look at the two pictures below in the order (①→②), what kind of story do you imagine? You might say that an *ogre *attacks a village and Momotaro fights him to help the village people. If you put these pictures in *reverse order (②→①), what might the story be like? You may say that Momotaro first attacks an ogre to take his treasures. Then, the ogre gets angry and goes to Momotaro's village to get them back. Media not only decide which information and pictures should be shown, but also decide how the story should be told.

①  ②

Every news story *reflects someone's point of view. ___4-c___, it is the *interpretation of the journalist. Think of drawing a picture in a class. When the students are asked to draw a picture of fruits on the center table, each picture will be drawn differently. That means an article on the ___5-b___ event will be different from reporter to reporter.

Media try to increase *sales or to get a larger *audience. ___4-d___, they make news more interesting, more exciting, and more impressive than straight facts. You need to make an effort to find out the true facts in news stories. Understanding the news is like doing a *jigsaw puzzle. You need many pieces to see the whole picture. To know what is really going on, it is important to collect a lot of information in many ways.

(注) directly　そのまま
statement　文
percentage　割合
relationship　関係
assumption　憶測(おくそく)
data　データ
impressive　印象的な
describe　説明する
ogre　鬼(おに)　attack　攻(せ)める
reverse　反対の
reflect　反映する
interpretation　解釈(かいしゃく)

sales　売上数
audience　視聴者(しちょうしゃ)
jigsaw puzzle　ジグソーパズル

〔問1〕 本文の流れに合うように，___1___の中に英語を入れるとき，最も適切なものを，次のア～オの中から一つ選べ。

ア．media sometimes forget to explain the situation

イ．media do not know where the news comes from

ウ．media alone can report almost all the daily events

エ．media do not understand how dangerous the news is

オ．media often make the news by deciding what to report

〔問2〕 (2)it is important to be able to tell the difference between facts and assumptions とあるが，次のア～オの英文の中からassumptionと思われるものを一つ選べ。

> ア．The 2017 study shows that a lot of university students in Japan do not read books for fun．イ．Actually, 53.1 percent of the students say they do not read books at all．ウ．That number is thought to increase in a few years．エ．The study also finds that many students use smartphones for almost three hours a day．オ．However, no strong relationship was found between reducing the time for reading and increasing the use of smartphones.

〔問3〕 【Graph 2】について，正しく述べているものを，次のア～オの中から一つ選べ。

ア．The percentage of people in their twenties rose to about twenty percent in 2005.

イ．The percentage of people in their thirties fell to about ten percent by the year 2015.

ウ．The percentage of people in their forties in 2005 was about forty percent more than that in 2015.

エ．The percentage of people in their fifties did not change between 2005 and 2010.

オ．The percentage of people in every generation never went down from 1995 to 2015.

〔問4〕 ___4-a___ ～ ___4-d___ の中には，それぞれ次の①～⑤のいずれかの英語が入る。それぞれに入る英語を並べた組み合わせとして最も適切なものを，下のア～カの中から一つ選べ。

① As a result
② In addition
③ In any case
④ In other words
⑤ On the other hand

	4-a	4-b	4-c	4-d
ア	②	①	③	④
イ	②	⑤	①	③
ウ	②	⑤	④	①
エ	⑤	①	③	④
オ	⑤	②	①	③
カ	⑤	②	④	①

〔問5〕 本文の流れに合うように，___5-a___ と ___5-b___ の中に共通して入る最も適切な1語を書け。

〔問6〕　本文の内容に一致(いっち)するものを，次のア〜オの中から一つ選べ。

ア．It is not good to believe a news story without question, but if you know how it is created, it is safe to believe it.

イ．【Graph 2】 shows that the second statement about 【Graph 1】 is not an assumption because the number of people reading books is dropping.

ウ．News media try to report every news story and make it more impressive to increase sales or to get a larger audience.

エ．When media change the order of information, that change can influence an audience's interpretation of the situation.

オ．If you are good at putting a jigsaw puzzle together, you can collect information quickly to find out the true facts.

<東京都立新宿高等学校>

14 次の文章を読んで，あとの各問に答えなさい。
（＊印の付いている単語・語句には，本文のあとに(注)がある。）

David Miller, an English teacher at Tamadaira High School, studied *journalism when he was in university. He wrote this essay for the school newspaper to give his students some advice.

Where do you get your news and information? What *news source do you use to know what is happening in the world?　I think many of you go to the internet or other *social media. In the past, most people got their news from television, radio and newspapers.　[(1)]　According to a study in America, more people get their news from social media than from newspapers or TV news. In Japan, fewer and fewer people read newspapers each year. The same thing is happening in many parts of the world.

Why is this situation happening?　Why do more and more people get their news from social media, not from newspapers?　One of the [(2)-a] is that going to social media for news is faster and easier. With their [(2)-b], people can get almost any [(2)-c] anytime, anywhere. Maybe they just don't want to wait for [(2)-d] to be printed and delivered to their house any more. Sometimes they don't even have to search news by themselves. Why not?　Because they receive news *notifications from the websites they visited before. Maybe you have experienced the same type of situation. For example, imagine you are a big fan of a famous Japanese baseball player in America. One day you searched online for news about the player. Since then, the websites you (3)[① about　② and　③ him　④ keep　⑤ news　⑥ sending　⑦ visited　⑧ you]. Not only that, you receive *advertisements for the baseball player's products, such as T-shirts, books or magazines.

Another important reason is that many people go online not only to get information but also to connect to other people. It is easy to express their ideas and opinions with their smartphone. They can easily share what they think with anybody in the world. This is something they [(4)-a] do with newspapers. Social media are convenient and useful both for [(4)-b] and sending information. Also, they can be powerful tools for people working to solve world problems, such as *climate change and world health. By using social media, these people can easily and quickly spread their message to millions of people around the world.

However, some people worry that there are problems with getting information from the internet and other social media. Other people say that newspapers and other *print media are more *reliable news sources. And others even think that social media have changed our lives *negatively. Why do they think so?　*In order to explain their points, they often talk about something called an "echo chamber." Do you know (5)what it is and how it works?

Echo chambers can happen when people hear or read just one type of opinion and connect only to people with the same ideas and *points of view. Imagine you are in a small room and hearing the same sound again and again, like an *echo. Some people in an echo chamber don't try to listen to other people outside of their group and they don't even trust what others are saying. Now, this is becoming a serious problem all over the world. Do you know why this happens, especially on the internet?

You may not know this, but every activity you do online *is recorded. When you search information, when you watch your favorite videos, and even when you just *click a "like" *button, everything becomes *data. [(6)-a] [(6)-b] [(6)-c] [(6)-d] They choose what to recommend to you next. Do you remember what happened to you after searching news about that famous baseball player?　That is a good example of what algorithms do. You may think getting such information is useful and convenient.

However, have you ever thought about this?　The same situation is happening when you read something more serious online, such as world news and social problems. Why?　Because the news and other information you receive online is selected and sent to you by algorithms. And in most cases, they show you just what you will be interested in. Because of this, maybe you will not get facts and opinions you may not agree with. Some people see (7)problems with this. For example, when you read a news story about climate change and learn how dangerous it is, maybe it was written by someone *supporting just one side of the *argument. Many people today believe that climate change is getting more serious, but at the same time, as many people don't believe it is happening.

There is another important thing to [(8)-a] when you get news or information from online. You always have to be careful and check if they are facts. Today, a lot of people say that the internet is full of ⬚(8)-b information. It is sad this may be true. There is also something called "fake news." You have probably heard of it before. Thanks to the internet, anybody can ⬚(8)-c their ideas and opinions online so easily, and sometimes they don't *fact-check the information they *post. So, you have to ask yourself these questions: "Where does this information come from? Is the news source ⬚(8)-d enough?" Many people still believe that newspapers are more reliable than online news. Do you know why? Because, in most cases, newspapers are fact-checked before they are printed. Though it takes some time, it is a necessary and important thing for news media.

Finally, I'd like to tell you some points you should be careful about. They are very important when you receive and use news or information from social media. First, the most important thing is to check the news source. Don't forget to check where the information came from. Go back to the original source and try to find who wrote it, if you can. The second thing is to always check different sources. When you are not sure about the news, try to find the same information in other news sources. If you cannot find it anywhere else, it will probably be fake news. Also, (9)it is important to try to see both sides of an argument if you really want to understand the problem or the situation. Fake news and wrong information can easily spread online, especially among people in echo chambers. So, always be open to different ideas and opinions different from yours. Try to listen to and welcome them, even when you do not agree with them. Don't fall into an echo chamber. Please remember these things next time you go online.

(注) journalism　ジャーナリズム
　　　news source　情報源
　　　social media　ソーシャル・メディア
　　　notification　通知　advertisement　宣伝広告
　　　climate change　気候変動
　　　print media　活字メディア　reliable　信頼できる
　　　negatively　悪い方向に
　　　in order to ～　～するために　point of view　視点
　　　echo　こだま　is recorded　記録される
　　　click　クリックする　button　ボタン
　　　data　データ　supporting　賛同している
　　　argument　議論　fact-check　事実確認をする
　　　post　投稿する

〔問1〕　本文の流れに合うように，⬚(1) に英語を入れるとき，最も適切なものは次の中ではどれか。
　ア．So, people today still trust newspapers and television as news sources.
　イ．However, some of them saw problems with these news sources.
　ウ．However, people today don't use these news sources so often.
　エ．So, some of them hoped there would be other news sources.

〔問2〕　本文の流れに合うように，⬚(2)-a ～ ⬚(2)-d の中に，次の単語を入れるとき，その組み合わせとして，最も適切なものは次のア～カの中ではどれか。
　ア．(2)-a　problems　　　(2)-b　websites
　　　(2)-c　solution　　　(2)-d　televisions

イ．(2)-a　reasons　　　(2)-b　smartphones
　　(2)-c　information　(2)-d　newspapers
ウ．(2)-a　situations　　(2)-b　newspapers
　　(2)-c　solution　　　(2)-d　magazines
エ．(2)-a　problems　　　(2)-b　websites
　　(2)-c　expression　(2)-d　televisions
オ．(2)-a　situations　　(2)-b　newspapers
　　(2)-c　information　(2)-d　magazines
カ．(2)-a　reasons　　　(2)-b　smartphones
　　(2)-c　expression　(2)-d　newspapers

〔問3〕　(3)【　① about　　② and information　③ him　　④ keep　　⑤ news　　⑥ sending　⑦ visited　　⑧ you】．とあるが，本文の流れに合うように，【　】内の単語・語句を正しく並べかえたとき，2番目と4番目と6番目にくるものの組み合わせとして最も適切なものは次のア～カの中ではどれか。

	2番目	4番目	6番目
ア	④	⑥	②
イ	⑦	⑧	②
ウ	④	⑥	③
エ	④	⑧	②
オ	⑦	⑧	③
カ	④	⑧	①

〔問4〕　本文の流れに合うように，⬚(4)-a と ⬚(4)-b にそれぞれ英語1語を入れるとき，入れるべき英語1語は何か。

〔問5〕　(5)what it is and how it works?とあるが，このことに関する本文の記述として本文で述べられている内容と異なるものは次の中ではどれか。
　ア．Some people connect only to people who have the same idea and points of view, and they don't trust what other people outside of their group say.
　イ．Hearing the same ideas or opinions again and again in a small room is now becoming a serious problem.
　ウ．If you hear or read just one type of idea and opinion online, you may fall into an echo chamber.
　エ．People in an echo chamber often don't welcome ideas and opinions different from theirs.

〔問6〕　本文の流れに合うように，⬚(6)-a ～ ⬚(6)-d の中に，それぞれ次のA～Dの文を入れるとき，その組み合わせとして最も適切なものは次のア～カの中ではどれか。
　A．They can easily learn what kind of information you will like by using algorithms, a kind of computer program.
　B．And the data you create are sent to websites and other social media services.
　C．Algorithms, then, decide the information you will receive later.
　D．What do they do with the data they collect?

	(6)-a	(6)-b	(6)-c	(6)-d
ア	D	B	A	C
イ	B	D	C	A
ウ	B	A	D	C
エ	D	A	C	B
オ	D	C	A	B
カ	B	D	A	C

〔問7〕 (7)problems with thisとあるが，このことに関する本文の記述として最も適切なものは次の中ではどれか。

ア．Algorithms won't show you which side of the argument you should support, especially in the case of climate change.

イ．Algorithms will show you facts and opinions you may not agree with, only when they are about serious social problems.

ウ．Algorithms do not choose the type of news and information you will not agree with.

エ．Algorithms cannot select and send you news stories you may be interested in.

〔問8〕 本文の流れに合うように，(8)-a ～ (8)-d の中に，次の単語を入れるとき，その組み合わせとして最も適切なものは次のア～カの中ではどれか。

ア．(8)-a remember　(8)-b negative
　　(8)-c express　(8)-d convenient

イ．(8)-a know　(8)-b negative
　　(8)-c learn　(8)-d reliable

ウ．(8)-a explain　(8)-b reliable
　　(8)-c read　(8)-d useful

エ．(8)-a remember　(8)-b wrong
　　(8)-c express　(8)-d reliable

オ．(8)-a know　(8)-b reliable
　　(8)-c read　(8)-d useful

カ．(8)-a explain　(8)-b wrong
　　(8)-c learn　(8)-d convenient

〔問9〕 (9)it is important to try to see both sides of an argument if you really want to understand the problem or the situation.とあるが，その内容を次のように書き表すとすれば，　　　　の中に，どのような英語2語を入れるとよいか。

When you try to understand a problem or a situation, it is not a good idea to see 　　　　 side of the argument.

〔問10〕 本文の内容と合っているものを，次のア～カの中から二つ選びなさい。

ア．Today, algorithms choose and send people news and information they want to read, so they often don't have to search news by themselves.

イ．People who work hard to solve world problems still think newspapers and other print media are more reliable news sources.

ウ．Some people don't want to post and share their ideas and opinions with others because they may be fact-checked.

エ．It takes some time to read and understand the information you get from newspapers because they are fact-checked in most cases.

オ．Social media are convenient and useful in many ways, but at the same time there are some problems online, such as fake news and echo chambers.

カ．The best way to find fake news is to go back to the original news source and find out who wrote it.

＜東京都立八王子東高等学校＞

15 次の文章を読んで，あとの各問に答えなさい。なお，[1]～[10]は段落の番号を表している。
（＊印の付いている単語・語句には，本文のあとに(注)がある。）

[1] Have you ever been lost in the streets or in the mountains? Many of you will say yes, but some of you have *probably never got lost and may say, "If I've been to a place before and go back 10 years later, I will remember my way." Are such people really born with this special ability? The answer to that question is in *brain activity. They don't get lost because they have a much better ability to find out where they are and use *spatial memory.

[2] In the last few years, scientists (1)【 we / have / the brain / use / which / discovered / part / for / of 】 finding our way around an area. They say that we use two kinds of *cells in the brain. Place cells in the *hippocampus find out where we are, and grid cells outside the hippocampus help us to understand the spatial *relationship between that place and other places. With the help of place cells and grid cells in the brain, we can have a sense of place and use *way-finding abilities.

[3] Our brain can find the way by using either or both of these cells. Some people are really good at finding their way by remembering *objects in the environment. For example, they may say, "I'll go to the gas station and make a right turn." Other people may *depend on spatial memory and say, "I'll go 50 meters to the north, and then 50 meters to the east." Though we all depend on both kinds of memory, the brain may use one over the other.

[4] 　ア　 This kind of human way-finding ability was not well known for a long time, but in the 21st century, scientists began to understand more about this ability by doing research into the hippocampi of taxi drivers in London. 　イ　 Some taxi drivers drove for more than forty years and they had much more developed hippocampi. 　ウ　 If the taxi drivers spent more time on the job, the hippocampus began to develop more space for the large *amount of way-finding experience. 　エ　 This study shows that way-finding experience can have a direct influence on the brain itself. 　オ　

[5] These days, however, these kinds of way-finding skills are becoming lost in the world of GPS, or global positioning systems. GPS helps people to get to their *destination. More people are losing the ability to find their way in new places by themselves. Now let's take a look at one example.

　　　　　　　　　(3)

They say the growing use of such smartphones can lead to big problems because people depend too much on technology without understanding the world around them.

[6] In fact, scientists are afraid that the use of GPS can have bad *effects on brain activity. They

worry a lot about its effects on human memories. Because of such technology, people don't have to create spatial maps of new places in their *mind, so their *mental space for remembering and *observing their environment is becoming smaller. And if technology suddenly doesn't work at all, people will not be able to find out where they are by themselves.

[7]　Scientists have done studies to know how using GPS *affects people's ability to find their way through the environment around themselves. They asked two groups of people to find their way through a city on foot in different ways. One group used a smartphone with GPS, and the other group used a paper map and compass to reach their destination. The study found the GPS group walked slower, made more stops, and walked farther than the map group. The GPS group made more mistakes and took longer to reach their destination. After their walks, the people in the GPS group also did not clearly remember the shape of the land and their way to their destination when they were asked to draw a map. The map group did much better in this study. The GPS group was looking down at a smartphone a lot and not really looking around at their environment. However, the map group did not depend on technology, and using a map with a compass helped them to pay attention to the natural world around them and remember it. This *experiment found that the use of map reading and way-finding skills to move through a spatial environment can improve the brain and help some areas to grow. It also showed that the use of modern way-finding technology can have bad effects on the brain, especially on memory. This means that people need to practice map reading and way-finding skills, like any other thinking skill, to stop their brain from becoming weaker.

[8]　Scientists say that such brain training may help us even in our later years. In another experiment, some people found their way to a destination through a *maze on a computer just by learning the right way after repeating it until they remembered. And much older people did the same thing just by creating mental maps and getting a sense of place in their mind. The scientists found the older people's hippocampi grew through the experiment. Today, some people gradually lose the ability to think and do things in a normal way, with their brain and memory affected when they grow older. Brain training, like in the experiment, will help us to find new ways of stopping illnesses connected to human memory.

[9]　As we have seen, we can improve our way-finding ability by practicing these skills. If we get out more and go to places, it is better. We will never ▢▢▢▢(4)▢▢▢▢. Using our body improves the brain, and using our brain helps new cells in the brain to grow. We can use different skills for finding our way. The important thing is to

practice those skills and *tune in to the environment. Technology is a very useful *tool, but in the end the human brain is still the greatest map reader working at a higher, more difficult level.

[10]　Humans move from one place to another with or without purpose. When we find out where we are and our *connection to a place by using our own "GPS" in the brain, we feel safe and we feel we are really living. We should not forget how true this is.

> （注）probably　おそらく　　brain　脳(º³)
> 　　spatial　空間の　　cell　細胞
> 　　hippocampus　海馬（複数形はhippocampi）
> 　　relationship　関係　　way-finding　道を探す
> 　　object　物体　　depend on ～　～に頼る
> 　　amount　量　　destination　目的地　　effect　影響
> 　　mind　頭脳　　mental　内的な　　observe　観察する
> 　　affect　影響する　　experiment　実験
> 　　maze　迷路(めいろ)　　tune in to ～　～になじむ
> 　　tool　道具　　connection　つながり

〔問1〕　(1)【 we / have / the brain / use / which / discovered / part / for / of 】とあるが，本文の流れに合うように，【　　　】内の単語・語句を正しく並べかえなさい。

〔問2〕　次の英文は，[4]の段落の ▢ア▢ ～ ▢オ▢ のいずれかに入る。この英文を入れるのに最も適切な場所を選びなさい。

> They found that the drivers had many mental maps of the city in their memories and had larger hippocampi than other people.

〔問3〕　▢▢▢(3)▢▢▢ の中には，次のA～Dのうち三つの文が入る。本文の流れに合うように正しく並べかえたとき，その組み合わせとして最も適切なものは，下のア～クの中ではどれか。

A. Police told them to learn way-finding skills without depending only on smartphones with GPS.

B. The police thought that lost people in the mountains could not find their way without smartphones with GPS.

C. The police saved lost people in the mountains many times and thought that kind of advice was necessary to reduce the number of such people.

D. In some parts of England, many people walk long distances in the mountains.

ア．A→B→C　　イ．A→D→B
ウ．B→D→A　　エ．B→C→D
オ．C→A→B　　カ．C→B→D
キ．D→B→A　　ク．D→A→C

〔問4〕　本文の流れに合うように，▢▢▢(4)▢▢▢ の中に本文中の英語2語を書きなさい。

〔問5〕　本文の内容に合う英文の組み合わせとして最も適切なものは，下のア～コの中ではどれか。

① Many people can go back to a place because they have much better spatial memory and ability to realize where they are.

② Grid cells find out where we are, and place cells understand the spatial relationship between a place and other places.

③ All of us depend on grid cells and place cells for finding our way, but the brain may use either or both of these cells.

④ Scientists are worried about the effects of GPS on people because they reduce space in people's minds for memory and attention to their environment.

⑤ The GPS group needed more time to reach their destination than the map group but easily remembered the shape of the land and their way.

⑥ In an experiment using a maze on a computer, older people's hippocampi became larger through the repeated process of remembering the right way.

⑦ People can practice skills for finding their way, but it is actually difficult to know much about their environment.

⑧ We should not forget that our sense of place, created by mental maps in the brain, leads us to feel safe and experience life.

ア	①	⑤		イ	②	④	
ウ	③	⑤		エ	④	⑥	
オ	⑤	⑦		カ	⑥	⑧	
キ	①	④	⑥	ク	②	④	⑦
ケ	③	④	⑧	コ	③	⑥	⑦

〔問6〕　下の質問について，あなたの考えや意見を，40語以上50語以内の英語で述べなさい。「.」「,」「!」「?」などは，語数に含（ふく）めません。

Technology is a very useful tool, but sometimes has bad effects on us, like GPS, if we use it too much in our daily lives. What is another example of such technology, and why?

＜東京都立西高等学校＞

第3章 英作文問題

a．和文英訳

1 あなたは，英語の授業で，「インターネットショッピング(online shopping)」について，長所と短所を述べる立場に分かれて話し合いをしました。それぞれの人物のメモをもとに，実際に話し合いをしたときの会話文を完成させなさい。会話文の ① ， ② には，それぞれメモに即して，適切な英語を書きなさい。また， ③ には，インターネットショッピングの長所についてのあなたの考えを，次の《注意》に従って英語で書きなさい。ただし， ③ は，朝美(Asami)の意見とは違う内容とすること。

《注意》・文の数は問わないが，10語以上20語以内で書くこと。
・短縮形(I'mやdon'tなど)は1語と数え，符号(，や．など)は語数に含めないこと。

〈Asamiのメモ〉

長所	・家まで直接配送してもらえるため，商品を運ぶ必要がない。

〈Kenjiのメモ〉

短所	・インターネットの安全な使い方を知らない人もいるため，問題が起こるかもしれない。

〈実際に話し合いをしたときの会話文〉

Asami　I think that online shopping is good because you ①_____ goods from the shop. They are directly sent to your house.

Kenji　You may be right, Asami. But online shopping has a bad point, too. Some people don't ②_____ the Internet in a safe way. So some of them may have problems.

You　I see what you mean, Kenji. But I still think online shopping is good because
③_____

(注) directly　直接に

＜岐阜県＞

2 あなたは，あなたの両親と留学生のジョシュア(Joshua)と一緒に京都へ旅行する予定である。ジョシュアに，旅行についてメールで伝えることにした。次の【メモ】の内容を伝えるために(1)～(3)に英語を書き，【メール】を完成させなさい。ただし，( )を含む文がいずれも1文になるようにすること。

【メモ】

・私たちは佐賀(Saga)から京都(Kyoto)へ電車で行く。
・京都には古いお寺がたくさんある。
・清水寺(Kiyomizu-dera Temple)に行く。
・多くの人が清水寺を訪れる。
・清水寺は日本で最も有名な寺だと思う。

【メール】

✉

To Joshua,
Hi. I can't wait to travel with you. We (1).
(2) in Kyoto. We will visit Kiyomizu-dera Temple.
Many people visit Kiyomizu-dera Temple. I think (3).
If you want to know more, please ask me.
See you.

＜佐賀県＞

3 健司(Kenji)は留学生のマーク(Mark)を誘ってボランティア活動に申し込んだ後，マークから【メール1】を受け取った。健司は【広告】を見ながら返信として【メール2】を作成した。やりとりが成立するように【メール2】の下線部①，②のそれぞれについて，( )内の語に英語を書き加え，英文を完成させなさい。ただし，( )内は( )内の語を含めて，6語以上使用して書くこと。

【メール1】

Hi, Kenji. I want to ask you about the volunteer work at Blue Park. You told me that I should take a bus to the park, but how long does it take to walk there from Tamahama Station? If it is sunny, I want to walk. If it rains, I'll take a bus.

Mark

【メール2】

Hi, Mark. I will answer your question. ①(walk), so it's a long way. ②And if it rains, (park). We will learn about sea animals at Tamahama Station Hall. It's near the station!

Kenji

【広告】

ボランティア募集！
海辺の清掃で，地域に貢献してみませんか？

日時：6月25日(日曜日)10:00～12:00
場所：ブルーパーク

▲玉浜駅から市営バス「ブルーパーク行き」で約10分
▲玉浜駅から徒歩で約40分
募集人数：約30名(小学生以上)

☆雨天時は，ブルーパークでのボランティア活動の代わりに，玉浜駅ホール(南口を出てすぐ)で，海の生物についての勉強会を行います。

＜佐賀県＞

4 あなたは，英語の授業で，自分の関心のあることについて発表することになり，次のメモを作成しました。メモをもとに，原稿を完成させなさい。原稿の ① ，② には，それぞれメモに即して，適切な英語を書きなさい。また，③ には，【あなたが参加したいボランティア活動】をＡまたはＢから１つ選んで符号で書き，【その理由】について，あなたの考えを，次の《注意》に従って英語で書きなさい。

《注意》・文の数は問わないが，10語以上20語以内で書くこと。
・短縮形（I'mやdon'tなど）は１語と数え，符号（, や . など）は語数に含めないこと。

〈メモ〉

（導　入）	先週，ボランティア活動についてのポスターを見た。長い間ボランティア活動に興味があったので参加したい。
（活動内容）	Ａ．公園でゴミを拾う。Ｂ．図書館で，子どもたちに本を読む。【あなたが参加したいボランティア活動とその理由】
	あなたの考え
（まとめ）	参加の呼びかけ

〈原稿〉

Last week, I saw a poster about volunteer activities. I'd like to join one of them because ① _____ volunteer activities for a long time.

In the poster, I found two different activities, A and B. If I choose A, I will pick up trash in the park. If I choose B, I will ② _____ . I want to join ③

Would you like to join me?

（注）pick up trash　ゴミを拾う

③　I want to join ____ because ____

<福岡県>

5 健二（Kenji）は英語の授業で，インターネットを使った買い物について調べて発表するという課題に取り組んでいます。Ⅰは準備のためのメモで，Ⅱはそれをもとに作成した発表原稿の一部です。(1)，(2)の問いに答えなさい。

Ⅰ

導入	展開	結論
インターネットを使って買い物をする人の数が増えている。	○お店に行かずに，好きな時に買い物ができる。○価格を比較しやすい。▲家に届くまで商品の実物を見ることができない。	良い点も悪い点もあるが，インターネットを使った買い物は私たちの生活の一部になってきている。

Ⅱ

These days, the ① _____ people who use the Internet to buy things is increasing. We can buy things at any time without going to stores. Also, we can compare prices easily. But we can't see our goods until they arrive. There are not only good points but also bad points. But ② _____ .

(1) ① に入る適当な英語２語を書きなさい。
(2) ② に入る適当な英語を書き，文を完成させなさい。

<福島県>

6 中学生のRikuのクラスはオーストラリアの中学生のSimonとビデオ通話（video meeting）をすることになった。しかし，Simonがメールで提案してきた日は都合がつかなかったので，Rikuは次の内容を伝える返信メールを書くことにした。

① 提案してきた11月15日は文化祭（the school festival）のため都合がつかない。
② 代わりに11月22日にビデオ通話をしたい。

Rikuになったつもりで，次の《返信メール》の _____ に，上の①，②の内容を伝える20語程度の英語を書け。２文以上になってもかまわない。なお，あとの _____ の指示に従うこと。

《返信メール》

Dear Simon,

Thank you for sending me an email, but can you change the day of the video meeting? _____ Please write to me soon.

Your friend,
Riku

※短縮形（I'mやDon'tなど）は１語として数え，符号（, や？など）は語数に含めない。

<鹿児島県>

7 陸（Riku）は，英語の授業で，友人のアレックス（Alex）のスピーチを聞き，コメントを書いて渡すことになった。伝えたいことは，アレックスの国の祭りについて学べたので，アレックスのスピーチはとても良かったということと，私たちは地域の文化を尊重しなければならないということである。あなたが陸なら，これらのことを伝えるために，どのようなコメントを書くか。次の _____ の中に英語を補い，コメントを完成させなさい。

〈To Alex〉

〈From Riku〉

<静岡県>

8 翔太（Shota）は，カナダ（Canada）へ帰国することになった留学生のキャシー（Cathy）に，メッセージカードを渡すことにした。伝えたいことは，カナダの若者の間で流行している音楽を教えてくれたことに感謝しているということと，電子メール（Ｅメール）を送るから返信してほしいということである。あなたが翔太なら，これらのことを伝えるために，どのようなメッセージを書くか。次の _____ の中に英語を補い，メッセージを完成させなさい。

Dear Cathy,

Shota

<静岡県>

9 あとの各問いに答えなさい。

(1) 次のような状況(状況(じょうきょう))において，あとの①〜③のとき，あなたならどのように英語で表しますか。それぞれ4語以上の英文を書きなさい。

ただし，I'mなどの短縮形は1語として数え，コンマ(,)，ピリオド(.)などは語数に入れません。

【状況】

> あなたは，アメリカから来た留学生のSamと，休み時間に教室で話をしているところです。

① どんなスポーツが得意か尋(たず)ねるとき。
② 自分たちの野球チームが昨日試合に初めて勝ったことがうれしいと伝えるとき。
③ 次の土曜日，自分たちの練習に参加しないかと尋ねるとき。

(2) Wataruは，英語の授業で，お気に入りのものについて紹介(しょうかい)するために，自分のバイオリンの写真を見せながらスピーチをすることにし，下の原稿(げんこう)を準備しました。

あなたがWataruなら，①〜③の内容をどのように英語で表しますか。それぞれ4語以上の英文を書き，下の原稿を完成させなさい。

ただし，I'mなどの短縮形は1語として数え，コンマ(,)，ピリオド(.)などは語数に入れません。

【原稿】

> Hello, everyone. I'm going to tell you about my violin.
> ① 祖母が誕生日にくれたということ。
> ② 祖母が私にバイオリンの弾(ひ)き方を教えてくれるということ。
> ③ 昨日夕食を食べる前に，家族のために演奏したということ。
> Thank you.

<三重県>

10 あとの各問いに答えなさい。

(1) 次のような状況(状況(じょうきょう))において，あとの①〜③のとき，あなたならどのように英語で表しますか。それぞれ6語以上の英文を書きなさい。

ただし，I'mなどの短縮形は1語として数え，コンマ(,)，ピリオド(.)などは語数に入れません。

【状況】

> あなたは，オーストラリアから来た外国語指導助手(ALT)のMr. Greenと，学校の廊下(ろうか)で話をしているところです。

① 日本の文化に興味があるか尋(たず)ねるとき。
② 日本には訪れる場所がたくさんあると伝えるとき。
③ オーストラリアで撮(と)った写真を見せてほしいと伝えるとき。

(2) Ryotaは，英語の授業で，自分が住むあおぞら町(Aozora Town)について紹介(しょうかい)することになり，下の原稿(げんこう)を準備しました。

あなたがRyotaなら，①〜③の内容をどのように英語で表しますか。それぞれ4語以上の英文を書き，下の原稿を完成させなさい。

ただし，I'mなどの短縮形は1語として数え，コンマ(,)，ピリオド(.)などは語数に入れません。

【原稿】

> Hello, everyone. I am going to tell you about Aozora Town.
> ① あおぞら町はひかり山(Mt. Hikari)で有名だということ。
> ② 春にひかり山に登ったら，多くの美しい花を見ることができるということ。
> ③ ひかり山の近くのレストランはあおぞら町で一番人気があるということ。
> Thank you.

<三重県>

11 あとの各問いに答えなさい。

(1) 次のような状況(状況(じょうきょう))において，あとの①〜③のとき，あなたならどのように英語で表しますか。それぞれ4語以上の英文を書きなさい。

ただし，I'mなどの短縮形は1語として数え，コンマ(,)，ピリオド(.)などは語数に入れません。

【状況】

> あなたは，カナダから来た留学生のDavidと，週明けに学校で話をしています。

① 昨日は，雨が降っていたので，家で過ごしたと伝えるとき。
② 父にもらった本を読み終えたと伝えるとき。
③ 好きな小説家(author)は誰(だれ)かと尋(たず)ねるとき。

(2) Saoriは，オーストラリアに1年間留学していました。帰国後すぐに，オーストラリアにいる友人のEllenにEメールを書いています。あなたがSaoriなら，①〜③の内容をどのように英語で表しますか。それぞれ5語以上の英文を書き，下のEメールを完成させなさい。

ただし，I'mなどの短縮形は1語として数え，コンマ(,)，ピリオド(.)などは語数に入れません。

【Eメール】

> Hello Ellen,
> Thank you very much for everything you did for me when I was in Australia.
> ① 昨日の夜，自宅に到着(とうちゃく)したということ。
> ② 留学を通じて多くのことを学んだということ。
> ③ 異文化を理解することは大切だと思うということ。
> Your friend,
> Saori

<三重県>

b. 英作文

1 あなたは，英語の授業で，「最近買ったもの」について，クラスメートの聡史(そと)と英語で伝え合う活動を行うことになった。あなたなら何と言うか。下の条件にしたがい，英語で書きなさい。

条件

- ［ A ］には，何を買ったかについて2語以上の英語で書く。
- ［ B ］には，買ったものについての説明を4語以上の英語で書く。
- 短縮形(I'mやisn'tなど)は1語と数え，コンマ(，)などの符号は語数に含めない。

聡史　Did you buy anything recently?

Yes. I ［　　A　　］.
あなた

Oh, please tell me more.

［　　B　　］.

（注）recently　最近

<長崎県＞ — ※ ＜熊本県・選択問題Ａ＞

2 次の会話を読んで，あとの問いに答えなさい。なお，あとの（注）を参考にしなさい。

〔中学生の優希(*Yuki*)と日本に来たばかりの留学生のキム(*Kim*)が話をしています。〕

Yuki: The next class is music, so I'll take you to the music room. Come this way.

〈Poster〉
バレーボール部員募集!!

Kim: Thank you. Oh, I like the picture on this *Poster*. I can't read the *kanji*. What does it mean?

Yuki: The volleyball team ［　　A　　］.

Kim: I see. I want to play some sports in Japan.

Yuki: You can try.

(After the music class)

Yuki: Now it's lunch break.

Kim: Where do we eat lunch?　How do you spend your lunch break?

Yuki: We eat lunch in our classroom. After lunch we can do the things we like. For example, we ［　　B　　］.

Kim: I see. That sounds nice.

Yuki: I hope you will enjoy your school life here.

Kim: Thank you. I have always wanted to study in Japan. <u>Do you want to study in a foreign country in the future?</u>

（注）poster　ポスター　　*kanji*　漢字
　　　lunch break　昼休み

問1．会話の流れに合うように，［ A ］には3語以上，［ B ］には5語以上の英語を書け。

問2．会話中の下線部の質問に対して，あなたならどのように答えるか。Yes, I do.またはNo, I don't.のいずれかを選び，その理由を10語以上の英語で書け。なお，英語は2文以上になってもかまわない。ただし，コンマ（，）やピリオド（．）などは語数に含めない。

<長崎県＞

3 次の(1)，(2)について，それぞれの指示に従って英語で書け。ただし，(1)の①と②，(2)は，三つとも，それぞれ6語以上の1文で書くこと。（「．」「？」などの符号は語として数えない。）

(1) 次の①，②の質問に答える文を書け。
　① 日本のことをあまり知らない海外の人に対して，日本について説明する機会があるとすれば，あなたは，どのようなことを伝えますか。
　② また，そのことを伝えるための準備として，どのようなことをしますか。

(2) 英語の授業で，近隣の高校とビデオメッセージを通じて交流することになった。その高校の学校生活について，高校生に質問するとすれば，あなたは，どのような質問をするか。その高校生に尋ねる文を書け。

<愛媛県＞

4 次の(1)，(2)について，それぞれの指示に従って英語で書け。

(1) 次の①，②の質問に答える文を書け。ただし，①と②は，二つとも，それぞれ6語以上の1文で書くこと。（「,」「.」などの符号は語として数えない。）
　① あなたが今までの学校生活で学んだことのうち，特に大切に思うことについて，下級生に伝える機会があるとすればどのようなことを伝えますか。
　② また，なぜそのことが大切だと思うのですか。

(2) あなたのクラスでは，帰国するALT(外国語指導助手)のためのお別れ会を計画しており，下の案内状(invitation)を送ることになった。あなたは，クラスで，そのALTのためにどのようなことをするか。（　）に当てはまるように文を書け。ただし，8語以上の1文で書くこと。（「,」「.」などの符号は語として数えない。）

Invitation

Hello. We will have a party for you next Friday.
（　　　　　　　　　　　　　　　　）
We hope you will enjoy the party.

<愛媛県＞

5 吹奏楽部のMikaが〔日本語のメモ〕をもとに，日本に住む友人のJennyを吹奏楽部のコンサートに誘うメールを英語で作成します。〔日本語のメモ〕と英語のメールを読んで，問1～問3に答えなさい。

〔日本語のメモ〕

彩中学校　吹奏楽部コンサート
日付：５月13日(土)　開演：午後１時30分
場所：彩中学校体育館

・たくさんの有名な曲を演奏します。
・きっと知っている曲もあり，楽しんで聞いてもらえると思います。
・コンサートに来られますか。友達や家族と来てはどうでしょうか。

From: Mika
To: Jenny
Subject: Sai Junior High School Brass Band Concert

Hello Jenny,
How are you?
We have a brass band concert next weekend. Here's the information.

Date: Saturday, ___A___ 13   Start: 1:30 p.m.
Place: Sai Junior High School Gym

We're going to play a lot of ___B___ music. I'm ___C___ that you know some of the music, and you can enjoy listening to it. Can you come to the concert? ___D___ come with your friends and family, too?

Your friend,
Mika

問1. 〔日本語のメモ〕をもとに，空欄 ___A___ ～ ___C___ にあてはまる適切な１語を，それぞれ英語で書きなさい。なお，省略した形や数字は使わないものとします。

問2. 〔日本語のメモ〕をもとに，空欄 ___D___ に適切な３語以上の英語を書きなさい。

問3. 次は，Mikaからの誘いを断る，Jennyの返信メールです。あなたがJennyなら，どのような返信メールを送りますか。空欄 ___E___ に２文以上の英文を書きなさい。１文目はI'm sorry, butに続けて，「コンサートに行けない」ということを伝え，２文目以降は，【語群】の中の語を１語のみ使ってその理由を書きなさい。

From: Jenny
To: Mika
Subject: Re: Sai Junior High School Brass Band Concert

Hi, Mika! Thank you for your e-mail.
___E___
I hope I can go to your brass band concert next time.
Your friend,
Jenny

【語群】
・dentist
・family
・homework

<河> ＜埼玉県＞

6 次の英文は，彩香(Ayaka)とニック(Nick)との会話である。会話の流れが自然になるように，次の ___(1)___，___(2)___ の中に，それぞれ７語以上の英語を補いなさい。

Ayaka : Hi, Nick. You look nice in that shirt.
Nick　 : My mother got it for me on the Internet.
Ayaka : Buying clothes on the Internet is useful, because ___(1)___
Nick　 : Last week, I visited a store near my house and got a shirt. Buying clothes in stores is sometimes better than on the Internet, because ___(2)___
Ayaka : I see.

＜静岡県＞

7 留学生のティム(Tim)とホストファミリーのあなた(You)とが，次のような話をするとします。あなたならどのような話をしますか。あとの条件1・2にしたがって，(①)，(②)に入る内容を，それぞれ英語で書きなさい。文の数はいくつでもよい。

You : Hi, Tim. Next summer, you and I will go on a trip with my family, right? (　①　)
Tim : Yes. Now, I have two ideas: going to the beach, or going to the mountain. Both sound good to me, but I can't decide. Which place is better, the beach or the mountain? Please choose the better place and tell me what we can enjoy there.
You : OK. (　②　)
Tim : I see. I understand why it is better. I am excited.

（注）go on a trip　旅行に行く

〈条件１〉　①に，「その計画を一緒に作りましょう。あなたは何か考えがありますか。」と伝える文を，10語程度の英語で書くこと。
〈条件２〉　②に，前後のやり取りに合う内容を，20語程度の英語で書くこと。

＜大阪府・B問題＞

8 次のA，Bの各問いに答えなさい。

A. あなたは留学生のMaryと，英語の授業で「身の回りにある便利なもの」について発表するため，ショッピングセンター(shopping center)に調べに来ています。後の条件にしたがって，後の会話中の ___ に入る英語を書きなさい。

| the automatic door
自動ドア | the elevator
エレベーター | the shopping cart
ショッピングカート |

Mary : I think a lot of things are convenient in this shopping center.
You 　: Yes. Look at that. _____
Mary : I think so too. Let's find more.
　I think (the automatic door / the elevator / the shopping cart) is convenient. _____
_____

【条件】

① the automatic door / the elevator / the shopping cartのうち，1つを選ぶこと。
② 書かれている文に続けて，あなたが①で選んだものについて，便利な点を説明する文を主語と動詞を含む10語以上の英語で書くこと。
③ 英文の数はいくつでもよい。
④ 短縮形（I'mなど）は1語として数えることとし，ピリオド，コンマなどの符号は語数に含めないこと。

B．あなたの通っている中学校の英語部の発行している新聞に次のような投稿がありました。中学3年生のあなたはその投稿を読み，回答することにします。後の条件にしたがって，あなたの考えを英語で書きなさい。

Hello. I'm in the second year of this school. In April, I will start the last year of junior high school. To spend my days at school better, what should I do? Please tell me your idea.

条件

① 中学校での学校生活に関する内容を含んだあなたの考えを主語と動詞を含む15語以上の英語で書くこと。
② 英文の数はいくつでもよい。
③ 短縮形（I'mなど）は1語として数えることとし，ピリオド，コンマなどの符号は語数に含めないこと。

<大分県>

9 あなたのクラスでは，英語の授業で，10年後の自分にあてた手紙を書くことにしました。手紙では，現在のあなたをI，myやme，10年後のあなたをyouやyourと書くことにします。下の(1)，(2)の問いに答え，手紙を完成させなさい。

Dear （あなたの名前） in 2031,

Hello. How are you? You are enjoying your life, right?
I have a dream. ⬚ ① ⬚ Has my dream come true? I want to know about your life in 2031. I have two questions for you about my dream.

⬚ ② ⬚

Good luck.

（あなたの名前） in 2021

(1) 手紙の流れに沿うように，　①　に入る適当な英語を，5語以上で書きなさい。
(2) 手紙の流れに沿うように，　②　に入る適当な英語を，15語以上で書きなさい。ただし，文の数はいくつでもかまいません。

<岩手県>

10 次のA，Bの各問いに答えなさい。
A．外国の文化を学ぶことのよさについて，次の条件にしたがって，あなたの考えを英語で書きなさい。

条件

① 主語と動詞を含む10語以上の英語で書くこと。
② 英文の数はいくつでもよい。
③ 短縮形（I'mなど）は1語として数えることとし，ピリオド，コンマなどの符号は語数に含めないこと。

B．あなたのタブレット端末に，英語の先生から次のような課題が送られてきました。後の条件にしたがって，先生の課題に対するあなたの答えを英語で書きなさい。

Hello, everyone.
I want you to do something good for your town. You will have two hours to do it. What will you do? And why will you do it? Please write your idea.

条件

① 主語と動詞を含む15語以上の英語で書くこと。
② 英文の数はいくつでもよい。
③ 短縮形（I'mなど）は1語として数えることとし，ピリオド，コンマなどの符号は語数に含めないこと。

<大分県>

11 次の場面と状況を踏まえ，下の(1)，(2)の問いに答えなさい。
〔場面〕 あなたは英語の授業で，友人のマーク（Mark）にメッセージを伝える方法について，次のワークシートに自分の考えとその理由を書いています。
〔状況〕 アメリカに帰国した友人のマーク（Mark）が，ある試合に勝利しました。

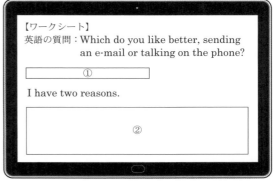

【ワークシート】
英語の質問：Which do you like better, sending an e-mail or talking on the phone?
⬚ ① ⬚
I have two reasons.
⬚ ② ⬚

(1) この〔状況〕で，あなたはどちらの方法を選びますか。ワークシートの英語の質問の答えとして，　①　に入る適当な英語を，6語以上で書きなさい。ただし，e-mailは1語として数えます。
(2) (1)で選んだ理由となるように，　②　に入る適当な英語を，20語以上で書きなさい。ただし，文の数はいくつでもかまいません。

<岩手県>

12 高校生の勇太と，来月オーストラリアに帰国予定の留学生のトムは，トムの帰国後，電子メールで連絡を取り合おうと考えています。勇太は英語と日本語のうち，どちらの言語を用いて電子メールのやり取りをするかについて，トムに提案するつもりです。あなたが勇太なら，トムに対してどのような提案をしますか。次の【勇太とトムの使用言語に関する情報】を参考にし，その提案を理由も含めて，20語程度の英文で書きなさい。なお，2文以上になっても構いません。

【勇太とトムの使用言語に関する情報】

・勇太とトムは，普段2人で会話をするとき，英語を用いている。
・トムは，日常的な話題については日本語で読み書きをすることができ，帰国後も日本語の学習を続けたいと考えている。

<広島県>

13 次の場面と状況を踏まえ，下の(1)，(2)の問いに答えなさい。

〔場面〕　あなたは英語の授業で，来週日本に来る留学生のアリス(Alice)のために，あなたの家で行う歓迎パーティーの食事について話し合っています。

〔状況〕　話し合いで，"get restaurant food"という案と"cook at home"という案があげられ，どちらが良いか意見を以下のワークシートにまとめることになりました。

【ワークシート】

英語の質問(ア)
　Which do you want to do, get restaurant food or cook at home?

　　　　　　　①

英語の質問(イ)
Why do you want to do so?

　　　　　　　②

(1)　この〔状況〕で，あなたはどちらの方法を選びますか。ワークシートの英語の質問(ア)の答えとして，　①　に入る適当な英語を，6語以上で書きなさい。
(2)　(1)であなたが選んだ理由となるように，英語の質問(イ)の答えとして，　②　に入る適当な英語を，20語以上で書きなさい。ただし，文の数はいくつでもかまいません。

<岩手県>

14 来週，あなたの所属する英語部に5名の新入生が入部します。その歓迎会で行う英語を使った活動について，担当のPaul先生に伝えることになりました。あなたは，どのような活動をしたいですか。次の条件にしたがって，書きなさい。

条件

○　次の2つの内容(ア・イ)を含む15語以上の英語で書くこと。
　　ア．活動の内容
　　イ．アの活動をしたい理由

○　2文以上の英文になってもよい。短縮形(I'mなど)は1語として数えることとし，ピリオド，コンマなどの符号は語数に含めないこと。

<大分県>

15 次の問いに答えなさい。英語の授業で，「私が大切にしているもの」をテーマにして発表原稿を書くことになりました。あなたが大切にしているものを1つ選び，その大切にしているものについて，15語以上35語以内の英語で書きなさい。なお，次の書き出しで始めることとし，書き出しの文は語数に含めません。

書き出し　I'm going to tell you about something important to me.

<滋賀県>

16 ALTのマイケル(Michael)先生が，英語の授業で次のような質問をしました。質問に対するあなたの考えを，あとの　　　　の指示に従って書きなさい。

マイケル先生

【A】 and 【B】 are two *wishes. If you could have one wish, which would you choose? And why would you choose it? Please write about it.

(注) wish 願い

【A】 meet a famous person in history

【B】 travel to the future

指示

・　　　　には，あなたが選んだ記号A，Bのいずれかを書く。
・あなたの考えを理由とともに25語以上の英語で書く。ただし，I would chooseで始まる1文は語数には含めない。
・英文の数は問わないが，前後つながりのある内容の文章にする。
・短縮形(I'm / don't など)は1語として数える。
・符号(, / . / ? / ! など)は，語数には含めない。

I would choose　　　　　．　　　　　　　　　

　　　　　　　　　　　　　　　　　　　　　　

　　　　　　　　　　　　　　　　　　　　　　

　　　　　　　　　　　　　　　　　25語

<富山県>

17 あなたは，英語の授業で，「中学生の時の思い出」について話すことになりました。次の　　　　に，30語以上の英語を書き，授業で話す原稿を完成させなさい。ただし，符号(. , ? ! など)は語数に含まないものとする。

Hello. I'll talk about one of my memories in my junior high school days.

　

Thank you.

（注）memories：memory（思い出）の複数形

<和歌山県>

18 次の英文は，香奈(Kana)さんの学級で英語のブラウン先生(Mr. Brown)が問いかけた内容です。あなたが香奈さんならどのように答えますか。問いかけに対する答えを，15語以上35語以内の英語で書きなさい。2文以上になってもかまいません。

【ブラウン先生の問いかけ】

Hello, everyone.
You will graduate soon. I think you have a lot of wonderful memories of your school life. Can you tell me about one of your best memories?

（注）memories：memory（思い出）の複数形

<滋賀県>

19 英語の授業で，次のテーマについて意見交換をすることになりました。ALTのナオミ・ブラウン(Ms. Naomi Brown)先生が以下のように発言し，意見交換が始まりました。

You've had school lunch in elementary and junior high schools. What a great school culture! I think we should have school lunch for high school students, too.

〈問い〉　ナオミ・ブラウン先生の考えに対し，<u>賛成または反対の立場</u>で，自分の考えを<u>20語以上30語程度の英文</u>で述べなさい。ただし，以下の[条件]に従って書くこと。

[条件]
(1) 賛成か反対かの立場を明確にする（agree, disagree どちらかを選ぶ）こと。
(2) 選んだ立場を説明する理由を2つ挙げること。まとまりのある内容にするため，"First, ～"，"Second, ～"等の表現を使用すること。
(3) 次の【英作文を書く際の注意事項】を参考とすること。

【英作文を書く際の注意事項】
① 主語と動詞を含む文で書くこと。
② 短縮形は1語と数える。ただし，ピリオド，コンマなどの符号は語として数えない。
③ 解答は各下線上に1語ずつ書くこと。
　　【記入例】　<u>No,</u> <u>I</u> <u>don't</u> <u>like</u> <u>it!</u>

I (agree / disagree) with Ms. Naomi Brown's idea.

.... 5
.... 10
.... 15
.... 20
.... 25
.... 30
.... 35

<沖縄県>

20 あなたは，英語の授業で，"An effective way to learn foreign cultures or customs"というテーマについて陽子と英語で意見交換をしている。次の陽子の発言に対するあなたの答えを，その理由とともに，25語以上35語以内の英語で書きなさい。ただし，短縮形(I'mやisn'tなど)は1語と数え，ピリオド(.)，コンマ(,)などの符号は語数に含めないものとする。

陽子の発言
　I think visiting other countries even for a few days is an effective way to learn foreign cultures or customs. Do you agree with me?

（注）effective　効果的な　　custom　習慣

<熊本県>

21 次は，KentaとALTのSmith先生との授業中の対話の一部である。あなたがKentaならば，来日したばかりのSmith先生に何を伝えるか。対話文を読んで，□□□にSmith先生に伝えることを書きなさい。ただし，あとの【注意】に従って書くこと。

Ms. Smith : It's very hot in Japan now, but I know Japan has other seasons, too. Can anyone tell me about the seasons in Japan?

Kenta : Yes. I'll tell you about the next season. It's autumn. It's a good season for going out.

Ms. Smith : OK. What can I enjoy when I go out in autumn?

Kenta : 　

Ms. Smith : Thank you. I'm looking forward to going out in autumn in Japan!

（注）autumn　秋　　go(ing) out　外出する
　　look(ing) forward to ～　～を楽しみにする

【注意】
① 対話の流れに合うように，20語以上30語以内の英語で書くこと。文の数はいくつでもよい。符号（. , ? ! など）は，語数に含めないものとする。
② 内容的なまとまりを意識して，具体的に書くこと。

<山口県>

22 次は，高校生のAyakoとシンガポールの高校生Judyが，オンラインで交流しているときの対話の一部である。あなたがAyakoならば，Judyに何を伝えるか。対話文を読んで，□□□にJudyに伝えることを書きなさい。ただし，下の【注意】に従って書くこと。

Ayako : When will you come to Japan, Judy?

Judy : I'm going to start studying in Japan next September. Oh, I only have five months to improve my Japanese!

Ayako : How long have you been studying Japanese?

Judy : For three years. I love reading Japanese, but speaking Japanese is still difficult for me. I want to speak Japanese better. What should I do?　Give me your advice.

Ayako : OK.

　

Judy : That's a great idea!　I'll try it. Thank you, Ayako.

（注）advice　助言

【注意】
① 対話の流れに合うように，20語以上30語以内の英語で書くこと。文の数はいくつでもよい。符号（．，？！など）は，語数に含めないものとする。
② 内容のまとまりを意識して，具体的に書くこと。

<山口県>

23 あなたは，アメリカから日本に来たばかりの留学生のサム（Sam）と仲良くなるために，今週末の計画を立てている。A，Bのうち，どちらの案を選ぶか，あなたの考えを【条件】にしたがって書け。
A．一緒にスポーツを観戦する。
B．一緒に料理をする。

【条件】
・最初の文は，I will choose _____.を用いること。その際，_____には，A，Bいずれかの記号を書くこと。
・二つの案について触れながら，あなたの考えを理由とともに書くこと。
・最初の文は語数に含めずに，30語以上の英語で書くこと。

<福岡県>

24 あなたの学校の英語の授業で，次の「コンピュータの画面」のように，ALTのライアン（Ryan）さんから一人一人のコンピュータに質問が示され，その質問について，それぞれが自分の考えを書き，クラスで共有することになりました。「コンピュータの画面」の_____に入るあなたの考えを，まとまりのある内容になるように，4文以上の英文で書きなさい。

コンピュータの画面

Ryan
My friend wants to come to our town in Japan. He has never visited Japan. He is asking me about the best season to come here. I have lived here for only three months, so I need your ideas. Which is the best season? And why?

Aiko

Kazuki

提出

(注)画面の中の□□□には，クラスの生徒が書いた考えが表示されている。

<山形県>

25 あなたは，英語の授業で，外国語の学習について陽子と英語で意見交換をしている。次の陽子の発言に対するあなたの答えを，その理由とともに，25語以上35語以内の英語で書きなさい。ただし，短縮形（I'mやisn'tなど）は1語と数え，ピリオド（.），コンマ（,）などの符号は語数に含めないものとする。

陽子の発言
Now we are studying English hard at school. In addition to English, I think it's good for us to learn another foreign language in the future. Do you agree with me?
（注）in addition to ～　～に加えて

<熊本県・選択問題Ｂ>

26 次の【メール】は交流をしているオーストラリアの中学生のMayがあなたに送ったものです。【メール】を読んで，Mayからの質問に対する答えを，説明を含めて25語以上の英文で，【返信】の中の_____に書きなさい。英文は2文以上になってもかまいません。ただし，【メール】，【返信】の中の○○○はあなたの名前が書かれているものとします。短縮形（I'mやdon'tなど）は1語と考え，符号（ピリオドなど）は語数に含めません。

【メール】

Hi, ○○○.
　How are you?　I'm going to visit Japan next month. I'm interested in Japanese schools. What do you like about your school life? Please tell me about one of your favorite things about school life.
Thanks,
May

【返信】

Dear May,
　Hello. Thank you for your e-mail. I'll answer your question.

　I hope you'll enjoy Japan.
Thanks,
○○○

<高知県>

27 あなたは，英語の授業で，ALT（外国語指導助手）にあなたが住んでいる町のお気に入りの場所を紹介することになりました。次の_____に，お気に入りの場所を1つ挙げ，理由や説明を含めて，30語以上の英語で書きなさい。ただし，符号（．，？！など）は語数に含まないものとする。

Hello. I'll talk about my favorite place, today.

Thank you.

<和歌山県>

28 あなたは，今年の夏，海外で1週間ホームステイをする予定である。ホームステイ先の家族から，どこへ一緒に行きたいかメールでたずねられた。あなたはどのような返事を書くか，行きたい場所を次の三つから一つ選び，【条件】にしたがって書け。
・a supermarket
・an art museum
・the sea

【条件】
・最初の文は，I want to go to ［＿＿＿］. を用いること。その際，［＿＿＿］には，行きたい場所のいずれかを書くこと。
・最初の文は語数に含めずに，選んだ理由とともに30語以上の英語で書くこと。

<福岡県>

29 次の質問に対するあなたの返答を，理由を含めて，30語以上の英語で書きなさい。ただし，符号（．，？！など）は語数に含まないものとする。

〔質問〕 Which month do you like the best?

<和歌山県>

30 以下の英文は，あなたが友人のマイク（Mike）からもらったメールの一部です。マイクの質問に対するあなたの答えを英語30語以上で書きなさい。符号（，．？！など）は，語数には含まないものとします。

【あなたがマイクからもらったメールの一部】

I am doing my homework and I have to write about "the most important thing in my life." For example, my father said that friendship is the most important in his life because he and one of his friends often helped each other when they *were in trouble. The most important thing in my life is my watch. My grandfather gave it to me when I entered junior high school. Now, I am more interested in this *topic and I want to know about other people's important things. What is the most important thing in your life? Why do you think so?

（注）be in trouble 困っている topic 話題，トピック
<茨城県>

31 次の英文を読んで，あなたの考えを，〔条件〕と〔記入上の注意〕に従って40語以上50語程度の英語で書きなさい。＊印のついている語句には，本文のあとに（注）があります。

Many people think that it is good to do many activities in *nature. So, many *organizations give children chances to spend time in nature. For example, schools hold many outdoor events to take children to places like mountains, rivers, lakes, or the sea. Museums or other *public facilities also hold events such as nature *observation classes or *farming activity classes. Children can do a lot of different activities in nature.

Some people say that elementary school children should spend more time in nature. Underline{What do you think about this?}

（注）nature 自然 organization 団体
public facilities 公共施設 observation 観察
farming 農業

〔条件〕 下線部の質問に対するあなたの考えを，その理由が伝わるように書きなさい。

〔記入上の注意〕
① 符号（，．？！など）は語数に含めません。
② 英文の数は問いません。

<埼玉県・学校選択問題>

32 次の英文を読んで，あなたの考えを，〔条件〕と〔記入上の注意〕に従って40語以上50語程度の英語で書きなさい。＊印のついている語句には，本文のあとに（注）があります。

It is important to consider what kind of place you want to live in. Some people *prefer living near the sea because they think the sea is better than mountains. Of course, other people like areas near mountains better than those near the sea. There are many things you have to think about when you decide where to live. Underline{Which do you prefer, living near the sea or mountains?}

（注）prefer 〜 〜を好む

〔条件〕下線部の質問に対するあなたの考えを，その理由が伝わるように書きなさい。

〔記入上の注意〕
① 符号（，．？！など）は語数に含めません。
② 英文の数は問いません。

<埼玉県・学校選択問題>

33 Read the following sentences and write your answer in English.

Suppose you have a goal to achieve, but you have difficulties to achieve the goal. In such cases, who or what helps you overcome those difficulties? Write who or what, and after that, from your experience or example, explain why you think so.

（注）suppose 考える achieve 達成する
overcome 乗り越える

<大阪府・C問題>

34 Read the following sentences and write your answer in English.

Some people say that reading books is important in our lives, and it helps us in many ways. How does it help us in our lives? Write your idea and after that, write some examples or your experiences to support your idea.

<大阪府・C問題>

35 Read the following sentences and write your answer in English.

Imagine that you are a member of a group of about 10 students. Each member of your group has a different character and opinion. When you choose a leader from the members, what kind of quality do you want the leader to have the most? Choose one of the following qualities, and write a reason for it. After that, write about your experience or an example to support your reason.

passion kindness creativity diligence
a sense of humor

（注）imagine 想像する quality 資質，性格
passion 情熱 kindness 優しさ
creativity 創造力 diligence 勤勉さ
humor ユーモア，笑い

<大阪府・C問題>

c．英作文（資料付き）

1 中学生のNaokiがALTのMs. Greenと会話をしています。会話の流れに合うように，会話中の(1)にはNaokiからMs. Greenへの質問を書きなさい。また，(2)，(3)にはMs. Greenからの質問に対するNaokiの答えを，絵を参考にして書きなさい。ただし，(1)〜(3)の下線部にはそれぞれ3語以上の英語を書くこと。

Hi, Naoki.

Ms.Green

Hi, Ms. Green.
(1)＿＿＿＿＿＿＿＿＿＿

Naoki

I'm fine, thank you. Oh, I saw you in the park yesterday. What were you doing there?

I lost my watch.
(2)So ＿＿＿＿＿＿＿＿＿＿

Did you find it?

Yes, I did.

Where did you find it?

(3)I ＿＿＿＿＿＿＿＿＿＿

Oh, that's good.

<〈群馬県〉>

2 次の(1)，(2)の絵において，2人の対話が成り立つように，□□□に主語と動詞を含む英文1文をそれぞれ書きなさい。

(1)

What did you do after dinner yesterday?

＿＿＿＿＿＿＿.

(2)

I can't find my phone! I'll be late. Please help me.

It's on the desk.

Thank you.

＿＿＿＿＿＿？

It's under the chair.

<〈北海道〉>

3 次のピクトグラム（pictogram　案内用図記号）を見て，あとの問いに答えなさい。

飲食禁止

説明文

Look at this pictogram.
You can see it anywhere in the library.
So you ［　　①　　］.
You should go outside, when you ［　　②　　］.
OK?

(問い)　校外学習で図書館へ行くため，あなたがクラスの外国人留学生にこのピクトグラムについて説明をすることになりました。説明文の ① には，このピクトグラムが示す禁止事項を， ② には，外国人留学生が屋外に出るべき具体的な場面を，それぞれ5語以上の英語で書き，英文を完成させなさい。

ただし， ① にはeat 〜（〜を食べる）， ② にはthirsty（のどのかわいた）を必ず使うこと。また，次の語を参考にしてもよい。

〈語〉
飲む，飲み物　drink　　～（の中）で　in ～
～を感じる　feel ～

＜愛知県・Aグループ＞

4 留学生のLindaがあなたにSNS上で相談している。添
付されたカタログを参考に，あなたがLindaにすすめ
たい方を選び，その理由を二つ，合わせて25～35語の英語
で書け。英文は2文以上になってもかまわない。

Linda
13:35

Hi! I want to buy a
bag. Which should I
buy, X or Y ? Please
give me your advice!

	X		Y
価格	~~3,600円~~ 4,300円		2,900円
特徴	化学繊維（防水）		綿（天然素材）
重さ	970g		590g
容量	30L		20L

You should buy (X ・ Y) because ＿＿＿＿＿＿

＜鹿児島県＞

5 次の(1)，(2)の絵において，2人の対話が成り立つよう
に，質問に対する答えを，主語と動詞を含む英文1文
でそれぞれ自由に書きなさい。

(1)

When is your birthday?

(2)

What do you think of this song?

＜北海道＞

6 中学生のTakuyaは，京都（Kyoto）を旅行中のLeoと
電話で会話をしています。Leoは，Takuyaの家にホー
ムステイしている留学生です。会話中の(1)～(3)には
TakuyaからLeoへの質問が入ります。会話の流れに合う

ような質問を，絵を参考にして書きなさい。ただし，(1)～
(3)の質問は，次の　　　　内からそれぞれ1語を使用し，3
語以上の英語とすること。

how	what	where	who	why

?

Takuya

(1) ＿＿＿＿＿＿＿＿＿＿＿＿＿＿＿＿

It's sunny here.
It's a wonderful day for the trip.

Leo

?

Oh, you're so lucky.
(2) ＿＿＿＿＿＿＿＿＿＿＿＿＿

I am going to visit a castle and a
famous temple today.

?

That sounds great.
You'll come home tomorrow, right?
(3) ＿＿＿＿＿＿＿＿＿＿＿＿＿

At two.
It will take about four hours by
Shinkansen.
So I'll come home at about six o'clock.

＜群馬県＞

7 留学生のエミリー（Emily）と純也（Junya）が話をし
ています。対話は①～⑤の順で行われています。④の
イラストは純也が話している内容です。自然な対話となる
ように，(1)，(2)の問いに答えなさい。

① Good morning, Junya. How are you?

Emily

② I'm hungry. I didn't ［　A　］ to eat
food this morning. I'm sleepy, too.

Junya

③ Oh, that's too bad. Why are you
sleepy?

④　Well, I often play video games for many hours at night and I played them last night, too. ☐B☐

⑤　You should. Also, you should make some rules with your family about playing video games.

(1)　☐A☐ に入る適当な英語2語を書きなさい。
(2)　イラストと対話の流れに合うように，☐B☐ に入る適当な英語を1文で書きなさい。

＜福島県＞

8　次のイラストと英文は，高校生の海斗と留学生のスーザンが，部活動について話したときのものです。①〜⑥の順に対話が自然につながるように，☐A☐〜☐C☐ にそれぞれ適切な英語を書いて，対話を完成しなさい。ただし，☐B☐ については，10語程度で書きなさい。

Yesterday...

①　Kaito, you look so happy today. What happened?

②　☐A☐ yesterday. so I'm happy.

③　That's great! I'm interested in club activities in Japan. What is a good point of them?

④　I think they have many good points. For example, we can ☐B☐ .

⑤　Oh, I see. I want to learn more.

⑥　We have many clubs in our school, so ☐C☐ .

＜広島県＞

9　達也（Tatsuya）さんは，留学生のジョージ（George）さんと話をしています。それぞれの場面に合う対話になるように（　　　）内に3語以上の英語を書きなさい。なお，対話は①から⑨の順に行われています。

1.　① How was your weekend?

② I went to Tokyo with my family. I had a good time there.

2.　③ (　　　　　　　　　　)?

④ I went to a *space museum. I learned many things and bought a book about space there.

⑤ That's good.

*space 宇宙

3.　⑥ This is for you. It's "Space Tea."

⑦ Wow, "Space Tea." (　　　　　　). Thank you.

4.　The next day

⑧ Hi, Tatsuya! The "Space Tea" was good. I became interested in space too. (　　　　　　)?

⑨ Of course.

＜富山県＞

10 次のＡ～Ｃのひとつづきの絵と英文は，ケイコ（Keiko）がオーストラリアを訪れていたときのある日のできごとを順番に表しています。Ａの場面を表す〈最初の英文〉に続けて，Ｂの場面にふさわしい内容となるように，　　　　　の中に適する英語を書きなさい。ただし，あとの〈条件〉にしたがうこと。

A.

〈最初の英文〉

　One day, Keiko tried to go to ABC Park alone. At the station, she asked a man, "Where is the *bus terminal?" The man answered, "It's by the *west exit of the station."

B.

　When she got to the bus terminal, there were three buses, a red one, a *blue one, and a *yellow one. Keiko asked a woman there, "I want to go to ABC Park. 　　　　　　　　the park?"

C.

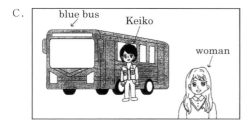

　"Yes, I do. The blue one. The fifth *stop from here is ABC Park. Have a nice day," the woman answered. "Thank you very much," Keiko said.

（注）bus terminal　バスターミナル　　west exit　西口
　　　blue　青い　　yellow　黄色い　　stop　停留所

〈条件〉

> ①　bus, goesとknowを必ず用いること。
> ②　①に示した語を含んで，　　　　内を７語以上で書くこと。
> ③　the park?　につながる１文となるように書くこと。
> ※短縮形（I'mやdon'tなど）は１語と数え，符号（，など）は語数に含めません。

＜神奈川県＞

11 次のＡ～Ｃのひとつづきの絵と英文は，ある日のできごとについてのユキコ（Yukiko）とレイカ（Reika）の会話を表しています。Ａの場面を表す〈最初の英文〉に続けて，Ｂの場面にふさわしい内容となるように，　　　　　の中に適する英語を書きなさい。ただし，あとの〈条件〉にしたがうこと。

A.

〈最初の英文〉

　Yukiko said, "I visited my grandfather last Sunday. He lives in Kamome *Village." Reika said, "I have never been to that village. How did you get there?"

B.

　Yukiko said, "I usually go to my grandfather's house with my family by car. But this time I went *by myself by train and bus." Reika asked, "　　　　　　　　get there when you used the train and the bus?"

C.

　Yukiko said, "Two hours. I enjoyed seeing the beautiful mountains from the bus. I talked about my trip with my grandfather. Next time, we can visit Kamome Village together." Reika said, "Oh, I'd like to!"

（注）Village　村　　by myself　ひとりで

〈条件〉

> ①　itとlongを必ず用いること。
> ②　①に示した語を含んで，　　　　内を６語以上で書くこと。
> ③　get there when you used the train and the bus?　につながる１文となるように書くこと。
> ※短縮形（I'mやdon'tなど）は１語と数え，符号（，など）は語数に含めません。

＜神奈川県＞

12 高校生の明子と留学生のエマは，SNS上で2人の住む地域の春祭りについてやり取りを行いました。次のやり取りはそのときのものです。上から順にやり取りが自然につながるように，　ア　・　イ　にそれぞれ適切な英語を書いて，やり取りを完成しなさい。ただし，　イ　については，15語程度で書きなさい。

Akiko

Hello, Emma. Can you come with me to the spring festival this Saturday, April 15?

What kind of festival is it?

Emma

Akiko

You can see beautiful flowers and enjoy watching some performances. Here is the timetable.

11:00 ～ 12:00 dance performance
12:00 ～ 13:00 karaoke performance
13:00 ～ 14:00 shamisen performance
14:00 ～ 15:00 dance performance
・All performances will be held rain or shine.

Cool! I've never watched a shamisen performance. Which one do you want to watch?

Emma

Akiko

　　　ア　　　 because one of my friends will perform. Her group will give a performance in the morning and repeat it in the afternoon.

Well, look at this weather information. I don't want to get wet in the rain. What should we do?

Emma

	Saturday, April 15				
Time	11	12	13	14	15
Weather					
Chance of rain (%)	70	50	20	0	0

Akiko

　　　イ　　　.

OK
Emma

(注) timetable　予定表　　be held　催される
　　　rain or shine　晴雨にかかわらず
　　　perform　上演する　　give　行う　　chance　可能性
　　　　　　　　　　　　　　　　　　　　　＜広島県＞

13 中学生のMikaは，英語の授業で留学先での体験談を発表することになりました。Mikaが準備した次のスライド(slide)と発表原稿をもとにして(1)，(2)の問いに答えなさい。

スライド1　　　　　　　　　スライド2

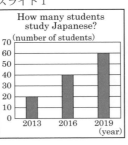

発表原稿

　This summer I studied at Green Junior High School for two weeks.

　In this school, there are some language classes.

　Slide 1 shows the number of students studying in the Japanese language class.

　In 2019, 　　　①　　　 than in 2016.

　Slide 2 shows what the students of the class in 2019 like about Japan.

　Traditional events are 　　　②　　　 the class.

　In the class, there is a special lesson called "Japan Day".

　I was invited to the lesson and talked about ③one Japanese traditional event.

(1) Mikaになったつもりで，発表原稿の　①　，　②　にそれぞれ4語の英語を書きなさい。
(2) Mikaになったつもりで，次の条件にしたがって，下線部③を説明する英文を書きなさい。
条件
○　次の2つの内容(ア・イ)を含む15語以上の英語で書くこと。
　　ア．one Japanese traditional eventの名称
　　　（ローマ字で書いても構わない）
　　イ．アの具体的な説明
○　2文以上の英文になってもよい。短縮形(I'mなど)は1語として数えることとし，ピリオド，コンマなどの符号は語数に含めないこと。

＜大分県＞

14 ひのき中学校の生徒Junと留学生のBenは，新聞部員です。二人は，近隣にあるやよい中学校のアンケート結果について，SNS（ソーシャルネットワーキングサービス）でやり取りをしています。二人のやり取りを読んで，(1)・(2)の問いに答えなさい。

19:21
Hi, Ben. I found an interesting graph. Please look at this.

 Jun

19:24

37% | 21% | 13% | 11% | 10% | 8%
複数回答なし

■ 公園や道路の清掃
▨ 地域のイベントの手伝い
▥ 高齢者施設での手伝い
▩ 幼稚園児や小学生の世話
▦ その他
□ ボランティアの希望なし

 Jun

19:25
This graph shows which volunteer work is popular among students at Yayoi Junior High School.

 Jun

 Ben
It's interesting. 　A　
19:27

19:30
Cleaning parks and roads is. Many students are interested in volunteer work. Only 8% of them don't want to do it.

Jun

 Ben
How about our school? What do they think about volunteer work?
19:32

19:33
I'm not sure. Let's find out.

Jun

 Ben
I have an idea. Why don't we ask students questions and show the results in our newspaper?
19:35

19:37
That's a good idea. 　B　

Jun

 Ben
We can ask them these questions. "Should junior high school students do volunteer work?" and "What kind of volunteer work do you want to do?"
19:40

（注）graph　グラフ　find out　調べる

(1) やり取りの内容から考えて，　A　・　B　に当てはまる適切な英文１文を，それぞれ書きなさい。ただし，英文は疑問詞と主語，動詞を含んだ文にすること。

(2) 下線部の質問"Should junior high school students do volunteer work?"について，あなたはどのように考えますか。あなたの考えを，理由を含めて25語以上の英文で答えなさい。英文は２文以上になってもかまいません。ただし，短縮形（I'mやdon'tなど）は１語と考え，符号（ピリオドなど）は語数に含めません。

<高知県>

15 友子(Tomoko)さんは，留学生のウェンディ(Wendy)さんと話をしています。それぞれの場面に合う対話になるように（　　）内に３語以上の英語を書きなさい。なお，対話は①から⑪の順に行われています。

1.
① Hi, Tomoko, I'm glad to see you here. Can you help me? I want a book about *Mozart.
② Of course. I know where it is. Let's go.
③ Thank you.

（注）Mozart　モーツァルト

2.
④ Wow, there are so many books about Mozart. （　　　　）?
⑤ How about this one? It also has a *bonus CD.
⑥ Sounds interesting! I'll buy this one.

（注）bonus CD　特典CD

3.
The next day
⑦ Hi, Wendy. Did you enjoy the book you bought yesterday?
⑧ Yes, I did. （　　　　）.

4.
⑨ Do you listen to Mozart?
⑩ Yes, and I often go to *classical concerts.
⑪ That's great. （　　　　）.

（注）classical concert　クラシックのコンサート

<富山県>

16 次の①～④は，ミホ（Miho）が，アメリカを訪れた時の出来事を描いたイラストです。③の場面で，ミホは何と言ったと思いますか。①～④の話の流れを踏まえ，□に入る言葉を英語で書きなさい。ただし，語の数は25語程度（．，？！などの符号は語数に含まない。）とすること。

〈千葉県〉

17 ALTのアーサー（Arthur）先生が，英語の授業で次のような話をしました。下の□の指示に従って英文を書きなさい。

> There are many problems in children's lives in the world. One of the biggest problems is "More than 121,000,000 children can't go to school." Please write what you think about this problem.

アーサー先生

More than 121,000,000 children can't go to school.

some reasons

working children | no schools | no teachers

指示

- アーサー先生の指示に従い，25語以上の英語で書く。
- 黒板を参考にしてもよい。
- 英文の数は問わないが，前後つながりのある内容の文章にする。
- 短縮形（I'm / don'tなど）は1語として数える。
- 符号（，/．/？/！など）は，語数には含めない。

〈富山県〉

18 次の①～④は，中学生のケンタ（Kenta）が，家の庭（yard）でマサト（Masato）とサッカーをしていた時のイラストです。④の場面で，ケンタは何と言ったと思いますか。①～④の話の流れを踏まえ，□に入る言葉を英語で書きなさい。

ただし，語の数は25語程度（．，？！などの符号は語数に含まない。）とすること。

〈千葉県〉

19 次の英文は，ある高校生が，英語の授業で，スマートフォンなどの機器(device)の利用について，自分の考えを書いたものです。あなたがその高校生になったつもりで，資料をふまえ，条件にしたがって，英文を完成させなさい。

英文

Devices such as smartphones are part of our life today. Actually, ＿＿＿(1)＿＿＿.

Such devices are very useful because we can do many things with them. For example, by using them, we can communicate with others, or we can ＿＿＿(2)＿＿＿.

However, we should be careful when we use them. ＿＿＿(3)＿＿＿ We need to learn how to use them well.

資料

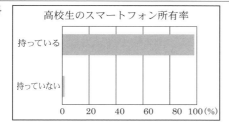

高校生のスマートフォン所有率

持っている
持っていない

0　20　40　60　80　100(%)

条件

・ (1) には，資料からわかることを，主語と動詞を含む英文1文で書きなさい。
・ (2) には，スマートフォンなどの機器を用いてできることについて，与えられた書き出しに続くように英語で自由に書きなさい。
・ (3) には，スマートフォンなどの機器を使用するときにすべきだと思うこと，または，すべきでないと思うことについて，あなたの意見とその理由を，24語以上の英語で自由に書きなさい。

〈北海道〉

20 次の各問いに英文で答えなさい。ただし，英文は主語・動詞を含む文であること。また，設問中に示された指示や条件を踏まえて解答すること。

〈場面設定〉新しいALTのブラウン先生（Mr. Brown）があなたの学校に来ました。生徒会役員のメンバーで，先生の歓迎会について話し合いをしています。

問1．ブラウン先生について書かれた次のメモをもとに，ブラウン先生を紹介する英文を2文書きなさい。

〈メ　モ〉　年齢：25歳　　出身：カナダ
　　　　　　誕生月：3月　　趣味：野球観戦

〈条　件〉・2つの文はどちらもメモにある情報について書くこと。
　　　　・2つの文は同じ内容にしないこと。

問2．ブラウン先生のことをもっとよく知るために質問を考えましょう。ブラウン先生に聞きたい質問を考え，英語で2文書きなさい。

〈条　件〉・質問文はいずれも疑問詞（What / When / Where / Who のいずれか）で始めること。
　　　　・2つの質問文は異なる内容にすること。
　　　　・問1のメモに示された内容について質問しないこと。

問3．次の2つの観光ツアーのどちらかをブラウン先生にすすめましょう。どちらか1つのツアーを選び，あなたがそのツアーをすすめたいと思う具体的な理由を含めて英文で書きなさい。

Okinawan Nature Tour

Time : 6:00 — 12:00　(6 hours)
Price : 1,000 yen
Activities : Visiting the beach and swimming

beach　　　　　swimming

Okinawan Food Tour

Time : 13:00 — 18:00　(5 hours)
Price : 1,500 yen
Activities : shopping and cooking

farmers' market　　cooking
（市場）

〈条　件〉・どちらのツアーをすすめたいかわかるように書くこと。
　　　　・そのツアーをすすめたい理由を具体的に説明すること。
　　　　・英文は2文以内で書くこと。

　Mr. Brown,
　　　　＿＿＿＿＿＿＿＿＿＿＿＿＿
　　　　I hope you enjoy this tour.

〈沖縄県〉

21 中学3年生のかずお(Kazuo)さんが，昼休みに教室で過ごしていると，オーストラリアからの留学生のスティーブ(Steve)さんがやってきました。絵1〜絵4は，そのときの二人の会話の様子を上から順に示したものです。これらの会話を読み，あとの各問いに答えなさい。

絵1

Hi, Kazuo. What are you reading?

Hi, Stave. I'm going to go to the summer camp at Mt. Daisen. This is a *flyer for it.

(注) flyer ちらし

絵2

(①)?

It's in the *western part of Tottori Prefecture.

(注) western part 西部

絵3
Can I see the flyer?
Of course. Here you are.

絵4
Oh, there are a lot of interesting things to do. And you can choose two of them. （　②　）?
I will ride a *horse and *go hiking. Are you interested in going to this summer camp too?
Summer Camp at Mt.Daisen
(注) horse 馬
　　 go hiking ハイキングに行く

問1．絵2の（　①　），絵4の（　②　）に入る英文を，それぞれ2語以上の一文で書きなさい。ただし，I'mのような短縮形は1語として数え，符号（，や．など）は語数に含めないこととします。

問2．次の発表は，夏休み後，かずおさんが，英語の授業でおこなった，サマーキャンプについてのスピーチの内容です。これを読み，発表の下線部の問いかけに対するあなたの考えを，あとの条件に従って20語程度の英語で書きなさい。ただし，I'mのような短縮形は1語として数え，符号（，や．など）は語数に含めないこととします。

発表

　　During summer vacation, I went to a summer camp with Steve. We rode on horses and went hiking. I met a high school student there. Her name was Tomoko. She was a volunteer and helped us when we did the *activities. I asked her, "Why did you decide to work as a volunteer?" She answered, "I wanted to do something useful for other people."
　　I think doing volunteer work will be a good experience, and it will help me to become a member of *society. What do you think? <u>What kind of volunteer work do you want to do?</u>

　　（注）activities：activity「活動」の複数形
　　　　　society　社会

条件

・主語・動詞を含む文で書くこと。
・自分の考えについて，その理由も書くこと。
・発表で述べられている例以外の内容とすること。

〈鳥取県〉

22 次の問いに英文で答えなさい。ただし，設問中に示された指示や条件を踏まえて解答すること。

〈場面設定〉　あなたの学校に来ているALTのジョシュ(Josh)先生が，春休みに離島への旅行を計画しています。ジョシュ先生は，離島への移動のために，飛行機(airplane)と船(ship)のどちらを利用したらよいか迷っています。

〈問い〉　以下の飛行機と船に関する情報をもとに，2つの移動方法のどちらかをジョシュ先生にすすめましょう。「どちらの移動方法をすすめるか」「その移動方法をすすめたい具体的な理由」がわかる英文を書きなさい。

飛行機(airplane)

①所要時間：50分
②便数：1日3便
（出発時刻：8 a.m./12 p.m./6 p.m.)
③運賃：12,000円

船(ship)

①所要時間：8時間
②便数：1日1便
（出発時刻：8 a.m.)
③運賃：4,000円

〈条　件〉
1．英文は主語・動詞を含む文であること。
2．英文は3文以内で書くこと。
3．どちらの移動方法をすすめたいかわかるように書くこと。
4．その移動方法をすすめたい具体的な理由を2つ書くこと。(理由はそれぞれ異なるものであること。理由は上に示した①所要時間，②便数，③運賃やイラストに示された情報にもとづくこと。)
5．示された英文（書き出し）に続けて書くこと。

Mr. Josh,
　I would like to give you advice for your trip.
＿＿＿＿＿＿＿＿＿＿＿＿＿＿＿＿＿＿＿
＿＿＿＿＿＿＿＿＿＿＿＿＿＿＿＿＿＿＿
＿＿＿＿＿＿＿＿＿＿＿＿＿＿＿＿＿＿＿
＿＿＿＿＿＿＿＿＿＿＿＿＿＿＿＿＿＿＿
I hope you have fun on your trip!

〈沖縄県〉

23 Hiroshiはあけぼの中学校の三年生です。今回社会科のグループ学習として，「あけぼの中学校の生徒がニュース情報を得る手段」を取り上げ，生徒にアンケートを取りました。その結果について留学生のTomと話し合っています。二人のやり取りを読んで，(1)・(2)の問いに答えなさい。

Hiroshi : Hi, Tom. We asked the students at this school, "<u>How do you usually get the news?</u>"
Tom : Thank you. 　　A　　
Hiroshi : 356 students did.
Tom : Oh good!　So many of them answered the question. 　　B　　
Hiroshi : I found that 88% of them watch TV.
Tom : Well, that's interesting. In the U.S., we usually use social media to get the news. How about this school?
Hiroshi : 70% of them answered they use social media.
Tom : Did many of them answer they read newspapers to get the news?
Hiroshi : No, only 32% of them do. Tom, how about you?
Tom : I use social media, but I think newspapers are also very useful.
　（注）social media　ソーシャルメディア

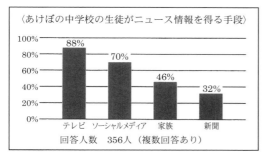

〈あけぼの中学校の生徒がニュース情報を得る手段〉

回答人数　356人（複数回答あり）

(1)　やり取りの内容から考えて，　A　・　B　に当てはまる適切な英文１文を，それぞれ書きなさい。ただし，英文は疑問詞と主語，動詞を含んだ文にすること。

(2)　下線部の質問 "How do you usually get the news?" について，あなたはどのように回答しますか。あなたの回答を，理由を含めて25語以上の英文で書きなさい。英文は２文以上になってもかまいません。ただし，短縮形（I'mやdon'tなど）は１語と考え，符号（ピリオドなど）は語数に含めません。

<高知県>

24 留学生のスティーブン(Steven)さんが，富山県の魅力を海外にアピールするポスターの案を２種類作成しました。下のＡとＢのポスターのうち，あなたがよいと思う方について，下の　　　　の指示に従って書きなさい。

【A】　　　　　　　【B】

指示

・　　　　　には，あなたが選んだポスターの記号Ａ，Ｂいずれかを書く。
・あなたの考えを理由とともに25語以上の英語で書く。ただし，I think 　　　　　 is better.の１文は語数には含めない。
・英文の数は問わないが，前後つながりのある内容の文章にする。
・短縮形（I'm / don'tなど）は１語として数える。
・符号（ , / . / ? / ! など）は下線部と下線部の間に書き，語数には含めない。

I think 　　　　　　　　 is better.　　　　　　

　　　　　　　　　　　　　　　　　　　　　　

　　　　　　　　　　　　　　　　　　　　　　

　　　　　　　　　　　　　　　　　　　　　　

　　　　　　　　　　　　　　　　　　　　　　

　　　　　　　　　　　　　　　　　　　25語

　　　　　　　　　　　　　　　　　　　　　　

<富山県>

25 中山先生(Ms. Nakayama)とマイケル(Michael)先生が，英語の授業のはじめに話をしています。絵１〜４は，そのときの２人の会話の様子を上から順に示したものです。これらの会話を読み，あとの各問いに答えなさい。

絵１

Hi, Michael. How was your weekend? — It was good!

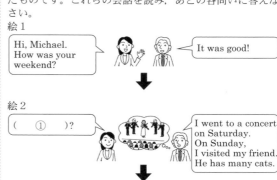

絵２

(①)? — I went to a concert on Saturday. On Sunday, I visited my friend. He has many cats.

絵３

(②)? — Five. Do you have any pets?

絵４

Yes. I have a dog, but it's a robot* dog. — Wow!

（注）robot　ロボット（の）

問１．絵２の（　①　），絵３の（　②　）にあてはまる英文を，それぞれ４語以上の一文で書きなさい。ただし，I'mのような短縮形は１語として数え，符号（，や．など）は語数に含めないこととする。

問２．絵１〜４の会話の後，マイケル先生が次のように生徒に問いかけました。マイケル先生からの問いかけの下線部に対するあなたの考えを，あとの条件に従って書きなさい。

マイケル先生からの問いかけ

Robots can solve many problems around us.
What kind of robot do you want?
What problem do you want to solve with your robot?

条件

・20語程度の英語で書くこと。
・主語・動詞を含む文で書くこと。
・会話で述べられている例以外の内容とすること。
・I'mのような短縮形は１語として数え，符号（，や．など）は語数に含めないこととする。

<鳥取県>

26 次は，中学生のHikariが昨日の下校中に体験した出来事を描いたイラストである。Hikariになったつもりで，イラストに合うように，一連の出来事を次の書き出しに続けて25〜35語の英語で書け。英文の数は問わない。

On my way home yesterday, _____

　　　　　　　　　　　　　　　　　　　＜鹿児島県＞

27 英語の授業で，「レジ袋の有料化」をテーマに調べたことや考えたことを書く活動を行いました。次の【資料】をもとに，あなたなら【ワークシート】の□□□にどのようなことを書きますか。後の《条件》に従って英語で書きなさい。

【資料】

買物した店舗でレジ袋を断った人の割合

（環境省ホームページにより作成）

【ワークシート】

Plastic bags are not *free now!

Before July 1, 2020, many stores in Japan gave free plastic bags to their customers who bought something there.
But now the bags are not free. If customers need a plastic bag, they have to buy one. Now many people _____

（注）free　無料の

《条件》
・【ワークシート】の□□□に，書き出しに続けて，【資料】から分かることと，「レジ袋の有料化」についてあなた自身が考えたことを，30語〜40語の英語で書くこと。
・英文の数はいくつでもよく，符号（ , . ! ? " " など）は語数に含めません。

　　　　　　　　　　　　　　　　　　　＜群馬県＞

28 あなたの町でテイラー先生（Ms. Taylor）が，次のA，Bの無料英会話クラスを開くことになった。どちらのクラスを受けたいか，あなたの考えを【条件】にしたがって書け。

クラスA

テイラー先生の英会話教室
日時： 毎週金曜日
　　　 16:30 〜 17:20
　　　 （50分間）
場所： 学校
形式： 4人グループ

クラスB

テイラー先生のオンライン英会話
日時： 毎週月曜日から木曜日
　　　 19:00 〜 20:30
　　　 （1日15分間，週3日まで）
場所： 自宅など
形式： インターネット
　　　 先生と1対1

【条件】
・最初の文は，I want to take Class □□□.を用いること。
　その際，□□□には，A，Bいずれかの記号を書くこと。
・二つのクラスについて触れながら，あなたの考えを理由とともに書くこと。
・最初の文は語数に含（ﾟ）めずに，30語以上の英語で書くこと。

（注）take　（授業などを）受ける

　　　　　　　　　　　　　　　　　　　＜福岡県＞

29 英語の授業で，国連が定める様々な記念日について調べ，ポスターにまとめて発表する活動を行いました。次の【ポスター】は，RioのグループがWorld Water Day（世界水の日）について調べたことをまとめたものです。後の《条件》に従って，　(A)　〜　(C)　に入る内容を英語で書きなさい。

【ポスター】

March 22 is World Water Day!

People cannot live without water. It is important for everyone in the world to get clean and safe water easily.

We need to realize:

1．Clean and safe water is necessary for our health.

Picture A	Picture B

We need clean and safe water for ☐(A)☐ , ☐(B)☐ , and so on.

2．<u>Getting water easily is also important for children's *education.</u>

In Japan, we ☐(C)☐

Picture C

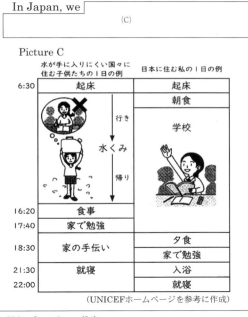

水が手に入りにくい国々に住む子供たちの１日の例　日本に住む私の１日の例

	水が手に入りにくい国々に 住む子供たちの１日の例	日本に住む私の１日の例
6:30	起床	起床
		朝食
	水くみ（行き・帰り）	学校
16:20	食事	
17:40	家で勉強	
18:30	家の手伝い	夕食
		家で勉強
21:30	就寝	入浴
22:00		就寝

(UNICEFホームページを参考に作成)

（注）education　教育

《条件》
・ ☐(A)☐ には１語， ☐(B)☐ には３語で，それぞれPicture A，Bに合う英語を書くこと。
・ ☐(C)☐ には，下線部の内容について，Picture Cの「水が入りにくい国々に住む子供たちの１日の例」と「日本に住む私の１日の例」を比較して分かることを，書き出しに続けて30語〜40語の英語で書くこと。ただし，英文の数はいくつでもよい。
・符号（，.！？""など）は語数に含めないこと。

<群馬県>

d．整序英作文

1 次の(1)，(2)の各対話文の文意が通るように，（　　）の中のア〜エを正しく並べかえて，左から順にその記号を書け。

(1) A：Soccer is becoming as （ア. baseball　イ. as　ウ. among　エ. popular）boys in my school.

B：Really? In my school, boys like baseball better than soccer.

(2) A：What's the Japanese name of this flower?

B：We （ア. in　イ. it　ウ. call　エ. *Himawari*）Japanese. It's one of my favorite flowers.

＜愛媛県＞

2 次の(1)，(2)の対話について，（　　）内の語句をすべて用い，意味がとおるように並べかえて，正しい英文を完成させなさい。ただし，文頭にくる語も小文字で示してあります。

(1) A：John will leave Japan next month.

B：Really? I'll miss him a lot. I（could / he / longer / stay / wish）.

(2) A：（called / this / is / flower / what）in English?

B：Sorry, I don't know.

＜宮崎県＞

3 次の(1)・(2)の対話文の〔　　〕内の語句を並べかえて，意味の通る英文を完成させなさい。ただし，〔　　〕内の語句を全部使うこと。

(1) Josh：Why did your brother go to Italy?

Beth：He went there〔cook / learn / to / to / how〕.

Josh：That's great!

(2) Kazuki：You look bored today, Jake.

Jake　：Today, we have no P.E. class.

Kazuki：Oh, I see. I think you have a lot of energy today.

Jake　：Yes. I〔every / P.E. class / wish / had / I〕day.

＜高知県＞

4 次の(1)，(2)，(3)の（　　）内の語句を意味が通るように並べかえて，(1)と(2)はア，イ，ウ，エ，(3)はア，イ，ウ，エ，オの記号を用いて答えなさい。

(1) A：Is Tom the tallest in this class?

B：No. He（ア. tall　イ. not　ウ. as　エ. is）as Ken.

(2) A：I hear so many （ア. be　イ. can　ウ. seen　エ. stars）from the top of the mountain.

B：Really? Let's go to see them.

(3) A：What sport do you like?

B：Judo! Actually I（ア. been　イ. have　ウ. practicing　エ. since　オ. judo）I was five years old.

＜栃木県＞

5 次は，AとBの対話です。（　　）内の語を正しく並べかえて，文を完成させなさい。

〔*At home*〕

A：Do you know what we should put in this emergency kit?

B：Look at this list. I think（what / will / you / it / show）you should put.

＜福島県＞

6 次は，AとBの対話です。（　　）内の語を正しく並べかえて，文を完成させなさい。

〔*At a teachers' room*〕

A：What is your plan for the farewell party for Alex?

B：First, we'll sing a song for him. After that, we'll（some / to / give / him / presents）.

＜福島県＞

7 次の(1)，(2)の対話について，（　　）内の語句をすべて用い，意味がとおるように並べかえて，正しい英文を完成させなさい。ただし，文頭にくる語も小文字で示してあります。

(1) A：Hello. May I speak to Tom, please?

B：Sorry. He's out now. I'll（you / him / call / to / tell）back.

(2) A：（be / what / like / the weather / will）tomorrow?

B：It'll be sunny.

＜宮崎県＞

8 次の各問いの会話文について，（　　）内のア〜オの語を正しく並べ替えて意味が通る文を完成させ，その並べ替えた順に記号をすべて書きなさい。

問1. A：I have a question about this math problem.

B：Oh, you should ask Yuji. He（ア. is　イ. very　ウ. math　エ. at　オ. good）.

問2. A：It is （ア. for　イ. to　ウ. write　エ. difficult　オ. me）English messages. I speak better.

B：That's true. You speak English well.

問3. A：Do you think Nana will come? She lives far from here.

B：I'm not sure, but I think she（ア. because　イ. come　ウ. it's　エ. won't　オ. raining）.

＜沖縄県＞

9 次の会話の下線部について，（　　）内の語を並べかえ，意味のとおる英文にしなさい。

Tomoki：What is that *building*? It looks old, but very beautiful.

Mary　：Oh, it is（was / built / temple / which / a）three hundred years ago.

(注) building　建物

＜鳥取県＞

10 次の(1)，(2)の各対話文の文意が通るように，（　　）の中のア～エを正しく並べかえて，その記号を書け。

(1) A：Do you （ ア．get　イ．she'll　ウ．when　エ．know ）to the station?
　　B：Yes. At 11:30.

(2) A：I want to practice the guitar. But I don't have one.
　　B：OK. You can use mine. I'll （ ア．it　イ．to　ウ．bring　エ．you ）tomorrow.

<愛媛県>

11 次の(1)，(2)，(3)の（　　）内の語句を意味が通るように並べかえて，(1)と(2)はア，イ，ウ，エ，(3)はア，イ，ウ，エ，オの記号を用いて答えなさい。

(1) Shall we （ ア．of　イ．in　ウ．meet　エ．front ）the station?

(2) My mother （ ア．to　イ．come　ウ．me　エ．wants ）home early today.

(3) The boy （ ア．tennis　イ．playing　ウ．is　エ．the park　オ．in ）my brother.

<栃木県>

12 次の(1)，(2)の対話について，（　　）内の語をすべて用い，意味がとおるように並べかえて，正しい英文を完成させなさい。ただし，文頭にくる語も小文字で示してあります。

(1) A：I'm going to go to Canada to study English next week.
　　B：Really?（ come / you / when / back / will ）to Japan?

(2) A：Have you decided the name of your new dog?
　　B：Yes. I （ Shiro / it / after / its / named ）color.

<宮崎県>

13 次の(1)・(2)の対話文の〔　　〕内の語句を並べかえて，意味の通る英文を完成させなさい。ただし，〔　　〕内の語句を全部使うこと。

(1) Meg　：Hey, Kenta. Can we go to the library together now?
　　Kenta：I'm still busy. I can't go with you.
　　Meg　：How 〔 been / have / playing / you / long 〕 that video game?
　　Kenta：For three hours.

(2) Daniel：What are you doing?
　　Fred　：I'm reading a Japanese novel. It 〔 by / written / writer / was / a famous 〕.
　　Daniel：Wow! Can you read Japanese?
　　Fred　：Yes.

<高知県>

14 次の1，2の会話について，それぞれの[　　]内の語を正しく並べかえて，英文を完成させなさい。

1．（家で）
Mother：Tom, are you still reading a book? It's time to go to bed! It's already 11:00 p.m.
Tom　：Yes, but this book is so interesting that I can't stop reading it.
Mother：Well, [been / long / you / have / how] reading it?
Tom　：Oh, for more than four hours. I should stop here and go to bed.

2．（休み時間の教室で）
Emi　　　：I heard you went to the zoo. Did you see the baby lion?
Ms. Baker：Yes. I'll show [it / you / some / of / pictures].
Emi　　　：Wow, it's so cute! I want to go and see it.

<岐阜県>

15 次の各問いの会話文について，（　　）内のア～オの語句を正しく並べ替えて意味が通る文を完成させ，その並べ替えた順に記号をすべて書きなさい。

問1．A：Do you remember （ ア．school festival　イ．held　ウ．when　エ．our　オ．was ）last year?
　　　B：No, I don't. Let's ask our teacher.

問2．A：Let's go shopping after school today.
　　　B：I'm sorry I can't. My mother （ ア．me　イ．come　ウ．to　エ．back　オ．told ）by 6 p.m.

問3．A：You have a nice camera.
　　　B：Thanks. This （ ア．the camera　イ．gave　ウ．is　エ．me　オ．my father ）on my birthday.

<沖縄県>

16 次の(1)，(2)，(3)の（　　）内の語句を意味が通るように並べかえて，(1)と(2)はア，イ，ウ，エ，(3)はア，イ，ウ，エ，オの記号を用いて答えなさい。

(1) A：What is your plan for this weekend?
　　B：My plan （ ア．shopping　イ．to　ウ．is　エ．go ）with my sister.

(2) A：This is （ ア．interesting　イ．most　ウ．movie　エ．the ）that I have ever watched.
　　B：Oh, really? I want to watch it, too.

(3) A：Do you （ ア．who　イ．know　ウ．drinking　エ．is　オ．the boy ）coffee over there?
　　B：Yes! He is my cousin. His name is Kenji.

<栃木県>

17 次の(1)～(3)の〔　　〕内の英語を正しく並べかえて，それぞれの対話文を完成させなさい。

(1) A：Do you study English at home every day?
　　B：Yes, I do. I also study French.
　　A：Why do you study English and French?
　　B：The two languages 〔 are / in / taught 〕 my country.

(2) A：What did you do last weekend?
　　B：I went to Hiraizumi and took some pictures there.
　　A：Can 〔 me / show / some / you 〕?
　　B：Of course. Here are the pictures.

(3) A：How many brothers or sisters do you have?
　　B：I have a sister. This is a picture of my family.
　　A：Which person is your sister in this picture?
　　B：Well, she is the girl 〔 a book / a cap / and / has / wears / who 〕 in her hand.

<岩手県>

18 次の(1)〜(3)の対話が成り立つように，それぞれ（　　）の中の単語を並べ替えて英文を完成させなさい。また，文のはじめは大文字で書きなさい。

(1) A : You look sleepy.
　　B : I got up at five thirty this morning.
　　A : Do (early / get / so / up / usually / you)?
　　B : No, only today. I wanted to try studying early in the morning.

(2) A : I have a cute cat. You can come to my house and play with my cat next Sunday.
　　B : Thanks. Can I ask Rio to come with me? She likes cats too.
　　A : (can / come / don't / I / she / think). She has a club activity every Sunday.

(3) A : Do you like watching baseball on TV?
　　B : Yes, I especially like high school baseball.
　　A : Have you ever been to *Koshien* to watch the baseball games?
　　B : No. (Hyogo / I / I / in / lived / wish). I would go to watch the baseball games every summer.

＜富山県＞

19 次の各問いの会話文について，（　　）内の語句を正しく並べ替えて意味が通る文を完成させ，その並べ替えた順に記号をすべて書きなさい。なお，（　　）内の語句は，文頭にくる場合も小文字で示しています。

問1. A : Sam, students must clean the classroom by themselves in Japan.
　　B : Really? I didn't know that. (ア. we　イ. to　ウ. don't　エ. clean　オ. have) our classroom in America.

問2. A : I've just arrived in Kyoto. I want to see everything!
　　B : Oh, how (ア. you　イ. long　ウ. going to　エ. stay　オ. are) here?
　　A : For seven days.

問3. A : Did you know (ア. are　イ. Canada　ウ. and French　エ. English　オ. spoken in)?
　　B : No, I didn't. That's interesting.

＜沖縄県＞

20 次の(1)・(2)の対話文の〔　　〕内の語を並べかえて，意味の通る英文を完成させよ。ただし，〔　　〕内の語を全部使うこと。

(1) *Shiho* : Mr. Yamada will visit your house today, right?
　　Jack : Yes, but I don't〔 when / arrive / he / know / will 〕.

(2) *Ms. Lee* : Hello?
　　Satoko : Hello. This is Satoko. May I speak to Kevin?
　　Ms. Lee : Sorry, he is out now. Do〔 you / call / him / to / want 〕you back?
　　Satoko : Yes, please. I'm at home all day today.

＜高知県＞

21 次の対話文の下線部について，あとのア〜カの語句を並べかえて正しい英文を完成させ，（　X　），（　Y　），（　Z　）にあてはまる語句を，それぞれ記号で答えなさい。

(1) *Cathy* : What did you do last weekend?
　　Jun : (　　　)（　X　）(　　　)（　Y　）（　Z　） her homework.
　　ア. stayed at　イ. and helped　ウ. home
　　エ. finish　オ. my sister　カ. I

(2) *Eri* : I want to (　　　)（　X　）(　　　)（　Y　）(　　　)（　Z　）for Jim.
　　Bob : I'm going to choose this blue one. I think he will like it.
　　ア. buy　イ. shirt　ウ. you
　　エ. which　オ. will　カ. know

＜山形県＞

22 次の対話文の下線部について，あとのア〜カの語句を並べかえて正しい英文を完成させ，（　X　），（　Y　），（　Z　）にあてはまる語句を，それぞれ記号で答えなさい。

(1) *Ted* : I went to Kyoto, Osaka and Hiroshima last month.
　　Masato : Did you? I think Kyoto (　　　)（　X　）(　　　)（　Y　）(　　　)（　Z　） cities.
　　ア. three　イ. the most　ウ. of
　　エ. is　オ. the　カ. popular

(2) *Kevin* : Have you ever been to the city library?
　　Takuma : No. We (　　　)（　X　）(　　　)（　Y　）(　　　)（　Z　） this city.
　　ア. of　イ. can't　ウ. a map
　　エ. there　オ. get　カ. without

＜山形県＞

23 次の対話文の下線部について，あとのア〜カの語句を並べかえて正しい英文を完成させ，（　X　），（　Y　），（　Z　）にあてはまる語句を，それぞれ記号で答えなさい。

(1) *Masaki* : I (　　　)（　X　）(　　　)（　Y　）(　　　)（　Z　） I borrowed. Did you see it?
　　Lily : No. I'll help you find it.
　　ア. been　イ. the book　ウ. have
　　エ. for　オ. which　カ. looking

(2) *Yoshie* : (　　　)（　X　）(　　　)（　Y　）(　　　)（　Z　） this computer?
　　David : Yes. He often writes e-mails with it.
　　ア. use　イ. can　ウ. you
　　エ. do　オ. your father　カ. think

＜山形県＞

24 次の(1)〜(3)の〔　　〕内の英語を正しく並べかえて，それぞれの対話文を完成させなさい。ただし，文頭に来る語も小文字で示してあります。

(1) A : We'll have a birthday party for my sister.
　　B : When?
　　A : Next Saturday. Why don't〔 join / us / you 〕?
　　B : Of course.

— 156 —

(2) A：I practiced baseball very hard.
　　B：Oh, did you?
　　A：I'm so tired. Could you give〔drink / me / something / to〕?
　　B：Sure.
(3) A：What's the matter?
　　B：I have lost my pen.
　　A：Is it in your bag?
　　B：No.〔am / for / I / looking / must / the pen〕be in my room.

＜岩手県＞

25 次の(1)～(3)の対話が成り立つように，それぞれ（　　）の中の単語や語句を並べ替えて英文を完成させなさい。また，文のはじめは大文字で書きなさい。

(1) A：I really like watching tennis games.
　　B：Oh, do you? Do you like playing tennis too?
　　A：No, I just like watching it.（do / play / sport / what / you）?
　　B：I play baseball every week.
(2) A：Yasuo sings very well, right?
　　B：Yes, but I think you can sing better.
　　A：Really?　（as / as / cannot / I / sing / well）Yasuo.
　　B：You can do it! I heard that you practiced singing after school.
(3) A：How did you like my presentation?
　　B：It was great.
　　A：Thank you. Actually（finish / helped / it / me / my friend）.
　　B：Oh, I see. It's nice to study with a friend.

＜富山県＞

26 次の(ア)～(エ)の対話が完成するように，（　　）内の六つの語の中から五つを選んで正しい順番に並べたとき，その（　　）内で3番目と5番目にくる語の番号をそれぞれ答えなさい。(それぞれ一つずつ不要な語があるので，その語は使用しないこと。)

(ア) A：We're going to watch a soccer game this Sunday. Is（1．to　2．anything　3．I　4．there　5．should　6．bring）?
　　B：You'll need something to drink because it will be hot.
(イ) A：Please tell（1．will　2．goes　3．you　4．come　5．me　6．when）back home.
　　B：Sure. I'll be at home at 7:00 p.m.
(ウ) A：Eri,（1．have　2．we　3．milk　4．are　5．any　6．do）left in the *bottle?
　　B：No, I drank it all.
(エ) A：Don't（1．afraid　2．asking　3．be　4．to　5．questions　6．of）if you have something you don't understand.
　　B：Thank you.
(注) bottle　瓶

＜神奈川県＞

27 次の(ア)～(エ)の対話が完成するように，（　　）の六つの語の中から五つを選んで正しい順番に並べたとき，その（　　）内で3番目と5番目にくる語の番号をそれぞれ答えなさい。(それぞれ一つずつ不要な語があるので，その語は使用しないこと。)

(ア) A：A lot of people use English all over the world.
　　B：Yes. English is（1．by　2．people　3．as　4．many　5．uses　6．spoken）their first language.
(イ) A：What（1．work　2．be　3．you　4．did　5．to　6．want）when you were a child?
　　B：A doctor. I was interested in helping many people.
(ウ) A：I'd like to buy a new computer, but I can't（1．should　2．I　3．one　4．to　5．which　6．decide）buy.
　　B：Oh, let me help you.
(エ) A：Can you play the piano?
　　B：Just a little. But I（1．better　2．wish　3．were　4．I　5．could　6．at）playing it.

＜神奈川県＞

28 次の(ア)～(エ)の対話が完成するように，（　　）内の六つの語の中から五つを選んで正しい順番に並べたとき，その（　　）内で3番目と5番目にくる語の番号をそれぞれ答えなさい。(それぞれ一つずつ不要な語があるので，その語は使用しないこと。)

(ア) A：Who is（1．tennis　2．the　3．of　4．best　5．in　6．player）the five?
　　B：Aya is. She won the city *tournament last month.
(イ) A：Do you know the（1．been　2．and　3．guitar　4．playing　5．girl　6．the）singing *over there?
　　B：Yes. That is Rumi, my sister's friend.
(ウ) A：Why do you like the book?
　　B：Because it（1．written　2．the　3．reading　4．eyes　5．through　6．is）of a little dog.
(エ) A：Do you（1．that　2．think　3．want　4．to　5．me　6．open）door?
　　B：Thank you. You are very kind.
(注) tournament　トーナメント　　over there　向こうで

＜神奈川県＞

29 留学生のエマ（Emma）が，クラスメイトのアズサ（Azusa）とタケル（Takeru）に次の2つのウェブサイトを見せながら旅行について相談しています。会話の流れに合うように，①～④の（　　）内の英語を並べかえて，記号で答えなさい。ただし，それぞれ不要な語(句)が1つずつあります。

Emma：Summer vacation starts next week! I'm going to *take a day trip with my friends next Wednesday. Which is better to do on the trip, wearing a *yukata* or *painting on a *wind chime?

Azusa : If I①(ア．I would　イ．choose　ウ． painting on a wind chime　エ．wearing a *yukata*　オ．were　カ．you,). Walking around the city *in traditional clothes sounds great!

Takeru : Painting on a wind chime sounds nice.

Emma : Why do you think so?

Takeru : Because you can take it home with you. You can enjoy the sound of the wind chime at home. The staff members ②(ア．wear　イ．you　ウ．will　エ．paint on　オ．show　カ．how to) a wind chime.

Azusa : Well, if you wear a *yukata* and take some pictures of yourself, you can enjoy them later, too.

Emma : That's true.... I can't decide which activity I should choose.

Takeru : Well... ③(ア．you　イ．do　ウ．a wind chime　エ．why　オ．don't　カ．paint on) in the morning?　Then you can wear a *yukata* in the afternoon.

Emma : That's a good idea. I'll do that. I don't ④(ア．my *yukata*　イ．clean　ウ．to　エ．want　オ．dirty　カ．make).

(注) take a day trip　日帰り旅行をする
paint on 〜　〜に絵をかく　　wind chime　風鈴
in 〜　〜を着て

〈茨城県〉

30 サトル(Satoru)と留学生のアイシャ(Aisha)，フェイロン(Fei Long)の３人が，休日にあおい町(Aoi Town)に出かける話をしています。下の二つのポスターを見ながら，会話の流れに合うように，①〜④の(　　　)内の英語を並べかえて，記号で答えなさい。ただし，それぞれ不要な語(句)が一つずつあり，文頭に来る語(句)も小文字で示されています。

Aoi Art Museum
【場所】　あおい駅から歩いて５分
【今月の特別企画】
*有名漫画家の原画を展示
*地元ゆかりの画家による絵画作品を郷土史とともに紹介

Aoi Science Museum
【場所】　あおい駅から歩いて20分
【今月の特別企画】
*サイエンスショー「エネルギー問題について考える」(世界の現状を3D映像で)
*写真展「海の不思議」(世界で活躍する写真家の作品を展示)

Satoru : Please look at the posters. We will go to Aoi Station by train, then walk to one of the museums. ①(ア．how　イ．want to　ウ．you　エ．which museum　オ．do　カ．visit)?　Aisha, you like the Aoi Art Museum, right?

Aisha : Yes, because ②(ア．famous cartoonists　イ．taken　ウ．many pictures　エ．by　オ．there are　カ．drawn) in this museum.

Fei Long : I see. Actually, my idea is different. I am interested in the science museum.

Satoru : Why?

Fei Long : Because we can learn many things about ③(ア．that　イ．have to　ウ．the amazing ocean　エ．energy problems　オ．solve　カ．we).

Aisha : But we can learn many things in the art museum, too. For example, the history of Aoi Town... Oh, also, ④(ア．takes　イ．to walk　ウ．it　エ．only 5 minutes　オ．only 20 minutes　カ．from) Aoi Station to the museum.

Satoru : Umm... It's very hard to decide.

〈茨城県〉

31 健(Ken)さんとキャシー(Cathy)さんの会話を読んで，あとの各問に答えなさい。

Cathy : Last weekend, I was sick in bed. Sachi was always with me and took care of me.

Ken : How kind!

Cathy : To say thank you to her, I gave her fish.

Ken : Fish?　Why?

Cathy : Oh, Sachi is my pretty cat. I had a fever, and she worried about me and stayed with me for a long time. ①(　　　)(　X　)(　　　)(　Y　)(　　　).

Ken : She can understand how you feel.

Cathy : Yeah. When I come back from work every day, she ②(　　　)(　X　)(　　　)(　Y　)(　　　). I say to her, "I'm home," and she always answers me.

Ken : Wow, she is very cute. I wish [　　　　]. But I can't. In fact, my father doesn't like animals.

Cathy : For me, Sachi is not an animal but an important part of my family.

Ken : I see. ③(　　　)(　X　)(　　　)(　Y　)(　　　) pets can be family members.

問１．下線部①〜③には，それぞれ次の【　　】内の語句を並べかえたものが入ります。ア〜オの語句を会話の意味が通じるように正しく並べかえて文を完成させるとき，(　X　)，(　Y　)にあてはまる語句はどれか，符号を書きなさい。ただし，文頭の文字も小文字で表されています。
① 【ア．better　イ．feel　ウ．helped　エ．me　オ．that 】
② 【ア．in front of　イ．is　ウ．me　エ．my house　オ．waiting for 】
③ 【ア．I　イ．know　ウ．my father　エ．to　オ．want 】
問２．[　　　]の中に入る３語〜６語の適切な内容の英語を書きなさい。

〈石川県〉

第4章 **リスニング問題**

a．5W1Hについて問われる問題

1　[音声 1]　これは，英語による説明を聞いて答える問題です。
ア．Can I lend you my dictionary?
イ．Can I use your dictionary?
ウ．Why don't you borrow a dictionary?
エ．Why don't you buy a dictionary?

〈岩手県〉

2　[音声 2]　No.1，No.2の会話を聞き，それぞれの英語の質問に対する答えとして，最も適切なものを，次のア〜エからひとつずつ選び，記号で答えなさい。会話は1回のみ放送します。
No.1 〈留学中の女子生徒(Maya)と現地の男子生徒(Alex)との会話〉
【質問】　What are they talking about?
　ア．Their school events.
　イ．Their plans for this weekend.
　ウ．Their favorite baseball teams.
　エ．The movies they like.
No.2 〈文化祭でダンスを披露する女子生徒(Emi)とブラウン先生(Mr. Brown)との会話〉
【質問】　When will Emi's dance finish?
　ア．About 11:00.　イ．About 11:10.
　ウ．About 11:15.　エ．About 11:25.

〈鳥取県〉

3　[音声 3]　HanakoとTaroの対話を聞いて，それに続く1番〜3番の質問の答えとして最も適当なものを，ア〜エから1つずつ選び，記号を書きなさい。
1番　ア．Taro thinks he should have only one pet.
　　　イ．Taro thinks his pet is good for his health.
　　　ウ．Taro thinks he doesn't have any ways to save his pet.
　　　エ．Taro thinks giving food to his pet every day is hard.
2番　ア．Some people stop keeping their pets for some reasons.
　　　イ．Some people think that pets are members of their family.
　　　ウ．Some people understand that pets are important for people's minds.
　　　エ．Some people take their pets to the hospital when they are sick.
3番　ア．They hope everyone will walk alone every day.
　　　イ．They hope everyone will keep at least two cats.
　　　ウ．They hope everyone will have many kinds of pets.
　　　エ．They hope everyone will be kind to their pets.

〈大分県〉

4　[音声 4]　これから読まれる英文は，美佐(Misa)と店員との会話である。あとに読まれるNo.1〜No.3の質問の答えとして最も適当なものをア〜ウの中から一つずつ選んで，その記号を書け。英文と質問は2回ずつ読まれる。
No.1 ア．To make T-shirts for her friends.
　　　イ．To look for popular food in the shop.
　　　ウ．To buy something for her family.
No.2 ア．Orange.　イ．Green.　ウ．Yellow.
No.3 ア．Two.　　イ．Three.　ウ．Four.

〈長崎県〉

5　[音声 5]　これから英文を読み，それについての質問をします。それぞれの質問に対する答えとして最も適当なものを，次のア〜エから一つずつ選び，その符号を書きなさい。
1．ア．On Sunday, November 22.
　　イ．On Monday, November 23.
　　ウ．On Tuesday, November 24.
　　エ．On Wednesday, November 25.
2．ア．Here you are.　　イ．How about you?
　　ウ．No, thank you.　エ．See you later.
3．ア．Baseball.　イ．Basketball.
　　ウ．Tennis.　　エ．Volleyball.
4．ア．Betty and her brother.
　　イ．Betty and her father.
　　ウ．Betty and her mother.
　　エ．Betty's father and mother.

〈新潟県〉

6　[音声 6]　これは英文を聞き取り，その内容について英語の質問に答える問題です。
あなたは海外研修旅行先のアメリカで，ある美術館を訪れています。これから放送するのは，その美術館の利用時のルールについて，ツアーガイドが説明している場面です。英文は1度だけ放送し，それに続けて英文の内容に関して二つの質問をそれぞれ2回放送します。質問の答えとして，最も適当なものをア，イ，ウの中から一つずつ選び，その記号を書きなさい。

Question 1　ア．Because it is important to talk about the rules.
　　　　　　イ．Because it is dangerous to run.
　　　　　　ウ．Because it is special to clean the museum.
Question 2　ア．You can talk on the smartphone in the museum.
　　　　　　イ．You can eat and drink in the museum.
　　　　　　ウ．You can take pictures in the museum.

〈山梨県〉

7　[音声 7]　これから，No.1からNo.4まで，四つの対話を放送します。それぞれの対話のあとで，その対話について一つずつ質問します。それぞれの質問に対して，最も適切な答えを，ア，イ，ウ，エの中から一つ選んで，その記号を書きなさい。

No.1 ア．Becky is.
　　 イ．Bob is.
　　 ウ．Kate is.
　　 エ．Becky and Bob are.
No.2 ア．Because she wanted to go shopping.
　　 イ．Because her family went shopping.
　　 ウ．Because the weather was bad.
　　 エ．Because she didn't want to go to the mountain.
No.3 ア．She can't ask where her dictionary is.
　　 イ．She can't tell where the table is.
　　 ウ．She can't find Kevin.
　　 エ．She can't find her dictionary.
No.4 ア．He will play in the tennis tournament next weekend.
　　 イ．He won all the games in the tennis tournament yesterday.
　　 ウ．He played tennis with Maki in the tournament.
　　 エ．He talked about tennis with Maki yesterday.
　　　　　　　　　　　　　　　　　　　　＜茨城県＞

8 音声 8 それぞれの質問に対する答えとして最も適当なものを，次の(ア)～(エ)から1つずつ選べ。
(1) (ア) She visited her grandfather and made a cake.
　　(イ) She played tennis with her friends.
　　(ウ) She watched TV at home.
　　(エ) She did her homework.
(2) (ア) Daisuke.　　(イ) Shota.
　　(ウ) Kumi.　　(エ) Lisa.
　　　　　　　　　　　　　　　　　　　　＜京都府＞

9 音声 9 放送による指示に従って答えなさい。
No.1 A．Three.　　B．Four.
　　 C．Five.　　D．Six.
No.2 A．Sam's father and mother.
　　 B．Sam and his sister.
　　 C．Sam's father and sister.
　　 D．Sam and his father.
　　　　　　　　　　　　　　　　　　　　＜千葉県＞

10 音声 10 会話を聞いて，その内容についての質問に答えなさい。それぞれ会話のあとに質問が続きます。その質問に対する答えとして適切なものを，次のa～dからそれぞれ1つ選びなさい。（会話と質問は2回読みます。）
No.1 a．Eggs.
　　 b．Dishes.
　　 c．Eggs and chopsticks.
　　 d．Chopsticks and dishes.
No.2 a．To her classroom.
　　 b．To the hospital.
　　 c．To Mike's house.
　　 d．To Mr. Brown's room.
No.3 a．He wants to graduate from school.
　　 b．He wants to introduce Japanese food.
　　 c．He wants to be the owner of a restaurant.
　　 d．He wants to travel all over the world.
　　　　　　　　　　　　　　　　　　　　＜兵庫県＞

11 音声 11 高校生の健(Ken)が英語の時間に行ったスピーチと，その内容について5つの質問を2回放送します。No.1～No.5の英文が質問の答えとなるように，　　　　に入る最も適切なものを，A～Dの中から1つずつ選び，その記号を書きなさい。
No.1 She started it about 　　　　　　　　.
　　 A．ten years ago　　　　B．twelve years ago
　　 C．fourteen years ago　　D．forty years ago
No.2 He was surprised because 　　　　　　　　 his grandmother's shop.
　　 A．so many customers came to
　　 B．so many foreign people came to
　　 C．there were only a few kinds of cakes in
　　 D．there were so many kinds of cakes in
No.3 She was 　　　　　　　　.
　　 A．Ken's mother
　　 B．Ken's teacher
　　 C．a customer at Ken's grandmother's shop
　　 D．a clerk at Ken's grandmother's shop
No.4 He usually goes to her shop 　　　　　　　　.
　　 A．in the morning
　　 B．after school
　　 C．on weekends
　　 D．on his birthday
No.5 He wants to 　　　　　　　　.
　　 A．meet Meg and her son again
　　 B．start his own shop in the future
　　 C．buy a birthday cake for his grandmother
　　 D．make his grandmother's shop more popular
　　　　　　　　　　　　　　　　　　　　＜和歌山県＞

12 音声 12 シドニーにホームステイ中のKazuyaと，語学学校講師のMs. Hillとの英語による対話を聞いて，それぞれの質問に対する答えとして，ア～エから最も適当なものを1つ選び，その記号を書きなさい。
No.1 ア．The zoo and the aquarium.
　　 イ．The zoo and the museum.
　　 ウ．The aquarium and the museum.
　　 エ．The zoo, the aquarium, and the museum.
No.2 ア．Ms. Hill will.
　　 イ．Kazuya will.
　　 ウ．Kazuya and Ms. Hill will.
　　 エ．Ms. Hill and her friends will.
No.3 ア．At 10:30.　　イ．At 11:15.
　　 ウ．At 11:30.　　エ．At 12:15.
　　　　　　　　　　　　　　　　　　　　＜三重県＞

13 音声 13 〔英語の対話とその内容についての質問を聞いて，答えとして最も適切なものを選ぶ問題〕
(1) ① ア．Because he has already practiced kendo in his country.
　　　　 イ．Because he can practice kendo even in summer.
　　　　 ウ．Because he has a strong body and mind.
　　　　 エ．Because he can learn traditional Japanese culture.
　　② ア．Four days a week.
　　　 イ．Five days a week.
　　　 ウ．Every weekend.
　　　 エ．Every day.

(2)

Lunch Menu

Happy Lunch

A　$3.00　　B　$4.50　　C　$4.50

Happy Jeff's Lunch　$7.00

Apple Pie: $3.00
Ice Cream: $2.00
French Fries: $2.00

Free Ticket!
or or

Happy Jeff's Hot Dogs

① ア．$4.00.
　イ．$5.00.
　ウ．$6.00.
　エ．$7.00.
② ア．A hot dog.
　イ．French fries.
　ウ．An ice cream.
　エ．A toy.

〈栃木県〉

14

音声 14　放送の指示に従って答える。

1．ア．Fifteen years old.
　イ．Twenty-three years old.
　ウ．Twenty-nine years old.
　エ．Thirty-two years old.
2．ア．Maki did.
　イ．Maki's father did.
　ウ．John's father did.
　エ．John's friend did.
3．ア．Because she wanted to improve her English.
　イ．Because she wanted to make him surprised.
　ウ．Because she wanted to talk about sports.
　エ．Because she wanted to learn Japanese.
4．ア．He wants them to learn more about world history.
　イ．He wants them to teach him Japanese after school.
　ウ．He wants them to play baseball together in his team.
　エ．He wants them to make many friends through English.

〈愛媛県〉

15

音声 15　サッカークラブに所属するボブと，姉で大学生のニーナとが電話で話をしています。二人の会話を聞いて，それに続く二つの質問に対する答えとして最も適しているものを，それぞれア～エから一つずつ選び，記号で答えなさい。

(1) ア．At the entrance of the house.
　イ．Inside the box in Bob's room.
　ウ．Around the table in the kitchen.
　エ．Under the lunch box inside Bob's bag.
(2) ア．She will clean the entrance to find Bob's shoes.
　イ．She will go to the stadium with Bob's soccer shoes.
　ウ．She will look for Bob's soccer shoes at home.
　エ．She will make a lunch for Bob and bring it to the stadium.

〈大阪府・A・B問題〉

16

音声 16　次のア～エの中から適するものをそれぞれ一つずつ選びなさい。

〈対話文1〉
　ア．To have a birthday party.
　イ．To write a birthday card for her.
　ウ．To make some tea.
　エ．To bring a cake.
〈対話文2〉
　ア．He was giving water to flowers.
　イ．He was doing his homework.
　ウ．He was eating lunch.
　エ．He was reading some history books.
〈対話文3〉
　ア．He got there by train.
　イ．He took a bus to get there.
　ウ．He got there by bike.
　エ．He walked there.

〈東京都〉

17

音声 17　（放送の指示にしたがって答える）

1．ア．Tom painted the picture in the art class.
　イ．Tom didn't think the picture Kana painted was really good.
　ウ．Tom was surprised that Kana painted a really good picture.
　エ．Tom didn't believe that Kana took the photo in the art class.
2．ア．Kana asked Tom how his uncle was.
　イ．Something good happened to Tom yesterday.
　ウ．Tom wasn't happy because he lost his ticket for the concert yesterday.
　エ．Kana knew that Tom got a ticket for his favorite singer's concert before she asked him what happened.
3．ア．Kana told Tom what he should eat.
　イ．The menu was written in both Japanese and English.
　ウ．Tom thought the pictures on the menu were helpful.
　エ．Kana thinks it would be easier to understand the menu if there were some pictures.
4．ア．Kana has a piano lesson on the 24th.
　イ．Kana has a piano lesson on the 25th.
　ウ．Both Kana and Tom were free on the 17th.
　エ．Both Kana and Tom are free on the 24th.
5．ア．Tom answered the interview in April.
　イ．All of the things Tom guessed about the interview were right.
　ウ．In the interview, 38 students chose "Making friends" as the thing they want to try harder.
　エ．In the interview, the number of students who chose "Club activities" as the thing they enjoy the most at school was the biggest.

〈大阪府・C問題〉

b．図表・グラフを用いた問題

1 音声 18 No.1～No.3の英文を聞き，それぞれの英文の内容を最もよく表しているものを，次のア～エからひとつずつ選び，記号で答えなさい。英文は1回のみ放送します。

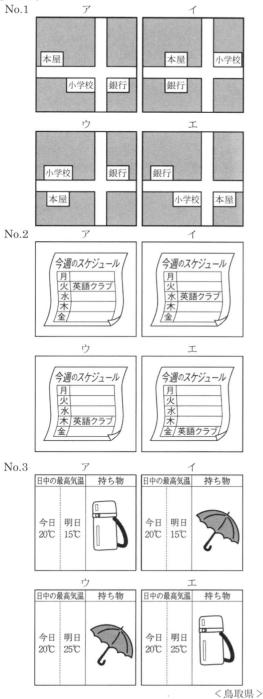

No.1

No.2

No.3

<鳥取県>

2 音声 19 これから，No.1とNo.2について，それぞれ2人の対話と，対話に関する質問が流れます。質問に対する答えとして最も適切なものを，それぞれの選択肢A～Dの中から選びなさい。

No.1

No.2

<群馬県>

3 音声 20 1番，2番の対話を聞いて，それぞれの質問の答えとして最も適当なものを，ア～エから1つずつ選び，記号を書きなさい。

1番

2番

ア．400 yen.　　イ．500 yen.
ウ．600 yen.　　エ．700 yen.

<大分県>

4

音声 21　放送の指示に従って答える。

ア．

1 2 3 4

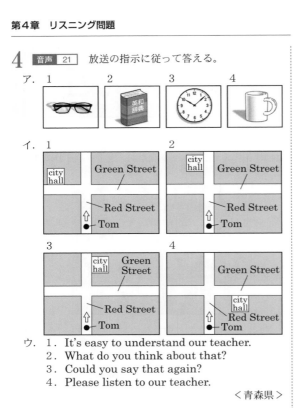

イ．

1 2

city hall　Green Street
Red Street　Tom

city hall　Green Street
Red Street　Tom

3 4

city hall　Green Street
Red Street　Tom

Green Street
city hall　Red Street　Tom

ウ．1．It's easy to understand our teacher.
　2．What do you think about that?
　3．Could you say that again?
　4．Please listen to our teacher.

〈青森県〉

5

音声 22　次のNo.1〜No.3について，それぞれ対話を聞き，その内容についての質問の答えとして最も適当なものを，それぞれア〜エから選びなさい。英文は1回読まれます。

No.1

ア　イ　ウ　エ

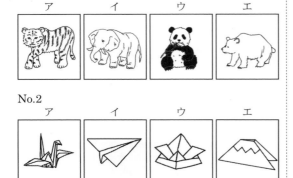

No.2

ア　イ　ウ　エ

No.3

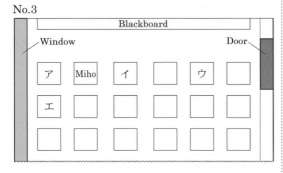

Blackboard
Window　　　　　　　Door
ア　Miho　イ　　　ウ
エ

〈北海道〉

6

音声 23　放送の指示に従って答えなさい。

ア　イ
ウ　エ

〈宮崎県〉

7

音声 24　あなたは留学先のアメリカで来週の天気予報を聞こうとしています。ア〜ウを報じられた天気の順に並べかえ，その記号を書きなさい。

ア　イ　ウ

〈鹿児島県〉

8

音声 25　話される英語を聞いて，それぞれの後の質問に対する答えとして最も適当なものを，アからエまでの中からそれぞれ1つ選びなさい。

1．ア　イ　ウ　エ

2．ア　イ　ウ　エ

3．ア　イ　ウ　エ

4．ア　イ　ウ　エ
　15ドル　20ドル　25ドル　30ドル

〈滋賀県〉

9

音声 26　次のNo.1〜No.3について，それぞれ対話を聞き，その内容についての質問の答えとして最も適当なものを，それぞれア〜エから選びなさい。

No.1

ア　イ　ウ　エ

No.2

No.3

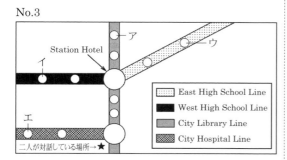

Station Hotel

East High School Line
West High School Line
City Library Line
City Hospital Line

二人が対話している場所→★

＜北海道＞

10 音声 27 外国人の観光客に，添乗員が市内観光について説明しています。これからその説明を放送します。その内容について，次の①，②の問いに答えなさい。

① この市内観光で訪れる場所を，訪れる順番に並べかえて，記号で答えなさい。

② 次の質問の答えになるように，（　　　）に適切な英語1語を書きなさい。

How long does this city trip take?
— It takes（　　　）hours.

＜茨城県＞

11 音声 28 ２つの場面の英文を読みます。それぞれの英文の後に質問を読みますから，ア～エの中から，質問の答えを表す絵として最も適切なものを１つ選び，その符号を書きなさい。

No.1

No.2

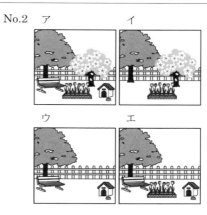

＜石川県＞

12 音声 29 これから読まれる英文は，太郎(Taro)がオーストラリアに行き，マイク(Mike)の家族と体験したことを話したものである。英文を聞き，No.1，No.2の問いに答えよ。英文は２回読まれる。

No.1 次の[質問]に対する[答え]の空所①，②に入る英語として最も適当なものをア～ウの中から一つずつ選んで，その記号を書け。
[質問] How old was Mike when Taro met him?
[答え] Mike was（　①　）.
ア．14 years old　　イ．16 years old
ウ．18 years old
[質問] Why was Taro nervous at first?
[答え] Because（　②　）.
ア．speaking English was difficult for Taro
イ．Mike didn't talk to Taro in English
ウ．Mike's English was always difficult for Taro

No.2 次は，[太郎の体験]を体験した順番に表したものである。①～④に入る適当な絵を下の[選択肢]ア～エの中から一つずつ選んで，その記号を書け。

＜長崎県＞

13 音声 30 放送の指示に従って答えなさい。

No.1

No.2

JohnさんとAyaさんが見ている表

	クラス	勝敗	順位
ア ——	3年1組	3勝1敗	2位
イ ——	3年2組	4勝0敗	1位
ウ ——	3年3組	1勝3敗	4位
	3年4組	0勝4敗	5位
エ ——	3年5組	2勝2敗	3位

〈山形県〉

14 音声 31 （放送の指示にしたがって答える）

No.1

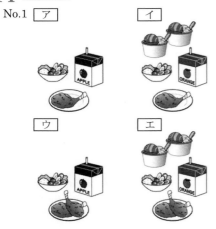

No.2

ア			イ		
	Schedule			Schedule	
Mon	Basketball Practice		Mon	Basketball Practice	
Tue	Piano Lesson		Tue		
Wed			Wed	Basketball Practice	
Thu	Basketball Practice		Thu	Library	
Fri	Basketball Practice		Fri	Basketball Practice	

ウ			エ		
	Schedule			Schedule	
Mon	Basketball Practice		Mon	Basketball Practice	
Tue	Library		Tue		
Wed			Wed	Basketball Practice	
Thu	Basketball Practice		Thu	Piano Lesson	
Fri	Basketball Practice		Fri	Basketball Practice	

〈石川県〉

15 音声 32 放送による指示に従って答えなさい。

No.1

A			B			C			D		
Fri.	Sat.	Sun.	Fri.	Sat.	Sun.	Fri.	Sat.	Sun.	Fri.	Sat.	Sun.

No.2

A				
B				
C				
D				

10　　20　　30　　40
Number of students

〈千葉県〉

16 音声 33 表を見て，質問に答える問題
※答えとして最も適当なものを表の中から抜き出して答えよ。

(1)

Enjoy Your Vacation in 2022!				
Course	A	B	C	D
How long	2 weeks	1 week	1 week	1 week
Where	London	Kyoto	Sydney	Okinawa
What to do				

(2)

Weekend Events at City Animal Park		
Day / Time	Saturday	Sunday
9:00～10:00	Birds	Cats
10:30～11:30		Dogs
13:00～14:00		Birds
14:30～15:30	Dogs	

〈福岡県〉

17 音声 34 由美(Yumi)とジョン(John)の会話を聞いて，質問の答えとして最も適切なものを選ぶ問題

A.

ア	イ	ウ	エ
国語	数学	英語	理科

B.

ア	イ	ウ	エ
ジョン　たかし	ジョン	はるな　ともこ	ともこ

C.

ア イ ウ エ labels for rows A組 B組 C組 D組

クラス	A組	B組	C組	D組	結果
ア A組		×	○	×	1勝
イ B組	○		○	○	3勝
ウ C組	×	×		×	0勝
エ D組	○	×	○		2勝

ドッジボール大会 対戦結果

D.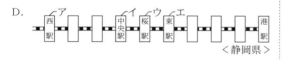

西駅 ア 中央駅 イ 桜駅 ウ 東駅 エ 港駅

〈静岡県〉

18 音声 35 放送の指示に従って答えなさい。

No.1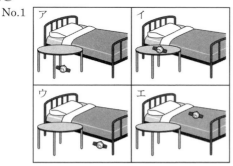

ア イ ウ エ

No.2

ア イ ウ エ

牛乳

No.3 ア． 8:15 a.m.
　　　イ． 8:30 a.m.
　　　ウ． 8:33 a.m.
　　　エ． 8:50 a.m.

〈宮崎県〉

19 音声 36 〔英語の対話とその内容についての質問を聞いて，答えとして最も適切なものを選ぶ問題〕

(1)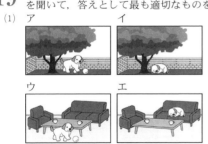

ア イ ウ エ

(2)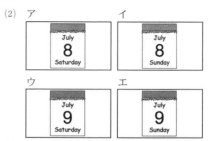

ア
July 8 Saturday

イ
July 8 Sunday

ウ
July 9 Saturday

エ
July 9 Sunday

(3) ア． Find the teacher's notebook.
　　 イ． Give her notebook to the teacher.
　　 ウ． Go to the teachers' room.
　　 エ． Play soccer with the teacher.

(4) ア． At Kate's house.
　　 イ． At the baseball stadium.
　　 ウ． At the bookstore.
　　 エ． At the museum.

〈栃木県〉

20 音声 37 ジョンとホストファミリーの恵子との会話を聞いて，恵子が住んでいる地域のごみの回収予定を表したものとして，次のア～エのうち最も適していると考えられるものを一つ選び，記号で答えなさい。

ア.

火曜日	水曜日	木曜日	金曜日
古紙	プラスチック ペットボトル		燃えるごみ

イ.

火曜日	水曜日	木曜日	金曜日
燃えるごみ	プラスチック ペットボトル		古紙

ウ.

火曜日	水曜日	木曜日	金曜日
燃えるごみ		プラスチック ペットボトル	古紙

エ.

火曜日	水曜日	木曜日	金曜日
燃えるごみ	古紙		プラスチック ペットボトル

〈大阪府・Ａ・Ｂ問題〉

21 音声 38 健(Ken)とリサ(Lisa)の会話を聞いて，質問の答えとして最も適切なものを選びなさい。

A.

ア イ ウ エ

B.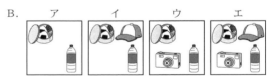

ア イ ウ エ

C.　ア　　　イ　　　ウ　　　エ

D.　　　ア　　　　　　　イ

ウ　　　　　　　エ

〈静岡県〉

22 音声 39　香織（Kaori）とベン（Ben）の対話を聞いて，質問の答えとして最も適当なものを，ア～エの中からそれぞれ一つずつ選びなさい。

No.1　ア　　　　　　　イ

ウ　　　　　　　エ

No.2　ア　　　　　　　イ

ウ　　　　　　　エ

No.3　ア　　　　　　　イ

ウ　　　　　　　エ

No.4　　　ア　　　　　　　　イ

ウ　　　　　　　　　エ

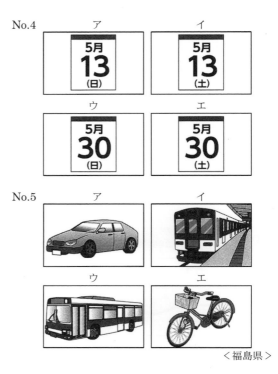

No.5　　ア　　　　　　　　イ

ウ　　　　　　　　エ

〈福島県〉

23 音声 40　これから，No.1～No.3まで，対話を3つ放送します。それぞれの対話を聞き，そのあとに続く質問の答えとして最も適切なものを，ア～エの中から選んで，その記号を書きなさい。

No.1

No.2

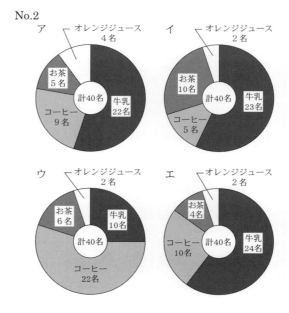

No.3　ア．He will clean his room.
　　　イ．He will cook dinner.
　　　ウ．He will go shopping.
　　　エ．He will practice the piano.

＜広島県＞

24 音声 41　放送される英文と問いを聞いて，問いに対する答えとして適切なものを選ぶ問題

No.1

ア

Nancy　　Bob　　Jack

イ

Bob
Nancy　　　　　Jack

ウ

Nancy　Bob　　Jack

エ

Nancy　Bob　　Jack

No.2

ア　イ　ウ ○○食堂　エ

No.3 ア

バスケットボール部：来週の予定						
曜日	月	火	水	木	金	土	日
練習場所		体育館		体育館	体育館の外	体育館	

イ

バスケットボール部：来週の予定						
曜日	月	火	水	木	金	土	日
練習場所	体育館		体育館		体育館		体育館

ウ

バスケットボール部：来週の予定						
曜日	月	火	水	木	金	土	日
練習場所		体育館		体育館	体育館の外	体育館	体育館

エ

バスケットボール部：来週の予定						
曜日	月	火	水	木	金	土	日
練習場所		体育館	体育館の外	体育館		体育館	

＜高知県＞

25 音声 42　放送はすべて英語で行われます。質問に対する答えとして最も適切なものを，A〜Dの中から一つずつ選び，その記号を書きなさい。各問題について英語は2回ずつ放送されます。

※Listen to each talk, and choose the best answer for each question.

No.1

A　　　　　B

C　　　　　D

No.2

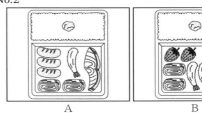

A　　　　　B

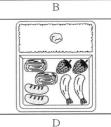

C　　　　　D

No.3

		A 月	B 火	C 水	D 木
1	8:50〜 9:40	国語	社会	数学	国語
2	9:50〜10:40	数学	体育	理科	理科
3	10:50〜11:40	理科	英語	体育	数学
4	11:50〜12:40	英語	国語	英語	英語
給食　／　昼休み					
5	13:40〜14:30	美術	技術・家庭	音楽	総合的な学習の時間
6	14:40〜15:30			社会	

＜埼玉県＞

ｃ．日本語で解答する問題

1 音声 43　あなたは，あるコンサート会場に来ています。これから放送されるアナウンスを聞いて，このコンサートホール内で禁止されていることをア～エの中から一つ選び，その記号を書きなさい。

ア．水やお茶を飲むこと
イ．写真を撮ること
ウ．音楽に合わせて踊ること
エ．電話で話すこと

〈鹿児島県〉

2 音声 44　これから，授業中の先生の指示を放送します。ア～エの中から，先生の指示にないものとして最も適当なものを一つ選び，その記号を書きなさい。

ア．発表の主題
イ．発表の長さ
ウ．発表する日
エ．発表で使うもの

〈鹿児島県〉

3 音声 45　放送の指示に従って答えなさい。

〈早紀さんのメモ〉

次の休日の予定について
　　ジョンさんと動物園に行く
　　・待ち合わせ場所：（　ア　）の近くの書店
　　　→そこから（　イ　）まで歩く
　　・待ち合わせ時刻：9時（　ウ　）分

〈山形県〉

4 音声 46　放送の指示に従って答えなさい。

〈史織さんが使っているホワイトボード〉

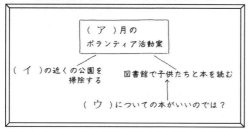

（　ア　）月の
ボランティア活動案

（　イ　）の近くの公園を
掃除する

図書館で子供たちと本を読む

（　ウ　）についての本がいいのでは？

〈山形県〉

5 音声 47　場面Ａ・Ｂにおける対話を聞いて，それぞれの質問に対する答えとして最も適するものを，ア～エから1つずつ選びなさい。

（場面Ａ）　ア．花屋　　イ．駅
　　　　　　ウ．病院　　エ．公園
（場面Ｂ）　ア．自転車の鍵　　イ．マンガ本
　　　　　　ウ．かばん　　　　エ．ソファー

〈徳島県〉

6 音声 48　放送される英文を聞いて，メモを完成させる問題

メモ

Happy Zoo のスペシャルイベント

〇開催日：　No.1
〇内容
　〈イベント1　No.2 〉
　　場所：ホースビレッジ
　　時刻：午前10時30分
　〈イベント2　赤ちゃんザルと一緒に記念撮影〉
　　場所：モンキーマウンテン
　　時刻：午後2時30分
　　＊ただし，No.3 人限定
　〈イベント3　赤ちゃんザルの名付け〉
　　当日，No.4 で応募する。

No.1　ア．4月5日　　イ．4月13日
　　　ウ．4月15日　　エ．4月30日
No.2　ア．馬にえさやり　　イ．馬と一緒に散歩
　　　ウ．乗馬体験　　　　エ．馬と一緒に記念撮影
No.3　ア．10　イ．20　ウ．30　エ．40
No.4　ア．動物園の入り口
　　　イ．モンキーマウンテン
　　　ウ．インフォメーションセンター
　　　エ．ウェブサイト

〈高知県〉

7 音声 49　それぞれの質問に対する答えとして最も適当なものを，(ア)～(エ)から1つずつ選べ。

(1)　(ア)　今月の14日　(イ)　今月の15日
　　　(ウ)　来月の14日　(エ)　来月の15日
(2)　(ア)　高校でバレーボールのチームに入っている。
　　　(イ)　サキと，週末にときどきバレーボールをしている。
　　　(ウ)　友達と，よくバレーボールの試合をテレビで見る。
　　　(エ)　小学生のとき，小さなトーナメントで最優秀選手に選ばれた。

〈京都府〉

8 音声 50　それぞれの質問に対する答えとして最も適当なものを，次の(ア)～(エ)から1つずつ選べ。

(1)　(ア)　学校　　　　　(イ)　レストラン
　　　(ウ)　エマの家　　　(エ)　スーパーマーケット
(2)　(ア)　アンの誕生日の前日に，ジェーンがプレゼントを買うことができなかったから。
　　　(イ)　アンの誕生日の前日に，アンが病気で病院に行くから。
　　　(ウ)　アンの誕生日に，ジェーンに他の用事が入ったから。
　　　(エ)　アンの誕生日に，エマがおじとおばに会う予定が入ったから。

〈京都府〉

d. 英作文をともなう問題

1 音声 51 放送の指示に従って答えなさい。
〈宮崎県〉

2 音声 52 あなたは，あなたの学校を訪問している海外の中学生と話をしているところです。相手の話をよく聞いて，最後の質問に対するあなたの返答を，英語で簡潔に書きなさい。
〈佐賀県〉

3 音声 53 放送される英文を聞いて，英文で答える問題
〈高知県〉

4 音声 54 これは，絵を見て答える問題です。

bus driver　Tom
〈岩手県〉

5 音声 55 あなたは，海外の中学生とのオンライン交流会の最後に，海外の中学生からのメッセージを聞いているところです。メッセージの内容を踏まえて，あなたのアドバイスを英語で簡潔に書きなさい。
〈佐賀県〉

6 音声 56 放送の指示に従って答えなさい。

〈宮崎県〉

7 音声 57 これから放送する対話は，留学生のジョンと高校生の春花が，ある話題に関して話したときのものです。下の【対話】に示されているように，まず①でジョンが話し，次に②で春花が話し，そのあとも交互に話します。⑤ではジョンが話す代わりにチャイムが1回鳴ります。あなたがジョンなら，この話題に関しての対話を続けるために，⑤で春花にどのような質問をしますか。⑤に入る質問を英文で書きなさい。
【対話】

John	①
Haruka	②
John	③
Haruka	④
John	⑤　チャイム

〈広島県〉

8 音声 58 あなたの学校に着任したばかりのALTの先生が英語の授業中に話したことを聞いて，あなたの答えを英文1文で書きなさい。
〈徳島県〉

9 音声 59 これから，OliviaとAkiraとの対話を放送します。その中で，OliviaがAkiraに質問をしています。Akiraに代わってあなたの答えを英文で書きなさい。2文以上になってもかまいません。書く時間は1分間です。
〈鹿児島県〉

10 音声 60 これから放送する英文は，留学生のキャシーが高校生の次郎に対して話したときのものです。キャシーの質問に対して，あなたならどのように答えますか。あなたの答えを英文で書きなさい。なお，2文以上になっても構いません。
〈広島県〉

11 音声 61 放送の指示に従って答える。
〈青森県〉

12 音声 62 渉(Wataru)が英語の授業で発表した内容を聞きながら，①〜⑤の英文の空欄に入る最も適当な英語1語を書きなさい。
① Though Wataru practiced tennis very hard, he couldn't (　　　　　　　) most of his games.
② Wataru (　　　　　　　) thought he didn't want to play anymore.
③ Wataru's teammate said to him with a (　　　　　　　), "You're doing your best."
④ The kind (　　　　　　　) from his teammate helped Wataru to start playing again.
⑤ Wataru was able to make lots of friends and he will (　　　　　　　) them forever.
〈福島県〉

13 音声 63 これから，留守番電話に録音された，ケビン(Kevin)からのあなたへのメッセージを再生します。そのメッセージについて，二つの質問をします。それぞれの質問の答えを，3語以上の英文で書きなさい。
〈新潟県〉

14 音声 64 （トムの話を聞き，その内容として適切なものを2つ選ぶ問題と，トムの最後の問いかけに対して，トムの話を踏まえ，1つの英文であなたの[質問]を書く問題）
ア. Tom has seven classes every day.
イ. Tom is good at Spanish and studies it hard.
ウ. Tom will learn Japanese because he likes Japanese comics.
エ. Tom has lunch in his classroom with his friends.
[質問] ＿＿＿＿＿＿＿＿＿＿＿＿＿＿＿＿＿ ?
〈秋田県〉

15 音声 65　健太の話を聞いて、質問に対する答えとなるように( )の中に適切な数字や語、語句を記入する問題

質問1. How long did Kenta's parents stay in Nagano?

They stayed there for ( ) days.

質問2. What did Kenta do with his sister before breakfast?

He (ⓐ) the (ⓑ) with his sister.

質問3. Why were Kenta's parents surprised when they came home?

Because Kenta ( ).

<静岡県>

16 音声 66　あなたは、3日間の「イングリッシュ・デイ」(英語に親しむイベント)に参加している。今から、そのイベント初日における先生の話を聞いて、その内容に合うように、【ワークシート】の下線部(A)、(B)、(C)に、それぞれ話の中で用いられた英語1語を書きなさい。また、下線部(D)には、先生の質問に対するあなたの返答を、4語以上の英語で書きなさい。

【ワークシート】

English Day

● Activities

Day1	English ___(A)___ activity and presentation
Day2	Going to a ___(B)___
Day3	Making our ___(C)___ short movie in English

● Q&A

| No.1 | I ___(D)___ . |

<山口県>

17 音声 67　放送を聞いて、「陽子のメモ」の ① ～ ③ に適当な英語を1語で書きなさい。また、「質問に対する答え」では、 ④ に適当な英語を2語で書き、答えとなる文を完成させなさい。英文は2回放送します。

「陽子のメモ」

・To get some Australian ① at a bank

・To bring some ② clothes

・To get some ③ books for our trip

「質問に対する答え」

She tells them to write down the things ④ and check them many times.

<熊本県・選択問題B>

18 音声 68　これから読む英文は、中学生の加奈(Kana)とブラウン先生(Mr. Brown)が話をしているときのものです。この英文を聞いて、(1)、(2)の問いに答えなさい。なお、英文は2回読みます。英文を聞く前に、まず、(1)、(2)の問いを読みなさい。

(1) 次の①～③に対する答えを、加奈とブラウン先生の話の内容に即して完成させるとき、( )に入る最も適切な英語を、1語書きなさい。

① Why is Mr. Brown surprised about the windows of Kana's house?

答え　Because they are ( ) of leaves.

② Who told Kana about energy problems?

答え　Her ( ) told her about them.

③ Why does Mr. Brown think that Kana's idea is good?

答え　Because she can ( ) electricity and eat vegetables.

(2) 加奈とブラウン先生の話の内容に合っているものを、ア～エから1つ選び、符号で書きなさい。

ア. Mr. Brown says that it's a good idea to talk about the colors of plants in English class.

イ. Mr. Brown says that the plants have not grown higher than the windows.

ウ. Kana says that she should use an air conditioner to keep the room cool for plants.

エ. Kana says that she can make the room a little cooler by using plants.

<岐阜県>

19 音声 69　エリ(Eri)さんが留学生のクリス(Chris)さんにインタビューをしています。インタビューを聞き、この後エリさんが書いた新聞記事を、下線部①、②に英語1語を入れて完成させなさい。また、このインタビューと新聞記事に関連した2つの質問を聞き、質問1は質問の答えとして最も適切なものをA、B、C、Dの中から1つ選び記号で答え、質問2は英語で答えなさい。

エリさんが書いた新聞記事

Surprisingly, Chris said it was ①_____ for him to sing "Daichi" in Japanese, and he actually sang it well. He seemed to enjoy the contest very much. His school doesn't have this kind of event. He wants to have it at his school in his country too because it is an event to ②_____ his classmates well.

質問1. A. Events in Chris's Country

B. Chris's Wonderful Classmates

C. Eri's Favorite Songs

D. Chris's First Chorus Contest

質問2. _____

<富山県>

e. そのほかの問題

1 音声 70 放送の指示に従って答える。

1. ア. No problem.　　イ. You're already home.
　 ウ. I'm so sorry.　　エ. Don't get angry.
2. ア. I want you to answer my question.
　 イ. You want to eat something.
　 ウ. I'm glad to hear you're feeling fine.
　 エ. You should go to a hospital.

＜愛媛県＞

2 音声 71 会話を聞いて答える問題です。最後の発言に対する受け答えとして最も適当なものを，ア〜エの中からそれぞれ一つずつ選び，記号を書きなさい。

1番　ア. Of course, they will.
　　 イ. They will move next month.
　　 ウ. It's in the south of Australia.
　　 エ. It will be rainy soon.
2番　ア. Yes, I bought it.
　　 イ. Yes, I heard it on Thursday.
　　 ウ. No, but I enjoyed it.
　　 エ. No, I didn't win.

＜佐賀県＞

3 音声 72 英語の短い質問や呼びかけを聞き，その後に読まれるア，イ，ウ，エの英語の中から，答えとして最も適当なものを一つずつ選ぶ問題
　※記号で答えよ。問題は3問ある。

＜福岡県＞

4 音声 73 放送を聞いて，それぞれのチャイムのところに入る対話の応答として，最も適当なものをア〜エから一つ選び，記号で答えなさい。<u>英文は1回ずつ放送します。</u>

1. 〈英語の授業での対話〉
　 ア. By car.
　 イ. We enjoyed fishing.
　 ウ. It took three hours.
　 エ. With my family.
2. 〈休み時間の対話〉
　 ア. Yes. I'll buy it.
　 イ. Yes. Almost every day.
　 ウ. No. I've never been there.
　 エ. No. Thank you for telling me.

＜熊本県＞

5 音声 74 放送による指示に従って答えなさい。

No.1　A. Yes, she is.　　　 B. Yes, I did.
　　　C. No, she doesn't.　D. No, I'm not.
No.2　A. Sure.　　　B. It's mine.
　　　C. I agree.　　D. It's on the table.
No.3　A. Dad was there.
　　　B. There were oranges.
　　　C. Mom says "OK."
　　　D. Yes, I ate cookies.

＜千葉県＞

6 音声 75 No.1〜No.3のそれぞれについて，英文A，B，Cが順番に読まれます。説明として正しいか，誤っているかを判断して，解答例のように○で囲みなさい。なお，正しいものはそれぞれ1つとは限りません。

解答例　A. ⓔ 誤　B. ⓔ 誤　C. 正 ⓔ

No.1

　 A. 正　誤　B. 正　誤　C. 正　誤

No.2

TYMショップタウン
定休日 毎月第2水曜日

フロアガイド

5階	レストラン
4階	本・文房具
3階	…………
2階	…………
1階	コーヒーショップ，花（入口）

　 A. 正　誤　B. 正　誤　C. 正　誤

No.3

スターシネマパーク☆

〔2月〕人気映画ランキング

タイトル	制　作・上映時間
1位 春の桜	（日　本・115分）
2位 天の河	（日　本・125分）
3位 サイレントシップ	（アメリカ・135分）
〃 ノレ	（韓　国・110分）

　 A. 正　誤　B. 正　誤　C. 正　誤

＜富山県＞

7 音声 76 2つの場面の英文を読みます。それぞれの英文の後に質問とその答えを読みますから，答えが正しいか，誤っているかを判断して，記入例のように○で囲みなさい。なお，各質問に対する正しい答えは1つです。

記入例　a. 正 ⓔ　b. 正 ⓔ　c. ⓔ 誤
No.1　a. 正　誤　b. 正　誤　c. 正　誤
No.2　a. 正　誤　b. 正　誤　c. 正　誤

＜石川県＞

8 音声 77 英語による対話を聞いて，それぞれの対話の最後の英文に対する受け答えとして，ア〜ウから最も適当なものを1つ選び，その記号を書きなさい。

No.1　ア. Here you are.　　 イ. You're welcome.
　　　ウ. It's perfect.
No.2　ア. This morning.　　 イ. Two hours later.
　　　ウ. Near the bed.
No.3　ア. About two hours ago.
　　　イ. At about seven in the evening.
　　　ウ. For about three minutes.

No.4　ア．When I was eight years old.
　　　イ．It was so difficult.
　　　ウ．My brother taught me.
＜三重県＞

9 音声 78 　これは，二人の対話を聞いて答える問題です。
(1)　ア．Around the station.
　　　イ．By taxi.
　　　ウ．From America.
　　　エ．With my dog.
(2)　ア．It is a big bird.
　　　イ．It is a blue bird.
　　　ウ．It is a small watch.
　　　エ．It is a white watch.
(3)　ア．I have been there three times.
　　　イ．I have just come here.
　　　ウ．I visited it last year.
　　　エ．I went there at three o'clock.
＜岩手県＞

10 音声 79 　放送による指示に従って答えなさい。
No.1　A．Yes, there is.　　B．No, I haven't.
　　　C．Yes, you have.　　D．No, there isn't.
No.2　A．Yes, I did.　　　B．Yes, you did.
　　　C．Sure.　　　　　　D．Good job.
No.3　A．One.　　　　　　B．Two.
　　　C．Four.　　　　　　D．Eight.
＜千葉県＞

11 音声 80 　No.1～No.3の順に，二人の対話をそれぞれ2回ずつ放送します。対話の最後にそれぞれチャイムが鳴ります。チャイムが鳴った部分に入る最も適切なものを，A～Dの中から1つずつ選び，その記号を書きなさい。
No.1　先生との対話
　　　A．I want to have fruit after lunch.
　　　B．I want to make delicious food and make people happy.
　　　C．Well, I haven't finished my breakfast yet.
　　　D．Well, I haven't looked at the menu yet.
No.2　友人との対話
　　　A．Wow, I want to listen to his music.
　　　B．Wow, I like drawing pictures.
　　　C．Well, I have lived in Japan for two years.
　　　D．Well, I'm playing the guitar with him now.
No.3　母親との対話
　　　A．Yes. Were you free at that time?
　　　B．Yes. You should go to bed because you are tired.
　　　C．Yes. Can you clean the table before cooking?
　　　D．Yes. We finished dinner today.
＜和歌山県＞

12 音声 81 　会話を聞いて，その会話に続く応答として適切なものを選びなさい。会話のあとに放送される選択肢a～cから応答として適切なものを，それぞれ1つ選びなさい。(会話と選択肢は1回だけ読みます。)
No.1　(場面)　翌日の天候について会話している
No.2　(場面)　図書館で会話している
No.3　(場面)　ミーティングを始める前に会話している
＜兵庫県＞

13 音声 82 　最初に，英語によるスピーチを聞きます。続いて，スピーチについての問いと，それに対する答えを聞きます。問いは問1と問2の二つあります。そのあと，もう一度，スピーチと問い，それに対する答えを聞きます。必要があればメモをとってもよろしい。問いの答えとして正しいものは「正」の文字を，誤っているものは「誤」の文字を，それぞれ答えなさい。正しいものは，各問いについて一つしかありません。
問1．a．正　誤　　b．正　誤
　　　c．正　誤　　d．正　誤
問2．a．正　誤　　b．正　誤
　　　c．正　誤　　d．正　誤
＜愛知県＞

14 音声 83 　会話を聞いて答える問題です。それぞれの会話の最後の文に対する応答として最も適切なものをア～エのうちから1つ選び，その記号を書きなさい。なお，会話の英文はそれぞれ1度だけ読まれます。選択肢ア～エの英文は読まれません。
問1．ア．Let's play baseball together.
　　　イ．That'll be nice.
　　　ウ．My favorite team won.
　　　エ．Yes, it was my first time playing baseball.
問2．ア．It takes ten minutes.
　　　イ．I went there by car.
　　　ウ．I was there at three o'clock.
　　　エ．At 5:00 p.m.
問3．ア．Yes, I think it will be sunny.
　　　イ．Well, I thought it was raining last weekend.
　　　ウ．Oh, I really like to go hiking.
　　　エ．Yes, I do.
＜沖縄県＞

15 音声 84 　チャイムのところに入るアキラの言葉として最も適するものを，次の1～4の中からそれぞれ一つずつ選び，その番号を答えなさい。
No.1　1．I ask the people working there about history.
　　　2．You can learn about the history of our city there.
　　　3．You can use the train to go to the library.
　　　4．The city library is not near the hospital.
No.2　1．Let's meet at nine thirty tomorrow.
　　　2．How about going to a museum?
　　　3．It will be fine tomorrow morning.
　　　4．Shall we go to the zoo tomorrow?
No.3　1．Yes. I am happy to meet your new dog.
　　　2．Yes. You need to call me when you get there.
　　　3．No. You have to keep the dog in the house.
　　　4．No. I am thinking about what to call him.
＜神奈川県＞

第2章 長文読解問題 ジャンル別トピックス一覧

5年 受験用 全国高校入試問題正解

野別過去問358題

英語 長文読解・英作文・リスニング

冊解答・解き方

旺文社

目 次

(注) 解答・解き方の中の（　）…省略可能を示す。
　　　　　　　　　　　［　　］…直前の語，または句の言い換え可能を示す。
　　　　　　　　　　　また，「go on foot［walk］」のようにカギのある時は go on foot と walk との言
　　　　　　　　　　　い換え可能を示す。

第1章 知識問題

a. 文中空欄の補充・選択

1 (ア) 3 (イ) 4 (ウ) 3
【解き方】文脈に合う単語を選ぶ。(ア)「とても重いので，テーブルを運ぶことができない」 (イ)「釣りに行くつもりなので，明日の天気は晴れになってほしい」 (ウ) 2文目以降は友人を紹介している。「私の友人を紹介させてください」

2 問1. (1) call (2) park 問2. [解答例] (1) be (2) mustn't [can't / cannot]
【解き方】問1. (1) call *A B*「AをBと呼ぶ」 (2) サッカーをする場所を選ぶ。問2. (1)「ここでは静かにしてください」命令文。Pleaseのあとに動詞の原形を続ける。(2) 右側の飲食禁止の表示を，「ここで食べてはいけません」とする。禁止を表す助動詞(1語)はmustn'tやcan't [cannot]。

3 (1) kind (2) popular
【解き方】(1) ルーシーは好きな音楽の種類を答えている。What kind of ～「どんな種類の～」 (2) is popular among ～「～の間で人気のある」

4 ① breakfast ② climb ③ March
【解き方】① 起きてから，朝食べるもの。② より高い所や最も高いところへ向かう。③ 1年で3番目の月。

5 ① arrive ② kitchen ③ vegetables
【解き方】①「到着する」の意味。空所のあとにatがあることに注意。助動詞のあとなので動詞の原形。②「料理をするのに使われる部屋」は「キッチン」。③「ジャガイモ，ニンジン，タマネギなど，人が食べる植物」は「野菜」。

6 (1) subject (2) usually
【解き方】(1) subject「教科」 (2) usually「ふだん」

7 1. ア 2. エ 3. イ 4. ウ
【解き方】(1)「これはだれの時計ですか」 3人称単数のbe動詞を入れる。(2) My father bought it for me.とあるので，mine「私のもの」が適切。(3) Bは最後の発言でat ～ Stationと場所を答えているので，whereが適切。(4) 空所直前のItはwatchを指している。過去分詞を入れて受動態の表現にする。

8 nothing
【解き方】シンの「土曜日はひまですか」という問いかけに，マーサはYesと答えている。やるべきことがnothing「何もない」とする。

9 (ア) 2 (イ) 4 (ウ) 3 (エ) 4
【解き方】(ア) One of the boysは3人称単数として扱うので，isが適切。(イ)「どの学校行事がいちばん好きか」という表現にする。(ウ) whichはa schoolを先行詞とする主格の関係代名詞。「1980年に建てられた学校」という意味になるように，〈be動詞＋過去分詞〉を続ける。(エ) 現在完了進行形の文。「午前10時からずっとこの本を読んでいる」という意味になるように，sinceを入れる。

10 問1. (1) down (2) help 問2. (1) zoo (2) colors 問3. (1) ago (2) present 問4. (1) most (2) July
【解き方】問1. (1) sit downで「座る」。(2)「いらっしゃいませ」と店員が客に使う決まり文句は，May I help you?。問2. (1) いろいろな動物を見学する場所は動物園。(2) 青，赤，緑は色の名前。問3. (1) two years agoで「2年前に」。(2) birthday presentで「誕生日のプレゼント」。問4. (1) 9月は降水量がいちばん多い(＝9月はいちばん多く雨が降る)。much「多い」の最上級はmost。(2) 降水量が約80mmの月は，3月と7月。

11 1. ウ 2. エ 3. イ
【解き方】1. take *A* to *B*「AをBに連れて行く」 2.「たった数分でそこに行ける」とあるので，「ここからいちばん近い」とする。 3.「ギターを弾いている男の子」playing the guitarが前の名詞the boyを修飾する構造。

12 問1. エ 問2. ア 問3. エ
【解き方】問1.「お寺に行って，写真をたくさん撮った」 問2.「マイクは，昨日は病気だったから学校に来なかったと思う」 問3.「それら(＝有名な画家が描いた複数の絵)を見たかったが，私の前に人が多くいたので見ることができなかった」

13 1. ア 2. ウ 3. イ
【解き方】1. 疲れているように見えるのは買い物袋が重そうだから。 2.〈I wish I could ＋動詞の原形〉「私は～できたらいいのに」は仮定法過去の文。 3.「先生に聞いてあとであなたに知らせます」 〈let＋O＋動詞の原形〉「Oに～させる」

14 問1. ア 問2. ウ 問3. エ
【解き方】問1. be happy to *do*「～してうれしい」 問2.「それはだれの自転車か」に対する答えには，「それは～のものです」が適切。問3. These girls dancing on the stage「ステージで踊っている女の子たち」は複数形。dancingは現在分詞の後置修飾で直前のgirlsを修飾する。

15 (ア) 1 (イ) 3 (ウ) 2 (エ) 4
【解き方】(ア) 文末に「私が子供のころ」とあるので，この文は過去の内容だと判断できる。(イ)「私は～の両方が好きなので，どちらかを選ぶことは難しい」 (ウ)「私は医師になって人々を助けたいのだが，あなたはどうか」とたずねら

れている。「私は将来何をしたいのか決めていない」が適切。
(エ)「なぜ英語の授業が好きか」と問われている。byのあとは動名詞のtalkingが適切。

「～を解決する」の目的語なので「～を」を表すthemが適切。themは前のtroublesを指す。(5)「音楽もわくわくする」とポジティブな内容が続くので、「ストーリーはすばらしい(fantastic)」が自然。(6)仮定法過去〈If＋主語＋動詞の過去形, 主語＋<u>would</u>＋動詞の原形〉のコンマ以下が疑問文。

16
(1) or　(2) umbrella　(3) instead
【解き方】(1)AかBかの選択を聞くときに使う接続詞。(2)雨の日の外出時に必要なもの。(3) instead of ～「～の代わりに」

17
1. エ　2. イ　3. ア　4. ウ
【解き方】1. 現在完了の疑問文。「あなたはもうこの映画を見ましたか」　2. 過去形の動詞sawに着目して過去を表す副詞句last week「先週」が適切。3.「すばらしかった」という返事に合わせて、<u>how was it?</u>「どうでしたか」とする。4.「すばらしかった」に続けて、「あなたも見るべきです」となるshouldが適切。should「～すべきである」

18
① カ　② ウ　③ ア
【解き方】①Aが「きみは英語の授業でのスピーキングテストは～だった？」とたずねた直後で「私には難しかった」と言い、それを受けてBは「私はうまくいった。きみは十分に準備した？」と言っている。空所には「どう」にあたる疑問詞が入る。②Bは次のスピーキングテストでAがうまくいくようにアドバイスしている。「私は英語をとても上手に話す友達がいる」となるように空所を補う。先行詞が人の場合に使われる、主格の関係代名詞が入る。③ when he was littleは過去を表す副詞節だから、現在完了は使えない。過去形の動詞を選ぶ

19
(1) ウ　(2) イ　(3) エ　(4) ア
【解き方】(1)主語のThose picturesが複数形なので、be動詞はare。(2) on New Year's Day this yearから過去形が適切。(3) the man wearing a *kimono*「着物を着ている男性」　現在分詞の後置修飾。(4) He's my mother's brother から my uncle「私のおじさん」とする。

20
1. エ　2. イ　3. ウ
【解き方】1. 空所の次に「電車を待っていた」とある。2.「100年以上も前に」とあるから過去形を使う。主語のItは本を指すので「～によって書かれた」と受動態になる。3. すべて準備できているから、何も持ってくる<u>必要はない</u>。don't have to ～「～する必要はない」

21
(ア) 2　(イ) 1　(ウ) 3　(エ) 4
【解き方】(ア) A or Bの2択なので、Whichを入れて「朝食にはご飯かパンのどちらを食べますか」とする。(イ)あとにgreatがあるので〈look＋形容詞〉「～に見える」が適切。(ウ)「学校に着いたとき」という過去の話なので過去形drankが適切。(エ)「私は彼に2か月間会っていない」という意味になるように、現在完了の否定文で表す。

22
(1) ウ　(2) イ　(3) ア　(4) ウ　(5) イ　(6) エ
【解き方】(1) like ～ing「～するのが好きだ」(2) Do you like ～?の質問に対して自分で返事をしている。Yes, I <u>do</u>.「はい、私は好きです」(3)「この物語は時空を超えた[タイムスリップした]少女に<u>ついての</u>ものだ」(4) solve

23
① ウ　② ア　③ イ
【解き方】①直後に「今日彼女から借りた」とあるので「これは私の姉[妹]のものです」とする。my sister'sは所有代名詞（～のもの）の形。②「もっと早く起きなさい、そうすればもっと時間があるわよ」〈命令文, and ～〉「…しなさい、そうすれば～」③「質問があれば、遠慮なく私に聞いてください」　feel free to ～「遠慮なく[気軽に]～する」

24
(1) エ　(2) ウ　(3) イ　(4) ア
【解き方】(1)「この町には図書館がありますか」となるように適語を補う。There is構文の疑問文。(2)「だから、パーティーには何も持って来なくてもいい」となるように適語を補う。〈don't have to＋動詞の原形〉「～する必要がない」(3)「彼女は先週からずっと病気です」となるように適語を補う。現在完了の文。have been ～ since …「…からずっと～」(4)「過去に戻れるなら何をしますか」　仮定法過去。

25
(1)(A) 4　(C) 2　(D) 3　(2) eaten
【解き方】(1)(A)「家族と祖母の家に行き、<u>そして</u>お雑煮のような特別な料理を食べる」。(C) call *A B*「<u>A</u>を<u>B</u>と呼ぶ」(D) take care of ～「～の世話をする」(2)過去分詞eatenにして経験の用法の現在完了の文を作る。

26
① エ　② イ　③ ウ
【解き方】① I'mから始まっているので現在進行形だと判断する。②相手の好物のカレーライスの「作り方」を教えてあげる、とするのが適切。③偶然に出会った2人の対話。Bの発言のMe, too.「僕もだよ」が対応するのはウの「ここで会うとは驚きだよ」のみ。

27
(1) イ　(2) ア　(3) ウ　(4) エ
【解き方】(1)「あなたは何をしましたか」(2) 7時に勉強を始めて9時半に入浴するので、「勉強したあとで入浴する」ことになる。(3) a dog called *Pochi*「ポチと呼ばれている犬」(4) take part in ～「～に参加する」

28
(1)(A) 1　(C) 3　(D) 2　(2) were
【解き方】(1)(A) arrive at ～で、「～に着く」という意味。(C)空所前後で、話のテーマが「日本の冬」から「ニュージーランドの道の名前」に転換している。By the way「ところで」が適切。(D)空所前後の内容から判断する。「それら（＝道の独特な名前）は、マオリの人々が話す言語に由来している」とするのが適切。(2)現在の事実と違う願望を表す仮定法過去の文。〈I wish＋主語＋(助)動詞の過去形〉で、be動詞は主語がIでもwereとする。

29
問1. No.1 How　No.2 turn　No.3 drink
問2. No.1 エ　No.2 イ

【解き方】問1. No.1 How about ～?「～はどうですか」 No.2 turn right「右に曲がる」 No.3 something to drink「飲み物」 問2. No.1「そこでは品物の値段が高くないので，エリカは図書館の隣の店で～するのが好きだ」 shopping「買い物をすること」が適切。No.2「昨日はそのテレビ番組を見たかった，～それを見る時間がなかった」but「しかし」が適切。

30
(1)イ　(2)ア　(3)エ　(4)ウ　(5)イ　(6)エ
【解き方】(1) the first time「初めて(のとき)」 (2) teach ～ how to do「～に…の仕方を教える」 過去形はtaught。 (3)「午前中，彼は多くの魚を釣ったが，私は一匹も釣れませんでした」 (4)前置詞のあとなので，目的格の代名詞。(5)〈比較級(～)＋than any＋単数名詞(…)〉「どの…よりも～」 (6) excited「(人が)興奮した」

31
① difficult, by　② help, learn　③ have, choose
【解き方】①次の文で「ホストファミリーの家の近くに電車の駅がいくつかあるので便利だ」と言っている。つまり，電車で移動するのは難しくない。It ～ to ...「…することは～だ」 ②次の文で「彼らのおかげで，たくさんの日本語の単語が理解できて～」と言っている。「彼らはよく，私が日本語を学ぶのを助けてくれる」とするのが適切。〈help＋人＋do〉「(人)が～するのを助ける」 ③前の文で「学校の制服は時間の節約になると思う」と言っている。毎朝，衣服を選ぶ必要がないからである。don't have to do「～する必要はない」

32
(1)エ　(2)ウ　(3)ア　(4)イ
【解き方】(1)一般動詞の過去形を用いた文 I got up at six this morning.に対して，「そうだったんですか」とあいづちを打つときは，did you?とする。(2) It's Tony's.「それはトニーのものです」という返事があるので，〈Whose＋無冠詞名詞 ～?〉「だれの～」とするのが適切。(3)受動態の English is shown on the screen.「英語がスクリーンに映し出される」の疑問文。(4)仮定法過去の文。「私があなたならば，医者に行くでしょうに」「～ならば」と現在の事実と異なることを仮定する条件を表す節の中では，主語が I や3人称単数の場合でも，ふつう be動詞は were を使う。

33
①ウ　②ア　③エ
【解き方】①「週末にピアノのレッスンがある」 on weekends「週末に」 ②「一緒に動物園へ行きたいけれど，行けません。私は宿題をしなくてはならないから」 have to～「～しなくてはならない」 do one's homework「宿題をする」 ③〈What (a)＋名詞!〉 形容詞がないタイプの感嘆文。What a surprise!「なんとまあ！」

34
(1)① wish　② both　③ practice
(2)④ written　⑤ easier　⑥ children
【解き方】(1)①仮定法過去の文で，I wish I could ～「私は～できたらいいのに」。②次に speaking and reading Japaneseとあることに着目。both A and B「AもBも」 ③ practice ～ing「～する練習をする」 (2)④「簡単な日本語で書かれた多くの本」となるよう過去分詞にする。written in easy Japanese が前の名詞 many books を修

飾する構造。⑤ than があるので比較級にする。⑥「それは子供だけでなく，おとなにもよい」という意味で，おとな全般を表す複数形 adults に対し，child も複数形にする。

35
(1)① Saturday　② library　③ popular　④ collect
(2)[解答例]① How did you　② most exciting of　③ me to go
【解き方】(1)①日曜日の前日。②本，新聞などがたくさん置いてある建物。③多くの人に好かれたり楽しまれたりする状態は「人気がある」ということ。④さまざまな場所からものを得るのは「集める」ということ。(2)①「電車で行った」と答えているので移動手段をたずねる疑問文を答える。過去形にすること。How ～?「どうやって～?」 ②「冬のスポーツの中でいちばんわくわくする」と最上級を用いた文にする。excitingの最上級は most exciting。③〈tell＋人＋to do〉で「(人)に～するように言う」。

36
問1. No.1 time　No.2 for　No.3 It
問2. No.1 ウ　No.2 ア
問3. [解答例] They were made
【解き方】問1. No.1「7時半に(起きた)」と答えているので，What time ～?「何時に～」とする。No.2 How long ～?は期間をたずねる表現で，現在完了(継続)の文。for five years「5年間」 No.3 It is ～ to do「…するのは～だ」の文。文末の it は That mountain を指す。問2. No.1 work「作動[機能]する」 No.2 次の文の「沖縄に行く」から，where to go「どこへ行くか」とする。問3. あとの by「～によって」に着目し，受動態〈be動詞＋過去分詞〉の文と判断する。主語は these cups を代名詞 They で表す。

37
問1. No.1 mine　No.2[解答例] speak　No.3[解答例] call　問2. No.1 イ　No.2 エ
問3. [解答例] We enjoyed
【解き方】問1. No.1 Is it yours?「それはあなたのものですか？」と聞かれて，Yesと答えているので，mineを入れて「はい，それは私のものです」とする。No.2 電話での会話であることをつかむ。May I speak to Yuto, please?「ユウトと話せますか？」 No.3 call O C「OをCと呼ぶ」 問2. No.1 前文に「いつも夕方に公園を散歩する。そのあと，夕食の料理を始める」とあるので，beforeを入れて「夕食の前に散歩することでおなかが減る」とするのが適切。No.2 must not do「～してはいけない」 禁止を表す。問3. enjoy doing「～することを楽しむ」

38
1. (1) long　(2) weather　(3) half　2. (1)エ　(2)イ
【解き方】1. (1)返事の「6歳から」から，期間をたずねる How long ～?が適切。現在完了進行形(have been ～ing)の疑問文。(2) sunnyやrainから，「昨日の京都の天気はどうだった？」とする。(3) 48パーセントは約半分である。2. (1)ケイトが昨日読んだ本をシンジはまだ読んでいない。ケイトが本がおもしろかった理由を話そうとして，シンジがPlease stop!「やめて！」と言う。その理由は，エ「明日それを読む」ので内容を知りたくないから。(2)サンドイッチを買いすぎたピーターがヒトミに「少し食べてくれる？」と言う。OK.に続く内容として，イ「1つ食べるけど，手伝ってくれるようほかの人にも頼んだほうがいい」が適切。one は a sandwich のこと。

39 (1)(a)エ　(b)ア　(2)(a)ウ　(b)エ　(c)ウ　(3)ウ→エ→ア→イ

【解き方】(1)(a)「姉[妹]はカレーライスがとても好きだ。しかし，私は好きではない」(b)「ブラウンさんは空いた時間があるときによく自分の車を洗車する」(2)(a)直後にYou can use it.「あなたはそれを使っていい」とあるので，「いいえ，使っていません」が適切。現在進行形への応答なのでbe動詞を用いる。(b)直後にAが「それでは家で映画を見ませんか」と言っているので，「私たちは予定を変えなければならない」が適切。Why don't we ～?「～しませんか」(c)直後で「それは多くの人々を救った医者についての実話だ」と本の内容を紹介しているので，「それはどんな種類の本ですか」が適切。(3)仮定法過去の文。主語がⅠや3人称単数の場合でもふつうbe動詞にwereを使う。「もし私があなたならば海外に行くでしょう」

40 (1)(a)ア　(b)エ　(2)(a)ウ　(b)イ　(c)ア　(3)エ→イ→ウ→ア

【解き方】(1)(a)event「行事，催し物」が適切。(b)京都での楽しい思い出に関することなので「決して忘れない」という気持ちが自然。forgetを入れる。(2)(a)疑問文の主語が複数であり，空所後の発言内容が肯定的であることから，ウのYes, we do.が適切。(b)Aが用いたa walking dictionaryという表現の意味を問う質問。meanは人を主語にして「～のことを言いたい」という意味になるのでWhat do you mean?で「(その表現で)何を言いたいのですか[どういう意味ですか]」という疑問になる。(c)昼食を一緒にという誘いを受けて，I'm sorry.と言ったうえで，明日はどうかと提案しているのでアの「昼食は食べたばかりだ」が自然。(3)knowの目的語としてthe manを選び，どのような男性かを説明する表現をtalking with your motherとすれば「あなたのお母さんと話をしている男性」という意味になる。

41 1. (1) seasons　(2) where　(3) daughter
2. (1)エ　(2)ウ

【解き方】1. (1)4つあり，その中でイチロウは春が，デイブは冬が好きだと言っている。(2)ナナミはテーブルをどこに持っていくのかを答えている。〈where to＋動詞の原形〉「どこに～すればよいか」(3)子供が男の子ならboy，女の子なら何と呼ぶかを答える。 2. (1)33人の生徒で4人の班を作れば，1つは5人の班を作らねばならなくなる。(2)ハルカがほんとうに新年会に参加したいと言っている理由として適切なものを選ぶ。ウの「昨年は病気で参加できなかった」が最適。

42 (1)ウ　(2)エ　(3)ア　(4)エ　(5)ウ　(6)イ

【解き方】(1) be glad to do「～してうれしい」，hear that SV「～だと聞く」。(2)「父が私にくれた本は，私が難しい数学の問題を解くのに役立った」 my father gave meというSVが主語The bookを修飾。〈help＋O＋動詞の原形〉「Oが～するのに役立つ」(3)「私にもっと練習時間があれば兄[弟]と同じくらい上手にバスケットボールができるのに」 仮定法過去の文〈I could＋動詞の原形～, if I＋動詞の過去形〉。(4) who is loved by many peopleという関係代名詞で導かれる節が主語The soccer playerを修飾。(5)「私たちのグループで共有されているアイデアはすばらしく思える」 shared in our groupという〈過去分詞＋語句〉が主語The ideaを修飾。〈sound＋形容詞〉「～に聞こえる[思える]」(6)「飛行機でロンドンに着くのに何時間かかるか知りたい」 間接疑問で〈how many hours＋SV〉の語順。〈it takes＋時間＋to do〉「～するのに(時間)かかる」

43 (1)ウ　(2)ア　(3)エ　(4)ウ　(5)エ　(6)ウ

【解き方】(1)「コンテストで2度優勝した少年は私の兄[弟]だ」 who won the contest twiceが前のThe boyを修飾。(2) were excited to do「～して興奮した」 a sleeping cat「眠っている猫」 beside「～のそばに」(3)「その歌手が毎日何時間練習しているかを知りたい」 間接疑問は〈疑問詞＋主語＋動詞〉の語順。(4)「彼女が私にくれたプレゼントは私が長い間ほしいと思っていたものだ」 she gave meが前のThe presentを，I wanted ～ for a long timeが前のthe oneを修飾。(5)「その本は海外旅行のために何を準備すべきかを知るのに十分な情報を私に与えてくれた」 give A B「AにBを与える」 what to do「何を～すべきか」(6)「試験が終わるまで私が見たいDVDを私から離しておこう」 keep A away from B「AをBから離しておく」 I want to watchが前のthe DVDsを修飾。

44 (1)ウ　(2)ア　(3)エ　(4)イ　(5)ア　(6)イ

【解き方】(1)「あなたが必要なものはすべてバッグに入っていますか」 everythingのあとに関係代名詞thatの節を続ける。(2) standing thereが前の名詞officerを修飾する形。which way to go「どちらの方向に行くべきか」(3)〈help＋O＋動詞の原形〉「Oが～するのを手助けする」(4)仮定法過去の文。I wish I could ～.「私は～できたらいいのに」 as fluently as ～「～と同じくらい流ちょうに」(5)文の骨格はThe letter was found in his house.で，letterのあとに関係代名詞whichの節が入った形。(6)〈ask＋O＋to do〉「Oに～するよう頼む」 〈let＋O＋動詞の原形〉「Oが～するのを許す」

45 A. イ　B. エ　C. ア　D. ウ

【解き方】A. 空所の直前に「あなたはそれ(＝ラグビーの試合)を見るべきだ」とあるので，イ「その試合はおもしろくなると思う」が適切。B. 空所の直前が「彼女は自分の部屋にいる」で，次のお母さんの発言が「彼女はその本にとても興味があるのね」なので，エ「彼女は3時間ずっと本を読んでいる」が適切。現在完了進行形は過去の一時点から現在までその動作が継続していることを表す。C. 空所に続く返事が「はい。気分がよくなり，よく眠ることができる」なので，ア「走ることに関してあなたにとっていい点はあるか」が適切。D. 空所の直後に「だから走るときには新しいものが発見できる」とあるので，ウ「私は毎日違ったコースを走る」が適切。

46 A. ア　B. イ　C. エ　D. ア

【解き方】A. 空所の直前に「シェリーについての大ニュース?」とあるので，ア「どういうことですか」が適切。B. 空所の直後に「はい，私たちは午前中にクラブ活動があるので，それがいいです」とあるので，イ「次の土曜日の午後はどうですか」が適切。How about ～?「～はどうですか」 C. 空所の直前に「それをどうやって知りましたか」という質問があり，直後に「そのとき彼女がそれについて私に話した」とあるので，エ「昨日，駅であなたの姉[妹]さんに会いました」が適切。D. 空所の直後に「なぜあなたはそのように考えられるのですか」という質問が続くので，ア「私があなたならばそのようには考えられないでしょう」が適切。仮定法過去の文。

b． そのほかの問題

1 ア．received　イ．swimming　ウ．lived
エ．sung　オ．send
【解き方】ア．「私はちょうどあなたのクリスマスカードを受け取りました」　I've は I have の短縮形で，現在完了。よって receive の過去分詞が適切。イ．主語の He はサンタクロースのこと。カードの絵でサンタは泳いでいるので，現在進行形 is swimming とする。ウ．「もし私がオーストラリアに住んでいたら私はあなたと海に行けるのに」という仮定法過去の文。〈If＋主語＋動詞の過去形〜，主語＋could＋動詞の原形〉で表す。エ．「オーストラリアで多くの人々に歌われている人気のあるクリスマスソング」の意味になるように，sing を過去分詞にする。sung by 〜 Australia の〈過去分詞＋語句〉が前の名詞を修飾する構造。オ．「もうすぐあなたに年賀状を送ります」　send A to B「A を B に送る」

2 問1．oldest　問2．written　問3．inviting
問4．heard
【解き方】問1．of the three「3 びきのうちで」と続くので最上級にする。問2．written in English「英語で書かれた」が a book を修飾する。問3．Thank you for 〜ing「〜してくれてありがとう」　問4．have never heard 〜「今までに一度も〜を聞いたことがない」　経験を表す現在完了。

3 問1．been　問2．hotter　問3．spoken
問4．could
【解き方】問1．have never been there「そこには一度も行ったことがない」　問2．気温の話をしている。「今日は昨日より暑い」　問3．「カナダではフランス語が話されていることを知っていましたか」　問4．仮定法過去。主節は〈主語＋助動詞の過去形＋動詞の原形〉の形をとる。

4 ① to practice　② finished　③ listening
【解き方】①　need to 〜「〜する必要がある」「スピーチコンテストに向けてしっかり練習する必要があった」　② finish 〜ing「〜し終える」「コンテストでようやく自分のスピーチを終えたとき，私はほっとした」　③ by 〜ing「〜することによって」　listen to 〜「〜を聞く」「クラスメートのスピーチを聞くことによって，次回でのよりよいスピーチの仕方を私は学んだ」

5 [解答例]⑴ I saw it　⑵ will be sunny
⑶ how to use
【解き方】⑴疑問文の you に対して主語を I（または We）にして，see を過去形の saw，the movie を代名詞 it に変える。⑵ tomorrow があるので，未来を表す表現 will be を使う。⑶ how to use 〜「〜の使い方」

6 問1．seen　問2．warmer　問3．playing
問4．be

【解き方】問1．現在完了（経験）。seen を入れて，「これほど美しい山を今までに一度も見たことがない」とする。問2．直後に than があるので比較級。warmer を入れて，「昨日より暖かいと思う」とする。問3．現在分詞（後置修飾）。直後に the guitar があるので playing を入れて，「ベンチでギターを弾いている男の人」とする。問4．助動詞を含んだ疑問文中の動詞は原形。be を入れて「明日は晴れるだろうか」とする。

7 ① found　② getting　③ gave　④ better
【解き方】① Where did you find it? と過去形で聞かれているので過去形 found にする。②主語は「その銘柄を手に入れること」。「手に入れること」は動名詞 getting か，不定詞 to get のどちらでも表現できるが設問に英語1語と指示があるので動名詞で答える。③ last month とあるので過去形 gave にする。④ than「〜より」という語があり，比較の文になっている。good の比較級は better。

8 [解答例]① I like them　② He has visited
③ It was built
【解き方】①「私はそれらの本が好きです」　history books を代名詞 them で表す。②「彼は（そこを）訪れたことがある」　my father を he にかえて主語にする。many times「何回も」があるので，「経験」を表す現在完了にする。③ the house を代名詞 it で表す。家は「建てられる」から受動態にする。250 years ago とあるので過去形。

9 1．① to cook　② gave　③ finishes [is finished]
2．① season(s)　② breakfast　③ color(s)
【解き方】1．① be going to do で，「〜するつもりだ」という意味。文脈から，cook と eat のどちらが適切かを判断する。② my grandmother 以降が vegetables を修飾している。③時を表す副詞節では，未来の内容でも動詞は現在形。2．①「季節」を意味する英語を入れる。②「食事」は，朝食，昼食，夕食など。③色を意味する英語を入れる。

10 ⑴ performance　⑵ would　⑶ウ→ア→オ→イ→エ　⑷オ→ウ→イ→エ→ア　⑸イ→オ→ア→エ→ウ
【解き方】⑴この文の主語となるので，名詞形の performance にする。⑵仮定法過去の文。助動詞 will は過去形の would にする。⑶ be good at 〜ing「〜することが得意である」に注目。(She) is good at making plans. ⑷ (Do you) know someone looking for a towel(?) look for 〜「〜を探す」　現在分詞 looking 〜 が someone を修飾している。⑸ (Will you) show me the pictures you (took on your trip?)「私にあなたが旅行で撮った写真を見せてくれますか」　〈show＋人＋もの〉「（人）に（もの）を見せる」。

11 ⑴ were　⑵ hottest　⑶オ→エ→ア→ウ→イ　⑷エ→ア→オ→イ→ウ　⑸ア→ウ→イ→エ→オ
【解き方】⑴ many trees が主語で，文末に 20 years ago とあるので，There were many trees 〜 とする。⑵直前に the があり，直後に of this month とあるので，hot の最上級 the hottest にする。英文の意味は，「明日は今月いちばん暑い日になると聞いている」。⑶ (To be a chef) is one of my dreams(.)「シェフになることは，私の夢の1つです」　⑷ (What) sports do you like to (watch on

TV?)「あなたは，テレビで何のスポーツを見るのが好きですか」 (5) (It) made me interested in recycling(.)「それ(＝その本)は，私にリサイクルへの興味を持たせた」 make O C「OをCにする」の構文。

12
(1) useful　(2) bought　(3)オ→イ→ウ→ア→エ
(4)ア→エ→オ→ウ→イ　(5)エ→オ→イ→ウ→ア
【解き方】(1)「それは，とても役に立ちます」 形容詞useful にする。(2)「母が先週，それを私に買ってくれた」 last weekとあるので過去形boughtにする。(3) How old is your sister(?)　年齢をたずねる疑問文は，How old ～? とする。(4) (I) was very surprised at the news(.)　be surprised at ～「～に驚く」(5) (Do) you know who they are(?)「あなたは，彼らがだれなのかを知っていますか」 間接疑問は，〈疑問詞＋SV〉の語順。

13
(1)① been　② memories　③ hotter
(2)④ August　⑤ take　⑥ bought
【解き方】(1)①現在完了の文。「～に行ったことがない」は beの過去分詞beenを使ってhave never been to ～とする。② a lot ofに続く可算名詞は複数形になる。③ than があるので比較級にする。hotはtを重ねてerをつける。 (2)④夏の話をしていることから，August「8月」が適切。 ⑤ take A to B「AをBに連れて行く」 ⑥ buy A for B「B にAを買ってあげる」 昨年の話なので過去形boughtにする。

14
(1)① seasons　② December　③ such
(2)④ heard　⑤ our　⑥ harder
【解き方】(1)① season「季節」 前にfourがあるので複数 形にする。②次の文のwinterがヒント。Dで始まる適切 な語はDecember。③あとにtennis and netballとスポーツの例があるので，sports such as tennis and netball「テニスやネットボールのようなスポーツ」とする。 (2)④直前にhave neverがあるので現在完了。過去分詞 heardにする。I have never heard ～「～を聞いたこと がない」 ⑤空所のあとに名詞teamがあることから，所有 格ourが適切な形。⑥直後のthanに着目し比較級にする。 harder than before「以前より一生懸命に」

15
(1) been　(2) a boy who couldn't speak
(3)(C) 4　(D) 1
【解き方】(1)直前にhaveがあるので過去分詞beenにして 現在完了を完成させる。(2)できあがった英文はyou found a boy who couldn't speak English well and you helped him.となる。関係代名詞で導かれる節who couldn't speak English wellが直前のa boyを修飾する。 (3)(C) It is ～ for ... to do「…が―するのは～だ」 (D) do my best「私のベストを尽くす」

16
(1) oldest　(2) when it was built　(3)(C) 3　(D) 1
【解き方】(1)直前にtheがあり，直後に比較の範囲を 表すin this city「この市の中で」があるので最上級oldestに する。(2)できあがった英文はDo you know when it was built?「あなたはそれがいつ建てられたか知っていますか」 となる。間接疑問の文。(3)(C) anyoneを修飾する現在分 詞の形容詞用法としてlivingを入れる。(D) S is known as ～「Sは～として知られている」

17
(1)① largest　② sold　③ talking　④ says
(2)① winter　② quiet　③ opinion　④ sleep
(3)[解答例]① How old is　② you show me
③ long have you
【解き方】(1)①「この町の書店でいちばん大きい」 largeを 最上級にする。②「多くの本が売られている」という受動態 で，sellを過去分詞にする。③ enjoy ～ing「～して楽し む」 ④主語のItに対して3人称単数現在形にする。この sayは「～と書いてある」の意。(2)①「冬休み中，日本では多 くの人が年賀状を送る」 秋と春の間の季節は「冬」。②「図 書館では静かにすることが大事だ」 大きな音や声がしな い様子はquiet「静かな」。③「あなたとは異なる意見があ る」 yoursはyour opinionということ。何かに関する考 えや気持ちはopinion「意見」。④「昨夜よく眠れなかった」 目を閉じて休むことはsleep「眠る」。(3)①年齢を答えてい るのでHow old is ～?「～は何歳ですか」とする。②「メ ニューを見せていただけますか」 Could you ～?「～して いただけますか」とshow A B「AにBを見せる」で表す。③ 「あなたはどのくらいの間スキーをしているのか」―「約4 時間」 How longで始め，現在完了進行形(have been ～ ing)の疑問文を続ける。

第2章 長文読解問題

a．スピーチ・発表原稿

① 日常・文化・社会

1 1．[解答例] did not[didn't] say 【別解】never said
2．修二が竜也にバドミントンで負けること。
3．[解答例] power　4．エ　5．ア
【解き方】 1．空所後の such words「そのような言葉」は，その前の竜也の言葉「僕は日本でバドミントンのチャンピオンになる」を受けている。「そんなことを言うのは恥ずかしいと思ったので」と続くので，「言わなかった」という否定文にするのが適切。2．「そんなにすぐにそれが起こるとは決して思わなかった」 that の内容は直前の2文から考える。3．直後の to reach は不定詞の形容詞用法で，「そのような言葉が目標に達する力を彼に与えた」などとする。4．本文は修二が竜也と対戦する直前で話が終わっているが，メールの内容から，修二が竜也に勝ったことがわかる。A は「初めてきみに勝ったときとてもうれしかったのを覚えている」。B は，本文最後の「僕は竜也に『今回は僕が勝つ。僕はチャンピオンになる』と言うつもりだ」を参考に，「きみが僕に『僕がチャンピオンになる』と言ったとき，驚いた」とする。5．第1段落とアが一致。竜也が修二に一生懸命練習するように頼んだ話はないのでイは不適。ウは，そのような記述は本文にないので不適。修二が竜也に目標を声に出すよう言ったのではないので，エも不適。
《大　意》 修二は7歳のときに竜也と出会い，同じバドミントンクラブに入った。竜也は上手ではなかったが，練習熱心で，いつも「僕はできる！　次は勝つ！　日本でバドミントンのチャンピオンになる！」と言っていた。修二は恥ずかしいのでそんなことを言わないが，いつも竜也に勝った。11歳のとき，初めて修二は竜也に負け，中学生になっても一度も勝てなくなった。とうとう，竜也は本当に日本のチャンピオンになった。竜也は，目標を声に出して言うと，その目標に向かって心と体が動き，自分を強くすると言う。これを聞いた修二も目標を口に出して練習し始めた。そして18歳の全国大会の決勝で竜也を打ち負かし，今度は修二がチャンピオンになった。

2 〔問1〕A．ウ　B．イ　〔問2〕ⓐ (After talking with my great-grandfather,) I began to learn about (wars in the world.)　ⓒ (Now my friends, my dream is to) make the world more peaceful(.)
〔問3〕外国の多くの高校生たちと平和について話し合い，お互いの考えを共有したこと。〔問4〕[解答例](1) There are seven members in her family.　(2) They have peace events at their school festivals.
〔問5〕エ → ウ → ア → イ　〔問6〕フォーラムに参加したり，平和のためのグループを作ったりすること。
【解き方】 〔問1〕A．空所のあとに奈菜の家族の人数，祖父母の父について書かれている。ウ「私の家族について話さ

せてください」が適切。〈let＋O＋動詞の原形〉「Oに～させる」　B．祖父母の父の話（第1段落の最後の3文）を聞き，世界の平和についてのウェブサイトを見たり，戦争についての新聞記事を読んだ。戦争について，もっと考えるべきだとわかった。イ「これは祖父母の父からの大事なメッセージだ」が適切。〔問2〕ⓐ begin to *do*「～し始める」　ⓒ make O C「OをCにする」　〔問3〕前の2文を参照。外国の多くの高校生と平和について話し合ったことと，考えを共有したことの2点を書く。〔問4〕(1)質問は「奈菜の家族は何人か」。空所Aの直後の文を参照。(2)質問は「いくつかの生徒のグループは文化祭で何をするか」。第4段落の最後から3文目を参照。〔問5〕エ．第1段落第7文。（数か月前の話）→ウ．第2段落第4文。（祖父母の父と話したあと）→ア．第3段落第3文。（先週のできごと）→イ．第4段落第4～6文。（先週のフォーラムに参加したあと）　〔問6〕下線部の前の2文を参照。the first action と my next action の2つの内容を具体的に書く。
《大　意》 私の祖父母の父は第二次世界大戦で戦った経験がある。数か月前，2人でテレビで戦争についてのニュースを見ていた。祖父母の父は，戦争はたくさんの人につらい思いをさせる，その悲しい気持ちを想像しようとしてみなさい，と私に話してくれた。それから私はウェブサイトや新聞記事で世界の平和や戦争について知り，多くの人が戦争のせいで悲しい思いをしていることを知って驚いた。私は先週，オンラインでの世界平和のための国際フォーラムに参加した。今，私の夢は世界をもっと平和にすることだ。それは高校生にはまだ難しいと考える人もいるかもしれない。でも高校生でも文化祭などのイベントを利用して小さな行動を起こすことはできる。フォーラムに参加するのは夢をかなえるための第1歩。次に，学校に平和のためのグループを作りたい。多くの人が努力すれば，小さな活動でも世界をよりよくすることができると思う。

3 問1．became　問2．[解答例] told me to　問3．ア　問4．イ，オ　問5．[解答例] give letters
【解き方】 問1．become ～で「～になる」。過去形 became にすることに注意。問2．〈tell＋人＋to *do*〉「(人)に～するように言う」　過去形 told にすることに注意。問3．that は前文にある加藤先生の発言を指す。問4．ア．武が忙しくて困ったのは，1年生ではなく2年生になってからなので内容に合わない。イ．第2段落より，内容に合う。ウ．紙に書いたのは加藤先生ではなく武なので内容に合わない。エ．第3段落参照。加藤先生は仕事に応じて時間帯も分別して行うことの合理性を教えてくれたので，内容に合わない。オ．第4段落参照。加藤先生の教えてくれた to-do list のおかげで時間を有効に使えるようになったので内容に合う。問5．卒業式の日に，自分の友達と先生に対して，これまでの感謝の気持ちを表すために何をするかを書く。不定詞の to で始まるので動詞の原形から書くことに注意。直後に to があるので give A to B「BにAをあげる」などがふさわしい。
《大　意》 中学生の武は2年生のとき，サッカー部のキャプテンと学級委員になった。やるべきことが多くて次第に忙しさを感じるようになった。担任の加藤先生に相談すると，時間の管理について話してくれた。やるべきことをまとめたリスト（to-do list）を作ること，その中から特に重要なものを選び，いつやるのかを考えることも大切だと教え

てくれた。それで毎日to-do listを作り，以前より上手に時間を使うことができるようになった。加藤先生のおかげで，武は再び学校生活について前向きになった。

4 (1)ウ，キ，ク　(2)ウ　(3)①イ　②ア
(4) became a little lighter
(5)① what her mother's　② they would become
【解き方】(1)ウは，第1段落空所アの前後の内容と合う。キは，第3，4段落から，ミキは図書館の女性スタッフからもらった本を2時間読み続け，ついに読み終わったので，一致。クは，第1段落最後の文から，ミキは中学生とわかる。また，第5段落で女性スタッフが「私はあなたと同じ年齢のときにこの町に引っ越してきた」と言っているので，一致。(2)挿入する文は「私は，彼女は私みたいだと思った」という意味。このsheは，空所ウの前のa girl who had to moveつまり「引っ越さなければならない女の子」のことなので，ウに入れるのが適切。(3)①第4段落の「彼女の話は私に大きな勇気を与えてくれた」などを参照。②第3，4段落は土曜日のできごとなので，第5段落冒頭のThe next dayは日曜日のこと。この日，ミキは図書館に行って本をくれた女性スタッフにお礼を言ったので，アが適切。(4)下線部のdidは直前の動詞became a little lighterを表す。引っ越し前に本の一部を売り，「本棚が少し軽くなった」→「私の心も少し軽くなった」ということ。〈become＋形容詞〉「～になる」 a little「少し」(5)①第6段落第1文のI understood my mother's words.の「母親の言葉」をwhat her mother's words meant「母親の言葉がどういう意味だったのか」と言い換える。②第7段落最後の文のI hoped that they would become someone else's treasures.「それら（＝私の本）がだれかほかの人の宝物になることを願った」を参照。
《大　意》　中学生のミキは外国に引っ越すことになった。ミキは読書好きで，本棚にあるたくさんの本は自分の宝物なので手放したくないと思っている。しかし全部は持って行けない。大好きだった図書館に別れを告げに行くと，お世話になった女性スタッフが1冊の本をくれた。それは引っ越さなければならない少女の話だった。ミキは勇気づけられ，本を手放す決心がついた。

5 (1)ⓐ felt　ⓑ written　(2)[解答例]① (They wanted to decide)(What kind of) Music to use for their dance.　② He was (just) listening to them.　(3)イ
(4)エ　(5)自分の意見を持ち，ダンスをよりよくするために，意見を言うことをおそれなかった様子。(6)あなたたちの助けなしに自分ができることは限られているということ。
(7)ウ
【解き方】(1)ⓐ前のbecameに合わせて過去形にする。ⓑ written in English「英語で書かれた」という〈過去分詞＋語句〉が，前の名詞a songを修飾する構造。(2)①「ダンスのリーダーたちは1回目の打ち合わせで何を決めたかったか」 第2段落第2文参照。what kind of music to～は「どんな種類の音楽を～するか」という意味。②「良は正太と亜希が話すのをやめる前，何をしていたか」 第3段落第2文参照。(3)空所Aの直前のthatは関係代名詞で，その前のfamous Japanese songの言い換えとして「すでに多くの生徒が知っている歌」とする。空所Bは，「日本のポピュラーソングを使ったら，ほかのクラスのダンスと同じになるかもしれない」の続きとして，「僕たちのダンスを個性的にするためにアメリカの古いロックを使いたい」とするのが適切。make O C「OをCにする」(4)良が指摘したのは，正太と亜希の意見の共通点。ここまでの正太と亜希の主張

から，エ「きみたちは2人とも，僕たちのダンスを見ている人々にそれを楽しんでもらいたいと思っている」とするのが適切。〈want＋O＋to do〉「Oに～してもらいたいと思う」(5)第6段落最後のThat influenced me.のThatが表す直前の文を日本語で表す。be afraid to do「～するのをおそれる」，improve「～をよりよくする」。(6)第7段落最後から2文目のI realized that ～を参照。realize that ～「～だと気づく」，without「～なしに」，are limited「限られている」，whichは関係代名詞。(7)この話のポイントは，正太と亜希には異なるアイデアがあり，どちらも意見を曲げなかったが，良が2人のアイデアを両方使うことでまとめたこと。よって，ウが適切。アは，打ち合わせは3人で行い，翌日にクラスメートに伝えたので，不一致。イは，良は正太と亜希のアイデアに具体的なコメントをしていないので，不一致。また，アメリカの古いロック（＝英語の歌）に反対した生徒はいたが，亜希と良が説得し，全員一致で，日本のポピュラーソングとアメリカの古いロックの両方を使うことに決まった。よって，エも不一致。
《大　意》　中学生の正太，亜希，良の3人は運動会で発表するダンスのリーダーである。ダンスにどんな音楽を使うか話し合ったところ，正太と亜希には異なるアイデアがあり，どちらも意見を曲げなかった。すると黙って聞いていた良が，どちらもダンスを見ている人に楽しんでもらいたいという気持ちは同じだとして，両方の意見を取り入れる別の案を出し，うまくまとめた。

6 1．エ　2．She met him at a pet shop ten years ago.　3．[解答例]communication
4．イ，オ　5．[解答例]think more about their lives and love them
【解き方】1．コロを飼うことになってどんな気持ちになったか。2．コロとの出会いは第1段落第4文に書いてある。コロは犬なのでitで受けることもできるが，ペットなど特別に愛情がある犬などはhim〔her〕で受けることが多い。3．次の文に「人と会って話をする」「写真を見せ合う」「情報交換する」とあるが，つまりこれらは「コミュニケーション」である。4．イ．第2段落第2文を参照。オ．最後の段落第2文を参照。5．最後の段落の終わりから3文目を10語以内にまとめる。
《大　意》　幼いころから犬のコロを飼っている絵里は，ペットを飼うことの利点を3つ挙げる。1．嫌なことがあったときや多忙で疲れているとき，ペットと接するとうれしい気持ちになり，リラックスできる。2．餌をやったり散歩させたり，ペットの世話をすることで責任感が養える。3．ペットを飼っている人たちとペットの写真を見せ合ったり情報交換したり，コミュニケーションが取れる。絵里は，すばらしい思い出が作れるのでペットを飼ってはいかがですか，と結んでいる。

7 問1．ウ　問2．朝食を食べることで体が温まる
問3．ア　問4．夕食を作る際に，朝食用に多めに料理を作ること。問5．長い時間おなかがすかないから。
【解き方】問1．下線部の直前にあるSo「だから」に着目して，下線部の直前2文に理由を求める。「その日，私は寝坊して，朝食を食べる時間がなかった。そうしたら，私は学校で勉強があまりよくできず，すぐに疲れてしまった」とあるので，ウ「ハルカは，朝食を食べなくて，学校でうまくいかなかったので」が最も適切。問2．下線部直後の文 Bodies get warmer by having breakfast, and we can play sports well without getting injured.から導く。〈get＋形容詞〉「～になる」 by ～ing「～することによっ

て」問3．第3段落第3文の「インターネットにある『朝食を食べることとテストの平均正答率』のグラフが，朝食を食べている生徒の国語の平均正答率が6つのうちで最も高かったと示している」より，(1)がJapanese「国語」のグラフである。第3段落第5文の「3教科のうちで，朝食を食べている生徒の平均正答率と朝食を食べていない生徒の平均正答率で，数学の差がいちばん大きい」より，(2)がMath「数学」のグラフである。よって，アが正解。問4．第4段落第3文にWhen you make dinner, it is good to make more food for breakfast.とある。it is good to make ～は形式主語構文。問5．第5段落最終文の後半but I don't get hungry for a long time when I eat it for breakfastから導く。このitは前文のa Japanese traditional breakfast「日本の伝統的な朝食」を指す。
《大意》毎日，朝食を食べることは健康にも学業成績にもいい。しかし，つい朝食を抜くことも多い。そんな人は，夕飯を作るときに翌朝の分も多めに作るなどの工夫をするとよい。また，長い時間おなかがすかないので，日本の伝統的な朝食がいちばんである。

8 1．①ウ ②ア ③イ 2．A．種類 B．健康によい C．季節 3．イ 4．Yes, they do. 5．ウ
【解き方】1．①空所のあとに「海外に多くの和食レストランがある」とあるので和食はとても人気があることがわかる。②食べ物の豊かな味わいを楽しめる。③空所以降は和食に季節を感じられる理由が書かれている。becauseは理由を表す接続詞。2．A．第2段落第1文のkindsは「種類」という意味。B．第3段落の第1文の is very good for our healthを日本語にする。C．第4段落第1文にwe can see the beautiful parts of nature and changing of the seasons in *washoku*とある。3．空所の前文が「すばらしい和食の文化があるのに和食の利点を忘れがちだ」という意味なので，それに続く文は，イの「このすばらしい文化を理解することが大切だ」が適切。4．第1段落終わりから3文目を参照。5．本文最後の文を参照。this great cultureは和食文化のこと。

9 (1)エ (2)ア (3)ウ (4)エ (5)[解答例]① share ideas about how to make his village better ② places with clean water (6)[解答例]Did you find any problems about our school?
【解き方】(1)「生徒会の一員として大切なことを学ぶ大きなチャンス」(2)「自分の考えが正しい答えかどうか確信していなかったから自分の考えを表現できなかった」(3)thatは直前の文の内容「私たちの地域社会を特別にしているものを失っていること」を指している。(4)ア．ワタナベ先生のためによりよい村にしたいとは書かれていない。イ．第2段落参照。20人のうち，10人が高校生，6人が中学生，残り（＝4人）が小学生。ウ．第3段落の最後を参照。「みんな自分のことを笑うだろう」は蔵之介が思ったことで，実際にそうなったわけではない。エ．最後から2文目の初めの2文に一致する。(5)①第1段落の空所Aを含む文の前文を参照。②第4段落の第4文参照。(6)蔵之介が「実際，問題はいくつかあります」と答えていること，また具体例として教室がきれいでないことを挙げていることに注目。スピーチの最後で蔵之介がI will try to find a problem about our schoolと言っているので，遥はそれを受けて質問したと考えられる。蔵之介がYes, I did.と答えているので，Did you ～?の疑問文であることにも注意。
《大意》生徒会に入った蔵之介は，ワタナベ先生にすすめられて村の生徒が集まる会合に参加した。ほかの生徒た

ちが自信をもって話す一方，蔵之介は自信がなく，自分の意見を言えなかったが，「次世代のためにどのように村をよりよい場所にするか」という問いに対して，ホタルが以前ほど見られなくなったことを発言した。蔵之介は笑われてしまうかと思ったが，その発言をきっかけにほかの生徒や村の職員たちが意見を続けた。蔵之介はこの経験から，問題を見つけてそれを周囲の人々と共有すれば，彼らが解決策を見つけるのを助けてくれることを学んだと言う。学校での問題を見つけて生徒会のメンバーと共有し，一緒に解決策を探るつもりだと述べてスピーチを締めくくった。

10 1．ア 2．エ 3．エ 4．ウ
5．(1)No, didn't (2)[解答例]started, faces
6．イ 7．③Sunday ④walk
【解き方】1．第3段落第1文に「翌朝は曇っていたが，登り始めてすぐあとに雨が降り出した」とあり，最終段落第3文に「晴れた空に虹が出ていた」とある。2．与えられた英文は「私は試合に負けたが，彼らとたくさんの経験をした」。このthemは空所エの直前にあるmy team membersと考えられる。3．単語の意味を推測する問題。"I don't want to go, because ～"に続くので，山登りに行きたくない理由として意味が通るのはエの「疲れている」しかない。4．空所の次の文に，「しかし今ではただ勝つためだけにソフトボールをしている」とあるので，ウ「私はただ友達とソフトボールをすることを楽しんでいた」が適切。5．(1)質問は，「久美は土曜日のソフトボールの試合に勝ちましたか」。第1段落第3文に「しかし私はその試合でうまくプレーできず，私たちは負けた」とある。(2)質問は，「山頂でお父さんと話しているときに，久美は何を思い出しましたか」。空所②の前で，「ソフトボールを始めたときのことを思い出した」と書いてあり，また，第3段落の空所エの前に「私はチームのメンバーの顔を思い出した」とある。6．イ．「久美のお父さんは雨でも山に登ることが好きだと言った」第3段落第8文に「雨でも晴れでも登るのを楽しむ」とあるのに一致。アは第2段落第7文に「行きたくない」とあるのに反する。ウは第3段落第4，6文から，昼食は山頂で食べた。エ．「久美のお父さんはいつでも試合に勝つのが大切だと考えた」という内容は本文にない。オは第4段落の内容に反する。7．③第1段落第1文から，久美のチームが試合に負けたのは土曜日で，その翌日である日曜日にお父さんと山に行った。④第3段落の空所エの3文前にwalk step by step「一歩一歩，歩く」という表現がある。
《大意》久美はうまくプレーできなかったためにソフトボールの試合に負けた。帰宅後，無念な気持ちをお父さんに話すと，お父さんは一緒に登山に行こうと誘ってくれた。山に登っているときに，久美はお父さんから大切なことを3つ教えられた。それは，成功するために全力を尽くすこと，ときどき立ち止まって自分がやってきたことについて考えること，状況を受け入れ一歩一歩進んでいくということだった。途中降り出した雨も上がり，空には美しい虹が出ていた。

11 1．①ウ ②イ 2．イ，エ 3．【1】ウ 【2】オ 【3】イ 【4】ア 【5】エ 4．ア 5．[解答例]A. problem B. interested C. bad D. without
6．[解答例]I can read books to children at my local library. It holds an event for children on Sundays, and students read books to children there. So, I want to join the event and share interesting books with them. I hope I can help children feel reading is fun. (48語)

【解き方】1.①第1段落最後の文を参照。this problemとはfood loss(食品ロス)のこと。②第2段落最後から4文目を見ると，日本では1年で約600万トンの食品ロスがあり，家庭から出るのはその半分，つまり300万トンである。2.イ.第2段落第3文に一致。エ.第3段落最後の文に一致。3.各段落の内容は次のとおり。【1】食品ロスについての導入部分。【2】世界や日本で起こっている食品ロスの実態。【3】食品ロスが起こってしまう理由。【4】食品ロスをなくすために私たちに何ができるか。【5】問題を解決し，困っている人を助けるためにできることをしよう。4.買い物に行く前にチェックしなければならないことは何か。5.A.第2段落第2文を参照。B.第2段落を参照。第3文で，最初は興味がなかったとあるが，その後，興味を持って調べている。C.第2段落最後の文を参照。D.第4段落最後の文を参照。6.「私ができる1つの小さなこと」をテーマに指定語数を使って書く。解答例の英文の内容は次のとおり。地元の図書館で子供たちに本を読むことができる。毎週日曜日に子供たちのためのイベントがあり，学生たちが本の読み聞かせをしている。私も参加して，おもしろい本を子供たちと読みたい。そして子供たちが読書は楽しいと感じてくれたらうれしい。

《大意》食品ロスとはまだ食べられる食べ物を無駄にすることだ。世界で800万人を超える飢えた人々がいる一方で食品ロスは毎年13億トンにも上る。日本では毎年600万トンの食品ロスがあり，その半分は家庭から出ている。食べ物が捨てられれば生産に使われた水やエネルギーも無駄になり，また，捨てられた食べ物を燃やして処理するのにCO$_2$が出て環境にも悪い。食品ロスをなくすには，買い過ぎない，注文し過ぎない，作りすぎないようにする。また，まだ食べられる食品を必要としている所に渡すフードバンクを利用するのもいい考えだ。食品ロスをなくすために，自分にできることから始めよう。

12 (1)(a) Yes, it is. (b) They decided to introduce the school buildings. (2)[解答例]Where is he from? (3)best (4)エ (5)ⓐイ ⓑothers (6)ア，ウ

【解き方】(1)(a)第2段落の田中先生の発言から，リアムが外国に住むのは初めてのことなので，肯定の答えとしてYes, it is.とする。(b)第4段落の第3文にMy group decided to introduce the school buildings.とあるので，参考にする。(2)リアムが男子であることが示されているので，疑問文の主語がheになることに注意。(3)butの前にvarious good ideasという表現があるので，goodの最上級のbestを入れると最も自然。(4)第5段落の第2文に最初のビデオをリアムが楽しんでくれたことが示してあり，その次に，He wanted to know about the town tooという記述が続いている。これが2番目のビデオを制作して送る理由となっているので，エの内容が合致する。(5)ⓐグレイス先生にスピーチのタイトルに関して助言を求めると，先生は「いちばん大事な部分に用いられている語を用いること」をすすめ，How about ～?の形で一例を紹介している部分。本文最終段落の最初にあるIt was great to think about Liam and work together with my group members.という部分がさやかの最も主張したい内容と考えられ，先生もその部分を強調しているのでイのWorking together for our new friendが適切なものと判断できる。ほかの選択肢は活動の一部だけに触れたものとなる。ⓑ最終段落の第3文にあるThrough this experience, I learned helping others makes us happy.の中のothers「他者」を選ぶ。(6)アは第1段落の描写と一致。イは最後のEita's feelingsはLiam's feelingsとすべきなので不一致。ウは第3段落後半の描写と一致する。エは第4

段落前半の描写と不一致。オは第4段落後半のグレイス先生の助言と不一致。カは第6段落後半のリアムの感想と不一致。よってアとウが正解。

《大意》中学生のさやかはアメリカからの留学生リアムを迎えるまでに取り組んだことをスピーチコンテストで発表するための原稿を示している。田中先生からの説明と助言でリアムが初めての日本での生活に順調に慣れる手助けになるようにビデオを作ることにし，また，ALTのグレイス先生の助言もあり，学校生活のさまざまな面を紹介するビデオをグループで分担することになった。発送後リアムからもビデオが送られてきて，さやかたちは彼がビデオを見て楽しんでくれたことを知りうれしくなった。そして彼の求めに応じて町のさまざまな施設の様子を紹介するビデオを撮り，送った。今リアムは日本にいて，私たちとともに学校生活を楽しんでいる。彼は私たちが作ったビデオのおかげで学校と町の様子を事前に知ることができて不安がなくなり，クラスの一員になれたことをうれしく思う，と私たちが喜ぶ感想を述べてくれた。リアムのことを考えグループで協力して活動し，彼が新たな生活に順調に慣れる手助けができたことはすばらしいことである。今回の経験を通して人の役に立つことで自分たちも幸せな気持ちになれるということを学ぶことができた。今後も人の手助けとなることを見つけ続けていくつもりだ。

13 (1)① met ⑥ began (2)(オ)→(エ)→(カ)→(ウ)→(ア)→(イ) (3)(エ) (4)(ア) (5)(a) nervous (b)(ア) (6)(ウ) (7)(イ) (8)(a)(エ) (b) make our future better

【解き方】(1)①現在完了〈have＋過去分詞〉。meetの過去分詞はmet。⑥直前の動詞wentに合わせて過去形beganにする。(2)We were surprised to hear that. be surprised to do「～して驚く」(3)「マウロの自己紹介の仕方」は，直前の文「流ちょうではなかったが，一生懸命に日本語を話そうとした」ことを指している。(4)マウロはわからない日本語があるとまわりの人たちに質問をした。質問の内容として，(ア)「この日本語は何という意味か教えてくれませんか」が適切。(5)(a)第5段落最後の文からnervousが適切。(b)涼真が，友達がいちばん大切であると考えた理由は3つある。第5段落，Third～以下を参照。「互いに意見を共有することができるので，友達と毎日話すことは大切だ」と言っている。(6)質問は，「マウロは，涼真の学校での最後の日，クラスメートに何と言いましたか」。第7段落最後の3文から(ウ)が適切。(7)(ア)「涼真はマウロが日本に1か月滞在することを先生から聞いた」　第2段落第3文に不一致。(イ)「涼真はマウロに会う前，マウロが何語を話すか知らなかった」　第2段落後半に一致。(ウ)「涼真はマウロが，一部の日本語の授業で一生懸命に勉強しているとは思わなかった」　第4段落第2文に不一致。(エ)「涼真は英語の授業でスピーチをした最後の生徒だった」　第6段落第1文に不一致。(8)(a)第6段落の中ほどのI thought everyone in the world had a chance to get education, but that was wrong.から，(エ)が適切。(b)第6段落終わりから2文目Education can help us make our future better.の下線部が適切。

《大意》高校生の涼真が，中学生のときの忘れられない友達，マウロについて書いた作文。外国から来たマウロは日本語の授業で一生懸命に勉強した。ある日，英語の授業で生徒全員がスピーチをしたが，マウロは，彼の人生において教育が最も大切である，と具体例を挙げながら話した。それを聞いた涼真は，教育がいかに大切か，教育が自分たちの未来をよりよいものにしてくれるということを理解した。

14 〔問1〕エ　〔問2〕never　〔問3〕ア　〔問4〕イ
〔問5〕〔解答例〕〔質問A〕She learned that pet animals have special powers. She now understands how much Snow helped the little girl in the car. (21語)　〔質問B〕It means that the kitten should belong to the little girl, not Lisa, and the cat is now at her side. (21語)　〔問6〕オ, カ　〔問7〕エ

【解き方】〔問1〕リサは子猫を失いたくなくて「どうして飼い主はちゃんと見ていなかったのか理解できないわ」と飼い主を批判するようなことを考え始めたのである。〔問2〕「私は両親にそのことについて一言も言わなかった」否定を表す語が入る。〔問3〕下線部は「スノーは何かおかしいと気づいた」という意味。子猫を手放すことになりそうでリサが不安になっていたので, そのように感じたのである。〔問4〕空所の前後は, 「私は『住所が間違っています』と彼女に言うこともできた。でも, それは遅すぎた。母がドアを開けてしまったのだ」という流れ。〔問5〕〔質問A〕本文第1段落の第5, 6文にある pet animals have special powers「ペットには特別な力がある」を参考にしながら, この経験では具体的に何が何の力になったのかを説明するとよい。〔質問B〕「子猫は今, 正しい場所にいる」とはどういうことなのか説明する。子猫は飼い主の女の子のところに戻ったことから考える。〔問6〕ア. リサが小さな友達と学校に行ったという内容はない。イ. リサがまだ子供で, 猫を飼うべきでないと両親が思ったという内容は本文にない。ウ. 電話をかけたのは母ではなくリサなので, 不一致。エ. 両親は女性からのお金を受け取らなかったので, 不一致。オ. リサがつけた名前がスノーで, 女の子がつけていた名前がルーシーなので一致。カ. 本文最後のほうにある女性の発言内容と一致。〔問7〕エのみ[ɑːr]で他はすべて[əːr]。

《大意》リサは15歳の中学生で, ある暖かい春の日, 学校の帰り道で, のら猫と思われるかわいい子猫を見つけた。その子猫は, 身元を示すしるしをつけておらず, リサのあとをずっと家までついてきた。両親にうそを言って飼おうとしたが, 両親はそのうそを見破り, リサに飼い主を見つけて返すべきだと言った。リサは町の新聞に告知を載せて飼い主を探そうと考えたが, 子猫を失うのが嫌でそれができずにいた。週末までにその子猫はすっかり家族の一員となり, 父も飼うことを認めてくれた。その翌週, 町の新聞の告知欄で, リサの自宅近くの女性が, 飼い猫が迷子になり探していることがわかった。その女性に電話すべきだったがそれができず, 両親にもその告知のことは言えなかった。リサは子猫にスノーと名づけ, 子猫はいつもリサのそばにいた。すべてが順調だったが, ただリサは新聞の告知欄のことが忘れられなかった。ある日, その女性のことを考え始め, 夜も眠れなくなってしまい, その翌朝, 両親にその告知のことを話し, 女性に電話した。すぐに女性がやって来て, スノーを見ると笑顔になり, 子猫をルーシーと呼んだ。子猫はとてもうれしそうで, 女性が飼い主であることは明らかであった。リサはスノーを抱えて逃げ出したかったが, 何とかこらえて作り笑顔で女性を迎えた。女性が外に出ると, 車の中に少女とその父親がいた。少女は子猫を見ると大きな笑顔を浮かべ, 子猫を呼び寄せた。女性の話によると, 少女はその女性の娘で, 一家は先月この町に引っ越してきたとのこと。少女は友達もいなくて毎日寂しがっていたので, 両親はその子猫を与えたのだ。子猫が少女の唯一の友達だった。その子猫がいなくなって, 少女はショックで一日中部屋に閉じこもり, ずっと泣いていたらしい。それを聞いて, リサは自分のことしか考えていなかったことに気づき, その少女のことに思いを至らせた。車が出て行くとき, リサは本物の笑顔になることができた。リサは正しいことをしたのだ。子猫はいるべき場所に戻ったのだ。リサは子猫からとても大切なことを学んだ。

---

② 自然・産業・科学技術

1 〔問1〕(1) ア　(2) ウ　〔問2〕A. ア　B. エ　C. イ　D. ウ　〔問3〕(1) エ　(2) 〔解答例〕What would you do

【解き方】〔問1〕(1)第1段落を参照。(2)第1段落第2文と最終段落の最後の2文参照。〔問2〕第2段落第4文よりVenusはEarthより小さい。第3段落最後から2文目より, Mercuryはいちばん小さい。第4段落第3文よりMarsは2番目に小さい。〔問3〕(1)武志の2番目の発言it's one of ～のitはエのto become a space scientistを指す。〈want＋人＋to do〉「(人)に～してほしいと思う」　(2)武志が「もし明日火星に行くことができたら, 火星から地球を見るのになあ」と答えている。「もし明日火星に行くことができたら, 何をしますか？」という意味の疑問文が適切。内容が現実的ではないので仮定法過去の疑問文にする。willではなくwouldを使うことに注意。仮定法過去は〈If＋主語＋(助)動詞の過去形, 主語＋would[could]＋動詞の原形〉の形で, 意味は「もし～なら, …だろうに」。

2 (1)ア. 新しいこと　イ. 食べた　ウ. 5月　(2)〔解答例〕1. It was written in 1969.　2. They can enjoy reading by putting their fingers into them.　【別解】They can put their fingers into them.　3. No, it wasn't.　(3)〔解答例〕My favorite thing is my watch because my grandfather gave it to me on my birthday last year. It is small and cute. (23語)　【別解】I like my bike. I always use it when I go out with my friends, so I could visit many places in my town. (24語)

【解き方】(1)ア. 第1段落第3文にIf you read it, you may feel that you want to try something new and improve yourself.とある。イ. 第2段落第5文にIt shows that the caterpillar has already eaten them.「それ(＝穴)はイモムシがすでにそれら(＝果物)を食べたことを示している」とある。ウ. 第3段落第2文にHe died last May「彼(＝エリック氏)は昨年5月に亡くなった」とある。(2)1.「原作はアメリカでいつ書かれたか」に答える。第1段落の第4文にThe original book was written in America in 1969.「原作はアメリカで1969年に書かれた」とある。2.「子供たちはどのように本についた穴で読むのを楽しめるか」　第2段落第7文Children can enjoy reading by putting their fingers into these holes.「子供たちはこれらの穴に指を入れることによって, 読むのを楽しむことができる」から答える。3.「アメリカでページの穴を作るのは簡単だったか」　第2段落第8文にThey were difficult to make in America.「それはアメリカでは作るのが難しかった」とある。このto makeは形容詞difficultの内容を限定する副詞用法の不定詞。(3)解答例は「私のお気に入りのものは腕時計です。昨年, 祖父が誕生日に私にくれました。それは小さくてかわいいです」という内容。別解は「私は自分の自転車が好きだ。友達と出かけるときにはいつもそれを使う。だから私の町の多くの場所を訪れることができた」という内容。

3 (1)B→A→C　(2)ア　(3)ウ　(4)・ライチョウの自然生息地をきれいに保つためにボランティア活動をすること。・ライチョウを助けるためにお金を集めること。

【解き方】(1)ライチョウは人々を火事や雷から守ってくれると信じていたので、長い間その数は減らなかった→B.しかし、ライチョウを捕まえて食べる人が出てきた→A.そのため、山にすむ数が減少した→C.そこで捕まえるのをやめるようにという命令が下った。(2) 第4段落の最後の3文に、ライチョウの生息数は1981年から1991年までに増加したが、2001年には減少し、その後増加したと書かれている。(3)ウ.第1段落の最後の2文に一致。(4)第5段落の第2、3文に書かれている。

《大意》 ライチョウは特別天然記念物で、立山など標高の高い山あいでしか生活できず、夏は茶色だが冬は白に変わる。江戸時代には火事や雷から守ってくれる鳥と信じられていたが、その後、人間が食用として捕まえるようになり、その数は減少した。気温の上昇のためにキツネなどが山を登って食べたことや、人が登山のときに捨てたビニール袋やペットボトルについていた細菌もその減少の原因である。人々は柵を作ったり、山をきれいにしたりして守ろうとしたが、その数が簡単に増加することはなかった。しかし、ライチョウの自然生息地を継続して掃除したり、彼らを救うためのお金を集めたりする努力は可能である。智也は、今年の夏は立山に行き、ライチョウの自然生息地を自分の目で見て、彼らについてもっと多くのことを知りたいと思っている。

4 (1)ア.3 イ.4 ウ.2 エ.1 (2)私たちは、どんなものからでも、どこでも、いつでも、すばらしいアイディア[考え]を手に入れることができるということ。
(3)ア.5 イ.2 ウ.6
【解き方】(1)ア.第1段落第1、2文に「私は5歳の妹の誕生日におもちゃをあげた。そうしたら彼女は二次元コードのついたおもちゃの箱を持ってきて、私に『これは何？ 私はいつも身の回りにこれを見かける』とたずねた」とあるので、3が適切。「コウスケが妹と二次元コードについて話したとき、彼女はそのいくつかを以前に見た」 イ.第2段落の終わりから2文目に「日常生活で、それ(＝二次元コード)のよりよい使い方を見つけようとした人々がいたということを、このことは示している」とあるので、4が適切。「二次元コードが人気になったのは、それを使う方法を見つけたいと思った人々がいたから」 ウ.第3段落第5文に「それ(＝身の回りの不便なことや単純な問題)への答えがとても簡単であることがときどきある」とあるので、2が適切。「コウスケが学んだことは、不便なことへの答えがとても簡単であることがときどきあるということだ」 エ.第4段落最終文に「(革新の)扉を開き私たちが想像したことのない方法で私たちの社会をよりよくするために、人々の『もし』を使いなさい」とあるので1が適切。「身の回りの『もし』に注目することによって、よりよい社会を作ることができると、コウスケは考えている」(2)直後の文We can get great ideas from anything, anywhere, and at any time.を日本語で表す。(3)ア.第2段落第4文を参照。have trouble in ～ing「～するのに苦労する」 イ.第4段落最終文参照。「自分の周りの社会をよりよくすることができるとコウスケは理解した。ここでのよく似た考え方とは日常生活の身の回りからすばらしいアイディアが見つかるという考え方のこと。ウ.「私たちは周りを見回して、古い考えだけを持ち続けずに、改善できることを見つけるべきだ」という内容は、第3段落最終文にある。
《大意》 二次元コードを生み出した日本人男性の例から、そのような革新的なアイディアは、身の回りの不便なことに対して「もし」と思考することによって思いつくことができるとコウスケは学んだ。そして自分も同じように将来世の中をよりよくしたいと考えた。

5 ①ウ ②イ ③ア ④[解答例] dangerous
【解き方】①第1段落の終わりから2文目のAdults need to sleep about 30% of the day.「大人は1日のおよそ30%の時間寝る必要がある」から、ウの7～8が正解。②第2段落の第6、7文のTigers and lions sleep ～. Tigers sleep a little longer than lions.から、睡眠時間が16時間のⓐにはTigers、14時間のⓑにはLionsが適切。続く第8文On the other hand, giraffes sleep for the shortest time ～.から、Giraffesの睡眠時間はいちばん短く、ⓓ2時間。残りのⓒ4時間がElephantsとなる。③「それらの動物(Giraffes or elephants)は食べ物を探すのに多くの時間が必要で～になるためにたくさん食べなければならない」「～」にはアのfullを入れ、「満腹になるために」とするのが適切。④前文のbecause other animals may try to eat them ～の内容から、空所にはdangerous「危険な」が適切。

6 1. (A)ウ (B)イ (C)ア 2. Wetlands are now getting smaller 3. ウ 4. エ 5. 湿地は水をきれいにし、二酸化炭素を保持できること。(25字)
6. [解答例]We can clean our town. We can ask our friends to clean our town together. (15語)
【解き方】1. 下線部のあと、3つのポイントについて、First, Second, Thirdと述べている。2. 第6段落第1文参照。3. ヒヨドリ、ウグイス、スズメの3種についての順位を比べる。ヒヨドリが最もひんぱんに観察された。1997年から2002年までウグイスよりスズメのほうがひんぱんに見ることができたが、2016年から2020年まではスズメが3位。これらから判断して適切なグラフはウ。4. ④第5段落第3～5文参照。湿地には植物が多く、多くの昆虫や魚が生息する。鳥はそれらを食べる。⑤直後の文のFor example,～で使い道の例が述べられている。飲むこと、農業、産業に使われるのはwater。5. 次の文から、First, Secondと2点述べられていることをまとめる。wetlands make water cleanはmake O C「OをCにする」の構文。6. 環境を守るために、自分たちができることを具体的に書く。解答例の意味は「私たちは町をきれいにできる。私たちは、一緒に町をきれいにしようと友達に頼むことができる」。
《大意》 日本にいる鳥とすむ場所について考えたい。日本でよく見られる鳥としてはヒヨドリ、ウグイス、スズメの3種類が挙げられる。鳥がすむのに好む場所が湿地だ。湿地は水が豊富なため、餌になる植物・昆虫・魚が豊富だ。しかし、世界の湿地は1970年以降50年で35%も減った。それは人間がその水を使うことと、地球温暖化によるものだ。湿地は水をきれいにし、また二酸化炭素を保持することができることから、地球温暖化を止めるのに役立つ。鳥と湿地を守るために一緒に何かしませんか。

7 (1)【1】オ 【2】ウ 【4】エ (2)ウ→イ→ア
(3)[解答例] work hard and help people (4)イ、オ
【解き方】(1)本文はコンビニの歴史で始まる。第1段落はできた当初の話なので、オが適切。第2段落は「今」の話に展開され、ウが適切。第3段落で社会の変化について述べたあと、第4段落はコンビニが抱える問題(a problem)について。よって、エが適切。(2)「30年ほど前は客の多くは若い人だった」(過去から今の話)→「でも今は高齢者の客が多い」(ウ)→「家の近くのコンビニは歩いて行けるので便利」(イ)→「また、彼ら(＝高齢者)はコンビニで食べ物を買えば、料理する必要がない」(ア) (3)「でもこの先、ロボットが増え、ロボットはコンビニで～するかもしれない」という文意に

合う内容を考える。解答例は「一生懸命働いて人々を助ける」。第4段落の「十分な労働者がいなければ閉業しなければならない」と，空所後の「そうすれば，コンビニは閉業しなくてよい」という流れから，ロボットが労働者不足の解決策になり得る点を押さえよう。(4)アは，コウジがニュースを見たのはテレビではなくインターネットなので不一致。イは，第1段落の「それら（＝おにぎり）を買う人はほんの少しだった」と一致。ウは，第2段落から，切手の販売や電気料金の支払いのサービスが始まったのは30年くらい前のこと。第1段落によると，日本初のコンビニは1972年ころ（1927年の約45年後）のことなので，不一致。エは，第4段落の「コンビニで働ける人が多くいない」と不一致。オは，ロボットは「日本のコンビニが今抱えている問題（＝労働者不足）」の解決策になり得るという話なので，一致。
《大意》　中学生のコウジはネットでコンビニについての興味深い記事を読んだ。コンビニは1927年にアメリカで始まり，45年ほどあとに日本に導入された。コンビニはおにぎりやお弁当などの食品の販売のほか，さまざまなサービスを提供していて，とても便利である。一方で，労働者不足という問題も抱えている。今，その解決策としてロボットが導入され始めている。

8　1. エ　2. ウ　3. A. エ　B. ア　C. イ
4. イ
【解き方】1. 「新しい魚群探知機は魚を捕るのにイルカのように音波を利用する」　第3段落第3文以降にイルカが音波を使って魚を捕まえていることが書かれており，第4段落第1文にそのイルカの技能が魚群探知機に応用されたことが書かれている。2. ②古い魚群探知機では，「漁師は魚群の場所しか見ることができなかった」。第1段落最終文および第2段落第2文参照。③「漁師はそれぞれの魚の大きさも見ることができる」　第4段落第4文参照。3. A. 「魚の数が減ったので，彼らはほんの少しの数の魚しか捕れなくなった」　第2段落最終文参照。B. 「漁師たちは魚の大きさを見ることができるので，彼らは捕りたい魚を選ぶことができる」　第4段落第4，5文参照。C. 「彼らは若い魚を捕らずにすむから，長年にわたり魚を捕り続けることができる」　第4段落最終文参照。4. 「ある日本人が，イルカが魚を捕まえる技能に注目することで新しい機械のヒントを得た」　最終段落第5文参照。
《大意》　かつての魚群探知機では魚の大きさまでは見極めることができず幼魚も乱獲してしまうこととなり，魚の数が減る原因となっていた。そこである日本人が，イルカの音波を使った狩りからその技術を学び，魚の大きさまでも認識できる新たな魚群探知機を開発した。おかげで今日では若い魚を捕ることなく，同じ場所で長年漁ができるようになった。

9　1. ［解答例］(1) Yes, he did.　(2) His father did.
2. ウ　3. ［解答例］eat　4. would be fun if I
5. ア，イ　6. ［解答例］I liked your speech very much. It's important to be interested in something. I hope I can find my dream like you. (22語)
【解き方】1. (1)第1段落第3文を参照。(2)第1段落中盤の I tried to ～ father stopped me. を参照。2. 下線部は，前文の「なぜヤコウタケは美しい緑色の光を放つのか」に対応している。「なぜ美しい緑色の光がヤコウタケから放たれるのかを，私たちは正確には知らない」が適切。3. 空所を含む段落から，次郎はキノコが昆虫や動物に対してメッセージを発していると感じていることがわかる。ベニテングタケのメッセージとして，適切な内容を考える。第4段

落の最終文に，「ベニテングタケは動物に食べられたくないのかもしれないとある」ので，eatなどが正解となる。4. 仮定法の文。「もし私がキノコが何について話しているのかがわかれば，楽しいだろう」という意味。5. ア「名前を持たないキノコはたくさんある」　第2段落第2文を参照。イ「ヤコウタケとベニテングタケは，次郎の好きなキノコだ」　第3段落の最初の2文，および第4段落第1文を参照。6. 「スピーチ全体への感想，キノコについて，興味があること，将来の夢」など，スピーチに関連した内容を列挙し，英文にできそうな内容を選んで，感想として書くとよい。
《大意》　私はキノコに興味がある。まだ幼かったころ，近所の森で初めてベニテングタケを見た。とてもきれいで，印象的だった。それ以来，キノコへの興味は尽きない。私が好きなのは，ヤコウタケとベニテングタケだ。ヤコウタケは美しい緑色の光を発する。ベニテングタケも赤いかさが美しいが，多くの動物には毒である。私は，このようなキノコたちは，昆虫や動物にメッセージを発しているのではないかと感じている。キノコ同士が電気信号を使って対話をしているという説を唱える科学者もいる。私は将来，世界中を回って，まだ見たことのないキノコを見つけたい。また，キノコのコミュニケーション方法についても学びたい。幼少期に抱いた好奇心が，私に将来の夢を与えてくれたのだ。

10　1. (A) borrowed　(B) making　2. ウ　3. small sea animals　4. ①卵を持つ魚　②稚魚　③人々に知ってもらう（①と②は順不同）　5. ア，カ　6. イ
【解き方】1. (A)　空所前の books，空所あとの from the library から borrow が適切。「私が先週図書館から借りた本」とする。last week とあるので，過去形にする。(B) by making the island's beach taller「島の砂浜をもっと高くすることによって」　make O C「OをCにする」　前置詞 by のあとなので，～ing（動名詞）にする。2. 空所ウの前文は「サンゴが赤土の下になると，しばしば死んでしまう」，空所のあとは「もし畑に強い根を張る植物で囲まれれば，赤土は畑にとどまることができる。多くの人がこのプロジェクトに参加してきた」とある。挿入文「それを止めるために，1人の中学生がそこの人々によい案を与えた」は，空所ウに入れると自然につながる。中学生の案は，畑に強い根を張る植物を植えること。3. 下線部(C)のある文の前の2文にも them があり，「それ（＝アマモ）はそれらに酸素を与える」「また，それらがより大きな海の動物に近づかないよう手助けする」「私たちは，それは安全な場所なのでそれらのすみかと言える」と述べている。いずれも空所イの前にある small sea animals を指している。4. 下線部の2文あとからの3文，So he doesn't catch ～ what he is doing. の内容をまとめる。①に該当するのは fish with eggs，②に該当するのは young fish，③は he visits a lot of places to let people know what he is doing の下線部が該当する。〈let＋O＋動詞の原形〉「Oに～させる」　5. ア. 第1段落の最初の4文の内容に一致。イ. 第2段落第2文に不一致。ウ. 第3段落空所イのあとの文に不一致。エ. 第4段落最終文に不一致。そのような内容は本文にない。オ. 空所ウの前文に不一致。カ. 空所ウの直後の文に一致。キ. そのような内容は本文にない。6. 健太が発表した英文は，海洋生態系を守ろうとするさまざまな例を挙げている。また，最終段落で If we work together, we can do more things to protect marine ecosystems. とある。イの Working together for better marine ecosystems「よりよい海洋生態系のために一緒に取り組むこと」が適切。
《大意》　健太は美しい海のそばで生まれ海が大好きだ。海のない生活は考えられない。しかし，今，海洋生態系は

いい状態とは言えない。オーストラリアでは，水面が上昇している。アオウミガメが産卵する浜辺を高くすることによって，アオウミガメを守ろうとしている。愛知では，小さな海の動物のすみかであるアマモの量が少なくなっているが，海底にアマモを植え始めている。千葉でも，ある漁師は，将来も東京近海の魚を人々に食べて楽しんでもらいたいと思い，持続可能な漁業に取り組んでいる。沖縄でも，台風のとき畑から流出する赤土でサンゴが死んでしまうのを止めるため，畑に強い根を張る植物を植え始めた。健太は自分自身のプロジェクトを始めることに興味がある。一緒に取り組めば，私たちは海洋生態系を守るためにより多くのことができると健太は考えている。

11 (ア)4　(イ)2　(ウ)2
【解き方】(ア)第3段落後半の「農家の数はより減少した」と，「60歳以上の農家の割合がより増えた」をもとに正答を選ぶ。(イ)空所前後の内容や接続詞を根拠に，つながりがよいものを選ぶ。①「このロボットは医者のように仕事をすることができるが，それにはできないことがある。それは医者に取って代わることはできない」②「ロボットと人間がまったく同じ仕事をできるとは思わない。しかし，ロボットは，人間が行ういくつかの仕事ができる。今日では，ロボットはとても重要になってきている」③「AI機器は収集した情報すべてを記憶することができるが，人間は機器にその使い方を教えなければならない。だから，私たちは常にそれらの効果的な使用方法について考えなければならない」(ウ)a.「カイトは，スピーチの中で，AI機器のある未来を聞き手に想像してほしいと思っている」第1段落の最終文を参照。e.「ロボットは農家が行うたいへんな仕事を代行することで，農家の生活を改善するだろう」第4段落の最後から2文目を参照。
《大　意》AI機器は大量の情報を収集・記憶し，それを用いて仕事をする。私はAI関連のイベントに参加し，2種類のロボットに出会った。1つは，医師のような仕事をするもので，個人に合わせて健康改善の提案をしてくれる。もう1つは，収穫時期を見きわめて，トマトを摘むロボットだ。日本の農業人口は減少傾向にあり，業界内の高齢化も進んでいる。ゆえに，農家の仕事を助けるロボットの存在は，重要性を増してきている。このように，便利で多様なAI機器が開発されているが，私たち人間にはそれらの効果的な扱い方を考える必要があることを，肝に銘じておくべきだ。AI機器が人類の役に立つことを期待している。

12 (1)ア　(2)understood how they could move
(3)エ　(4)other sea animals　(5)Have you tried to open　(6)イ　(7)エ　(8)イ　(9)① Yes, they are.
② We can use the power of the strong muscle.
【解き方】(1)「ホタテガイがすばやく動けると知らなかったので私はとても驚いた」(2)「それらがどのようにして動くことができるのか」を間接疑問で表す。〈疑問詞＋S＋V〉の語順に注意。(3)「ホタテガイは進みたい方向と逆の方へすばやく水を押し出すことで動くことができる」(4)「ホタテガイは自分の命を守るためにほかの海洋動物から泳いで離れる」(5)「～したことがありますか」は経験を表す現在完了の疑問文で表す。「～しようとする」はtry to do.(6)空所は「2枚の殻を手で開けるのが簡単ではないとわかった」に続く部分。(ii)「(初めて開けようとしたとき)すごくたいへんで時間がかかり，結局できなかった」→(i)「この経験(＝iiの内容)を思い出し，なぜ貝は殻を閉じ続けられるのか知りたいと思った」→(iii)「そこで，図書館に行って何冊か本を読み，この疑問への答えを見つけた」→空所後の「その本によ

ると～」につながる。(7)仮定法過去の文。貝には殻を閉じ続けられる強い筋肉があるという話のあとなので「もし私たちに2枚の殻がある貝と同じ筋肉があれば，重いかばんを長時間持って疲れることはないだろう」が適切。(8)ア．テレビではなく本で読んだ。イ．第2段落の最後から2文目と一致。ウ．第4段落と不一致。エ．第3段落のHowever, shellfish with two shells don't become tired.などを参照。貝は筋肉に含まれる特殊なタンパク質のために疲れない。(9)①「ホタテガイは2枚の殻がある貝類で最も活動的か」第2段落の最終文を参照。②「将来，科学技術がさらに発達したら，私たちは何が使えるか」第4段落の第4文を参照。

13 問1．[解答例]Because they were light and cool.
問2．日本は湿度が高く，ぬれると乾くのに時間がかかるから。問3．A. show B. broken 問4．①ウ ②カ ③エ 問5．I imagine what umbrellas will be like in 問6．[解答例](1) using them (2) different ideas (3) give us
【解き方】問1．「明治時代以降，なぜ西洋の傘が日本で人気になったか」理由は第5段落最後の文のbecause of their light weight and cool design「その傘の軽さとかっこいいデザインのために」にある。Because they were light and their designs were cool.などでもよい。問2．第8段落では，日本と他国の傘を使う頻度の違いについて，湿度に着目している。マユミの意見はIn my opinion，～にある。「日本人が他国の人々と比べて傘を使う頻度が高い」理由は，soの前の部分を日本語で表すとよい。問3．A. were usedは受動態で，to　A　は不定詞「～するために」。「その傘は所有者の権威を示すために使われたようである」B.「傘は開閉できたが，重く，簡単に壊れた」were brokenという受動態が適切。問4．①この段落は西洋の傘が人気になったあと，日本が独自の折りたたみ傘や透明のビニール傘を作るようになった話なので，ウ「(こうして)いくつかのタイプの傘が日本の製造業者によって作られた」が適切。②直前の「雨期は，雨が突然降り，まもなくするとやむ」から，カ「雨はすぐにやむので傘を使わない」が適切。③「ニュージーランドでは，日本と同じくらい雨が降るのに，人々は雨が降ってもあまり傘を使わない」though「～だけれども」問5．「ときどき私は，将来傘がどんなふうになるかを想像する」間接疑問〈疑問詞＋主語＋動詞〉の語順に注意。be like「～のように」in the future「将来」問6．(1)第4段落第1文から，「日本の人々は江戸時代中期以降に傘を使い始めた」とする。using umbrellasでもよい。(2)日本は他国と比べ湿度が高く乾きにくいので他国よりも傘を使う。ここも日本と他国の違いを表す文になるように，fromに着目して〈different＋名詞＋from ～〉「～と異なる(名詞)」とするのが適切。(3)本文最後に「傘の歴史について学ぶことで新しい傘を生み出すヒントが得られるかもしれない」とある。設問の文は主語がWeではなくlearningなので，get a hintをgive ～ a hint「～にヒントを与える」で表す。
《大　意》高校1年生のマユミが傘の歴史について調べて書いた文章。日本で傘が使われた最も古い形跡は古墳時代。調査によると，江戸時代中期以降に傘を使い始めたが，高価だったので多くの人は，みのとすげがさを使っていた。その後，傘を作る方法が広がったが，ペリー提督が来たころ(江戸時代後期)に西洋の傘が入ってきて，その軽さとデザイン性から日本中に広まった。20世紀になると，日本は独自の傘を作るようになった。マユミは日本人が外国と比べてよく傘をさす理由は，日本では湿度が高く，雨で一度ぬれると乾きにくいからだと考えた。

b．Eメール・手紙文

1 エ
【解き方】マイケルのメールに，「ニュージーランドでやってみたいことを教えてください」とある。この回答として，エ「地元の人々と一緒に伝統的な踊りをやってみたい」が適切。

2 ウ
【解き方】里穂のメールに「今日の英語の授業で，先生は発表について話した。私たちは3人か4人のグループを作り，テーマとして1つの国を選ばなければならない」とある。ウ「英語の授業の発表で，それぞれのグループは1つの国について話す」が適切。

3
(1)何を学ぶかを決める前に，自分の将来の仕事を決めるべきかどうかということ。(2)[解答例] I can improve my skills　(3) You don't know what will be useful in the future.　(4)ア　(5)[解答例]① No, she hasn't. ② She decided her goal first.　③ They sometimes make their own stories.　(6)[解答例] You helped me a lot. I decided to follow my heart. Though I don't know what I will do in the future, I can learn something important through art history.

【解き方】(1)ヒカリが悩んでいる問いとは，【ヒカリからフレッドへのメール】の最終文にある Should I decide my future job before I decide what to study? に集約されている。このメールの第2段落では，この問いを持つに至った経緯としてユリとのやり取りが書かれている。(2)【フレッドからヒカリへのメール】では，フレッドは最終文で You can improve some skills by doing so.「そうする（＝自分の好きな教科を勉強する）ことでいくつかの能力を向上させることができる」とアドバイスしている。空所を含む文は，このアドバイスを受けてヒカリが考えたことである。(3)ナイチンゲールは看護師であったが，人々の命を守るには衛生的な環境が必要であることを，数学や統計学の知識を用いて示した。記事がこの例で伝えたいことは，Do you understand what this story means? から始まる次の段落に示されており，第2文の「将来何が役に立つかはわからない」がその中心的な内容。(4)ユリのように目標のために学んだり，フレッドの言うように能力を高めるために学んだり，そして記事に書かれているように何が役に立つかはわからずとも学ぶことを楽しむなど，学ぶ理由は人それぞれであるということを示すアが適切。(5)①【ヒカリからフレッドへのメール】の第2段落中ほどを参照。②【ヒカリからフレッドへのメール】の第2段落最終文を参照。③【フレッドからヒカリへのメール】の第2段落後半参照。(6)本文全体を通して読み取れる方向性を踏まえて書きたい。解答例では，将来何をするかはわからないが，芸術の歴史を学ぶことで何か大切なことが学べるとしている。フレッドが紹介してくれた記事の内容に触れて書いてもよい。

《大意》【ヒカリからフレッドへのメール】　友達のユリと将来について話していた。私は芸術の歴史に興味があり，高校を終えたあと，それについて学びたいが，ユリは「教師や研究者になりたいの？」と聞いてきた。私は将来の職業についてまだ何も決められていない。ユリは，何を学ぶか決める前に，まず自分の目標を決めたそうだ。フレッド，あなたは医者になるために勉強を頑張っているのですよね。私も何を勉強するか決める前に将来を決めるべきでしょうか。

【フレッドからヒカリへのメール】　難しい問題だね。私は，今は目標のために勉強しているが，医者になったあとも勉強し続けるつもりだ。それに，自分の夢には関係のない教科を勉強することも好きだ。たとえば，私は演劇の授業も好きだ。創作をして新しいことをつくり出せるようになったり，はっきり話せるようになる。私の兄は大学で数学を学んでいるが，音楽の授業でチームワークを学べると言う。好きな教科を学ぶことで，能力を向上させることができるよ。

【ウェブサイトの記事】　好きな教科だけを勉強していればいいのだろうか。ナイチンゲールの例をご紹介しましょう。彼女は世界で最も有名な看護師の1人だ。彼女は衛生的な病院を作りたいと思っていた。彼女は数学や統計学の知識があったので，その知識を使って，環境が汚いと人々の命がおびやかされてしまうことを示した。このように，将来何が役に立つかはわからないのだ。もし役に立たなくとも，新しいことを学ぶのは楽しいものだ。自分の世界を広げられる。私の父は理科の教員だが，75歳にして大学で古典文学を学んでいる。新しいことを学べてとてもうれしいと言っている。

4
(1)レオは日本語をうまく話せず，ときどきカナたちの日本語を理解できないということ。(2)ア
(3)[解答例] talk with them in Japanese　(4)エ
(5)[解答例]① Yes, they can.
② Because he doesn't look so happy when Kana and her classmates talk to him.　③ They can share ideas with people in the world.　(6)[解答例] (Hello,) Kana(. I'm ＊＊＊.) Why don't you ask him what he really wants?　For example, he may like talking in Japanese because he is studying in Japan.　You are kind, so you can help him better.　【別解】(Hello,)　Leo(. I'm ＊＊＊.)　Your classmates will understand you if you tell them your true feelings. When I had an experience like yours and told my friends my feelings, we became better friends.

【解き方】(1)下線部を含む文の前文が that の内容にあたる。設問に「具体的に」とあるので He と our がそれぞれだれを指すかを明確にすること。(2)カナの手紙の終わりから2番目の段落に書いてある最後の文を見ればわかるとおり，レオはカナたちが英語ができないので困っていると，カナは考えている。(3)2文前の Some friends talked to me in English を参照。レオの手紙を見ると最後から2番目の段落の終わりのほうに同じようなことが書かれている。つまり，レオも先生も同じ経験をしていた。(4)4つの選択肢の動詞を見るといずれも現在形で，現在の状況を伝えている。カナはレオが自分たちのせいで元気がないのかも知れないと心配し，レオは本当の気持ちを言うとみんなを傷つけてしまうかもしれないと不安になっている。これはお互いのことを思いやっているということだ。(5)①最初の段落の第4文を参照。②カナの手紙の第2段落最後から2文目を参照。we を Kana and her classmates と書き換えることに注意する。③レオの手紙の第4段落第3文を参照。(6)解答例の意味は次のとおり。〔カナへの返事〕レオにどうしてもらいたいか聞くといいよ。たとえば，彼は日本で勉強してるのだから日本語で話すのを望んでいるのかもしれない。あなたは親切なのでもっとうまくレオを手助けできる

よ。〔レオへの返事〕ほんとうの気持ちを言ったらクラスメートはわかってくれるよ。僕もきみと同じ経験をしたとき、自分が思っていることを友達に言ったらもっと仲よくなれたよ。

《大意》 マイク先生は生徒と交流するために質問箱を設置していて、ある日2通の手紙を受け取った。1通はカナダからでフランス人留学生のレオのことが書かれてあった。「ここのところレオは話しかけても元気がありません。レオの英語は速くて聞き取れないときがあるし、私たちもすべてを英語で話すことはできません。英語がもっと上手になればいいのかな？」 もう1通はレオからだった。「先生なら僕の気持ちがわかってくれると思います。友達は僕に英語で話しかけてくるけど、ほんとうは日本語で話したい。日本語を勉強しに来ているわけだし、ゆっくり話してもらえれば多少は理解できる。でもこのことを言ったらみんなを傷つけるかな」 マイク先生も昔レオと同じ経験をしたことを思い出した。双方ともお互いを思いやっての手紙で2人はきっとよい友達になるだろうと思いながら返事を書き始めた。

5 (1)ア (2)〔解答例〕(She used it because) she wanted to remember the time with Tomomi. (3)イ (4) English books
【解き方】(1)トモミのメールの第3段落第1, 2文から、電車に乗って、窓から美しい海の風景を楽しんだことがわかる。(2)質問は「なぜフサコは、その手紙を書くのに、トモミがあげたペンを使ったのですか」。フサコの手紙の第3段落第4文の後半(because I want to 〜)を参照。「トモミと過ごした時間を思い出したいから」という理由が述べられている。(3)ア.「トモミはコンピューターを買って、それをフサコに送った」 トモミのメールの第2段落第1文に不一致。イ.「フサコはずいぶん前に外国で働いた」 トモミのメール第2段落第3文に一致。ウ.「トモミは小学生のとき、英語をよく理解した」 トモミのメールの第3段落第4文に不一致。エ.「フサコはトモミがメールを送るとき、しおりが便利だと思っている」 フサコの手紙の第3段落第5, 6文に不一致。(4)トモミはメールの第3段落第3文以降で、フサコの家で見た many books written in English を話題にしている。次にフサコの家に行くときに英語でそれら(＝本)を読みたいと言っているので、空所には English books を入れるのが適切。

6 (1)ア (2)エ (3)〔解答例〕 Indonesia can develop more
【解き方】(1)空所の直前の文に「私の国では日本語が書いてある電車をよく見ます」とあり、次の太一の発言が、「ほんとうに？ その電車はどうですか」なので、ア「それに、私はその電車を実際に利用したことがある」が適切。(2)下線部の発言のあとの太一のスピーチ原稿を見る。最後の2文「新聞によると、インドネシアは電車を輸入するのをやめる。インドネシアは自国で作られた電車を使おうとしているとも書いてある」から、エ「インドネシアは自国で作られた電車を使おうとしている」が適切。(3)空所②がある太一の発言は Me too. で始まっていることに着目。直前のレオの発言最終文にある I hope Indonesia can develop more. の下線部「インドネシアはもっと発展できる」を入れる。

c．グラフ・資料

① グラフ・表

1 1．エ 2．〔解答例〕wanted to try new things
【解き方】1．①グラフを参照。「外国の人と友達になりたい」は51.9％＝more than half である。②グラフを参照。「外国での生活や勉強に関心がある」が40.2％＝about forty percent である。③表を参照。一番人気ではないが、900人より少し多い国は、カナダ。2．このあとの発言「約38％の人が(自分と)同じ考えでうれしい」は、グラフの「新しいことに挑戦したい」に該当する。よって、(Because I) wanted try new things(.)「新しいことに挑戦したかった(から)」などとする。

2 1．エ 2．ウ 3．イ
【解き方】1．キャンプ場の数を示した表(table)を説明した第2段落参照。北海道はキャンプ場が200以上あり、表のAにあたる。Bは2位の長野。「山梨は岐阜より少し多い」ので、Cが山梨、Dが岐阜。2．本文とグラフを照合していくと、第一次キャンプブームの1994年のあと、1999年にかけて数が減った。2009年は1994年の約半数だった。2009年から2019年にかけて、数は再び増加し続けた。3．第4段落第5文(Second, 〜)とイが一致。アは、1994年〜2009年の間キャンプ人口は減少したので、never decreased が不適。ウは、第4段落最後の My father is one of them. は、春樹の父親は、第一次キャンプブームを経験し、親になってからまた子供とキャンプに行き始めた世代の1人ということ。よって、「この夏初めてキャンプに行った」は不一致。エは、第4段落第3, 4文から、「キャンプのアニメや有名人のビデオ」が理由でキャンプ人気が高まったのは、第一次キャンプブームではなく今のことなので、不一致。

3 1番目．ウ 2番目．エ
【解き方】1番目．本文の中ほどに「2011年に約1500万人が電車を利用した」とある。グラフでそれを示しているのはウ。2番目．終わりから3文目を見ると「バスの利用者の数はほぼ毎年減った」とある。グラフが右下がりなのはエ。

4 〔問1〕エ 〔問2〕Ⓐ ア Ⓑ エ Ⓒ ウ Ⓓ イ 〔問3〕ア 〔問4〕(1)〔解答例〕 make posters (2)イ
【解き方】〔問1〕第2段落第2, 3文(Every Friday, 〜, I recorded the sales there.)から、エが適切。〔問2〕Ⓐ第3段落第3文(In those months, we sold vegetables the most.)から、vegetables が適切。Ⓑ第3段落第4文(In June, the percentage of processed products was higher than fruits and flowers.)から、processed products(加工製品)が適切。Ⓒ第3段落第6文(Compared to June, the percentage of fruits became higher)から fruits が適切。Ⓓ同じく第6文の後半(the percentage of flowers was the same)から、flowers が

適切。〔問3〕最終段落の内容より，ア「由衣は，よりよい品物を作りたいと思っている」が適切。〔問4〕(1)由衣の「もっと多くの人に（駅に買いに）来てもらいたい」に対し，トムが「それについて，どんなことができますか」と聞いている。make posters「ポスターを作る」，pass out fliers「チラシを配る」などが考えられる。(2)ア．「由衣は日曜日にいくらかのフルーツを買うことができた」　このような内容は対話にない。イ．「由衣は人々に品物をおいしく食べてもらいたい」　最初の由衣の発言（People look happy when they buy our products. So I become happy.）に一致。ウ．「トムは由衣のスピーチを聞いて悲しかった」　トムの最初の発言（That was a wonderful speech.）に不一致。エ．「トムは，フルーツについて質問がある」　トムはフルーツについて質問していないので，不一致。

5

1．X．フランス　Y．ドイツ　Z．スペイン
2．ミラさんがイギリスで使っていた日本語の教科書。
3．ウ，オ
【解き方】1．まず，「2018年，私の国（＝イギリス）はドイツよりも多くの人が日本語を学んだ」（ミラの最初の発言）から，ドイツはYまたはZ。「2015年から2018年の間にフランスは学習者が3,000人以上増えた」（健の2番目の発言）から，フランスはXまたはZ。「スペインは2015年，日本語学習者の数が5か国で最も少なかった」（ミラの2番目の発言）から，スペインはZなので，Yがドイツ，Xがフランスに決まる。2．下線部①のitは，前のミラの発言のthe Japanese-language textbook I used in the U.K.を指す。3．表を見ると，イギリスの学習者数は2018年よりも2015年のほうが多いので，ウが一致。ミラは3番目の発言で「アニメの大ファンだったから日本語を学び始めたが，まもなくして日本語そのものにも興味を持った」と言っている。よって，オが一致。

6

1．ア　2．shorter　3．イ
【解き方】1．第2段落の終わりから2文目に，「インドの人々はアメリカの人々とほぼ同じ長さの時間眠ります」とあるのでBはAmerica。2．2007年，2015年を比べると，人々の平均睡眠時間は以前よりshorter「短く」なっている。この単語は第2段落最終文にある。3．イ「真衣は，特に若いときに人々はより長く眠る必要があると言っている」は，最終段落第2文に一致する。

7

(1)ア　(2)イ　(3)イ
【解き方】(1)表を見ると，半数以上がTo send or read messagesを選んだ年齢層は，50.6%の18-29歳。(2)表を見ると，全年齢層で60-84歳が最も高い回答率だったのは13.3%のTo play a game.。(3)第1段落の内容から，アンケート回答者は1,000人，「歩きスマホをするか」に332人がYesと答え，その他は全員Noと答えた。つまり，半数以上がNoと答えたので，イが適切。ウは，表のWithout thinking anythingの欄を見ると10%以上の年齢層が複数あるので，less than 10%が不適。エは，最終段落の内容から，didn't chooseがchoseなら正しい。

8

(1)イ　(2)イ　(3)ア
【解き方】(1)直前に「各年齢層とも，最も高い割合と最も低い割合の2項目が同じ」とあり，表を見るといちばん上のtasteといちばん下のhow easy and convenientである。(2)表から，20－29歳と40－49歳の2番目に高い割合

はprice。(3)全項目のうち，年齢層間で最も大きな差（38.7）がある項目はどれか。freshnessの60－69歳の71.5と20－29歳の32.8の差が38.7になる。1つずつ計算する時間的余裕はないので，低い数値と高い数値が含まれる項目に目星を付ける。

9

(1)ウ　(2)イ　(3)エ　(4)ウ→ア→エ　(5)〔解答例〕We shouldn't ride too fast.
【解き方】(1)ウ「自転車のあるよりよい生活」が適切。ほかの選択肢の内容は，本文全体を通して言及されていない。(2)アヤの発言の中盤以降を参照。「市の人口の約半分は，自転車を利用する」「次に多いのが車の利用者」「人口の18%は，バスか電車を利用する」「残りの人は，徒歩で通勤通学する」とある。(3)エミは自転車専用道路などを例に，コペンハーゲンが自転車利用者にとって便利な市であることを説明している。エ「コペンハーゲンには，自転車利用者を支援する方策があることを学んで，エミは驚いた」が適切。(4)ユウタの発言を参照。ウ：序盤The first slide ～ the environment. → ア：中盤The second slide ～ to exercise. → エ：終盤：The last slide ～ of sightseeing. (5)下線部⑤のあとにWhat should you do?とあるのを参考に，We shoud [shouldn't]で書き始めるとよい。

10

1．ウ　2．イ　3．エ　4．い
5．a．イ　b．ア　c．エ　d．ウ
【解き方】1．空所のあとの文を参照。多くの家庭が現金を使用していない状況が読み取れるので，「キャッシュレス決済は，母国スウェーデンではとても人気がある」が適切。2．空所前の1文に「日本では，多くの人が今でも現金を使っていると思う」とあるので，「現金のない生活が想像できない」が適切。3．前の文に「日本では，キャッシュレス決済が増えていることを示している」とあるので，グラフ1について言及していることがわかる。グラフ1によると，キャッシュレス決済が30%を超えているのは，2021年だとわかる。4．英文の意味は「彼らは自分の国から大量の紙幣と硬貨を持参する必要がない」となる。空所の前文で，訪日外国人にとってのキャッシュレス決済の利便性に言及しているので，空所いに入れると文脈に合う。5．キャッシュレス決済のよい点と悪い点をまとめている。a．エリックの4番目の発言に，「支払うときに，時間があまりかからない」とある。b．エリックの5番目の発言に，「つり銭の用意や，レジの現金確認が不要なので，従業員は時間を節約できる」とある。c．太郎の最後から3番目の発言に，「スマートフォンやデビットカードをなくしたら，見つけた人がお金を使ってしまうかもしれない」とある。d．エリックの最後の発言に，「特に子供は金銭感覚を持つことができないかもしれない」とある。

11

1．ウ　2．エ　3．ア
【解き方】1．第3段落第3文に，1963年も2013年もカナダの食料自給率が最も高いとあり，また第4文に，「1963年にはアメリカの食料自給率はフランスより高いけれども，2013年にはフランスとアメリカの食料自給率はほぼ同じです」とあるので表のCはフランスである。2．お好み焼きの材料である豚肉やエビは輸入品が多いので，お好み焼きは日本の料理であるけれども，エ「国際的な」食べ物でもあると言える。3．ア．第2段落最終文に「私たちはそれら（＝豚肉やエビ）をとても多くのさまざまな国から輸入しているのに驚きました」とあるのに一致。イ．第1段落の

最終文に「日本の食料自給率が半分に満たないと学校で学んだ」とあるのに反する。ウ．右のグラフによるとエビの19.5パーセントをベトナムから輸入しているが半分ではない。エ．第3段落第2文にある「これは1963年と2013年の4か国における食料自給率に関するものです」という説明に反する。

12 問1．エ 問2．イ 問3．same 問4．インドの人々が出すプラスチックごみの量はなぜ少ないのかという（30字） 問5．エ 問6．ウ
【解き方】問1．エ．「魚は海中のプラスチックを餌だと思う」 ジョンの最初の発言の最後Small pieces of plastic look like food to fish, so a lot of fish eat the plastic. と一致。問2．ジョンの2番目の発言の後半部，China, as a country, produced the most amount of plastic waste.より中国が(A)，America is second.よりアメリカが(B)とわかる。さらになおやの4番目の発言In India, people produced the least amount of plastic waste as a country and per person.より(C)がインドとわかる。問3．空所を含む文の主語Itは前文のabout 8 million tons of plastic wasteを指しており，Graph 1で示されている日本の値と同じである。問4．下線部のitは前のなおやの発言「インドでは，国単位で見ても個人単位で見てもプラスチック廃棄量が最も少ない」を指している。問5．空所④に入るのは相変わらずレジ袋を使い続けている人の発言であるから，エ「なぜレジ袋の使用を止めるべきなのか？」が適切。問6．ウ．「自分のバッグを店に持っていくことは小さなことかもしれないが，もしみんなが行えば変化が起きるでしょう」 スピーチの最終段落の内容と一致。

13 1．ウ，オ 2．エ 3．wonder how to find it 4．Who 5．[解答例]He has worked for twenty-five years. 6．ア 7．[解答例]get more knowledge
【解き方】1．Chart 1を確認すると，Flight Attendant「客室乗務員」とPilot「パイロット」がある。ウ「1970年に人気があったいくつかの仕事は，飛行機に関係している」は正しい。また，第4段落の最後から2文目に，「新しい経験をすれば，あなたの夢は変わるかもしれない」とある。よって，オ「田中先生は新しい経験が夢を変えるかもしれないと信じている」は適切。2．空所前の内容を確認する。「入院中，寂しく感じていたときに，看護師が話しに来てくれて，気分が落ち着いた」と翔太は回想している。「私は彼のやさしさを忘れないだろう」とするのが適切。3．wonderは「～だろうか」という意味の動詞。〈how to＋動詞の原形〉で「～の仕方」という意味。完成する文は，「私はどうやってそれ（＝自分の目標）を見つけたらよいだろうか」という意味。4．空所直後，七海は「父に聞くつもり」と答えている。「だれにインタビューするつもりですか」という文意にするのが適切。5．第1段落の最終文を参照。「父は25年間警察官を続けてきた」とある。6．第1段落の終わりに「私は，父がこの仕事を選んだ理由を知らなかった」とあるので，第2段落は，この理由について言及していると推測できる。「助けが必要な人を助けられるとき，私はうれしく感じる。彼らの笑顔は私をいつも幸せにしてくれるから，私はこの仕事をしている」とするのが適切。7．第3段落を参照。「夢が見つからない」と言う七海に，父親はYou should get more knowledge, ～と助言している。この助言と，空所を含む文が対応していると考えて，「私は夢を見つけるために，もっと知識を身につけようと思う」とする。

14 1．[解答例](1) Yes, it does(.) (2) The rice was(.)
2．ア 3．many people who suffer from hunger around 4．エ 5．ウ 6．[解答例]I agree with Kenta because we can get fresh vegetables in season. (12語)
【解き方】1．(1)質問は「日本は国内の食べ物の60％超を外国から輸入しているか」。第2段落第2，3文，および，Graph 1を参照。(2)質問は「知美さんの朝食の中で，日本で生産された食品は何か」。第2段落中盤，The rice was grown in Japanを参照。2．文脈から，「この米は日本で育てられたが，この魚は外国で捕まえられた」という意味になると推測できる。3．(There are) many people who suffer from hunger around (the world.)「世界中には，飢えに苦しむ人々が大勢いる」。4．Graph 3を参照。エ「家庭から出る食品廃棄物は，食品廃棄物全体のほぼ半分だ」が適切。5．第3段落に，a lot of fuel is used when the food is transported「食品輸送には大量の燃料が使用される」，If we buy locally produced food, we don't use much fuel.「地元でつくられた食べ物を買えば，あまり燃料を使わなくてすむ」とあるので，ウ「地元でつくられた食べ物は，輸入された食べ物と比較して燃料をあまり必要としない，と知美さんは言っている」内容と一致。6．下線部は「私たちの地元でつくられた食べ物を買うのはよいことだと思う」。条件を守って，誤りのない英文を書くように心がける。

15 問1．エ 問2．ア→ウ→エ→イ 問3．ア 問4．ウ 問5．[解答例]I met in the store on [along] the beach
問6．A．カ B．ア C．オ D．イ 問7．(a)ウ
(b)[解答例]I can stop buying things I do not need. Today, there are many products that look useful or interesting, and I sometimes buy them without thinking about using them. After buying them, I often realize that I do not use them in my daily life and throw them away. To stop buying such things, I should know what is really necessary for me.
【解き方】問1．look like～で，「～のように見える」という意味。問2．ア「その中で『海洋生物の惨事』という表現を見つけた」→ウ「それは，海中で食べるプラスチックごみのために，海洋動物や魚がどんどん死んでいるという意味だ」→エ「記事にはまた，2050年には魚よりもプラスチックごみのほうが多くなるだろう，とあった」→イ「『これを止めなければ，海洋動物も魚もいなくなるだろう』と続いていた」問3．第3段落の第3文より，2020年7月，日本では，ビニール袋が有料化されたとわかる。これを踏まえてグラフ1を見るとビニール袋の有料化後，買い物時にビニール袋を入手する人は減ったとわかる。また，このシステムは成功していると言える。問4．グラフ2の内容と，文脈から判断する。空所前では，プラスチックごみ削減に向けて取り組んでいる例が示され，Howeverと続く。ウ「40％以上の人々は，まだ行動を起こしていない」が適切。問5．空所直後の内容から，空所前のThe womanは，第1段落で登場した女性だと推測できる。剛の視点で，この女性を説明する。問6．「それを解決するには長い時間を要するので，継続できることをやるべきだ。私たちの行動は小さいかもしれないが，より多くの人が加われば，海の未来は変わるだろう」問7．(a)空所直後に，「その理由のために，きみは学校で『スポごみ運動』を行うんだね」とある。この運動について，最終段落第2文に「みんながプラスチックごみの問題に興味を持ってくれることを願っている」とあるので，ウが適切。(b)環境保全のためにできることを書く。

《大　意》　剛は浜辺の小さな店に立ち寄った。店内で出会った女性は，プラスチックごみの問題に危機意識を持っており，店内の芸術作品はこの女性がプラスチックごみを使って作ったものだった。日本では，ビニール袋有料化を契機に，多くの人々が問題解決に向けて動き始めたが，いまだに行動しない人も多い。剛は，だれもが楽しめる方法で，多くの人々にプラスチックごみ削減運動に参加してもらうことが先決だと考え，ゲーム形式のごみ回収運動を企画した。

---

②　ポスター・案内など

1
(1)ア　(2)ウ

【解き方】(1) Dreaming of Traveling の第1文，および Sally の第3文を参照。ア「ホテルからの眺め」が適切。(2) Good Dad Eric の第2文を参照。浜辺はホテルの前にあることがわかるので，ウ「浜辺に行くためにタクシーに乗らなければならない」は不適切。

2
ア，カ

【解き方】ア.広告にある ONLINE CONVERSATION COURSE の Place / Time「場所／時間」欄に every day「毎日」とある。カ.広告のいちばん下に〈MORE INFORMATION〉として電話番号とメールアドレスが掲載されているので，「このイベントについてもっと情報がほしければ，電話をしたりメールを送ることができる」は内容に合う。イ. ONLINE CONVERSATION COURSE は 5,000円とあるので広告の内容に合わない。ウ. BUSINESS COURSE の Content and Fee「内容と料金」欄2番目に「少なくとも3回レッスンに参加しなければならない」とあるのに不一致。have to ～「～しなければならない」 at least「少なくとも」 エ. CULTURE COURSE の Place / Time 欄に11:00—14:00とあるので，in the evening「夕方に」は広告の内容に不一致。オ. BUSINESS COURSE の Age「年齢」欄に over 18 years old「18歳より年上の人」とあるので，15歳の人は参加できない。

3
1．ア　2．①ウ　②ウ

【解き方】1．サッカーチームの勧誘ポスター。タイトル下の「サッカーの経験は不要」から，アが適切。イは予定表の下の「サッカーシューズを持参してください」と合わない。ウはサポーターとしても参加できるので不適切。エは直接練習を見に行ってもよいので不適切。2．トムは月曜日と水曜日，ケンタは土曜日が都合が悪い。残る練習日は金曜日で，場所はリバータウンスタジアム。

4
(1) cheaper　(2) 3　(3) 1，6

【解き方】(1)ウェブサイトの The Type of Photo Books の料金表を見るとどのサイズも Hard Cover より Soft Cover のほうが cheap「安い」。ここでは比較級にする必要がある。(2)ナミの2番目の発言に「私は中サイズのフォトブックを注文しようと思う」とあり，ナミの3番目の発言に「私は厚手の表紙のフォトブックを選ぶ($30)。それをつや出し加工してもらう(Option＋$5)」とある。(3) 1.「人々はインターネットでフォトブックを注文できる」ウェブサイトの冒頭にある「このウェブサイトからフォトブックを注文してください！」に一致する。6.「人々はお店でフォトブックを受け取れる」は，ウェブサイトの下にある「私たちのお店に来ていただければより早く受け取れます」に一致。2.「写真を送ることがフォトブックを作る第1段階である」にはウェブサイトの Step 1 には「大きさを選ぶ」とある。3.「フォトブックには4つの異なるサイズがある」 Size は Small, Medium, Large の3種類である。4.「人々が注文できるすべてのフォトブックは30ページある」 ウェブサイトの The Type of Photo Books の表には 20 pages とある。5.「フォトブックを作り終えるのに，お

店は1週間を必要としている」 ウェブサイトの下のほうに「フォトブックを印刷して作るには私たちには3日必要です」とあるのに不一致。

5 (1) 70(ドル) (2) 13(時)55(分)
【解き方】(1)ケイの2番目の発言から,科学博物館に行くケイの家族は,ケイの父・母・弟・ケイの4人とわかる。これに由佳を加えた入場料を求める。曜日:ケイの1,2番目の発言から,科学博物館に行くのは土曜日。年齢:ケイの父・母は大人料金。ケイの弟は,ケイの2番目の発言から10歳で,ケイと由佳は,由佳の2番目の発言から中学生とわかる。以上から,週末の大人2人,子供3人の料金を計算する。(2)ケイの最後の発言から,レストランでの昼食のあとに,バーチャル宇宙旅行に参加することがわかる。ポスターから,このイベントに参加するには,開始5分前に会場へ行く必要があるとわかる。また,レストランの営業時間を考慮すると,②の時間帯に参加すると推測できる。

6 問1.エ 問2.エ 問3.ウ,オ
【解き方】問1.予定表の最初に11月18日から20日までとある。問2.直後で,マサは「でも子供たちに上手に本が読めるかが心配だ」と言っている。City Libraryでは10:30から「子供たちへの読み聞かせ」が行われる。問3.ウ.Sakura Nursery Schoolでは昼食は11:30からで,4つの体験場所の中でいちばん早い。オ.South Fire Stationでは8:30から「路上ランニング」が行われる。

7 1.twice 2.エ 3.②ア ③ウ 4.900
【解き方】1.質問は,「この市では何回,燃やせるごみが回収されますか」。表にBurnable GarbageはMonday and Fridayとあるので,答えはIt's collected twice a week.となる。2.空所①は大きい椅子について話しているところなので案内の下の2つ目の〇の項目を参照。処分するためには,椅子の上に特別なカードを張って,エ「この番号に電話をする」。3.②空所の前に「今日は木曜日」とあるので,明日(=金曜日)はburnable garbageの回収日。③木曜日に出せるごみは,表からplasticsである。4.表から,one card(special card)は500円,one large size packは400円で合計900円となる。

8 (1)①ウ ②ア ③ウ ④エ ⑤イ (2)[解答例]We can't play basketball on Monday(s)
【解き方】(1)①話題はスポーツ公園でバスケットボールをすることなので,ウの「公園にはバスケットボールのコートが2面ある」が適切。②ウェブサイトの終わりに「(公園に)ボールやラケットはありません」とあることと,空所直後に「ボールを持ってる?」と続くことから,アが適切。③公園に行くのは土曜日で,空所前のクリスの発言は「公園が開くときに公園の入口の前で会おう」という意味。ウェブサイトのOpening Hours(開園時間)を見ると,土曜日は9:00に開くことから,ウが正解。④1時に駅に行かなければならないタクヤにクリスは何と助言するか。ウェブサイトのBus(時刻表)を見ると,「公園→駅」のバスは所要時間約20分で,12:30発のバスに乗れば1時前に駅に着く。よって,エが適切。このあとにあるクリスの「3時間プレーできるね」という発言も参考にする。⑤ウェブサイトのHow much(料金)を見ると,バスケットボールのコートは1時間あたり1,000円で,3時間使用するので合計3,000円。会話の前半から,参加するのは10人なので,1人あたり300

円となる。(2)タクヤが「今度の月曜日は?」と言うが,ウェブサイトによるとそれはできない。because it's closed「閉まっているので」につながる内容にする。We can't go on Monday(s)などでもよい。

9 (1) too (2)(ア) (3)(ウ) (4)(イ)
【解き方】(1)①ジーナは2番目の発言で1冊を推せんし,直前の発言でもう1冊を推せんしている。Then, I'll buy it, too.「では,私はそれも買います」 ③ Oh, I think I chose too many books.「ああ,私はあまりにも多くの本を選んでしまったと思う」 (2)その前で,まみとジーナは「Septemberは『7番目の月』という意味」「Septemberは1年の9番目の月でしょう?」というやりとりをしている。(ア)「その理由を述べるために,その歴史について話をさせてください」とするのが適切。(3)会話から,まみが買うことにした本はジーナとの会話の順に,(ア)Lily,(ウ)The Blue Sky,(イ)Our Memoryの3冊。ジーナは下線部④の本について,「買う必要はない。学校の図書館にある。最初読んだときから,ずっとこの本が好きだ」と言っている。(ア)(イ)(ウ)の本の中でジーナが読んだことがあるのは,(ウ)のThe Blue Sky。ジーナの3番目の発言を参照。(4)(ア)「まみはスミス先生からそのリストをもらったので,英語の本を読み始めようとした」 まみの最初の発言に不一致。先月から読んでいて,スミス先生によい本を教えてと頼んだら昨日リストをもらった。(イ)「The Blue Skyの筆者は日本で人気があり,ジーナはまみと話す前にそのことを知っていた」 ジーナの3番目と4番目の発言に一致。(ウ)「本のコメントを通してスミス先生は,The Pastにはいくつかの難しい単語があると,まみに伝えた」 The Pastのコメントに不一致。難しい単語があるのは,Our Memory。(エ)「筆者によって撮られた多くの写真は,人々がThe White Seaの話の状況を理解する助けとなる」 リストのThe White Seaのコメントに不一致。筆者が描いた絵についてコメントしている。pictureには「絵」と「写真」の2つの意味があるがtake picturesでは「写真を撮る」,draw picturesでは「絵を描く」。

③ 複合資料

1 (ア) 4 (イ) 4

【解き方】(ア)どのような基準で, ミキが天ぷら料理店を選んだかを確認する。ベッキーの1回目の発言から「日曜日に営業していること」。ベッキーの2回目の発言と, 続くミキの発言から「割引を含めて, 最も安く昼食を食べられること」。ベッキーの3回目の発言から「地元の野菜天ぷらを食べられること」。以上3つの基準に最も合致するものをリストから選ぶ。(イ)ダイスケの最後の発言から, 空所を含むリストは, グリーン先生との会話のあとで, ダイスケがスピーチコンテストに向けてやるべきことをまとめたものだと推測できる。グリーン先生の4回目の発言に「あなたは最初に原稿を書くべきだ。原稿を書き終えれば, 概要を速く書ける」とあり, ダイスケは同調しているので, ①(オ), ②(イ)となる。また, グリーン先生の5回目の発言に「音声録音の前に, 英語を話す練習をするべきだ。2回戦用の音声録音を送ったあとで, ジェスチャーの練習をするべきだ」とあり, ダイスケはこの意見にも同調しているので, ③(ア), ④(エ), ⑤(ウ)となる。

2 1. How long 2. [解答例] (1) it will rain 【別解】 it is going to rain (2) The story was written by 【別解】 The person who wrote the story is (4) is easy for them 3. イ 4. ツバメの巣が人に壊されたり, ひなが巣から落ちたりすること。(29字) 5. ア 6. [解答例] When I become a high school student, I will go to school by bike every day. Using cars is not good for the earth. I think using buses and trains is good, too. Also, I will turn off the light when I leave a room. I hope my action will save the earth. 【別解】 I usually try to reduce trash [garbage]. For example, using plastic bags is bad for the earth. So, I always use my own bag when I go to a supermarket. I also want to use things again and again.

【解き方】1. アリスがfor more than three weeksと答えているので, その期間をたずねていると推測できる。2. (1)図1より, 「ツバメが地上を低く飛ぶと, 雨が降る」という言い伝えの内容を英語で書く。(2)図2より, 「その話は, オスカー・ワイルドによって書かれた」という内容を英語で書く。(4)空所を含む文は, 文頭にSoとあるので, 前文の日本家屋に関する話が続いていると推測できる。図4から, 「ツバメがすむ場所(巣)を作りやすい」という内容を英語で書く。3. 下線部のあとの内容を確認する。only 9,500 swallows were found in 2020「2020年には9,500羽しか発見されなかった」, the number of houses has been growing for these 35 years「この35年間で, 住宅の数は増え続けている」とある。4. 下線部のあとの内容を確認する。Their nests are sometimes broken by people.「彼らの巣は人に壊されることがある」, baby swallows fall from their nests「ひなが巣から落ちる」とある。5. 文脈判断。空所の前の文に, 「私たちの町は大きくなり, 多くの場所で自然が失われた」とある。「食べ物を見つけられないので, ツバメにとってこの町で生活することは簡単ではない」と続けるのが適切。6. 解答例では, これから行おうとしていることを助動詞willを使って表している。別解では, 普段行っていることをI usually 〜やI always 〜と表している。

3 1. ウ 2. ア 3. (1)イ

(2)[解答例] My grandfather and I often go to a park near my house. He enjoys seeing trees and flowers there. The park gives us a chance to have a good time together.

【解き方】1. 空所(A)のあとで, リクが「グラフでパーセンテージがいちばん低い」と答えているので, (A)にはA place for eating(食事のための場所)が入る。空所(B)のあとで, トニーが「パーセンテージがA place for exercise and sports(運動とスポーツのための場所)とA hub for the community(地域社会の拠点)より少し低い」と言っているので, (B)にはA place for children to play(子供が遊ぶ場所)が入る。2. トニーは1, 2番目の発言からCity Planning(都市計画)の基本の講義を受講したいことがわかる。木曜日午後は都合が悪いので, 残った火曜日午後の講義が受講できる。リクはその後の発言から, Making Parks in Towns(町に公園を作ること)の発展の講義を受講したいことがわかる。午前が都合いいので, 水曜日午前の講義が受講できる。3. (1)ア. 生活をよりよくするのはオンライン講義ではなく公園。イ. 第2段落第3, 4文と一致。ウ. 公園について調べたのはトニーの姉[妹]ではなくトニー。また姉[妹]がオンライン講義を受けたという話もない。エ. トニーの姉[妹]が公園のイベントで話をして楽しむのはトニーとではなく来場した人々とである。(2)「町に公園があることについてあなたにとってよい点は何か」という質問に対する答えを書く。I'll tell you one good point.から, よい点を1つに絞って書くこと。解答例は, 「私と祖父はよく家の近くの公園に行く。彼はそこの木々や花を見るのを楽しむ。公園は私たちに一緒に楽しい時を過ごす機会を与えてくれる」という意味。ほかには, 本文の内容を参考にして, スポーツの場, 子供が遊ぶ場, くつろぐ場, コミュニケーションの場, イベントを行う場などの観点で答えることができるだろう。

4 問1. (1)イ (2)①ア ②ウ 問2. エ 問3. (1)ウ (2)イ

【解き方】問1. (1)読書が好きな1年生の人数(85人)は3年生(72人)よりも多いのでイが適切。アは, 3年生は72人なので, More than 80 percentと言えない。ウは, 1年生→3年生の順に人数が減っているので不適。エは, 2年生は3年生よりも人数が多いので不適。not as 〜 as ...「…ほど〜ない」 (2)①「その理由を選んだ生徒はたった5%」という情報から, 「部活動」が入る。② 20%以上の生徒が選んだのは「友達と遊ぶ」(28%)である。問2. 「先生の結論」の情報のなかで, 「短くて簡単なルート」と「海や山などの自然の写真を撮りたい」の両方を満たすルートはどれかを考える。まず, 「Bは最も長い」「Aは難しい」から, AとBを消去する。「CとDはAより短い」「Dも海が見える」から, Dが正解。Cは「道中に(自然ではなく)たくさんの有名な古い建物がある」が不正解の決め手になる。問3. (1)項目1の内容とウが合う。イは, 項目5から, 作った防災マップを見せるのは家族(your family)なので, your friendsが不適。(2)「グリーン先生のための防災マップ」では, 項目3にある「家から避難所までの避難ルート」が示されていない。よって, 先生のアドバイスとしてイが適切。ア, ウ, エはどれも防災マップで示されている。

5 1. エ 2. ウ 3. (1)ア (2)[解答例] I think it is very nice to wear kimono. In Tokyo, there are places to try them on and learn about the history of kimono. I know one of those places, and I want to

take you there when you come to Japan.
【解き方】1.(A)は，空所後で鳥の観察や階段の話をしている。パンフレットを見るとPark Areaの内容に合う。(B)は，マイクがMountain AreaとOnsen Areaに興味があり，温泉は日帰り旅行の最後に楽しめると言っているので，先に行くのはMountain Areaである。2.(A)は，新鮮な野菜が買え，焼き魚が食べられる場所。また，グラフで最も人気がある場所はFarmers' Marketである。(B)は，マイクが歴史に興味があることと，その建物は江戸時代に建てられたことから，Town Museumがあてはまる。3.(1)メールの第2段落第3，4文とアが合う。(2)マイクはメールの最後で，日本の伝統文化を楽しむのに，何をすればよいかアイデアを求めている。解答は「アイデアを1つ教えてあげよう」に続く部分。アイデアを1つ考えて3文で書く。解答例は「着物」を取り上げている。

d．会話文

1
(1)ウ　(2)ア　(3)イ
【解き方】(1)Ⅰ．クリス博士の3番目の発言の第3文参照。宇宙空間に食べ物を運ぶのには莫大（ばくだい）なお金がかかる。Ⅱ．クリス博士の6番目の発言の第2文参照。夜には太陽光はあたらないが，ベジーを使えば1日中光があたる。(2)晴の最後から4番目の発言の第3文とクリス博士の最後から4番目の発言の第3文参照。レタスは調理が不要で，生育が早い。(3)最後から2番目の晴の発言の第2文参照。「将来宇宙空間で生活しやすくなるなら，僕はいつか宇宙空間に住めるだろう」を受けてクリス博士が「きみはそうする人になれるよ」と答えている。

2
問1．エ　問2．(1)イ　(2)イ　問3．ウ　問4．エ
【解き方】問1．サキナ先生は最初の発言の最後で，Maybe, a rainbow was a bad sign ～ to them.と言っている。問2．(1)ナターシャ先生は最後から2番目の発言で虹は「赤，オレンジ，黄，緑，青，紫」と数えている。全部で6色。(2)サキナ先生は最後から2番目の発言の最後のほうで，「アフリカのある人たちには虹は8色が見える」と言っている。問3．入れる英文の「虹についてほかに何か興味深い情報が見つかりましたか」に続くものとして最も適切なのは，ウのあとの，「えーと，そうねえ。この記事には，虹には何色あるかについて書かれているわ」。問4．2人の会話をまとめた表現とあるので，エ「虹に関するさまざまな考えや印象」が最適。それ以外は本文中に書かれているが，一部を表しているに過ぎない。

3
(1)A．ア　B．ウ　C．ア　(2)ⓐイ　ⓑエ　ⓒウ
(3)イ→ア→オ→ウ→エ　(4)[解答例] Would you like to go there next Sunday?　(5) understand Japanese culture
【解き方】(1)A．直前のジュディの発言「それはとてもきれいだったので，ホストファミリーのみんなに見せたのよ」に対して，アの「それを聞いてうれしいわ」が適切。B．「ビデオ？　もっと詳しく説明してください」　C．直前にあるジュディの質問「和紙を自分で作ったってこと？」に対して，ア「そのとおりよ」が適切。(2)ⓐ a variety of ～「さまざまな～」　ⓑ「日本の長い歴史を学ぶことができる」　ⓒ if I were you「もし，私があなたなら」　仮定法過去の文。(3)(It was fun to) think about how I could create (a great nengajo.)「どうやったらいい年賀状が作れるかと考えることは楽しかった」　(4)直後のYes, of course.「ええ，もちろんよ」という応答に合う英文を考える。(5)空所ⓑのあとに出てくるI'm happy I can understand Japanese culture more. を参照。

4
(1)A．イ　E．エ　(2)日本の文化と自分たちの文化は異なると思っていたのに，同じような種類の伝統行事があったから。(3)C．help me make　G．if I were you
(4)ウ　(5)野菜を植えるときに，環境にとって安全な方法の例。(6)ウ，オ
【解き方】(1)A．「先祖がマリーゴールドの香りのために帰ってくる」　because of ～「～のために(理由)」　E．「マ

リーゴールドを使うことが１つのよい方法だ」　文の主語になるように動名詞（〜ing形）にする。(2)直前の文の内容をまとめる。(3)C.「マリーゴールドは私が安全な菜園を作るのを助けてくれる」〈help＋O＋(to＋)動詞の原形〉で「Oが…するのを助ける」。E.if I were you「私があなたなら」　現在の事実と異なることを述べる仮定法過去の基本表現。(4)「トマトの葉を食べる昆虫が（マリーゴールドの）においが好きでないので」に続くのは、ウ「それら（＝昆虫）がトマトの葉を食べに来ない」が自然。(5)直前の文およびそれまでのやり取りでケイタは、マリーゴールドを使うことで農薬を使わずにすみ、そのようにして「野菜を植えるときに環境にとって安全な方法を選びたい」と言っている。それに対しての「ほかの例を教えてくれますか」。(6)ア.ルイスの３番目の発言参照。メキシコで墓に飾られるのはトマトではなくマリーゴールド。イ.ルイスの２番目の発言参照。メキシコでは先祖が帰ってくる行事は11月に行われる。ウ.空所Eを含むケイタの発言に一致する。エ.語群G付近のやり取り参照。ルイスが農家であるケイタの友人に会うのは、野菜を植える際の環境に安全な方法を学ぶためであり、おいしい野菜の育て方を学ぶためではない。オ.ルイスの最後から２番目の発言に一致する。

5 (1)b.エ　d.イ　(2)① than　② bad　(3)エ
(4)X.share　Y.important
【解き方】(1)a.次の智の発言It's about smartphones.から、ウの「もちろん。レポートは何についてですか」が適切。b.次に智がYes,と答えているから、そのあとに続く文「スマートフォンは今日（ <ruby>今<rt>こん</rt></ruby>日）とても人気がある」とbは同じような内容になると推測できる。エ「おもしろそうですね。多くの人が日常生活でスマートフォンを使っているのを知っている」が適切。c.アマンダが「（スマートフォンには）よい点と悪い点があると思う」に続く発言としては、ア「そうですね。よい点について、まず知りたい」が適切。d.空所の前はスマートフォンでインターネットを使うこと、空所のあとではそのほかの使い方が書かれているので、イ「わかりました。生徒たちはスマートフォンを使って、ほかに何ができますか」が適切。e.アマンダのスマートフォンについての意見を聞いて、お礼の言葉を言う。オ「あなたの意見を聞かせてくれてありがとう。とても役に立ったよ」が適切。(2)①空所の前は比較級 more convenient なので、そのあとに than「〜より」がくる。than before「以前より」　②下線部の前にはgood pointsが述べられ、あとにはbad pointsが述べられているので、空所にはbadが適切。(3) makeを入れ、「その状況はほかの人たちを不愉快にさせる」とする。make A B「AをBにする」　(4)X.アマンダの５番目の発言第３文を参照。share A with B「AをBと共有する」　Y.智の最後の発言「（スマートフォンの）適切な使い方を知るべきだ」を「適切に使うことは重要だ」にする。〈it is 〜 for＋人＋to do〉「（人）にとって…することは〜だ」

6 1.ⓐイ　ⓑア　ⓒエ　2.[解答例]Do you remember you saw me last Friday?
3.[解答例]A.for　B.let　C.one　4.①イ　②エ　③ウ　5.始めの２語：each country　終わりの２語：and living　6.[解答例]Can you tell us about this in class?　7.[解答例]① why　② drawn　③ stop
【解き方】1.ⓐ空所の前文を見る。急いでいる理由は、イ「図書館がまもなく閉館になる」から。ⓑ空所のあとに「彼は〜と言った」とあるので、ア「その生徒は何と言ったの？」が適切。ⓒ空所の前に「イギリスでは雨の日が多いが、すぐ

にやむ」とあるので、エ「だから多くの人はたいてい傘を使わない」と続く。2.「会ったことを覚えている」は、解答例のようにremember (that) SVで表せる。会ったのは過去なのでsawと過去形にすること。you saw meはyou met meでもよい。remember 〜ingを使ってもよい。3.A.Thank you for 〜ing「〜してくれてありがとう」　ここでは「来てくれてありがとう」の意味。B.let me knowは「私に知らせる[教える]」という意味。〈let＋O＋動詞の原形〉で「Oに〜させてやる」。C.one of 〜「〜のうちの１人」「僕は雨にぬれるのを気にしないアメリカ人の１人なんだ」という意味。4.①直後のvery longに着目。長いのは傘の歴史。② 動名詞の主語は単数扱いなので、エが適切。③前後を見る。「日本はよく傘を使う国だ」と「傘をあまり使わない国もある」の２文をつなげるには、ウのOn the other hand「一方で」が適切。5.直前のひろきの発言の、終わりから２文目を参照。ひろきは、傘の使用状況は国によって異なるという事例をもとに「どの国も独自の考え方と生活の仕方がある」ことに気づいた。6.解答例のthisはそれまでひろきがジョーンズ先生に伝えたこと（本やウェブサイトや留学生を通して学んだこと）を指す。7.①間接疑問〈疑問詞＋SV〉。ひろきはなぜジョーンズ先生が傘を使わないのか知りたかった。②過去分詞の形容詞用法は「〜された」という意味になる。古代の壁画に描かれた傘。③ stop 〜ing「〜することをやめる」

7 問1.ア　問2.エ　問3.イ　問4.ウ
問5.イ,エ　問6.[解答例]*sushi*を選んだ場合：(You should try *sushi* because) it is the most famous Japanese food and you can eat many different kinds of fish in Nagasaki(.) (18語)　【別解】(You should try *sushi* because) Nagasaki is famous for delicious fish. It is not so expensive in Nagasaki(.) (13語)
*ramen*を選んだ場合：(You should try *ramen* because) Japanese *ramen* is popular in the world now and you can find nice *ramen* shops in Nagasaki(.) (17語)　【別解】(You should try *ramen* because) you will feel warm if you eat it [*ramen*] in winter(.) (10語)
【解き方】問1.空所の前で「あなたはいろいろな食べ物が好きなのですね。でもあなたはアメリカ出身ですよね」とあり、空所直後では「もちろん好きですよ」とあるので、ア「アメリカ料理はどうですか」が適切。問2.空所直後の文に「アメリカに来れば、もっとおいしいサンドイッチが食べられますよ」とあるので「日本のサンドイッチはアメリカのほどおいしくない」が適切。not as 〜 as ...「…ほど〜でない」　問3.スミス先生の５、６番目の発言から読み取る。問4.空所直前に「違ったことをやってみると、興味深いものを見つけられる」とあるので、空所を含む文は「新しいことをやってみることはわくわくする」と考えられる。問5.ア.スミス先生は冒頭のやりとりでどれがいちばん好きか選べないと言っているので、日本料理よりもタイ料理が好きであるとは言えない。イ.ヒロの４番目の発言と一致する。ウ.スミス先生の最後から２番目の発言参照。アジアを旅行したのはスミス先生である。エ.*Comments*でのマリアの投稿内容に一致する。オ.デイビッドは「ルンダンを作ろうとしたが難しかった」と投稿している。問6.*Comments*でのビリーの投稿から、冬に長崎を訪れるつもりであり、すしとラーメンのどちらを食べてみるべきか悩んでいることを読み取る。どちらをすすめるか、適切な理由を書く。

8 (1)A. ウ　B. イ　(2)①C　② chicken　(3)ア，オ
【解き方】(1) A. 次のノラが「牛肉は食べられない。それに，卵アレルギーです」と言っているので，ウ「何か食べられない物はありますか」が適切。B. お父さんが「二次元コードを思いついたとき，彼は白と黒の石を使う伝統的なボードゲームをしていた。それは何というゲームかわかりますか？」と聞き，アヤが「碁」と答えたので，イ「正解です」が適切。(2)ノラの4番目の発言から，the hottest one「いちばん辛いカレー」で，ice cream があって，drink がないセットとわかる。よって，①Cセットが適切。②いちばん辛いのは，メニューでvery hotと表現されているchicken。(3)ア. ノラの5番目の発言から，内容に一致。イ. アヤの2番目の発言を参照。アヤはアイスクリームとアップルジュースを望んでいるからDセットになるので，不一致。ウ. 空所Bの前にあるアヤのお父さんの発言参照。日本人の技術者が二次元コードを思いついたのは碁をしているときで，テレビを見ているときではないので，不一致。エ. 空所Bのあとのアヤのお父さんの発言の最後の文を参照。barcodeと2D codeが反対なので，内容に不一致。オ. ノラとアヤの最後の発言参照。内容に一致。

9 問1. ウ　問2. イ　問3. ア　問4. イ　問5. ウ，オ
【解き方】問1. ウ. アダムの2番目の発言で，母親がジェームズに，アダムにボールを投げないようにと言っているのにやめないので腹を立てたことが書かれている。問2. アダムの4番目の発言で，ジェームズとペットのリッキーは部屋の角にいたことがわかる。問3. アダムの4番目の発言の後半に，ジェームズはリッキーの耳をなで，やさしく自分のほうに引き寄せたとある。問4. itの内容は直前のsee and talk with them(＝my friends in Japan)の部分。問5. ウ. アダムの4番目の発言中のジェームズの様子の記述と一致。オ. 桜の最後の発言の最後の1文と一致。

10 (ア)5　(イ)1　(ウ)5
【解き方】(ア)①下線部を含むマサオの発言に「2000年の1人あたりの米消費量は，1962年の量の約55%だった」とある。グラフから，1962年の消費量は約118kgとわかる。約118(kg)×0.55＝約65(kg)より，グラフBが適切。②(a)下線部を含むアユミの発言に「パンが最も人気だった」とあるので，正答をY・Zにしぼることができる。マサオの5回目の発言に「40人のうち，50%超が朝食にパンを食べる」とあるので，正答はYに決まる。(イ)空所前後の内容をもとに，つながりがよいものを選ぶ。「外国から十分な小麦が輸入されなければ，何が起こるだろうか」との問いに，ホワイト先生は「小麦食品の価格が高騰すると思う」と答えている。「しかし，日本人の食生活は大きく変化しており，多くの日本人が小麦粉の食品を食べているので，彼らが小麦粉の食品を食べるのをやめられるとは思わない」と続ける。(ウ) c. 「マサオはボランティア活動の経験を生かして，日本の米について発表することにした」　マサオの4回目の発言の最終文を参照。e. 「より多くの米粉のパンを食べることは，日本の米の消費量を増やすよい方法だと，マサオは考えている」　マサオの5回目の発言の最終文を参照。

11 〔問1〕エ　〔問2〕イ　〔問3〕ア　〔問4〕ア　〔問5〕ウ　〔問6〕イ　〔問7〕ウ
【解き方】〔問1〕下線部(1)は，直前のルミの発言を受けて，「私も，物の前に(数を表す)言葉を付け加えるのを忘れることが多い」という意味。〔問2〕スティーブが，下線部(2)の前で，ホームステイ先の母親の発言に対して「担任のムラタ先生の姿が見えると思った」と言い，あとでケンタが，「お母さんはムラタ先生が来ると言いたかったんだよ」と言っている。〔問3〕あらたまった状況では，Thank you for your help.の代わりにI am grateful for your help.という表現を使うという流れを受けて，似たようなほかの表現に話題が展開していく。〔問4〕アイカが日本語と英語の両方であらたまった表現を学ぶべきだと思うと言い，ルミがスティーブに対してそういったあらたまった表現を使ったほうがいいのかと問いかけ，ケンタがそうは思わないと言っている。〔問5〕アイカがスティーブに，「もっと英語を教えてもらえませんか」と頼み，ルミとケンタも私たちにも教えてくださいと同調したのに対し，スティーブが「喜んでそうするよ」と答えている。〔問6〕下線部(4)のあとのスティーブのAnd the speed of speakingで始まる発言の中に，ルミとアイカがゆっくりとわかりやすい(simple)表現を使ってくれて，そのおかげでスティーブが会話を楽しんでいるとある。〔問7〕ルミの3番目の発言の中で，「スティーブ，日本語についてあなたにとって難しい表現が(数字のあとに付ける枚や冊の)ほかにありますか」と聞いているので，(A)にはaskedが入る。スティーブの2番目の発言の中で，ホームステイ先の母親が「ムラタ先生がみえる」と言ったとき，その意味がわからなかったことが述べられている。母親の発言は日本語によるものだったので，Japaneseが入る。また，後半のI also have realizedで始まるケンタの発言の中で，スティーブに日本語を教えているうちに日本語が興味深いことに気づいた旨が述べられており，最後のほうのInterestingで始まるスティーブの発言の中で，ルミやアイカに日本語の表現をもっと教えてくれるよう頼んでいる。

12 (1)イ　(2) some interesting information　(3)エ　(4)イ　(5) If I had a picture　(6)ア　(7)ウ　(8) am glad that I could　(9)イ，オ
【解き方】(1) look for ～「～を探す」　(2) according to ～は「～によると」で，itは直前のsome interesting information「興味深い情報」を指す。(3)「あなたがおっしゃるのはつまり～ということですね？」という文意で，空所には前のグリーン先生の発言内容と合うエが適切。(4)広志とグリーン先生が世界各国の発酵大豆食品について話しているところにインドネシア出身のサリが登場し，グリーン先生が「彼女も(発酵大豆食品について)何か知っているかもしれない」と言う。イ「彼女に聞いてみたらどう？」が空所後にうまくつながる。広志のI'll do so.のdo soはask herということ。(5)空所後のI could show ～ のcouldに着目して，「もし私が…なら～できるでしょうに」を仮定法過去〈If I＋動詞の過去形…，I could＋動詞の原形～〉で表す。(6)挿入文は「そして，それもねばねばしていなかった」で，itが指すものは直前にあるはず。納豆はねばねばしているが，テンペはねばねばしていないという話のあと，空所アに入れると，「広志にタイ産の発酵大豆食品を食べたと話した」→「それもねばねばしていなかった」→「だから納豆を初めて食べたときびっくりした」と流れに合う。(7)広志の応答「この近所でテンペが買えるとは思わない」につながるのはイ。(8)「～できてうれしい」be glad that S can[could] ～　(9)グリーン先生の2番目の発言のHowever, ～とイが一致。広志の最後の発言のI think learning ～とオが一致。

13 〔問1〕(a)イ　(b)ア　(c)オ　(d)エ　(e)ウ
〔問2〕1番目：キ　4番目：カ　8番目：ウ
〔問3〕オ　〔問4〕(a) time　(b) together　(c) without

(d) safe

【解き方】〔問1〕(a)直前の発言でリサがダイアンとジョージに窓側の席を譲り，「お2人が美しい景色が見られるといいわね」と言ったことに対して，ダイアンがお礼を述べた。(b)直前のa top speed of 285 kilometers per hour「最高時速285キロ」を受けて，アの「ほんとうなの？　それは速い！」。(c)直前にあるダイアンの「新横浜に時間びったりに着いたわ」を受けて，オの「日本の電車はほとんど遅れないと聞いたよ」。(d)直後に「富士山はきれいだね」とあるので，エの「ちょっと外を見て」が適切。(e)直後でダイアンは「新幹線はほんとうに安全な旅行手段だね」と安全面について話していることから考える。〔問2〕(They thought that to) increase speed and reduce noise the shape of the front of the shinkansen needed to be very similar to (the beak).「スピードを増加させ騒音を減らすためには，新幹線の前部の形は鳥のくちばしにとても似たものになる必要があると彼らは考えた」〔問3〕①ジョージにとっても新幹線は初めてのことなので，不一致。②窓側の席に座ったのはジョージとダイアンなので，不一致。③フランスは15分遅れで正式な遅延となる。イギリスは10分遅れで正式な遅延となる。よってイギリスのほうが遅延に対する意識は高いと言えるので，不一致。④空所(d)の前のジョージの発言より，一致。⑤掃除は毎回行い，座席スペースは広いので，不一致。⑥東京駅を8:30に出発して名古屋に10:10に到着したので，不一致。⑦新幹線は50年の歴史の中で10億人以上(over one billion)の人の輸送をしてきたというリサの説明があるので，不一致。hundreds of millions of ～は「何億もの～」の意味。⑧最後から2番目のリサの発言内容と一致。〔問4〕(a) on time「定刻に」(b) work together「協力する」(c) without worrying about delays「遅延を心配せずに」(d)「最後に，新幹線は安全である」

14 〔問1〕エ　〔問2〕ウ　〔問3〕ア　〔問4〕イ　〔問5〕カ　〔問6〕カ　〔問7〕エ　〔問8〕ク　〔問9〕[解答例]
Cows are the most useful animals for people. There are two reasons. First, milk is so good for people's health that many people drink it every day. Second, people can get a lot of energy from beef. There are a lot of restaurants serving beef. People need them the most. (50語)

【解き方】〔問1〕(1)-a　CのThat's new to me.は「それは初耳です」という意味。直前にあるケントによるクラゲの泳ぎ方の話を聞いたあとのリカの発言。(1)-b 直前にあるリカの質問に対してナカ先生がD「それはいい質問ですね」と答えた。(1)-c 直前にあるナカ先生の「博物館に行ってクラゲについての特別展を見よう」という提案に対して，Aの「それはおもしろそうですね」。(1)-d 直前にある「理科の発表のためにもクラゲを捕まえられるといいね」というミックの発言に対して，リカがB「冗談でしょ？」と答えた。〔問2〕下線部の直後に続くミックの発言から判断する。〔問3〕直後でミックが「僕がやってみましょう」と言って，タマネギを例に説明していることから考える。アの「より簡単な例を示して，その化学反応を説明できる人はいませんか」が適切。〔問4〕直後に2つの物質の説明があり，タマネギが細かく切られることにより化学反応が起こることが述べられている。イの「タマネギが細かく切られる前にそこには2つの異なる物質がある」が適切。〔問5〕(Why) does the special substance change the raw material into something really different(?)「その特別な物質はなぜその原料をまったく違うものに変えてしまうのか」 change A into B「AをBに変える」〔問6〕(6)-a「GFPの何が特別

なのですか」(6)-b「蛍光物質と酵素が同じ場所にあるのです」(6)-c「オワンクラゲは光るとき，別の場所から酵素を得る必要がありません」(6)-d「ウミホタルは蛍光物質と酵素を体の別々の場所に持っています」〔問7〕空所の3つ前のケントの「科学者は，GFPを使ってタンパク質(の移動)をたどるときに何が必要でしょうか」という質問からの話の流れをつかむ。ミック「それは特別なタンパク質なの？」→ケント「いいや，違うよ。ふつう太陽から来るものさ(B)」→リカ「日常生活で目に見えないものでしょ？(D)」→ケント「もちろん，見えないさ(A)」→リカ「わかったわ。紫外線ね(C)」，という流れ。〔問8〕①ミックは8月の集まりでリカの話を聞いてからクラゲについて発表することを提案しているので，不一致。②ケントがクラゲが大好きだという内容は本文にない。③なぜ光らないウミホタルがいるのかを理解しているのはケントなので，不一致。④例を用いて説明したのはミックなので，不一致。⑤博物館でのサキとの対話の最初の部分から一致。⑥空所(6)のある部分のサキとケントのやりとりから一致。⑦GFPが以前はあまり利用されなかったという内容は本文にない。⑧本文のいちばん最後のミックの発言より，一致。〔問9〕人々にとって最も有益と思われる動物を挙げて，その理由を説明する。理由は2つくらい挙げると必要な語数でうまくまとめられるだろう。

e．説明文

① 日常・文化・社会

1 1．イ　2．[解答例]different　3．ゾウの耳や鼻の中に入ることができ，ゾウはそれを嫌がる（26字）　4．ウ
【解き方】 1．後半の「だから，たくさんの人がじゃんけんを楽しむことができる」から，「その（＝じゃんけんの）ルールを理解するのは簡単だ」とするのが適切。It is ～ to *do*「…するのは～だ」　2．1つ目の空所は，第2，3段落で各国のじゃんけんの違いが説明されているので，「他国では，人々は日本で使われている手ぶりと異なる手ぶりを使う」とする。be different from ～「～と異なる」，the onesは hand gesturesのこと。2つ目の空所は「手ぶりとその意味が違っても人々はそれを楽しめる」。3．「小さなアリが大きなゾウを打ち負かす理由は想像できるか」。その理由は次の文にある。4．選択肢から，「そうすれば，それはよい～になるかもしれない」という文意だとわかる。主語のthatは，その前の「外国に行くことがあれば，現地の人たちのじゃんけんのやり方をたずね，あなたの[日本の]じゃんけんも紹介してみてはどうか」という内容を受けている。よって，ウが適切。

2 1．(1)エ　(2)ウ　(3)ウ　2．① living　② spoken　3．イ　4．ア　5．grow healthy vegetables
6．[解答例]our soccer team won the game
【解き方】 1．(1)第2段落の最後2文から，エ「彼と弟たちが両親不在で夕飯を食べなければならなかったとき，智明は悲しく感じた」。(2)第4段落第3文以下から，ウ「智明の両親から日本の農業について学ぶために，外国人学生の集団が農場に来た」。(3)第4段落に含まれる会話の内容から，ウ「智明の両親は，子供たちともっと多くの時間を過ごしたかったので，新しい機械を買った」。2．① living in the townが能動の意味でpeopleを修飾して「町に住む人々」となる。②直前にあるwasと結び付いて受動態になり，「英語が農場で話された」となる。3．空所の直後に「智明は週末に家族と一緒に外出できないので」という理由があるので，イ「智明は両親の仕事が好きではなかった」が適切。4．students（人）を先行詞とする主格の関係代名詞whoが適切。5．空所の直後に「そして，それらを売ることによって多くの人々を幸せにする」のthemが指すものを考えて，grow healthy vegetables「健康によい野菜を栽培する」を入れる。この表現は第1段落第3文にある。6．解答例は「私たちのサッカーチームが試合に勝ったとき，私は幸せに感じた」。
《大　意》 智明の両親は農業を営んでいて，家の隣にある大きな農場で健康によい野菜を栽培している。彼らの野菜はおいしくて町に住む人たちにも評判がよい。しかし，両親は週末も朝から晩まで働いているため，智明は家族と週末を楽しむことがなく，両親と一緒に夕飯を楽しむことができないこともあり，悲しく思っていた。両親は地元の農家の人々と健康によい野菜を栽培するための農業技術について話し合うための会合を開くことがよくあった。ある日，日本の農業技術を学ぶ外国人と両親が英語で話していた。父親が外国人に新しく購入した農業機械について，それを

使って節約できた時間を子供たちと過ごすために使うと言っているのを聞いて驚き，うれしくなった。その後，両親と楽しい時間を過ごすようになり，農業にも興味が出て，農業の手伝いをするようになった。現在，智明は両親のことを誇りに思い，両親のような農家になろうと，農業高校に進学するために熱心に勉強している。高校入学後は世界の人々と農業技術を共有できるように，英語も熱心に勉強しようと考えている。

3 (1)ウ　(2)(a) 3　(b) 1　(c) 4　(d) 2　(3) talk with his heart
【解き方】 (1)与えられた文は「短歌を作ることはそれほど難しくない」。空所ウに入れると，その直後にある文「自由に短歌を作ることができる」と自然につながる。(2)(a)質問は「マサトとトムはいつも何を一緒に楽しむか」。第2段落第2文に「マサトもそれ（＝マンガ）が好きで，彼らはよくそのストーリーについて話すのを楽しむ」とあるので，3「マンガについて話すこと」が適切。(b)質問は「なぜマサトとトムは国語の授業の宿題を一緒にすることが多いのか」。第3段落第3文に「国語の授業の宿題を1人でやるのはトムにはまだ難しかった。だから彼らはそれをしばしば一緒にやり，マサトがトムを手伝ってあげた」とある。したがって，1「トムはそれをやるのにマサトの助けが必要だったから」が適切。(c)質問は「オカ先生がよい短歌を作るということをマサトはどうやって知ったか」。空所イの3文後に「マサトはときどき学校新聞で先生のよい短歌を見た」とあるので，4「学校新聞を読むことによって」が適切。(d)質問は「マサトは何についての短歌を作ることに決めたか」。第5段落の最後から2文目に，「マサトはこの気持ちについての短歌を作ることに決めた」とある。this feelingとはこの段落にある，トムと多くのことを楽しんだことや，トムが帰ってしまうのは寂しいけれど，自分たちの将来のためにそれぞれの場所で成長しなければならないことを表す。したがって，2「トムとの思い出と自分たちの将来について」が正しい。(3)質問は，「オカ先生によるとよい短歌を作るためにマサトは何をすべきか」。第4段落の最後の2文で「自分の心と会話をしなさい。そうすればよい短歌を作れます」と言っている。
《大　意》 マサトとトムは友人同士で，一緒に剣道の練習をしたりマンガのストーリーについて話したり，マサトはトムが国語の宿題をするのを手伝うような間柄だった。短歌を作る宿題があったが，マサトにとっても短歌を作るのは簡単ではなかった。剣道の先生であるオカ先生は短歌の名人で，よい短歌を作るのには自分の心と会話するとよいと教えてくれた。マサトはトムへの自分の気持ちを込めた短歌を贈った。

4 (1)ウ　(2)エ　(3) shared
【解き方】 (1)下線部を含む文全体の意味は「何人かの子供たちは通りで遊べないとわかっていたが，彼らはときどきそれをした」。(2)ア．市役所の職員とは話せなかったので不一致。イ．ルークはポスターを作るのをやめていないので不一致。ウ．第4段落の第5文より，不一致。エ．最後の段落の内容と一致。(3)「公園はみんなのためのものなので，ルークはいつも公園を彼らと一緒に使った」　第2段落の最後の文の中にあるsharedを参照。share O with ～「Oを～と共有する，一緒に使う」

5 1．エ　2．ウ　3．エ　4．イ
【解き方】 1．質問は「ハルキのおじいさんはハルキの

— 27 —

英語について何と言ったか」。第2段落最後の文から、この
まま練習し続けると上手になると言った。エの「練習す
ることによって英語を上達させることができると言った」が
適切。2. 質問は「学校祭の当日、何が起こったか」。第6段
落第3〜5文から、ハルキがスクリーンに映っているデイ
ビッドたちを紹介している。3. 質問は「デイビッドについ
て正しいのはどれか」。第7段落の第3文から、エが適切。
4. 質問は「ハルキはこの経験のあとで今、何を信じている
か」。最終段落最後の2文より、イ「心配するよりも努力し
続けることのほうが大切だ」が適切。

《大意》　高校生のハルキには、アメリカに高校生の友達
がいる。名前はデイビッドで、知り合ってまだ6か月。い
つも彼とはオンラインで会話するが、自分の英語が下手で
通じるのか心配だった。ハルキは今度の学校の文化祭では
ダンスに出演する予定だ。そのダンスの曲をデイビッドが
作ってくれることになった。実際にその曲を聞いてみると、
ダンスチームのみんなはとても気に入って一生懸命練習に
励んだ。文化祭当日、ハルキは見に来てくれた人たちにス
クリーンでデイビッドとそのバンドを紹介した。日米合同
のパフォーマンスは大成功のうちに終わった。次の日、ハ
ルキはデイビッドに曲のお礼を言い、デイビッドは作曲を
楽しんだと言った。彼はまた、英語のミスを気にするハル
キに、ハルキの英語は十分理解できて楽しんでいると言っ
てくれた。ハルキは心配事が解消されてうれしかった。ハ
ルキは、小さなミスを怖がらないで努力し続けることが大
事だと思った。

6 (1)ウ　(2)エ　(3)インドでは、他国出身の人々は施設に
入ることができなかったから。
(4)a. blue　b. brown　(5)イ、エ　(6)①オ　②イ
【解き方】(1)エミーは自分の目の色が茶色ではなく青色
だったらいいのにと願っていた。前の晩に「青色の目をくだ
さい」と神に祈ったので、翌朝青目が青色になっていると期
待して鏡を見たのである。anticipationは「予想、期待」。
(2) thisは直前の内容を受けている。エミーは施設から逃
げ出した少女と出会った。少女は空腹で弱っていて、「施設
には私のような子供がほかにもたくさんいる」と言った。
エミーはこれを聞き、子供たちを助けようと決めた。よっ
て、エ「その施設には多くのおなかをすかせた子供たちがい
た」が適切。(3)下線部は「彼女が彼(＝施設長)と会うのは困
難だった」という意味で、その理由は次の文にある。enter
「〜に入る」　(4)エミーは目が茶色で、インド人も茶色。外
国人は施設に入れないので、エミーは肌の色を変えてイン
ド人の服を着ることでインド人を装ったが、目の色は変え
る必要がなかったという点を押さえる。aは、仮定法過去
の文では事実に反する内容を表すので、「もし私が青い目を
していたら、インド人のようになれないだろう」とし、bは
「彼女の茶色い目のおかげで、インドの子供たちをたくさん
救うことができた」となる。(5)エミーは母親のような青い
目にあこがれたので、イが一致。エミーは施設長に会うた
めにコーヒーの粉で肌の色を変えたのでエも一致。アは、
エミーは最年長で、外で危険な遊びをするのが好きだった
ので不一致。ウは、インドに渡ったのは27歳のときでa
little girlは不適。オは、エミーが本に書いたのはインドの
施設の子供たちについてなので、to以下が不適。カは、最
終段落から、エミーは生涯をインドで過ごしたので不一致。
(6)①第7段落のエミーの発言「私は自分自身と自分の目の
色を誇りに思う」を参考に、「エミーは強く、自分のすべて
を受け入れられるようになった」が適切。②「エミーは困難
な状況でも子供を助けることをやめなかった」　stop　〜
ing「〜するのをやめる」

《大意》　インドで活躍したイギリス人のエミー・カーマ

イケルさんの話。エミーは幼いころ、自分の目が茶色では
なく青色だったらいいのにと思っていた。27歳で宣教師と
してインドに渡ったエミーは、施設で困難な状況にある子
供たちのことを知った。施設長に会って話したいと思った
が、外国人は施設に入れない。そこでエミーは、コーヒー
粉で肌の色を変えてインド人の服を着ることでインド人を
装って会うことができた。このとき目の色は変える必要が
なかったので、自分の茶色の目に感謝するのであった。エ
ミーは生涯をインドで過ごし、千人以上の子供を救った。

7 (1)ウ、オ、ク　(2)2　(3)① He joined five lessons.
② He thought he should change his ways of
learning. (4)[解答例]① I think his experience was
wonderful because he found better ways of learning
English. (14語)　② I usually listen to English songs
every morning and I talk to my English teacher
after school. (17語)
【解き方】(1)アは、オーストラリアではなくアメリカなので
不一致。イは、第1段落に「カズマは興味をもった」とある
ので不一致。ウは、第1段落の「世界各地から来る学生と一
緒に英語を学ぶ」や、第2段落の「世界各地から来た25人の
生徒と一緒に勉強した」と一致する。エは、カズマが意見を
言えるようになったのは1週間以上たってからのことなの
で不一致。オは、第3段落でカズマの先生の1人が「この学
校には学生を支援する特別な先生方がいる」と言って、彼ら
に相談するよう提案したことから、一致。カは、カズマは
特別な先生に悩みを相談したので不一致。キは、スミス先
生がカズマの先生と話したという内容は本文にないので不
一致。クは、第4段落でスミス先生と話したあと、カズマ
は授業でうまくいくようになったので一致。本文最後の1
文も手がかりになる。(2)挿入する文は「しかし、彼は自分の
意見が持てずに何も言わなかった」という意味。空所2の
前に They had their own opinions and shared them
during the lessons. Kazuma understood what other
students said.「彼らは自分自身の意見を持っていて、授業
中それを共有した。カズマはほかの生徒が言っていること
はわかった」に着目する。空所2に入れるのが適切。続く
「彼は孤独に感じた」ともうまくつながる。(3)①「アメリカ
の高校での初日、カズマはいくつの授業を受けたか」　第2
段落第2文に On the first day of the program,
Kazuma joined five lessons「プログラム初日、カズマは
5つの授業を受けた」とある。②「カズマはスミス先生と話
したときどう思ったか」　第4段落の When he talked
with Ms. Smith, Kazuma thought 〜 の文の Kazuma
を He に変えてその後をそのまま書けばよい。(4)①カズマ
のアメリカでの経験をどう思うかを自分なりに考えて書
く。自分の意見を書くときは、I think 〜 で始めるとよい。
②自分自身が英語力を伸ばすのにふだんしていることを書
く。I usually 〜 で始めるとよい。

《大意》　高校生のカズマは英語を一生懸命勉強していて、
学校でも英語がよくできる。ある日、先生から夏にアメリ
カの高校で行われる特別英語学習プログラムについて聞い
た。英語に自信があったのでとても楽しみに参加した。し
かし、世界各地から来たほかの生徒のように自分の意見を
持ってお互いに話すことができず、すっかり自信を失うの
だった。先生と話し、勉強の仕方を変える必要があると考
えた。その後、自分の考えを持つように、より注意深く本
を読むようにした。それで、授業で自分の意見を言えるよ
うになり、再び自信を取り戻した。

8 問1．［解答例］sad［alone］　問2．イ　問3．ウ　問4．ア　問5．以前のようにはピアノを弾けなくなったが，ルークと出会い再び弾けるようになった（から。）(38字)　問6．［解答例］I learned that we should not give up our dreams. (10語)

【解き方】問1．空所①は左手が動かなくなったルークが感じたことであるから sad「悲しい」が適切。空所⑤は，ルークとメアリーが2人でピアノを弾き始めた部分。sadを入れ，「彼らはもう悲しくなかった」とするのが適切。問2．イ．「彼女は夢をあきらめたくなかったから」　下線部直後の「彼女はまだピアノの教師になりたかった」が該当箇所。問3．あとに続くメアリーの発言「ピアノを聞いて思い出がよみがえってきました。将来の夢だったことを思い出したのです」が該当箇所。問4．第2段落よりルークは左手が動かない。そして第3段落よりメアリーは右手が使えないことがわかるので，ルークが左手を使っているアが適切。問5．下線部は「1つの扉が閉まっても，また別の扉が開く」という意味。「1つの扉が閉まった」は右手が使えなくなりピアノが弾けなくなったこと，「別の扉が開く」はルークと出会い再びピアノが弾けるようになったことを表している。問6．解答例は，最後のルークの発言「夢をあきらめなければ，ほんとうにやりたいことを見つけることができる」という内容から，「夢をあきらめるべきではないということを学んだ」とした。

《大意》　メアリーとルークは有名な音楽家である。彼らの音楽は美しく特別なのだが，その理由は何だろう？ルークはオーストラリアの高校生だったときからピアノを熱心に練習していたのだが，ある日通学中に事故にあい，左半身が動かなくなった。「もうピアノが弾けない」彼は世界の終わりのように感じ，とても悲しかった。メアリーはピアノの教師になることを夢見ており，熱心にピアノの練習をしていた。15歳のとき，病気になり3か月の入院を余儀なくされ，医師から右手が使えないかもしれないと告げられた。彼女は医師の言葉が信じられなかった。それでもピアノの先生になりたかった。数年がたち，メアリーはコミュニティセンターを訪れた。何かできることを探していたのだ。センター長に案内してもらっていると，ピアノの音色が聞こえてきて，メアリーは泣き出した。「思い出がよみがえってきました。将来の夢だったことを思い出したのです」　メアリーはそのピアノを片手だけで演奏し美しい音色を奏でているルークを見て驚いた。「初めまして，ルーク。私の名前はメアリーといいます。ポロネーズ第7番幻想を知っていますか？」とメアリーがたずねると，「はい，大好きな曲です。一緒に弾くのはどうですか？」とルークは答えた。メアリーがルークと一緒にピアノを弾いてみると，とても美しい音色が奏でられた。2人とももう悲しい気持ちにはならなかった。メアリーはこう言う，「1つの扉が閉まっても，また別の扉が開く。音楽を失ったけど，ルークと出会えた。そして今また音楽を得たの」。ルークはこう言う，「人生ってのは，ときに難しいね。だけど，夢をあきらめなければ，ほんとうにやりたいことを見つけられるはずさ」。

9 1．イ　2．［解答例］They didn't have enough time to talk with each other.　3．エ　4．笑顔で話せば相手もうれしく感じ，親切にすれば相手もやさしくしてくれるということ。(40字)　5．［解答例］Thank you for everything you've done for me. You're the best mother in the world. (15語)　6．イ，ウ

【解き方】1．イの絵を見ると，観客席でサラの母が応援している。しかし本文ではサラが母を自分のサッカー試合に誘ってはいるが，「仕事で行けない」と断られているから内容に合わない。第5段落第3文参照。2．質問の意味は「サラの母がサラに話しかけたとき，母が寂しそうな顔をしていたのはなぜか」。第4段落第1文から抜き出す。そこではWe don't have ～と書かれているが，解答はThey don't have ～と書くこと。3．サラが母にサッカーの試合に来てくれるかと頼んだとき，仕事のため行けないと断られてしまい，つい意地悪な言葉をかけてしまった。しかし，母は励ましの言葉をサラのためにホワイトボードに書いてくれていた。意地悪な言葉を母にかけた自分が好きでなかったのだ。第5段落の最後の2文と下線部②の前の2文参照。4．第8段落第5，6文参照。5．次の文に，「サラは母の幸せそうな顔を見たいと思った」とある。それに合うメッセージを考える。解答例の意味は「これまで私にしてくれたすべてのことに感謝します。お母さんは世界一の母親ですよ」。6．ア．from the beginning「始めから」が内容に合わない。第1段落第2文参照。イ．第2段落第1文と第3段落を参照。中学生になってサッカーで忙しくなる前は，サラは家で両親の手伝いをよくしていたので，内容に合う。ウ．第8段落第1文より，内容に合う。エ．第11段落第2文より，内容に合わない。オ．最後の段落第1文より，内容に合わない。

《大意》　両親が看護師をしていたサラの家には母だけが使うホワイトボードがあった。両親は忙しかったので，サラは家の手伝いをよくしていた。中学年になってサッカー部に入ったサラはとても忙しくなり，母は話す時間が十分になく悲しそうだった。サッカーの試合が近づいてきたとき，仕事が重なって応援に行けないと言う母にサラは意地悪なことを言った。しかし当日の朝，ホワイトボードを見ると母の応援メッセージが書いてあった。それを見て，サラはいやみを言った自分が嫌になった。その後，病院で職場体験があったとき，サラは看護師のジョンに「患者と接するときは笑顔と親切が大事である」と教えてもらい，これまでの母とのできごとを思い返した。そこでサラはホワイトボードに初めて母にメッセージを書いた。すると母から「書いてくれてうれしい」と返事をもらった。今ではサラと母は以前よりもよく話をするようになったが，ホワイトボードの書き込みも続けている。サラはいつか自分の本心をホワイトボードなしで伝えられるようになりたいと願っている。

10 (1)①ア　②エ　(2)A．products　B．talking　(3)イ　(4)ウ，カ

【解き方】(1)①空所の前後を見る。英語でヒカリ市のビデオを作るのはどうかとの意見に，ア「それはいい考えだ」とみんなが賛成し部長も承諾した。②作ったビデオを市役所のスタッフに見せて，エ「あなたたちが，私たちのビデオに興味を持ってくださると，私たちはうれしい」と部長が言った。(2)A．such as ～は「たとえば～のような」で，ジュースやかばんを含めてproducts「製品」という。第3段落第2文に該当の単語がある。B．第4段落最後の文を参照。市場の人と話すことでより多くの情報を得た。前置詞byのあとは動名詞にする。第2段落に該当の単語がある。(3)ビデオの内容は第2段落に書かれている。当時の英語クラブのメンバーはヒカリ城やヒカリフラワーパークやヒカリ日曜市場をビデオに収めようと話し合った。(4)ウ．第2段落最後から7文目(One of my classmates ～)に一致。カ．最終段落第1文と第5文に一致。

《大意》　リョウタの住むヒカリ市はとてもよい町だが，海外からの観光客が少ない。リョウタが所属する英語クラブで観光客を呼び寄せるビデオを英語で作ろうということになった。そしてみんなで手分けしてヒカリ市の観光スポットに出向き情報を仕入れることにした。リョウタは

オーストラリア人留学生のメアリーとともに市場へ出かけた。屋台の人と話をしたり，トマトジュースを買ったり，市場を楽しみながら情報を得ることができた。完成したビデオを市役所の担当者に見せたところ，気に入ってもらえて外国人観光客向けのウェブサイトで使ってくれることになった。10年後，リョウタは市役所で観光客相手の仕事をしていた。メアリーは帰国していたが，お互い連絡を取り合っていた。久しぶりにメアリーが来日することになり，2人は再び市場を訪れた。メアリーは外国人観光客が大勢いるのを見て驚いた。そして10年前に飲んだトマトジュースがまだあるのを知って懐かしく思った。

11
〔問1〕イ　〔問2〕エ→イ→ア→ウ　〔問3〕(1)ア　(2)エ　(3)イ　〔問4〕(1)エ　(2)ウ

【解き方】〔問1〕ハルトの感情は，第3段落の下線部の3文前のHaruto spokeで始まる文とその次の文の内容の結果生じたもの。〔問2〕エ．第1段落中に書かれている。イ．第4段落の最後から2文目参照。ア．第5段落の第3～6文参照。ウ．最終段落の第1，2文参照。〔問3〕(1)第1段落の最後のほうのDo you really think ～?　I'm not sure. を参照。(2) One week passed.で始まる第4段落第2～5文参照。(3) On Wednesdayで始まる第6段落中ほどのWill you help me? ～ That made Haruto happy.を参照。〔問4〕(1)最後から2番目の段落の第3文を参照。(2) The next weekで始まる第5段落の後半と，続く第6，7段落を参照。

《大意》　アヤカは毎週水曜の放課後，児童館でボランティア活動をしていて，それにオリビアとハルトが協力することになった。3人が児童館を訪ねると職員のササキさんが歓迎してくれた。遊戯室に入ったとき，ハルトは1人の少年，カズヤに一緒に遊ぼうと声をかけたが，彼は嫌だと答え，絵を描き続けるのだった。1週間後，2度目の訪問のとき，ハルトはカズヤに一緒にサッカーをしようと誘ったが，反応は前と同じだった。一方，アヤカやオリビアは子供たちと楽しそうに過ごしていた。その翌週，ハルトはカズヤに声をかけなかったが，その夜アヤカから電話があり，カズヤがハルトから声をかけてもらえなかったので寂しがっていたという話を聞いた。ハルトは，どうやったらカズヤと友達になれるかを考えた。その次の水曜日，ハルトがカズヤに紙芝居作りを手伝ってくれるように声をかけると，カズヤはいいよと言い，手伝うことになった。紙芝居の絵を描きながら，ハルトとカズヤはコミュニケーションをとることができた。2週間後，紙芝居は完成し，オリビアが子供たちに紙芝居を見せることになった。職員のササキさんはハルトとカズヤが仲よくなったことを喜んだ。

12
(1)イ　(2)ア　(3)ウ　(4)ア　(5)エ　(6)ウ

【解き方】(1)ナッジ理論に関する説明文。第1段落第2文はnudge「そっと突く」の文字どおりの意味で，ナッジ理論についてはAccording to the theory, ～の部分で説明される。その内容から，nudgingとは，イ「人がすべきことをするための一助となる特別な状況を作ること」である。(2)「目覚まし時計が寝床に近いと，寝床から出ずに簡単に止めることができる」 close to ～「～に近い」と3文後のfar from ～「～から遠くに」が対比。(3)第3段落は，目覚まし時計を寝床から手の届く場所に置いた場合と，遠くに置いた場合の比較で，空所には遠くに置いた場合どうなるかの説明が入る。(iii)「目覚まし時計を止めるのに，寝床から出て行かなければならない」→(i)「目覚まし時計を止めたあと，隣にある教科書を見て勉強しなければならないこと

を思い出す」→(ii)「それから，寝床に戻らず，勉強を始める」(4)「nudgingは，その状況に少し影響を与えることだが，人の行動に大きな影響を与える場合がある」という文意。but以下のhave a great influenceの対比でmake a small difference「小さな変化をもたらす，少し影響を与える」とする。(5)第2段落のIn convenience store B, if shoppers ～から，コンビニBは，無料のレジ袋をもらいたい人は会計時に「要求カード(Request Card)」を渡す（→イとウは不正解）。その結果はHowever, in convenience store B, the number became ～にあり，このthe numberは，前文から「無料のレジ袋をもらわなかった人の数」のこと。その数が「以前より明らかに増えた」のだから，エが適切。(6)本文最後の2文とウが合う。第2段落第2文から，政府の調査の意図はレジ袋の削減なので，エは不適。

《大意》　ナッジ理論に関する説明文。nudgeは「(注意を引くために)そっと突く」という意味の語で，ナッジ理論では，やるべきことに対して，（強制的ではなく）小さなきっかけを作ることで，人の行動に影響を与えることができる。たとえば，朝5時に起きて登校前に1時間勉強したいとしよう。目覚まし時計が寝床の近くにあれば，すぐに止めることができ，二度寝してしまう。一方，目覚まし時計を寝床から遠くに置いて隣に教科書を置けば，起き上がって止めにいかなければならず，教科書に気づいて勉強を始めることができる。この場合，「目覚まし時計を遠くに置く」という「小さなきっかけ」が行動に影響を与えたことになる。今，多くの人がこのナッジ理論でさまざまな問題を解決する方法を模索している。

13
〔問1〕ウ　〔問2〕イ　〔問3〕[解答例]It means you cannot find anyone to help you and you don't know what to do in a new situation. (20語)
〔問4〕me to write about the Lincoln cent together
〔問5〕[解答例]The cherry blossoms around the Lincoln Memorial are best now. I have never been there before, so can you take me there some time in April? (26語)　〔問6〕始めの2語：If there　終わりの2語：it together　〔問7〕エ　〔問8〕sad　〔問9〕ウ

【解き方】〔問1〕一家でアメリカに行くことをためらう息子に対して母親が事情の説明をするもので，(However, she) told me that my father wanted her and me to go (together.)という文になる。父親が2人と一緒に行きたいと思っている，という内容。ウの順番が正解となる。〔問2〕「ものごとは起こるべくして起こるものだ」ということで，これからのことをあれこれ心配しても仕方がない，成り行きにまかせるしかない，という楽観的な意味合い。イに合致する。〔問3〕森の中を1匹で歩く小鹿のような孤立無援の立場，ということ。表現の意味合いを一般の人の立場で述べるならIt means you cannot find anyone to help you and ～などと，文中の時制と主語に合わせてIかheの立場で述べるならばIt means I [he] felt very helpless and ～などと書き始めるのが妥当。それに「新たな環境でどうしたらいいのかわからない[わからなかった]」という要素を入れればいいだろう。〔問4〕「すぐに彼の考えに同意した」ということ。his ideaが指す具体的な依頼の内容を盛り込んだ本文最後から2段落目のジュンの回想部分にある，he askedに続く8語を入れる。〔問5〕リンカーン記念館に行こうとジャックを誘った，ということなので桜を主とした，その地の魅力と具体的な訪問時期を示した勧誘の表現にする。〔問6〕「問題が生じても，何か解決策はあるものだ」という趣旨の表現を文中から探し出す。第2段落下線部(1)のあとで，母親がジュンにアメリカ行き

を説得する場面にある，If there is a difficulty, I am sure we can solve it together. という発言がほぼ同義。最初のIf there と最後のit together を答えることになる。〔問7〕本文で紹介されている2人のレポートで1セント硬貨のデザインの描写がある。レポートの最初の段落の最後に，表のリンカーンの顔は「右側を向いている」と説明され，次の段落で，裏は「リンカーン記念館」であること，そして最後の文で「（そのまま）左右に裏返すと（リンカーン記念館が）上下逆になっている」という描写がある。これに合致するのはエの組み合わせと判断できる。〔問8〕2人がどのようなときにびんに硬貨を入れたのかは，レポートのあとの2段落目にwhen we have a happy day という表現で示されているので，入れなかったのはhappy ではなかった日ということになる。第4段落前半の，2人が共同作業を始める場面のジャックの表情の描写He looked sad, の〜sad を入れるのが適切。〔問9〕数字や肯定，否定にかかわる表現を中心に各選択肢を吟味する。本文の記述と一致するのはウのみで，第4段落第5文中のジャックの発言内容から読み取れる。つまり，ジャックは長い間ジュンと話をしたいと思っていたが，どのように話しかけたらいいのかわからなかったのである。

《大意》 春になると私はワシントンD.C.のポトマック川沿いの桜を思い出す。9歳のときに父親の転勤に合わせ，前向きな考えの両親の説得を受けて，不安をかかえながら現地に住み始めたのだった。しかし予想に反して現地の小学校は私をやさしく迎えてくれた。少したったとき，歴史の授業でジャックとともにレポートを書くことになったが，近所で私の顔を知っている彼は私と前から話をしたかったと言ってくれた。私も彼と話す機会を求めていた。私たち2人は互いのことをよく理解し，レポートでは，独特のデザインで変遷を経てきたリンカーン大統領記念コインを扱うことにした。私たちはこの活動で国民の尊敬を受けるリンカーンの特異で偉大な生涯とコインの変遷をまとめ上げた。そしてますます親交を深め，楽しいことがあった日は，貧しい人々のためにびんにコインを貯めていく活動も始めた。突然，家族で5月に帰国することが決まり，そのことをジャックに伝えるために4月に彼を周辺の桜で有名なリンカーン記念館へ誘った。私の帰国を知った彼は悲しんでくれ，私は彼に感謝の気持ちを述べた。そのときの美しい桜のことは脳裏に残っている。私は米国で大切な友人を得て，貴重な経験もできた。彼とは今でもメールで交流し，隣人のように感じている。私はこの経験を通じてさまざまな面で成長し，どのような問題も必ず解決できること，ものごとはやってみるまで成否はわからないこと，自分を信じ最善を尽くすことの大切さを学んだのだ。

14 〔問1〕オ 〔問2〕ウ 〔問3〕イ 〔問4〕オ 〔問5〕ア 〔問6〕thief 〔問7〕イ，オ 〔問8〕[解答例] Rakugo is traditional Japanese storytelling of funny stories. It is usually about ordinary people living everyday lives like us, so we can empathize with the characters. Through their mistakes or weaknesses, we can learn that no one is perfect. Please enjoy Rakugo in Japan. (44語)
【解き方】〔問1〕話題は「だれが最初の落語家だったか」。DのThey はBのmany Rakugo storytellers を指すので，B→D。Dで三笑亭可楽が紹介され，Cの「可楽以前には〜」とつながるので，D→C。Aのthat old style とはCの「落語が路上や寿司やおそばの店内で演じられた」ことを指すので，C→A。〔問2〕第5段落の第6文より，ウの「落語の登場人物が金持ちであるためにときどき問題を解決するから」が不適切。金持ちだからではなく，「たくましく，賢

い(tough or clever)」ので問題を解決するのである。〔問3〕第7段落にある立川談志の発言の後半にあるSome people may say 〜 such a strong will. を参照。〔問4〕(At the end of my speech,) I would like to introduce one of the most famous Rakugo stories (to you.) 〔問5〕(5)-a「俺は泥棒だぞ。おまえ，怖いだろう？」「いいや。俺は怖くない」 (5)-b「この時点で，男はこの泥棒はあまり賢くないことがわかった」 (5)-c「彼はいい考えを思いついた。大声で話し続けたのである」 (5)-d「男は静かになって，泥棒は彼にお金をあげた」 〔問6〕とんだ目に遭った泥棒の言葉。「ほんとうに俺たちのどっちが泥棒なんだろう？」 〔問7〕ア. 通りの人々の注意を引きつけるために楽器を使ったのは上方落語なので，不一致。イ. 第5段落の第3文より一致。ウ. 講談は，落語と違って，偉人についての話なので，不一致。エ. 本文には「病気で寝ていた」とうそを言ってその襲撃に参加しなかったとあるので，不一致。オ. 第8段落の最後の文より，一致。カ. 布団に寝ている男に気づいたので，泥棒がその家に入ろうと決めたという内容は本文にない。〔問8〕落語とは何であるのかをまず説明して，そのあとでその魅力を具体的に説明したい。本文で述べられている内容をうまく利用してまとめるのがコツ。落語の魅力については，本文の第5段落を参照するとよい。
《大意》 落語は長い歴史を持ち，1623年に安楽庵策伝によって書かれた『醒睡笑』が始まりだと言われているが，最初の落語家がだれであるのかははっきりしていない。落語には，上方落語と呼ばれる関西のものと，江戸落語と呼ばれる東京のものがあり，両者にはいくつかの違いがある。たとえば，上方落語では見台を使うが，江戸落語では使わない。落語が最初に誕生したのは関西で，江戸落語は上方落語のよい点を採り入れている。その1つが出囃子（でばやし）である。これは，大正時代に京都に行った東京の落語家が持ち帰ったものである。落語は400年の歴史があるが，その魅力は落語がふつうの人々の生活についての話であり，多くの人がその話に共感するからである。また，落語は人々の失敗や弱さを扱うことが多い。多くの人は，落語を聞くと，完璧な人などいないとわかってほっとするのである。落語と講談は似ているが異なる。落語と違い，講談はふつう偉人についての話で，聞く者にそういう人物のように生きることを奨励する。よって，講談は江戸時代，侍の間で人気だった。また，子供たちに侍の歴史や作法を教えるのに利用された。その一例が忠臣蔵である。この話について落語家の立川談志は，「忠臣蔵の四十七士のほかに，うそをついたりして，襲撃に参加しなかった侍もいただろう。彼らは忠誠心がなかったのではなく，強い意志が持てなかったのだ。落語は，そんな完璧ではない人間の側面を扱うものだ」と言う。落語は完璧ではないふつうの人を扱い，それを聞いて，私たちは自分の弱さを笑い飛ばし，完璧でなくても大丈夫だとわかるのである。最後に，有名な落語の1つを紹介する。ある夏の夜，男が寝ているところに泥棒が入る。泥棒が男に金を出すように脅すが，男はそれに動ずることなく，「俺は大工だが，道具を売り払ってしまい，もう仕事に行けない」と大声で叫ぶ。泥棒は男に静かにするように言うが，男は大声で話し続ける。とうとう泥棒は，大工道具を買い戻すお金をあげることを条件にして，男を黙らせる。どっちが泥棒だか？

②　自然・産業・科学技術

1

1．ア　2．③エ　④ウ　⑤オ　⑥ア　3．エ

【解き方】 1．①は，前の「列車が定刻に来ない」を受けて，「それ（＝列車）がどれくらい遅れるか」とする。②は，前のa train is coming to the stationのcomingをarrivingに言い換える。2．③前の部分で，電光掲示板で情報を「見る」ことと，スピーカーから流れる情報を「聞く」ことが説明されていることから考える。④「情報を得るには，周りの人を見て，それから何をすべきかを判断しなければならない」　⑤空所前のthis machineは第3，4段落から，乗客にメッセージを伝える機械のことで，「この機械が日本のほかの駅にも広がることを願う」とする。⑥ある学生の願いが鉄道会社に届き，状況が改善したというこの文章の趣旨を踏まえ，「さまざまな意見を受け入れ尊重すれば，社会をよりよくすることができると思う」とする。3．第3段落：Thank you for using our train（A）→画面に閉まるドアの音（プシュー）が見えた（C）の順。第4段落：列車が動いているとき画面にその音の文字（ガタンゴトン…）が見える（D）→英語（Your attention, please.）が示されているので外国人にも理解しやすい（B）の順。

《大　意》 鉄道の駅では，情報を確認するのに，電光掲示板を見たり，スピーカーから流れる放送を聞いたりする。しかしある日，1人の学生がスピーカーの音が聞こえにくく，情報を聞き逃し，列車に乗り込む途中にドアが閉まるという危険な目にあった。その学生は，音を文字と絵にして画面で示してくれたらいいのにと願った。その学生の願いが鉄道会社に届き，ホームに機械が設置された。機械の画面にはドアが閉まる様子や列車が近づいてくる様子が文字や絵で示され，子供や外国人にもわかりやすい。この経験から，学生は，さまざまな意見を受け入れ尊重すれば，社会をよりよくすることができると思った。

2

(1)ウ　(2)ア　(3)イ　(4)ウ　(5)①ア　②エ

【解き方】 (1) I wonder where[who/whatなど]で「どこで[だれが/何を]〜かしら（と思う）」。(2) aは「水を蓄える施設」があとに続くので，like dams「ダムのような」のイ。bは2文後の「雨のときは雨水を吸収して地面をしっかり保つ」から，ア「森林は地面を安全に保つ」が適切。keep O C「OをCに保つ」　cは「その主な理由の1つは二酸化炭素」が続くので，ウ「森林は地球温暖化を止める」が適切。次の文One of the main causes of itのitはglobal warmingを指す。(3)第2段落のRainwater goes into 〜「雨水は森林の地中を通って，きれいな水に変わっていく」と，第1段落のForests release water and we use it for 〜「森林は水を放出し，私たちはそれを工業や農業，また日常生活に使う」を参照。(4)ア．第2段落参照。森林の木は水を作っているのではなく，貯蔵・浄化しているので内容と一致しない。イ．第2段落の最後の文を参照。ダムではなく，森林に降る雨のことを話しているので内容と一致しない。ウ．第3段落最後の文に一致する。エ．最終段落最後から2文目を参照。one yearが誤りなので内容と一致しない。(5)①第4段落参照。②第4段落最後の文を参照。環境を守るとあり，第4段落は地球温暖化を防ぐ木の役割について書かれていることに着目する。

《大　意》 日本は国土の3分の2が森林だ。森林には水を蓄え，放出するというダムと同じ働きがある。雨水は森林の地下を通ってきれいになり，ゆっくりと川に流れ出る。また森林は雨水を吸収して，木々の根が地面をしっかり押

さえる働きもしている。また，地球の温暖化を防ぐためにも役立っている。今，地球は二酸化炭素の影響で気温が上がっているが，木々はこれを吸収して酸素を出しているのだ。また切られた木にも同じ効果が期待できるので，木材を使うことは環境を守るために大いに貢献していることになる。もし森林がなければ，将来，より多くの山崩れや環境の問題を心配しなければならなくなるだろう。水を得るのももっと難しくなる。林業は，育成，伐採，植樹を50年から100年の周期で繰り返し，森林を安全に保っている。

3

(1)Ⓐイ　Ⓑア　(2)① hungry　②エ

【解き方】 (1)Ⓐ 1日に15,000回まばたきをし，まばたき1回が0.3秒とすると，15,000×0.3で4,500秒，つまり1日に75分間目を閉じていることになる。close (our eyes)とするのが適切。Ⓑ第4文（Most of us blink 〜）は「私たちの多くは1分間におよそ15回まばたきをし，何かに集中しているときは，それほど頻繁にまばたきをしない」という意味。友達と話しているときより，本を読んでいるとき（＝集中しているとき）はまばたきが少なくなるので，15より少ない10 (times)とするのが適切。(2)①第6文の後半had nothing to eatを1語で表すとhungryとなる。②ア．「トマトはもともとヨーロッパから来たもので，アンデス山脈にもたらされた」　第2，3文に不一致。イ．「ヨーロッパの人々は16世紀前にトマトを食べることを楽しんだ」　第3，4文に不一致。ウ．「16世紀にトマトが初めて日本にもたらされた」　第9文に不一致。エ．「毎日トマトを食べることによって私たちの寿命が延びたと言う人々もいる」　終わりから2文目に一致。

4

問1．[解答例] He used the Internet.　問2．イ　問3．（トシコの農園の）果樹に水を与えること。　問4．ウ，オ　問5．[解答例] I use the Internet to talk with foreign people.

【解き方】 問1．「ヒロシはトシコと話すために何を使ったか」　第2段落第1文に「数日後，ヒロシはその計画について，インターネットでトシコと話した」とある。問2．「利点」とは「いい点」のこと。続くトシコの話の内容からも判断できる。問3．同じ文の主節にあるgive water to my fruit treesのこと。問4．ウ．「新しい科学技術を使うことによって，トシコは果樹農家としての自分の働き方を変えた」　第2段落の第4文以下の内容に一致。オ．「アスカの意見では，トシコのウェブサイトを見る人々は農業に関するトシコの考えに影響を受けるでしょう」　第3段落の終りから2文目の内容に一致。問5．解答例は，「私は外国の人々と話をするためにインターネットを使う」という意味。問題の指示に従って文法的に正しい文を書くことが大切である。

《大　意》 中学生のヒロシにはトシコという祖母がいる。彼女は最新の科学技術を使いこなして，果物の栽培を効率よく行い，さらに収穫した果物をインターネットを通じて販売している。このように新しい科学技術を有効に使うことで多くの人々の生活が変わってきている。

5

(1)ウ　(2)(a)1　(b)4　(c)3　(3)(a) made by　(b) become an engineer

【解き方】 (1)空所前後の文脈から判断する。ウに入れて，「彼らは博物館をおよそ2時間歩き回った。しかし，少年たちには夢のようだったので，疲れを感じなかった」とするのが適切。(2)(a)第2段落を参照。1「彼女は彼らのために，ヨーク行きの電車の切符を買った」が適切。(b)第3段落終

盤のSurprisingly, 〜 *Shinkansen*, too.を参照。4「博物館滞在中，彼らは日本の列車を見た」が適切。(c)第4段落最後の3文Masaru learned a 〜made him happy.を参照。make O C「OをCにする」　3「日本はイギリスと協力していたことを学んだから」が適切。(3)(a)第4段落前半のDavid answered, "It's a train made by a Japanese company.を参照。(b)最終段落の第2文Now he has a dream of becoming an engineer.を参照。答えの文はToで始まっているので動詞の原形を続ける。

《大意》 マサルはロンドンでホームステイをした。ステイ先には，デイビッドという少年がいた。2人は電車好きで，すぐに意気投合した。2人は，デイビッドの母の計らいで，電車でヨークに出かけることになった。ヨークでは，鉄道博物館を訪れた。館内には，約300の列車が保存されており，イギリスの鉄道について多くのことを学ぶことができた。帰りは，日本の会社が作った列車に乗った。マサルは，日本の鉄道が開通した150年前から，日本とイギリスが鉄道技術の発展において協力関係にあることを知った。帰国後，マサルはエンジニアになるために勉強している。彼は将来，イギリスの鉄道にかかわる仕事に携わりたいと考えている。

6 (1)エ　(2)エ　(3)ウ　(4)ア
(5) losing something very important
【解き方】(1)空所を含む文の次に，「将来それら（＝文化や慣習）を失うかもしれない」とあるので，最新のテクノロジーは文化や慣習をchange「変える」かもしれない。(2)第2段落の最後から5文目に，「もう1つの例は前もって自然災害についての情報を手に入れられるということだ」とあるので，エ「人々は自然災害が起こる前に，それについて知ることができる」が適切。(3)下線部の前の2文に，「多くの人々が自分の住んでいる場所から新しい場所へと引っ越した。だから地域によっては人口減少が問題になったところもある」とあり，第2段落にはテクノロジーを使って新しい生活を作り出すことが書いてあるので，ウ「そこで生活するほうが楽なので，多くの人々が新しいテクノロジーのある新しい場所に移動した」が適切。(4)④「生活をよりよくするために，新しいテクノロジーを使って新しい生活を作り出すのが重要だ」　⑤「また伝統的なものを保持することも重要である」　(5)「新しいものと生活するならば，losing something very important（何かとても重要なものを失う）という問題について考えなければならないと現在わかっているからだ」　この表現は第2段落最終文にある。

7 (1)エ　(2)エ　(3)イ　(4)[解答例] they will look more beautiful　[別解] we can use them again　(5)ウ
【解き方】(1)段落②で言われていることは，第1文に要約されている。ある会社が頑張っているのは，伝統的な技法を使って，古い衣服を捨てずに再利用することで，その技法とは黒く染めることである。(2)もとは黒以外の色だったが今は黒い色になったお気に入りの服を捨てずに着続けられることがすばらしいという文脈。(3) the *kintsugi* experienceについては，段落③の第3，4文に書かれている。金継ぎとは皿や茶碗などの壊れたものを修復する技法で，皿の壊れた部分をくっつけるのに漆と金粉が使われる。(4)段落③の最後から2文目の「金継ぎを施したあと，茶碗はより美しく見える」や段落④の第3文「金継ぎの技法を使えば，古いものや壊れたものを再利用できる」が参考になる。(5)タイトルづけの問題では，本文と関係ないもの，本文中に述べられているが部分的な記述のものを除外し，本文中の全体で語られることを反映しているものを選ぶ。ア，

エは無関係で，イは部分的な記述になっている。
《大意》 京都には古いものや壊れたものを修理する，また，伝統的な日本の文化を守ろうとする会社がある。その1つは，100年の歴史を持つ，紋付を黒く染める会社で，2013年に古い服や汚れた服を黒く染めなおす事業を始めた。多くの人々は黒く染められたお気に入りの服を捨てずに着続けられる。2つ目は，金継ぎと呼ばれる，漆と金粉を使って，壊れた皿や茶碗を修理する技術を持った漆器の会社である。その会社は金継ぎ道具一式も販売していて，動画を見ればその使い方がわかる。このように，日本の伝統的技法を使えば，古いものや壊れたものを捨てずに再利用できるのである。

8 問1．イ　問2．父親に新しいカップを買わなくてもいい（18字）　問3．エ　問4．①あおい焼のカップをもらった（13字）　②あおい焼の作り方を学ぶ（11字）　問5．エ→ウ→ア→イ　問6．イ，オ　問7．①エ　②ア　③ウ
【解き方】問1．下線部の前の母親から絵美への発言内容を読み取る。問2．下線部は直前の絵美の発言I will buy a new cup for you.に対するもの。問3．第1段落の最後に「絵美は（あおい焼を）ただの昔ながらの陶器だとしか思わず，どうしてそんなに有名なのかわからなかった」とある。校外学習であおい焼について学ぼうと思ったのはエ「あおい焼の何がそんなによいのか」を理解したかったからと考えられる。問4．第4段落の内容，特にジョンの発言についてまとめる。問5．本文が時系列にそって書かれているので，書かれている順番に並べればよい。エは第1段落，ウは第2段落，アは第3，4段落，イは第6段落にそれぞれ書かれている。問6．ア．第1段落で絵美は父に謝っている。イ．第3段落の中ほどを参照。新しいあおい焼が大都市のレストランで使われ，愛されているとある。ウ．第4段落の前半に「ジョンが見せてくれたカップは，彼女（＝絵美）には特別には見えなかった」とある。エ．父親が絵美にあおい焼について教えたという記述はない。オ．第6段落最後を参照。「校外学習で訪れた場所」とはナオとジョンの陶器製造所のこと。問7．①ナオは新しい種類の陶器を作ろうとしている。第3段落前半を参照。②ジョンによれば，あおい焼の色は見る角度によって変わる。第4段落の中ほどを参照。③あおい焼は絵美の住む町のすばらしい文化である。第6段落前半参照。
《大意》 絵美は父が大事にしていたあおい焼のゆのみを割ってしまった。あおい焼は絵美の住む町で作られる陶器だが，なぜそんなに有名なのかわからない絵美は，校外学習であおい焼について学ぶことにした。校外学習では，まずナオという若い女性が新しい種類のあおい焼を作っていることを知った。また，ニュージーランドから来たジョンは，かつてあおい焼を誕生日にもらったことからその美しさにひかれ，あおい焼の作り方を学びにこの町に来ていたのだった。絵美は，あおい焼には人の人生を変える力があるのだと知った。彼女は校外学習で学んだことを父に話し，2人は週末にナオとジョンのところで新しいあおい焼のゆのみを買う予定をたてた。

9 (1)ア　(2)エ　(3)イ　(4)エ　(5)イ
【解き方】(1)アサガオは朝に咲く花なので「暗くなってから約10時間後に開花する」が適切。(2)「多くの人はほとんどの植物は葉に気孔があると知っているが，彼女はアサガオには花びらにも気孔があることを発見した」(3)下線部後の「花びらの気孔は暗い時間に開いた」「葉の気孔は明るい時間，主に光合成のために開いた」から考える。(4)「暗くなって花びらの気孔が開くと，水が茎から花びらに吸い上

げられ，花びらが十分な水を得ると開花する」(5)生徒は，アサガオの花びらの白い部分に小さい穴（気孔）があることを発見し，さらなる研究でなぜアサガオが朝に咲くのかという疑問の糸口を見つけた。よって，イが適切。

10〔問1〕イ　〔問2〕エ　〔問3〕produce　〔問4〕amount　〔問5〕need to show the government how safe cultured meat is　〔問6〕オ　〔問7〕(A)キ　(B)ク

【解き方】〔問1〕第3段落の第1文が答えの最初の部分となるような疑問文が適切。つまり，「ではなぜ一部の人々は代替肉(fake meat)を食べ始めたのだろうか」というイが適切。〔問2〕「一部の人々はこのようなふるまいに反対している」という意味の文であり，最後のthis behaviorが指すものが先行する文になければならない。to take livestock's lives and eat their meat「家畜の命を奪いそれらの肉を食べること」を受けると考えられるエの空所が適切となる。〔問3〕目的語がそれぞれ1 kilogram of beef，a lot of methaneとなっているので「生産する，発生させる」という意味のproduceが適切となる。〔問4〕cultured meat「培養肉」を作り出す過程などの話題であり，それをほんの少量作り出すだけでもお金と時間がかかる，ということを述べた文。肉などは「量」でとらえるので，前の段落の最後から2番目の文にあるamountを選ぶ。just a tiny amount (of cultured meat)「ほんの少量（の培養肉）」ということ。〔問5〕前の文にあるneed，次の文のneed to ～との関連でneed to show ～という表現から始まると判断したい。the government how safe cultured meat isとSVOOの語順にすれば，「また，科学者たちは政府に培養肉がいかに安全かを示す必要がある」という文ができあがる。how以下の間接疑問の語順に注意したい。〔問6〕(6)-aには「かなり多くの～」という意味の形容詞，(6)-bには「だれも～でない」，(6)-cには「私たちのだれもが～」という意味の代名詞が入ると判断したい。just a fewは「ほんの少数の～」という意味で，意外にも「多数」を表すquite a fewとは反対の表現であることに注意。〔問7〕(A)①は第1段落の第2文の記述に一致。②はthe easiest and most effective wayという表現が本文と不一致。③はpigs，sheepに関しては述べられていないので不一致。④は第3段落の最後に述べられている内容と一致する。(B)①は第4段落の内容と不一致。②は第4段落のa lot of artificial ingredients and additivesのことを述べた文と一致。③は第5段落の記述と一致する。④は「培養肉」に関しては「一般的な」ものという記述はないので不一致となる。

《大意》　最近多くの国で本物の肉ではなく「代替肉(fake meat)」に対する関心が高まりつつあり，30年以内にタンパク質摂取の主流になるだろうという報告もある。この流れには健康面，倫理面，そして環境面などのいくつかの理由がある。家畜の肉を食べすぎることで健康に害があり，生き物である動物の命を奪ってその肉を食べることは倫理に反し，牛などの家畜を育てるために多くの水，穀物，土地を費やし，地球温暖化に悪影響のある大量のメタンガスの排出も問題だという考えである。代替肉には2種類あり，1つは大豆などを原料にする植物由来の肉，もう1つは動物の細胞を採取し体外で育てる培養肉である。ただ植物由来の肉には人工的な添加物が含まれるという問題点，培養肉を作るにはかなりの費用がかかり，実際の代用肉になるにはかなりの時間がかかるという問題点はある。かなりの人々が代用肉に関心を持っているのは事実だが，実際に将来本物の肉の代用品になりえるかは未知である。

11(1)ウ　(2)エ　(3)ア　(4)ウ　(5)イ　(6)エ

【解き方】(1)「世界中の多くの科学者がこの興味深い生物を何年も研究し続けている」　現在完了進行形(have been *doing*)の文。(2)「変形菌は，何個かに切り分けられると，その1個1個は別々に生き，えさを探索することができる」(3)第3段落と図を参照。変形菌は，自らの形を変えて2か所にあるえさまで動いていき，最後には1つの線になって栄養を吸収した。(4)迷路の実験内容を考える。(ii)「変形菌を多くに切り分け，迷路のさまざまな場所に置いた」→(i)「（切り分けられた）変形菌が迷路の中でそれぞれ探索を始め，ほかの変形菌と出会うと融合した」→(iii)「数時間後，そのような動作(= iの内容)を何度も繰り返すことで変形菌は1つになった」(5)ア.迷路は実験で使用したのであって，変形菌が住む場所とは関係がない。イ.Picture 1とPicture 2の実験ではいずれも，変形菌は形を変えて動き，2か所にあるえさにたどり着くことを示しているので，適切。ウ.迷路の実験で多くに切り分けられた変形菌は順に融合し，最後には1つになる。よってimpossibleが不適。エ.ほかの生物が栄養を取る方法に関する内容は本文中にない。(6)ア.第1段落第3文と不一致。イ.変形菌は効率よく動いて栄養を取るという趣旨の文章なので，「困難な状況では何もしないのが効率よい」は不適。ウ.最終段落第1文と不一致。エ.第4段落最後の文と一致。

《大意》　変形菌は変わった仕組みで生きている。科学者がある実験を行った。ケースの中に変形菌を入れ，離れた2か所にえさを置き，変形菌がどうやってえさまでたどり着くかを観察した。結果，変形菌は自ら形を変えて広がり始め，2か所のえさまで動いていき，最後には2点を結ぶ1つの線になった。また別の実験では，迷路を用いた。まず変形菌を多く切り分けて迷路のあちこちに置いた。すると変形菌は自ら形を変えて動き回り，別の変形菌に会うと融合し，数時間後には1つにつながった。2か所にえさを置くと，またしても2点を結ぶ最短の1つの線になった。いずれの実験でも，変形菌は自ら最短経路を見つけ，2か所にあるえさから一度に栄養を取り入れたことから，非常に効率よく体形を変えることがわかった。

12〔問1〕イ　〔問2〕ウ　〔問3〕ア　〔問4〕how it looks　〔問5〕エ　〔問6〕human activity　〔問7〕エ

〔問8〕〔解答例〕We should stop cutting down trees in the forests. Many species of animals and plants live there, so if we continue, more of them will lose their homes. If we stop cutting down trees, many species will be safe, and we will stop destroying their environment. (46語)

【解き方】〔問1〕与えられた文中にあるsuch evolution「そのような進化」とは空所イの前文の内容を指す。空所イの直後の文中にはhowever「しかしながら」があり，前文の内容と対照的な内容になっていることにも注意する。〔問2〕下線部のあとの記述を参照。その蛾(が)の羽の色が黒っぽくなったのは，大気汚染で木の樹皮に生えていたlichenが死んで，樹皮の色が黒っぽくなったからである。lichenが生えている樹皮は本来は白っぽい。〔問3〕「dark moths(黒っぽい蛾)」の数の減少が少ないところが工場地域であることから判断する。〔問4〕how it looks「それがどのように見えるか」は第10段落の最終文にある。〔問5〕Bの質問の答えはCではないことに注意する。空所直後の文Why has this happened?のthisはAの内容を指す。〔問6〕the influence that human activity is having on it「人間の活動がそれ(=地球上の生物)に与えている影響」human activityは第1段落の後ろから2番目の文中にあ

る。〔問7〕①第1段落の第2文より，不一致。②人間は生物の変化のスピードを速めたので，不一致。③第4段落の内容と一致。④蛾が環境を変えたという内容は本文中にないので，不一致。⑤そのような内容は本文にないので，不一致。⑥薬草成分は球根の中にあるので，不一致。⑦第10段落の内容と一致。⑧そのような内容は本文にないので不一致。〔問8〕人間の地球環境への影響を減らすためにやるべきことを1つ挙げて，なぜそれが大事なのかを説明する。

《大意》　地球の歴史の中で今の時代はthe Anthropocene「人新世(じんしんせい)」と呼ばれるが，そのように呼ばれるのは人間の活動が地球環境に大きな影響を与えているからである。あらゆる生物は長い時間をかけて進化しているが，この「人新世」以来，人間の活動のためにその進化のスピードを速めている種がある。その一例はオオシモフリエダシャクと呼ばれる蛾である。この蛾はヨーロッパに生息し，その羽は霜降り模様の白色である。ところが，19世紀になると，イングランドの工場地域のこの蛾の羽の色が黒っぽくなった。なぜこの変化が起こったのだろうか。19世紀の初期，多くの工場が建てられ，工場からの黒い煙による大気汚染のために，工場近くの木々の樹皮に生息するコケが死んでしまい，樹皮の色が黒っぽくなった。そのためにそこに生息する蛾が天敵の鳥から身を守るために羽の色を黒っぽくしたのである。実際，工場のない田舎に生息する蛾の羽の色は白っぽいままであった。人間の活動が影響を及ぼした植物もある。フリティラリア・デラバイというバイモである。この植物は中国に生えていて，かつて，その花の色は明るい黄色，葉の色は明るい緑色だけであった。この植物の球根には薬草成分があり，2,000年にわたり薬として採取されてきた。ところが，20世紀の終わりになってこの薬の需要が高まり，以前よりも多く採取されるようになった。すると，その植物の花と葉の色が黒っぽくなったのである。それは山の岩や石の多いところで育つが，そのような場所では黒っぽい色のほうが目立たないからである。中国での6年以上にわたる研究によると，人が行きにくい場所に育つものは元の明るい色のままであったが，人が行きやすい場所のものは色が黒くなっているということである。生物の進化には多くの要因が影響しているが，今日，人間の活動がそれに与えている影響は以前よりも大きくなっている。

13 〔問1〕オ　〔問2〕ウ　〔問3〕イ　〔問4〕カ　〔問5〕same　〔問6〕エ

【解き方】〔問1〕「ニュースは常に集められ，そのまま報道される」という文に続き，In fact「実際には」で始まる内容。次の文のhow it is createdにもつながるのはオの「メディアはしばしば報道内容を決定することでニュースを作り出している」というもの。ほかの選択肢は文脈に合わない。〔問2〕assumption「憶測」とはデータから直接読み取れない内容なのでbe thought to ～「～だと思われる」という表現を用いたウが該当する。〔問3〕グラフが示す数値と合致するのはイの30代の人々に関する記述のみ。アはrose，ウはabout forty percent，エはdid not change，オはnever went downの部分が合致しないと判断できる。〔問4〕選択肢から見て4－aには②か⑤が入ると判断できる。【Graph 1】から【Graph 2】に視点を変えるところなのでOn the other hand「その一方で」が適切。4－bには「追加情報」を示す②のIn addition「それに加えて」，4－cには，前の表現を別の表現で言い換える働きのものがふさわしいので④のIn other words「言い換えれば」が入る。ここでカが正解と判断できるが，4－dには前の表現の結果が続くので①のAs a result「その結果」が適切とわかる。〔問5〕2つの空所それぞれのあとに続くdifferentと対比

される表現，つまりsameが入ると判断する。〔問6〕アは後半のbut以下の記述が，イは後半のis not an assumption以下の記述が，ウはtry to report every news storyという記述がそれぞれ本文と合わない。エは第5段落の内容と一致する。オはたとえとしてのjigsaw puzzleが条件として扱われている点で不適切。

《大意》　人は新聞，テレビ，インターネットなどのメディアを通じて情報を得るが，伝えられるとおりに内容を信じてしまうのは危険である。たとえば，Graph 1は，20代の若者が年を追うごとに新聞を読まなくなっていることを示しているが，その理由を「若者が本を読みたがらないからだ」と結論づけることはできない。これは具体的なデータに基づかない，伝える側の「憶測」である。事実と憶測はしばしば混在するので読む側は区別することが必要となる。同じデータに基づいて上の世代の数値の変動を含めたGraph 2のような示し方をすれば，新聞を読む時間の減少は，20代に限ったことではなく，それほど急激ではないという違った印象になるとわかるだろう。メディアがどのような伝え方をするかでニュースの印象も違ってくる。桃太郎の物語も，村人を困らせる鬼の絵と，桃太郎が鬼を退治する絵を順番に見せれば，桃太郎が村人を助けたことになるが，見せる絵の順番を逆にすれば，桃太郎に攻撃された鬼が仕返しに桃太郎の村を襲う，という違った物語になる。メディアは伝える内容だけでなく，どのように伝えるかも決めているのだ。授業で真ん中のテーブルに置かれた果物を写生すると生徒によって違う絵になるようにできごとも伝える者によって違うものになる。メディアは多くの視聴者を獲得するためにニュースをおもしろく，印象的なものにする傾向があるので，ほんとうに起こっているのは何かを知るにはジグソーパズルを完成させるためにピースを埋めていくような視聴者側の多様な情報収集が重要となる。

14 〔問1〕ウ　〔問2〕イ　〔問3〕エ　〔問4〕[解答例] (4)－a. can't　(4)－b. getting[receiving]　〔問5〕イ　〔問6〕カ　〔問7〕ウ　〔問8〕エ　〔問9〕[解答例] just[only] one　〔問10〕ア，オ

【解き方】〔問1〕ウのthese news sourcesが空所前のtelevision, radio and newspapersを指し，「昔はほとんどの人がテレビ，ラジオ，新聞からニュースを得ていた」→ウ「しかし，今日の人々はこれらの情報源を使わない」という流れが適切。〔問2〕人々が新聞ではなくネットやその他ソーシャルメディアからニュースを得るようになった理由を説明した部分。その理由の1つはソーシャルメディアのほうが速くて簡単だから。スマートフォンを使っていつでもどこでもほぼどんな情報も入手できる。単に新聞が印刷・配達されるのを待ちたくないだけかもしれない。wait for A to do「Aが～するのを待つ」のto不定詞が受動態になっている。〔問3〕(Since then, the websites you) visited keep sending you news and information about him(.)「それ以降，あなたが訪れたウェブサイトは，彼に関するニュースや情報をあなたに送り続ける」 you visitedが前の主語the websitesを修飾する構造。動詞はkeep ～ing「～し続ける」で，send A B「AにBを送る」のBをnews and information about himとする。himは「あなた」がネットで検索したアメリカの有名な日本人野球選手のこと。〔問4〕(4)－aは「これ(＝世界中のだれとでも簡単に意見交換すること)は新聞ではできないことだ」。(4)－bは「ソーシャルメディアは情報の受信と発信の両方にとって便利で役に立つ」。〔問5〕下線部のitは"echo chamber"を指す。次の段落によると，「エコーチェンバー」とは，同じような意見ばかり聞いたり読んだりするとき，また同じ考えや視点を持った人とばかり接していると，

ほかの考えや視点が入りにくくなる現象のこと。これが世界中で深刻な問題になりつつあるとは書かれているが，Imagine you are in a small room〜「狭い部屋にいるとしよう」のin a small roomは単に仮の話であるので，イは本文と述べられていることが異なる。〔問6〕空所前は，情報検索したり好きなビデオを見たり「いいね」ボタンをクリックすると，それが全部データになるという趣旨で，これに続くのは，B「そしてそのデータはウェブサイトやソーシャルメディアサービスに送られる」。次にDのtheyはBのwebsites and other social media servicesを受けており，「それらは集めたデータをどうするのか」と問いかけ，その答えとして，A「それら（＝Bのtheyと同じ）はアルゴリズム（一種のコンピュータープログラム）を使うことで，あなたがどんな情報が気に入りそうかを容易に把握する」→C「それから，アルゴリズムがのちにあなたが受け取るだろう情報を決める」が続く。〔問7〕thisの指す内容は前にある。あなたが受信するニュースや情報はアルゴリズムによって選別・送信されている＝興味のありそうなものだけが示される＝共感しないだろう事実や意見は示されないという趣旨。これと似た意味になるウが適切。〔問8〕(8)-a. ネットでニュースや情報を得るときに覚えておくべき重要なことがもう1つある。(8)-b. ネットは間違ったニュースであふれている。(8)-c. ネットのおかげでだれでも考えや意見を表現することができる。(8)-d. その情報源は十分に信頼できるか。〔問9〕「議論の両面を見るのが重要」＝「議論の片面だけを理解するのはよくない」〔問10〕第2段落の空所(2)-dの次の文と，第7段落のアルゴリズムの説明がアと一致。ソーシャルメディアが便利で役立つことは第3段落にあり，一方でfake news(第8段落)やecho chambers(第4，5段落)などの問題点も述べていることから，オが一致。イは，第8段落でネットよりも新聞を信頼する人に言及しているが，これは「世界の問題を解決する努力をしている人」に限定されない。エは，新聞は事実確認されるため印刷まで多少時間がかかるが，情報を読んで理解するのに時間がかかるわけではない。カは，第9段落にもとの情報源に戻りだれが書いたかを調べる重要性が書かれているが，これは偽ニュースを見つける(find fake news)方法というより，情報が真実か否かを見きわめるための方法である。

《大　意》　大学でジャーナリズムを学んだ高校の英語教員が，生徒へのアドバイスとして学校新聞に寄稿したエッセイ。一昔前，情報源はテレビやラジオ，新聞だったが，今ではインターネットやスマートフォンのおかげで速く容易に情報を入手できる。ソーシャルメディアは便利だが，問題もある。たとえば，エコーチェンバー現象だ。アルゴリズム技術により，好きなビデオを見たり「いいね」をクリックするたびにその人のデータが集まり，好みを把握し，似たような考えや意見，気に入りそうな情報を示し続ける。その結果，視野が狭くなりほかの意見や視点が入らなくなる。また，ソーシャルメディアではだれでも簡単に事実確認を行わずして情報を共有したり自分の考えや意見を発信できるため，間違った情報が拡散されるという問題もある。

15 〔問1〕have discovered which part of the brain we use for　〔問2〕イ　〔問3〕ク　〔問4〕get lost　〔問5〕ケ　〔問6〕[解答例]Internet communication tools are an example. They help us with sending messages but can have bad effects on our communication skills. If we use such tools too much, we will not be able to communicate well when we meet or talk to someone on the telephone.（46語）

【解き方】〔問1〕「（科学者はある地域の道を理解するのに）私たちが脳のどの部分を使っているのかを見つけ出した」現在完了の文にする。〔問2〕与えられた文の冒頭にあるTheyはイの前文にあるscientists「科学者」を指す。また，与えられた文の具体的な内容がイの直後にある2文で説明されている。〔問3〕空所の直前の文は「さて，1つの例を見てみよう」という意味で，ここではある事例が説明されている。最初に状況説明を表すDがくる。Aの文中のthemがDのmany peopleを指すと考えられるので，D→A。Cのthat kind of adviceとはAにある「GPSのついたスマートフォンに頼らずに道を探すスキルを身につけること」という助言だと考えて，A→C。〔問4〕第1段落の最後の文を参照。〔問5〕①第1段落の内容から，Many peopleとは言えないので不一致。②第2段落より，Grid cellsとplace cellsの説明が逆なので不一致。③第2段落および第3段落の第1文より，一致。④第6段落の後半の内容と一致。⑤第7段落の第6文より，不一致。⑥第8段落前半の内容と不一致。⑦そのような内容は本文にないので不一致。⑧最後の段落の第2文より，一致。〔問6〕科学技術はとても役に立つツールだが，使いすぎると私たちに悪影響を与えることがある。そのような科学技術の例を挙げて，どうしてそうであるのかを説明する。解答例では，インターネットでのコミュニケーションツールを例に挙げた。

第３章 英作文問題

a．和文英訳

1 ［解答例］① don't have to carry ② know how to use ③ you can shop anytime you want. You don't have to care about opening hours of stores. (16語)【別解】you can buy things that are not sold near your place. For example, you can buy things from abroad. (19語)

【解き方】①朝美のメモの「商品を運ぶ必要がない」の部分を英語で表す。「〜する必要がない」はdon't have[need] to 〜。②ケンジのメモの「インターネットの安全な使い方を知らない人もいる」の部分を英語で表す。空所後のin a safe wayは「安全な方法で」という意味で、「〜の使い方」を〈how to＋動詞の原形〉で表す。③書く内容はインターネットショッピングの長所で、becauseのあとなので〈主語＋動詞〉で表す。解答例のようにもう１文補足して10〜20語にするとよい。別解のようにFor exampleを用いて具体例を書く方法もある。ネットショッピングの長所としては、解答例の「店の営業時間を気にせずいつでも買い物ができる」や別解の「近くで売っていないもの、たとえば外国から買える」のほか、「交通費がいらない」「買った人の意見が見られる」「ネットのほうが商品の数が多い場合がある」なども考えられる。

2 ［解答例］(1) will go to Kyoto from Saga by train 【別解】are going to use trains from Saga to Kyoto (2) There are many old temples 【別解】We can see a lot of old temples (3) it is the most famous temple in Japan 【別解】it is more famous than any other temple in Japan

【解き方】(1)メモの１番目の内容を英文にする。未来の予定について述べるため、willやbe going toなどを用いる。go to A from B「BからAへ行く」(2)メモの２番目の内容を英文にする。「〜に…がある」はThere is[are] ... in 〜を使って表す。(3)メモの最後の内容を英文にする。「最も有名な〜」はthe most famous 〜や〈more famous than any other＋名詞の単数形〉で表せる。

3 ［解答例］① You must walk for forty minutes 【別解】It takes 40 minutes to walk there ② we won't go to the park 【別解】they will not have the volunteer work at the park

【解き方】① how long does it take to walk there from Tamahama Station?「玉浜駅からそこ（＝ブルーパーク）まで、徒歩でどれぐらいかかるか」への返事を書く。【広告】に、「玉浜駅から徒歩で約40分」とある。②空所前にif it rainsとあるので、雨天時について説明する。【広告】に、「ブルーパークでのボランティア活動の代わりに」とあるので、「雨天時は公園でのボランティア活動が中止になる」ことがわかる。

4 ［解答例］① I have been interested in ② read books for children in the library ③A (because) I like spending my time outdoors and moving my body. (10語) 【別解】B (because) I like reading books and spending my time with children. (10語)

【解き方】① be interested in 〜「〜に興味がある」 長い間興味があったのは、現在までの状態の継続なので現在完了で表す。② read 〜 for ...「…に〜を読む」 ③解答例は、外で過ごすことと体を動かすことが好きだからAに参加したい、別解は、本を読むことと子どもたちと過ごすのが好きなのでBに参加したいとしている。

5 (1) number of (2)［解答例］buying things on the Internet is becoming a part of our lives

【解き方】(1) the number of 〜「〜の数」(2) buy 〜 on the Internet「インターネットで〜を買う」という表現を動名詞を用いて主語にする。shopping on the Internet 〜でもよい。「〜になる」という意味のbecomeやgetは現在進行形にすると「〜になりつつある」という意味を表す。

6 ［解答例］November 15 is not good for our class because we have the school festival on that day. How about November 22?

【解き方】①の「（〜にとって）都合がつかない」はnot good for 〜などと表せる。②はほかにCan we have the meeting on November 22 instead?などと表せる。insteadは「（その）代わりに」の意味の副詞。

7 ［解答例］Your speech was great because I could learn about the festivals in your country. I learned that we must respect our local culture.

【解き方】書くべきポイントは、「あなたの国の祭りについて知ることができたので、あなたのスピーチはとてもよかった」と、「私たちは地域の文化を尊重しなければならない」の２つ。２つ目の内容はスピーチで学んだことと考えて、解答例ではI learned that 〜と表している。

8 ［解答例］Thank you for telling me about the songs which are popular among young people in Canada. I would like to send an e-mail to you, so could you please answer it?

【解き方】Thank you for 〜ing.「〜してくれてありがとう」 Could you please 〜 ?「〜してくれませんか」

9 ［解答例］(1)① What sport are you good at? 【別解】What sports can you play well? / Tell me the sport you are able to play well. ② I'm glad that our baseball team won a game for the first time yesterday. 【別解】I'm happy because my baseball team won for the first time yesterday. / Our team won the baseball game for the first time yesterday, so I'm pleased. ③ Can you join our practice next Saturday? 【別解】Why don't you take part in our practice this Saturday? / Let's practice on Saturday. (2)① My grandmother gave it to me for my birthday. 【別解】I got this violin from my grandmother as a birthday present. / It's a birthday present from my grandma. ② She teaches me how to play the violin. 【別解】I'm learning the way to play it from my grandmother. / She's my violin teacher. ③ I played the violin for my family before we had dinner yesterday. 【別解】I played it in front of my family before eating dinner yesterday. / Before dinner yesterday, I played it for my family.

【解き方】(1)①「どんなスポーツ」はwhat sport(s)やwhat kind(s) of sports。②「~ということがうれしい」は，I'm happy [glad / pleased] that[because] ~などで表せる。「初めて」は，for the first time。win「~に勝つ」の過去形はwon。③相手を誘っていると考えてWhy don't you ~?やLet's ~ .で表すこともできる。(2)①主語を祖母にするか自分にするかプレゼントにするかで動詞が変わってくる。②「弾き方」はhow to playやthe way to playと不定詞を使うとよい。③接続詞beforeを使うとやったことの順番を示せる。「家族のために」はfor my family。

10 [解答例](1)① Are you interested in Japanese culture? 【別解】Is Japanese culture interesting for you? / Do you have an interest in the culture of Japan? ② There are a lot of places to visit in Japan. 【別解】My country has many spots you should visit. / In our country, we have lots of good places to see. ③ Will you show me the pictures you took in Australia? 【別解】Can I see some photos taken in Australia? / I want you to show me a picture which was taken in your country. (2)① It's famous for Mt. Hikari. 【別解】Aozora Town has a famous mountain called Mt. Hikari. / Many people know Mt. Hikari in my town. ② If you climb it in spring, you can see many beautiful flowers. 【別解】You will find a lot of pretty flowers when you go up Mt. Hikari in the spring. / In spring, people can see lots of lovely flowers on the mountain. ③ The restaurant near Mt. Hikari is the most popular in Aozora Town. 【別解】The restaurant by the mountain is the most popular of all restaurants in the town. / The restaurant near Mt. Hikari is more popular than any other restaurant in my town.

【解き方】(1)①「~に興味がある」はbe interested in ~という熟語を使って表現できる。②「訪れる場所」は不定詞の形容詞用法を使ってa lot of places to visitとしてもいいし，関係代名詞を使ってmany spots which you should visitなどとしてもよい。この場合，whichは目的格なので省略できる。③「見せてほしい」とお願いする表現は，Will you ~?「~してくれませんか」，Can [May] I ~?「~してもいいですか」，I want [would like] you to ~「私はあなたに~してほしい」などがある。(2)①「~で有名だ」はbe famous for ~。②「あなたは春に山に登る」と「あなたは花を見ることができる」という2つの文をつなげる接続詞は，if「もし~たら」やwhen「~するとき」などが適当である。③「一番人気」は，popular「人気がある」の最上級(most popular)を使って表現するとよい。

11 [解答例](1)① It rained yesterday, so I stayed home. 【別解】I was at home because it was rainy[raining] yesterday. / I stayed at home yesterday because of (the) rain. ② I finished reading the book (that[which]) my father gave me. 【別解】I finished reading a book given by my father. / I've finished the books my father gave to me. ③ Who is your favorite author? 【別解】Can you tell me which author you like? (2)① I arrived at my house last night. 【別解】I came back here yesterday at night. / Last night, I got home. ② I learned many things through studying in Australia. 【別解】I could learn a lot of things by studying abroad. / I was able to learn a lot through studying in your country. ③ I think it's important to understand other cultures. 【別解】It's important for me to understand different culture. / In my opinion, understanding another culture is important.

【解き方】(1)①「昨日は雨が降っていた」は無生物主語のitを用いてIt rained[was raining / was rainy] yesterdayなどと表す。「~なので…」は，~, so …または…because ~と表す。別解のようにbecause of (the) rain「雨のために」としてもよい。「家で過ごした」はI stayed (at) homeやI spent time at homeなど。②「私は本を読み終えた」はI finished (reading) the book(s)。I've[have] finished ~ と現在完了でもよい。これに「父にもらった」という情報を付け加えるには，the book(s) (that[which]) my father gave (to) me「父が私にくれた本」とするとよい。目的格の関係代名詞は省略するほうが自然。父から「与えられた」という受動態で表してもよい。例：the book(s) (that[which] was) given (to me) by my father。③「あなたの好きな小説家は誰ですか」という疑問文はWho's your favorite author?。別解のCan you tell me ~?「~を教えてくれますか」では間接疑問になるので〈which + 主語 + 動詞〉の語順。(2)①「昨日の夜」はlast night。「自宅に到着した」はarrived at my house, came back home, got (back) homeなど。メールの前の文の~ in Australiaからのつながりとして「(オーストラリアではなく)日本の自宅」と考えてarrived at my house in Japanなどとしてもよい。②「留学を通じて」はthrough studying abroad [overseas]やby studying abroad「留学することによって」。ここでは具体的にはオーストラリア留学のことなので，through studying in Australia [your country]などとしてもよい。「(私は)多くのことを学んだ」はlearned many [a lot of] things。③「~だと思う」はI think (that) S V。In my opinion「私の意見では」という表現も可。「~するのは大切だ」はit is [it's] important to do，または別解のように動名詞「~すること」を主語にして表すこともできる。「異文化」はother [different] culturesやanother culture。

b．英作文

1 ［解答例］A．bought a bag
B．I want to use it for shopping
【解き方】A．Did you buy 〜?と過去形で聞かれているので，〈I bought＋もの.〉で答える。B．買ったものの詳細や，何のために買ったか，何に使うかなどを書くとよい。

2 ［解答例］問1．A．needs new members 【別解】is looking for some members / wants someone to join it　B．go to the library and read books 【別解】can play basketball in the gym / just talk with our friends in the classroom　問2．Yes, I do.を選んだ場合：I am interested in other cultures and want to communicate with people in other countries. (15語) No, I don't.を選んだ場合：I want to go to a university in Japan and study Japanese history. (13語)
【解き方】問1．A．「部員募集」は，メンバーを「必要としている」や「探している」などで表現できる。B．昼休みに昼食後にしてもいいことを書く。5語以上で書かなければならないので，どこでそれをするのかなどの情報を入れるとよい。問2．質問は「あなたは将来，外国で勉強したいですか」。

3 ［解答例］(1)① Japan has its own food culture.
② I will read books about traditional Japanese food.　(2) What school events does your school have?
【解き方】(1)①「文化」「食べ物」「季節」などが考えられる。②準備として「本やインターネットで調べる」「ポスターに情報をまとめる」などがあげられる。(2)「学校行事」「部活動」などが質問事項として考えられる。

4 ［解答例］(1)① We should study English hard every day.　② Because we can talk with many foreign people.　(2) We will sing your favorite songs in English together.
【解き方】(1)①学校で特に力を注ぐべきことなどを書く。②①についての理由を書く。(2)パーティーの催しものを英語で書く。解答例は，「私たちは，みんなで英語であなたの好きな歌を歌うつもりです」。

5 問1．A．May　B．famous　C．sure
問2．［解答例］Why don't you
問3．［解答例］(I'm sorry, but) I can't go to the concert. I have to go to the dentist.
【解き方】問1．A．日本語メモの「5月13日」を参照。B．「たくさんの有名な曲」を参照。C．「きっと知っている曲もあり」を参照して，I'm sure that 〜「きっと〜だと思います」で表す。問2．「友達や家族と来てはどうでしょうか」を参照して，Why don't you 〜?などの提案表現で表す。疑問文であることと，空所後が動詞の原形comeである点に注意。問3．I'm sorry, but 〜は「すみませんが〜」という意味で，「コンサートに行けない」はI can't go to the concert.と表せばよい。理由は，語群のhomeworkを使って，I have a lot of homework to do.「やらなければなら

ない宿題がたくさんある」なども考えられる。

6 ［解答例］(1) we can buy them〔clothes〕even late at night（8語）【別解】we don't have to go to stores to buy them〔clothes〕(10語)　(2) we can try on the clothes we want to buy (10語)【別解】shopping in stores with friends is much more fun（9語）
【解き方】(1)インターネットで服を買うことが便利であることの理由を書く。the clothes we buy on the Internet are often cheaper「インターネットで買う服のほうが安いことがよくある」などでも可。(2)店で購入するほうがインターネットで購入するよりもよい理由を書く。

7 ［解答例］① Let's make the plan together. Do you have any ideas? (10語)
② I think the mountain is better because we can enjoy climbing it together. We can make our friendship stronger there. (20語)
【解き方】①「一緒に〜しましょう」Let's 〜 together.「あなたは何か〜がありますか」Do you have any 〜?
②夏の旅行先として，「海と山のどちらがいいか」「そこで何を楽しめるか」を書く。解答例のように，I think the beach（またはthe mountain）is better because we can enjoy 〜.で表すとよい。

8 ［解答例］A．(I think) the automatic door (is convenient.) We don't have to use our hands to open it. (10語)【別解】(I think) the elevator (is convenient.) We can go to other floors fast with many people. (10語) / (I think) the shopping cart (is convenient.) We can carry many things easily even though they're heavy. (10語)　B．If you don't understand some subjects, you should ask your teachers how to study them. (15語)
【解き方】A．便利な点について，英語で説明できるものを選んで書くとよい。B．4月に中学3年に進級する生徒に対して，よりよい学校生活を送るためのアドバイスを考える。

9 ［解答例］(1) I want to be a doctor.　(2) Are you a doctor now?　Are you going to work in a foreign country someday? (15語)【別解】(1) I'd like to teach English.　(2) Did you learn English in America or in Canada?　Do you enjoy teaching English now? (15語) / (1) I am going to visit many countries.　(2) Which countries have you been to?　Can you tell me what your favorite country is? (15語)
【解き方】(1) Iを主語にして，これからの10年を見越したうえで，現在の自分の夢を書く。(2)その夢に関して，youを主語にして，10年後の自分にたずねたい質問を2つ書く。

10 ［解答例］A．We can learn some different ideas that we don't know. (10語)
B．I will pick up trash in the park because many people use it every day. (15語)
【解き方】A．解答例は「私たちが知らない，違った考え方が学べる」。「外国の文化を学べば，その文化のすばらしさがわかる」や「外国の文化を知ることで自国の文化のすばらし

さが再認識できる」などとも答えられる。B. 先生からの課題は「あなたたちに，町にとって何かよいことをしてほしいと思う。それをするのに２時間あります。あなたは何をしますか。またなぜそうするのですか。あなたの考えを書いてください」というもの。解答例は，「公園のごみを拾う」ことを提案し，理由は「毎日たくさんの人がそこを利用するから」。「近くの老人ホーム(an old people's home)に行く」ことを提案し，理由は「お年寄りの話を聞けば，彼らが喜んでくれるだろうから」などとすることもできる。

11 [解答例](1) I like sending an e-mail better. (6語)　(2) First, I think talking on the phone is more expensive. Second, Mark can read my e-mail when he has time. (20語)　【別解】(1) Talking on the phone is better. (6語)　(2) One reason is that I can tell my message quickly. The other reason is that I can hear his voice. (20語)
【解き方】(1)解答例は「私はメールを送るほうがより好きだ」，別解は「電話で話すほうがいい」という意味。(2)解答例は「第一に，電話で話すことはとても料金がかかる。第二に，マークは時間があるときに私のメールを読むことができる」，別解は「１つの理由は，自分のメッセージをすぐに伝えることができることだ。もう１つの理由は，彼の声を聞けることだ」。語数制限を守って，内容に整合性がある，文法的に正しい文を書くのが大切である。

12 We should send e-mails in Japanese because you can practice Japanese and I can help you. (16語)
【解き方】英語と日本語のどちらを提案してもよい。与えられた情報をもとに，理由が書きやすいほうを選ぶとよい。

13 [解答例](1) I want to get restaurant food. (6語)　(2) Getting restaurant food is faster than cooking at home. We can do other things like talking about Japan with Alice. (20語)　【別解】(1) Cooking at home is a better way. (7語)　(2) I can show Alice how to cook Japanese food and cook together. It'll be more exciting than getting restaurant food. (20語)
【解き方】(1)「レストランの料理を出すか」，「家で料理をするか」のどちらの立場かを自分の知っている英語を使って，端的に表現する。(2)まず，選んだ立場だと何がいいのか，何ができるのかを書き，その結果どんなふうになるのか，どんなことができるかを書くとよい。

14 [解答例]I want to sing English songs together because we can learn the sound of English.(15語)
【解き方】「私は〜したい」は，I want to do.で表現する。理由はbecauseという接続詞を使う。becauseのあとには主語と動詞を含む文を続ける。

15 [解答例]The most important thing to me is the camera that my father gave me last year. He took wonderful pictures with it. I want to become a good photographer like him. (31語)
【解き方】大切にしているものの例をいくつか考えて，そこから英文として書けそうなものを選ぶとよい。ある程度の

語数が必要なので，「大切にしている理由」「大切にしているものの説明」など，話をふくらませられるかどうかで，判断する。

16 [解答例](I would choose) A(.) If I could meet Dazai Osamu, I would ask many questions about my favorite book "Run, Melos!" Then I would like to ask him to take pictures together. (28語)
【別解】(I would choose) B(.) I wish I could see the world without war. I want to know how people in the future stopped wars. Then I want to talk about it with my friends to make a better world. (35語)
【解き方】A(歴史上の有名な人物に会う)と，B(未来に行く)のどちらの願いをかなえたいかを選び，その理由を書く。いずれも非現実的な願いなので，仮定法で書く。

17 [解答例]I liked our English classes in junior high school. I enjoyed speaking English in many activities and games. I was very happy because our teacher often gave me some good advice. (31語)
【解き方】授業，クラブ活動，生徒会活動，友達とのことなどから選ぶことができる。活動内容や楽しかったこと，頑張ったことなどを書くとよいだろう。解答例は，「私は中学校で英語の授業が好きだった。たくさんの活動やゲームで英語を話すことを楽しんだ。私たちの先生はしばしばよいアドバイスをくれたので，私はとてもうれしかった」という内容。

18 [解答例]Our field trip is my best memory. We visited the castle in our city last year. It was interesting for me to study the history of our city. (28語)
【解き方】【ブラウン先生の問いかけ】は「学校生活のすばらしい思い出がたくさんあると思います。いちばんの思い出の１つについて私に話してください」という内容。解答例は「校外見学が私のいちばんの思い出です。昨年，私たちは町にある城を訪れました。町の歴史を勉強するのは私にとって興味深いことでした」。

19 [解答例](I) agree (with Ms. Naomi Brown's idea.) First, I don't want my mother to get up early to cook my lunch. Second, I like to eat lunch at the school cafeteria while chatting with my friends. (29語)　【別解】(I) disagree (with Ms. Naomi Brown's idea.) First, I belong to the baseball club. The school lunch is too small, so I can't get enough calories. Second, lunch boxes are healthier than school lunch served at the school cafeteria. (32語)
【解き方】条件(1)に従い，agree, disagreeのいずれかを選び，条件(2)には，理由を２つ挙げることとあるので，それらを"First, 〜", "Second, 〜"などの表現を使って書く。

20 [解答例]I agree. When you want to learn foreign cultures and customs, just reading books or watching videos is not enough. Eating local food or talking to local people is great experiences. (31語)

【解き方】質問は「数日間でも外国を訪れることは，外国の文化や習慣を学ぶ効果的な方法だと思います。私に賛成ですか」。解答ではまず，賛成か反対かをI agree.やI disagree.などで簡潔に表し，理由を続ける。解答例は賛成の立場で，「賛成です。外国の文化や習慣を学ぶには，本を読んだり動画を見たりするだけでは不十分です。現地の食べ物を食べたり現地の人と話したりするのはいい経験になる」という意味。賛成の場合は，外国に行くことが効果的である理由を述べるので，日本国内ではできないことを書くと説得力があるだろう。

21 [解答例]You can enjoy taking pictures on a mountain. In autumn, many trees on a mountain become colorful. Yellow and red trees are very beautiful, so you can take good pictures.(30語)
【解き方】空所の前でスミス先生が「秋に外出するとき何を楽しめますか」と質問しており，空所後で「日本で秋に外出するのを楽しみにしています」と言っているので，秋の外出について外国人にすすめたいことを書く。解答例は「山で写真を撮るのを楽しめる。秋には山の多くの木が色鮮やかになる。黄色や赤い木はとても美しい。だからよい写真が撮れる」という内容。内容的にまとまりがあるか，具体的か，書いたあとで確認すること。

22 [解答例]You should watch Japanese movies. You can learn various Japanese words used in our daily lives. If you practice using these words with your friends, you can speak Japanese better.(30語)
【解き方】外国人に，日本語をうまく話せるようになるための助言をする。「日本語の映画を見る」「日本語を話す人と練習をする」など，うまく話せるようになるための手段をいくつか挙げ，英文として書きやすいものを選ぶとよい。

23 [解答例]I will choose A. I want to watch a Japanese baseball game with Sam. We can talk about our favorite players from our countries. We can cook Japanese food together if it rains then.(30語) **【別解】**I will choose B. I want to cook Japanese food Sam likes and enjoy eating it with him. I can't [won't] talk much if we watch sports, so we can talk more by cooking together.(30語)
【解き方】解答例はA（一緒にスポーツを観戦する）を選んで，「私はサムと野球の試合を見たい。私たちは自分の国の大好きな選手について話すことができる。そのとき雨が降ったら，一緒に日本料理を作れる」という内容。別解はB（一緒に料理をする）を選んで，「私はサムと一緒に彼が好きな日本料理を作り，それを食べるのを楽しみたい。スポーツを見ると私はあまり話せない。だから一緒に料理をすることによってより多く会話できる」という内容。

24 [解答例]Summer is the best season. In summer, we have exciting festivals. Your friend can try our traditional dance with a dance group. He can also eat many kinds of local food.
【解き方】英文から，日本に初めて来るライアンさんの友達が，自分たちの町に来るのにいちばんよい季節を知りたがっているという状況を押さえる。解答ではまず，Which is the best season?に対する直接的な答えとして，四季の

中から季節を1つ選び，〜 is the best season.やThe best season (to come here) is 〜.と書く。そしてその理由を3文以上書く。その季節特有の情報（行事や風景，できることや見られるものなど）を考えよう。情報は解答例の「お祭り」のように1つにしぼってくわしく書いてもいいし，異なる情報を複数書いてもよい。

25 [解答例]No, I don't. We have many things to do every day, such as homework and club activities. So we don't have time to learn another language. We should study only English. (31語)
【解き方】解答例の英文は反対の立場で「宿題や部活など毎日やることがたくさんあるので学ぶ外国語は英語だけでよい」という意見。

26 [解答例]My favorite thing is the baseball club. We practice three days a week after school. We visit other schools and have a baseball game several times a year. (28語)
【解き方】自分が学校生活の中で好きなことを現在形で書く。Mayのメール中の表現を利用して，one of my favorite things is 〜やI'm interested in 〜などとしてもよい。

27 [解答例]My favorite place is a library in my city. I like the library because it has a lot of interesting books. My friends and I often go there to borrow books. (31語)
【解き方】最初に好きな場所を述べ，そのあとに理由を続ける。becauseを使うほか，I have two reasons. First 〜. Second ....のように述べてもよい。

28 [解答例](I want to go to) a supermarket(.) I'm interested in unique food. Supermarkets in your country have many vegetables I've never seen in Japan. I'd like to ask you about them and learn about your food culture. (30語)
【解き方】解答例は，「私はスーパーマーケットに行きたい。私は珍しい食べ物に興味があります。あなたの国のスーパーマーケットには日本では見たことのない多くの野菜があります。私はそれらについてあなたにたずねて，あなたたちの食文化について学びたいと思います」という意味。

29 [解答例]I like November (the best). I have two reasons. First, food in fall is delicious. Second, nature in November is beautiful. I often visit parks near my house to see beautiful trees. (30(32)語)
【解き方】質問の内容は「あなたは（1年のうちで）何月がいちばん好きですか」。自分が書きやすい月を選ぶとよい。理由を書くことと，語数指定に注意する。

30 [解答例]The most important thing in my life is the camera that my father gave me on my birthday last year. My father took wonderful pictures with it, so I want to take beautiful pictures like him.(36語) **【別解】**The most important thing in my life is my family. We always help each other and talk a lot about many things. When I feel sad, they always talk to me and listen to me carefully. When they look busy, I try to help them and they thank me. That makes me happier. My family is very important to me.(60語)

【解き方】「人生で最も大事なものは何か」を、理由を含めて書く。メールにある friendship「友情」と watch「腕時計」の例を参考にするとよい。解答例は「カメラ」、別解は「私の家族」についてで、このように、The most important thing in my life is ～で書き始めるとよい。

31 [解答例] I agree with this. Activities in nature are very fun, and children learn many things by doing them. For example, if they go camping, they will enjoy looking at beautiful views, fishing or cooking with their friends. By experiencing these activities, children will learn that working together is very important.(50語)

【解き方】自然の中での活動はよいことであると考える人が多く、子供たちに自然の中で過ごす機会を与えようと、学校では子供たちを山や川などに連れて行き、博物館などの公共施設でも自然観察や農業体験の講座を開いている。こうした現状を踏まえたうえで、小学生が自然の中で過ごす時間をもっと増やすべきであるかどうかについて自分の意見を英語でまとめるのが問題。まず、賛成であるか反対であるかを述べ、そのあとでその理由を書くとよい。

32 [解答例] I want to live near mountains. I can feel the changing seasons, and there is clean air and water in a quiet environment. In summer, I can enjoy swimming in the river, and in winter, I can enjoy skiing. I want to relax in nature and eat fresh fruits.(49語)

【解き方】「あなたは、海の近くに住むのと山の近くに住むのでは、どちらのほうを好むか」という質問。解答の第1文では、海・山のどちらかを選び、want や would like、prefer を使って「～を好む」と表す。理由については、解答例を参考に、海(または山)の利点や、I can ～を使ってそこでできることなどを書くとよい。

33 [解答例] I think making an effort helps me. In my experience, I become very nervous when I don't practice or prepare well. For example, I made several mistakes in a speech contest because I didn't practice hard. However, when I practice many times with my friends, I don't become nervous. I need to practice and prepare well to overcome my nervous feeling and do my best. Making an effort encourages me to try the things I need to do to achieve my goal.

【解き方】達成するのが難しい目標があるとき、だれ、もしくは何がその困難を乗り越える手助けをしてくれるか。それがだれ、もしくは何かを書いたあと、自身の経験や具体例からそう思う理由を説明する。in my experience「私の経験では」、for example「たとえば」、however「しかしながら」などの表現を用い、論理展開のわかりやすい英文を書くこと。

34 [解答例] I think it helps us learn many things that we didn't know before. For example, by reading a book about people's lives in the old days, I can understand how they lived at that time. To know the difference between the things they had and the things we have now is interesting. In addition, by reading a book written by a sport player, I can learn what effort the player has made. It makes me become more interested in the sport. In this way, reading books helps us know new things.

【解き方】問題は「本を読むことは私たちの生活の中で重要なことで、多くの点で私たちを助けてくれると言う人がいる。読書は私たちの生活の中でどう私たちを助けてくれるか。あなたの考えを書き、その考えを支持する具体例や経験を書きなさい」という意味。まず、自分の意見を I think ～で簡潔に書く。その後、具体例は For example, ～、体験談は From my experience, ～、情報の追加は Also, ～や In addition, ～など、文頭のつなぎ言葉をうまく使って論理的な文章にしよう。最後は In this way, ～「このようにして」、For these reasons, ～「これらの理由から」、Therefore, ～「したがって」などを使って自分の意見を再確認することもできる。

35 [解答例] I want a leader to have kindness the most because if the leader is kind, other members can give their opinions easily. Last year, my soccer team lost a game, and we had a meeting on what to do for winning the next game. Then, our leader listened to everyone's opinion very carefully, and he said something nice to everyone. So, we could relax and share our feelings. After that, I felt our team became a better team with one goal. From the experience, I think a good leader needs kindness the most.

【解き方】場面設定・設問は「あなたは10人ほどの学生グループの1員だとする。各メンバーには異なる性格や意見がある。メンバーの中からリーダーを選ぶ際、リーダーにはどんな資質を最も持ってもらいたいか。下記から1つ選び(①)、その理由を書け(②)。そのあとで、理由を裏づけるために自分の経験または具体例を書け(③)」。解答の英文に①～③の3つを含めること。①②は I want a leader to have (選んだ資質) the most で書き始め、その理由を because でつなげるとよい。解答例のように、条件の「各メンバーには異なる性格や意見がある」という点を踏まえた理由になるとなおよい。③は解答例では自分の経験を書いている(Last year 以下)。①②と違って、過去の経験は過去形で表すこと。結論を書くことは求められていないが、解答例ほどの長さの意見文を書くときは、最後に再び意見(どの資質が最も重要か)を書いて文章を締めると構成がしっかりした文章になる。解答例は「その経験から、よいリーダーにはやさしさが最も必要だと思う」と締めくくっている。

ｃ．英作文（資料付き）

1 ［解答例］(1) How are you?　(2) I was looking for it.　(3) found it on a bench.
【解き方】(1)グリーン先生の I'm fine, thank you.「元気です，ありがとう」に合う質問は How are you?「お元気ですか」や How are you doing? など。(2)「腕時計をなくした。それで，<u>それを探していた</u>」→「見つかった？」の流れが適切。What were you doing there? に対し，過去進行形で答える。(3)「どこでそれ（＝腕時計）を見つけたの？」と聞かれている。絵を参考に，I found it on a bench.「私はそれをベンチの上に見つけた」などとする。

2 ［解答例］(1) I watched TV(.)　(2) Where's my cap(?)
【解き方】(1)昨日の夕食後のことをたずねられているので，主語は I，動詞は過去形で書く。(2) on the desk は my phone のある場所。It's under the chair. に続くように，帽子のある場所をたずねるのが自然。

3 ［解答例］① must not eat or drink there　② are thirsty in the building　【別解】① can't eat or drink in the building　② feel hungry or thirsty there
【解き方】5語以上という指示に注意。①「飲食禁止」は，「（あなたは）そこで食べたり飲んだりしてはいけない」や「建物の中では，食べたり飲んだりできない」と表せる。②外に出たほうがいいのは，どんなときか。thirsty は必ず使うとあるので，「建物内でのどがかわいた（とき）」や「そこで，おなかがすいたり，のどがかわいた（とき）」とする。

4 ［解答例］(You should buy) X (because) it is bigger than Y. You can carry a lot of things in the bag. Also, you don't have to worry about the things in the bag if it starts to rain. (32語)
【解き方】リンダにすすめる方を選び，その理由（よい点など）を2つ書く。Xのよい点として，「大きい」，「防水」，「50％の割引」などが考えられる。Yのよい点として，「軽い」，「安い」，「小さくてかわいい」などが考えられる。

5 ［解答例］(1) It's July 4.　(2) It's nice.
【解き方】(1)「誕生日はいつですか」の答えを書く。It is のあとに月，日を順に書く。解答例は「7月4日」。(2)「この歌をどう思いますか」の答えを書く。It is のあとに続ける。解答例は「すてきだね」。

6 ［解答例］(1) How is the weather in Kyoto?　(2) Where are you going to visit today?　(3) What time will you leave Kyoto?
【解き方】(1)レオが It's sunny here. と答えているから，京都の天候を聞いている。(2)レオが，今日，訪れる場所を答えている。(3)「2時」と答えているから，京都を出発する時刻［新幹線の出発時刻］を聞いている。What time ～「何時に～」　leave Kyoto「京都を出発する」

7 ［解答例］(1) have time　(2) I should go to bed by ten and get up early to have breakfast.
【解き方】(1)「おなかがすいている」のあとに，「食事をする時間がなかった」と続くのが自然。(2)③で眠い理由を聞かれ，④で理由を説明しているが，⑤の You should.「そうすべきね」という応答なので，空所Bには「これからは～しなければ」という決意の表現を I should から始めて示すのが適切。イラストでは，「10時には寝て，朝は早く起きて朝食を食べる」ことが示されている。

8 ［解答例］A. I won the game　B. make many friends and enjoy our school life together　C. you should visit some of them
【解き方】A. 昨日起こったうれしいこととして，上の吹き出しに海斗がバドミントンのラケットとトロフィーを手に持っている様子が描かれている。解答例の「昨日，僕は（バドミントンの）試合に勝った」や，I won a badminton tournament「トーナメント戦で優勝した」などが考えられる。試合は match でもよい。B. 日本の部活動のよい点を考えて書く。C.「僕たちの学校にはクラブがたくさんあるので，～」に続く内容を考える。解答例のほか，you can try one you are interested in「きみが興味のあるものに挑戦できるよ」など。

9 ［解答例］③ Where did you go in Tokyo(?)　【別解】What did you do there(?)　⑦ I'll drink it tonight(.)　【別解】I have never had it(.)　⑧ Can I borrow the book you bought in Tokyo(?)　【別解】Will you tell me about it(?)
【解き方】③話題は達也の東京旅行で，④で宇宙博物館に行って何をしたかを答えていることから考える。⑦おみやげに Space Tea をもらったジョージは何と言うか。Thank you. と続くので，Space Tea に関する内容にする。⑧「僕も宇宙に関心を持った」のあとに何と言うか。達也の Of course.「もちろん，いいよ」に合うよう，宇宙に関するお願い・提案・誘いなどの表現を入れるのがよい。

10 ［解答例］Do you know which bus goes to
【解き方】女性は Yes, I do. と答えているので，空所を含む文は，Do you で始まる疑問文だと判断できる。また，空所前後の英文から，ケイコは「（3台のバスのうち）どのバスが ABC 公園に行くのか」をたずねていると推測できる。

11 ［解答例］How long did it take to
【解き方】Cの場面で，ユキコが「2時間」と答えていることから，空所を含むレイカの質問は，「電車とバスを利用した場合は，そこに到着するのに<u>どれぐらい時間がかかったか</u>」という内容だとわかる。

12 ［解答例］ア. I want to watch the dance performances
イ. Let's watch the shamisen performance and the dance performance in the afternoon (12語)
【解き方】2人のやり取りをもとに，明子の発言を考える。ア. 空所前後のやり取りから，明子は友人が参加する公演を見たいのだと推測できる。空所後の発言から，友人のグループは，午前と午後に1回ずつ公演を行うことがわかる

ので，このグループはダンスの公演を行うことがわかる。
イ. 前問から，「明子はダンス公演が見たい」ことがわかっ
ているが，エマの3番目の発言に「雨にぬれたくない」とあり，
天気予報では，午前のダンス公演の時間帯は降水確率が高
い。また，エマの2番目の発言から，「エマは三味線（しゃみ
せん）の公演を見たい」ことがわかる。これらを踏まえて，エマの
OK. に合うよう，Let's 〜. などを用いて提案する。

13 (1)① more students study[studied]Japanese
② the most popular in
(2)[解答例]In February, we have an event called
setsubun. We throw beans and we eat them.(15語)
【解き方】(1)①スライド1を見ると2016年より2019年のほ
うが，日本語を勉強する生徒が多い。②スライド2から，伝
統行事はいちばん人気があるとわかる。(2)解答例は「2月
に節分という行事がある。私たちは豆を投げ，それを食べ
る」という意味。

14 [解答例](1)A. Which volunteer work is the
most popular?　B. What questions can we
ask them?
(2) I think they should. It is because they can do
something to help people and make people happy.
Also, they can make friends with people outside
school. (27語)
【解き方】(1)A. 次にジュンが「公園や道路の清掃だ」と答え
ている。アンケート結果では37%で1位なので，ベンは「い
ちばん人気のあるボランティア活動は何ですか」と質問し
ている。the most popular「いちばん人気がある」　B. ベ
ンが「彼らにこういう質問ができる」と例を挙げて答えてい
るので，ジュンは「彼らにどんな質問ができるだろうか」と
質問している。(2)中学生はボランティア活動をすべきかど
うかについて自分の意見を書く。次にその答えの理由とな
る自分の考えを書く。解答例は「賛成である。理由は人を
助けて幸せにできることと，自分も学校外に友達ができる
から」。

15 [解答例]④ Which one is the best(?)　【別解】
Will you show me the most popular one(?)
⑧ I learned a lot about Mozart(.)　【別解】The CD
was great(.)　⑪ Let's go together next time(.)　【別
解】I want to go with you(.)
【解き方】④状況を確認する。「本がたくさんある」と言う
ウェンディに，友子は「これはどう？」と1冊の本を提案し
ている。おすすめの本をたずねる表現を入れるとよい。⑧
昨日買った本について話が進んでいる。ウェンディは，本
を楽しんだので，その本について，肯定的な感想や説明を
書くとよい。⑪空所前で，友子は「クラシックのコンサート
によく行く」と話し，ウェンディは「それはいいね」と答えて
いる。「一緒に行きたい」など，流れに合う内容を考える。

16 [解答例]I want to go to ABC Hotel, but I don't
know where I am now. Could you tell me the
way to get there, please? (25語)　【別解】May I ask
you a question? I am looking for ABC Hotel. Is it
near here? Would you show me how I can get
there? (25語)
【解き方】ミホはホテルへの行き方を知りたい様子である
ことがわかる。解答例は，「ABCホテルに行きたいのです

が，現在地[今，私がどこにいるのか]がわかりません。そ
こへの行き方を教えてくださいませんか」という意味。
Could[Would] you show[tell] me the way[how] to
get 〜?は，道順をたずねるときによく使われる表現。別解
は，「おたずねしたいのですが。私はABCホテルを探して
います。それはこの近くですか。そこへの行き方を教えて
くださいませんか」という意味。look for 〜「〜を探す」
how I can get there「どのようにそこに行くか，そこへの
行き方」

17 [解答例]I think it is important for children to
study. I learn many useful things at school
every day. I want to learn a lot about this problem
and think about how to help them. (34語)
【解き方】世界には学校に行けない子供が1億2,100万人以
上いる。この問題についてどう思うかを書く。解答例では
学校で学ぶことの重要性を書いているが，黒板に書かれた
学校に行けない理由「働かなければならない」「学校がなく，
先生もいない」を利用してもよいし，問題の解決策を書いて
もよいだろう。

18 [解答例]I'm sorry. When we were playing
soccer in my yard, our soccer ball went into
your yard. Will you get and bring it for us? (25語)
【別解】Our ball flew into your yard when we were
playing soccer in my yard. It's in the tree. Can I go
in and get it? (25語)
【解き方】ケンタが家の庭で友達とサッカーをしていて
蹴ったボールがアレンさんの庭に入ってしまったので，そ
のおわびを言い，ボールを取ってもらう表現を考える。2，
3文で書けば，指定の25語でまとめられる。「木の上にボー
ルがのっかった」と言う場合は，on the treeでなく，in the
treeとすることに注意。

19 [解答例](1) (Actually,) most high school students
have smartphones(.)
(2) (〜, or we can) get some information we need(.)
(3) I think we shouldn't use our smartphones for
many hours. We forget the time easily and don't
have enough time to do other things. (24語)
【解き方】(1)「資料からわかること」は，「高校生のほとんど
がスマートフォンを持っている」ということ。(2)できること
は，前文で「ほかの人とコミュニケーションがとれる」と
書いてあるので，それ以外の用途を書く。解答例は「必要な
情報を入手できる」。(3)解答例は「私たちはスマートフォン
を長時間も使うべきではないと思う。簡単に時間を忘れ，
ほかのことをする時間がなくなってしまう」という内容。

20 [解答例]問1. Mr. Brown is twenty-five years
old. He comes from Canada.【別解】Mr. Brown
likes watching baseball games. His birthday month
is March.　問2. What sports do you play? When
did you come to Japan?【別解】Where do you want to
go in Japan?　Who is your favorite singer?　問3. I
think you will like Okinawan Nature Tour because
the beach is really beautiful and you will be able to
enjoy swimming. It costs 1,000 yen for six hours,
and it finishes at noon.【別解】I think you should
choose Okinawan Food Tour because cooking

Okinawan food will be a good experience. You will also have a chance to shop at the farmers' market.

【解き方】問1. 与えられたメモの情報を用いて2文を答える。必ずしも情報のすべてを使う必要はない。問2. 与えられた条件から疑問詞で始まる疑問文を2つ答える。〈疑問詞＋doなどの助動詞＋you＋動詞の原形〉の語順に注意したい。問3. 「すすめる」という動詞にこだわると難しい。I think you will like AやI think that you should do の形を使うとよい。条件にあるように, どちらのツアーをすすめたいかわかるように書く。また, そのツアーをすすめる具体的な理由を書く。答えは2文以内にする。

21

[解答例]問1. ① Where is it [Mt. Daisen](?) ② What will you do(?)【別解】Which do you want to choose(?) 問2. I want to clean the park near my house because it will make the park nicer for people to enjoy. (20語)

【解き方】問1. ①かずおが「鳥取県の西部にあるよ」と答えているので, 場所をたずねる疑問文を作る。②かずおが「乗馬とハイキングをするよ」と答えているので, 何をするつもりかたずねる疑問文を作る。問2. どんな種類のボランティア活動をしたいかという問いに対する答えを書く。理由にはbecauseを使うとよいが, becauseの前にピリオドを置いて, Because 〜 . と文を独立させてはならないことに注意。

22

[解答例]I think you should take an airplane. You can get there in less than an hour. Besides, you can get up later and pack your bag on the day you leave, and this can be more relaxing.【別解】I think you should choose a trip in a ship. If you take a ship, you can enjoy nice lunch and a beautiful ocean view, too. In addition, you have to pay only 4,000 yen, and this is a reasonable price.

【解き方】まず, 与えられた書き出しにうまく続け, 飛行機と船のどちらの移動方法をすすめるかを書く。次に, 所要時間, 便数, 運賃などから理由を2つ書く。それぞれの移動日の過ごし方や, 空からの景色, 海の景色が楽しめることなどもイラストから推測できる。

23

[解答例](1)A. How many students answered the question? B. What did you find? (2) I usually use social media because I can receive the news of the world quickly on my mobile phone. I can also watch videos about the news. (27語)

【解き方】(1)A. 空所の直後に「356人の生徒がした」とある。アンケート結果を見ると, 「回答人数　356人」とある。「何人の生徒がその質問に答えたか」という意味の英文を入れるとよい。B. 空所の直後で, ヒロシは「彼らの88%はテレビを見ていることがわかった」と, アンケート結果からわかったことを答えている。「(アンケート結果から)何がわかったか」という意味の英文を入れるとよい。(2)質問は, 「いつもは, どのようにしてニュースを得ているか」という意味。本文中に, ニュース情報を得る手段の例が挙げられているので, この中から理由が書きやすいものを選ぶとよい。解答例は「携帯電話ですばやく世界のニュースを受け取ることができるから, 私はふだんソーシャルメディアを使う。そのニュースについて動画を見ることもできる」という意味。

24

[解答例](I think) A (is better.) Toyama has many places to visit. For example, we can see the Kurobe Dam. We can also see the Takaoka Daibutsu. Both are big and wonderful. I think foreign people can enjoy them. (33語)【別解】(I think) B (is better.) Toyama has a lot of good food. Toyama is especially famous for sushi because we can get fresh fish all year. I think foreign people can enjoy eating it. (29語)

【解き方】二重下線にAかBを忘れず記入し, 選んだ理由を書く。Aのポスターには観光名所が描かれているので, 解答例はToyama has many places to visit. で始め, その例を2つ挙げ, 最後の文でI think 〜 can enjoy them. とまとめている。Bのポスターにはスイカやカニといった名産品が描かれている。別解ではToyama has a lot of good food. で始め, 1年じゅう新鮮な魚がとれるので, すしが特に有名だ, と例を挙げている。そして, I think 〜 can enjoy eating it. とまとめている。

25

[解答例]問1. ① What did you do(?) ② How many cats does he have(?) 問2. It is difficult for my grandmother to carry heavy things, so I want a robot that will help her. (19語)

【解き方】問1. ①土曜日と日曜日に何をしたかを答えているので, 「あなたは何をしましたか」とする。②「彼は猫をたくさん飼っている」→「彼は何匹の猫を飼っているのですか」→「5匹」の流れ。問2. どんなロボットがほしいか, そのロボットでどんな問題を解決したいか, の2点を含むこと。ほしいロボットを先に書いて, because SV「(なぜなら)〜だから」でつなげてもよい。

26

[解答例]I found a crying girl. She said she couldn't find her father. So I took her to the police station. Then, her father came. Finally, she met her father. We were very happy. (33語)

【解き方】ヒカリになったつもりで書くので, 主語をIにする。以下の内容を簡単な英語で書く。1. 「泣いている女の子に会った。その子は父親がいなくて泣いていた」　2. 「その子を警察(police station)に連れて行った」　3. 「そこに父親が来た」　4. 「ついにその女の子は父親に会えた。みんなうれしかった」

27

[解答例]don't buy plastic bags at stores. They bring their own bags when they go shopping. This is good because we don't have to use too much plastic. I think many people got plastic bags they didn't need before. (38語)

【解き方】まず, グラフから, レジ袋を有料化したあと, レジ袋を断った人が大幅に増えたことを読み取ろう。ワークシートを読むと, 以前無料だったレジ袋が, 今は有料であることが書かれている。「今, 多くの人は〜」という書き出しなので, まずはグラフを踏まえて「レジ袋を断る」という内容を続け, その後, レジ袋を買わない理由や, その結果どうなるかなどを書くとよい。

28

[解答例](I want to take Class) A. I want to practice speaking English with other students because I can enjoy English more with my friends. In Class B, I can only talk with the teacher

in English. (30語)【別解】(I want to take Class) B. I play soccer on a team after school on Friday, so I can't practice English in Class A. I like Class B better because I'm free at night after dinner. (30語)
【解き方】提示されたものには，日時，場所，形式の違いがあるので，それらと自分の生活や考え方と比較して書く内容を決める。内容はその理由がはっきりしているものを選ぶのがよい。まず，AかBを選び，そのクラスを受けたい理由を書き，そのあとでもう１つのクラスの欠点や選べない理由を付け加えるとよい。

29 (A) drinking　(B) washing our hands
(C)[解答例] can get water easily and study at school. However, there are children who cannot go to school in some countries. They have to walk for many hours to get water, so they don't have time to study at school. (39語)
【解き方】(A)(B)「私たちには(A)や(B)などのために清潔で安全な水が必要だ」という意味の文で，for のあとには名詞や動名詞を続ける。Picture A と Picture B を参照し，drinking「飲むこと」と washing our hands「手を洗うこと」を入れるとよい。(C)両者の主な違いは，日本の子供が学校に行っている間，水が手に入りにくい国々の子供たちは水くみのため学校に行けないこと。与えられた書き出しは In Japan, we なのでまず日本について書く。そして However「しかしながら」などを用いて「水が手に入りにくい国々の子供たち」について書く。解答例の第３文「彼らは水を得るのに何時間も歩かなければならないため，学校で勉強する時間がない」は，They can't go to school because it takes many hours to get clean and safe water.「彼らは清潔で安全な水を得るのに何時間もかかるので学校に行くことができない」などの表現も可能。

d．整序英作文

1 (1) エ→イ→ア→ウ　(2) ウ→イ→エ→ア
【解き方】(1) as ～ as ...「…と同じぐらい～だ」among は「～の間で」という意味。(2) call A B で，「AをBと呼ぶ」という意味。in Japanese「日本語で」

2 (1) wish he could stay longer
(2) What is this flower called
【解き方】(1)〈I wish＋主語＋過去形の(助)動詞～〉「～ならいいのに」　現在の事実に反する願望を表す。完成した英文の意味は「彼がもっと長くいられればいいのに」。(2) call A B「AをBと呼ぶ」の受動態の疑問文。「この花は英語で何と呼ばれていますか」

3 (1) to learn how to cook
(2) wish I had P.E. class every
【解き方】(1) to learn「学ぶために」　不定詞の副詞用法。〈how to＋動詞の原形〉で，「～の仕方」という意味。(2)仮定法過去の文。〈I wish＋主語＋動詞の過去形〉で，「～であればなあ」という意味。現在の事実と違う願望を表す。

4 (1) エ→イ→ウ→ア　(2) エ→イ→ア→ウ
(3) イ→ア→ウ→オ→エ
【解き方】(1) not as ～ as ...「…ほど～でない」　(2)主語は so many stars「とても多くの星」で，動詞は受動態 can be seen になる。(3)「５歳のときから柔道をやっている」を現在完了進行形 have been ～ ing で表す。

5 it will show you what
【解き方】Aの発言は「この防災セットに何を入れればいいかわかる？」　答えは (I think) it will show you what (you should put.)「それが何を入れるべきか教えてくれると思う」it は直前の this list「このリスト，一覧」を指す。〈show＋人＋もの〉で「(人)に(もの)を教える，示す」「もの」にあたる部分に what you should put という間接疑問の形が来ている。

6 give some presents to him
【解き方】「私たちは彼にいくつかプレゼントをあげます」〈give＋もの＋to＋人〉「(人)に(もの)をあげる」

7 (1) tell him to call you
(2) What will the weather be like
【解き方】(1)「あなたに電話をかけ直すように，彼に言っておきます」　(2)「明日はどんな天気になるだろうか」

8 問１．ア→イ→オ→エ→ウ　問２．エ→ア→オ→イ→ウ　問３．エ→イ→ア→ウ→オ
【解き方】問１．be good at ～「～が得意だ」　問２．〈It is difficult for A to＋動詞の原形〉「～するのはAにとって難

しい」　問3. because it's raining「雨が降っているから」

9 (Oh, it is) a temple which was built (three hundred years ago.)
【解き方】「それは，300年前に建てられた寺だ」　関係代名詞which（主格）を使ってa templeを説明する。

10 (1)エ→ウ→イ→ア　(2)ウ→ア→イ→エ
【解き方】(1) (Do you) know when she'll get (to the station?)「あなたは彼女がいつ駅に着くか知っていますか」　(2) (I'll) bring it to you (tomorrow.)「明日それをあなたのところに持って行ってあげましょう」　bring *A* to *B*「AをBに持って行く」

11 (1)ウ→イ→エ→ア　(2)エ→ウ→ア→イ
(3)イ→ア→オ→エ→ウ
【解き方】(1) (Shall we) meet in front of (the station?) Shall we ～?「～しましょうか」　in front of ～「～の前で」　(2) (My mother) wants me to come (home early today.) 〈want＋人＋to *do*〉「（人）に～してもらいたいと思う」　(3) (The boy) playing tennis in the park is (my brother.)　playing tennis in the parkはThe boyを修飾する現在分詞句。

12 (1) When will you come back
(2) named it Shiro after its
【解き方】(1)疑問詞whenが最初で未来を表す助動詞willが続く。「あなたはいつ日本に戻ってきますか」　(2) named it Shiro「それをシロと名づけた」　after its color「その色にちなんで」　name *A B* after *C*は「Cにちなんで，AをBと名づける」の意味。

13 (1) long have you been playing
(2) was written by a famous writer
【解き方】(1)「そのビデオゲームをどのくらいやっているの?」　How long ～?「どのくらいの（時間・長さ）か」　現在完了進行形。have been ～ing「ずっと～し続けている」　(2)「それは有名な作家によって書かれた」　受動態。was written by ～「～によって書かれた」

14 1. how long have you been
2. you some pictures of it
【解き方】1. トムの応答「4時間以上」から，「どのくらいの間それを読んでいるの?」という文を作る。how longで始め，現在完了進行形〈have been ～ing〉の疑問文を続ける。2. 語群のitはthe baby lionを指す。「あなたにそれ（＝ライオンの赤ちゃん）の写真を何枚か見せましょう」という文を作る。〈show＋人＋もの〉「（人）に（もの）を見せる」

15 問1. ウ→エ→ア→オ→イ　問2. オ→ア→ウ→イ→エ　問3. ウ→ア→オ→イ→エ
【解き方】問1. (Do you remember) when our school festival was held (last year?)「昨年いつ，うちの学校の文化祭が行われたかを覚えていますか」　間接疑問の語順に注意。問2. (My mother) told me to come back (by 6 p.m.)「母は私に6時までにうちに帰って来なさいと言っ

た」　〈tell＋人＋to *do*〉「（人）に～するように言う」　問3. (This) is the camera my father gave me (on my birthday.)「これは父が私の誕生日にくれたカメラです」　my father gave meがthe cameraを修飾する形。「父が私にくれたカメラ」

16 (1)ウ→イ→エ→ア　(2)エ→イ→ア→ウ
(3)イ→オ→ア→エ→ウ
【解き方】(1) (My plan) is to go shopping (with my sister.)「私の計画は姉[妹]と一緒に買い物に行くことだ」　(2) (This is) the most interesting movie (that I have ever watched.)「これは，私が今まで見た中で最もおもしろい映画だ」　(3) (Do you) know the boy who is drinking (coffee over there?)「あそこでコーヒーを飲んでいる少年を知っているか」

17 (1) are taught in　(2) you show me some
(3) who wears a cap and has a book
【解き方】(1)「私の国では，2つの言語が教えられている」　受動態。(2)「いくつか見せてもらえますか」　show *A B*「AにBを見せる」　第4文型。(3)「彼女は帽子をかぶっていて，手に本を持っている女の子だ」　最後のin her handの直前はhas a bookであるべき。whoは主格の関係代名詞。

18 (1) (Do) you usually get up so early(?)
(2) I don't think she can come(.)
(3) I wish I lived in Hyogo(.)
【解き方】(1)朝5時30分に起きたと言う相手に対し，「あなたはいつもそんなに早く起きるのですか」とする。「いいえ，今日だけです」とあとの流れにも合う。(2)「リオも私と一緒に行くか聞いてもいい?」に対し，「彼女は来ることができないと思う」とする。「私は～ないと思う」はI don't think SVの語順。(3)「私は兵庫に住んでいたらいいのに」　〈I wish I＋動詞の過去形〉（仮定法過去）は，非現実的な現在の願望を表す。

19 問1. ア→ウ→オ→イ→エ　問2. イ→オ→ア→ウ→エ　問3. エ→ウ→ア→オ→イ
【解き方】問1. We don't have to clean (our classroom in America.)　don't have to *do*「～しなくてもよい」　問2. (Oh, how) long are you going to stay (here?)　how longは期間をたずねる疑問文。問3. (Did you know) English and French are spoken in Canada(?)　know (that) ～「～だと知っている」　受動態は〈be動詞＋過去分詞〉。

20 (1) know when he will arrive
(2) you want him to call
【解き方】(1)「私は彼がいつ到着するのかを知らない」　〈when＋主語＋動詞〉は間接疑問で名詞節になっている。主語と動詞の語順に注意。(2)「彼に電話をかけ直してほしいですか」　〈want＋人＋to *do*〉「（人）に～してほしいと思う」

21 (1)X. ア　Y. イ　Z. エ
(2)X. エ　Y. ウ　Z. ア
【解き方】(1) I stayed at home and helped my sister

finish (her homework.)「家にいて妹が宿題を終わらせる
のを手伝った」〈help＋O＋動詞の原形〉「Oが〜するのを
手伝う」(2)(I want to) know which shirt you will
buy (for Jim.)「あなたがジムにどのシャツを買うか知り
たい」 間接疑問は，〈疑問詞＋S V〉の語順で，疑問詞に
which shirtがくる形。

22 (1)X. イ Y. ウ Z. ア
(2)X. オ Y. カ Z. ア
【解き方】(1)(I think Kyoto) is the most popular of
the three (cities.) ＜the＋最上級＋of the＋名詞の複数
形＞「〜の中で最も…だ」(2)(We) can't get there
without a map of (this city.) can't do without「〜な
しには…できない」

23 (1)X. ア Y. エ Z. オ
(2)X. ウ Y. オ Z. ア
【解き方】(1)(I) have been looking for the book which
(I borrowed.)「私は借りた本をずっと探しています」 現
在完了進行形の文。「(ずっと)〜し続けている」(2)Do
you think your father can use (this computer?)「あなた
は，あなたのお父さんはこのコンピューターを使うこと
ができると思いますか」

24 (1)you join us (2)me something to drink
(3)The pen I am looking for must
【解き方】(1)Why don't you 〜?は人を何かに誘うときに
用いる表現で，「〜しませんか」。(2)〈give＋人＋もの〉で
「(人)に(もの)を与える」。something to drinkは「何か飲
み物」。(3)「私が探しているペンは私の部屋にあるにちがい
ない」という意味になる文を作る。penとIの間に関係代名
詞の目的格が省略されている。

25 (1)What sport do you play(?)
(2)I cannot sing as well as (Yasuo.)
(3)(Actually) my friend helped me finish it(.)
【解き方】(1)「あなたは何のスポーツをしますか」(2)「私は
ヤスオほど上手に歌うことはできない」(3)「私の友人がそ
れを終わらせるのを手伝ってくれた」〈help＋人＋動詞
の原形〉で，「(人)が〜するのを手伝う」という意味。

26 (3番目，5番目の順に)(ア)3，6 (イ)3，4 (ウ)1，
3 (エ)6，5
【解き方】(ア)(Is) there anything I should bring(?)「私
が持っていくべきものはあるか」 I should bring が
anythingを後置修飾している。(イ)(Please tell) me
when you will come (back home.)「いつ帰宅するのか
教えてください」 間接疑問を含む文。(ウ)(Eri,) do we
have any milk (left in the bottle?)「エリ，びんの中に牛
乳は残っていますか」 過去分詞left以降がmilkを後置修
飾している。(エ)(Don't) be afraid of asking questions
(〜.)「わからないことがあるなら，質問をすることを恐れ
てはいけない」 be afraid of 〜ingで，「〜することを恐
れる」という意味。

27 (3番目，5番目の順に)(ア)4，3 (イ)6，2 (ウ)3，
1 (エ)3，6
【解き方】(ア)(English is) spoken by many people as
(their first language.)「英語は第1言語として多くの
人々に話されている」 usesが不要。(イ)(What) did you
want to be (when you were a child?)「子供のころは何
になりたかったですか」 workが不要。(ウ)(〜, but I
can't) decide which one I should (buy.)「〜だが，どれ
を買うべきか決められない」 toが不要。(エ)(But I) wish
I were better at (playing it.)「しかし，私はそれをもっと
上手に弾けたらなあ」 仮定法過去の文。couldが不要。be
good at 〜ing「〜するのが上手だ」の比較級。

28 (3番目，5番目の順に)(ア)1，3 (イ)6，2 (ウ)5，
4 (エ)4，1
【解き方】(ア)(Who is) the best tennis player of (the
five?)「5人の中でだれが最もすぐれたテニス選手ですか」
inが不要。(イ)(Do you know the) girl playing the
guitar and (singing over there?)「向こうでギターを弾
いて歌っている女の子を知っていますか」 beenが不要。
playing 〜とsinging 〜の2つが前の名詞the girlを後ろ
から修飾している。(ウ)(Because it) is written through
the eyes (of a little dog.)「それは小犬の目を通して書か
れているからです」 readingが不要。(エ)(Do you) want
me to open that (door?)「私にあのドアを開けてもらいた
いですか[あのドアを開けてあげましょうか]」 thinkが
不要。〈want＋人＋to do〉「(人)に〜してもらいたいと思
う」

29 ①オ→カ→ア→イ→エ ②ウ→オ→イ→カ→エ
③エ→オ→ア→カ→ウ ④エ→ウ→カ→ア→オ
【解き方】① (If I) were you, I would choose wearing a
yukata(.)の語順。仮定法過去の文。If I were you, I
would 〜「もし私があなたなら〜するだろう」。続く「伝統
的な服を着て」は浴衣(ゆかた)のことなので，ウではなくエを選
ぶ。② (The staff members) will show you how to
paint on (a wind chime.)の語順。show A how to do「A
に〜の仕方を教える」 ③ Why don't you paint on a
wind chime (in the morning?)の語順。Why don't you
〜?「〜してはどうですか」 両方の体験ができるように，午
前中に風鈴の絵付け，午後に浴衣を着てはどうかと提案し
ている。④ (I don't) want to make my *yukata* dirty(.)
の語順。「私は浴衣を汚したくない」という意味。make O
C「OをCにする」

30 ①エ→オ→ウ→イ→カ ②オ→ウ→カ→エ→ア
③エ→ア→カ→イ→オ ④ウ→ア→エ→イ→カ
【解き方】①疑問詞で始まる文。Which museum do you
want to visit？ howが不要。②〈there are＋名詞の複
数形〉の文型。(Yes, because) there are many pictures
drawn by famous cartoonists (in this museum.)
takenが不要。③ Aoi Science Museumのポスターに，
「エネルギー問題について考える」とある。(Because we
can learn many things about) energy problems that
we have to solve(.) the amazing oceanが不要。④所
要時間を表す言い方。(Oh, also,) it takes only 5
minutes to walk from (Aoi Station to the museum.)
only 20 minutesが不要。

31 問1．①(X)ウ　(Y)イ　②(X)オ　(Y)ア　③(X)オ　(Y)エ
問2．[解答例]I could have a cat　【別解】to have a cat

【解き方】問1．① That helped me feel better.「それは私がよりよい気分になるのを助けた」〈help＋O＋動詞の原形〉「Oが〜するのを助ける」　② She is waiting for me in front of my house.「彼女は私の家の前で私を待っている」　現在進行形の文。ここでの「彼女」はキャシーの飼い猫。wait for 〜「〜を待つ」　in front of 〜「〜の前で」　③ I want my father to know 〜.「私は父にペットも家族の一員になり得ると知ってもらいたいと思う」〈want＋O＋to *do*〉「Oに〜してもらいたいと思う」　問2．キャシーが飼っている猫の話を聞いて，「私も猫を飼えたならいいのに」という文が適切。空所後に「しかし飼えない。実は，父が動物を好きではない」と続いていることに注目。〈I wish＋主語＋(助)動詞の過去形〜〉は，「〜が…ならいいのに」と実現不可能な願望を表す。別解のようにwish to *do*「〜するのを願う」を用いてもよい。

第4章 リスニング問題

a. 5W1H について問われる問題

1 イ
【解き方】友達と勉強していてわからない単語があった。その意味を知りたいときにその友達に対して言う言葉。イ「きみの辞書使ってもいい？」が適切。

放送内容

You are studying English with your friend. You want to know the meaning of a word.
Question : What will you say to your friend?

2 No.1 イ No.2 エ
【解き方】No.1 最初のアレックスの発言Are you going to do anything this weekend?を聞き取る。No.2 エミの発言Our dance starts at 11:15.とIt will be about 10 minutes.を聞き取る。

放送内容

No.1
Alex : Are you going to do anything this weekend?
Maya : Maybe I'll just watch movies at home. How about you?
Alex : If it is sunny on Sunday, my brother and I will go to see a baseball game.
Maya : That's nice.
No.2
Mr. Brown : Hi, Emi. I heard your dance will start at 11:00.
Emi : No, actually the first dance group starts at 11:00. Our dance starts at 11:15.
Mr. Brown : OK. How long will it be?
Emi : It will be about 10 minutes.

3 1番 イ 2番 ア 3番 エ
【解き方】1番 タロウは最初の発言でLiving with pets is good for our health.と言っている。2番 ハナコが2回目の発言でSome people give up keeping their pets.と言っている。3番 ハナコが最後の発言でWe should try to do the things our pets need when we live together.と言い、タロウも最後にI think so, too.と応じている。エ「彼らは、みんながペットにやさしくすることを望んでいる」が適切。

放送内容

Hanako : I have two cats. They're so cute. I enjoy living with them. They always make me happy. Living with pets is good for people's minds.
Taro : I take a walk with my dog every day and play in the park. Living with pets is good for our health.
Hanako : I heard some sad news about having pets. Some people give up keeping their pets.
Taro : I'm sorry to hear that. I think pets are members of our family. We should give food to them and take them to the hospital when they are sick.
Hanako : You are right. We should try to do the things our pets need when we live together.
Taro : I think so, too.
　1番 What does Taro think about his pet?
　2番 What news did Hanako hear?
　3番 What do Hanako and Taro hope?

4 No.1 ウ No.2 ア No.3 イ
【解き方】No.1 美佐の1番目の発言を聞き取る。No.2 美佐の3番目の発言を聞き取る。No.3 父と母に加え、最後の美佐と店員とのやりとりから妹[姉]にも買うことがわかる。

放送内容

店員 : May I help you?
美佐 : I'm looking for something to give to my family in Japan.
店員 : Oh, we have T-shirts in many different colors.
美佐 : Well, my father likes green, but this green T-shirt is too small for him.
店員 : I'm sorry, but we only have a bigger one in orange, red, and yellow. This summer orange is very popular.
美佐 : Well, then, I'll get the orange one for him and the green one for my mother.
店員 : Good. Do you want anything else?
美佐 : If you have a smaller one in yellow, I'll buy it for my sister.
店員 : OK, we have one.
　No.1 Why did Misa come to the shop?
　No.2 What color did Misa choose for her father's T-shirt?
　No.3 How many T-shirts will Misa buy?

5 (1) 1. イ 2. ア 3. ウ 4. ア
【解き方】(1) 1. 11月24日(火)の前日。2. 「あなたの辞書を使ってもいいですか」とたずねられ、了承するときの応答。Here you are.「はい、どうぞ」 3. バスケットボールは野球とバレーボールより人気。テニスはバスケットボールより人気。4. Betty asked her brother to come there with herとあり、ベティーは兄に美術館に付き添ってくれるように頼んだことがわかる。

放送内容

1. Today is Tuesday, November 24. My sister Yuzuki went to Kyoto yesterday.
Question : When did Yuzuki go to Kyoto?
2. You are doing homework with Hiroki. He says to you, "Can I use your dictionary?"
Question : What will you say to Hiroki if you want him to use your dictionary?
3. Yamato asked his classmates about their favorite sports. Baseball, basketball, tennis, and volleyball were popular in his class. Basketball was more popular than baseball and volleyball, and tennis was more popular than basketball.
Question : Which sport was the most popular in Yamato's class?
4. Betty wanted to go to the museum last Sunday. Her father and mother were too busy to go there, so Betty asked her brother to come there with her. They enjoyed looking at beautiful pictures in the museum.
Question : Who went to the museum last Sunday?

6 Q.1 イ　Q.2 ウ
【解き方】Q.1 利用時のルールを４つ言っているがその１つ目。Q.2 ルール４つのうちの最後に(Finally)，ふだんは撮影禁止なのだが，今日は特別な日なので許可すると言っている。

放送内容

Hello, everyone. Now I'd like to tell you the rules of this art museum. First, you can't run in the museum. It is dangerous to do so here, so please walk slowly. Second, people want to look at pictures in a quiet room, so you must not make any big sounds. Of course, don't use your smartphone to talk with your friends, either. Third, please don't eat or drink in the museum. It is very important to keep the museum clean. Finally, in this museum, usually, you can't take pictures. But today is a special day for this museum, so you can take pictures today only. Now, please enjoy the museum.
Question 1 : Why do you have to walk slowly in this museum?
Question 2 : What can you do in this museum today only?

7 No.1 ア　No.2 ウ　No.3 エ　No.4 イ
【解き方】No.1 今，本を読んでいるのは This is a book ～ と説明しているベッキー。No.2 リサが家にいた理由は雨が降っていたから(because it was raining)で，これを「天気が悪かったから」と言い換えたウが適切。No.3 エイミーは冒頭で「私の辞書がどこか知らない？」と聞いており，エ「辞書が見つからない」が適切。No.4 I have great news.に続く説明の部分を聞き取る。get first prizeは「１等賞を取る，優勝する」という意味で，正解イでは「全試合に勝った」と表している。

放送内容

No.1 A : What are you reading, Becky?
B : Hi, Bob. This is a book about Japanese history.
A : I'm interested in it. Can I borrow the book after you finish?
B : I borrowed this from Kate. So please ask her.
Question : Who is reading a book?
No.2 A : I went shopping with my family last weekend. How about you, Risa?
B : I wanted to go to the mountain with my family, but we couldn't because it was raining.
A : Uh... then, what did you do?
B : We stayed home during the weekend.
Question : Why did Risa stay home?
No.3 A : Kevin, do you know where my dictionary is? I can't find it.
B : Well... I think it's under the table, Amy.
A : I have already checked there.
B : Then you can ask Mom.
Question : What is Amy's problem?
No.4 A : Hi, Tom, you look so happy.
B : Hi, Maki. I have great news. I got first prize in the tennis tournament yesterday.
A : Really? I didn't know you were a good tennis player.
B : I have played tennis for ten years. Shall we play tennis next weekend?
Question : What is Tom's good news?

8 (1)(イ)　(2)(ウ)
【解き方】(1)質問は「マナは先週の土曜日，何をしましたか」。マナの２番目の発言 I played tennis with my friends on Saturdayを聞き取る。(2)質問は「写真の中でいちばん若いのはだれですか」。４人のうちダイスケは最年長，話し手のリサはショウタより若い，リサはクミより年上。したがって，いちばん若いのはクミ。

放送内容

(1) A : Hi, Ami. What did you do last weekend?
B : On Saturday, I visited my grandfather and made a cake with him. On Sunday, I watched TV at home. I had a nice weekend. How about you, Mana?
A : I played tennis with my friends on Saturday and did my homework on Sunday.
B : You had a good weekend, too!
Question : What did Mana do last Saturday?
(2) A : Hi, Lisa. Do you have any brothers or sisters?
B : Yes, I do. Look at this picture. There are four people in the picture. These boys are my brothers, Daisuke and Shota. This girl is my sister, Kumi, and this is me. Daisuke is the oldest of the four. I am younger than Shota.
A : I see. Are you older than Kumi?
B : Yes, I am.
Question : Who is the youngest in the picture?

9 No.1 B　No.2 C

【解き方】No.1 質問は「来週末，その公園にはいくつの博物館があるでしょうか」。その公園には an art museum, a history museum, a sports museum に加えて，来週金曜日に a computer museum ができるので，4つとなる。No.2 質問は「サムの祖父の家からだれが早く帰宅しましたか」。サムの最後の発言，～so she (= my sister) and my father had to go back home earlier ～から，C の Sam's father and sister. が適切。

No.1　Do you want to find something new or interesting?　Our park is the best for you. Now there are an art museum, a history museum, and a sports museum in our park. Next Friday, a new museum will open. It will be a computer museum, and it will be the biggest museum in the city. It will have many kinds of computers. I think that you have never seen some of them before. The park is in front of Aozora Station, and it takes only 5 minutes from there. We hope you will visit our park soon!
　　Question：How many museums will the park have next weekend?
No.2　Meg：Hi, Sam. How was your weekend?
　　　Sam：It was fun. I went to see my grandfather and stayed at his house.
　　　Meg：Good. Did you go there with someone?
　　　Sam：I went there with my family.
　　　Meg：Sounds nice! Your grandfather was happy to see you, right?
　　　Sam：Yes, but my sister had dance practice on Sunday, so she and my father had to go back home earlier than my mother and I.
　　　Question：Who went back home early from Sam's grandfather's house?

10 No.1 a　No.2 d　No.3 c

【解き方】No.1 最初のほうではルーシー（女性）がコンビニで卵と箸と皿を買う流れだが，男性がルーシーにスーパーで卵を買うよう頼み，自分は箸と皿を買うと言う。よって，ルーシーが買うのは卵だけである。No.2 キャシーは頭痛で顔色の悪いマイクに家に帰るよう言うが，マイクはブラウン先生に理科のレポートを持って行かなければならない。キャシーの「昼休みに私がそれ（＝マイクの理科のレポート）を先生の部屋に持って行ってあげる」から，d が適切。his room の his はブラウン先生のこと。No.3 コウジは「海外でレストランのオーナーになるためにビジネスを学びたい」と言っている。

No.1〔A：男性，B：女性〕
A：Lucy, we need some eggs, chopsticks and dishes for tomorrow's party.
B：I'll buy them at the convenience store.
A：Can you buy the eggs at the supermarket in front of the station?　There is a sale today.
B：OK.
A：Then, I'll buy the chopsticks and dishes.
B：Thank you. See you later.

　　（Question）　What is Lucy going to buy?
No.2〔A：女性，B：男性〕
A：You look pale, Mike.
B：Hi, Kathy. I have a headache.
A：Oh, really?　You need to go home.
B：I have to take my science report to Mr. Brown.
A：I'll take it to his room during the lunch break.
B：Thank you. Here is my report.
　　（Question）　Where will Kathy go for Mike during the lunch break?
No.3〔A：男性，B：女性〕
A：Emily, what will you study after you graduate from high school?
B：I'm going to study Japanese food because I want to introduce it to the world. How about you, Koji?
A：I'd like to study business to be the owner of a restaurant overseas.
B：Sounds great!　Then, you should keep studying English.
A：You're right. English will be useful.
B：You can do it!
　　（Question）　Why does Koji want to study business?

11 No.1 D　No.2 A　No.3 C　No.4 B　No.5 D

【解き方】No.1 質問は「健の祖母はいつお店を始めたか」。She started the shop about forty years ago. を聞き取る。No.2 質問は「昨年の夏，なぜ健は驚いたのか」。I was surprised because so many customers came to the shop. を聞き取る。No.3 質問は「メグとはだれか」。She came to the shop to buy her son's birthday cake. を聞き取る。No.4 質問は「ふつう健はいつ祖母のお店に行くか」。I usually go to her shop after school と言っている。No.5 質問は「健は何をしたいと思っているか」。I want to make the shop more popular. を聞き取る。

　　Today, I will talk about my grandmother's cake shop. She started the shop about forty years ago. It is small and old. She works alone in the shop, so she can't make many kinds of cakes. But her cakes are delicious and I wanted to learn how to make them. So, I helped her in her shop last summer. I was surprised because so many customers came to the shop.
　　One day, I met a woman. Her name was Meg. She came to the shop to buy her son's birthday cake. She told me that she bought a birthday cake for him in my grandmother's shop every year. I was glad to hear that everyone in her family likes my grandmother's cakes.
　　Now, I usually go to her shop after school. When I see the happy faces of my grandmother and her customers, I also feel happy. I love her shop. I want to make the shop more popular.
　　Question No.1：When did Ken's grandmother start her shop?
　　Question No.2：Why was Ken surprised last summer?

Question No.3 : Who was Meg?
Question No.4 : When does Ken usually go to his grandmother's shop?
Question No.5 : What does Ken want to do?

12　No.1 ア　No.2 イ　No.3 イ

【解き方】No.1 カズヤは週末について「動物園に行った」「水族館にも行った」「博物館に行きたかったが時間がなかった＝行かなかった」と言っている。No.2 カズヤは明日帰国する前に，昼食においしい魚が食べたいと言い，先生のすすめる空港のレストランで食べることにした。つまり，空港でランチを食べるのはカズヤ。No.3 質問は，明日カズヤが空港に到着する時刻。駅発の10:30のバスに乗って空港まで45分かかることから，到着時刻は11:15。

放送内容

Kazuya : Hi, Ms. Hill.
Ms. Hill : Hi, Kazuya. How was your weekend?
Kazuya : It was great. I went to the zoo, and I liked it very much.
Ms. Hill : It's very popular among tourists.
Kazuya : It was interesting to learn about animals that are only in Australia. I also went to the aquarium and enjoyed the dolphin show.
Ms. Hill : That's nice.
Kazuya : I wanted to go to the museum, but I didn't have time for that.
Ms. Hill : You can go there next weekend.
Kazuya : No, I can't. I will leave Sydney tomorrow afternoon. Today's English lesson was the last lesson for me. It was fun to learn English from you.
Ms. Hill : I'm glad you had a good time in my class.
Kazuya : I stayed here for two weeks, but I think it was too short.
Ms. Hill : What time are you going to leave here tomorrow?
Kazuya : At 2:30. I want to eat a nice fish for lunch before that. Do you know a good restaurant?
Ms. Hill : Yes. How about a restaurant in the airport? I often enjoy eating there with my friends when we travel. If you go to the airport early, you will have time to enjoy eating some delicious fish.
Kazuya : That's a good idea. It takes 45 minutes from the station to the airport by bus, so I will take a bus at 10:30 or 11:30.
Ms. Hill : You should take a bus at 10:30 in the morning because there will be less people.
Kazuya : OK. I will.
No.1 Where did Kazuya visit on the weekend?
No.2 Who will have lunch at the airport tomorrow?
No.3 What time will Kazuya arrive at the airport tomorrow?

13　(1)①エ　②ア　(2)①ウ　②イ

【解き方】(1)①質問は，「ボブはなぜ剣道部に入りたいのですか」。ボブの3番目の発言にI want to learn traditional Japanese culture, so I'll join the kendo club!「僕は日本の伝統文化を学びたいので剣道部に入ります」とあるので，エ「日本の伝統文化が学べるから」が適切。②質問は，「ボブは週に何日剣道の練習をしますか」。カトウ先生が4番目の発言でwe practice from Tuesday to Saturday「私たちは火曜日から土曜日まで練習しています」と言っているのに対してボブがI want to spend weekends with my host family, so I can't come on Saturdays.「週末はホストファミリーと過ごしたいので土曜日は来られません」と言っているので，ア「週に4日」練習する。(2)①質問は，「男性はいくら支払いますか」。I'll order the cheapest Happy Lunch, and an apple pie.「いちばん安いハッピーランチとアップルパイを注文します」と言っている。ハッピーランチの中でいちばん安いAが3ドル，アップルパイが3ドル，合計はウ「6ドル」になる。②質問は，「男性は，何を無料でもらいますか」。最後に男性がmy little brother likes cars, but ...I'll have French fries today.「弟は車が好きですが，今日はフレンチフライをいただきます」と言っている。

放送内容

(1) Ms. Kato : Hi Bob, which club are you going to join?
Bob : Hello Ms. Kato. I haven't decided yet. I've seen practices of some sports clubs, like soccer and baseball, but I've already played them before.
Ms. Kato : Then, join our kendo club!
Bob : Kendo! That's cool!
Ms. Kato : Kendo is a traditional Japanese sport. You can get a strong body and mind.
Bob : I want to learn traditional Japanese culture, so I'll join the kendo club! Do you practice it every day?
Ms. Kato : No, we practice from Tuesday to Saturday.
Bob : OK..., but do I have to practice on weekends? I want to spend weekends with my host family, so I can't come on Saturdays.
Ms. Kato : No problem! Please come to see our practice first.
Bob : Thank you!
① Why does Bob want to join the kendo club?
② How many days will Bob practice kendo in a week?
(2) Clerk : Welcome to Happy Jeff's Hot Dogs! May I help you? Here's a lunch menu.
A man : Thank you. Um..., I'd like to have a hot dog, and... an ice cream.
Clerk : How about our apple pie? It's very popular.
A man : Ah, it looks really good.
Clerk : Then, how about Happy Jeff's Lunch? You can have both an apple pie and an ice cream.
A man : Well, I don't think I can eat both, so... I'll order the cheapest Happy Lunch, and an apple pie.
Clerk : OK. Is that all?

A man : Yes. Oh, I have a free ticket.

Clerk : Then you can get French fries, an ice cream, or a toy for free. Which do you want?

A man : Um…, my little brother likes cars, but… I'll have French fries today.

Clerk : OK.

① How much will the man pay?

② What will the man get for free?

----

14 1．ウ 2．イ 3．ア 4．エ

【解き方】 1．冒頭部分で「私は32歳だ。3年前に英語教師として日本に来た」とある。ウ「29歳」が適切。2．中盤で「ある日，キムラさんと私は，スタジアムに野球の試合を見に行った。(中略)キムラさんには，マキという子供がいた」と言っている。ジョンと一緒にスタジアムで野球を見たのは，イ「マキの父親」である。3．中盤で「彼女(＝マキ)は英語が好きで，もっと上手に英語を話したかった。だから，彼女は何度も私に英語で話しかけた」と言っている。ア「英語を上達させたかったから」が適切。4．終盤で「あなたたちが英語を使って，多くの友人を作ることを望んでいる」と言っている。エ「彼は彼ら(＝生徒たち)に，英語を通して多くの友人を作ってほしいと思っている」が適切。

放送内容 --

Hello, everyone. My name is John. I'm from America. I'm thirty-two years old. I came to Japan three years ago as an English teacher. This is my second time to stay in Japan. Today, let me tell you about my first time.

When I was fifteen, I came to Japan with my father. My father has a friend who lives in Japan. His name is Mr. Kimura. We stayed at his house for three weeks. His favorite sport is baseball, and I love it, too. I talked a lot about baseball with him. One day, Mr. Kimura and I went to a stadium to watch a baseball game. That was my best experience.

Mr. Kimura has a child, Maki. She liked English and wanted to speak English better. So she talked to me in English many times. She also helped me learn Japanese. By using some Japanese, I made many friends in Japan.

It's fun to learn foreign languages. I hope you'll try to use English and make a lot of friends. That will make your life more exciting. Please enjoy English classes.

〔質問〕

1．How old was John when he came to Japan as an English teacher?

2．Who watched a baseball game with John at a stadium?

3．Why did Maki try to talk to John a lot?

4．What does John want the students to do?

----

15 (1)エ (2)イ

【解き方】 (1)ボブはサッカーの試合でスタジアムにいるが，ユニフォームが見つからない。電話で家にいるニーナに探してもらうが，家でも見つからない。ニーナが

もう一度バッグの中を見るように言うと，ボブは「弁当箱の下にあった！」と言う。よって，エが正解。(2)ボブがシューズを家に忘れてしまい，ニーナが「車で10分後に持って行ってあげる」と言う。よって，イが正解。

放送内容 --

Bob : Nina? I need your help. Are you at home now?

Nina : Yes, Bob. What's the matter?

Bob : Well, I'm at the soccer stadium. Practicing before the match will start in 20 minutes. But, I can't find my soccer uniform.

Nina : What? Today's match is very important and you prepared well last night, right?

Bob : Yes, I think so. But my uniform is not here. Can you go and look around my room? Its color is blue.

Nina : Of course, Bob. Please wait… OK, I'm in your room, now.

Bob : I guess I put my uniform inside the box by the door. Please open it.

Nina : …No, there is no uniform here. Any other places?

Bob : Oh, around the table in the kitchen! When I took my lunch box there, I had the uniform with me.

Nina : …Around the table? No, it's not here. Bob, are you sure that you left it?

Bob : What do you mean?

Nina : I think you are excited now. How about looking inside your bag once again?

Bob : OK… …Wow! Sorry, you are right! It's here under the lunch box!

Nina : I knew it. Please relax, Bob. Now, you are ready.

Bob : Yes. Thank you very much.

Nina : You're welcome. Please try your best! I'll go and watch your match soon. …Oh? Here are your soccer shoes at the entrance.

Bob : Oh no! I forgot to bring my soccer shoes!

Nina : Don't worry, Bob. I will bring these shoes to you in 10 minutes by car.

Bob : Thank you again, Nina. I'll wait for you.

Nina : No problem. See you soon.

Question 1 : Where was Bob's soccer uniform found?

Question 2 : What will Nina do next?

----

16 〈対話文1〉ア 〈対話文2〉エ 〈対話文3〉ウ

【解き方】 〔問題A〕〈対話文1〉質問は「なぜタロウは祖母の家に行ったか」で，選択肢は to 不定詞「〜するために」。タロウの最初の発言「誕生日会をするために祖母の家に行った」に答えがある。〈対話文2〉1回目の放送で質問の John と one o'clock をしっかり聞き取り，2回目の放送でジョンの発言に集中する。「昼食後図書室に行き(12時50分ごろ)，歴史の本を読み(20分間)，教室に戻った(1時15分)。〈対話文3〉質問は「今日，ボブはどうやって家からコンサートに行ったか」で，I came by bike from home. に答えがある。家に帰る手段を話した部分にまどわされないように。

放送内容

〈対話文1〉

Meg　：Hi, Taro. What did you do last Sunday?

Taro　：Hi, Meg. I went to my grandmother's house to have a birthday party.

Meg　：That's nice.

Taro　：In the morning, I wrote a birthday card for her at home. Then I visited her and gave her the card. She looked happy. After that, she made some tea for me.

Meg　：That sounds good.

Taro　：In the evening, my sisters, mother, and father brought a cake for her.

Meg　：Did you enjoy the party?

Taro　：Yes, very much.

　　Question：Why did Taro go to his grandmother's house?

〈対話文2〉

Satomi：Hi, John. I've been looking for you. Where were you?

John　：I'm sorry, Satomi. I was very busy.

Satomi：I went to your classroom in the morning and during lunch time. What were you doing then?

John　：Early in the morning, I gave water to flowers in the school garden. After that, I did my homework in my classroom.

Satomi：Oh, you did. How about during lunch time? I went to your room at one o'clock.

John　：After I ate lunch, I went to the library. That was at about twelve fifty. I read some history books there for twenty minutes and came back to my room at one fifteen.

　　Question：What was John doing at one o'clock?

〈対話文3〉

Jane　：Hi, Bob. I'm happy that I can come to the concert today.

Bob　：Hi, Jane. Yes. Me, too.

Jane　：How did you get here today?

Bob　：Why?　I came by bike from home.

Jane　：This morning, I watched the weather news. I think it'll be rainy this afternoon.

Bob　：Oh, really?　I'll have to go home by train and bus. What should I do with my bike?

Jane　：After the concert, I will keep it at my house. We can walk to my house.

Bob　：Thank you.

Jane　：You're welcome. And you can use my umbrella when you go back home from my house.

　　Question：How did Bob get to the concert from home today?

- -

17　1．ウ　2．イ　3．ウ　4．エ　5．ウ

【解き方】1．トムはカナが描いた絵を見て，驚き（Wow），ほめている（really good!）ので，ウが適切。2．トムは，うれしそうにしている理由をたずねられ，Yesterday，～と昨日のできごとを説明する。よって，イが適切。3．トムの発言の These pictures on the menu help me choose what to eat.「メニューのこれらの写真が，僕が何を食べるかを選ぶのに役立つ」から，ウが適切。

〈help＋O＋動詞の原形〉「Oが～するのに役立つ」　4．トムは土曜日（24日）ひまで，土曜日に行こうと誘うが，カナは毎週土曜日はピアノのレッスンがある（ので行けない）と言う。しかしそのあと，17日の土曜日が今年最後のレッスンだと思い出し，「今度の土曜日はあいている」と言う。今度の土曜日は24日なので，エが適切。5．「もっと頑張りたいと思うことは何か」の質問について，「最も多くの生徒が『友達を作る』を選んだと思う」→「38人の生徒がそれを選んだ」の流れから，ウが一致。トムの答えは2つともはずれたのでイは不一致。「学校で何がいちばん楽しいか」の質問に対して最も回答が多かった選択肢は述べられていないが，「クラブ活動」よりも「友達と話す」のほうが選んだ生徒数が多かったので，エは不一致。

放送内容

In this part of the listening test, you will hear five conversations between Kana and Tom. After listening to each conversation, you will hear a question. Each question will be read only once and you must choose one answer. Now begin.

1．Kana：Tom, look at this. I painted this picture in the art class.

　Tom　：Wow, the picture is really good!　It looks like a photo! I can't believe you painted this, Kana.

　Question：What does Tom mean?

2．Kana：Hi, Tom. What happened?

　Tom　：Why do you ask that, Kana?

　Kana：Because you look happy. I guess something good happened to you.

　Tom　：Well, actually, you're right. Yesterday, I got a ticket from my uncle for my favorite singer's concert.

　Kana：That makes sense.

　Question：Which is true about this conversation?

3．Kana：Tom, have you decided what to eat?　If you need my help, I'll explain in English what is written on the menu.

　Tom　：Oh, I'm OK, Kana. These pictures on the menu help me choose what to eat. They look delicious!

　Kana：If this menu were written in both Japanese and English, it would be easier for you to understand it.

　Question：Which is true about this conversation?

4．Tom　：Hi, Kana. Some members of the music club will hold a concert on the stage in the park near our school.

　Kana：It sounds fun, Tom. When will it be held?

　Tom　：It will be held this Saturday, December the 24th and this Sunday, December the 25th. I'll be free on Saturday. How about going with me on Saturday?

　Kana：Well... I have a piano lesson every Saturday. How about the 25th?

　Tom　：I'll go to the theater with my host family on the 25th.

　Kana：I see. Oh, now I remember Saturday the 17th was the last piano lesson of this year, so I'll be free on this Saturday.

　Tom　：Oh, great!

　Question：Which is true about this conversation?

5.　Tom　：Hi, Kana. What are you doing?
　　Kana：I'm making a report about the interview I did at school in April.
　　Tom　：Interview?　Sounds interesting!
　　Kana：Yes, it is. I asked several questions to 100 students in the first grade. And, they chose one answer from three choices.
　　Tom　：What did you ask them?
　　Kana：First, I asked them, "What is the thing you want to try harder?". The choices are "Studying," "Making friends" and "Club activities." Can you guess which was chosen by the most students?
　　Tom　：Well... I guess the most students chose "Making friends."
　　Kana：Well, 38 students chose that. But more students chose "Studying."
　　Tom　：I see. What was another question?
　　Kana：I asked, "What is the thing you enjoy the most at school?". And, the choices are "Studying," "Talking with friends" and "Club activities."
　　Tom　：I guess the most students chose "Club activities."
　　Kana：That answer was chosen by the first grade students who joined a club activity. But many first grade students haven't joined a club activity yet. So, more students chose "Talking with friends."
　　Tom　：I understand.
　Question：Which is true about this conversation?

- -

b. 図表・グラフを用いた問題

1　No.1 イ　No.2 ア　No.3 エ
【解き方】No.1 in front of ～「～の前に［で］」
No.2 before thenは「水曜日の前に」ということ。No.3 明日は晴れで，今日よりも暑いことから，気温が下がることを示すアとイ，傘を持って行くウは消去できる。エの水筒はsomething to drinkを表している。

放送内容
No.1　A bookstore is in front of the bank.
No.2　The English club teacher will be busy on Wednesday this week. So, let's have English club before then.
No.3　Tomorrow will be sunny and hotter than today. So, you don't need to bring an umbrella but you should bring something to drink.

- -

2　No.1 D　No.2 C
【解き方】No.1 トムのI played tennis with my sister.を聞き取る。No.2 ケンタのI have a dog and two cats.を聞き取る。

放送内容
No.1
A：Saki, what did you do last Sunday?
B：I went to a piano concert after shopping. How about you, Tom?
A：I played tennis with my sister.
B：That's nice.
　質問します。　What did Tom do last Sunday?
No.2
A：Hi, Nancy. Oh, you have two dogs. They are cute. Do you often come to this park?
B：Hi, Kenta. Yes. They like walking here. Do you have any pets, too?
A：Yes. I have a dog and two cats.
B：Oh, really?　I want to see them.
　質問します。　Which pets does Kenta have?

- -

3　1番 イ　2番 ウ
【解き方】1番 娘は音楽好きの父に，音楽を聞くときに使うものをプレゼントした。2番 女の子はハンバーガーとオレンジジュースとフライドポテトを注文したが，ハンバーガーを買うとドリンクは無料になる。

放送内容
1番　Father：Thank you for giving me a birthday present, Meg.
　　　Meg　：You are welcome, Dad.
　　　Father：Why did you choose this?
　　　Meg　：You are interested in music, so I want you to use it when you listen to music.

Question: What did Meg buy for her father?

2番　Man：May I help you?
　　　Girl：I'd like to buy a hamburger.
　　　Man：Sure. If you buy a hamburger, you don't have to pay for a drink.
　　　Girl：Oh, really? Orange juice, please.
　　　Man：OK. Anything else?
　　　Girl：French fries, please. That's all.
　　　Question：How much will this girl pay?

----

4 ア．2　イ．1　ウ．3
【解き方】ア．You want to know what a word means.「ある単語が何の意味なのかを知りたい」ときに使うものは2の辞書。イ．最初にTom is walking on Red Street to visit the city hall.「トムは市役所を訪れるためにレッドストリートを歩いている」、次にHe will go to Green Street and turn left.「グリーンストリートに行き左に曲がる」、Then, he will find the city hall on his right.「そうすると右手に市役所が見つかる」とあるので1の地図が内容に合う。ウ．You are talking with a teacher from Australia in English, but you didn't hear what he said.「あなたはオーストラリア出身の先生と英語で話しているが、彼が言ったことが聞き取れなかった」と言っている。そんなときは、3「もう一度言ってくださいますか」と言う。

放送内容 ----------------------

ア．You want to know what a word means. What will you use?
イ．Tom is walking on Red Street to visit the city hall. He will go to Green Street and turn left. Then, he will find the city hall on his right. Which picture shows this?
ウ．You are talking with a teacher from Australia in English, but you didn't hear what he said. What will you say to him?

----

5 No.1 ア　No.2 ウ　No.3 ア
【解き方】No.1 ジョンはI like tigersと言っている。No.2 日本の昔の帽子の一種で、大きい紙で作ればかぶることができる。No.3 ケンの机は、黒板の近く・ミホの隣・窓のそば。

放送内容 ----------------------

No.1
A：John, there are many kinds of animals in this zoo.
B：Yes, Mary. I like tigers, so I want to see them first.
A：OK. I want to see elephants after that.
　Question：What animal does John like?
No.2
A：What are you making with origami paper, Kumi? It looks like a mountain.
B：This is a kind of old Japanese hat, Mike. If you make one with bigger paper, you can wear it on your head.
A：That's very interesting! I'll try to make one.
　Question：What is Kumi making?

No.3
A：Where is your desk in your classroom, Ken?
B：Now I sit near the blackboard, and Miho is next to me.
A：Do you like your place?
B：Yes. It's so bright because my desk is by the window.
　Question：Where is Ken's desk?

----

6 イ→ウ→エ→ア
【解き方】「それから私たちは川へ泳ぎに行った」（イ）、「泳いだあとで、父が夕飯を作り、私たちはそれを楽しんだ」（ウ）と続き、さらに「夜には私たちは空に美しい星を見た」（エ）と言っている。翌日の話になり、「私たちは出発する前に、その場所を掃除した」（ア）と言っている。

放送内容 ----------------------

I went camping with my family last weekend. First, we set up the tent. Then we went swimming in the river. The water was a little cold but I had a lot of fun. After swimming, my father cooked dinner and we enjoyed it. At night, we saw beautiful stars in the sky. On the next day, before we left, we cleaned the area. On the way home, we sang songs in the car. It was a very nice weekend.

----

7 ウ→イ→ア
【解き方】明日の月曜日と次の日は雨、水曜日から金曜日は晴れ、週末は強風。

放送内容 ----------------------

Here is the weather for next week. Tomorrow, Monday, will be rainy. You'll need an umbrella the next day too, because it will rain a lot. From Wednesday to Friday, it will be perfect for going out. You can go on a picnic on those days if you like. On the weekend, the wind will be very strong. You have to be careful if you wear a hat. I hope you will have a good week.

----

8 1．エ　2．ア　3．ウ　4．イ
【解き方】1．質問は「ユキへのプレゼントは何ですか」。I will use it when I drink coffee at home.「家でコーヒーを飲むときに使います」と言っているのでエのカップが正解。2．質問は「今、カメラはどこにありますか」。He put it on the chair.「彼はそれを椅子の上に置きました」と言っているのでアが正解。3．質問は「ジョンは何をしますか」。Can you clean the table?「テーブルをきれいにしてくれませんか」と言われている。4．質問は「今日はTシャツ2枚でいくらですか」。All the T-shirts are usually 15 dollars, but they are only 10 dollars today.「いつもはすべてのTシャツが15ドルですが、今日はたったの10ドルです」と言っているので、今日は2枚を20ドルで買える。

放送内容

No.1　A：Happy birthday, Yuki. This is a present for you. Please open it.

　　　B：Thank you. Wow, it's nice. I will use it when I drink coffee at home.

　　Question：What is the present for Yuki?

No.2　A：Mom, do you know where my camera is?

　　　B：Dad used it to take pictures of flowers this morning.

　　　A：Oh, it's over there. He put it on the chair.

　　Question：Where is the camera now?

No.3　A：John, are you busy now?

　　　B：No, I'm just watching TV.

　　　A：I'm cooking dinner now. Can you clean the table?

　　　B：Sure.

　　Question：What is John going to do?

No.4　A：May I help you?

　　　B：Yes, please. I'm looking for some T-shirts.

　　　A：The T-shirts are here. All the T-shirts are usually 15 dollars, but they are only 10 dollars today.

　　　B：That's nice. I'll take these two.

　　Question：How much are two T-shirts today?

9　No.1 エ　No.2 イ　No.3 ウ

【解き方】No.1 ケイティーが先週末したのはバドミントン。No.2 デイブは I can't find my dictionary. と言っている。No.3 City Library Line に乗って，Station Hotel で降りる。次に East High School Line に乗り換えて2つ目の駅で降りる。

放送内容

No.1

A：Satoshi, how was your weekend?

B：It was great!　I went fishing with my father. What did you do last weekend, Katie?

A：I played badminton with my sister.

　Question：What did Katie do last weekend?

No.2

A：What are you doing, Dave?

B：I can't find my dictionary. I usually put it in my school bag, but it isn't there. Did you see it, Mom?

A：No. Why don't you look around your desk?

B：OK, I will.

　Question：What is Dave looking for?

No.3

A：Excuse me. Could you tell me how to get to the art museum?

B：Sure. First, take the City Library Line to the Station Hotel.

A：So, you mean I should get off at the Station Hotel, right?

B：Yes. And change to the East High School Line and get off at the second bus stop from the Station Hotel. The art museum is in front of the bus stop. This is the easiest way to get there.

　Question：Where should the woman get off to visit the art museum?

10　①ア→エ→イ→ウ　② eight

【解き方】① First, ～から，最初は市立美術館（ア）に行く。次に In the afternoon, ～で市立庭園へ行くと言うが，Before we visit the garden, ～からその前に昼食を食べる。よって，エ→イの順。そして Finally, ～から，最後に行くのは音楽ホール（ウ）。②市内観光ツアーの所要時間は，最初のほうの「今9時です」と最後の「本日のツアーは午後5時に終わります」から，8時間である。

放送内容

Welcome to our city trip. Today we'll visit some famous places by bus. It's nine o'clock now. First, we'll arrive at the City Museum in 20 minutes. We'll have one and a half hours to see many famous pictures there. In the afternoon, we'll go to the City Garden. During this season we can see beautiful flowers. Oh, I forgot to say. Before we visit the garden, we'll have lunch at Aoi restaurant. Finally, we'll go to the Music Hall and enjoy some wonderful music. Today's trip will be over at five in the afternoon.

11　No.1 ア　No.2 エ

【解き方】No.1 質問は「アレックスは明日の朝，何をするか」。明日のことについて，アレックスは2番目の発言で，「僕は朝，ギターの練習をする」と言っている。No.2 質問は「彼らは庭に何が見えるか」。「庭にきれいな花があるね」「日曜日には，私はその大きな木の下のベンチに座って，本を読むのを楽しむ」「私は桜の花が好きだが，ここにはそれがない」「ああ，なんてかわいい犬小屋でしょう」と言っている。これらの発言から判断する。

放送内容

〔No.1〕

A：Alex, will you clean this room in the afternoon?

B：Sorry, Mom. I have to do my homework. After that, I'm going to go shopping with my friend.

A：What about tomorrow?

B：I'll practice the guitar in the morning, but I can clean the room in the afternoon.

A：Thank you.

　Question：What will Alex do tomorrow morning?

〔No.2〕

A：Welcome to my garden!

B：Wow!　There're beautiful flowers in your garden.

A：Thank you. On Sundays, I sit on that bench under the big tree and enjoy reading books.

B：Nice!

A：I'm thinking about planting a cherry blossom tree next month. I like cherry blossoms, but I don't have one here.

B：I like that plan. Oh, what a pretty dog house! Do you have a dog?

A：Yes. He loves to play in the garden.

　Question：What do they see in the garden?

12　No.1 ①ウ　②ア　No.2 ①ウ　②イ　③エ　④ア

【解き方】No.1 ① Mike was ～. と He was 18

years old. を聞き取る。② At first, I was very nervous because I couldn't speak English very well. を聞き取る。No.2 英文の後半の内容を聞き取る。

放送内容 -

I'm Taro. I went to Australia last summer when I was 16 years old. I stayed with Mike's family. Mike was a high school student. He was 18 years old. At first, I was very nervous because I couldn't speak English very well. However, Mike was very kind and talked to me in easy English, so I enjoyed communicating with him. I found that both Mike and I loved music and we became good friends. I spent the weekends with his family. On the first weekend, Mike and I went shopping in the afternoon. We enjoyed looking for a nice guitar. In the evening, we went to a concert together and got so excited. On the next weekend, I went fishing with Mike and his mother. I didn't know how to catch fish, but she taught it to me. And I got one big fish! Mike said, "Great, Taro! We can cook it together." Mike and I made dinner. It was fun. I stayed in Australia for only two weeks but I had a lot of wonderful memories.

- -

13 No.1 ウ No.2 ア
【解き方】No.1 中盤で,お母さんは息子に卵を買いに行くように言っている。No.2 中盤でジョンが,自分のクラスは2勝で,アヤのクラスがより多く勝っていると言っている。また,最後のほうでアヤが,自分のクラスが全部の試合に勝ってほしかったとも言っている。

放送内容 -

No.1
Mother : Have you finished your homework? Please help me cook dinner.
Boy : Sure. Mom, I will wash the vegetables.
Mother : I've already done it. Can you go to the store to buy eggs?
Boy : OK.
Question : What is the boy going to do to help his mother?
No.2
John : We had four basketball games, and I played in all of them.
Aya : You were playing very well, John. How many games did your class win?
John : Two. Your class won more games than my class, Aya. The members of your class played very hard.
Aya : Yes. But I wanted my class to win all of the games.
Question : Which is Aya's class?

- -

14 No.1 ウ No.2 イ
【解き方】No.1 質問の意味は,「女性は何を買うか」。フライドチキンを2ピース,サラダ,リンゴジュースのウが適切。No.2 質問の意味は,「対話後の今週のマークのスケジュールはどれか」。I have <u>basketball practice</u>

on Monday, Wednesday and Friday と,I have time on Thursday after school. と,I'll meet you in the library を聞き取る。

放送内容 -

〔No.1〕 A : I'd like two pieces of fried chicken and a salad, please.
B : Would you like anything to drink?
A : Do you have apple juice?
B : Yes.
A : I'll take it.
B : That'll be eight dollars in total.
Question : What will the woman buy?
〔No.2〕 A : Mark, would you like to go to the library to study with me this week?
B : Hi, Emi. Well, I have basketball practice on Monday, Wednesday and Friday. How about Tuesday?
A : I'm sorry. I have a piano lesson on Tuesday.
B : OK, well... I have time on Thursday after school.
A : Thank you. I'll meet you in the library, then.
Question : Which one is Mark's schedule for this week after the dialog?

- -

15 No.1 D No.2 A
【解き方】No.1 質問の意味は「どれが金曜日から日曜日までの天候を示しているか」。会話では,金曜日は曇り,土曜日は雨,日曜日は晴れ,と言っているので,Dが正解。No.2 質問の意味は「どれが歩いて学校に来る生徒の人数を示しているか」。いちばん多いのは自転車通学,2番目に多いのが電車通学,バス通学が20名。残りのAが徒歩通学の人数を表している。

放送内容 -

No.1 Girl : Hi! It's sunny today!
Boy : I'm thinking of going to Sky Park this weekend.
Girl : Sounds great.
Boy : Are you busy this weekend? How about going together?
Girl : OK! What day are you going to go there? I'm free on Saturday.
Boy : I'm going to go on Sunday. The weather will be sunny on Sunday but it's going to be rainy on Saturday.
Girl : Mmm.... How about Friday? It will be cloudy on Friday, but it won't be rainy.
Question : Which shows the weather for Friday to Sunday?
No.2 I asked 100 students "How do you come to school?" I found the number of students who come by bicycle was the largest of all. The number of students who use the train was second. 20 students come by bus. The other students walk to school.
Question : Which shows the number of students who walk to school?

- -

16

(1) (Course) B　(2) 10:30

【解き方】 (1)質問は「彼にとっていちばんよいコースはどれか」。前半に「タクヤは今年の夏，旅行に1週間とっている」「日本を旅したいと思っている」と言っていて，中ほどで「彼はそのとき1人で有名な場所を歩いて回るのを楽しんだ。だから同じように次の旅も楽しみたいと思っている」と言っているので，期間は1週間で京都を1人で歩いて回るBがよい。(2)質問は「彼が参加するイベントは何時に始まるか」。「彼は家でネコを飼っている。だから彼はほかの種類の動物と遊びたいと思っている」と言っていて，後半で「彼は日曜日の午前中にしか公園へ行けない」とあるので，日曜日の10:30に始まるイベントに参加する。

放送内容

(1) Takuya has one week for a trip this summer. He wants to travel around Japan because he went abroad last summer. He enjoyed walking around famous places by himself then, so he wants to enjoy the next trip in the same way. Which is the best course for him?

(2) This weekend, Kenji will join an event at City Animal Park to play with animals. He has a cat at home, so he wants to play with another kind of animal. He can go to the park only on Sunday morning. What time does the event he will join start?

17

A. イ　B. エ　C. ア　D. イ

【解き方】 A. 質問はジョンが昨日勉強した教科であることに注意する。中ほどでジョンが I studied math yesterday. 「僕は昨日数学を勉強した」と言っている。B. 最後に由美が So, I only went with Tomoko. 「それで，私はトモコだけと一緒に行った」と言っている。C. 中ほどの由美の発言に My class won just one game「私のクラスは1試合だけ勝った」とあるので，表より1勝のクラスを選ぶ。D. 目的地は東駅で，今乗っている電車は途中で中央駅にしか停車しない。東駅に行くには，その中央駅で乗り換える。

放送内容

A. John : Hi, Yumi. What subject did you study yesterday?
　Yumi : I studied Japanese. Did you study it, too?
　John : No. I studied math yesterday. Well, what are you doing now?
　Yumi : I'm doing my English homework. It's really difficult.
　John : I will finish my science homework first. After that, I'll help you.
　質問　What subject did John study yesterday?

B. John : Yumi, you have wanted to see this movie, right? I will see the movie with Takashi tomorrow. Why don't you come with us?
　Yumi : Thank you, but I saw the movie last Sunday.
　John : Really? Who did you go with? With Haruna and Tomoko?
　Yumi : Haruna had a piano lesson and couldn't go on that day. So, I only went with Tomoko.
　John : I see.
　質問　Who went to the movie with Yumi last Sunday?

C. Yumi : All of the games have finished. How many games did your class win?
　John : We didn't win all of them, but we won two games. How about your class?
　Yumi : Not good. My class won just one game, so two classes were better than mine. I wanted to win more games.
　John : Don't be so sad. You had a good time, right?
　Yumi : Of course.
　質問　Which is Yumi's class?

D. Yumi : Our train has just left Nishi Station. We will be at Higashi Station in twenty minutes.
　John : Can we get there without changing trains?
　Yumi : No, we can't. This train only stops at Chuo Station before arriving at Minato Station.
　John : Then, how can we get to Higashi Station?
　Yumi : We will change trains at the next station.
　John : OK.
　質問　Where will Yumi and John change trains?

18

No.1 ウ　No.2 イ　No.3 エ

【解き方】 No.1 質問は「マイクはどこで自分の時計を見つけましたか」。母の「ベッドの下を見たら，マイク？」に対して，マイクが「ああ，あった」と答えている。No.2 質問は「ジュディは，けさ，朝食に何を食べましたか」。ジュディが2番目の発言で，「たいていトーストと牛乳を食べますが，けさはリンゴも食べました」と言っている。No.3 質問は「電車は何時にサクラ駅に着きますか」。ヒナタ駅8時30分発の電車に乗り，サクラ駅まで20分かかるので，サクラ駅には8時50分に着く。

放送内容

No.1
M : Mom, I put my watch on the table by the bed. But I couldn't find it.
F : How about looking under the bed, Mike?
M : OK. Oh, I've found it.
F : I'm glad I could help.
　Question : Where did Mike find his watch?

No.2
F : What did you have for breakfast this morning, Kazuya?
M : Let's see. I had rice, miso soup, and sausages. How about you, Judy?
F : I usually have some toast and milk. This morning I also had an apple.
M : Oh, you had a lot this morning.
　Question : What did Judy have for breakfast this morning?

No.3
M : What time shall we meet at Hinata Station to go

to the zoo?
F：How about 8:15 a.m.? We can take the train that leaves at 8:30 a.m.
M：OK. How long does it take from Hinata Station to Sakura Station near the zoo?
F：Well, it takes 20 minutes to get there.
Question：What time does the train get to Sakura Station?

----

19 (1)ア (2)エ (3)イ (4)ウ

【解き方】(1)「庭の木の下でハチ(犬)を見た」「ボールで遊んでいた」 (2)「7月9日の日曜日はどう？」→「午前は時間がある」 (3)サラの「彼(＝スズキ先生)にノートを渡さなくてはいけない」を聞き取る。(4)コウジは「博物館近くの書店で僕を待っててくれる？ すぐにそこに会いに行くよ」と言っているので、コウジとケイトが会うのは「書店」。

放送内容

(1) A：Hi, Cathy. Welcome to my house. Did you see my dog, Hachi, outside?
B：Hi, Kazuma. Yes, I saw Hachi under the tree in your garden.
A：Really? He is so quiet today. Was he sleeping?
B：No, he was playing with a ball.
Q：What was Hachi doing when Cathy came to Kazuma's house?

(2) A：Hi, Tomoki. We have to finish our report by July 19th. How about doing it together next Saturday?
B：You mean July 8th? Sorry, Meg. I'll be busy on that day. How about Sunday, July 9th?
A：Oh, I have a piano lesson in the afternoon every Sunday, but I have time in the morning.
B：OK. See you then!
Q：When will Tomoki and Meg do their report together?

(3) A：Hi, Satoshi. Did you see Mr. Suzuki? I went to the teachers' room, but he wasn't there.
B：Hi, Sarah. He is on the school grounds. Why do you want to see him?
A：I have to take my notebook to him because I couldn't give it to him yesterday.
B：I see. I'm sure he's still there.
Q：What does Sarah have to do?

(4) A：Hello, Koji. This is Kate. Where are you now?
B：Hi, Kate. I'm at home. I'm watching a baseball game on TV.
A：What? We are going to go to the museum today. Did you forget that?
B：Oh no! I'm so sorry. Can you wait for me at the bookstore near the museum? I'll meet you there soon.
Q：Where will Koji meet Kate?

----

20 イ

【解き方】燃えるごみは今日(＝火曜日)、古い雑誌と新聞は古紙扱いで金曜日、ペットボトルは明日(＝水曜日)。

放送内容

John ：Good morning, Keiko. I cleaned my room last night and I put the trash in this plastic bag. What should I do now?
Keiko：Good morning, John. The trash can be burned, right? It's Tuesday today, so please put the bag in front of our house. The bags will be collected later today.
John ：OK, can I put these old magazines and newspapers in the same bag?
Keiko：No, we should recycle them. The day for them is Friday.
John ：I will keep that in mind. Oh, there are some plastic bottles here. Do you have another bag for them? Plastic bottles can also be recycled, right?
Keiko：Yes, but the day for plastic things is tomorrow. This is the bag for them. Here you are.
John ：Thank you, Keiko.

----

21 A. エ B. ウ C. ウ D. イ

【解き方】A. 長い鉛筆1本と花3輪を手に持っている。B. リサが「帽子、お弁当、飲み物を忘れないでね」と言うが、健は「バスで行くので帽子はいらない」と言っている。次のリサの「カメラを持って来てくれる？」にSure.と応じているので、健が持って行くのは、お弁当、飲み物、カメラ。C. 健にクッキーをすすめられたリサは、「この大きいのを今食べてもいい？」と聞く。健は「食べる前に手を洗って」と言うが、リサは「もう洗ったよ」と答えているので、このあとリサはクッキーを食べると考えられる。D. 選択肢から、東京の天気を聞き取る。「東京は昨日からずっと雨が降っている」と「明日まで雨はやまない」から、イが正解。最後のI wish ～「今日東京は晴れたらいいのに」は仮定法過去で事実に反する願望を表す。

放送内容

A.
Lisa：Hi, Ken. Look at this picture. This is my favorite movie character.
Ken：Oh, she has a long pencil in her hand. Why does she have it?
Lisa：Because she loves studying. She also likes plants, so she holds three flowers in her other hand.
Ken：I see.
　質問　Which is Lisa's favorite movie character?
B.
Ken：We're going to visit the science museum tomorrow. I'm so excited.
Lisa：Me, too. Don't forget your cap, lunch, and something to drink.
Ken：I see, but we'll go there by bus. So we don't need a cap.
Lisa：You're right. Oh, if you have a camera, can you bring it?
Ken：Sure. I have a good one.

質問 What will Ken bring to the science museum?

C.
Ken : Lisa, have you finished your tennis practice?
Lisa : Yes, it was hard.
Ken : Would you like to eat some cookies? I made them yesterday.
Lisa : Wow, your cookies look delicious. Can I eat this big one now?
Ken : Of course, but wait. Before eating it, wash your hands.
Lisa : Oh, I've already done it.
Ken : OK, here you are.
　質問　What will Lisa do next?

D.
Lisa : Good morning, Ken. Why do you have an umbrella? It's cloudy now, but it will be sunny here in Shizuoka this afternoon.
Ken : I'm going to see my grandmother in Tokyo. This morning, the TV news said, "It has been raining in Tokyo since yesterday."
Lisa : Oh, I watched that, too. It will not stop raining there until tomorrow, right?
Ken : Yes. I wish it would be sunny in Tokyo today.
　質問　Which TV news did Ken and Lisa watch?

----

22 No.1 イ　No.2 エ　No.3 ア　No.4 イ　No.5 ウ
【解き方】対話文と質問が読まれる前にイラストに描かれているものに目を通しておくと解答しやすい。No.1 ベンの2番目の発言のvisit the zooで判断。No.2 ベンの3番目の発言のlike pandasで判断。No.3 香織が4番目の発言でpractice the pianoと言っている。No.4 コンサートについて，香織はon Saturday, May 13thと答えている。SaturdayとSunday，thirteenthとthirtiethを聞き違えないことが重要。No.5 take a busという香織の発言で判断。

放 送 内 容 ------------------------------

Kaori : Hi, Ben.
Ben : Hi, Kaori.
Kaori : We'll have the "Golden Week" holidays soon. Do you have any plans for them?
Ben : Yes. I'm going to visit the zoo with my host family.
Kaori : That's nice! Do you like animals?
Ben : Yes. I especially like pandas very much. They are so cute. How about your plans?
Kaori : I'm going to practice the piano for my music club's concert.
Ben : Wow! Does your music club have a concert? When is it?
Kaori : It's on Saturday, May 13th at Central Hall. Do you want to come?
Ben : Yes, but how can I get there?
Kaori : You can take a bus from the station to the hall. It takes about 15 minutes.
Ben : Great! I'm looking forward to the concert. Good luck!
Kaori : Thank you. See you later!
　Question No.1　Where is Ben going to go during his Golden Week holidays?

Question No.2　What is Ben's favorite animal?
Question No.3　What is Kaori going to do during her Golden Week holidays?
Question No.4　When is the concert of Kaori's music club?
Question No.5　How can Ben get to Central Hall?

----

23 No.1 イ　No.2 エ　No.3 ウ
【解き方】No.1「トムのカギはどこにあるか」という質問。最後の「机の下に何かあるよ」に対して，Oh, it's my key!と言っている。No.2「朝食で何を飲むか」を表したグラフ。「牛乳がいちばん人気」「コーヒーはお茶より人気が高い」「オレンジジュースを飲む生徒はたった2人」という情報から，エが正解。No.3「ジェームズは宿題を終えたあと，まず何をするか」という質問。宿題のあとの予定を聞かれたジェームズは「部屋の掃除をする」と答えるが，「買い物に行ってくれる？」と言われて「宿題が終わったらすぐに行くよ」と答えている。よって，ウが正解。soon after SV「〜したらすぐに」

放 送 内 容 ------------------------------

No.1
A : Tom, what are you looking for?
B : I'm looking for my key. I usually put it on the desk, but it's not there.
A : Well, I have seen it on the bed or by the window before.
B : I have already checked those places.
A : Look. There is something under the desk. What's that?
B : Oh, it's my key! Why is it there?
　Question No.1 : Where is Tom's key?
No.2
A : Mr. Jones, look at this graph. I asked my classmates what they drink with breakfast.
B : Milk is the most popular, right?
A : Yes. I didn't think milk would be so popular.
B : Kana, what do you drink?
A : I drink tea, but coffee is more popular than tea. What do you drink?
B : I drink orange juice.
A : In my class, only two students drink orange juice.
B : I see.
　Question No.2 : Which graph are Mr. Jones and Kana looking at?
No.3
A : James, have you finished your homework?
B : No, I haven't, but I will finish it soon.
A : Do you have any plans after that?
B : Yes, I'm going to clean my room. Then I'm going to practice the piano. What's the matter, Mom?
A : I'm cooking dinner and need more eggs. Can you go shopping?
B : Sure. I'll go soon after I finish my homework. Is there anything else you need?
A : Yes. I also need some apples.
B : OK. I'll buy them, too.
　Question No.3 : What will James do first after he finishes his homework?

----

24 No.1 ウ　No.2 エ　No.3 ア

【解き方】No.1 ナンシーはボブと同じぐらいの背丈で，ボブはジャックよりも背が高い。No.2 質問は，「お城に行く前にどこに行ったか」。前半で「お寺に行った。次にお城に行った」と言っている。No.3 バスケットボール部は，火曜日，木曜日，土曜日に体育館で練習し，金曜日には外で走る。

放送内容 ----------------------------

No.1 Bob has a sister and a brother. His sister, Nancy is as tall as Bob. Bob is taller than his brother, Jack.

Question : Which picture shows this?

No.2 Taro and Mike went out together on Saturday. First, they went to a temple which is famous for its tower. Next, they went to a castle. Mike was happy to see the nice view from the top of it. After that, they became very hungry. So, for lunch, they went to a restaurant and enjoyed Udon noodles together. After they had lunch, they went to an old bridge in town and walked across it.

Question : Where did Taro and Mike go before they went to the castle?

No.3 The plan of the basketball team for next week has changed. We, the basketball team, are going to share the gym with the volleyball team next week. Because volleyball games will be held on Sunday, the volleyball team will use the gym on Monday, Wednesday and Friday. We will practice in the gym on Tuesday, Thursday and Saturday. On Friday, we will go outside and run around the gym.

Question : Which is the plan of this basketball team for next week?

----

25 No.1 B　No.2 A　No.3 C

【解き方】No.1「競技場でサッカーを見ていたときに撮った」に合うのはB。No.2 トニーの発言「ソーセージがおいしそう」と，エリカの返事「イチゴは入っていない」より，Aが適切。No.3 話者の感想ではなく「いつ何の科目があったか」を中心に聞く。「給食のすぐ前に英語があった」「数学のほうがおもしろかった」「数学のすぐあとの理科もおもしろかった」「午後の音楽を楽しんだ」　この最後の情報だけからでもCが選べる。

放送内容 ----------------------------

Look at No.1 to No.3. Listen to each talk, and choose the best answer for each question. Let's start.

No.1

A : Nancy, look at this picture. It's me. My friend took it when we were watching a soccer game in the stadium.

B : Oh, you look very excited, Yuji.

A : Yes. I really enjoyed watching my favorite soccer player.

B : That's great.

Question : Which picture are they talking about?

No.2

A : Your lunch looks good, Erika. The sausages look delicious.

B : Thank you, Tony. Yours looks good, too. It has strawberries, but I don't have any.

A : Actually, I bought them at the supermarket yesterday. They are so sweet.

B : That's nice. I like strawberries, so I'll buy some later.

Question : Which is Erika's lunch?

No.3

A : Today, we had English class just before lunch, and we sang an English song. It was fun.

B : Yes. But for me, math class was more interesting.

A : Oh, really? For me, science class right after math class was also interesting.

B : I know you like science, but you like music the most, right? You enjoyed music class in the afternoon.

Question : What day are they talking about?

C. 日本語で解答する問題

1 エ
【解き方】you cannot talk on the phone in this hall と言っている。

　Welcome to "Starlight Concert"! To enjoy the concert, please remember some rules. You can drink water or tea. You can take pictures and put them on the Internet if you want to. You can enjoy dancing to the music. But you cannot talk on the phone in this hall. We hope you will enjoy the concert and make good memories. Thank you.

2 イ
【解き方】First, Second, Third に注目する。1.来週金曜日にスピーチをする。2.地球のためにできることについてスピーチする。3.話すとき図（写真）を使う。

　You learned about problems of the Earth this week. Now I want you to make a speech. First, give your speech next Friday. Second, make a speech about something you can do for the Earth. Third, please use some pictures with your speech. Do you have any questions?

3 ア. 郵便局　イ. 駅　ウ. 15
【解き方】ア. the bookstore near the post office を聞き取る。イ. we can walk to the station を聞き取る。ウ. why don't we meet at 9:15? を聞き取る。

Saki：John, we're going to go to the zoo on the next holiday. I can't wait!
John：Saki, I don't know much about this city. Can I meet you at the bookstore near the post office and go to the zoo together?
Saki：OK. Let's meet at the store. Then we can walk to the station. I want to take the train that leaves at 9:40, so why don't we meet at 9:15?
John：Sure!

4 ア. 10　イ. 病院　ウ. 動物
【解き方】ア. 最初に史織が10月のボランティア活動として何ができるかを問いかけている。イ. 真奈が病院の近くの公園の掃除を提案している。ウ. ウィリアムの図書館で子供たちと一緒に本を読むという提案に、史織が動物に関する本がいいのではと言っている。

Shiori：We are going to do a volunteer activity in October. What can we do, Mana?
Mana：The park near the hospital is used by many people, so it's a good idea to clean it. How about you, William?
William：I want to read books together with little children at the library.
Shiori：Interesting. I think books about animals are good for children.

5 場面A. ア　場面B. イ
【解き方】場面A. Is there a flower shop around here?「このあたりに花屋さんはありますか」とたずねているので、この女性が行きたいのは「花屋」。場面B. I can't find my comic book.「私のマンガ本が見つからない」と言っているので、ケイトが探しているのは「マンガ本」。

場面A
F：Excuse me. Is there a flower shop around here?
M：Yes. Can you see that small shop over there?
F：Oh, the building between the station and the hospital?
M：Yes. It's new and they sell many kinds of flowers.
　Question　Where does the woman want to go?
場面B
M：Are you looking for your bike key again, Kate?
F：No. I can't find my comic book. I think I put it in my bag.
M：You left it on the sofa last night after reading it.
F：Oh, now I remember!　Thanks, Dad.
　Question　What is Kate looking for?

6 No.1 エ　No.2 ア　No.3 イ　No.4 ウ
【解き方】No.1 on April 30を聞き取る。No.2 you can give food to horsesを聞き取る。No.3 Only 20 people can join this event.を聞き取る。No.4 We will put a box in the information center以降を聞き取る。その箱に名前を書いたカードを入れて応募するのである。

　Welcome to Happy Zoo. It is April 5. Today, we have good news. Happy Zoo will be 15 years old on April 30. On that day, we will have three special events. In the first event, you can give food to horses. If you want to join it, please come to Horse Village at 10:30 a.m. It's in the north of the zoo. In the second event, you can take pictures with a baby monkey. She was born last month. If you want to take a picture with her, please come to Monkey Mountain at 2:30 p.m. It's in the south of the zoo. Only 20 people can join this event. Don't miss it! In the third event, you can name the baby monkey. She doesn't have a name. If you have a good idea, please give her a name. We will put a box in the information center on that day. Please write a name on a card and put it into the box. You can see the monkey's name on our website next month. We hope you'll enjoy the special events!

----

7 (1)(イ) (2)(ウ)

【解き方】(1)質問は「サキは大事なサッカーの試合がいつあるか」。エマが2番目の発言で,サキに参加してくれないかと言っているバレーボールの試合は,今月の14日。サキはそれに対して,I have an important soccer game the next day と言っている。(2)質問は「サキの姉について言える1つのこととは何ですか」。会話の後半でサキが she sometimes plays volleyball with her friends on weekends. She often watches volleyball games on TV with them, too. と言っている。

放送内容 ------------------------------

Emma : Hi, Saki. Do you like playing volleyball?
Saki : Yes, Emma. Why?
Emma : I'm on the local volleyball team and we have a small tournament on the 14th (fourteenth) this month. But one of our members can't come. Can you join our team?
Saki : I'm sorry, but I can't. I have to practice soccer that day because I have an important soccer game the next day.
Emma : I see.
Saki : Well, I have a sister, so I will ask her. She is a high school student and she likes playing volleyball.
Emma : Thank you. Is your sister on the volleyball team at her school?
Saki : No. But when she was a junior high school student, she was on the volleyball team at her school.
Emma : Does she play volleyball now?
Saki : Yes, she sometimes plays volleyball with her friends on weekends. She often watches volleyball games on TV with them, too.
Emma : Does she play volleyball well?
Saki : Yes. She was chosen as the best player in a small tournament when she was a junior high school student.
Emma : Wow, I'm sure your sister will help our team a lot.
Question (1) : When does Saki have the important soccer game?
Question (2) : What is the one thing we can say about Saki's sister?

----

8 (1)(エ) (2)(イ)

【解き方】(1)「エマは現在どこにいますか」　前半の,ジェーンの「エマをお願いします」に対して,エマの母親は She is in a supermarket と答えている。(2)「ジェーンとエマは,なぜアンの誕生日パーティの日にちを変えなければならないのか」　中ほどでジェーンが Ann is sick and will go to a hospital soon today と言っている。

放送内容 ------------------------------

Mother : Hello?
Jane : Hello. This is Jane. May I speak to Emma?
Mother : Hi, Jane. Sorry. She is in a supermarket now because I told her to buy food for dinner. Do you want to talk to her about the birthday party for your school friend tomorrow?
Jane : Yes, I have an important message about the party. Can you give it to her, please?
Mother : Sure. What is it?
Jane : Emma and I had a plan for a birthday party for Ann in a restaurant tomorrow because tomorrow is her birthday. We have already bought the presents for her. But Ann is sick and will go to a hospital soon today. So, it is difficult for us to have the party tomorrow. We have to change the date. I think next Sunday is the best. I'm free on that day, but I want to ask Emma what she thinks.
Mother : OK. I'll tell her that. Oh! I remember my family has another plan for next Sunday. Her uncle and aunt will come to our house on that day.
Jane : I see.
Mother : I'll tell her to call you again when she comes home.
Jane : Thank you.
Question (1) : Where is Emma now?
Question (2) : Why do Jane and Emma have to change the date for Ann's birthday party?

----

d. 英作文をともなう問題

1 [解答例] I like spring because flowers are beautiful.
【解き方】好きな季節とその理由を英文で答える問題。解答例は「花がきれいなので春が好きだ」。

Japan has four seasons. Which season do you like the best? And why do you like it?

2 [解答例] I walk to school. 【別解】By bike.
【解き方】質問は「あなたはどうやって学校に来るか」。最初のHowを聞き逃さないこと。

放送内容

I am very surprised that there is no school bus at your school. In my country, most students come to school by bus, so we have a lot of school buses. How do you come to school?

3 [解答例] I want to go to Okinawa to enjoy swimming and learn about the unique nature there.
【解き方】質問は,「日本で1週間旅行するとしたら, どこに行きたいか, またその理由は」というもの。質問文を利用してI want to go to ～「私は～へ行きたい」などと答えるとよい。理由については, 解答例では to 不定詞の副詞用法を使っているが, because I ～の形でもよい。

放送内容

I went to Hokkaido to ski for one week during this winter vacation. If you can travel in Japan for one week, where do you want to go and why?

4 [解答例] Is this bus going to the zoo?
【別解】Does this bus go to the zoo?
【解き方】トムは動物園に行きたいと思っているので, バスが動物園へ行くかどうかをたずねる疑問文を作る。運転手がYes.と答えているので, yesかnoで答えられる疑問文を作ることもポイント。

放送内容

Look at the picture. Tom wants to go to the zoo by bus. What should Tom say to the bus driver in this picture?

5 [解答例] Making Japanese friends is the best way.
【別解】You should watch Japanese movies.

【解き方】日本語の勉強方法を提案する。

放送内容

I was so happy today because I talked with you. I have been interested in the Japanese language, and now I want to learn about it more! What is the best way to study it? Please tell me!

6 [解答例] I will look it up in a dictionary.
【解き方】放送文は「あなたは今, 本を読んでいます。しかし知らない難しい単語に出会います。あなたは, その単語の意味を理解するためにどうしますか」。解答例は「私はそれ(＝知らない単語)を辞書で調べます」。

放送内容

You are reading a book now. But you find a difficult word you don't know. What will you do to understand the meaning of the word?

7 [解答例] Why did you take a bus today?
【解き方】対話の内容から,「ジョンは通学中のバス内で春花に出会い, 彼女から, ふだんは自転車通学をしていることを聞かされた」状況である。通学方法についての対話が続くような質問を考える。

放送内容

John : Good morning, Haruka.
Haruka : Oh, good morning, John! We're on the same bus!
John : I have never seen you on the bus.
Haruka : Well, I usually go to school by bike.
John : (チャイム)

8 [解答例] You should try *okonomiyaki*.
【解き方】発言に出てきたもの以外の日本食をすすめること。また疑問文が What Japanese food should I try? なので, You should try ～と表現するのが自然となる。

放送内容

I like eating and I've already had *sushi*, *tempura*, and *sukiyaki* since I came to Japan. They were all delicious, but I want to eat something different next time. What Japanese food should I try?

9 [解答例] I started cooking for my family.
【解き方】新しいことを始めたと言うがそれはどんなことか, 自由に書く。

放送内容

Olivia : During the winter vacation, I started reading English books.
Akira : Oh, really? I also started doing something new.
Olivia : What did you do, Akira?

Akira :（ ）.

---

10 ［解答例］I agree. If you ask him what he wants, he can get the things he wants and will be happy.

【解き方】キャシーは父親の誕生日に何をあげたらいいかわからないので友達に相談すると，「お父さんに何がほしいかをたずねるべきだ」と言われた。質問は「この考えについてどう思うか。なぜそう思うか」という意味で，まず，その考えについて賛成か反対かをI agree.またはI disagree.などで簡潔に答え，そのあとに理由を続けよう。

```
放送内容
```

It's my father's birthday soon. I'd like to give him something, but I don't know what he wants. So I asked one of my friends what I should give him. She said, "You should ask him what he wants for his birthday." What do you think about this idea? And why do you think so?

---

11 ［解答例］I will read many books written in English. 【別解】I want to talk with an English teacher every day.

【解き方】質問は，「あなたは高校で英語力を向上させるために何をしますか」。解答例は「英語で書かれた本をたくさん読む」，別解は「毎日，英語の先生と話をしたい」。

```
放送内容
```

Hi, everyone. You have only a few weeks before graduating. I remember all the school days I've had with you. My best memory is enjoying the English classes with you. Your English is getting better. So, I want to ask you. What will you do to improve your English in high school?

---

12 ① win ② once ③ smile ④ message ⑤ remember

【解き方】①第2文を聞き取る。「ほとんどの試合で勝つことができなかった」と言っている。②第3文を聞き取る。「もうテニスをしたくないと思ったこともあった」と言っている。once「かつて，一度」 ③第4文を聞き取る。with a smile「微笑んで」 ④第5文で，「チームメートからの親切なメッセージのおかげで，またテニスができるようになった」と言っている。⑤最後の文を聞き取る。remember 〜「〜を忘れずに覚えている」

```
放送内容
```

I belonged to the tennis club for three years. Though I practiced tennis very hard, I couldn't win most of my games. I once thought I didn't want to play anymore. At that time, one of my teammates said to me with a smile, "You're doing your best." The kind message from my teammate helped me to start playing again. In my school life, I was able to make lots of friends and I will remember them forever.

---

13 ［解答例］Q.1 Yes, they do.
Q.2 It is in front of the library.

【解き方】Q.1 メッセージの前半部分を聞き取る。This is Kevin. Are you free next Saturday? I'm going to go out with Saki. We'll be glad if you can join us. Q.2 The restaurant is in front of the library.

```
放送内容
```

Hello. This is Kevin. Are you free next Saturday? I'm going to go out with Saki. We'll be glad if you can join us. We'll meet at the station at ten o'clock and then go shopping. After that, we're going to have lunch at my favorite restaurant. The food is good, so you'll like it. The restaurant is in front of the library. Please call me back later. Bye.

Question 1. Do Kevin and Saki want to go out with you next Saturday?
2. Where is Kevin's favorite restaurant?

---

14 ア，ウ
［質問］［解答例］How do you go to school(?)
【別解】Do you wear a school uniform(?)

【解き方】授業は午前中に4つ，午後に3つあるので，アが一致。Next year, 〜の文とウが一致。トムの問いかけは「僕の学校生活について質問はありますか」。通学手段や制服などトムが話さなかった内容を考えよう。

```
放送内容
```

Hello, everyone. Today, I'll talk about my school life. I have four classes in the morning and three in the afternoon every day. At my school, the students can learn some languages. I study Spanish. I'm not good at it, but I study it hard because I want to go to Spain someday. Next year, I'm going to study one more language, Japanese, because I like Japanese comics. At lunch time, I eat my favorite food at the school cafeteria with my friends. Pizza and sandwiches are popular. Now, do you have any questions about my school life?

---

15 質問1．7［seven］
質問2．ⓐ cleaned ⓑ house
質問3．made a cake for them

【解き方】質問1．最初のほうに出てくるLast summer, my parents 〜 stayed there for seven days.を聞き取る。質問2．中ほどに出てくるBut we cleaned the house together before breakfast.を聞き取る。質問3．最後のほうに出てくるWhen my parents came home, they were surprised because I made a cake for them.を聞き取る。

```
放送内容
```

質問1．How long did Kenta's parents stay in Nagano?
質問2．What did Kenta do with his sister before breakfast?
質問3．Why were Kenta's parents surprised when they came home?

I live with my father, mother, and sister. My parents and my sister work hard every day.

Last summer, my parents went to Nagano to meet their friends and stayed there for seven days. My sister and I didn't go with them. When my parents stayed in Nagano, we did different things in our house. I cooked breakfast and dinner. My sister washed the dishes. But we cleaned the house together before breakfast. Life without our parents was hard but fun.

When my parents came home, they were surprised because I made a cake for them. They ate the cake and told me it was very good. So, I was happy.

Now I sometimes cook dinner for my family.

16
(A) writing　(B) river　(C) original
(D) [解答例] want to visit Australia

【解き方】(A) Today, we'll have an English writing activity in the morning.「今日は午前中に英作文活動をします」と言っている。(B) Tomorrow, we'll go to a river.「明日は川に行きます」と言っている。(C) On the last day, we'll make a short movie. You'll write your original story and make the movie in English.「自分たちのオリジナルの物語を書いて英語の映画を作ります」と言っている。(D) 質問は「どこの国を訪れたいですか」。〈I want to visit＋国名〉の形で答えればよい。

放送内容 ------------------------------------

Good morning, everyone. Now, I'll tell you about what we're going to do during our English Day. Today, we'll have an English writing activity in the morning. In the afternoon, you'll have a presentation. Tomorrow, we'll go to a river. I'll show you how to catch big fish! On the last day, we'll make a short movie. You'll write your original story and make the movie in English. Let's have a good time together, and make your English better!

OK then, let's start the writing activity now. Enjoy writing and sharing your ideas in a group. First, I'll ask you some questions, so write your ideas on the paper. Question number one. What country do you want to visit? Write your answer now.

17
① money　② warm　③ [解答例] useful
④ [解答例] they need

【解き方】① please get some Australian moneyと言ったあと，そのお金を日本の銀行(bank)で入手するよう指示している。② please bring some warm clothesを聞き取る。③ 図書館か書店に行き，旅行に使える本を入手するよう言っている。解答例はuseful「役に立つ」。④ 質問は「ブラウン先生は話の最後の部分で，生徒たちに何をするよう言っているか」。please write down ~を聞き取る。the necessary things「必要なもの」をthe things they needに言い換える。the studentsをtheyと表す点に注意。

放送内容 ------------------------------------

Ms. Brown：You're planning to travel to Australia

this August, and you have only one month before leaving. Now, I'll tell you three things to do for the trip.

First, please get some Australian money. Two or three hundred dollars will be fine, and you can get it at a bank in Japan. You may use it for lunch or shopping.

Second, please bring some warm clothes because it's winter in Australia. It's a little cold, so you may need a jacket or a coat.

Third, please go to a library or a bookstore and get some books you can use for your trip. It's important for you to get information about the country you'll visit before going there.

You have many things to get for the trip in one month, so please write down the necessary things and check them many times. Have a nice weekend!

質問します。　What does Ms. Brown tell the students to do in the last part of her talk?

18
(1)① full　② sister　③ save　(2) エ

【解き方】(1)① ブラウン先生のOh, I'm surprised! The windows are full of leaves.を聞き取る。be full of ~「~でいっぱいだ」　② 加奈のMy sister told me about energy problems.を聞き取る。③ 加奈のI can save electricity in my houseやブラウン先生のYou can both save electricity and eat vegetables.が手がかり。(2) 加奈の説明によると，グリーンカーテン(Green Curtains)は，窓をおおう植物(plants)が日光を遮って部屋を少し涼しくするので，節電につながる。よって，エが適切。

放送内容 ------------------------------------

Kana　　　：Hello, Mr. Brown. Do you have time now?

Mr. Brown：Hi, Kana. What's up?

Kana　　　：I'm preparing for the presentation in English class. I want to talk about "Green Curtains". Could you tell me what you think about my topic?

Mr. Brown：Green Curtains?

Kana　　　：Yes. Please look at this picture.

Mr. Brown：Oh, I'm surprised! The windows are full of leaves. The plants have grown higher than the windows.

Kana　　　：These are called Green Curtains. I make them at my house every year.

Mr. Brown：I see. Why did you become interested in them?

Kana　　　：My sister told me about energy problems. Then, I learned that making Green Curtains is one way to save energy.

Mr. Brown：Great. Can you tell me more about Green Curtains?

Kana　　　：Of course. Because of Green Curtains,

the sun light doesn't come into the room so much, and that makes the room a little cooler. So I don't have to use the air conditioner a lot. It means I can save electricity in my house.

Mr. Brown : Wow, that's nice. And these are cucumbers, right?

Kana : Yes. Cucumbers are popular vegetables for making Green Curtains.

Mr. Brown : Your idea is good. You can both save electricity and eat vegetables. Your classmates will be interested in your topic.

Kana : Thank you, Mr. Brown.

Mr. Brown : You're welcome.

----

19 ① easy　② know　質問1．D

質問2．[解答例] What song do you want to sing at the next chorus contest?

【解き方】①中盤に，"It is a very difficult song to sing, isn't it?" "Actually, I could sing it easily." とある。it is［was］〜 for *A* to …の構文で，easily を形容詞 easy に書き換える。②後半を参照。クリスは合唱コンクールについて，This kind of contest is a chance to <u>know</u> each other. と言っている。質問1．新聞記事の内容は「クリスは合唱コンクールを楽しみ，母国の学校でも開催したいと思っている」というもの。D「クリスの初めての合唱コンクール」が適切。質問2．エリがたずねたものを除き，合唱コンクールに関連したクリスへの質問を考える。

　　放送内容　-------------------

A : Hi, Chris. I'm Eri. I'm writing the school's newspaper. Do you have time to talk?

B : Sure.

A : I'd like to ask you some questions about yesterday's chorus contest. Do you have a chorus contest at your school in your country?

B : No, we don't. So it was my first one.

A : Oh, really?　Did you enjoy the contest?

B : Yes, very much.

A : What song did you sing?

B : We sang "*Daichi*."

A : It is a very difficult song to sing, isn't it?

B : Actually, I could sing it easily. It's my favorite singer's song, so I have sung it many times before. I think I could sing well at the contest too.

A : That's nice. Do you want to have a chorus contest at your school too?

B : Yes, of course. In my country, we don't join a school event with all classmates. This kind of contest is a chance to know each other.

A : I agree with you. Thank you very much for your time. This will be in the school's newspaper.

B : You're welcome. I'm excited to read it.

　質問1．Choose the best title for Eri's writing.

　質問2．If you ask another question about the chorus contest to Chris, what else do you want to ask?　Write one question in English.

----

e．そのほかの問題

1　1．ア　2．エ

【解き方】1．「ありがとう」と言っているので，アの No problem.「いいんですよ」が適切。2．「（今）寒気がする。何も食べたくない」と言っているので，エ「病院に行くべきだ」が適切。

　　放送内容　-------------------

1．A : It's raining now. So I'll take you home by car.
　　B : You're so kind. Thank you.
　　A : (チャイム)

2．A : Sayaka, you said you were not feeling fine this morning. How are you feeling now?
　　B : I'm feeling cold. And I don't want to eat anything.
　　A : (チャイム)

2　1番 イ　2番 ウ

【解き方】1番「彼らはいつ日本を去るか」に対して，イ「彼らは来月引っ越す」が適切な応答。2番「あなたは試合に出たか？」に対して，ウ「いいえ。でも私はそれを楽しんだ」が適切な応答。

　　放送内容　-------------------

1番　A : Did you know that Keita's family is going to move to Australia?
　　　B : Really?　I didn't know that. When will they leave Japan?

2番　A : I heard your baseball team won the game yesterday.
　　　B : Yes, it was great.
　　　A : Did you play in the game?

3　(1)イ　(2)エ　(3)イ

【解き方】(1)質問は，「これはだれの自転車ですか」なので，イ「私のものです」が適切。(2)「昨日はどうやって家に帰りましたか」と質問されて，エ「バスです」が適切。(3)「いつ日本語を学び始めましたか」という質問に対して，イ「15歳のときです」と答える。

　　放送内容　-------------------

(1)　Wow, look!　That's a cool bike. Whose bike is it?
　　ア．It's blue.
　　イ．It's mine.
　　ウ．It's near the park.
　　エ．It's ten years old.

(2)　Lucy, how did you go home yesterday?
　　ア．To cook dinner.
　　イ．In the evening.
　　ウ．About one hour.
　　エ．By bus.

(3)　Ms. Green,　when　did　you　start　learning

Japanese?
ア．By listening to music.
イ．When I was fifteen.
ウ．Because I was interested in it.
エ．For three hours.

---

4 1．イ 2．イ
【解き方】1．「そこ（＝天草）で何をしたの？」―イ「魚釣りを楽しんだ」 2．「よくそこ（＝図書館）に行くの？」―イ「うん。ほぼ毎日（行くよ）」

放送内容

No.1 M：Where did you go last weekend?
　　　F：Well, I visited my cousin in Amakusa.
　　　M：Sounds great. What did you do there?
　　　F：（チャイム）
No.2 M：The book you're reading looks difficult. Is it yours?
　　　F：No. I borrowed it from the school library.
　　　M：Do you often go there?
　　　F：（チャイム）

---

5 No.1 C No.2 D No.3 A
【解き方】No.1「彼女はあなたの家の近くに住んでいるのですか」に対する受け答えは，Cの No, she doesn't. が適切。No.2「僕はノートを探しているけれど見つからない」に対する受け答えは，D「テーブルの上にありますよ」が適切。No.3「だれがキッチンにいましたか」と聞いているので，A「お父さんが（そこに）いました」が適切。

放送内容

No.1 Woman：Where did you go last Sunday?
　　　Man　：I visited my grandmother.
　　　Woman：Does she live near your house?
No.2 Bob　：Where is it? … Oh, hi Mary.
　　　Mary：Hi, Bob. What are you doing?
　　　Bob　：I'm looking for my notebook, but I can't find it.
No.3 Girl：Someone ate my cake!
　　　Boy：Oh, it wasn't me.
　　　Girl：Who was in the kitchen?

---

6 No.1 A．正 B．誤 C．正 No.2 A．誤 B．正 C．正 No.3 A．正 B．正 C．誤
【解き方】問題A．No.1 ぞうきんは「何かをきれいにするときによく使う」のでAは正しい。「洗って何度も使う」のでCも正しい。No.2 本を売る店があるのでBは正しい。定休日は毎月第2水曜日＝月に1回水曜日閉店でCも正しい。No.3 アメリカの映画（3位）は日本の映画（1位と2位）ほど人気がないのでAは正しい。アメリカの映画（135分）は韓国の映画（110分）よりも長いのでBも正しい。

放送内容

No.1　A．You often use it to clean something.
　　　B．You always need it to make a T-shirt.
　　　C．You usually wash it and use it many times.

No.2　A．You must go up if you want to buy flowers.
　　　B．There is a shop that sells books in TYM Shop Town.
　　　C．TYM Shop Town is closed on Wednesday once a month.
No.3　A．The American movie was not as popular as the Japanese ones in February.
　　　B．You need a longer time to watch the American movie than the Korean one.
　　　C．It takes more than 2 hours to watch each movie.

---

7 No.1 a．誤 b．正 c．誤
　　No.2 a．正 b．誤 c．誤
【解き方】A．No.1 質問は「ティムは次に何と言うか」。最後の発言が「私は来週，野球の試合に行くんだ」なので，b「それは楽しそうだね」が適切。No.2 質問は「マークはパーティーに何を持ってくるか」。マークは最初の発言で，「彼女は甘いものが好きだ。だから，私は彼女のためにチョコレートケーキを作る」と言っている。

放送内容

〔No.1〕
A：Hi, Tim! Do you like baseball?
B：Yes, it's my favorite sport. Why?
A：I'm going to a baseball game next week.
　Question：What will Tim say next?
　Answer　：a．It was a great game.
　　　　　　b．That sounds fun.
　　　　　　c．You look sad.
〔No.2〕
A：This Friday is Susan's birthday. Let's have a birthday party, Mark!
B：Yes, let's. She likes sweet things, so I'll make a chocolate cake for her.
A：That's nice. Then, I'll get some drinks.
B：Thank you. Susan likes donuts, too. Can you bring some?
A：Sure. I can.
　Question：What will Mark bring to the party?
　Answer　：a．A chocolate cake.
　　　　　　b．Some donuts.
　　　　　　c．Some drinks.

---

8 No.1 ウ No.2 ア No.3 イ No.4 ウ
【解き方】No.1 How about ～?「～はどうですか」店員にこの大きい帽子はどうかと聞かれて，ウ「ぴったりだ」と答える。No.2「腹痛はいつ始まったの？」と聞かれて，ア「今日の朝」と答える。No.3「彼は何時に戻りますか？」と聞かれて，イ「夜7時ごろです」と答える。No.4「どうやって～を覚えたの？」と聞かれて，ウ「兄が教えてくれた」と答える。

放送内容

No.1　A：May I help you?
　　　B：Yes, I'm looking for a cap. I like this one, but it's a little small for me.
　　　A：OK. How about this bigger one?

No.2 A：Good morning, Bob. Oh, what's wrong?
　　 B：I feel sick and I have a stomachache.
　　 A：Oh, no. When did the stomachache start?
No.3 A：Hello, this is Harry. May I speak to Jack, please?
　　 B：Sorry, he isn't at home now. Any messages?
　　 A：No, thank you. What time will he come back?
No.4 A：Nick, what are you doing?
　　 B：I'm drawing a picture with a computer.
　　 A：Wow, it's beautiful. How did you learn about drawing pictures with a computer?

----

9 (1)イ　(2)エ　(3)ア
【解き方】(1)最後の How did you come here?「どのようにしてここに来たのですか」を聞き取る。(2)腕時計が話題で，最後に What color is it? と色をたずねている。(3)最後の How many times have you been there?「そこへは何回行ったことがありますか」を聞き取る。three times「3回」

放送内容

(1) A：Why were you late?
　　B：I missed the train.
　　A：How did you come here?
　　B：（チャイム）
(2) A：Do you have a watch?
　　B：Yes. I like it very much.
　　A：What color is it?
　　B：（チャイム）
(3) A：Have you ever been to Hiraizumi?
　　B：Yes. And I want to visit Hiraizumi again.
　　A：How many times have you been there?
　　B：（チャイム）

----

10 No.1 B　No.2 C　No.3 A
【解き方】No.1 Have you been there?「そこに行ったことがありますか」に対する受け答えは，B の No, I haven't. が適切。No.2「明日はそれ（＝本）を忘れないでね」に対する受け答えは，C の Sure. が適切。No.3「では 3 の前に来る数字は何か」に対する受け答えは，この number game では奇数が並んでいることから考えると，A の One. が適切。

放送内容

No.1 Man 　：Are there any big supermarkets near here?
　　 Woman：A new big supermarket opened last week.
　　 Man 　：Really?　Have you been there?
No.2 Girl：Did you bring the book you bought yesterday?
　　 Boy：I'm sorry but I forgot it.
　　 Girl：Oh, don't forget it tomorrow.
No.3 Woman：Let's play a number game!　Three, five, seven. What number comes next?

Boy 　：Nine!
Woman：That's right. Then, what number comes before three?

----

11 No.1 B　No.2 A　No.3 C
【解き方】No.1 先生の，「なぜ自分のレストランを持ちたいのか」の問いに対する応答である。No.2 有名な音楽家の写真を見せられての応答である。No.3「一緒に料理をしましょうか」の問いに対する応答である。

放送内容

No.1 先生との対話
　先　生：What do you want to do in the future, Yuka?
　生　徒：I want to have my own restaurant.
　先　生：Why do you want to have your own restaurant?
　生　徒：〈チャイム音〉
No.2 友人との対話
　男の子：Look at this picture. Do you know the man playing the guitar?
　女の子：No. Who is he?
　男の子：He is Takeshi, a famous musician in Japan.
　女の子：〈チャイム音〉
No.3 母親との対話
　男の子：I'm hungry, Mom.
　母　親：Dinner is not ready.
　男の子：Shall we cook together?
　母　親：〈チャイム音〉

----

12 No.1 b　No.2 a　No.3 c
【解き方】No.1 明日雨だと聞いて，「えー！　明日テニスをしたいのに」と言う。これに対し，b「残念ね」が適切。No.2 女性は本の貸出期間をたずねている。How long 〜? に対し，a「5日間」が適切。No.3 ミーティングを始めるのにトムがいない。「遅れると言っていたよ」に対し，c「じゃあ，（トムがいなくても）始めよう」が適切。

放送内容

No.1 〔A：男性，B：女性〕
A：What's the weather tomorrow?
B：The news says that it will rain.
A：Oh, no!　I want to play tennis tomorrow.
　 a．I'd love to.
　 b．That's too bad.
　 c．It's my turn.
No.2 〔A：女性，B：男性〕
A：Excuse me. Can I borrow five books?
B：Sorry, only three books at a time.
A：I see. How long can I keep them?
　 a．For five days.
　 b．About five books.
　 c．On the fifth floor.
No.3 〔A：男性，B：女性〕
A：Now, it's time to start today's club meeting.
B：Wait, Tom isn't here.
A：It's OK. He said he would be late.
　 a．Then, he didn't attend the meeting.
　 b．Then, he must be on time.

c．Then, let's begin.

----

13 問1．a．誤　b．誤　c．誤　d．正
　　　問2．a．誤　b．誤　c．正　d．誤
【解き方】問1．先月，コウタはお年寄りの男性に市役所への行き方を英語でたずねられ，道案内ができた。問2．スピーチの最後のほうでThen I decided to study English harder.と言っている。

■放送内容■ ---------------------------

Hello, I'm Kota. About five years ago, I began to study English at school. At that time, I was too shy to speak English. Last month, an old man asked me the way to City Hall in English. At first I felt nervous, but I was very satisfied when I could show the way. Then I decided to study English harder. Thank you.
問1．What happened last month?
　a．Kota went to school with the old man.
　b．Kota asked the way to City Hall in English.
　c．Kota began to study English for the first time.
　d．Kota showed the old man the way to City Hall.
問2．What is the best title of this speech?
　a．Why I was shy at school
　b．My English about five years ago
　c．Why I study English hard
　d．The way to study English

----

14 問1．ウ　問2．エ　問3．ア
【解き方】問1．見に行った野球の試合はどうだったかという質問に対する答えを選ぶ。問2．郵便局が何時に閉まるかという質問に対する答えを選ぶ。問3．浜辺に行くかハイキングに出かけるのによい天候になるかという質問に対する答えを選ぶ。

■放送内容■ ---------------------------

問1．A：Hi, Sarah. How was your day?
　　　B：It was fun!　I went to a baseball game.
　　　A：That's great. How was the game?
　　　B：(　　　　　)
問2．A：Excuse me, do you know how to get to the post office?
　　　B：Sure. Go two blocks that way, then turn right, and it will be on your left.
　　　A：Thank you so much!　Do you know what time it will close?
　　　B：(　　　　　)
問3．A：What are your plans for this weekend?
　　　B：I haven't decided yet. I want to go to the beach or go hiking.
　　　A：That sounds fun. Will the weather be good for those activities?
　　　B：(　　　　　)

----

15 ㈦ No.1 3　No.2 2　No.3 4
【解き方】㈦ No.1 学校から図書館への行き方を聞かれて，「電車で行ける」と答えている3が適切。No.2 明日は雨で，動物園以外の場所として，博物館を提案している2が適切。No.3 祖母からもらった犬について「名前はあるの？」と聞かれて，4「いや。なんと呼ぶか考えているんだ」が適切。

■放送内容■ ---------------------------

No.1　Sarah：I want to go to the city library after school, Akira. I'm going to learn about the history of our city there. Do you know where the library is?
　　　Akira：Yes, Sarah. It's not near our school. It's by the hospital. It has a lot of interesting books about our city. I like the library.
　　　Sarah：That's nice!　How can I get there from school?
　　　Akira：（チャイム）
No.2　Sarah：Akira, let's take your little brother to the zoo tomorrow.
　　　Akira：Oh, but it will be rainy tomorrow. Let's visit another place.
　　　Sarah：OK. Where will we go?
　　　Akira：（チャイム）
No.3　Sarah：I heard you got a dog. Are you happy, Akira?
　　　Akira：Yes, I am. He is very cute. My grandmother gave him to me yesterday.
　　　Sarah：That's wonderful!　I want to meet him soon. Does he have a name?
　　　Akira：（チャイム）

Obunsha